Readings in
Microeconomics

ECONOMIC SERIES
Under the Editorship of
Clark W. Reynolds
Stanford University

Readings in Microeconomics, second edition
edited by William Breit, *University of Virginia*
and Harold M. Hochman, *The Urban Institute, Washington, D.C.*

Readings in Labor Market Analysis
edited by John F. Burton, Jr., Lee K. Benham,
William M. Vaughn, III, and Robert J. Flanagan
All of the University of Chicago

Modern Political Arithmetic
Bruce F. Davie and Bruce F. Duncombe
Georgetown University

Readings in Macroeconomics, second edition
edited by M. G. Mueller
University of Glasgow

Economic Analysis and Industrial Structure
Douglas Needham
State University of New York, Brockport

Readings in the Economics of Industrial Organization
edited by Douglas Needham
State University of New York, Brockport

Readings in the History of Economic Theory
edited by Ingrid H. Rima
Temple University

Readings in Microeconomics

Second Edition

Edited by
William Breit
University of Virginia

Harold M. Hochman
The Urban Institute, Washington, D.C.

DRYDEN PRESS
HINSDALE, ILLINOIS

Preface

Price theory, unlike Picassos, chamber music, or giraffes, is not a phenomenon to be admired for its own sake. Rather, it is something ultilitarian that, like hammers, screwdrivers, and wrenches, makes up, in Mrs. Joan Robinson's apposite phrase, " a box of tools." The purpose of our book is to familiarize the student with these tools, as the professional economist uses them. These tools have long been used in dealing with the traditional policy issues of poverty and income distribution, as well as in the explanation of such otherwise mysterious values as the price of caviar. In recent years, however, the instrumental power of microeconomics has been demonstrated, first in such areas as defense analysis and operations research, and then in those areas dealing with such social problems as crime, environmental pollution, the provision of public goods, and human resources development.

The excellent response to our first edition, including its translation into Italian, confirms our conviction that conventional textbooks, however clearly written and thorough, can satisfy but part of the needs of economic education. Seasoned students of economics must be thoroughly familiar with original articles in the professional literature, material which is all too often very limited in its availability. Our book, therefore, tries to alleviate the necessity of obliging our students to spend countless hours in a reserve book room and restless nights under the threat of fine for failure to return reserve books by 9:00 A.M.—for most of us a depressing reminiscence.

The papers reprinted in this volume, as in the first edition, focus on the logic, methodology, and applications of microeconomics. We have, for the most part, selected articles that emphasize conceptual rather than empirical material and articles that can be readily understood without significant formal training in any mathematics more advanced than geometry and, in a few cases, elementary calculus. With but two exceptions the selections have been reprinted in their entirety.

Devising the table of contents, both for the first edition and for this one, posed many difficult problems of choice. No book can be all-inclusive. Thus, we had to omit some articles that are on every economist's "must" list, including the editors', in order to effect a sometimes reluctant reconciliation of competing claims to limited space. For example, we decided simply to exclude a number of classic and well-known articles that have already been reprinted and are available in the volume *Readings in Price Theory* published by the American Economic Association. Since the substantive content of such articles is fully assimilated in major textbooks, our judgment was that it would be redundant to reprint them. The omission of Professor Viner's "Cost Curves and Supply Curves," the Sweezey and Stigler article on the "Kinky Oligopoly Demand Curve," and the many other important pieces reprinted in the AEA volume is in no way an oversight. We view this volume as a complementary and not a competing product.

In revising the book, ten selections have been added and six of the original articles have been omitted. The additions reflect our desire to strengthen certain sections of the book and to add some material that has become available since the publication of the first edition. In particular, we wanted to strengthen the section of the book concerned with alternative market structures. We also wanted to incorporate selections which describe some of the recent applications of price theory to allocation problems (Becker's paper on crime and punishment and Hirshliefer's paper on transfer prices are examples) and to present some discussion of recent developments in the theory of the firm (Alchian's paper on management of the firm) and the extension of price theory to public choice (the articles by Buchanan and Samuelson). The omission of six of the articles included in the first edition in no way reflects upon their merit. We simply felt that the articles that have been added are essential to the specific purposes of the book, and in light of this fact and the constraint on space, it was necessary for us to engage in selective pruning.

We have, of course, incurred many obligations in the preparation of this volume. All of our colleagues at the University of Virginia and the Urban Institute have been generous in their support, encouragement, and, most of all, in their constructive criticism of our plans. Many users of the book—students and teachers alike—have made valuable suggestions, many of which are reflected in the changes made. Mrs. Grace Dawson has devoted a considerable amount of time (and an ample quota of good humor) to the administrative effort that this revision entailed. As in the case of the first edition, Mrs. Merle E. Hochman's enthusiasm encouraged us to see the work through to completion. Our main obligation, however, is to the many authors and publishers who so graciously permitted us to reprint their material. We, and the students who will use this book are grateful to them. Formal acknowledgments of sources and brief biographical sketches of the authors are to be found at the beginning of each contribution.

APRIL 1971

William Breit
Charlottesville, Virginia

Harold M. Hochman
Washington, D.C.

Introduction

Microeconomics is that branch of economic theory concerned with the behavior of individual households and firms in the process of constrained choice. In working out the implications of this process, the theory explains how scarce resources are allocated among competing uses. There are two major subdivisions of microeconomics: one which explains the pricing of final products and another which explains the pricing of factors of production. The first deals with the division of output among consumers and the division of its production between firms and industries, while the second is concerned with the distribution of income. Taken together, they constitute the subject matter of microeconomics.

Microeconomics is sometimes called "price theory" because of its emphasis on how relative prices are determined and the crucial role that such prices play in solving the problems of production and distribution. So important, in fact, are relative prices in organizing production and distribution that an economy which is primarily reliant upon them to solve these problems is appropriately called a "price system."

The theory of price is one of the most challenging and rewarding subjects offered in a university curriculum. The student, in mastering its fundamentals, is enabled to sort out the considerations relevant to evaluation of the vast mass of policies that affect the allocation of resources. The papers collected in this volume were chosen on the basis of their ability to enable the student to learn and to apply the basic logic of this approach.

Part I, The Nature of an Economic System, contains a classic paper by Frank H. Knight in which the author defines the scope of economics and sets forth the five main functions of an economic system. He also provides an overview of the types of economic organizations that have attempted to perform these essential functions.

The two papers in Part II, The Method of Economic Analysis, are excursions into the domain of philosophy of social science. Friedman's essay on methodology makes the important distinction between positive and normative economics. The author argues that undue emphasis on the descriptive "realism" of assumptions has caused economists to neglect the really crucial factor in the construction of good economic theory, namely, does the theory enable us to predict accurately how consumers and producers will behave? To what extent are the implications of the theory borne out in practice? This, of course, implies that any adequate scientific theory must be put into the form of testable (conceivably refutable) hypotheses. Nagel, an eminent philosopher of science, argues that the central thesis of Friedman's methodology discussion is correct but nevertheless contains some ambiguities in that theories have an explanatory function in addition to their predictive one.

Part III, Demand, covers two major areas in the subject matter of demand theory: (1) utility theory and consumers' surplus and (2) analysis of the shape and slope of the demand curve itself. Alchian's essay discusses the measurability of utility and clarifies the meaning of many concepts typically used in utility theory. It also provides an admirable review of the literature from Slutsky and Hicks through Friedman, Savage, and Markowitz. Machlup provides a detailed review of the recent contributions of Hicks to the theory of consumer demand. In so doing, Machlup carefully and precisely analyzes, through the use of indifference curve techniques, the four measures of consumer's surplus.

The second paper by Friedman suggests that the usual conception of the demand curve does not meet the positivist test of conceivable refutability, inasmuch as the existence of the income effect allows the demand curve to slope either positively or negatively. Friedman, in seeking an operational tool, derives a hypothetical constant-real-income demand curve in which he eliminates the income effect of a change in price. Thus, with Friedman's characteristic skill and ingenuity, the law of demand becomes an operational proposition. Bailey however, points out that Friedman's construction does not take into account the overall fixity of resource supply. The various points along the constant-real-income demand curve may not represent available alternatives. Bailey, therefore, fixes the production possibilities of the community and derives a demand curve reflecting genuinely available alternatives. Leibenstein's essay analyzes the implications of effecting a transition from individual to collective demand curves. In so doing, it incorporates various external or "spill-over" effects into the traditional theory of consumer demand.

The papers in Part IV are concerned with the theory of supply. Stigler's essay is a modern rigorous statement of the famous principle expounded by Adam Smith that "the division of labor is limited by the extent of the market." Stigler argues that Adam Smith's famous dictum implies a theory of the functions of the firm and industry, and he presents a geometrical analysis of the effect of the gains from specialization on the firm's cost curves. The second paper by Alchian proposes a reformulation of the firm's cost function. Alchian makes a sharp distinction between the rate of output and the volume of output. He indicates that marginal cost is an increasing function of the rate of output, the volume being held constant; it is a falling function of the volume of output, the rate being held constant. The significance of this curiously neglected distinction is that (among other things) it provides a theoretical explanation for the existence of quantity discounts. De Alessi's paper relies heavily on Alchian's approach to cost in showing that the use of a wealth-maximizing approach to firm behavior, in place of a profit-maximizing approach, gives pertinent predictions regarding the behavior of the firm in the short run. It also contains an examination of the "uneconomic" regions of the production function. Dorfman presents a nonmathematical exposition of the techniques of linear programming in which the firm's production function consists of alternative fixed proportions activities or processes. The article illustrates the significance of this powerful tool for economic theory as well as for solutions of practical business and governmental problems.

The articles in Part V, Market Structures, are divided into two sections. The first covers the full spectrum of degrees of rivalry among firms, from perfect competition, which Joan Robinson carefully defines and analyzes, to monopoly, under which market power, as Professor Lerner demonstrates, can be measured by the excess of price over marginal cost. Professor Lerner's famous articles does much more than its title indicates. Included is a discussion of the meaning of an "optimum" position (clarified with the device of production and consumption indifference curves) that provides an introduction to the subject of "welfare economics."

The papers in the section on imperfect competition handle the theoretical apparatus and discuss the implications of imperfectly competitive market structures for resource allocation. Cassels' essay provides a capsule summary of Chamberlin's theory of monopolistic competition. It gives a detailed exposition of the meaning of "excess capacity," a term which must be used with utmost care in order to avoid the kinds of erroneous conclusions that are too often drawn from Chamberlin's analysis. The paper by the late N.S. Buchanan presents a diagrammatic solution to the theoretical problem of rationalizing advertising expenditures, a topic which received its impetus from Chamberlin's analysis of selling costs. Nutter's note is critical of the Chamberlin approach to product differentiation and shows that, under quite reasonable assumptions, product differentiation is completely consistent with competitive behavior and traditional utility theory. Demsetz carries this line of attack even further. He utilizes a technique similar to that developed in Buchanan's paper, in which price and quantity produced are allowed to vary simultaneously with selling cost, to show that excess capacity is not a necessary result of monopolistic competition, even if all the assumptions of Chamberlin's model are granted. An analysis of the behavior of multiple-plant firms, as contrasted with the more conventional one-firm-one-plant model, is provided by Patinkin. He suggests that a cartel model is the best approach to understanding the forces at work in imperfectly competitive markets. In addition to its substantive content, Patinkin's article provides a brisk exercise in the use of the geometry of price theory.

The analysis by Fellner is taken from a chapter of his classic work, *Competition Among the Few*. In these pages he gives a summary analysis of the contribution of Heinrich von Stackelberg to oligopoly theory and explains how the technique of the Stackelberg indifference map extends oligopoly analysis into related market structures. Stackelberg introduced the recognition of interdependence into oligopoly analysis and showed that, under some rather restrictive assumptions, chaotic markets usually result if each firm attempts to establish a leadership position. One of the most important recent contributions to oligopoly theory, that of Sylos-Labini, is discussed by Needham. Sylos-Labini showed how firms in an oligopolistic industry might price their output if they wished to discourage entry by new firms. Needham demonstrates that under certain specific assumptions made by Sylos, long-run price cannot exceed average cost by more than an amount which is determined by economies of scale and absolute cost differences between existing firms and potential entrants. The third paper by Alchian explores some recent contributions to the theory of firm behavior in imperfectly competitive markets, including a critical discussion of the contributions of Baumol, Marris, and Williamson. Alchian argues that the utility-maximizing approach has implications consistent with the available evidence regarding managerial behavior.

The papers in Part VI provide some applications of the techniques of price theory to resource allocation. Hirshleifer examines the problem of pricing commodities that are exchanged by the various divisional organizations within a single firm and indicates the pricing policies that would maximize total profit of the corporation as a whole. Eckaus shows how to use the tool of the production function to analyze the problem of structural disequilibrium in underdeveloped areas. He also makes use of the method of linear programming developed in the above paper by Dorfman. Becker ingeniously applies the tools of microeconomics, in particular, the analysis of choice, to determine the optimal level of law enforcement activity in a society. Kessel's theoretical and empirical study applies the model of the discriminating monopolist to explain the pricing of medical services. He indicates how the implications of such a model might be consistent with the observed behavior of physicians and the American Medical Association.

The five papers in Part VII, Microeconomics of Income Distribution, are concerned with a special case of the theory of price: the pricing of factors of production. The articles show that the same principles and tools which explain pricing of final products also explain factor prices. Joan Robinson's essay provides a neat summary of the attempts of economists to answer the following question: If each factor is paid its marginal product, how do we know that we exhaust the total product? This is the famous "adding up" problem of distribution theory, and Mrs. Robinson extends the traditional analysis to the case of imperfect competition. Bronfenbrenner utilizes the tool of indifference curves to explore and interpret the present state of profit theory, from the Knightian formulation to the more recent approaches of Simons and Baumol. Dewey applies similar techniques to clarify and simplify the theory of interest. This note was a precurser of the more detailed exposition later published in his book, *Modern Capital Theory*. The paper by Rottenberg describes the structure of the baseball players' labor market and the rules of that market. He points out the implications of the current rules for resource allocation and indicates that some players receive less than they would be worth in a market unimpaired by the present constraints; in a free market each player would receive the value of his marginal product and the current "exploitation" would not occur. The article by Rees is both an empirical and theoretical approach to the impact of labor unions on the allocation of resources. The author develops a technique for estimating the loss in real output that results from the effect of collective bargaining on the structure of wages and from direct restrictions on output.

The final selections in Part VIII are concerned with general equilibrium, welfare economics, and public goods. Bator's "Simple Analytics of Welfare Maximization" performs a veritable tour de force, because in a relatively few pages it summarizes most of welfare economics within the framework of the static and stationary neoclassical model. Its treatment of such theory is, moreover, nonmathematical. The reader will find this a most helpful review of almost all aspects of microeconomics. The next paper in the volume takes up the question of the nature of costs and explores the famous Pigouvian distinction between private and social costs. Coase's paper, a classic work on the nature of social cost, comes to the rather surprising conclusion that private and social costs are equal under perfect competition. Since the manner in which our legal system assigns liability for damage does not affect private marginal costs of production, it has no effect on the composition of output. Bator's "Anatomy of Market Failure" is a summary exposition of the conditions under which governmental intervention becomes appropriate in the face of "market failure." He shows that unless production functions exhibit certain very specific characteristics (for example, decreasing returns) or if externalities of production and tastes are present, it might be possible to make everyone better off by intervention. Samuelson's classic paper treats private consumption goods and public consumption goods as extreme polar cases in order to provide a neat geometrical treatment of the theory of public expenditure. In the final reading, Buchanan constructs a model to explain the optimal size of membership organizations or "clubs" in which exclusion is possible. Since such organizations involve aspects of "privateness" and "publicness," Buchanan's technique helps to bridge the gap between Samuelson's polar cases of private and public goods.

Contents

Part I

THE NATURE
OF AN ECONOMIC
SYSTEM

1. Social Economic Organization*

FRANK H. KNIGHT

Frank H. Knight (B.S. and A.M., Tennessee, 1913; Ph.D., Cornell, 1916) was born in McLean County, Illinois, in 1885. Most of his academic career has been spent at the University of Chicago, where he is the Morton D. Hall Distinguished Service Professor, Emeritus, of Social Science and Philosophy. Knight is one of the world's leading economists, having made significant contributions to many problems of both economic theory and social philosophy. He is best known for his *Risk, Uncertainty and Profit,* a monumental study of the role of the entrepreneur in economic life. In 1950 he was president of the American Economic Association and in 1957 the recipient of its coveted Francis A. Walker Award, given "not more frequently than once every five years to the living [American] economist who in the judgment of the awarding body has during his career made the greatest contribution to economics."

SOCIAL ECONOMIC ORGANIZATION AND ITS FIVE PRIMARY FUNCTIONS

It is somewhat unusual to begin the treatment of a subject with a warning against attaching too much importance to it; but in the case of economics, such an injunction is quite as much needed as explanation and emphasis of the importance it really has. It is characteristic of the age in which we live to think too much in terms of economics, to see things too predominantly in their economic aspect; and this is especially true of the American

* Reprinted from *The Economic Organization* by Frank H. Knight by permission of Harper & Row, Publishers. Copyright 1933, 1951 by Frank H. Knight, pp. 3–30.

people. There is no more important prerequisite to clear thinking in regard to economics itself than is recognition of its limited place among human interests at large.

Common Definitions of Economics Much Too Broad, though the Economic Conception of Life Is Too Narrow

In modern usage, the term economic has come to be used in a sense which is practically synonymous with intelligent or rational. This is the first and broadest conception of the term, within which we have to find by narrowing it down progressively, a definition which will describe the actual subject-matter of the science of political economy. It is in accord with good linguistic usage to think and speak of the whole problem of living as one of economy, the economical use of time, energy, etc.— *resource* of every sort. Many definitions of economics found in text books fall into this error of including virtually all intelligent behavior. One writer has actually given as his definition of economics the "science of rational activity." Others find its subject matter is "man's activity in making a living," or "the ordinary business of life." Such definitions come too near to saying that economics is the science of things generally, of everything that men are for practical reasons interested in. Such a definition is useless and misleading. It is necessary to devote a little time to making clear the restrictions which mark off the modestly limited domain of economic science within the inclusive sphere of knowledge as a whole.

In the first place, it should be understood that economizing, even in this broad sense of rational activity, or the intelligent use of given means in achieving given ends, does not include all human interests, and that the kind of knowledge on which such activity rests does not exhaust the field of human knowledge. It is, as we have said, one of the errors, not to say vices, of an age in which the progress of natural science and the triumphs of its application to life have engrossed men's attention, to look upon life too exclusively under this aspect of scientific rationality. It is requisite to a proper orientation to economic science itself as well as necessary to a sound philosophy of life, to see clearly that life must be more than economics, or rational conduct, or the intelligent accurate manipulation of materials and use of power in achieving results. Such a view is too narrow. It implies that the results to be achieved are to be taken for granted, whereas in fact the results themselves are often quite as much in question as the means and procedures for achieving results. Living intelligently includes more than the intelligent use of means in realizing ends; it is fully as important to select the ends intelligently, for intelligent action directed toward wrong ends only makes evil greater and more certain. One must have intelligent tastes, and intelligent opinions on many things which do not directly relate to conduct at all. Not only are the objectives of action in fact a practical problem, as well as the means of achievement, but intelligent discussion of the means cannot be separated from the discussion of the ends.

Living is an art: and art is more than a matter of a scientific technique, and the richness and value of life are largely bound up in the "more." In its reaction from the futility of medievalism and mystical speculation, the modern Western world has gone far to the other extreme. It loses much of the value of life through neglect of the imponderables and incommensurables, and gets into a false conception of the character of social and individual problems. Our thinking about life-values runs too much in terms of material prerequisites and costs. It is an exaggeration which may be useful to say that economic goods as a class are predominantly "necessary" rather than truly valuable. The importance of economic provision is chiefly that of a prerequisite to the enjoyment of the free goods of the world, the beauty of the natural scene, the intercourse of friends in "aimless" camaraderie, the appreciation and creation of art, discovery of truth and communion with one's own inner being and the Nature of Things. Civilization should look forward to a day when the material product of industrial activity shall become rather its by-product, and its primary significance shall be that of a sphere for creative self-expression and the development of a higher type of individual and of human fellowship. It ought to be the first aim of economic policy to reduce the importance of economic policy in life as a whole. So it ought to be the highest objective in the study of economics to hasten the day when the study and the practice of economy will recede into the background of men's thoughts, when food and shelter, and all provision for physical needs, can be taken for granted without serious thought, when "production" and "consumption" and "distribution" shall cease from troubling and pass below the threshold of consciousness and the effort and planning of the mass of mankind may be mainly devoted to problems of beauty, truth, right human relations and cultural growth.

The Actual Subject
Matter of Economics

What is discussed in the science of economics includes a relatively small fraction of the economic side of life taken in the broad sense. It has nothing to do with the concrete processes of producing or distributing goods, or using goods to satisfy wants. The study of these matters comes under the head of technology, including engineering, business management, and home economics. Economics deals with the *social organization* of economic activity. In practice its scope is much narrower still; there are many ways in which economic activity may be socially organized, but the predominant method in modern nations is the price system, or free enterprise. Consequently it is the structure and working of the system of free enterprise which constitutes the principal topic of discussion in a treatise on economics.

The Meaning
of Organization

Everyone is familiar with the idea of division of labor—by which is really meant specialization of labor—and many econo-

mists have taken it as their point of departure in expounding the science of economics. This was the procedure of Adam Smith, for example, whose book, *The Wealth of Nations*, published in the year 1776, ranks as the first modern treatise on economics.

Modern economic society is often compared with a living body or "organism" and the comparison is certainly suggestive. The essential similarity and the fundamental idea for our purpose is precisely that of division of labor or specialization. But the expression "division" of labor, does not tell us enough. The idea is rather division into different *kinds* of labor. A number of men hoeing in a field or nailing shingles on a roof exemplify "division" of labor, but not organization. The problems of organization arise only when *different things are being done*, in the furtherance of a *common end*, and in definite relations to each other, i.e., in *coordination*. A single man in raising a crop or building a house shows division of labor in another sense, since he does many different things, but this is not yet organization in the sense with which we are concerned. The human body shows organization in the true sense, since the various "organs" not only perform different functions, but must all act in a substantially continuous manner and in proper adjustment to each other. Again, organization must be distinguished from cooperation; it involves cooperation, but more. If a group of men lift a stone which is too heavy for one to move alone, they cooperate, and increase their power by cooperation; their action is cooperative, but they are not organized, since they are all doing the same thing.

It is obvious enough that the economic or living-making activities of the modern world are very elaborately organized. We need not pause to comment on the number of persons who have contributed, and in what different ways, in supplying the wants of the humblest citizen today. The authorities of the federal census prepare a catalogue or classification of occupations which lists many thousands of these economic functions for the working population of the United States alone and which yet makes no pretense of distinguishing all specialized functions. For instance, farm laborers are classed together though different individuals work at the production of a wide variety of crops. It is evident also that the accomplishment of the ultimate purpose of it all, the provision for the needs and desires of the people, depends upon these various operations being carried on with a fair degree of continuity and tolerable co-ordination. The problem of organization, which sets the problem of economic science, deals with the concrete means or mechanism for dividing the general function of making a living for the people into parts and bringing about the performance of these parts in due proportion and harmony.

More specifically, it is a problem of the social machinery for accomplishing *five fairly distinct functions*. Every system of organization must perform these tasks, and it is its success or failure in discharging these functions which determines its value as a system. Back of the study of economics is the practical need of making the organization better, and we can hope for success in this task only if we proceed to it intelligently, which is to say on the basis of an understanding of the nature of the work which a system of organization has to perform, and of the alternatives open in the way of possible types of organization machinery.

THE FIVE MAIN FUNCTIONS OF AN ECONOMIC SYSTEM

The general task of organizing the economic activity of society may be divided into a number of fundamental functions. These are in fact very much inter-connected and overlapping, but the distinction is useful as an aid to discussing the existing economic order both descriptively and critically, its structure as well as its workings. These functions fall into a more or less logical sequence. The first is to decide what is to be done, that is, what goods and services are to be produced, and in what proportions. It is the function of setting standards, of establishing a social scale of values, or the function of social choice; the second is the function of organizing production, in the narrow sense, of getting done the things settled upon as most worth doing; third is distribution, the apportioning of the product among the members of society; the fourth is really a group of functions having to do with maintaining and improving the social structure, or promoting social progress.

1. The Function of Fixing Standards; The Notion of Efficiency

In a world where organizations were absent, where each individual carried on his life activities in isolation and independence of all others, the matter of standards would be simply a matter of individual choice. But when the production of wealth is socialized, there has to be a *social* decision as to the relative importance of different uses of productive power, as to which wants are to be satisfied and which left unsatisfied or to what extent any one is to be satisfied at the expense of any other. In the case of an individual, choice need be made only among his own wants; but in a social system, the wants of different individuals also come into conflict. As far as this is a quantitative question merely, of how far the wants of one are to be gratified at the expense of the wants of another, or left ungratified in favor of another, the problem is one of *distribution*, and will be noticed under another heading (the third function). But to a large and increasing extent, society finds it necessary or advisable further to regulate the individual's regulation of his own want-satisfaction, to enforce a community standard of living. As a matter of fact, these two problems are closely interlaced, the question of *whose* wants and that of *which* wants are to be given preference, and in what measure. It is important to observe that they are largely the same question. The difference in the "amount" consumed by different persons is not mainly a difference in the amounts of the same commodities; different persons consume different things, which are quantitatively compared only through the agency of the value scale itself. Nevertheless there seems to be ample justification for a logical separation of the questions of what is to be produced from that of who is to get the product, and for discussing separately the relations between the two phases of organization.

A point of fundamental importance in connection with the question of standards is that of the origin or ultimate source of wants. The system of social organization does more than reduce individual values to a common denominator or scale of equivalence. In large part the individual wants themselves are *created* by social intercourse, and their character is also largely dependent upon the form of organization of the economic system upon which they are dependent for their gratification. The workings of the economic organization in this connection form a problem too large and complex to be discussed at any length in a small book like this one. Indeed, the subject of wants is not only vast in scope but apparently cannot be reduced to scientific terms, except within rather narrow limits, falling rather in the field of art. The scientific discussion of economics has to be restricted in the main to the analysis of the organization of want-satisfaction. In the science of economics the wants are

largely taken for granted as facts of the time and place, and the discussion of their origin and formation is left for the most part to the distinct studies of social psychology and cultural anthropology.[1]

The problem of standards or values occupies a key position in Economics. The practical objective of economics, it must be kept in mind, is that of improving the social organization and increasing its efficiency. There is a common misconception that it is possible to measure or discuss efficiency in purely physical terms. The first principles of physics or engineering science teach that this is not true, that the term efficiency involves the idea of value, and some measure of value as well. It is perhaps the most important principle of physical science that neither matter nor energy can be created or destroyed, that whatever goes into any process must come out in some form, and hence as a mere matter of physical quantity, the efficiency of all operations would equal one hundred per cent. The correct definition of efficiency is the ratio, not between "output" and "input" but between *useful* output and total output or input. Hence efficiency, even in the simplest energy transformation, is meaningless without a measure of usefulness or value. In any attempt to understand economic efficiency, the notion of value is more obviously crucial since most economic problems are concerned with a number of kinds both of outlay and of return, and there is no conceivable way of making comparisons without first reducing all the factors to terms of a common measure. It will appear in due course that the science of economics is largely taken up with description and analysis of the process by which this common denominator of

---

[1] The deliberate creation or changing of wants for specific commodities as by advertising, is to some extent an exception, but in the main such activities must be regarded as creating a *knowledge of* certain *means* of satisfying wants rather than as changing ultimate *wants*.

things consumed and produced by the economic system is arrived at, that is, with the *problem of measuring values.*

2. The Function of Organizing Production

The second step, logically speaking, after the ranking and grading of the uses to which productive power may be put, is that of actually putting them to use in accordance with the scale of values thus established. From a social point of view, this process may be viewed under two aspects, (a) the assignment or *allocation* of the available productive forces and materials among the various lines of industry, and (b) the effective *coordination* of the various means of production in each industry into such groupings as will produce the greatest result. The second of these tasks properly belongs to technological rather than to economic science, and is treated in economics only with reference to the interrelations between the organization of society as a whole and the internal organization of the industries.

3. The Function of Distribution

This third function would not exist at all in an unorganized world. Each individual, acting independently of all others, would simply consume what he produced. But where production is socialized, the separate productive contribution of one participant in the process cannot be directly identified or separated. It is apparent that a modern factory operative, say one who spends all his time putting buttons on shoes or nailing the covers on packing cases, cannot live on his own product, physically interpreted. When we further consider that different individuals contribute to production in fundamentally different ways, many by furnishing land or other "natural resources" or material equipment or money or managerial or supervisory services, or by selling goods, and in other ways which make

no identifiable physical change in any product, it is manifest that if everyone is to get a living out of the process some *social mechanism* of distribution is called for.

In this connection should be recalled the close relation between distribution and the control of production. The decision as to what to produce is closely bound up with the decision for whom to produce. There is also a close relation between the third function and the second. In our social system distribution is the chief agency relied upon to control production and stimulate efficiency. Ours is a system of "private property," "free competition" and "contract." This means that every productive resource or agent, including labor power, typically "belongs" to some person who is free within the legal conditions of marketing, to get what he can out of its use. It is assumed, and the course of the argument will show at length why it is true, that there is in some effective sense a real positive connection between the productive contribution made by any productive agent and the remuneration which its "owner" can secure for its use. Hence this remuneration (a distributive share) and the wish to make it as large as possible, constitute the chief reliance of society for an incentive to place the agency into use in the general productive system in such a way as to make it as productive as possible. The strongest argument in favor of such a system as ours is the contention that this direct, selfish motive is the only dependable method, or at least the best method, for guaranteeing that productive forces will be organized and worked efficiently. The argument assumes that in spite of the difficulty above referred to of identifying the particular contribution to the social product made by any person or piece of property, it is possible to separate it out, and measure it, in terms of value and that the distributive system does this with accuracy enough to make remunerations vary in accord with product. If this were not true in the main, remuneration could not really afford an incentive to productive efficiency, and an economic order based on individualism would not function.

4. Economic Maintenance and Progress

There is no moral connotation in the term progress; it refers to any persistent cumulative change, whether regarded as good or bad. The principal forms of economic progress include, (1) growth of population and any cumulative change in its composition or education which affects either its productive powers or its wants; (2) the accumulation of material aids to production or "capital" of all kinds, including such permanent sources of satisfaction as newly discovered natural resources and also works of art;[2] (3) improvements in technical processes or changes in the form of business organization. It is to be noted especially that progress has two sorts of significance for the economic organization. First, it is one of the products or values created by the latter, at a cost; i.e., it involves using productive power for this purpose and sacrificing its use for other purposes; and second, it affects and changes the character of the economic system itself and the conditions under which the system works.

This fourth function of organization, especially the provision for progress, cuts across all the other three. It is a matter of standards or values to decide how much progress society can afford or cares to have at the cost of sacrificing present values, and what forms it shall take; it is a matter of productive organization to utilize the determined share of available productive power to bring about progress in the amount and of the kinds decided upon, and it is a problem of distribution to apportion the burdens and benefits of progress among

[2] Destruction and exhaustion of resources not replaced is also a progressive change.

the members of society. We may be reminded also that it is true of progress as of all other lines of human action that it comes within the field of economics just in so far as it is related to the organized system of producing and distributing the means of want-satisfaction.

The first three of these functions (or four, since No. 2 is really double, involving two aspects) are relatively "short-time" in character. They are all aspects of the general problem of an economic society working under "given conditions," in contrast with the fourth function which relates to the problem of improving the given conditions through the course of time. The first three therefore make up the problems of what may be called the "stationary economy." If society either could not or did not try to grow and progress and make improvements, its economic problem would be entirely within this field. But since economic societies do in fact face problems of growth and improvement, and make some effort to solve them intelligently, we have to add the fourth function, or group of functions. Such problems are frequently referred to under the head of "dynamic" economics; for reasons which cannot be given in detail here, this is a seriously misleading use of language, and they should be called simply problems of progress or historical problems.

The "given conditions" of the stationary economy are included under the three heads of *resources, wants,* and *technology,* which may be subdivided and classified in more elaborate ways. The separation is based on the plain and simple fact that with reference to social calculations and plans which look ahead only a few years, these factors, resources, wants and the technological system will not change enough to affect the argument or plans seriously. But looking ahead over historical time they do change, to an indefinite extent, and the production and guidance of changes in them becomes the dominant character of the social economic problem. In the "short-run" (of a few years), however, the problem is to utilize in the best way the existing resources and technology in the satisfaction of existing wants.

A Fifth Function: To Adjust Consumption to Production within Very Short Periods

For completeness, this survey of functions should point out that within *very short* periods society faces still another set of "given conditions," hence still another type of problem, and in consequence its economic organization has still another task or function to perform, though this fifth function is rarely distinguished sharply from those of the "stationary economy" point of view. From this latter point of view, the problem is to adjust production to consumption under the given conditions. But in many cases, production cannot be adjusted quickly, while demand conditions do change rapidly; and in addition, production in many fields is subject to fluctuations from causes beyond control. In consequence, the supply of many commodities is fixed for considerable periods of time, on a level more or less divergent from the best possible adjustment to existing conditions of demand. The supply on hand is of course the result of productive operations in the past, and has to suffice until it can be changed. In agriculture this is conspicuously true. The crop of a given year has to last until the next year's crop is produced (except in so far as other parts of the world having different crop seasons can be drawn upon). In the case of manufactured goods, production is not definitely periodic, but it is still true that the rate of production frequently cannot be changed in a short time, to meet changes in demand, at least not without enormous cost.

It follows that over short periods consumption has to be controlled and distributed with reference to an existing supply or current rate of production, at the same time that adjustment of production to consumption requirements is being made as rapidly as practicable. The existing supply of wheat or potatoes, for example, must be distributed (a) over the season for which it has to suffice and (b) among the different consumers and their different needs. Thus there is a fifth function of organization, the opposite in a sense, of number two in the four above discussed, namely the short-run adjustment of consumption to past or current production.[3]

ADVANTAGES AND DISADVANTAGES OF ORGANIZED ACTION

The Reasons for Organizing Activity

As previously remarked, a high degree of organization in human activity is a fairly recent development in the world's history, and is still restricted mainly to what we call the European peoples or cultures. The urge behind its development can be stated in the single word *efficiency*. The object of industrial activity is to utilize an available fund of productive agencies and resources in making the goods and services with which people satisfy their wants. Organized effort enables a social group to produce more of the means of want-satisfaction than it could by working as individuals. During the course of history, the possibility of increased efficiency has led to an ever greater degree of specialization, which in turn has constantly called for a more elaborate and effective mechanism of coordination and control, just as the higher animals require an enormously more complex nervous and circulatory system than the lower. It will be worth while to carry the analysis a little beyond the general notion of efficiency and see some of the reasons why specialized effort yields larger or better results. We must then turn to the other side

[3] It is rather typical of economic phenomena that cause and effect relations are apt to run in opposite directions in the short-run and the long-run. This is a common source of difficulty in the reasoning, as will appear more fully in the treatment of the forces which fix prices.

of the picture and note some of the disadvantages of organization.

The Gains from Specialization[4]

The largest gain which the higher animals secure in comparison with lower, less organized forms, arises from the adaptation of structure to function. In the most primitive animals the same kind of tissue has to perform all the divergent functions of locomotion, seizing and ingestion of food, digestion, assimilation, excretion of waste and reproduction, while in the mammalian body the specialization of tissues and organs for the various functions and the increased efficiency with which all are consequently performed, are too evident to need extended comment. Some social insects produce physically divergent types of individuals adapted by structure to perform different functions. In the familiar case of the bees, the bulk of the community is made up of "workers" and the reproductive function is specialized in the queens and drones. Certain species of ants and termites present a very complex social structure containing a dozen or more structurally specialized types of individuals. One of the most interesting facts in regard to human society is the absence of definite structural specialization of individuals. Human organization is an artificial thing, a culture product. Natural differences undoubtedly exist among human beings, and are taken advantage of, more or less, in fitting individuals to specialized functions; but the differences seem to be accidental, and unpredictable. Certainly human beings do not become fused into a super-organism in the manner of the cells in an animal body. It is in fact a matter of the greatest uncertainty and one of the most disputed

questions in the whole field of knowledge, as to how far observed differences in kinds and degrees of capacity are innate and how far they are the result of "nurture" and the subtle influences of environment and social suggestion. The tendency of scientific study at the present time is to place more and more emphasis on the environment and less upon congenital structure. In any case, human differences are not so definitely transmitted by inheritance as to be predictable in advance; they have to be discovered and developed and the individual fitted to his place in the system by some artificial means. There is no mechanical solution of the human social problem, as in the case of the animal organism or even of insect societies; human beings have to form themselves into an organization as well as to control and operate it when constructed.

1. Utilization of Natural Aptitudes; Especially Those of Leaders and Followers However, we are safe in asserting that there are some innate individual differences in human capacities and aptitudes, and the first in the list of gains from organization results from taking advantage of them. One social problem is to discover such differences and utilize them as far as possible. They can never be predicted with any certainty before the birth of the individual, in fact they cannot usually be discerned at any time in life from clear external marks; and in the course of the development of the individual they become so largely overlaid with acquired traits that they can never be separated from the latter. The most important natural differences of which we can be reasonably sure are those of physical stature and dexterity and (with much less certainty) of general mental activity. The most important differentiation in function, or division of labor, between individuals is the separation between direction and execution, or the specialization of *leadership*. It may well be true that able leaders are in general also more competent workers or

---

[4] It will be recalled that we are using the word "specialization" instead of the familiar "division of labor," not only is labor divided, but it is differentiated and co-ordinated, and the other elements or factors in production are likewise "specialized"—often more extensively and vitally than the human factor.

operatives, but the gain from superior direction is so much more important than that from superior concrete performance that undoubtedly the largest single source of the increased efficiency through organization results from having work planned and directed by the exceptionally capable individuals, while the mass of the people follow instructions.

2. Development and Utilization of Acquired Skill and Acquired Knowledge The principal quality in man which gives him superiority over the animals is his ability to learn, including learning to know and learning to do. But even in man this capacity is exceedingly limited in scope in comparison with the whole range of acquired human knowledge and activity, and a large part of the gain from organizing activity comes from the increase in the efficiency of learning which is connected with reducing the field in which an individual must exercise his learning ability. Even the specialization of leadership undoubtedly rests as much upon acquired as upon innate differences. In truth, the fundamental innate difference among men is in the capacity to learn itself. In other fields than leadership—fields of specialized knowledge and skill in the narrower sense—it is still more clearly impossible to separate the factor of innate capacity from that of acquired powers, and still more evident that the innate capacity itself is a capacity to learn rather than directly to perform. Even in the case of genius, what is inherited is an extraordinary capacity to learn, or learn to do, certain things, and the amount of actual specialization in the original bent is highly uncertain. In modern machine industry, where the operative is restricted to repetition of a few simple movements, an incredible increase of speed as compared with that of an untrained worker may be achieved in a short space of time. The operations generally involve movements very different from any which are natural to man as an animal, movements such as setting type, playing a musical instrument, or sorting mail matter

into boxes; but they can be learned by any normal person, and when mastered they make possible the employment of a technology vastly more efficient than that of primitive industry. (See No. 5 below.)

3. Changing Pieces of Work Cheaper, Within Limits, Than Changing Jobs The saving of time and effort in changing from one operation to another is the third gain from specialization. It is true that if a man performs the same operation repeatedly, he must change from one object, or piece of work, to another. But by the use of mechanical conveyers, scientific routing and the like, it is found that, *within limits,* the process of bringing to the workman a procession of shoes, automobile cylinders, or hog carcasses is far less costly than having him make the changes in position, changes in tools used, etc., involved in performing successively on any one of them the various operations necessary to complete the making of a product, as was done under old handicraft conditions. This gain is evidently rather closely connected with that arising from specialized skill. It is to be especially emphasized, because so commonly overlooked, that in this connection there are offsetting costs, which only within limits are exceeded by the gains. Not only must the cost of changing jobs be compared with the cost of changing pieces of work as within a given factory. If each man completed a product, the workers would not have to be brought together into factories at all, a feature which also involves large costs, and neither would the materials have to be assembled from such a vast area or the product distributed back over a market perhaps nation-wide or even world-wide in extent. The costs of bringing together vast quantities of materials and of distributing the product tend in fact to offset very considerably the gains of large scale production. These costs include not merely actual transportation, but marketing costs in the form of profits, risks and losses from inaccurate forecasting of demand, idleness due to over-production, storage, insurance and the like. The public has been educated by apologists for monopoly to over-estimate seriously the real gains from large-scale factory methods; these offsetting losses are rarely appreciated to the full.

4. Natural Advantages in the Case of "Natural Resources" However uncertain we may be as to the innate differences in men, there can be no question that the natural resources of different regions are suited to widely divergent employments. In such extreme cases as mineral deposits, for example, specialization to regions is absolute, since minerals can only be extracted where they exist, and this is quite commonly in places where any other industry is virtually out of the question. Also, "geographical" or "territorial" specialization is almost a physical necessity as between different climatic zones. Other industries may be carried on in different regions, but usually some locations offer greater or lesser advantages over others, which may or may not be sufficient to offset transportation costs and other costs of specialization. The question of political interference with territorial specialization, through "tariffs," bounties, subsidies and the like, has formed an important political issue in all modern nations. Such measures practically always reduce the gains from specialization and the arguments used to support them are fallacious from a purely economic point of view. In some cases a political unit can profit at the expense of others, but this is rarely possible and still more rarely achieved by the policies adopted, and is always to the disadvantage of the world as a whole.

5. Artificial Specialization of Material Agents. Division of Operations Leads to Invention and Use of Machinery Even natural resources are never used in their natural state. The process of developing and adapting them to particular uses is generally more or less of a specializing process and may be compared to the "education" of a human being. When we turn to the forms of produc-

tive equipment usually classed as artificial —tools, machines, buildings and the like, it is evident that specialization goes very far indeed. A tool or machine is usually much more specialized than a human being can ever be, and its efficiency in a particular task is connected with the degree of its specialization. Many things can be done, after a fashion, with a hammer; only one with an automatic printing-press or a watch-screw machine; but that one thing is done with wonderful precision and speed. Perhaps the very largest single source of gain from the specialization of labor is that it makes possible the development and use of machinery, the effectiveness of which is almost entirely a matter of its specialization to limited and relatively simple operations.

6. Minor Technical Gains The gains from natural and artificial adaptation of men and things to tasks, plus that due to changing pieces of work instead of tasks (our No. 3 above) do not exhaust the economies of specialization. There is an economy in coordination due to the fact that a specialized worker need have access only to the tools used for the operations he continuously performs, and not to all those used in making the article. This is practically rather an incidental matter, subordinate to the specialization of equipment. In primitive industry little is invested in tools, and a large investment carries with it specialization of both workers and equipment. We may note also as a final consideration in connection with this whole subject, that in many cases any sort of effective work involves the performance of different operations simultaneously, which of course necessitates specialization.

Social Costs of Specialization

All the gains from specialization are summed up in the one word, *efficiency;* it enables us to get more goods, or better; its advantages are *instrumental.* On the other hand, specialization in itself, is an evil, measured by generally accepted human ideals. It gives us more products, but in its effects on human beings as such it is certainly bad in some respects and in others questionable. In the nature of the case[5] it means a narrowing of the personality; we like to see people of all-around, well-developed powers and capacities. In extreme instances, such as the monotonous work of machine-tending, or repetitive movements at a machine-forced pace, it may be ruinous to health and maddening to the spirit. In this connection it is especially significant that the most important source of gain also involves the most important human cost. The specialization of leadership means that the masses of the people work under conditions which tend to suppress initiative and independence, to develop servility as well as narrowness and in general to dehumanize them.

Technical Costs of Organization

We have already mentioned the fact that there is another side to the technical advantages of specialization, namely the costs of assembly and distribution. This aspect of the situation is hinted at in the famous saying of Adam Smith that the division of labor is limited by the extent of the market, that is, really, by distribution costs. To these we must add the broader category of costs of organization in general. The existing social organization is called an "automatic" system, and in some respects it is such. But any system of bringing large numbers of people into intercommunication and coordinating their activities must involve enormous costs in actual human and physical energy. Organizations are like water-drops, or snow-balls or

stones, or any large mass; the larger they are the more easily they are broken into pieces, the larger *in proportion* is the amount of energy that must be consumed in merely holding them together. The larger the army the bigger the proportion of officers, and the more unwieldly the aggregate, even then. The losses from this source in the modern world are stupendous; the number of persons, and still more the amount of brain power, which must be entirely taken up with passing on directions and keeping track of what is being done and "oiling the machinery" in one way and another is truly appalling. And the opportunity for persons to secure private gain by dislocating the organization machinery leads to still greater waste and loss.

Interdependence

A final important disadvantage of organized production and distribution is the resulting interdependence of persons and groups. This interdependence is supposed to be mutual, in the long run; but for the time being, the persons who perform such functions as coal mining and transportation are very much more necessary to, say, school teachers or farmers than the latter are to them. Strikes or failures to function due to accidental causes produce a kind of suffering unknown in unorganized society, or even in small groups within which the pressure of public opinion is much more powerful. A phase of this interdependence manifests itself acutely in the ebb and flow of prosperity, particularly the recurrence of business crises bringing widespread distress.

TYPES OF SOCIAL ORGANIZATION ECONOMICS AND POLITICS

Social Organization and Biological Organism: Analogy and Contrast

As an introduction to the survey and classification of forms of social organization it will be useful to revert briefly to

---

[5] Statements of this kind need a good deal of interpretation. In reality everything depends on the alternative system used as a basis of comparison. The idyllic system of universal craftsmanship certainly never existed historically; perhaps it could not exist; but we think we can imagine its existence.

the comparison between economic society and the human body—especially to emphasize the fundamental difference. In this comparison the human individual is said to correspond to the "cell," the ultimate unit of biological structure. Individuals, like the cells in an animal body, are aggregated into "tissues" and "organs," which carry on the elementary life functions, seizing nourishment, transforming it into a condition suitable for use or digestion, distribution, disposal of waste, etc. The analogy is indeed obvious, and no doubt useful within limits, if it is kept on the level of analogy and not pressed too far. However, reasoning from analogy is always dangerous, and the conception of the "social organism" has probably produced more confusion than enlightenment. The differences between society and an animal organism are practically more important than the similarities, for it is in connection with the differences that the social problems arise.

The division of labor between the organs of the body is based on an innate differentiation of physical structure, and the coordination of their activities is automatic and mechanical. The cells or tissues do not choose what positions they will take up or what functions they will perform, nor can they change from one position or function to another. They do not meet with any of the problems which make the study of human organization a practical concern; they have no separate interests which may conflict with each other or with those of the body as a whole, and there can be no competition among them in any but a figurative sense.

Human society is the opposite of all this. Definite machinery has to be deliberately designed to reconcile or compromise between the conflicting interests of its members, who are separate purposive units; the organization as a whole has no value in itself or purpose of its own, according to the dominant theory of democracy at least,

but exists solely to promote the interests of its members. In the same way, as we have seen, planned provision must be made in human society for working out the division of labor, assigning the separate tasks to the various persons and apportioning productive equipment among them, for distributing the fruits of the activity, and even for determining the character of its own future life and growth.[6]

Types of Organization

1. "Status" and Tradition, or the Caste System The nearest approach to a mechanical division and coordination of activity which is reached or can be conceived of in human society would be a universal system of *status* or "caste." It is possible to imagine a social order in which elaborate specialization of activities is achieved on a purely customary basis, and some approximation to such an ideal is found in the caste system of India. We can suppose that rigid social custom might fix all the details of the division of occupations and technique of production, the assignment of individuals to their tasks being determined by birth, while tradition would also set the details of the standard of living for everyone. Such a society would have to be nearly unprogressive, though slow change in accordance with unconscious historical forces is compatible with the hypothesis.

There are two reasons for ascribing considerable theoretical importance to caste as a system of organization. It serves to bring out by contrast the characteristics of the modern Western system based on property and competition, a contrast made famous by Sir Henry Maine's theory that the transition from a régime of status to one of contract is a fundamental historical law. In the second place there is a large element of status in the freest society; so-

[6] See also the discussion of insect societies (above p. 11) to which the observations made in regard to the animal organism will largely apply though in a lesser degree.

cial position, character of work and standard of living are determined even in America today, perhaps nearly as much by the "accident" of birth as by conscious or unconscious selection in accord with innate personal traits. Moreover, any society based on the natural family as a unit tends toward progressively greater rigidity of stratification. With the passing of the frontier and the special conditions of a new country, rapid change in this direction has come to be a conspicuous feature of American life, though political and social motives have led us to set up opposing forces such as free education.

2. The Autocratic or Militaristic System
The first step away from a caste system in the direction of increasing freedom is represented by a centralized, autocratic system most briefly described by comparing it with the organization of an army. In such a social order, worked out to logical completeness, the whole structure of society, the division of labor, determination of policies, and allocation of burdens and benefits, would be dictated by an absolute monarch. The individual need not be asked what he wants or thinks good for him in the way of either his consumption or his share in production. The idea of organization itself might be worked out to any degree of intricacy, and coordination might indeed be highly effective. In practice, such a system would have to contain a large element of caste, unless the family were abolished entirely, as in Plato's scheme for an ideal republic. The organizing principle in an autocratic system is personal authority resting upon "divine," or prescriptive, right.

It is to be observed that this principle, while theoretically reduced to a minimum in modern society, is actually, like that of tradition and caste, very much in evidence. The exercise of "authority," while limited in degree, is as real as either "free" exchange or persuasion, within the family,

in the internal organization of business units and in the "democratic" system of government itself. In an autocratic system worked out to ideal perfection, the population as well as all material goods would be the *property* of the monarch; the political and economic systems, as we habitually understand the terms today, would be completely fused, the ideas of sovereignty and property identified. A picture of such a social order may be found in the story of Joseph in Egypt, in the book of Genesis, after first the chattels of the people and then their persons were turned over to Pharaoh in exchange for the grain stored up by Joseph against the lean years. The theory of medieval European feudalism may be regarded as a combination of the principles of caste and of autocracy. This means that under feudalism also, there is no separation between the economic and political aspects of the social organization. The contrast in meaning between the two in the modern world will presently be looked into.

3. Anarchism as a Possible System In the third type of organization mechanism to be considered, we swing to the extreme opposite of the two preceding, from rigorous control by tradition or arbitrary authority to absolute freedom, or purely voluntary association. Whether such a system is possible, may well be doubted, as most of the world does doubt; but it is at least conceivable, and many cultivated and noble minds have, as is well known, advocated attempting it as a practical program. The idea is simple enough; it is contended that if inequality and all hope or thought of exploiting or exercising authority over other men were abolished, people might agree voluntarily as to what were best to be done in the various contingencies of social life and the best method for doing it, and proceed accordingly, without any giving or taking of orders, or any threat of compulsion or restraint by force. It is not necessary to suppose that everyone would have to be all-knowing in regard to every sort of question. It is fully consistent with the theory of anarchy to have recourse to expert opinion; it must be assumed only that the experts would be able to agree, or that the mass of people would agree on which expert to recognize and follow. The theorists of philosophic anarchism who have attracted serious attention assign a large rôle to custom and the force of social opinion. There is no doubt that custom has in fact played the leading part in both originating and enforcing laws, especially in early times. But the case for anarchism in the sense of voluntary agreement through rational deliberation—that is, for this system as opposed to a caste and custom organization—is much less plausible. Apparently insuperable difficulties stand in the way of the elimination of compulsion in an intricate machine civilization subject to the stresses of rapid material progress.

4. Democracy or Democratic Socialism The two systems remaining to be considered represent combinations of or compromises between systems already named. The first, democratic socialism, is a compromise between the authoritarian and the anarchistic. The nearest approach to the freedom of anarchy which we even theoretically reach on any extended scale is the rule of the majority. In its main structural features a society organized entirely on this principle would resemble the autocratic, authoritarian system. The difference is that the controlling authority, instead of being an absolute autocrat, would itself be under the control of "public opinion," that is, the will of the majority of the citizens, expressed through some "political" apparatus. Again, the economic and political organizations would be fused and identified. This is the type of social structure advocated in the main by persons calling themselves "socialists" though by no means

to the exclusion of other types of organization machinery, especially that of free bargaining. Custom could not of course be excluded in any case, and competitive characteristics would undoubtedly appear, since few socialists would absolutely prohibit market dealings. The exercise of personal authority—beyond that involved in the majority taking precedence over the minority in cases of disagreement as to policy—would be reduced to the minimum. It is hardly necessary to mention the fact that the activities of modern societies are to a considerable and increasing extent organized "socialistically," that an increasing fraction of their activities are carried on under the mandatory direction of agencies selected by majorities and as far as practicable made subject to the will of the majority. Examples are the postal system, the schools, streets and highways, the central banks and an increasing proportion of public utility services.

5. The Exchange System The last type of organization machinery to be distinguished is the one especially characteristic of modern Western nations, in which the whole system is worked out and controlled through exchange in an impersonal competitive market. It is variously referred to as the competitive system, the capitalistic system, the system of private property and free exchange, individual exchange cooperation, and so on. Its most interesting feature is that it is automatic and unconscious; no one plans or ever planned it out, no one assigns the participants their rôles or directs their functions. Each person in such a system seeks his own satisfaction without thought of the structure of society or its interests; and the mere mechanical interaction of such self-seeking units organizes them into an elaborate system and controls and coordinates their activities so that each is continuously supplied with the fruits of the labor of one vast and unknown multitude in return for performing some service for another multitude also large and unknown to him. Although the actuality diverges in many respects from such a simple idealized description, the results which are in fact achieved by this method are truly wonderful. Like the other systems described, it does not exist and can hardly be thought of as existing in a pure form. But so large a part of the ordinary work of the modern world is organized in this way that such expressions as "the present social system" or the "existing economic order," are commonly understood to refer to the organization of provision for the means of life through buying and selling.

Two Sub-types
of Exchange Organization

(A) *Handicraft and* (B) *Free Enterprise* The first step in the description of the free exchange system must be to distinguish between two forms of it which differ in fundamental respects. That would be in the proper sense an exchange system or society, in which each individual produced a single commodity and exchanged his surplus of this, directly or through the medium of money, for the various other things required for his livelihood. Some approximation to this system existed in the handicraft organization of the medieval towns, and of course the farmers and a few city craftsmen of today typically produce concrete things to sell. We call this a "handicraft" system.

But such is by no means the characteristic form of modern economic organization. In modern industry in its most developed form no individual or small group can be said to "produce" anything. As it is sometimes put, we have gone beyond division of occupations to the division or subdivision of tasks. Typically, each individual merely performs some operative detail in the making of a commodity, or furnishes to some productive organization a part of the natural resources or capital it employs. But

this difference in technology, as compared with a system where each person makes an entire article, is not so important as the difference in the personal relations, in the system of organization itself. In a handicraft system each one lives by producing and selling goods, and generally owns the material upon which he works and the article he makes when it is finished, as well as his shop or work place—most naturally in his home—and the tools or equipment used in performing his work.

In the modern free enterprise system, as exemplified in the large-scale industries, the relation of the individual to the system is of a quite different sort. As the worker produces nothing and owns nothing, he can exchange nothing, so far as want-satisfying goods are concerned. The individual in fact gets his living, not by selling and buying or exchanging *goods*, but by selling *productive services* for *money* and buying with the money the *goods* which he uses. And of course he does not carry out this exchange with other individuals, since they are in the same situation as himself, but typically with *business units*.

A business unit, or enterprise, is made up of individuals (among whom the man who sells to or buys from it may himself be included) but is distinct from these individuals and constitutes a fictitious person, company, a firm or typically a corporation. Production is now commonly carried on by such units. They are, of course, controlled by natural persons, but these "officers" act for the organization and not as individuals. Various separate persons (possibly with other business units as intermediaries) own and ultimately control any one business unit. The business unit itself partly owns but largely hires or leases from individuals (in some cases again indirectly) the productive power with which it operates, including the services of human beings and those of "property," natural and artificial.

It is a fact familiar to every reader of

such a book as this that in the modern world economic activity has typically become organized in this form: *business units* buy productive services and sell products; *individuals or families* sell productive services and buy products. Hence the study of economics in our society is mainly the study of free enterprise.

Part II

THE METHOD
OF ECONOMIC
ANALYSIS

2. The Methodology
of Positive Economics*

MILTON FRIEDMAN[1]

Milton Friedman (A.B., Rutgers, 1932; M.A., Chicago, 1933; Ph.D., Columbia, 1946) was born in Rahway, New Jersey, in 1912. He is one of the most vigorous and able exponents of the free enterprise system. He is the Paul Snowden Russell Distinguished Service Professor of Economics at the University of Chicago, where he has had a distinguished academic career that has included publication of such major books as *Essays in Positive Economics*, *A Theory of the Consumption Function*, *Price Theory*, *A Monetary History of the United States, 1867–1960* (with Anna J. Schwartz), *The Optimum Quantity of Money and Other Essays*, and *Dollars and Deficits*. In 1951 Friedman was awarded the John Bates Clark Medal by the American Economic Association. This award is made "every two years to that American Economist under the age of 40 who is adjudged to have made a significant contribution to economic thought and knowledge." During 1967 he was president of the American Economic Association. The clarity of style and dialectical skill for which Milton Friedman is known are abundantly evident in the following selection. His preeminence as a teacher is attested to by his pervasive influence on young scholars.

In his admirable book on *The Scope and Method of Political Economy*, John Neville Keynes distinguishes among "a *positive science* . . . [,] a body of systematized knowledge concerning what is; a *normative* or *regulative science* . . . [,] a body of systematized knowledge discussing criteria of what ought to be . . . ; an *art* . . . [,] a system of rules for the attainment of a given end"; comments that "confusion between them is common and has been the source of many mischievous errors"; and urges the importance of "recognizing a distinct positive science of political economy."[2]

This paper is concerned primarily with certain methodological problems that arise

* Reprinted from *Essays in Positive Economics* by Milton Friedman by permission of The University of Chicago Press. Copyright, 1935, pp. 3–43.

[1] I have incorporated bodily in this article without special reference most of my brief "Comment" in *A Survey of Contemporary Economics*, Vol. II, B. F. Haley, ed. (Chicago: Richard D. Irwin, Inc., 1952), pp. 455–57.

I am indebted to Dorothy S. Brady, Arthur F. Burns, and George J. Stigler for helpful comments and criticism.

[2] (London: Macmillan & Co., 1891), pp. 34–35 and 46.

in constructing the "distinct positive science" Keynes called for—in particular, the problem how to decide whether a suggested hypothesis or theory should be tentatively accepted as part of the "body of systematized knowledge concerning what is." But the confusion Keynes laments is still so rife and so much of a hindrance to the recognition that economics can be, and in part is, a positive science that it seems well to preface the main body of the paper with a few remarks about the relation between positive and normative economics.

I. THE RELATION BETWEEN POSITIVE AND NORMATIVE ECONOMICS

Confusion between positive and normative economics is to some extent inevitable. The subject matter of economics is regarded by almost everyone as vitally important to himself and within the range of his own experience and competence; it is the source of continuous and extensive controversy and the occasion for frequent legislation. Self-proclaimed "experts" speak with many voices and can hardly all be regarded as disinterested; in any event, on questions that matter so much, "expert" opinion could hardly be accepted solely on faith even if the "experts" were nearly unanimous and clearly disinterested.[3] The conclusions of positive economics seem to be, and are, immediately relevant to important normative problems, to questions

of what ought to be done and how any given goal can be attained. Laymen and experts alike are inevitably tempted to shape positive conclusions to fit strongly held normative preconceptions and to reject positive conclusions if their normative implications—or what are said to be their normative implications—are unpalatable.

Positive economics is in principle independent of any particular ethical position or normative judgments. As Keynes says, it deals with "what is," not with "what ought to be." Its task is to provide a system of generalizations that can be used to make correct predictions about the consequences of any change in circumstances. Its performance is to be judged by the precision, scope, and conformity with experience of the predictions it yields. In short, positive economics is, or can be, an "objective" science, in precisely the same sense as any of the physical sciences. Of course, the fact that economics deals with the interrelations of human beings, and that the investigator is himself part of the subject matter being investigated in a more intimate sense than in the physical sciences, raises special difficulties in achieving objectivity at the same time that it provides the social scientist with a class of data not available to the physical scientist. But neither the one nor the other is, in my view, a fundamental distinction between the two groups of sciences.[4]

Normative economics and the art of economics, on the other hand, cannot be independent of positive economics. Any

[3] Social science or economics is by no means peculiar in this respect—witness the importance of personal beliefs and of "home" remedies in medicine wherever obviously convincing evidence for "expert" opinion is lacking. The current prestige and acceptance of the views of physical scientists in their fields of specialization—and, all too often, in other fields as well—derives, not from faith alone, but from the evidence of their works, the success of their predictions, and the dramatic achievements from applying their results. When economics seemed to provide such evidence of its worth, in Great Britain in the first half of the nineteenth century, the prestige and acceptance of "scientific economics" rivaled the current prestige of the physical sciences.

[4] The interaction between the observer and the process observed that is so prominent a feature of the social sciences, besides its more obvious parallel in the physical sciences, has a more subtle counterpart in the indeterminacy principle arising out of the interaction between the process of measurement and the phenomena being measured. And both have a counterpart in pure logic in Gödel's theorem, asserting the impossibility of a comprehensive self-contained logic. It is an open question whether all three can be regarded as different formulations of an even more general principle.

policy conclusion necessarily rests on a prediction about the consequences of doing one thing rather than another, a prediction that must be based—implicitly or explicitly—on positive economics. There is not, of course, a one-to-one relation between policy conclusions and the conclusions of positive economics; if there were, there would be no separate normative science. Two individuals may agree on the consequences of a particular piece of legislation. One may regard them as desirable on balance and so favor the legislation; the other, as undesirable and so oppose the legislation.

I venture the judgment, however, that currently in the Western world, and especially in the United States, differences about economic policy among disinterested citizens derive predominantly from different predictions about the economic consequences of taking action—differences that in principle can be eliminated by the progress of positive economics—rather than from fundamental differences in basic values, differences about which men can ultimately only fight. An obvious and not unimportant example is minimum-wage legislation. Underneath the welter of arguments offered for and against such legislation there is an underlying consensus on the objective of achieving a "living wage" for all, to use the ambiguous phrase so common in such discussions. The difference of opinion is largely grounded on an implicit or explicit difference in predictions about the efficacy of this particular means in furthering the agreed-on end. Proponents believe (predict) that legal minimum wages diminish poverty by raising the wages of those receiving less than the minimum wage as well as of some receiving more than the minimum wage without any counterbalancing increase in the number of people entirely unemployed or employed less advantageously than they otherwise would be. Opponents believe (predict) that legal minimum wages increase poverty by increasing the number of people who are unemployed or employed less advantageously and that this more than offsets any favorable effect on the wages of those who remain employed. Agreement about the economic consequences of the legislation might not produce complete agreement about its desirability, for differences might still remain about its political or social consequences; but, given agreement on objectives, it would certainly go a long way toward producing consensus.

Closely related differences in positive analysis underlie divergent views about the appropriate role and place of trade-unions and the desirability of direct price and wage controls and of tariffs. Different predictions about the importance of so-called "economies of scale" account very largely for divergent views about the desirability or necessity of detailed government regulation of industry and even of socialism rather than private enterprise. And this list could be extended indefinitely.[5] Of course, my judgment that the major differences about economic policy in the Western world are of this kind is itself a "positive" statement to be accepted or rejected on the basis of empirical evidence.

If this judgment is valid, it means that a consensus on "correct" economic policy depends much less on the progress of normative economics proper than on the progress of a positive economics yielding con-

[5] One rather more complex example is stabilization policy. Superficially, divergent views on this question seem to reflect differences in objectives; but I believe that this impression is misleading and that at bottom the different views reflect primarily different judgments about the source of fluctuations in economic activity and the effect of alternative countercyclical action. For one major positive consideration that accounts for much of the divergence see "The Effects of a Full-Employment Policy on Economic Stability: A Formal Analysis," *infra*, pp. 117–32. For a summary of the present state of professional views on this question see "The Problem of Economic Instability," a report of a subcommittee of the Committee on Public Issues of the American Economic Association, *American Economic Review*, XL (September, 1950), 501–38.

clusions that are, and deserve to be, widely accepted. It means also that a major reason for distinguishing positive economics sharply from normative economics is precisely the contribution that can thereby be made to agreement about policy.

II. POSITIVE ECONOMICS

The ultimate goal of a positive science is the development of a "theory" or "hypothesis" that yields valid and meaningful (i.e., not truistic) predictions about phenomena not yet observed. Such a theory is, in general, a complex intermixture of two elements. In part, it is a "language" designed to promote "systematic and organized methods of reasoning." [6] In part, it is a body of substantive hypotheses designed to abstract essential features of complex reality.

Viewed as a language, theory has no substantive content; it is a set of tautologies. Its function is to serve as a filing system for organizing empirical material and facilitating our understanding of it; and the criteria by which it is to be judged are those appropriate to a filing system. Are the categories clearly and precisely defined? Are they exhaustive? Do we know where to file each individual item, or is there considerable ambiguity? Is the system of headings and subheadings so designed that we can quickly find an item we want, or must we hunt from place to place? Are the items we shall want to consider jointly filed together? Does the filing system avoid elaborate cross-references?

The answers to these questions depend partly on logical, partly on factual, considerations. The canons of formal logic alone can show whether a particular language is complete and consistent, that is,

whether propositions in the language are "right" or "wrong." Factual evidence alone can show whether the categories of the "analytical filing system" have a meaningful empirical counterpart, that is, whether they are useful in analyzing a particular class of concrete problems.[7] The simple example of "supply" and "demand" illustrates both this point and the preceding list of analogical questions. Viewed as elements of the language of economic theory, these are the two major categories into which factors affecting the relative prices of products or factors of production are classified. The usefulness of the dichotomy depends on the "empirical generalization that an enumeration of the forces affecting demand in any problem and of the forces affecting supply will yield two lists that contain few items in common." [8] Now this generalization is valid for markets like the final market for a consumer good. In such a market there is a clear and sharp distinction between the economic units that can be regarded as demanding the product and those that can be regarded as supplying it. There is seldom much doubt whether a particular factor should be classified as affecting supply, on the one hand, or demand, on the other; and there is seldom much necessity for considering cross-effects (cross-references) between the two categories. In these cases the simple and even obvious step of filing the relevant factors under the headings of "supply" and "demand" effects a great simplification of the problem and is an effective safeguard against fallacies that otherwise tend to occur. But the generalization is not always valid. For example, it is not valid for the day-to-day fluctuations of prices in a primarily speculative market. Is a rumor of an increased excess-profits tax, for example, to be regarded as a factor operating pri-

---

[6] Final quoted phrase from Alfred Marshall, "The Present Position of Economics" (1885), reprinted in *Memorials of Alfred Marshall*, ed. A. C. Pigou (London: Macmillan & Co., 1925), p. 164. See also "The Marshallian Demand Curve," *infra*, pp. 56–57, 90–91.

[7] See "Lange on Price Flexibility and Employment: A Methodological Criticism," *infra*, pp. 282–89.

[8] "The Marshallian Demand Curve," *infra*, p. 57.

marily on today's supply of corporate equities in the stock market or on today's demand for them? In similar fashion, almost every factor can with about as much justification be classified under the heading "supply" as under the heading "demand." These concepts can still be used and may not be entirely pointless; they are still "right" but clearly less useful than in the first example because they have no meaningful empirical counterpart.

Viewed as a body of substantive hypotheses, theory is to be judged by its predictive power for the class of phenomena which it is intended to "explain." Only factual evidence can show whether it is "right" or "wrong" or, better, tentatively "accepted" as valid or "rejected." As I shall argue at greater length below, the only relevant test of the *validity* of a hypothesis is comparison of its predictions with experience. The hypothesis is rejected if its predictions are contradicted ("frequently" or more often than predictions from an alternative hypothesis); it is accepted if its predictions are not contradicted; great confidence is attached to it if it has survived many opportunities for contradiction. Factual evidence can never "prove" a hypothesis; it can only fail to disprove it, which is what we generally mean when we say, somewhat inexactly, that the hypothesis has been "confirmed" by experience.

To avoid confusion, it should perhaps be noted explicitly that the "predictions" by which the validity of a hypothesis is tested need not be about phenomena that have not yet occurred, that is, need not be forecasts of future events; they may be about phenomena that have occurred but observations on which have not yet been made or are not known to the person making the prediction. For example, a hypothesis may imply that such and such must have happened in 1906, given some other known circumstances. If a search of the records reveals that such and such did happen, the prediction is confirmed; if it reveals that such and such did not happen, the prediction is contradicted.

The validity of a hypothesis in this sense is not by itself a sufficient criterion for choosing among alternative hypotheses. Observed facts are necessarily finite in number; possible hypotheses, infinite. If there is one hypothesis that is consistent with the available evidence, there are always an infinite number that are.[9] For example, suppose a specific excise tax on a particular commodity produces a rise in price equal to the amount of the tax. This is consistent with competitive conditions, a stable demand curve, and a horizontal and stable supply curve. But it is also consistent with competitive conditions and a positively or negatively sloping supply curve with the required compensating shift in the demand curve or the supply curve; with monopolistic conditions, constant marginal costs, and stable demand curve, of the particular shape required to produce this result; and so on indefinitely. Additional evidence with which the hypothesis is to be consistent may rule out some of these possibilities; it can never reduce them to a single possibility alone capable of being consistent with the finite evidence. The choice among alternative hypotheses equally consistent with the available evidence must to some extent be arbitrary, though there is general agreement that relevant considerations are suggested by the criteria "simplicity" and "fruitfulness," themselves notions that defy completely objective specification. A theory is "simpler" the less the initial knowledge needed to make a prediction within a given field of phenomena; it is more "fruitful" the more precise the resulting prediction, the wider the area within which the theory yields predictions, and the more additional lines for further research it suggests. Logi-

[9] The qualification is necessary because the "evidence" may be internally contradictory, so there may be no hypothesis consistent with it. See also "Lange on Price Flexibility and Employment," *infra*, pp. 282–83.

cal completeness and consistency are relevant but play a subsidiary role; their function is to assure that the hypothesis says what it is intended to say and does so alike for all users—they play the same role here as checks for arithmetical accuracy do in statistical computations.

Unfortunately, we can seldom test particular predictions in the social sciences by experiments explicitly designed to eliminate what are judged to be the most important disturbing influences. Generally, we must rely on evidence cast up by the "experiments" that happen to occur. The inability to conduct so-called "controlled experiments" does not, in my view, reflect a basic difference between the social and physical sciences both because it is not peculiar to the social sciences—witness astronomy—and because the distinction between a controlled experiment and uncontrolled experience is at best one of degree. No experiment can be completely controlled, and every experience is partly controlled, in the sense that some disturbing influences are relatively constant in the course of it.

Evidence cast up by experience is abundant and frequently as conclusive as that from contrived experiments; thus the inability to conduct experiments is not a fundamental obstacle to testing hypotheses by the success of their predictions. But such evidence is far more difficult to interpret. It is frequently complex and always indirect and incomplete. Its collection is often arduous, and its interpretation generally requires subtle analysis and involved chains of reasoning, which seldom carry real conviction. The denial to economics of the dramatic and direct evidence of the "crucial" experiment does hinder the adequate testing of hypotheses; but this is much less significant than the difficulty it places in the way of achieving a reasonably prompt and wide consensus on the conclusions justified by the available evidence. It renders the weeding-out of unsuccessful hypotheses slow and difficult.

They are seldom downed for good and are always cropping up again.

There is, of course, considerable variation in these respects. Occasionally, experience casts up evidence that is about as direct, dramatic, and convincing as any that could be provided by controlled experiments. Perhaps the most obviously important example is the evidence from inflations on the hypothesis that a substantial increase in the quantity of money within a relatively short period is accompanied by a substantial increase in prices. Here the evidence is dramatic, and the chain of reasoning required to interpret it is relatively short. Yet, despite numerous instances of substantial rises in prices, their essentially one-to-one correspondence with substantial rises in the stock of money, and the wide variation in other circumstances that might appear to be relevant, each new experience of inflation brings forth vigorous contentions, and not only by the lay public, that the rise in the stock of money is either an incidental effect of a rise in prices produced by other factors or a purely fortuitous and unnecessary concomitant of the price rise.

One effect of the difficulty of testing substantive economic hypotheses has been to foster a retreat into purely formal or tautological analysis.[10] As already noted, tautologies have an extremely important place in economics and other sciences as a specialized language or "analytical filing system." Beyond this, formal logic and mathematics, which are both tautologies, are essential aids in checking the correctness of reasoning, discovering the implications of hypotheses, and determining whether supposedly different hypotheses may not really be equivalent or wherein the differences lie.

But economic theory must be more than a structure of tautologies if it is to be able to predict and not merely describe the consequences of action; if it is to be something

[10] See "Lange on Price Flexibility and Employment," *infra, passim.*

different from disguised mathematics.[11] And the usefulness of the tautologies themselves ultimately depends, as noted above, on the acceptability of the substantive hypotheses that suggest the particular categories into which they organize the refractory empirical phenomena.

A more serious effect of the difficulty of testing economic hypotheses by their predictions is to foster misunderstanding of the role of empirical evidence in theoretical work. Empirical evidence is vital at two different, though closely related, stages: in constructing hypotheses and in testing their validity. Full and comprehensive evidence on the phenomena to be generalized or "explained" by a hypothesis, besides its obvious value in suggesting new hypotheses, is needed to assure that a hypothesis explains what it sets out to explain—that its implications for such phenomena are not contradicted in advance by experience that has already been observed.[12] Given that the

hypothesis is consistent with the evidence at hand, its further testing involves deducing from it new facts capable of being observed but not previously known and checking these deduced facts against additional empirical evidence. For this test to be relevant, the deduced facts must be about the class of phenomena the hypothesis is designed to explain; and they must be well enough defined so that observation can show them to be wrong.

The two stages of constructing hypoth-

[11] See also Milton Friedman and L. J. Savage, "The Expected-Utility Hypothesis and the Measurability of Utility," *Journal of Political Economy,* LX (December, 1952), 463–74, esp. pp. 465–67.

[12] In recent years some economists, particularly a group connected with the Cowles Commission for Research in Economics at the University of Chicago, have placed great emphasis on a division of this step of selecting a hypothesis consistent with known evidence into two substeps: first, the selection of a class of admissible hypotheses from all possible hypotheses (the choice of a "model" in their terminology); second, the selection of one hypothesis from this class (the choice of a "structure"). This subdivision may be heuristically valuable in some kinds of work, particularly in promoting a systematic use of available statistical evidence and theory. From a methodological point of view, however, it is an entirely arbitrary subdivision of the process of deciding on a particular hypothesis that is on a par with many other subdivisions that may be convenient for one purpose or another or that may suit the psychological needs of particular investigators.

One consequence of this particular subdivision has been to give rise to the so-called "identification" problem. As noted above, if one hypothesis is consistent with available evidence, an infinite number are. But, while this is true for the class of hypotheses as a whole, it may not be true of the subclass obtained in the first of the above

two steps—the "model." It may be that the evidence to be used to select the final hypothesis from the subclass can be consistent with at most one hypothesis in it, in which case the "model" is said to be "identified"; otherwise it is said to be "unidentified." As is clear from this way of describing the concept of "identification," it is essentially a special case of the more general problem of selecting among the alternative hypotheses equally consistent with the evidence—a problem that must be decided by some such arbitrary principle as Occam's razor. The introduction of two substeps in selecting a hypothesis makes this problem arise at the two corresponding stages and gives it a special cast. While the class of all hypotheses is always unidentified, the subclass in a "model" need not be, so the problem arises of conditions that a "model" must satisfy to be identified. However useful the two substeps may be in some contexts, their introduction raises the danger that different criteria will unwittingly be used in making the same kind of choice among alternative hypotheses at two different stages.

On the general methodological approach discussed in this footnote see Tryvge Haavelmo, "The Probability Approach in Econometrics," *Econometrica,* Vol. XII (1944), Supplement; Jacob Marschak, "Economic Structure, Path, Policy, and Prediction," *American Economic Review,* XXXVII (May, 1947), 81–84, and "Statistical Inference in Economics: An Introduction," in T. C. Koopmans (ed.), *Statistical Inference in Dynamic Economic Models* (New York: John Wiley & Sons, 1950); T. C. Koopmans, "Statistical Estimation of Simultaneous Economic Relations," *Journal of the American Statistical Association,* XL (December, 1945), 448–66; Gershon Cooper, "The Role of Economic Theory in Econometric Models," *Journal of Farm Economics,* XXX (February, 1948), 101–16. On the identification problem see Koopmans, "Identification Problems in Econometric Model Construction," *Econometrica,* XVII (April, 1949), 125–44; Leonid Hurwicz, "Generalization of the Concept of Identification," in Koopmans (ed.), *Statistical Inference in Dynamic Economic Models.*

eses and testing their validity are related in two different respects. In the first place, the particular facts that enter at each stage are partly an accident of the collection of data and the knowledge of the particular investigator. The facts that serve as a test of the implications of a hypothesis might equally well have been among the raw material used to construct it, and conversely. In the second place, the process never begins from scratch; the so-called "initial stage" itself always involves comparison of the implications of an earlier set of hypotheses with observation; the contradiction of these implications is the stimulus to the construction of new hypotheses or revision of old ones. So the two methodologically distinct stages are always proceeding jointly.

Misunderstanding about this apparently straightforward process centers on the phrase "the class of phenomena the hypothesis is designed to explain." The difficulty in the social sciences of getting new evidence for this class of phenomena and of judging its conformity with the implications of the hypothesis makes it tempting to suppose that other, more readily available, evidence is equally relevant to the validity of the hypothesis—to suppose that hypotheses have not only "implications" but also "assumptions" and that the conformity of these "assumptions" to "reality" is a test of the validity of the hypothesis *different from* or *additional to* the test by implications. This widely held view is fundamentally wrong and productive of much mischief. Far from providing an easier means for sifting valid from invalid hypotheses, it only confuses the issue, promotes misunderstanding about the significance of empirical evidence for economic theory, produces a misdirection of much intellectual effort devoted to the development of positive economics, and impedes the attainment of consensus on tentative hypotheses in positive economics.

In so far as a theory can be said to have "assumptions" at all, and in so far as their "realism" can be judged independently of the validity of predictions, the relation between the significance of a theory and the "realism" of its "assumptions" is almost the opposite of that suggested by the view under criticism. Truly important and significant hypotheses will be found to have "assumptions" that are wildly inaccurate descriptive representations of reality, and, in general, the more significant the theory, the more unrealistic the assumptions (in this sense).[13] The reason is simple. A hypothesis is important if it "explains" much by little, that is, if it abstracts the common and crucial elements from the mass of complex and detailed circumstances surrounding the phenomena to be explained and permits valid predictions on the basis of them alone. To be important, therefore, a hypothesis must be descriptively false in its assumptions; it takes account of, and accounts for, none of the many other attendant circumstances, since its very success shows them to be irrelevant for the phenomena to be explained.

To put this point less paradoxically, the relevant question to ask about the "assumptions" of a theory is not whether they are descriptively "realistic," for they never are, but whether they are sufficiently good approximations for the purpose in hand. And this question can be answered only by seeing whether the theory works, which means whether it yields sufficiently accurate predictions. The two supposedly independent tests thus reduce to one test.

The theory of monopolistic and imperfect competition is one example of the neglect in economic theory of these propositions. The development of this analysis was explicitly motivated, and its wide acceptance and approval largely explained, by the belief that the assumptions of "perfect competition" or "perfect monopoly" said

---

[13] The converse of the proposition does not of course hold: assumptions that are unrealistic (in this sense) do not guarantee a significant theory.

to underlie neoclassical economic theory are a false image of reality. And this belief was itself based almost entirely on the directly perceived descriptive inaccuracy of the assumptions rather than on any recognized contradiction of predictions derived from neoclassical economic theory. The lengthy discussion on marginal analysis in the *American Economic Review* some years ago is an even clearer, though much less important, example. The articles on both sides of the controversy largely neglect what seems to me clearly the main issue—the conformity to experience of the implications of the marginal analysis—and concentrate on the largely irrelevant question whether businessmen do or do not in fact reach their decisions by consulting schedules, or curves, or multivariable functions showing marginal cost and marginal revenue.[14] Perhaps these two examples, and the

[14] See R. A. Lester, "Shortcomings of Marginal Analysis for Wage-Employment Problems," *American Economic Review*, XXXVI (March, 1946), 62–82; Fritz Machlup, "Marginal Analysis and Empirical Research," *American Economic Review*, XXXVI (September, 1946), 519–54; R. A. Lester, "Marginalism, Minimum Wages, and Labor Markets," *American Economic Review*, XXXVII (March, 1947), 135–48; Fritz Machlup, "Rejoinder to an Antimarginalist," *American Economic Review*, XXXVII (March, 1947), 148–54; G. J. Stigler, "Professor Lester and the Marginalists," *American Economic Review*, XXXVII (March, 1947), 154–57; H. M. Oliver, Jr., "Marginal Theory and Business Behavior," *American Economic Review*, XXXVII (June, 1947), 375–83; R. A. Gordon, "Short-Period Price Determination in Theory and Practice," *American Economic Review*, XXXVIII (June, 1948), 265–88.

It should be noted that, along with much material purportedly bearing on the validity of the "assumptions" of marginal theory, Lester does refer to evidence on the conformity of experience with the implications of the theory, citing the reactions of employment in Germany to the Papen plan and in the United States to changes in minimum-wage legislation as examples of lack of conformity. However, Stigler's brief comment is the only one of the other papers that refers to this evidence. It should also be noted that Machlup's thorough and careful exposition of the logical structure and meaning of marginal analysis is called for by the misunderstandings on this score that mar Lester's paper and almost conceal the evidence he presents that is relevant

many others they readily suggest, will serve to justify a more extensive discussion of the methodological principles involved than might otherwise seem appropriate.

III. CAN A HYPOTHESIS BE TESTED BY THE REALISM OF ITS ASSUMPTIONS?

We may start with a simple physical example, the law of falling bodies. It is an accepted hypothesis that the acceleration of a body dropped in a vacuum is a constant—g, or approximately 32 feet per second per second on the earth—and is independent of the shape of the body, the manner of dropping it, etc. This implies that the distance traveled by a falling body in any specified time is given by the formula $s = \frac{1}{2} gt^2$, where s is the distance traveled in feet and t is time in seconds. The application of this formula to a compact ball dropped from the roof of a building is equivalent to saying that a ball so dropped behaves *as if* it were falling in a vacuum. Testing this hypothesis by its assumptions presumably means measuring the actual air pressure and deciding whether it is close enough to zero. At sea level the air pressure is about 15 pounds per square inch. Is 15 sufficiently close to zero for the difference to be judged insignificant? Apparently it is, since the actual time taken by a compact ball to fall from the roof of a building to the ground is very close to the time given by the formula. Suppose, however, that a feather is dropped instead of a compact ball. The formula then gives wildly inaccurate results. Apparently, 15 pounds per square inch is significantly different from zero for

to the key issue he raises. But, in Machlup's emphasis on the logical structure, he comes perilously close to presenting the theory as a pure tautology, though it is evident at a number of points that he is aware of this danger and anxious to avoid it. The papers by Oliver and Gordon are the most extreme in the exclusive concentration on the conformity of the behavior of businessmen with the "assumptions" of the theory.

a feather but not for a ball. Or, again, suppose the formula is applied to a ball dropped from an airplane at an altitude of 30,000 feet. The air pressure at this altitude is decidedly less than 15 pounds per square inch. Yet, the actual time of fall from 30,000 feet to 20,000 feet, at which point the air pressure is still much less than at sea level, will differ noticeably from the time predicted by the formula—much more noticeably than the time taken by a compact ball to fall from the roof of a building to the ground. According to the formula, the velocity of the ball should be gt and should therefore increase steadily. In fact, a ball dropped at 30,000 feet will reach its top velocity well before it hits the ground. And similarly with other implications of the formula.

The initial question whether 15 is sufficiently close to zero for the difference to be judged insignificant is clearly a foolish question by itself. Fifteen pounds per square inch is 2,160 pounds per square foot, or 0.0075 ton per square inch. There is no possible basis for calling these numbers "small" or "large" without some external standard of comparison. And the only relevant standard of comparison is the air pressure for which the formula does or does not work under a given set of circumstances. But this raises the same problem at a second level. What is the meaning of "does or does not work"? Even if we could eliminate errors of measurement, the measured time of fall would seldom if ever be precisely equal to the computed time of fall. How large must the difference between the two be to justify saying that the theory "does not work"? Here there are two important external standards of comparison. One is the accuracy achievable by an alternative theory with which this theory is being compared and which is equally acceptable on all other grounds. The other arises when there exists a theory that is known to yield better predictions but only at a greater cost. The gains from greater

accuracy, which depend on the purpose in mind, must then be balanced against the costs of achieving it.

This example illustrates both the impossibility of testing a theory by its assumptions and also the ambiguity of the concept "the assumptions of a theory." The formula $s = \frac{1}{2} gt^2$ is valid for bodies falling in a vacuum and can be derived by analyzing the behavior of such bodies. It can therefore be stated: under a wide range of circumstances, bodies that fall in the actual atmosphere behave *as if* they were falling in a vacuum. In the language so common in economics this would be rapidly translated into: the formula assumes a vacuum. Yet it clearly does no such thing. What it does say is that in many cases the existence of air pressure, the shape of the body, the name of the person dropping the body, the kind of mechanism used to drop the body, and a host of other attendant circumstances have no appreciable effect on the distance the body falls in a specified time. The hypothesis can readily be rephrased to omit all mention of a vacuum: under a wide range of circumstances, the distance a body falls in a specified time is given by the formula $s = \frac{1}{2} gt^2$. The history of this formula and its associated physical theory aside, is it meaningful to say that it assumes a vacuum? For all I know there may be other sets of assumptions that would yield the same formula. The formula is accepted because it works, not because we live in an approximate vacuum—whatever that means.

The important problem in connection with the hypothesis is to specify the circumstances under which the formula works or, more precisely, the general magnitude of the error in its predictions under various circumstances. Indeed, as is implicit in the above rephrasing of the hypothesis, such a specification is not one thing and the hypothesis another. The specification is itself an essential part of the hypothesis, and it is a part that is peculiarly likely to be revised and extended as experience accumulates.

In the particular case of falling bodies a more general, though still incomplete, theory is available, largely as a result of attempts to explain the errors of the simple theory, from which the influence of some of the possible disturbing factors can be calculated and of which the simple theory is a special case. However, it does not always pay to use the more general theory because the extra accuracy it yields may not justify the extra cost of using it, so the question under what circumstances the simpler theory works "well enough" remains important. Air pressure is one, but only one, of the variables that define these circumstances; the shape of the body, the velocity attained, and still other variables are relevant as well. One way of interpreting the variables other than air pressure is to regard them as determining whether a particular departure from the "assumption" of a vacuum is or is not significant. For example, the difference in shape of the body can be said to make 15 pounds per square inch significantly different from zero for a feather but not for a compact ball dropped a moderate distance. Such a statement must, however, be sharply distinguished from the very different statement that the theory does not work for a feather because its assumptions are false. The relevant relation runs the other way: the assumptions are false for a feather because the theory does not work. This point needs emphasis, because the entirely valid use of "assumptions" in *specifying* the circumstances for which a theory holds is frequently, and erroneously, interpreted to mean that the assumptions can be used to *determine* the circumstances for which a theory holds, and has, in this way, been an important source of the belief that a theory can be tested by its assumptions.

Let us turn now to another example, this time a constructed one designed to be an analogue of many hypotheses in the social sciences. Consider the density of leaves around a tree. I suggest the hypothesis that the leaves are positioned as if each leaf deliberately sought to maximize the amount of sunlight it receives, given the position of its neighbors, as if it knew the physical laws determining the amount of sunlight that would be received in various positions and could move rapidly or instantaneously from any one position to any other desired and unoccupied position.[15] Now some of the more obvious implications of this hypothesis are clearly consistent with experience: for example, leaves are in general denser on the south than on the north side of trees but, as the hypothesis implies, less so or not at all on the northern slope of a hill or when the south side of the trees is shaded in some other way. Is the hypothesis rendered unacceptable or invalid because, so far as we know, leaves do not "deliberate" or consciously "seek," have not been to school and learned the relevant laws of science or the mathematics required to calculate the "optimum" position, and cannot move from position to position? Clearly, none of these contradictions of the hypothesis is vitally relevant; the phenomena involved are not within the "class of phenomena the hypothesis is designed to explain"; the hypothesis does not assert that leaves do these things but only that their density is the same *as if* they did. Despite the apparent falsity of the "assumptions" of the hypothesis, it has great plausibility because of the conformity of its implications with observation. We are inclined to "explain" its validity on the ground that sunlight contributes to the growth of leaves and that hence leaves will grow denser or more putative leaves survive where there is more sun, so the re-

[15] This example, and some of the subsequent discussion, though independent in origin, is similar to and in much the same spirit as an example and the approach in an important paper by Armen A. Alchian, "Uncertainty, Evolution, and Economic Theory," *Journal of Political Economy*, LVIII (June, 1950), 211–21.

sult achieved by purely passive adaptation to external circumstances is the same as the result that would be achieved by deliberate accommodation to them. This alternative hypothesis is more attractive than the constructed hypothesis not because its "assumptions" are more "realistic" but rather because it is part of a more general theory that applies to a wider variety of phenomena, of which the position of leaves around a tree is a special case, has more implications capable of being contradicted, and has failed to be contradicted under a wider variety of circumstances. The direct evidence for the growth of leaves is in this way strengthened by the indirect evidence from the other phenomena to which the more general theory applies.

The constructed hypothesis is presumably valid, that is, yields "sufficiently" accurate predictions about the density of leaves, only for a particular class of circumstances. I do not know what these circumstances are or how to define them. It seems obvious, however, that in this example the "assumptions" of the theory will play no part in specifying them: the kind of tree, the character of the soil, etc., are the types of variables that are likely to define its range of validity, not the ability of the leaves to do complicated mathematics or to move from place to place.

A largely parallel example involving human behavior has been used elsewhere by Savage and me.[16] Consider the problem of predicting the shots made by an expert billiard player. It seems not at all unreasonable that excellent predictions would be yielded by the hypothesis that the billiard player made his shots *as if* he knew the complicated mathematical formulas that would give the optimum directions of travel, could estimate accurately by eye the an-

[16] Milton Friedman and L. J. Savage, "The Utility Analysis of Choices Involving Risk," *Journal of Political Economy,* LVI (August, 1948), 298. Reprinted in American Economic Association, *Readings in Price Theory* (Chicago: Richard D. Irwin, Inc., 1952), pp. 57–96.

gles, etc., describing the location of the balls, could make lightning calculations from the formulas, and could then make the balls travel in the direction indicated by the formulas. Our confidence in this hypothesis is not based on the belief that billiard players, even expert ones, can or do go through the process described; it derives rather from the belief that, unless in some way or other they were capable of reaching essentially the same result, they would not in fact be *expert* billiard players.

It is only a short step from these examples to the economic hypothesis that under a wide range of circumstances individual firms behave *as if* they were seeking rationally to maximize their expected returns (generally if misleadingly called "profits")[17] and had full knowledge of the data needed to succeed in this attempt; *as if,* that is, they knew the relevant cost and demand functions, calculated marginal cost and marginal revenue from all actions open to them, and pushed each line of action to the point at which the relevant marginal

[17] It seems better to use the term "profits" to refer to the difference between actual and "expected" results, between *ex post* and *ex ante* receipts. "Profits" are then a result of uncertainty and, as Alchian (*op. cit.,* p. 212), following Tintner, points out, cannot be deliberately maximized in advance. Given uncertainty, individuals or firms choose among alternative anticipated probability distributions of receipts or incomes. The specific content of a theory of choice among such distributions depends on the criteria by which they are supposed to be ranked. One hypothesis supposes them to be ranked by the mathematical expectation of utility corresponding to them (see Friedman and Savage, "The Expected-Utility Hypothesis and the Measurability of Utility," *op. cit.*). A special case of this hypothesis or an alternative to it ranks probability distributions by the mathematical expectation of the money receipts corresponding to them. The latter is perhaps more applicable, and more frequently applied, to firms than to individuals. The term "expected returns" is intended to be sufficiently broad to apply to any of these alternatives.

The issues alluded to in this note are not basic to the methodological issues being discussed, and so are largely by-passed in the discussion that follows.

cost and marginal revenue were equal. Now, of course, businessmen do not actually and literally solve the system of simultaneous equations in terms of which the mathematical economist finds it convenient to express this hypothesis, any more than leaves or billiard players explicitly go through complicated mathematical calculations or falling bodies decide to create a vacuum. The billiard player, if asked how he decides where to hit the ball, may say that he "just figures it out" but then also rubs a rabbit's foot just to make sure; and the businessman may well say that he prices at average cost, with of course some minor deviations when the market makes it necessary. The one statement is about as helpful as the other, and neither is a relevant test of the associated hypothesis.

Confidence in the maximization-of-returns hypothesis is justified by evidence of a very different character. This evidence is in part similar to that adduced on behalf of the billiard-player hypothesis—unless the behavior of businessmen in some way or other approximated behavior consistent with the maximization of returns, it seems unlikely that they would remain in business for long. Let the apparent immediate determinant of business behavior be anything at all—habitual reaction, random chance, or whatnot. Whenever this determinant happens to lead to behavior consistent with rational and informed maximization of returns, the business will prosper and acquire resources with which to expand; whenever it does not, the business will tend to lose resources and can be kept in existence only by the addition of resources from outside. The process of "natural selection" thus helps to validate the hypothesis—or, rather, given natural selection, acceptance of the hypothesis can be based largely on the judgment that it summarizes appropriately the conditions for survival.

An even more important body of evidence for the maximization-of-returns hypothesis is experience from countless applications of the hypothesis to specific problems and the repeated failure of its implications to be contradicted. This evidence is extremely hard to document; it is scattered in numerous memorandums, articles, and monographs concerned primarily with specific concrete problems rather than with submitting the hypothesis to test. Yet the continued use and acceptance of the hypothesis over a long period, and the failure of any coherent, self-consistent alternative to be developed and be widely accepted, is strong indirect testimony to its worth. The evidence *for* a hypothesis always consists of its repeated failure to be contradicted, continues to accumulate so long as the hypothesis is used, and by its very nature is difficult to document at all comprehensively. It tends to become part of the tradition and folklore of a science revealed in the tenacity with which hypotheses are held rather than in any textbook list of instances in which the hypothesis has failed to be contradicted.

IV. THE SIGNIFICANCE AND ROLE OF THE "ASSUMPTIONS" OF A THEORY

Up to this point our conclusions about the significance of the "assumptions" of a theory have been almost entirely negative: we have seen that a theory cannot be tested by the "realism" of its "assumptions" and that the very concept of the "assumptions" of a theory is surrounded with ambiguity. But, if this were all there is to it, it would be hard to explain the extensive use of the concept and the strong tendency that we all have to speak of the assumptions of a theory and to compare the assumptions of alternative theories. There is too much smoke for there to be no fire.

In methodology, as in positive science, negative statements can generally be made with greater confidence than positive statements, so I have less confidence in the following remarks on the significance and role of "assumptions" than in the preceding remarks. So far as I can see, the "assumptions of a theory" play three different, though related, positive roles: (a) they are often an economical mode of describing or presenting a theory; (b) they sometimes facilitate an indirect test of the hypothesis by its implications; and (c), as already noted, they are sometimes a convenient means of specifying the conditions under which the theory is expected to be valid. The first two require more extensive discussion.

A. The Use of "Assumptions" in Stating a Theory

The example of the leaves illustrates the first role of assumptions. Instead of saying that leaves seek to maximize the sunlight they receive, we could state the equivalent hypothesis, without any apparent assumptions, in the form of a list of rules for predicting the density of leaves: if a tree stands in a level field with no other trees or other bodies obstructing the rays of the sun, then the density of leaves will tend to be such and such; if a tree is on the northern slope of a hill in the midst of a forest of similar trees, then . . . ; etc. This is clearly a far less economical presentation of the hypothesis than the statement that leaves seek to maximize the sunlight each receives. The latter statement is, in effect, a simple summary of the rules in the above list, even if the list were indefinitely extended, since it indicates both how to determine the features of the environment that are important for the particular problem and how to evaluate their effects. It is more compact and at the same time no less comprehensive.

More generally, a hypothesis or theory consists of an assertion that certain forces are, and by implication others are not, important for a particular class of phenomena and a specification of the manner of action of the forces it asserts to be important.

We can regard the hypothesis as consisting of two parts: first, a conceptual world or abstract model simpler than the "real world" and containing only the forces that the hypothesis asserts to be important; second, a set of rules defining the class of phenomena for which the "model" can be taken to be an adequate representation of the "real world" and specifying the correspondence between the variables or entities in the model and observable phenomena.

These two parts are very different in character. The model is abstract and complete; it is an "algebra" or "logic." Mathematics and formal logic come into their own in checking its consistency and completeness and exploring its implications. There is no place in the model for, and no function to be served by, vagueness, maybe's, or approximations. The air pressure is zero, not "small," for a vacuum; the demand curve for the product of a competitive producer is horizontal (has a slope of zero), not "almost horizontal."

The rules for using the model, on the other hand, cannot possibly be abstract and complete. They must be concrete and in consequence incomplete—completeness is possible only in a conceptual world, not in the "real world," however that may be interpreted. The model is the logical embodiment of the half-truth, "There is nothing new under the sun"; the rules for applying it cannot neglect the equally significant half-truth, "History never repeats itself." To a considerable extent the rules can be formulated explicitly—most easily, though even then not completely, when the theory is part of an explicit more general theory as in the example of the vacuum theory for falling bodies. In seeking to make a science as "objective" as possible, our aim should be to formulate the rules explicitly in so far as possible and continually to widen the range of phenomena for which it is possible to do so. But, no matter how successful we may be in this attempt, there inevitably will remain room for judgment in applying the rules. Each occurrence has some features peculiarly its own, not covered by the explicit rules. The capacity to judge that these are or are not to be disregarded, that they should or should not affect what observable phenomena are to be identified with what entities in the model, is something that cannot be taught; it can be learned but only by experience and exposure in the "right" scientific atmosphere, not by rote. It is at this point that the "amateur" is separated from the "professional" in all sciences and that the thin line is drawn which distinguishes the "crackpot" from the scientist.

A simple example may perhaps clarify this point. Euclidean geometry is an abstract model, logically complete and consistent. Its entities are precisely defined— a line is not a geometrical figure "much" longer than it is wide or deep; it is a figure whose width and depth are zero. It is also obviously "unrealistic." There are no such things in "reality" as Euclidean points or lines or surfaces. Let us apply this abstract model to a mark made on a blackboard by a piece of chalk. Is the mark to be identified with a Euclidean line, a Euclidean surface, or a Euclidean solid? Clearly, it can appropriately be identified with a line if it is being used to represent, say, a demand curve. But it cannot be so identified if it is being used to color, say, countries on a map, for that would imply that the map would never be colored; for this purpose, the same mark must be identified with a surface. But it cannot be so identified by a manufacturer of chalk, for that would imply that no chalk would ever be used up; for his purposes, the same mark must be identified with a volume. In this simple example these judgments will command general agreement. Yet it seems obvious that, while general considerations can be formulated to guide such judgments, they can never be comprehensive and cover

every possible instance; they cannot have the self-contained coherent character of Euclidean geometry itself.

In speaking of the "crucial assumptions" of a theory, we are, I believe, trying to state the key elements of the abstract model. There are generally many different ways of describing the model completely —many different sets of "postulates" which both imply and are implied by the model as a whole. These are all logically equivalent: what are regarded as axioms or postulates of a model from one point of view can be regarded as theorems from another, and conversely. The particular "assumptions" termed "crucial" are selected on grounds of their convenience in some such respects as simplicity or economy in describing the model, intuitive plausibility, or capacity to suggest, if only by implication, some of the considerations that are relevant in judging or applying the model.

B. The Use of "Assumptions" As an Indirect Test of a Theory

In presenting any hypothesis, it generally seems obvious which of the series of statements used to expound it refer to assumptions and which to implications; yet this distinction is not easy to define rigorously. It is not, I believe, a characteristic of the hypothesis as such but rather of the use to which the hypothesis is to be put. If this is so, the ease of classifying statements must reflect unambiguousness in the purpose the hypothesis is designed to serve. The possibility of interchanging theorems and axioms in an abstract model implies the possibility of interchanging "implications" and "assumptions" in the substantive hypothesis corresponding to the abstract model, which is not to say that any implication can be interchanged with any assumption but only that there may be more than one set of statements that imply the rest.

For example, consider a particular proposition in the theory of oligopolistic behavior. If we assume (a) that entrepreneurs seek to maximize their returns by any means including acquiring or extending monopoly power, this will imply (b) that, when demand for a "product" is geographically unstable, transportation costs are significant, explicit price agreements illegal, and the number of producers of the product relatively small, they will tend to establish basing-point pricing systems.[18] The assertion (a) is regarded as an assumption and (b) as an implication because we accept the prediction of market behavior as the purpose of the analysis. We shall regard the assumption as acceptable if we find that the conditions specified in (b) are generally associated with basing-point pricing, and conversely. Let us now change our purpose to deciding what cases to prosecute under the Sherman Antitrust Law's prohibition of a "conspiracy in restraint of trade." If we now assume (c) that basing-point pricing is a deliberate construction to facilitate collusion under the conditions specified in (b), this will imply (d) that entrepreneurs who participate in basing-point pricing are engaged in a "conspiracy in restraint of trade." What was formerly an assumption now becomes an implication, and conversely. We shall now regard the assumption (c) as valid if we find that, when entrepreneurs participate in basing-point pricing, there generally tends to be other evidence, in the form of letters, memorandums, or the like, of what courts regard as a "conspiracy in restraint of trade."

Suppose the hypothesis works for the first purpose, namely, the prediction of market behavior. It clearly does not follow that it will work for the second purpose, namely, predicting whether there is enough evidence of a "conspiracy in re-straint of trade" to justify court action. And, conversely, if it works for the second purpose, it does not follow that it will work for the first. Yet, in the absence of other evidence, the success of the hypothesis for one purpose—in explaining one class of phenomena—will give us greater confidence than we would otherwise have that it may succeed for another purpose—in explaining another class of phenomena. It is much harder to say how much greater confidence it justifies. For this depends on how closely related we judge the two classes of phenomena to be, which itself depends in a complex way on similar kinds of indirect evidence, that is, on our experience in other connections in explaining by single theories phenomena that are in some sense similarly diverse.

To state the point more generally, what are called the assumptions of a hypothesis can be used to get some indirect evidence on the acceptability of the hypothesis in so far as the assumptions can themselves be regarded as implications of the hypothesis, and hence their conformity with reality as a failure of some implications to be contradicted, or in so far as the assumptions may call to mind other implications of the hypothesis susceptible to casual empirical observation.[19] The reason this evidence is indirect is that the assumptions or associated implications generally refer to a class of phenomena different from the class which the hypothesis is designed to explain; indeed, as is implied above, this seems to be the chief criterion we use in deciding which statements to term "assumptions" and which to term "implications." The weight attached to this indirect evidence depends on how closely related we judge the two classes of phenomena to be.

Another way in which the "assump-

---

[18] See George J. Stigler, "A Theory of Delivered Price Systems," *American Economic Review,* XXXIX (December, 1949), 1143–57.

[19] See Friedman and Savage, "The Expected-Utility Hypothesis and the Measurability of Utility," *op. cit.,* pp. 466–67, for another specific example of this kind of indirect test.

tions" of a hypothesis can facilitate its indirect testing is by bringing out its kinship with other hypotheses and thereby making the evidence on their validity relevant to the validity of the hypothesis in question. For example, a hypothesis is formulated for a particular class of behavior. This hypothesis can, as usual, be stated without specifying any "assumptions." But suppose it can be shown that it is equivalent to a set of assumptions including the assumption that man seeks his own interest. The hypothesis then gains indirect plausibility from the success for other classes of phenomena of hypotheses that can also be said to make this assumption; at least, what is being done here is not completely unprecedented or unsuccessful in all other uses. In effect, the statement of assumptions so as to bring out a relationship between superficially different hypotheses is a step in the direction of a more general hypothesis.

This kind of indirect evidence from related hypotheses explains in large measure the difference in the confidence attached to a particular hypothesis by people with different backgrounds. Consider, for example, the hypothesis that the extent of racial or religious discrimination in employment in a particular area or industry is closely related to the degree of monopoly in the industry or area in question; that, if the industry is competitive, discrimination will be significant only if the race or religion of employees affects either the willingness of other employees to work with them or the acceptability of the product to customers and will be uncorrelated with the prejudices of employers.[20] This hypothesis is far more likely to appeal to an economist than to a sociologist. It can be said to "assume" single-minded pursuit of pecuniary self-in-

terest by employers in competitive industries; and this "assumption" works well in a wide variety of hypotheses in economics bearing on many of the mass phenomena with which economics deals. It is therefore likely to seem reasonable to the economist that it may work in this case as well. On the other hand, the hypotheses to which the sociologist is accustomed have a very different kind of model or ideal world, in which single-minded pursuit of pecuniary self-interest plays a much less important role. The indirect evidence available to the sociologist on this hypothesis is much less favorable to it than the indirect evidence available to the economist; he is therefore likely to view it with greater suspicion.

Of course, neither the evidence of the economist nor that of the sociologist is conclusive. The decisive test is whether the hypothesis works for the phenomena it purports to explain. But a judgment may be required before any satisfactory test of this kind has been made, and, perhaps, when it cannot be made in the near future, in which case, the judgment will have to be based on the inadequate evidence available. In addition, even when such a test can be made, the background of the scientists is not irrelevant to the judgments they reach. There is never certainty in science, and the weight of evidence for or against a hypothesis can never be assessed completely "objectively." The economist will be more tolerant than the sociologist in judging conformity of the implications of the hypothesis with experience, and he will be persuaded to accept the hypothesis tentatively by fewer instances of "conformity."

V. SOME IMPLICATIONS FOR ECONOMIC ISSUES

The abstract methodological issues we have been discussing have a direct bearing on the perennial criticism of "orthodox"

[20] A rigorous statement of this hypothesis would of course have to specify how "extent of racial or religious discrimination" and "degree of monopoly" are to be judged. The loose statement in the text is sufficient, however, for present purposes.

economic theory as "unrealistic" as well as on the attempts that have been made to reformulate theory to meet this charge. Economics is a "dismal" science because it assumes man to be selfish and money-grubbing, "a lightning calculator of pleasures and pains, who oscillates like a homogeneous globule of desire of happiness under the impulse of stimuli that shift him about the area, but leave him intact";[21] it rests on outmoded psychology and must be reconstructed in line with each new development in psychology; it assumes men, or at least businessmen, to be "in a continuous state of 'alert,' ready to change prices and/or pricing rules whenever their sensitive intuitions . . . detect a change in demand and supply conditions";[22] it assumes markets to be perfect, competition to be pure, and commodities, labor, and capital to be homogeneous.

As we have seen, criticism of this type is largely beside the point unless supplemented by evidence that a hypothesis differing in one or another of these respects from the theory being criticized yields better predictions for as wide a range of phenomena. Yet most such criticism is not so supplemented; it is based almost entirely on supposedly directly perceived discrepancies between the "assumptions" and the "real world." A particularly clear example is furnished by the recent criticisms of the maximization-of-returns hypothesis on the grounds that businessmen do not and indeed cannot behave as the theory "assumes" they do. The evidence cited to support this assertion is generally taken either from the answers given by businessmen to questions about the factors affecting their decisions—a procedure for testing economic theories that is about on a par with testing theories of longevity by asking octogenarians how they account for their

long life—or from descriptive studies of the decision-making activities of individual firms.[23] Little if any evidence is ever cited on the conformity of businessmen's actual market behavior—what they do rather than what they say they do—with the implications of the hypothesis being criticized, on the one hand, and of an alternative hypothesis, on the other.

A theory or its "assumptions" cannot possibly be thoroughly "realistic" in the immediate descriptive sense so often assigned to this term. A completely "realistic" theory of the wheat market would have to include not only the conditions directly underlying the supply and demand for wheat but also the kind of coins or credit instruments used to make exchanges; the personal characteristics of wheat-traders such as the color of each trader's hair and eyes, his antecedents and education, the number of members of his family, their characteristics, antecedents, and education, etc.; the kind of soil on

---

[21] Thorstein Veblen, "Why Is Economics Not an Evolutionary Science?" (1898), reprinted in *The Place of Science in Modern Civilization* (New York, 1919), p. 73.

[22] Oliver, *op. cit.*, p. 381.

[23] See H. D. Henderson, "The Significance of the Rate of Interest," *Oxford Economic Papers*, No. 1 (October, 1938), pp. 1–13; J. E. Meade and P. W. S. Andrews, "Summary of Replies to Questions on Effects of Interest Rates," *Oxford Economic Papers*, No. 1 (October, 1938), pp. 14–31; R. F. Harrod, "Price and Cost in Entrepreneurs' Policy," *Oxford Economic Papers*, No. 2 (May, 1939), pp. 1–11; and R. J. Hall and C. J. Hitch, "Price Theory and Business Behavior," *Oxford Economic Papers*, No. 2 (May, 1939), pp. 12–45; Lester, "Shortcomings of Marginal Analysis for Wage-Employment Problems," *op. cit.*; Gordon, *op. cit.* See Fritz Machlup, "Marginal Analysis and Empirical Research," *op. cit.*, esp. Sec. II, for detailed criticisms of questionnaire methods. I do not mean to imply that questionnaire studies of businessmen's or others' motives or beliefs about the forces affecting their behavior are useless for all purposes in economics. They may be extremely valuable in suggesting leads to follow in accounting for divergencies between predicted and observed results; that is, in constructing new hypotheses or revising old ones. Whatever their suggestive value in this respect, they seem to me almost entirely useless as a means of *testing* the validity of economic hypotheses. See my comment on Albert G. Hart's paper, "Liquidity and Uncertainty," *American Economic Review*, XXXIX (May, 1949), 198–99.

which the wheat was grown, its physical and chemical characteristics, the weather prevailing during the growing season; the personal characteristics of the farmers growing the wheat and of the consumers who will ultimately use it; and so on indefinitely. Any attempt to move very far in achieving this kind of "realism" is certain to render a theory utterly useless.

Of course, the notion of a completely realistic theory is in part a straw man. No critic of a theory would accept this logical extreme as his objective; he would say that the "assumptions" of the theory being criticized were "too" unrealistic and that his objective was a set of assumptions that were "more" realistic though still not completely and slavishly so. But so long as the test of "realism" is the directly perceived descriptive accuracy of the "assumptions"—for example, the observation that "businessmen do not appear to be either as avaricious or as dynamic or as logical as marginal theory portrays them"[24] or that "it would be utterly impractical under present conditions for the manager of a multi-process plant to attempt . . . to work out and equate marginal costs and marginal revenues for each productive factor"[25]—there is no basis for making such a distinction, that is, for stopping short of the straw man depicted in the preceding paragraph. What is the criterion by which to judge whether a particular departure from realism is or is not acceptable? Why is it more "unrealistic" in analyzing business behavior to neglect the magnitude of businessmen's costs than the color of their eyes? The obvious answer is because the first makes more difference to business behavior than the second; but there is no way of knowing that this is so simply by observing that businessmen do have costs of different magnitudes and eyes of different color. Clearly

it can only be known by comparing the effect on the discrepancy between actual and predicted behavior of taking the one factor or the other into account. Even the most extreme proponents of realistic assumptions are thus necessarily driven to reject their own criterion and to accept the test by prediction when they classify alternative assumptions as more or less realistic.[26]

The basic confusion between descriptive accuracy and analytical relevance that underlies most criticisms of economic theory on the grounds that its assumptions are unrealistic as well as the plausibility of the views that lead to this confusion are both strikingly illustrated by a seemingly innocuous remark in an article on business-cycle theory that "economic phenomena are varied and complex, so any comprehensive theory of the business cycle that can apply closely to reality must be very complicated."[27] A fundamental hypothesis of science is that appearances are deceptive and that there is a way of looking at or interpreting or organizing the evidence that will reveal superficially disconnected and diverse phenomena to be manifestations of a more fundamental and relatively simple structure. And the test of this hy-

---

[24] Oliver, *op. cit.*, p. 382.
[25] Lester, "Shortcomings of Marginal Analysis for Wage-Employment Problems," *op. cit.*, p. 75.
[26] E.g., Gordon's direct examination of the "assumptions" leads him to formulate the alternative hypothesis generally favored by the critics of the maximization-of-returns hypothesis as follows: "There is an irresistible tendency to price on the basis of average total costs for some 'normal' level of output. This is the yardstick, the shortcut, that businessmen and accountants use, and their aim is more to earn satisfactory profits and play safe than to maximize profits" (*op. cit.*, p. 275). Yet he essentially abandons this hypothesis, or converts it into a tautology, and in the process implicitly accepts the test by prediction when he later remarks: "Full cost and satisfactory profits may continue to be the objectives even when total costs are shaded to meet competition or exceeded to take advantage of a sellers' market" (*ibid.*, p. 284). Where here is the "irresistible tendency"? What kind of evidence could contradict this assertion?
[27] Sidney S. Alexander, "Issues of Business Cycle Theory Raised by Mr. Hicks," *American Economic Review*, XLI (December, 1951), 872.

pothesis, as of any other, is its fruits—a test that science has so far met with dramatic success. If a class of "economic phenomena" appears varied and complex, it is, we must suppose, because we have no adequate theory to explain them. Known facts cannot be set on one side; a theory to apply "closely to reality," on the other. A theory is the way we perceive "facts," and we cannot perceive "facts" without a theory. Any assertion that economic phenomena *are* varied and complex denies the tentative state of knowledge that alone makes scientific activity meaningful; it is in a class with John Stuart Mill's justly ridiculed statement that "happily, there is nothing in the laws of value which remains [1848] for the present or any future writer to clear up; the theory of the subject is complete." [28]

The confusion between descriptive accuracy and analytical relevance has led not only to criticisms of economic theory on largely irrelevant grounds but also to misunderstanding of economic theory and misdirection of efforts to repair supposed defects. "Ideal types" in the abstract model developed by economic theorists have been regarded as strictly descriptive categories intended to correspond directly and fully to entities in the real world independently of the purpose for which the model is being used. The obvious discrepancies have led to necessarily unsuccessful attempts to construct theories on the basis of categories intended to be fully descriptive.

This tendency is perhaps most clearly illustrated by the interpretation given to the concepts of "perfect competition" and "monopoly" and the development of the theory of "monopolistic" or "imperfect competition." Marshall, it is said, assumed "perfect competition"; perhaps there once was such a thing. But clearly there is no longer, and we must therefore discard his theories. The reader will search long and hard—and I predict unsuccessfully—to find in Marshall any explicit assumption about perfect competition or any assertion that in a descriptive sense the world is composed of atomistic firms engaged in perfect competition. Rather, he will find Marshall saying: "At one extreme are world markets in which competition acts directly from all parts of the globe; and at the other those secluded markets in which all direct competition from afar is shut out, though indirect and transmitted competition may make itself felt even in these; and about midway between these extremes lie the great majority of the markets which the economist and the business man have to study." [29] Marshall took the world as it is; he sought to construct an "engine" to analyze it, not a photographic reproduction of it.

In analyzing the world as it is, Marshall constructed the hypothesis that, for many problems, firms could be grouped into "industries" such that the similarities among the firms in each group were more important than the differences among them. These are problems in which the important element is that a group of firms is affected alike by some stimulus—a common change in the demand for their products, say, or in the supply of factors. But this will not do for all problems: the important element for these may be the differential effect on particular firms.

The abstract model corresponding to this hypothesis contains two "ideal" types of firms: atomistically competitive firms, grouped into industries, and monopolistic firms. A firm is competitive if the demand curve for its output is infinitely elastic with respect to its own price for some price and all outputs, given the prices charged by all other firms; it belongs to an "industry" defined as a group of firms producing a single "product." A "product" is defined as a collection of units that are per-

[28] *Principles of Political Economy* (Ashley ed.; Longmans, Green & Co., 1929), p. 436.

[29] *Principles*, p. 329; see also pp. 35, 100, 341, 347, 375, 546.

fect substitutes to purchasers so the elasticity of demand for the output of one firm with respect to the price of another firm in the same industry is infinite for some price and some outputs. A firm is monopolistic if the demand curve for its output is not infinitely elastic at some price for all outputs.[30] If it is a monopolist, the firm is the industry.[31]

As always, the hypothesis as a whole consists not only of this abstract model and its ideal types but also of a set of rules, mostly implicit and suggested by example, for identifying actual firms with one or the other ideal type and for classifying firms into industries. The ideal types are not intended to be descriptive; they are designed to isolate the features that are crucial for a particular problem. Even if we could estimate directly and accurately the demand curve for a firm's product, we could not proceed immediately to classify the firm as perfectly competitive or monopolistic according as the elasticity of the demand curve is or is not infinite. No observed demand curve will ever be precisely horizontal, so the estimated elasticity will always be finite. The relevant question always is whether the elasticity is "sufficiently" large to be regarded as infinite, but this is a question that cannot be answered, once for all, simply in terms of the numerical value of the elasticity itself, any more than we can say, once for all, whether an air pressure of 15 pounds per square inch is "sufficiently" close to zero to use the formula $s = \frac{1}{2}gt^2$. Similarly, we cannot compute cross-elasticities of demand and then classify firms into industries according as there is a "substantial

gap in the cross-elasticities of demand." As Marshall says, "The question where the lines of division between different commodities [i.e., industries] should be drawn must be settled by convenience of the particular discussion." [32] Everything depends on the problem; there is no inconsistency in regarding the same firm as if it were a perfect competitor for one problem, and a monopolist for another, just as there is none in regarding the same chalk mark as a Euclidean line for one problem, a Euclidean surface for a second, and a Euclidean solid for a third. The size of the elasticity and cross-elasticity of demand, the number of firms producing physically similar products, etc., are all relevant because they are or may be among the variables used to define the correspondence between the ideal and real entities in a particular problem and to specify the circumstances under which the theory holds sufficiently well; but they do not provide, once for all, a classification of firms as competitive or monopolistic.

An example may help to clarify this point. Suppose the problem is to determine the effect on retail prices of cigarettes of an increase, expected to be permanent, in the federal cigarette tax. I venture to predict that broadly correct results will be obtained by treating cigarette firms as if they were producing an identical product and were in perfect competition. Of course, in such a case, "some convention must be made as to the" number of Chesterfield cigarettes "which are taken as equivalent" to a Marlborough.[33]

On the other hand, the hypothesis that cigarette firms would behave as if they were perfectly competitive would have been a false guide to their reactions to price control in World War II, and this would doubtless have been recognized before the event. Costs of the cigarette firms must have risen during the war. Under

---

[30] This ideal type can be divided into two types: the oligopolistic firm, if the demand curve for its output is infinitely elastic at some price for some but not all outputs; the monopolistic firm proper, if the demand curve is nowhere infinitely elastic (except possibly at an output of zero).

[31] For the oligopolist of the preceding note an industry can be defined as a group of firms producing the same product.

[32] *Principles*, p. 100.

[33] Quoted parts from *ibid.*

such circumstances perfect competitors would have reduced the quantity offered for sale at the previously existing price. But, at that price, the wartime rise in the income of the public presumably increased the quantity demanded. Under conditions of perfect competition strict adherence to the legal price would therefore imply not only a "shortage" in the sense that quantity demanded exceeded quantity supplied but also an absolute decline in the number of cigarettes produced. The facts contradict this particular implication: there was reasonably good adherence to maximum cigarette prices, yet the quantities produced increased substantially. The common force of increased costs presumably operated less strongly than the disruptive force of the desire by each firm to keep its share of the market, to maintain the value and prestige of its brand name, especially when the excess-profits tax shifted a large share of the costs of this kind of advertising to the government. For this problem the cigarette firms cannot be treated *as if* they were perfect competitors.

Wheat farming is frequently taken to exemplify perfect competition. Yet, while for some problems it is appropriate to treat cigarette producers as if they comprised a perfectly competitive industry, for some it is not appropriate to treat wheat producers as if they did. For example, it may not be if the problem is the differential in prices paid by local elevator operators for wheat.

Marshall's apparatus turned out to be most useful for problems in which a group of firms is affected by common stimuli, and in which the firms can be treated *as if* they were perfect competitors. This is the source of the misconception that Marshall "assumed" perfect competition in some descriptive sense. It would be highly desirable to have a more general theory than Marshall's, one that would cover at the same time both those cases in which differentiation of product or fewness of numbers makes an essential difference and those in which it does not. Such a theory would enable us to handle problems we now cannot and, in addition, facilitate determination of the range of circumstances under which the simpler theory can be regarded as a good enough approximation. To perform this function, the more general theory must have content and substance; it must have implications susceptible to empirical contradiction and of substantive interest and importance.

The theory of imperfect or monopolistic competition developed by Chamberlin and Robinson is an attempt to construct such a more general theory.[34] Unfortunately, it possesses none of the attributes that would make it a truly useful general theory. Its contribution has been limited largely to improving the exposition of the economics of the individual firm and thereby the derivation of implications of the Marshallian model, refining Marshall's monopoly analysis, and enriching the vocabulary available for describing industrial experience.

The deficiencies of the theory are revealed most clearly in its treatment of, or inability to treat, problems involving groups of firms—Marshallian "industries." So long as it is insisted that differentiation of product is essential—and it is the distinguishing feature of the theory that it does insist on this point—the definition of an industry in terms of firms producing an identical product cannot be used. By that definition each firm is a separate industry. Definition in terms of "close" substitutes or a "substantial" gap in cross-elasticities evades the issue, introduces fuzziness and undefinable terms into the abstract model where they have no place, and serves only to make the theory analytically meaningless—"close" and "substantial" are in the

[34] E. H. Chamberlin, *The Theory of Monopolistic Competition* (6th ed.; Cambridge: Harvard University Press, 1950); Joan Robinson, *The Economics of Imperfect Competition* (London: Macmillan & Co., 1933).

same category as a "small" air pressure.[35] In one connection Chamberlin implicitly defines an industry as a group of firms having identical cost and demand curves.[36] But this, too, is logically meaningless so long as differentiation of product is, as claimed, essential and not to be put aside. What does it mean to say that the cost and demand curves of a firm producing bulldozers are identical with those of a firm producing hairpins?[37] And if it is meaningless for bulldozers and hairpins, it is meaningless also for two brands of toothpaste—so long as it is insisted that the difference between the two brands is fundamentally important.

The theory of monopolistic competition offers no tools for the analysis of an industry and so no stopping place between the firm at one extreme and general equilibrium at the other.[38] It is therefore incompetent to contribute to the analysis of a host of important problems: the one extreme is too narrow to be of great interest; the other, too broad to permit meaningful generalizations.[39]

---

[35] See R. L. Bishop, "Elasticities, Cross-elasticities, and Market Relationships," *American Economic Review*, XLII (December, 1952), 779–803, for a recent attempt to construct a rigorous classification of market relationships along these lines. Despite its ingenuity and sophistication, the result seems to me thoroughly unsatisfactory. It rests basically on certain numbers being classified as "large" or "small," yet there is no discussion at all of how to decide whether a particular number is "large" or "small," as of course there cannot be on a purely abstract level.

[36] *Op. cit.*, p. 82.

[37] There always exists a transformation of quantities that will make either the cost curves or the demand curves identical; this transformation need not, however, be linear, in which case it will involve different-sized units of one product at different levels of output. There does not necessarily exist a transformation that will make both pairs of curves identical.

[38] See Robert Triffin, *Monopolistic Competition and General Equilibrium Theory* (Cambridge: Harvard University Press, 1940), esp. pp. 188–89.

[39] For a detailed critique see George J. Stigler, "Monopolistic Competition in Retrospect," in *Five Lectures on Economic Problems* (London: Macmillan & Co., 1949). pp. 12–24.

VI. CONCLUSION

Economics as a positive science is a body of tentatively accepted generalizations about economic phenomena that can be used to predict the consequences of changes in circumstances. Progress in expanding this body of generalizations, strengthening our confidence in their validity, and improving the accuracy of the predictions they yield is hindered not only by the limitations of human ability that impede all search for knowledge but also by obstacles that are especially important for the social sciences in general and economics in particular, though by no means peculiar to them. Familiarity with the subject matter of economics breeds contempt for special knowledge about it. The importance of its subject matter to everyday life and to major issues of public policy impedes objectivity and promotes confusion between scientific analysis and normative judgment. The necessity of relying on uncontrolled experience rather than on controlled experiment makes it difficult to produce dramatic and clear-cut evidence to justify the acceptance of tentative hypotheses. Reliance on uncontrolled experience does not affect the fundamental methodological principle that a hypothesis can be tested only by the conformity of its implications or predictions with observable phenomena; but it does render the task of testing hypotheses more difficult and gives greater scope for confusion about the methodological principles involved. More than other scientists, social scientists need to be self-conscious about their methodology.

One confusion that has been particularly rife and has done much damage is confusion about the role of "assumptions" in economic analysis. A meaningful scientific hypothesis or theory typically asserts that certain forces are, and other forces are not, important in understanding a particular class of phenomena. It is frequently convenient to present such a hypothesis by stating that the phenomena it is desired to predict behave in the world of observation *as if* they occurred in a hypothetical and highly simplified world containing only the forces that the hypothesis asserts to be important. In general, there is more than one way to formulate such a description—more than one set of "assumptions" in terms of which the theory can be presented. The choice among such alternative assumptions is made on the grounds of the resulting economy, clarity, and precision in presenting the hypothesis; their capacity to bring indirect evidence to bear on the validity of the hypothesis by suggesting some of its implications that can be readily checked with observation or by bringing out its connection with other hypotheses dealing with related phenomena; and similar considerations.

Such a theory cannot be tested by comparing its "assumptions" directly with "reality." Indeed, there is no meaningful way in which this can be done. Complete "realism" is clearly unattainable, and the question whether a theory is realistic "enough" can be settled only by seeing whether it yields predictions that are good enough for the purpose in hand or that are better than predictions from alternative theories. Yet the belief that a theory can be tested by the realism of its assumptions independently of the accuracy of its predictions is widespread and the source of much of the perennial criticism of economic theory as unrealistic. Such criticism is largely irrelevant, and, in consequence, most attempts to reform economic theory that it has stimulated have been unsuccessful.

The irrelevance of so much criticism of economic theory does not of course imply that existing economic theory deserves any high degree of confidence. These criticisms may miss the target, yet there may be a target for criticism. In a trivial sense, of course, there obviously is. Any theory is

necessarily provisional and subject to change with the advance of knowledge. To go beyond this platitude, it is necessary to be more specific about the content of "existing economic theory" and to distinguish among its different branches; some parts of economic theory clearly deserve more confidence than others. A comprehensive evaluation of the present state of positive economics, summary of the evidence bearing on its validity, and assessment of the relative confidence that each part deserves is clearly a task for a treatise or a set of treatises, if it be possible at all, not for a brief paper on methodology.

About all that is possible here is the cursory expression of a personal view. Existing relative price theory, which is designed to explain the allocation of resources among alternative ends and the division of the product among the co-operating resources and which reached almost its present form in Marshall's *Principles of Economics*, seems to me both extremely fruitful and deserving of much confidence for the kind of economic system that characterizes Western nations. Despite the appearance of considerable controversy, this is true equally of existing static monetary theory, which is designed to explain the structural or secular level of absolute prices, aggregate output, and other variables for the economy as a whole and which has had a form of the quantity theory of money as its basic core in all of its major variants from David Hume to the Cambridge School to Irving Fisher to John Maynard Keynes. The weakest and least satisfactory part of current economic theory seems to me to be in the field of monetary dynamics, which is concerned with the process of adaptation of the economy as a whole to changes in conditions and so with short-period fluctuations in aggregate activity. In this field we do not even have a theory that can appropriately be called "the" existing theory of monetary dynamics.

Of course, even in relative price and static monetary theory there is enormous room for extending the scope and improving the accuracy of existing theory. In particular, undue emphasis on the descriptive realism of "assumptions" has contributed to neglect of the critical problem of determining the limits of validity of the various hypotheses that together constitute the existing economic theory in these areas. The abstract models corresponding to these hypotheses have been elaborated in considerable detail and greatly improved in rigor and precision. Descriptive material on the characteristics of our economic system and its operations have been amassed on an unprecedented scale. This is all to the good. But, if we are to use effectively these abstract models and this descriptive material, we must have a comparable exploration of the criteria for determining what abstract model it is best to use for particular kinds of problems, what entities in the abstract model are to be identified with what observable entities, and what features of the problem or of the circumstances have the greatest effect on the accuracy of the predictions yielded by a particular model or theory.

Progress in positive economics will require not only the testing and elaboration of existing hypotheses but also the construction of new hypotheses. On this problem there is little to say on a formal level. The construction of hypotheses is a creative act of inspiration, intuition, invention; its essence is the vision of something new in familiar material. The process must be discussed in psychological, not logical, categories; studied in autobiographies and biographies, not treatises on scientific method; and promoted by maxim and example, not syllogism or theorem.

3. Assumptions
in Economic Theory*

ERNEST NAGEL

Ernest Nagel (B.S., City College of the City University of New York, 1923; A.M., Columbia University, 1925; Ph.D., 1931) was born in Czechoslovakia in 1901. He is one of the world's most distinguished philosophers of science. Nagel has served on the faculty of Columbia where he has been John Dewey Professor of Philosophy since 1936. Before that he taught at the City University of New York. He was editor of the journal *Philosophy of Science* from 1956–1959 and is a Fellow of the American Academy of Arts and Sciences. He is the author of *Sovereign Reason, Logic Without Metaphysics,* and *The Structure of Science.* *The Scientific American,* in a review of his book *Sovereign Reason,* called Professor Nagel "One of the clearest of contemporary thinkers . . . he brings to his task a sense of humor and an admirable gift for plain talk."

Sound conclusions are sometimes supported by erroneous arguments, and the error is compounded when a sound conclusion is declared to be mistaken on the ground that the argument for it is mistaken. This general observation must serve as my *apologia* for venturing to discuss an important and much debated methodological issue in economics, though not myself an economist. In his well-known essay, "The Methodology of Positive Economics," [1] Professor Milton Friedman defends

* Reprinted from *American Economic Review* (May 1963) by permission of the publisher, pp. 211–219.
[1] It is published in his *Essays in Positive Economics* (Chicago, 1953). All page references, unless otherwise noted, are to this book.

the use of abstract (and in particular, neoclassical) theory in economic analysis, in effect by defending the principle that the adequacy of a theory must be judged, not by assessing what he calls the "realism of its assumptions," but rather by examining the concordance of the theory's logical consequences with the phenomena the theory is designed to explain—a principle which many economists continue to reject, frequently because arguments similar to his seem to them mistaken. I also think that his argument provides no firm support for this principle; and, indeed, my paper is a critique of his defense of it. However, the relevance of my paper is not, I think, limited to Professor Friedman's essay, for I hope to show that despite the inconclusiveness of his argument his conclusion is sound.

I

Since the notions of theory and assumption are central in discussions of the principle at issue, it is convenient to begin by noting some distinctions.

1. The word theory is often used in the social sciences (including economics) rather loosely, to designate almost any general statement, however narrow its intended range of application may be. Thus, the label is commonly given to empirical generalizations (often stated in the form of equations obtained with the help of techniques of curve fitting) that are simply extrapolations from observed statistical regularities, and are asserted to hold only for behaviors occurring in a given community during some particular historical period. On the other hand, many economists (including Professor Friedman) employ the word far more selectively, and approximately in the sense associated with it when it occurs in such phrases as "the Newtonian theory of motion."

It is in this second sense that theory will be used in this paper. Accordingly, an economic theory (e.g., the neoclassical theory of consumer choice) is a set of statements, organized in a characteristic way, and designed to serve as partial premises for explaining as well as predicting an indeterminately large (and usually varied) class of economic phenomena. Moreover, most if not all the statements of a theory have the form of generalized conditionals, which place no spatiotemporal restrictions on the class of phenomena that may be explained with their help. For example, the law of diminishing returns can be expressed in this form: If the quantity of a factor of production is augmented by equal increments, but the quantities of all other factors are kept constant, then the resulting increments in the product will eventually diminish. Space is lacking for discussing adequately the anatomy of theories, but a few additional features distinctive of them must be briefly mentioned.[2]

2. In a given codification of a theory, the statements belonging to it can be divided into three subgroups. The first consists of statements which count as the fundamental ones, and are often called the theory's "assumptions" (or basic "hypotheses"); the second subgroup contains the statements that are logically deducible as theorems from statements in the first. However, the term "assumption" is sometimes also used to refer to the antecedent clause of a conditional theoretical statement in either of these subgroups. This is the way Professor Friedman seems to use the word when, in discussing Galileo's law for freely falling bodies (i.e., "if a body falls toward the earth in a vacuum, its instantaneous acceleration is constant"), he asks whether this law does in fact "assume" that bodies actually fall through a vacuum.

The third subgroup of theoretical statements can also be readily characterized, if we recall that many (and perhaps all) statements in the first two subgroups contain expressions which designate nothing actually observable and are not explicitly definable in terms of expressions that do. Familiar examples of such expressions (for easy reference I will call them "theoretical terms") are "vacuum" in Galileo's law, "gene" in biological theory, and "elasticity of demand at a point" in neoclassical economic theory. Theoretical terms signify either various entities that cannot be specified except by way of some theory which postulates their existence, or certain ideal limits of theoretically endless processes. It

[2] A more detailed analysis is contained in my *The Structure of Science* (New York, 1961), especially Chaps. 5 and 6.

is therefore evident that statements containing such terms cannot possibly explain or predict the course of actual events, unless a sufficient number of theoretical terms (but not necessarily all of them) are coordinated with observable traits of things. Thus, although the theoretical terms "instantaneous acceleration" and "perfectly divisible commodity" describe nothing that can be identified in experience, the expressions do in fact correspond to empirically determinable features in certain actual processes as a consequence of various rules employed (usually tacitly) by physicists and economists. In addition to the two subgroups already mentioned, a theory will in general therefore also contain a third subgroup of statements (though commonly not fully formulated) that indicate among other things such correspondences. It must be emphasized, however, that these statements do not define theoretical terms by way of terms signifying observable traits, so that theoretical terms cannot be eliminated from formulations in which they occur with the help of these statements.[3]

3. One further point deserves mention in this connection. In most disciplines, theoretical formulations (particularly those in the first two subgroups) are normally treated as statements about some subject matter, so that as in the case of other statements questions about the truth or falsity of such formulations are regarded

[3] This point is of major importance. Professor Friedman also recognizes a category of statements in a theory roughly equivalent to the third subgroup of theoretical statements distinguished above; but he appears to believe that theoretical terms can be eliminated with the help of statements in this category. The point at issue cannot be adequately discussed in short compass, but an example will perhaps make clear why such a belief is dubious. Quantum theory is stated in terms of various theoretical terms, referring to such elementary particles as electrons. However, although physicists are certainly able to apply quantum theory to observable processes with the aid of statements in the third subgroup, such statements of correspondence do not permit the elimination of terms like "electron" from quantum theory.

as significant though difficult to answer. On the other hand, theoretical formulations are sometimes denied the status of "genuine" statements and are said to be simply rules which are instrumental for drawing inferences from genuine statements but which cannot be properly characterized as true or false. It is impossible in the space available to examine the merits of these opposing views on the status of theories. I have mentioned them to call attention to the fact that a defense of the methodological principle under discussion is intelligible only on the supposition that economic theory is a set of genuine statements, so that considerations of their truth or falsity are not irrelevant to the objectives of economic analysis.

II

Professor Friedman rests his argument for the methodological principle on some general reflections concerning the nature of theories *überhaupt*. He notes that a theory cannot explain a class of phenomena, unless it abstracts a small number of "common and crucial elements" (in terms of which the phenomena may be predicted) from the mass of differing circumstances in which the phenomena are embedded. Accordingly, the assumptions of a satisfactory theory are inescapably "descriptively false" or "unrealistic," so that it is pointless to assess the merits of a theory by asking whether or not its assumptions are realistic. The relevant question is whether or not the theory yields predictions which are "sufficiently good approximations for the purpose at hand."[4]

However, an assumption may be unrealistic in at least three senses important for the argument, though Professor Friedman does not distinguish them.

1. A statement can be said to be unrealistic because it does not give an "exhaustive" description of some object, so that it

[4] Pp. 14–15.

mentions only some traits actually characterizing the object but ignores an endless number of other traits also present. However, no finitely long statement can possibly formulate the totality of traits embodied in any concretely existing thing; and it is difficult to imagine what a statement would be like that is not unrealistic in this sense, or what conceivable use such a statement could have. But in any event, it is with this rather trivial sense of the word in mind that Professor Friedman seems frequently to defend the legitimacy of unrealistic assumptions in economic theory;[5] and although it is not clear whether any economists have maintained a contrary thesis, his defense is fully conclusive.

2. A statement may be said to be unrealistic because it is believed to be either false or highly improbable on the available evidence. Such lack of realism can sometimes be established on the basis of what Professor Friedman calls a "directly perceived descriptive inaccuracy"; but in general, statements can be shown to be false only "indirectly," by first deducing from them some of their logical consequences (or implications), and then comparing the latter with "directly" observed matters of fact. Since it is usually not possible to establish the falsity of theoretical statements directly, Professor Friedman correctly stresses the relevance of this indirect procedure for ascertaining whether a theory is unrealistic. Nevertheless, as he recognizes and even illustrates,[6] the distinction between an assumption and its implications is a sharp one only in a given formulation of a theory—an implication of some assumption in one formulation may in another formulation be a premise implying that assumption. Accordingly, his repeated claim that an assumption can be rightly tested for its realism only indirectly obviously needs qualification.

[5] Pp. 18, 25, 32, 35.
[6] Pp. 26–27.

But in any event, if by an assumption of a theory we understand one of the theory's fundamental statements (i.e., those belonging to the first of the three subgroups previously noted), a theory with an unrealistic assumption (in the present sense of the word, according to which the assumption is false) is patently unsatisfactory; for such a theory entails consequences that are incompatible with observed fact, so that on pain of rejecting elementary logical canons the theory must also be rejected. On the other hand, a universal conditional neither asserts nor presupposes that the conditions explicitly stated in its antecedent clause are actually realized; accordingly, a theoretical statement having this logical form is not proved to be false by showing that the specifications in its antecedent are not embodied in some given spatiotemporal region (or for that matter, in any region). Professor Friedman is therefore quite right in maintaining that a theory is not necessarily erroneous merely because its assumptions are unrealistic—provided that he is taken to mean by an "assumption of a theory," as he sometimes appears to mean, an antecedent clause of some theoretical statement. However, a theory whose assumptions are in this sense unrealistic for a given domain is simply inapplicable in that domain, though it may be applicable in another. But what is to be said of a theory whose assumptions are ostensibly unrealistic for every domain? The aspect of this question that is especially relevant to Professor Friedman's essay is best treated after the third sense of unrealistic has been explained.

3. In many sciences, relations of dependence between phenomena are often stated with reference to so-called "pure cases" or "ideal types" of the phenomena being investigated. That is, such theoretical statements (or "laws") formulate relations specified to hold under highly "purified" conditions between highly "idealized"

objects or processes, none of which is actually encountered in experience. For example, the law of the lever in physics is stated in terms of the behavior of absolutely rigid rods turning without friction about dimensionless points; similarly, a familiar law of pricing in economics is formulated in terms of the exchange of perfectly divisible and homogenous commodities under conditions of perfect competition. Statements of this kind contain what have previously been called "theoretical terms," which connote what are in effect the limits of various non-terminating series and which are not intended to designate anything actual. Such statements may be said to be unrealistic but in a sense different from the two previously noted. For they are not distinguished by their failure to provide exhaustive descriptions, nor are they literally false of anything; their distinguishing mark is the fact that when they are strictly construed, they are applicable to nothing actual.

However, laws of nature formulated with reference to pure cases are not therefore useless. On the contrary, a law so formulated states how phenomena are related when they are unaffected by numerous factors whose influence may never be completely eliminable but whose effects generally vary in magnitude with differences in the attendant circumstances under which the phenomena actually recur. Accordingly, discrepancies between what is asserted for the pure case and what actually happens can be attributed to the influence of factors not mentioned in the law. Moreover, since these factors and their effects can often be ascertained, the influence of the factors can be systematically classified into general types; and in consequence, the law can be viewed as the limiting case of a set of other laws corresponding to these various types, where each further law states a modified relation of dependence between the phenomena because of the influence of

factors that are absent in the pure case. In short, unrealistic theoretical statements (in the third sense of the word) serve as a powerful means for analyzing, representing, and codifying relations of dependence between actual phenomena.

III

Professor Friedman's discussion of unrealistic assumptions in examples of theoretical statements drawn from physics and biology sheds important light on his defense of such assumptions in economic theory. It will therefore be useful to examine his account of one of these examples.

1. In his discussion of Galileo's law, Professor Friedman notes that the law is stated for bodies falling in a vacuum, but also declares that the law "works" in a large number of cases (i.e., it is in sufficiently good agreement for certain purposes with the actual behavior of bodies in these cases), though not in others. He therefore suggests that the law can be restated to read: Under a wide range of circumstances, bodies that fall in the actual atmosphere behave *as if* they were falling in a vacuum. Indeed, he seems to think that the law can be rephrased without mentioning a vacuum, as follows: Under a wide range of circumstances, the distance a body falls in a specified time is given by the formula $s = \frac{1}{2} gt^2$. Accordingly, he maintains that the circumstances in which the law works (and is therefore acceptable) must be specified as "an essential part" of the law, even though this specification (and in consequence also the law) may need revision in the light of further experience.[7]

However, as has already been indicated, the term "vacuum" is a theoretical one, so that Galileo's law in its standard version is formulated for pure cases of falling bodies. Professor Friedman's proposed par-

[7] Pp. 18–19.

aphrase which omits all mention of a vacuum thus rests on the supposition that theoretical terms can in general be replaced by nontheoretical ones, without altering the meaning and function of the statements containing them. But the possibility of such a replacement is dubious on formal grounds alone; and what is more important, the suggestion that unless theoretical terms can thus be eliminated the statements containing them are scientifically otiose, overlooks the rationale for stating laws in terms of pure cases. In point of fact, the proposed paraphrase mistakenly assumes that Galileo's law can be assigned the functions actually performed by statements of correspondence (belonging to the third subgroup of theoretical statements) without impairing the effectiveness of the standard formulation for achieving systematic generality in theoretical physics.

2. The example Professor Friedman uses for the most part in his defense of unrealistic assumptions in economics is the familiar "rational maximization of returns" hypothesis in the theory of the firm. However, he states it as follows: "Under a wide range of circumstances, individual firms behave *as if* they were seeking rationally to maximize their expected returns and had full knowledge of the data needed to succeed in this attempt." [8] He freely admits that as a rule businessmen lack such knowledge and do not perform the intricate calculations required for ascertaining the indicated maximum. Indeed, he declares that "the apparent immediate determinants of business behavior" could be anything at all; e.g., ingrained habit or a chance influence. He nevertheless claims that these admitted facts do not affect the validity of the hypothesis. The relevant evidence, according to him, is the large set of facts in good agreement with various implications of the hypothesis, including

the fact that firms whose actions are markedly inconsistent with it do not survive for long.

It is pertinent to ask, however, whether the operative premise from which these implications really follow is perhaps the supposition, suggested by Professor Friedman's discussion, that is rendered by: "Under a wide range of circumstances, the behavior of individual firms brings them returns approximately equal to a certain magnitude (called the maximum of expected returns by economists)"; or whether the operative premise is the hypothesis as he formulates it. On the first alternative, most of the matters mentioned in his "as if" formulation are irrelevant to the substantive content of the hypothesis. In particular, the hypothesis must then not be understood as either asserting or implying that firms conduct their affairs in order to achieve some objective. To be sure, the statement of the hypothesis contains the expression "the maximum of expected returns"; nevertheless, this expression simply designates a set of rules used by economists rather than by firms for calculating a certain magnitude. In short, the hypothesis in this case is a somewhat loosely expressed empirical generalization about the returns firms actually receive as the outcome of their overt behavior, and it specifies no determinants in explanation of that behavior.[9] Accordingly, although the hypothesis is not an exhaustive description of anything, it is not clear in what sense other than this trivial one the hypothesis is in this case unrealistic if, as Professor Friedman claims, it is in good agreement

[8] P. 21.

[9] In particular, the hypothesis does not include the assumption, integral to many formulations of neoclassical theory, that firms are purposive agents, whose decisions are based on rationally formed estimates of the relative advantages and risks associated with alternative courses of action open to them. See, for example, Frank H. Knight, *Risk, Uncertainty and Profit* (London, 1957), and Paul A. Samuelson, *Foundations of Economic Analysis* (Cambridge, Mass., 1947), Chap. III.

with experience. On the second alternative, however, it is difficult to avoid reading the hypothesis as saying that firms do seek to maximize their returns in a rational manner, since otherwise it appears to be asserting nothing whatsoever. But the hypothesis must then be understood as dealing with pure cases of economic behavior, requiring the use of theoretical terms in its formulation which cannot be replaced by nontheoretical expressions. Accordingly, the various facts Professor Friedman freely admits but thinks are irrelevant may in this case be quite pertinent in assessing the merits of the hypothesis.

Professor Friedman's essay does not indicate explicitly which alternative renders the hypothesis as he understands it. In consequence, the essay is marked by an ambiguity that perhaps reflects an unresolved tension in his views on the status of economic theory. Is he defending the legitimacy of unrealistic theoretical assumptions because he thinks theories are at best only useful instruments, valuable for predicting observable events but not to be viewed as genuine statements whose truth or falsity may be significantly investigated? But if this is the way he conceives theories (and much in his argument suggests that it is), the distinction between realistic and unrealistic theoretical assumptions is at best irrelevant, and no defense of theories lacking in realism is needed. Or is he undertaking that defense in order to show that unrealistic theories cannot only be invaluable tools for making predictions but that they may also be reasonably satisfactory explanations of various phenomena in terms of the mechanisms involved in their occurrence? But if this is his aim (and parts of his discussion are compatible with the supposition that it is), a theory cannot be viewed, as he repeatedly suggests that it can, as a "simple summary" of some vaguely delimited set of empirical

generalizations with distinctly specified ranges of application.[10]

Curiously enough, something like the notion that theories can be viewed in this manner underlies one criticism of Professor Friedman's defense of the maximization-of-returns hypothesis. Thus Professor Koopmans argues that if (as Professor Friedman holds) the fact that firms whose behavior diverges from it are not likely to survive is a basis for accepting the hypothesis, "we should postulate that basis itself and not the profit maximization which it implies in certain circumstances."[11] This seems like a recommendation that since a basis for accepting Newtonian gravitational theory is the fact that observed regularities in the motions of the planets are in agreement with various special laws deduced from the theory, we should postulate those regularities rather than the theory—a recommendation that would replace the theory by the empirical evidence for the theory. Such a proposal not only rejects the conception that theories have an explanatory function; it also overlooks the irreplacable role theories have in scientific inquiry in suggesting how empirical generalizations may need to be corrected, as well as in directing and systematizing further empirical research. Unless I have seriously misunderstood Professor Friedman's essay, he would reject a proposal of this sort. Nevertheless, at various points in his argument he seems to construe theoretical statements in a manner that is almost indistinguishable from what is implied by such a proposal. I have therefore tried in this paper to show where his argument lacks cogency, as well as to indicate why the main thesis he is ostensibly defending is nonetheless sound.

[10] P. 24.
[11] Tjalling C. Koopmans, *Three Essays on the State of Economic Science* (New York, 1957), p. 140.

Part III

DEMAND

Utility Theory and Consumers' Surplus

4. The Meaning of Utility Measurement*

ARMEN A. ALCHIAN[1]

Armen A. Alchian (A.B., Stanford, 1936; Ph.D., 1944) was born in Fresno, California, in 1914. Since 1946 he has served on the faculty of the University of California (Los Angeles), where he is now Professor of Economics. Since 1947 he has been a member of the Economics Division of the RAND Corporation. He is famous for his work in price theory and for research on inflation and the economic theory of property rights. His textbook, *University Economics* (with William R. Allen), is noteworthy for the rigor and clarity of its exposition.

Economists struggling to keep abreast of current developments may well be exasperated by the resurgence of measurability of utility. After all, the indifference curve analysis was popularized little over ten years ago amidst the contradictory proclamations that it eliminated, modified, and strengthened the rôle of utility. Even yet there is confusion, induced partly by careless reading and exposition of the indifference curve analysis and partly by misunderstandings of the purposes and implications of utility measurement. This paper attempts to clarify the rôle and meaning of the recent revival of measurement of utility in economic theory and of the meaning of certain concepts and operations commonly used in utility theory.

Measurement in its broadest sense is the assignment of numbers to entities. The process of measurement has three aspects which should be distinguished at the outset. First is the purpose of measurement, second is the process by which one measures something, *i.e.*, assigns numerical values to some aspect of an entity, and the third is the arbitrariness, or uniqueness, of the set of numerical values inherent in the purpose and process. In the first part of this paper we briefly explore the idea of

* Reprinted from *American Economic Review* (March 1953) by permission of the publisher, pp. 26–50.

[1] The author is associate professor of economics at the University of California, Los Angeles. He wishes to acknowledge gratefully the aid of Norman Dalkey and Harry Markowitz, both of The RAND Corporation. The patient explanations of Dalkey in answering innumerable questions overcame early impulses to abandon the attempt to understand recent utility literature. Markowitz detected several ambiguities and errors in earlier drafts of this exposition. Since neither has seen the final draft they must be relieved of responsibility for remaining errors and ambiguities.

arbitrariness or uniqueness of numbers assigned by a measurement process. In Part II we state some purposes of utility measurement. In Part III we examine a method of measuring utility, the purpose of the measurement and the extent to which the measurement is unique. In Part IV we look at some implications of the earlier discussion.[2]

I. DEGREE OF MEASURABILITY

The columns of Table 4.1 are sequences of numbers illustrating the concept of the "degree of measurability." The entities, some aspect of which we wish to measure, are denoted by letters. Later we shall discuss the meaning of these entities. Our first task is to explain the difference between monotone transformations and linear transformations.

We shall begin with monotone transformations and then come to linear transformations via two of its special cases, additive and multiplicative constants.

Monotone Transformations

Let there be assigned a numerical magnitude (measure) to each entity concerned. For example in Table 4.1, for the ten en-

[2] The explanation assumes no mathematical background and is on an elementary level. This paper is not original in any of its ideas, nor is it a general review of utility and demand theory. It is merely a statement of some propositions that may help the reader separate the chaff from the wheat. It may even make clear to the reader, as it did to the writer, one meaning of utility. Most of the material presented here is contained in J. Marschak, "Rational Behavior, Uncertain Prospects and Measurable Utility," *Econometrica* (April 1950), XVIII, 111–141, an article written for the mathematically mature. A bibliography is included, to which those who might wish to read more deeply should refer. Excellent starting points are M. Friedman and L. J. Savage, "The Utility Analysis of Choices Involving Risk," *Jour. Pol. Econ.* (Aug. 1948), LVI, 279–304, and J. Marschak, "Why 'Should' Statisticians and Businessmen Maximize 'Moral Expectation'?", *Proceedings of the Second Berkeley Symposium on Mathematical Statistics and Probability* (Berkeley, University of California Press, 1951), pp. 493–506.

TABLE 4.1

ILLUSTRATION OF TYPES OF MEASUREMENT

Entities	Alternative measures of "utility"								
	1	2	3	4	5	6	7	8	9
A	1	2	6	11	2	6	5	6	3
B	2	4	7	12	4	12	7	10	7
C	3	5	8	13	6	18	9	14	13
D	4	8	9	14	8	24	11	18	21
E	5	11	10	15	10	30	13	22	31
F	7	14	12	17	14	42	17	30	43
G	11	22	16	21	22	66	25	46	57
H	14	28	19	24	28	84	31	58	73
I	16	33	21	26	32	96	35	66	91
J	17	34	22	27	34	102	37	70	111

tities, A–J, listed in the extreme left-hand column, nine different sets of numbers are utilized to assign nine different numbers to each of the entities. If two sets of numbers (measures) result in the same ranking or ordering of the entities (according to the numbers assigned), then the two sets are *monotone transformations* of each other. In Table 4.1 it will be seen that all nine measures give the same ranking, thus all nine measures are monotone transformations of each other. If this property holds true over the entire class of entities concerned, then the two measures are monotone transformations of each other for that class of entities. The possible set of monotone transformations obviously is very large.

Linear Transformations: Additive Constants

We shall approach the linear transformation by considering two special forms. Look at the numbers in column 3. They are the same as those in 1 except that a constant has been added, in this case 5, *i.e.*, they are the *same "up to"* (except for) an *additive constant*. The measure in column 4 is equivalent to that in column 1 with 10 added. Columns 1, 3 and 4 are *transforms* of each other "up to" (by means of) *additive constants*. This can also be expressed by saying they are equivalent except for an additive constant. The term "up to" implies that we may go through some simpler types. For example, all the transforms up to an additive constant are also contained in the larger, less restricted class of possible transforms known as monotone transforms. An additive constant is a quite strong restriction, even though it may not seem so at first since there is an unlimited number of available constants. But relative to the range of possibilities in the general linear transformations this is very restrictive indeed.

Linear Transformations: Multiplicative Constants

Now look at column 5. It is equivalent to column 1 except for multiplication by a constant, in this case, 2. Column 5 is a monotone transform of column 1, and it is also a "multiplicative by a constant" transform of column 1. Column 6 is column 1 multiplied by 6. Thus, while columns 1, 5 and 6 are monotone transforms of each other, they are also a more particular type of transform. They are transforms up to a multiplicative constant. These are special cases of linear transformations which we shall now discuss.

General Linear Transformations

The numbers of column 7 are equivalent to column 1 except for multiplication by 2 and addition of 3. Letting y denote the numbers or "measures" in column 7 and x those of column 1, we have $y = 2x + 3$. Column 8 is derived similarly from column 1; the multiplier is 4 and the added constant is 2. Column 8 is given by $4x + 2$, but a little inspection will show that column 8 can be derived from column 7 by the same process of multiplying and adding. In this case column 8 is obtained from column 7 by multiplying by 2 and adding −4. Columns 1, 7 and 8 are thus "linear

transforms" of each other. This is also expressed by saying that they are the same measures "up to a linear transformation"; that is, any one of these measures can be obtained from any other one by simply selecting appropriate constants for multiplication and addition.

There is a particular property of the linear transformation that has historical significance in economics. Look at the way the numbers change as one moves from entity to entity. For example, consider columns 1 and 7. The numerical change from entity E to entity F has a value of 2 in the measure of column 1, while in the measure of column 7, it has a numerical value of 4. From F to G the change is 4 in measure 1, and in measure 7 it is 8. If the increment is positive, it will be positive in all sequences which are linear transforms of this particular sequence. But this is true also for all monotone transformations—a much broader class of transformations or measures. Of greater significance, however, is the following attribute of linear transforms: if the differences between the numbers in one of the sequences increases (or decreases) from entity to entity, then the differences between the numbers of these same entities in all of its *linear* transformations will also be increasing (or decreasing). In general, the property of increasing or decreasing increments is not affected by switching from one sequence of numbers to any linear transformation of that given sequence. In mathematical terms, the sign of the second differences of a sequence of numbers is invariant to linear transformations of that sequence.[3] The significance of invariance will be discussed later, but we should note that this property of increasing (or decreasing) differences between the numbers assigned to pairs of entities is nothing but increasing marginal utility— if one christens the assigned numbers "utilities."

[3] In monotonic transformations the sign of the *first* differences only are necessarily left undisturbed.

II. PURPOSE OF MEASUREMENT

Order

In the nine columns of Table 4.1 are nine "different" measures of some particular aspect of the entities denoted A, B, C, . . . J. How different are they? We have already answered this. Which is the "right" one? This depends upon what one wants to do with the entities and the numbers. It would be more useful to ask which one is a *satisfactory* measure, for then it is clear that we must make explicit for what it is to be satisfactory.[4] For example, if my sole concern were to predict which of the entities would be the heaviest, the next heaviest, etc., I could, by successively comparing pairs in a balancing scale, completely order the entities. [Having done so, I could then assign the numbers in *any* one of columns 1 through 9] so long as I assign the biggest number to the heaviest, and so on down. This means that for the purpose of indicating *order*, any one of the monotone transforms is acceptable.

The remaining task is to determine whether the order is "correctly" stated; the fact that the order is the same, no matter which one of the above transforms is used, does not imply that the order is correct. What do we mean by "correctly"? We mean that our stated or predicted order is matched by the order revealed by some other observable ordering process. You could put the entities on some new weighing scales (the new scales are the "test"), and then a matching of the order derived from the new scales with our stated order is a verification of the correctness (predictive validity) of our first ordering. Any monotone transform of one valid ordering number sequence is *for the purpose* in this

[4] A pause to reflect will reveal that there is a second problem besides that of deciding what "satisfactory" means. This second problem, which we have so far begged, is: "How does one assign numbers to entities?" It is deferred to the following section.

illustration *completely equivalent* to the numbers actually used. That is, any one of the possible monotone transformations is just as good as any other.

We may summarize by saying that, given a method for validly ordering entities, any monotone transformation of the particular numerical values assigned in the ordering process will be equally satisfactory. We may be technical and say that "all measures of order are equivalent up to (except for being) monotone transformations." Or, in other words, a method of validly denoting *order* only, is not capable of uniquely identifying a particular set of numbers as *the* correct one. Any monotonic transformation will do exactly as well. The degree of uniqueness of an ordering can also be described by saying it is only as unique as the set of monotone transformations. Thus, we often see the expression that "ordering is unique up to a monotone transformation."

Ordering Groups of Entities

But suppose our purpose were different. Suppose we want to be able to order *groups* of entities according to their weights. More precisely, suppose we want to assign numbers to each of the component objects so that when we combine the objects into sets or bundles we can order the weights of the composite bundles, knowing only the individually valid numbers assigned to each component, by *merely adding* together the numbers assigned to each component. And we want to be able to do this for any possible combination of the objects. Fortunately, man has discerned a way to do this for weights. The numbers which are assigned by this discovered process are arbitrary up to a multiplicative constant (of proportionality), so that the numbers could express either pounds, ounces, tons or grams. That is, we can arbitrarily multiply all the numbers assigned to the various components by any constant we please, without destroying the validity of our resulting numbers for this particular purpose. But we can not use any monotone transformation as we could in the preceding case where our purpose was different.

If we were to add an arbitrary constant to each component's individually valid numerical (weight) value we would not be able to add the resulting numbers of each component in order to get a number which would rank the composite bundles. Thus, the numbers we can assign are rather severely constrained. We can not use any linear transformation, but we can use a multiplicative constant, which is a special type of linear transformation. And if we were to "measure" lengths of items so as to be able simply to "add" the numbers to get the lengths of the items laid end to end, we would again find ourselves confined to sequences (measures) with a multiplicative constant as the one available degree of arbitrariness.

Utility
and Ordering of Choices

The reader has merely to substitute for the concept of weight, in the earlier example about weight orders, the idea of "preference" and he is in the theory of choice or demand. Economics goes a step further and gives the name "utility" to the numbers. Can we assign a set of numbers (measures) to the various entities and predict that the entity with the largest assigned number (measure) will be chosen? If so, we could christen this measure "utility" and then assert that choices are made so as to maximize utility. It is an easy step to the statement that "you are maximizing your utility," which says no more than that your choice is predictable according to the size of some assigned numbers.[5] For analytical convenience it is customary to postulate that an individual

seeks to maximize something subject to some constraints. The thing—or numerical measure of the "thing"—which he seeks to maximize is called "utility." Whether or not utility is some kind of glow or warmth, or happiness, is here irrelevant; all that counts is that we can assign numbers to entities or conditions which a person can strive to realize. Then we say the individual seeks to maximize some function of those numbers. Unfortunately, the term "utility" has by now acquired so many connotations, that it is difficult to realize that for present purposes utility has no more meaning than this. The analysis of individual demand behavior is mathematically describable as the process of maximizing some quantitive measures, or numbers, and we assume that the individual seeks to obtain that combination with the highest choice number, given the purchasing power at his disposal. It might be harmless to call this "utility theory."[6]

Three Types
of Choice Predictions

Sure Prospects Before proceeding further it is necessary to indicate clearly the types of choice that will concern us. The first type of choice is that of selecting among a set of alternative "riskless" choices. A riskless choice, hereafter called a sure prospect, is one such that the chooser knows exactly what he will surely get with each possible choice. To be able to predict the preferred choice means we can assign numbers to the various entities such that the entity with the largest assigned number is the most preferred, the one with the second largest number is the next most preferred, etc. As said earlier, it is customary to christen this numerical magnitude with the name "utility."

[5] The difficult (impossible?) psychological, philosophical step of relating this kind of utility to some *quantity* of *satisfaction, happiness, goodness* or *welfare* is not attempted here.

[6] The author, having so far kept his opinions submerged, is unable to avoid remarking that it would seem "better" to confine utility "theory" to attempts to explain or discern why a person chooses one thing rather than another—at equal price.

An understanding of what is meant by "entity" is essential. An entity denotes any specifiable object, action, event, or set or pattern of such items or actions. It may be an orange, a television set, a glass of milk, a trip to Europe, a particular time profile of income or consumption (*e.g.*, steak every night, or ham every night, or steak and ham on alternate nights), getting married, etc. Identifying an entity exclusively with one single event or action would lead to unnecessary restrictions on the scope of the applicability of the theorem to be presented later.[7]

Groups of Sure Prospects A second problem of choice prediction would be that of ordering (predicting) choices among riskless *groups* of entities. A riskless group consists of several entities all of which will be surely obtained if that group is chosen. The problem now is to predict the choice among riskless groups knowing only the utilities assigned to the individual entities which have been aggregated into groups. Thus if in Table 4.1 we were to assemble the entities A through J into various groups, could we predict the choice among these groups of entities knowing only the utility numbers that were assigned to the component entities for the purpose of the preceding choice problem? Of course we ask this question only on the assumption that the utilities previously assigned to the component entities were valid predictors of choice among the single sure prospects.[8]

Uncertain Prospects A third type of

problem is that of ordering choices among risky choices, or what have been called uncertain prospects. An uncertain prospect is a group of entities, only one entity of which will be realized if that group is chosen. For example, an uncertain prospect might consist of a fountain pen, a radio and an automobile. If that uncertain prospect is chosen, the chooser will surely get one of the three entities, but which one he will actually get is not known in advance. He is not completely ignorant about what will be realized, for it is assumed that he knows the probabilities of realization attached to each of the component entities in an uncertain prospect. For example, the probabilities might have been .5 for the fountain pen, .4 for the radio and .1 for the automobile. These probabilities sum to 1.0; one and only one of these entities will be realized. An uncertain prospect is very much like a ticket in a lottery. If there is but one prize, then the uncertain prospect consists of two entities, the prize or the loss of the stake. If there are several prizes, the uncertain prospect consists of several entities—the various prizes and, of course, the loss of the stake (being a loser).

But there is another requirement that we want our prediction process to satisfy. Not only must we be able to predict the choices, but we want to do it in a very simple way. Specifically, we want to be able to look at each component separately, and then from utility measures assigned to the elements, as if they were sure prospects, we want to be able to aggregate the component utility measures into a group utility measure predicting choices among the uncertain prospects. For example, suppose the uncertain prospects consisted of a pen, a radio and an automobile as listed in Table 4.2.

Are there utilities which can be assigned to the pen, the radio and the automobile, so that for the purpose of comparing these four uncertain prospects the same num-

[7] For example, see H. Wold, "Ordinal Preferences or Cardinal Utility? (With Additional Notes by G. L. S. Shackle, L. J. Savage, and H. Wold)"; A. S. Manne, "The Strong Independence Assumption-Gasoline Blends and Probability Mixtures (with Additional Notes by A. Charnes)"; P. Samuelson, "Probability, Utility, and the Independence Axiom"; E. Malinvaud, "Note on Neumann-Morgenstern's Strong Independence Axiom," *Econometrica* (Oct. 1952), XX, 661–79.

[8] For an illustration of this problem of rating a composite bundle by means of the ratings of the ratings of the components, see A. S. Manne, *op. cit.*

bers could be used in arriving at utility numbers to be assigned to the uncertain prospects? In particular, can we assign to the pen, the radio and the automobile numbers such that when multiplied by the associated probabilities in each uncertain prospect they will yield a sum (expected utility) for each uncertain prospect, and such that these "expected utilities" would indicate preference?

TABLE 4.2

EXAMPLES OF UNCERTAIN PROSPECTS

Uncertain prospect	Probabilities of getting		
	Pen	Radio	Automobile
1	.5	.4	.1
2	.58	.30	.12
3	.85	.0	.15
4	.0	.99	.01

Before answering we shall briefly indicate why choices among uncertain prospects constitute an important class of situations. Upon reflection it will be seen to be the practically universal problem of choice. Can the reader think of many cases in which he *knows* when making a choice, the outcome of that choice with absolute certainty? In other words, are there many choices—or actions—in life in which the *consequences* can be predicted with absolute certainty? Even the act of purchasing a loaf of bread has an element of uncertainty in its consequences; even the act of paying one's taxes has an element of uncertainty in the consequences involved; even the decision to sit down has an element of uncertainty in the consequence. But to leave the trivial, consider the choice of occupation, purchase of an automobile, house, durable goods, business investment, marriage, having children, insurance, gambling, etc. ad infinitum. Clearly choices among uncertain prospects constitute an extremely large and important class of choices.

III. METHOD OF MEASUREMENT

So far we have discussed the meaning and purpose of measurement. We turn to the method of measurement recognizing that for each type of choice prediction the method of measurement must have a rationale as well as a purpose. For a moment we can concentrate on the rationale which is properly stated in the form of axioms defining rational behavior.

Sure Prospects

Let us start with a rationale for the first type of choice. We postulate that an individual behaves consistently, *i.e.*, he has a consistent set of preferences; that these preferences are transitive, *i.e.*, if B is preferred to A, and C to B, then C is preferred to A; and that these preferences can be completely described merely by attaching a numerical value to each. An implication of these postulates is that for such individuals we can predict their choices by a numerical variable (utility). Asking the individual to make pairwise comparisons we assign numbers to the sure prospects such that the choice order will be revealed by the size of the numbers attached. The number of pairwise comparisons that the individual must make depends upon how fortunate we are in selecting the pairs for his comparison. If we are so lucky as first to present him a series of pairs of alternatives of sure prospects exactly matching his preference order, the complete ordering of his preferences will be obtained with the minimal amount of pairwise comparisons. Any numbering sequence which gives the most preferred sure prospect the highest number, the second preferred sure prospect the second highest number, etc., will predict his choices according to "utility maximization." But any other sequence of numbers could be used so long as it is a *monotone transformation* of the first sequence. And this is exactly the meaning of the statement that utility is *ordinal* and not cardinal. The transitivity postulate enables this pairwise comparison to reveal the complete order of preferences, and the consistency postulate means he would make his choices according to the prediction. Thus if he were to be presented with any two of ten sure prospects, we would predict his taking the one with the higher utility number. If our prediction failed, then one of our postulates would have been denied, and our prediction method would not be valid. A hidden postulate is that the preferences, if transitive and consistent, are stable for the interval involved.[9] Utility for this purpose and by this method is measurable up to a monotonic transformation, *i.e.*, it is ordinal only.

Groups of Sure Prospects

The second type of choice, among *groups* of sure prospects, can be predicted using the same postulates only if we treat each group of sure prospects as a sure prospect. Then by presenting pairs of "groups of sure prospects" we can proceed as in the preceding problem. But the interesting problem here is that of predicting choice among groups of sure prospects (entities) only by knowing valid utility measures for choices among the component sure prospects. Can these utility numbers of the component entities of the group of sure prospects, which are valid for the entities by themselves, be aggregated to obtain a number predicting choice among the groups of sure prospects? In general the answer is "no." Hence, although utility was meas-

urable for the purpose of the kind of prediction in the preceding problem, it is not measurable in the sense that these component measures can be aggregated or combined in any known way to predict choices among *groups* of sure prospects. Utility is "measurable" for one purpose but not for the other.[10]

Uncertain Prospects

We want to predict choices among uncertain prospects. And we want to make these predictions solely on the basis of the utilities and probabilities attached to the elements of the uncertain prospects.

Without going into too many details an intuitive idea of the content of the axioms used in deriving this kind of measurability will now be given.[11] For expository convenience the statement that the two entities A and B are equally desirable or indifferent will be expressed by $A = B$; if however A is either preferred to or indifferent to B, the expression will be $A \geq B$.

---

[9] Some problems involved in this assumption and in its relaxation are discussed by N. Georgescu-Roegen, "The Theory of Choice and the Constancy of Economic Laws," *Quart. Jour. Econ.* (Feb. 1950), LXIV, 125–38.

[10] It is notable that the usual indifference curve analysis is contained in this case. Any *group* of sure prospects (point in the xy plane of an indifference curve diagram) which has more of each element in it than there is in another group of two sure prospects, will be preferred to the latter. And further, if one group of sure prospects has more of one commodity than does the other group of sure prospects, the two groups can be made indifferent by sufficiently increasing the amount of the second commodity in the other group of sure prospects. The indifference curve (utility isoquant) approach does not assign numbers representing utility to the various sure prospects lying along either the horizontal or the vertical axis and then from these numerical values somehow obtain a number which would order choices among the groups of prospects inside the quadrant enclosed by the axes.

[11] This is the method developed by J. von Neumann and P. Morgenstern, *The Theory of Games and Economic Behavior* (Princeton University Press, 1944). A very closely analogous method was suggested in 1926 by F. Ramsey, *The Foundations of Mathematics and Other Logical Essays* (The Humanities Press, N. Y., 1950), pp. 166–90. The neatest, but still very difficult, exposition is by J. Marschak, *op. cit.* Still another statement of essentially the same set of axioms is in Friedman and Savage, *op. cit.*

1. For the chooser there is a transitive, complete ordering of all the alternative possible choices so far as his preferences are concerned. That is if $C \geq B$ and $B \geq A$, then $C \geq A$.

2. If among three entities, A, B, and C, $C \geq B$, and $B \geq A$, then there is some probability value p, for which B is just as desirable as the uncertain prospect consisting of A and C, where A is realizable with probability p, and C with probability 1-p. In our notation: if $C \geq B$ and $B \geq A$, then there is some p for which $B = (A, C; p)$, where $(A, C; p)$ is the expression for the uncertain prospect in which A will be realized with probability p, and otherwise, C will be realized.

3. Suppose $B \geqq A$, and let C be any entity. Then $(B, C; p) \geqq (A, C; p)$ for any p. In particular, if $A = B$, then the prospect comprising A and C, with probability p for A and 1-p for C, will be just as desirable as the uncertain prospect comprised of B and C, with the same probability p for B, and 1-p for C.

4. In the uncertain prospect comprising A and B with probability p for A, it makes no difference what the process is for determining whether A or B is received, just so long as the value of p is not changed. Notationally, $(A, B; p_1), B; p_2) = (A, B; p_1 p_2)$.

To help understand what these axioms signify we give an example of behavior or situation that is inconsistent with each, except that I can think of no totally unreasonable behavior inconsistent with the first axiom. Behavior inconsistent with the second axiom would be the following: Suppose C is two bars of candy, B is one bar of candy, and A is being shot in the head. Form an uncertain prospect of C and A with probability p for C. If there is no p, however small or close to zero, which could possibly make one indifferent between the uncertain prospect and B, the one bar of candy, he is rejecting axiom (2). Are such situations purely hypothetical?

The third axiom, sometimes called the "strong independence assumption," has provoked the most vigorous attack and defense. So far no really damaging criticism has been seen. It takes its name from the implication that whatever may be the entity, C, it has no effect on the ranking of the uncertain prospects comprised of A or C and B or C. This kind of independence has nothing whatever to do with independence or complementarity among groups of commodities. Here one does not receive both A and C, or B and C. He gets either A or C in one uncertain prospect, or he gets either B or C in the other. Even if A and C were complements and B and C were substitutes, the ordering would not be affected—this is what the postulate asserts.[12]

Axiom 3 is inconsistent with a situation in which the utility of the act of winning itself depends upon the probability of winning, or more generally if probability itself has utility. For example, at Christmas time, one does not want to know what gift his wife is going to give him; he prefers ignorance to any hints or certainty as to what his gift will be. This is a type of love for gambling. Conversely, one may be indifferent to whether he gets roast beef or ham for dinner, but he does want to know which it will be purely for the sake of knowing, not because it will affect any prior or subsequent choices.

Axiom 4 is inconsistent with a concern or difference in feeling about different ways of determining which entity in an uncertain prospect is actually received even though the various systems all have the same probability. For example, suppose an uncertain prospect had a probability of .25 for one of the entities. It should make no difference whether the probability is based on the toss of two successive coins with heads required on both, or whether it is based on the draw of one white ball from an urn containing one white and three

---

[12] See the literature listed in footnote 7.

black. But consider the case of the slot machine. Why are there three wheels with many items on each wheel? Why not one big wheel, and why are the spinning wheels in sight? One could instead have a machine with covered wheels. Simply insert a coin, pull the handle and then wait and see what comes out of the machine. Does seeing the wheels go around or seeing how close one came to nearly winning affect the desirability? If observation or knowledge of the number of steps through which the mechanism must pass before reaching the final decision makes any difference, even if the fundamental probability is not subjectively or objectively affected, then axiom 4 is denied.

Implied in the stated axioms is a method for assigning numerical utility values to the various component entities. The method is perhaps explained best by an illustration of the method using the entities of Table 4.1. Take one entity, *A*, and one other, say *B*, as the two base entities. Between these two entities you choose *B* as preferable to *A*. Now I *arbitrarily* assign (*i.e.*, choose any numbers I wish so long as the number for *B* exceeds that for *A*) the number 2 to *B* and some smaller number, say 1, to *A*. You then consider entity *C*, which you assert you prefer to *A* and to *B*. The next step is rather involved; I now form an uncertain prospect consisting of *C* and *A*. You are now offered a choice between *B*, a sure prospect, and the uncertain prospect comprised of "*A* or *C*," where you get *A* or *C* depending upon the outcome of a random draw in which the probability of *A* is *p*, otherwise you get *C*.

You are asked to, and you do, select a value of *p* which when contained in the uncertain prospect leaves you indifferent between *B* and the uncertain prospect, "*A* or *C*." [13] If *p* were set at nearly zero, you would choose the uncertain prospect, since

C is assumed here to be preferred to *A*; choosing the uncertain prospect would mean that you would almost surely get *C*. The converse would be the outcome if *p* were set at nearly 1. Therefore, some place in between there is a value of *p* which would leave you indifferent between *B* and the uncertain prospect of "*A* or *C*." After you indicate that value of *p*, I assign to the uncertain prospect the same number, 2, I did to *B* since they are equally preferred by you.

Now we may determine a number for *C* by the following procedure. Treat the probability *p*, and its complement *1-p*, as weights to be assigned to the numbers for *A* and *C* such that the weighted sum is equal to the number 2, which has been assigned to the uncertain prospect. If, for example, you were indifferent when *p* was equal to .6, then we have the following definitional equation, where we let *U(A)* stand for the number assigned to *A*, *U(B)* for the number assigned to *B*, and *U(C)* for the number assigned to *C*:

$$U(B) = p \cdot U(A) + (1\text{-}p) \cdot U(C)$$
$$\frac{U(B) - p \cdot U(A)}{(1\text{-}p)} = U(C) = 3.5.$$

Using this convenient formula we can assign numbers to the entities *D, E, F* by appropriately forming uncertain prospects and letting you determine that value of *p* which produced indifference. These revealed numbers will completely order the entities. If *E* has a larger number than *G*, *E* will be preferred over *G*. This assignment of numerical value is made without ever comparing *E* and *G* directly. Each has been compared with a base entity. A brief pause to reflect will reveal that in this paragraph we have been specifying a convenient method for manipulating, or combining the "utilities" or "choice indicator numbers" as well as specifying a process of attaching numbers (utilities) to the entities.

It happens that if we insist on using the simple formula above, rather than some more complicated one, the numerical mag-

[13] It is important to notice that the sure prospect must not be preferred to both of the components of the uncertain prospects, for in that event no probability value would induce indifference.

nitudes assigned by this process are unique up to a linear transformation. For example, suppose that by our process of assigning numbers we obtained the set of numbers in column 3 of Table 4.1 for entities *A* to *J*. Now, instead of assigning 7 and 6 to *B* and *A*, had we decided in the first place to assign a value of 7 to entity *B* and a value of 5 to entity *A*, we could have obtained instead the sequence in column 7. Column 7 is a linear transformation of column 3. In other words, we may arbitrarily, at our complete discretion, assign numbers to *two* of the entities; once that has been done, our method will determine the remaining unique numbers to be assigned. But all the various *sets* of numbers (utilities) that could have been obtained, depending upon the two initial numerical values, are linear transformations of each other. Thus, our measurement process is unique "up to" a linear transformation.

If the preceding method of assigning numbers does predict correctly the choice a person actually makes among uncertain prospects, then we have successfully assigned numbers as indicators of choice preferences. We have successfully measured utility and have done it with the convenient computational formula above. Furthermore, every linear transformation of our predicting numbers, "utilities," would be equally valid—or invalid.

In summary, (1) we have found a *way* to assign numbers; (2) for the way suggested, it so happens that the assigned numbers are unique up to linear transformations; (3) the numbers are convenient to manipulate. All this was implicit in our set of postulates. Before asking whether the numbers predict actual behavior, we shall discuss some side issues.

Diminishing or Increasing Marginal Utility

Recalling our earlier exposition of the mathematical properties of linear transformations, we see that in all of the columns (except 2 and 9 which are not linear transformations of the others) the pattern of *increments* between the numbers assigned to entities is similar. For example, between pair *H* and *I* on scale 7 the increment is 4 and between pair *I* and *J* it is 2. Moving from *H* through *I* to *J* we have a diminishing increment in the numerical magnitudes assigned. In more familiar terminology we have diminishing marginal utility among *H*, *I* and *J*.[14] Similarly, all the linear transforms of scale 7 will retain this diminishing marginal utility over the range of entities *H*, *I* and *J*. And the suggested way of assigning numbers to the component entities assigns numbers (utilities) which are equivalent up to a linear transformation; that is, any one of the linear transformations will be just as good—for our purposes—as any other of them. By implication we can determine whether there is diminishing or increasing marginal utility.

Maximization of Expected Utility

By this method of assigning utilities we have ordered all the entities. However, our purpose was more than this; otherwise the uniqueness of the numbers up to a linear transformation would have been an unnecessary restriction. As we know, any monotonic transformation would leave order unaffected. The linear transformation restriction is imposed by our desire to predict choices among uncertain prospects from the utilities and probabilities of the component entities and to do it in a convenient form, *viz.*, according to maximization of expected utility.[15]

Implied in our set of postulates is not only the preceding method of assigning numbers for utilities but also (in fact the

[14] More strictly we should also have some scale for measuring the amount of *H*, *I* and *J*, either in weight or volume, etc. While the process for assigning these scales also is a complex one, we may pass over it in order to concentrate upon the "utility" measure.

[15] It is not dictated by any nostalgia for diminishing marginal utility.

two are merely two aspects of the same implication) a method for combining the utilities of the component entities into a utility number for the uncertain prospect.

This method is based on the implication that a person who behaves according to the axioms will choose among uncertain prospects according to expected utility. Expected utility is merely the sum of the weighted utilities of the components of the uncertain prospects where the weights are the probabilities associated with each component. In symbolic form

$$U(A \text{ or } B, p) = pU(A) + (1\text{-}p)U(B)$$

where the expression $U(A \text{ or } B, p)$ denotes the utility of the uncertain prospect of entities A and B in which A will be received with probability p, and B otherwise. For example, we could from any one of our measures in Table I (except columns 2 and 9) predict what one would do when faced with the following choice: he is presented first with an uncertain prospect containing entities B and C. If he chooses this prospect, his probability of getting B is one-half; otherwise, he will get C. The other uncertain prospect which he is offered contains entities A and E, and if he chooses this prospect his probability of getting F is one-fourth—otherwise, he gets A. Our individual will choose the first prospect, no matter which of our acceptable measures we use. We obtain this prediction by multiplying (weighting) the "utility" measures of each entity in each prospect by the probability of that entity. If we use the utility measure of column 8, we have for the first prospect $(\frac{1}{2} \times 14) + (\frac{1}{2} \times 10) = 12$, and for the second prospect, $(\frac{3}{4} \times 6) + (\frac{1}{4} \times 22) = 10$. The first prospect has the larger expected "utility" and will be chosen.[16] How can we justify this procedure of adding

the products of probabilities and "measures of utilities" of entities in an uncertain prospect and calling the result "the utility" of the uncertain prospect? The axioms of human behavior on which it is based are those which earlier gave us the procedure for "measuring utility" up to a linear transformation.[17]

Another way to express this implication that a rational person chooses among uncertain prospects so as to maximize expected utility is in terms of the implied shapes of indifference curves in the plane of *probabilities* of the various components of the uncertain prospects.

Suppose that I am indifferent between receiving a watch and receiving $30.00. In Figure 4.1(a), the horizontal scale measures the probability with which I will get $30.00 and the vertical axis measures the probability with which I will get the watch. The origin represents the point at which I am sure to get nothing. The point W on the vertical axis presents the situation in which I am sure to get the watch and not get the $30.00. The point M on the horizontal axis represents the situation in which I am sure to get the money and am sure not to get the watch. A straight line drawn from W to M represents all the various uncertain prospects in which I might get the watch or I might get the money, where the probabilities are given by the horizontal distance for the money

---

[16] If column 9 had been used, the chooser would have been declared indifferent, *i.e.*, the two combinations have equal utility. This is inconsistent with the utility value and predictions derived from the measures in the other columns.

[17] If our task is merely to order choice among the uncertain prospects, we could, after obtaining the expected utility of the prospect, obviously perform any monotonic transformation on it without upsetting the order of choices among the uncertain prospects. However, there seems little point in doing so, and there is good reason not to do so. In particular one might wish to predict choices among groups of uncertain prospects where, in each group of prospects, the entities are themselves uncertain prospects. This combination of several uncertain prospects into one resultant uncertain prospect is a consistent operation under the preceding postulates, and the utility measures attached to it will have an implied validity if the utility measures attached to the component prospects, derived in the manner indicated earlier, are valid.

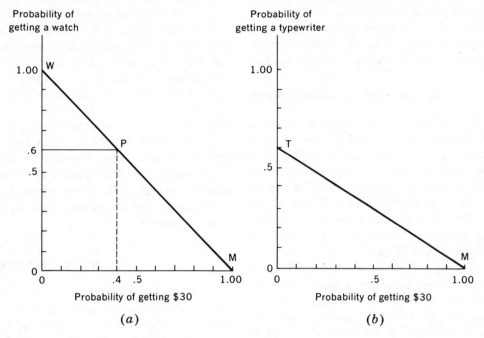

FIGURE 4.1

and the vertical distance for the watch. Thus, the point P represents the prospect in which I will get the watch with probability ⅔ or otherwise the money (with probability ⅓). The preceding axioms imply that this straight line is an indifference line or utility isoquant. In other words, the utility isoquant is a *straight* line in the space of probabilities, in this case a straight line from one sure prospect (the watch with certainty) to the other equally sure prospect (the $30.00 with certainty).

The straight line utility isoquants need not go from sure prospect to sure prospect, as can be seen from a second example. Suppose that I am indifferent between receiving $30.00 with certainty (sure prospect of $30.00) and the uncertain prospect in which I will get a particular typewriter with probability .6 and nothing with probability .4. In Figure 4.1(*b*), this latter uncertain prospect is *T* on the vertical axis. Since I am indifferent between this uncertain prospect *T* and the $30.00

with certainty (point *M*) a straight line, *TM*, is a utility isoquant, and all prospects represented by the points on that line are indifferent to me—have the same utility. In summary, in any such figure, a straight line through any two equally preferred prospects will also contain all prospects (certain and uncertain) that are equally preferred to the first two. This can be generalized into three and more dimensions in which case the straight line becomes a plane surface in three or more dimensions.

The additivity of the simple weighted (by probabilities of the components of the entities) "utilities" enables us to call this composite utility function a linear utility function. This means that the measure of "utility" of uncertain prospects (in a probability sense) of entities is the sum of the "expectation" of the "utilities" of the component entities; it does not mean that our numerical numbers (measuring utility) assigned to the entities are linear functions of the physical amounts (*e.g.*, weights or counts) of the magnitude entities. Here linearity means that the utility of the uncertain prospects is a linear function of the utility of the component entities; incidentally the utility function is also a linear function of the probabilities of the entities.

IV. VALIDITY OF MEASUREMENT

Has anyone ever succeeded in assigning numbers in this way and did the sequence based on past observations predict accurately the preferences revealed by an *actual* choice among new and genuinely available prospects? The only test of the validity of this whole procedure, of which the author is aware, was performed by Mosteller and Nogee.[18]

The essence of the Mosteller-Nogee experiment was to subject approximately 20 Harvard students and National Guardsmen to the type of choices (indicated above on pages 65–67 required to obtain a utility measure for different entities. In the experiment, the entities were small amounts of money, so that what was being sought was a numerical value of utility to be attached to different amounts of money. After obtaining for each individual a utility measure for various amounts of money, Mosteller and Nogee predicted how each individual would choose among a set of uncertain prospects, where the entities were amounts of money with associated probabilities. Although some predictions were incorrect, a sufficiently large majority of correct predictions led Mosteller and Nogee to conclude that the subjects did choose among uncertain prospects on the basis of the utilities of the amounts of money involved and the probabilities associated with each, *i.e.*, according to maximized expected utility. Perhaps the most important lesson of the experiment was the extreme difficulty of making a really good test of the validity of the implications of the axioms about behavior.

[18] F. Mosteller and P. Nogee, "An Experimental Measurement of Utility," *Jour. Pol. Econ.* (Oct. 1951), LIX, 371–404.

Whether this process will predict choice in any other situation is still unverified. But we can expect it to fail where there are pleasures of gambling and risk-taking, possibly a large class of situations. Pleasures of gambling refers not to the advantages that incur from the possibility of receiving large gains, but rather to the pleasure of the act of gambling or act of taking on extra risk itself. There may be an exhilaration accompanying sheer chance-taking or winning per se as distinct from the utility of the amount won. Even worse, the preference pattern may change with experience.

V. UTILITY OF INCOME

We can conclude our general exposition with the observation that although the preceding discussion has referred to "entities" we could have always been thinking of different amounts of income or wealth. The reason we did not was that we wanted to emphasize the generality of the choice problem and to emphasize that utility measures are essentially nothing but choice indicators. However, it is useful to consider the utility of income. How do the numerical values (utilities) assigned by the preceding method vary as income varies? Now this apparently sensible question is ambiguous, even after our preceding discussion which we presume to have eliminated confusion about the meaning of "measurability of utility." For the question still remains as to whether the utility measure assumes (1) a utility curve that stays put and along which one can move up and down as income varies; or, (2) a utility curve whose shape is definable only on the basis of the current income as a reference point for change in levels of income. The former interpretation emphasizes dependence of utility on levels of income, while the latter emphasizes the dependence of utility on the changes in income around one's present position.

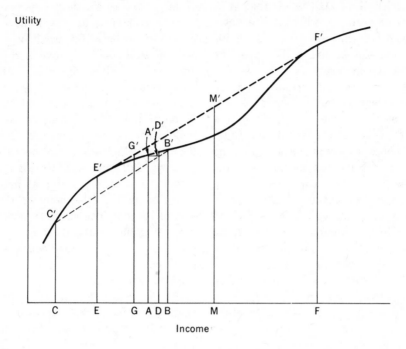

FIGURE 4.2

The most common type of utility curve has been one whose shape and position is independent of the particular income actually being realized at the time the curve of utility of income is constructed. For example, Friedman and Savage draw a utility curve dependent primarily upon levels of income rather than upon changes in income, and it is presumed that individuals choose as if they were moving along that curve.[19] The generic shape of the curve postulated by Friedman and Savage is shown in Figure 4.2.[20] This shape is supposed to explain the presence of both gambling and insurance. How does it do this?

Reference back to our method of predicting choices among uncertain prospects reminds us that choices will be made so as to maximize expected utility. A graphic interpretation is very simple. In Figure 4.2, let the income position now existing be A;

let the individual be faced with a choice of staying where he is, or of choosing the uncertain prospect of moving to income position B with probability .999 or of moving to income position C with probability .001. Position A represents paying fire insurance, while positions C and B form the uncertain prospect where C is the position if a fire occurs with no insurance and B is the position if no fire occurs with no insurance. Will he choose the uncertain prospect or the sure position A? The basis for the choice as implied in our postulates can be described graphically as follows: From point B' draw a straight line to point C'. This straight line gives the expected utility of all uncertain prospects of the incomes B and C as the probability attached to C varies from zero to one. The point on this straight line yielding the expected utility of our uncertain prospect can be found by computing the expected *income*, D, and then rising vertically to point D' on the straight line $B'C'$. The ordinate DD' is the expected utility of the uncertain pros-

[19] *Op. cit.*
[20] The utility curve is unique up to a linear transformation.

pect. If the length of DD' is less than AA', as it is in our example, where AA' denotes the utility of the income after taking insurance, then the person will choose the insurance and conversely.

It is apparent that if the utility curve were always convex as in the first and last part of the curve in Figure 4.2, a person would never choose an uncertain prospect whose expected income was no greater than the insured income position. And if the curve were concave, a person would always choose the uncertain prospect where the expected income was at least equal to the present insured position.

If the curve has the shape postulated by Friedman and Savage, it is possible to explain why a person will take out insurance and will at the same time engage in a gamble. To see how the latter is possible, suppose a person were at position A. At the same time that he might be willing to take out insurance he may also be willing to gamble by choosing an uncertain prospect of ending up at E or F, despite its lower expected income at G, because the expected utility GG' of the uncertain prospect is larger than the utility AA' of position A. Friedman and Savage tentatively attempt to lend some plausibility to this shape of utility curve by conjuring that economic society may be divisible into two general income level classes, the lower one being characterized by the first convex part of the curve and the higher one by the upper convex section. An intermediate group is in the concave section.

H. Markowitz has pointed out certain unusual implications of the Friedman-Savage hypothesis.[21] A person at the point M would take a fair bet with a chance to get to F. This seems unlikely to be verified by actual behavior. Secondly, if a person is at a position a little below F, he will not want insurance against small probabilities

of large losses. Further, any person with income greater than F will never engage in any fair bet. But wealthy people do gamble. Is it solely the love of risk taking? To overcome these objections, Markowitz postulates that utility is related to *changes* in the level of income and that "the utility function has three inflection points. The middle one is at the person's "customary" income level, which except in cases of recent windfall gains and losses is the present income. The income interval between the inflection points is a nondecreasing function of income. The curve is monotonically increasing but bounded; it is at first concave, then convex, then concave, and finally convex.

Markowitz's hypothesis is consistent with the existence of both "fair" (or slightly "unfair") insurance and lotteries. The same individual will both insure and gamble. The hypothesis implies the same behavior whether one is poor or rich.

Markowitz recognizes that until an unambiguous procedure is discovered for determining when and to what extent current income deviates from customary income, the hypothesis will remain essentially nonverifiable because it is not capable of denying any observed behavior. The Markowitz hypothesis reveals perhaps more forcefully than the Friedman-Savage hypothesis, that utility has no meaning as an indicator of a level of utility. Utility has meaning only for changes in situations. Thus while I might choose to receive an increase in income rather than no increase, there is no implication that after I have received it for a while I remain on a higher utility base—however interpreted—than formerly. It may be the getting or losing, the rising or the falling that counts rather than the actual realized position. In any event Markowitz's hypothesis contains no implications about anything other than changes in income.

Our survey is now completed. We

[21] H. Markowitz, "The Utility of Wealth," *Jour. Pol. Econ.* (April 1952), LX, 151–58.

started with developments after the Slutsky, Hicks, Allen utility position in which utility is measured up to monotone transformations only. This meant exactly no more and no less than that utility is ordinal. In other words, the numerical size of the increments in the numbers in any one measure (column of numbers in Table I) is without meaning. Only their signs have significance. Utility translation: marginal utility has meaning only in being positive or negative, but the numerical value is meaningless, *i.e.*, *diminishing* or *increasing* marginal utility is completely arbitrary since one can get either by using the appropriate column.[22]

The first postwar development was the Neumann and Morgenstern axioms which implied measurable utility up to a linear transformation, thus reintroducing diminishing or increasing marginal utility,[23] and which also implied a hypothesis or maxim about rational behavior. This was followed by the Friedman and Savage article and Marschak's paper. These papers are essentially identical in their postulates and propositions although the presentation and exposition are so different that each contributes to an understanding of the other. The Friedman and Savage paper however contains an added element: they attempt to prophesy the shape of the curve of utility of income that would be most commonly revealed by this measurement process. Mosteller and Nogee then made a unique contribution in really trying to verify the validity and applicability of the postulates. Most recently, Markowitz criticized the Friedman and Savage conjecture about the shape of utility of income curve,

with his own conjecture about its dependence upon income changes. And that is about where matters stand now.

A moral of our survey is that to say simply that something is, or is not, measurable is to say nothing. The relevant problems are: (1) can numerical values be associated with entities and then be combined according to some rules so as to predict choices in stipulated types of situations, and (2) what are the transformations that can be made upon the initially assigned set of numerical values without losing their predictive powers (validity)? As we have seen, the currently proposed axioms imply measurability up to a linear transformation. Choices among uncertain prospects are predicted by a simple probability-weighted sum of the utilities assigned to the components of the uncertain prospect, specifically from the "expected utility."

And now to provide emotional zest to the reader's intellectual activity the following test is offered. Imagine that today is your birthday; a friend presents you with a choice among three lotteries. Lottery A consists of a barrel of 2000 tickets of which 2 are marked $1000 and the rest are blanks. Lottery B consists of another barrel of 2000 tickets of which 20 are marked $100 and the rest are blanks. Lottery C consists of a barrel of 2000 tickets of which 1 is marked $1000 and 10 are marked $100. From the chosen barrel one ticket will be drawn at random and you will win the amount printed on the ticket. Which barrel would you choose? Remember there is no cost to you, this is a free gift opportunity. In barrel A the win of $1000 has probability .001 and the probability of getting nothing is .999; in barrel B the probability of winning $100 is .01 and getting nothing has probability .99; in barrel C $1000 has probability .0005, $100 has probability .005 and wining nothing has probability .9945. For each barrel the mathematical expectation is $1.00. The

---

[22] It is a simple task—here left to the reader—to find current textbooks and articles—which will be left unnamed—stating that the indifference curve analysis dispenses with the concept of utility or marginal utility. Actually it dispenses only with *diminishing* or *increasing* marginal utility.

[23] Incidentally, the *Theory of Games* of Neumann and Morgenstern is completely independent of their utility discussion.

reader is urged to seriously consider and to make a choice. Only after making his choice should he read the footnote.[24]

CONCLUSION

1. Some readers may be jumping to the conclusion that we really can use *diminishing* or *increasing* marginal utility and that the "indifference curve" or "utility isoquant" technique has been superfluous after all. This is a dangerous conclusion. The "indifference curve" technique is more general in not requiring measurability of utility up to a linear transformation. But

[24] Only the reader who chose C should continue, for his choice has revealed irrationality or denial of the axioms. This can be shown easily. He states he prefers C to A and to B. First, suppose he is indifferent between A and B; he doesn't care whether his friend chooses to give him A or B just so long as he gets one or the other. Nor does he care how his friend decides which to give. In particular if his friend tosses a coin and gives A if heads come up, otherwise B, he is still indifferent. This being so, a 50–50 chance to get A or B is equivalent to C, as one can see by realizing that C is really equivalent to a .5 probability of getting A and a .5 probability of getting B. Thus if A and B are indifferent there is no reason for choosing C.

Second, the reader choosing C may have preferred A over B. We proceed as follows. Increase the prize in B until our new B, call it B', is now indifferent with A. Form the uncertain prospect of A and B' with probability of .5 for A. This is better than C since C is nothing but an uncertain prospect composed of A and the old B, with probability of .5 for A. Where does this leave us? This says that the new uncertain prospect must be preferred to C. But since the new uncertain prospect is composed of .5 probability for A and .5 for B', the chooser of C must be indifferent between the uncertain prospect and A. (In axiom 3 let A and B be indifferent, and let C be identically the same thing as A. In other words, if the two entities in the uncertain prospect are equally preferred, then the uncertain prospect is indifferent to one of the entities with certainty.) The upshot is that A is just as desired as the new uncertain prospect which is better than C. Thus A is preferred to C, but the chooser of C denied this. Why? Either he understood and accepted the axioms and was irrational in making a snap judgment, or else he really did not accept the axioms. He may now privately choose his own escape. This example is due to Harry Markowitz.

its greatest virtue is th "partial" analysis of commodity the indiffe by using an extra dim tercommodity analyses analyses. But does the of measurement give ordinal measurement have seen, measurabil transform" both impli the possibility of pred uncertain prospects, tion.

2. Nothing in the measurable utility— numbers—enables us among groups of sure prospects. The "utility" of a group of sure prospects is not dependent on *only* the utility (assigned number) of the *entities* in the combination. It is dependent upon the particular *combination of entities; i.e.,* we do not postulate that the utility of one sure element in a group of sure things is independent of what other entities are included. We think it obviously would not lead to valid predictions of actual choices. Therefore, it must be realized that nothing said so far means that we could measure the total utility of a market basket of different entities by merely adding up the utilities of the individual component entities. No method for aggregating the utilities of the component entities for this purpose has been found; therefore, for this purpose we have to say that utility is not measurable.

3. Is the present discussion more appropriate for a journal in psychology or sociology? If economists analyze the behavior of a system of interacting individuals operating in field of action—called the economic sphere—by building up properties of the system from the behavior aspects of the individuals composing the system, then the economists must have some rationale of behavior applicable to the individuals. An alternative approach is to consider the whole system of individuals

and detect predictable properties of the system. The classic example of this distinction is in physics. One approach postulates certain laws describing the behavior of individual molecules, or atom particles, while the other starts with laws describing the observable phenomena of masses of molecules. Apparently, most economists have relied upon the former approach, the building up from individuals—sometimes referred to as the aggregation of microeconomic analysis into macro-economic analysis. On the other hand, those who are skeptical of our ability to build from individual behavior find their haven in postulates describing mass behavior. The current utility analyses aid the former approach.

4. The expression "utility" is common in welfare theory. For demand theory and the theory of prediction of choices made by individuals, measurability of the quantity (called "utility") permits us to make verifiable statements about individual behavior, but there is as yet no such happy development in welfare theory. "Measurability up to a linear transformation" does not provide any theorems for welfare theory beyond those derivable from ordinality. I mention this in order to forestall temptations to assume the contrary. The social welfare function as synthesized by Hicks and Scitovsky, for example, does not require the "utility" (choice-ordering numbers) of each individual to be measurable up to a linear transformation. It is sufficient that the individual's utility be measurable up to a monotone transformation—or, in other words, that it have merely ordinal properties. Ordinal utility is adequate in this case because orderings are made of positions or states in which, as between the two states compared, everyone is better off in one state than in the other. The welfare function does not enable a ranking of two states in one of which some people are worse off.[25] This

would require an entirely different kind of measure of utility for each person because of the necessity of making interpersonal aggregations of utilities. As yet no one has proposed a social welfare function acceptable for this purpose, nor has anyone discovered how, even in principle, to measure utility beyond the linear transformation. Even more important, the various elements in the concept of welfare (as distinct from utility) have not been adequately specified. In effect the utility whose measurement is discussed in this paper has literally nothing to do with individual, social or group welfare, whatever the latter may be supposed to mean.

5. A brief obiter dictum on interpersonal utility comparisons may be appropriate. Sometimes it is said that interpersonal utility comparisons are possible since we are constantly declaring that individual A is better off than individual B. For example, "a rich man is better off than a poor man." But is this really an interpersonal utility comparison? Is it not rather a statement by the declarer that he would prefer to be in the rich man's position rather than in the poor man's? It does not say that the rich *man* is happier or has more "utility" than the poor *man*. Even if the rich man has a perpetual smile and declares himself to be truly happy and the poor man admits he is sorrowful, how do we know that the rich *man* is happier than the poor *man*, even though both men prefer being richer to being poorer? If I were able to experience the totality of the poor man's situation and the rich man's, and preferred the rich man's, it would not constitute an interpersonal comparison; rather it would be an *intrapersonal*, intersituation comparison.

---

[25] Absolutely nothing is implied about taxation.

For example, justification of progressive income taxation by means of utility analysis remains impossible. The best demonstration of this is still E. D. Fagan, "Recent and Contemporary Theories of Progressive Taxation," *Jour. Pol. Econ.* (Aug. 1938), XLVI, 457–98.

It is hoped that the reader now has at his command enough familiarity with the meanings of measurability to be able to interpret and evaluate the blossoming literature on utility and welfare, and that this exposition has made it clear that welfare analysis gains nothing from the current utility analysis, and conversely.

5. Professor Hicks' Revision of Demand Theory*

FRITZ MACHLUP

Fritz Machlup (Dr. rer. pol., University of Vienna, 1923) was born in Wiener-Neustadt, Austria, in 1902. He has taught at Harvard University, the University of Buffalo, and Johns Hopkins University, and since 1960 has been Walker Professor of Economics and International Finance at Princeton University. Machlup is well-known for his defense of marginalism and has written extensively in the fields of economic theory, international trade, and industrial organization. Many of his articles on international economics are collected in the volume *International Payments, Debts, and Gold.* Among other works, he is the author of *Involuntary Foreign Lending, Remaking the International Monetary System,* and *Education and Economic Growth.* He is, in a sense, the economics profession's ambassador to the academic community and was elected President of the American Association of University Professors for the term 1962–1964. During 1966 he was President of the American Economic Association.

The "demand theory" which Hicks is revising in his new book[1] is that of the first three chapters of his *Value and Capital,*[2] published in 1939. The original version was 42 pages long, the revision covers 194 pages. The new version goes deeper into the "foundations" and is more than patient in its "elaborations."

Among the chief reasons for undertaking the revision are the ascendancy of Samuel-son's "revealed preference" approach (about which Hicks is sceptical), certain developments in the mathematical set theory of "strong" and "weak ordering" (of which Hicks gives a presentation which avoids mathematics), the discovery of a more closely reasoned derivation of the law of demand from a few simple propositions of logic, and the realization of some mistakes in his earlier treatment of consumer's surplus and complementarity.

The book falls into three parts: I. "Foundations"; II. "The Demand for a Single Commodity"; III. "The General Theory of Demand." There is no treatment of the "welfare side" of demand theory,

* Reprinted from *American Economic Review* (March 1957) by permission of the publisher, pp. 119–135.

[1] J. R. Hicks, *A Revision of Demand Theory* (Oxford: Clarendon Press. 1956. Pp. vii, 196. $3.75.)

[2] J. R. Hicks, *Value and Capital* (Oxford, 1939).

nor of its empirical-statistical side, the book being confined to the deductive aspects of what Hicks calls "Plain Economics." He promises to present us with a statement of welfare economics at some later time. But empirical demand analysis, being "concerned with the statistical application of the theory rather than with the theory itself," is regarded by Hicks as outside his field (pp. vi–vii). Yet, "econometric application" is to him an important test, for "a theory which can be used by econometrists is to that extent a better theory than one which cannot" (p. 3).

A brief chapter is devoted to the rejection of (even hypothetically) measurable utility. Hicks holds that in the more elementary parts of the theory the assumption of cardinal utility neither helps nor hinders, but "in the more difficult branches cardinal utility becomes a nuisance" (p. 9). If one rejects, as one probably is forced to by rather simple reflection, the hypothesis of independent utilities, and if one grants the usefulness and possibility of dividing the effects of price changes into those of substitution and of changes in income, one has in effect eliminated cardinalism from the argument (pp. 11–15). Perhaps Hicks wanted to go further, for he eliminated even the word "utility" from most of the rest of the book. But is this more than a terminological gesture? The pages are full of "levels of indifference," which after all are not really different from levels of satisfaction or utility; several times the term "real income" is used as an equivalent (*e.g.*, p. 80); and finally there is much discussion of "the consumer's valuation" of units of goods, "average valuation" as well as "marginal valuation," of the practical unimportance of "cases of increasing marginal valuation," of the position of equilibrium where the consumer's marginal valuation of a good is equal to its price (pp. 89–90), of the theorem of the "Additivity of Marginal Valuations" and the "generalized law

of Diminishing Marginal Valuation" (p. 153). I cite this list without any critical intent; on the contrary, I approve the introduction of new terms where it is desired to avoid some of the connotations associated with old terms. But the old-fashioned utility theorists, cardinal, semi-cardinal, as well as ordinal, may note with a sense of satisfaction that the "newfangled" techniques are not so very far removed from their good old ways.

The methodological position underlying Hicks' approach is eminently sound. He is free from positivist-behavioristic restrictions on the study of consumers' behavior, and he also avoids contentions about the supposedly empirical assumptions regarding rational action. Instead, he starts from a fundamental postulate, the "preference hypothesis." Faced with factual data about quantities of commodities purchased and with the task of explaining changes in these quantities, the economist has at least three possibilities: explanations in terms of nonprice data, explanations in terms of effects of current price changes, and explanations in terms of lagged effects of price changes. No matter which of the explanations seems most pertinent, one "needs a technique for separating out the current-price effects from the others," and for this purpose one needs a theory "which will tell us something about the ways in which consumers would be likely to react if variations in current prices and incomes were the only causes of changes in consumption." Thus we must proceed "by postulating an *ideal consumer*, who by definition is only affected by current market conditions. . . . The assumption of behaviour according to a scale of preferences comes in here as the simplest hypothesis . . ." (p. 17). No direct test of the preference hypothesis is practically possible (pp. 17 and 58). It is a postulate accepted because of its fertility in deduced "consequences that can be empirically applied" in the sense that they are successful in aiding "the arrangement of empirical data in meaningful ways" (pp. 17–18).

I. THE LOGIC OF WEAK ORDERING AND THE ELEMENTARY LAW OF DEMAND

Since the "demand theory, which is based upon the preference hypothesis, turns out to be nothing else but an economic application of the logical theory of ordering" (p. 19), the reader will first have to take the lesson Hicks offers on the "logic of order." He must learn the difference between *strong* ordering, where each item has a place of its own in the order, and *weak* ordering, where some items may be clustered in a group *within* which none can legitimately be put ahead of the others. (The indifference curve, he is told, implies weak ordering inasmuch as all the points on that curve are *equally* desirable, whereas the "revealed preference" approach implies to Hicks that the positions between which choice is actually made can be strongly ordered.) Hicks teaches this lesson in logic in a relatively painless way, using chiefly examples involving the consistency and transitivity of propositions about the spatial positions of certain things to the left or right of one another. Without graphical support, his examples of "items left of *P*" and "items right of *P*" (pp. 26–35) may trouble readers who are alert to the possibility that *Q* may be left or right of *P* depending on the position of the observer or on the direction in which *P* or *Q* is facing. Forgetting this relativity of right and left, readers may learn, as Hicks wants them to, the distinctions between, and applications of, "two-term consistency conditions" and "transitivity conditions." And the most flexible, studious and docile of the readers may actually keep these conditions in mind ready to be produced to demonstrate certain theorems of demand theory. Older teachers of theory, including

the present reviewer, will probably forget enough of these lessons to force them to stick with their accustomed didactic techniques.

In the explanation of the consumer's choice between two goods which are available only in discrete units, the theory of strong ordering seems superior. But where the choice is between any good which may be imperfectly divisible and money which is finely divisible, the possibility of equally desired combinations must be accepted and "strong ordering has to be given up" (p. 41). Weak ordering implies that rejected positions need not be inferior to a position actually chosen, but may have been indifferent; hence, actual choice fails to reveal definite preference. But, adopting the weak-ordering approach, committing ourselves to some degree of continuity (justified by the divisibility of money or general buying power), we must make two additional basic assumptions "to get any farther": that the consumer will always prefer a larger amount of money to a smaller amount and that his preference order is transitive. Hicks has no objections to these assumptions, and I have none either.

From the logic of weak ordering and the two additional assumptions just stated all major propositions of the theory of consumer's demand can be deduced. Hicks proceeds to do this first for the demand for a single commodity, that is, for the behavior of a consumer "confronted with a market in which the price of no more than one good is liable to change" (p. 47). The primary task is to derive the law of demand, that is, "the principle that the demand curve for a commodity is downward sloping" (p. 59). The technique chosen is that "of dividing the effects of a price-change into two parts": income effect and substitution effect. The latter "can be deduced from consistency theory." The income effect, according to Hicks, rests on observation; but he might just as well have said that it rests on the definitions of "normal" and "inferior" goods. (Observation comes in only to support the proposition that the income- elasticities of demand are nonzero for most goods, and positive if the goods are broadly defined.) The substitution effect, as Hicks demonstrates, tends to increase the consumption of a good at a reduced price. The income effect will do the same, except for inferior goods. Hence, an exception to the law of demand—the Giffen case—can occur only when the good is inferior ("with a negative income-elasticity of significant size"), the substitution effect is small, and the proportion of income spent upon the inferior good is large (pp. 66–67).

II. A FAMILY OF HYPOTHETICAL INCOME VARIATIONS

The division of the effects of a price-change into substitution and income effects is arbitrary to the extent that the income effect is the hypothetical effect of a hypothetical change in income by an amount deemed commensurate to the price change. For separating out the two effects Hicks presents two alternative methods, neither of which corresponds to the one he presented in his earlier book. Since, to follow him, we have to manipulate three different income effects and two related concepts of consumer's surplus, a catalogue of the alternative concepts of relevant income variations and a graph showing the relevant indifference curves and budget lines will be useful. (Figure 5.1 uses indifference curves, which Hicks avoids in his book. There are no indifference curves in any of his 22 graphs, though there are points that are defined as representing "indifferent positions.") Since the relative magnitudes of the various hypothetical variations of income depend on whether the good whose price is reduced or increased is a normal or an inferior one, we must state what we assume: we assume the good to be normal.

ALTERNATIVE CONCEPTS OF INCOME VARIATIONS MEASURING SOME RELEVANT EFFECTS OF PRICE CHANGES UPON THE CONSUMER

Pertaining to price reductions

The *cost difference* L [for Laspeyre] (shown as FG in Figure 5.1) equals the amount of a lump-sum *tax* which the consumer, following a reduction in the price of X, would have to pay in order to be able to purchase just the same quantities, and no more, of X and of all other goods that he purchased before the price reduction.

The *compensating income variation* (shown as FH in Figure 5.1) equals the amount of a lump-sum *tax* which the consumer, after a reduction in the price of X has caused him to purchase a larger quantity of X at the lower price, would have to pay in order to be pushed back to the same indifference level that he had attained when he purchased a smaller quantity of X at the higher price—provided that he is permitted after paying the tax to adjust again (reduce by $B'C'$) the quantity of X purchased.

The *compensating consumer's surplus* (shown as FS in Figure 5.1) equals the amount of a lump-sum *tax* which the consumer, after a reduction in the price of X has caused him to purchase a larger quantity of X at the lower price, would have to pay in order to be pushed back to the same indifference level that he had attained when he purchased a smaller quantity of X at the higher price—provided that he is *not* permitted after paying the tax to adjust again (reduce) the quantity (OB') of X purchased.

The *equivalent income variation* (shown as FI in Figure 5.1) equals the amount of a lump-sum *subsidy* which the consumer, after purchasing a certain quantity of X at a given price, would have to receive in order to be lifted up to the same indifference level that he would attain if a reduction in the price of X caused him to purchase a larger quantity of X at the lower price—provided that he is permitted after receiving the subsidy to adjust (increase by $A'E'$) the quantity of X purchased.

The *equivalent consumer's surplus* (shown as FT in Figure 5.1) equals the amount of a lump-sum *subsidy* which the consumer, after purchasing a certain quantity of X at a given price, would have to receive in order to be lifted up to the same indifference level that he would attain if a reduction in the price of X caused him to purchase a larger quantity of X at the lower price—provided that he is *not* permitted after receiving the subsidy to adjust (increase) the quantity (OA') of X purchased.

Pertaining to price increases

The *cost difference P* [for Paasche] (shown as FJ in Figure 5.1) equals the amount of a lump-sum *subsidy* which the consumer, following an increase in the price of X, would have to receive in order to be able to purchase just the same quantities, and no less, of X and of all other goods that he purchased before the price increase.

The *compensating income variation* (shown as FI in Figure 5.1) equals the amount of a lump-sum *subsidy* which the consumer, after an increase in the price of X has caused him to purchase a smaller quantity of X at the higher price, would have to receive in order to be lifted back to the same indifference level that he had attained when he purchased a larger quantity of X at the lower price—provided that he is permitted after receiving the subsidy to adjust again (increase by $A'E'$) the quantity of X purchased.

The *compensating consumer's surplus* (shown as FT in Figure 5.1) equals the amount of a lump-sum *subsidy* which the consumer, after an increase in the price of X has caused him to purchase a smaller quantity of X at the higher price, would have to receive in order to be lifted back to the same indifference level that he had attained when he purchased a larger quantity of X at the lower price—provided that he is *not* permitted after receiving the subsidy to adjust again (increase) the quantity (OA') of X purchased.

The *equivalent income variation* (shown as FH in Figure 5.1) equals the amount of a lump-sum *tax* which the consumer, after purchasing a certain quantity of X at a given price, would have to pay in order to be pushed down to the same indifference level that he would attain if an increase

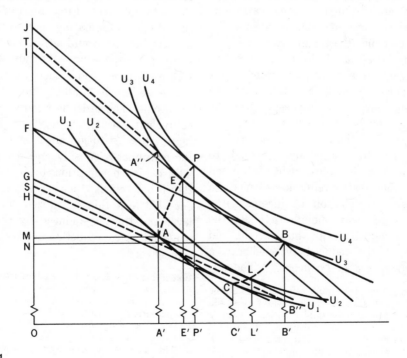

FIGURE 5.1

in the price of X caused him to purchase a smaller quantity of X at the higher price—provided that he is permitted after paying the tax to adjust (reduce by $B'C'$) the quantity of X purchased.

The *equivalent consumer's surplus* (shown as FS in Figure 5.1) equals the amount of a lump-sum *tax* which the consumer, after purchasing a certain quantity of X at a given price, would have to pay in order to be pushed down to the same indifference level that he would attain if an increase in the price of X caused him to purchase a smaller quantity of X at the higher price—provided that he is *not* permitted after paying the tax to adjust (reduce) the quantity (OB') of X purchased.

We have here five different income variations relevant to price reductions, and five relevant to price increases; since four of the latter have counterparts among the former of equal size (though of opposite signs) we have six different magnitudes. Let us defer the discussion of the four consumer's surpluses—of two sizes—and deal first with the three pairs of income variations called "cost differences," "compensating variations," and "equivalent variations." (All these terms are of Hicksian coinage.)

A. The Three Pairs of Income Effects and Substitution Effects

First of all, why, for the case of a price reduction, are two of the income variations visualized as taxes and one as a subsidy? The point is that the imaginary subsidy is to be given *instead* of the price reduction —hence, an *"equivalent* variation of income." The two imaginary taxes, on the other hand, are to be imposed, *after* the price reduction becomes effective, in order to undo some of the effects of that reduction, the one by taking away enough to offset the gain in total utility obtained through the price reduction—hence, a *"compensating* variation of income"—the other to take away enough to offset the money saving made in buying the old quantity at the reduced price—hence a *"cost difference à la Laspeyre."*[3] The rel-

ative sizes of the three income variations should now be clear (for the case of a price reduction of a normal good). The cost difference is the smallest; the compensating variation must be bigger in order to offset the gain the consumer could make through adjusting his purchases after paying the cost-difference tax; the equivalent variation must be bigger still because no price reduction and no substitution have yet taken place.

The income effect of a price reduction of a "normal" good is, of course, positive. How then can imaginary taxes, or income reductions, describe it? The trick is that the imaginary taxes are to be thought of as immediately followed by imaginary tax refunds, and these refunds are regarded as the income effect. First we tax the consumer (thus eliminating the income effect) and see how he would adjust his purchases to the price reduction—the substitution effect in isolation—and then we refund the tax to see how he would spend this increase in income. The order is reversed when the equivalent variation is used: we first eliminate the substitution effect and, by giving the consumer a subsidy and watching him adjust his consumption to it, we isolate the income effect; then we take the difference between this subsidized consumption level and the one induced by the uncompensated price reduction as the substitution effect.[4]

---

[3] Since the latter tax would seize only what the consumer could save if he purchased the old collection of goods, and would thus leave it open to him still to improve his position (by substituting more of the cheapened good for other goods), it was once referred to as an *"undercompensating* variation of income." See P. A. Samuelson, "Consumption Theorems in Terms of Overcompensa-

tion rather than Indifference Comparisons," *Economica,* Feb. 1953, N.S. XX, 1–9.—Samuelson discussed a price increase and, hence, an "overcompensating" variation of income, since the Paasche cost difference would be larger than the compensating variation.

[4] This asymmetry in procedure is apt to cause confusion regarding the signs of the income effects. It is already a little strange that we, follow-

The three methods trace three different paths from position A to position B (see Figure 5.1). The equivalent variation sends us *via E*, the compensating variation *via C*, and the cost difference *via L*. Students of Hicks' *Value and Capital* may remember that they were told to take the E-route.[5] In my review article of 1940 I proposed the L-route.[6] Strangely enough, Hicks forgot both my directions and his own. He now (p. 61) attributes the L-route to a 1953 article by Samuelson,[7] and states that he himself had adopted the C-route.[8] He recommends the C and L routes as alternatives, though he finds the C-route less convenient in relation to the income effect and more convenient in relation to the substitution effect (p. 69). The E-route, once the only one described in this context, he now finds least convenient (p. 80).

The effect of the price reduction upon the consumption of X is invariably $A'B'$, but with the different imaginary intermediate points the substitution effects are

$A'C'$, $A'L'$, or $E'B'$, respectively, and the respective income effects are $C'B'$, $L'B'$, or $A'E'$. If we reverse the direction of change and describe the effects of a price increase, we see that the equivalent variation will be found through C as the intermediary point, and the compensating variation through E, while the cost difference, now *à la Paasche*, will have a new point, P, as a half-way place. The relative sizes of the income variations are rather different from what they were before: the equivalent variation is now the smallest, the compensating variation is bigger, and the cost difference is the biggest (this time deserving the Samuelson designation as "overcompensating" variation). The substitution effects upon the consumption of X will now be $B'E'$, $B'P'$, or $C'A'$, the income effects $E'A'$, $P'A'$, or $B'C'$.

B. The Four Consumer's Surpluses

In *Value and Capital* the compensating variation in income figured as the consumer's surplus. "But this was a mistake," which Hicks corrected in his article on "The Four Consumer's Surpluses"[9] and corrects now again (p. 96). The "mistake" is easy to make and hard to clear up. There are, as Hicks now takes pains to explain, two angles from which demand theory can be viewed: one may ask either what quantities would be consumed at certain prices, or what maximum prices would be paid for certain quantities. Hicks accordingly distinguishes "price-into-quantity analysis" and "quantity-into-price analysis" (p. 83). The former is best understood by visualizing the consumer as a pure competitor in the market, free to purchase at a given price any quantity he chooses. For the

---

ing Hicks, speak of a positive income effect when a negative change of price causes a positive change in the consumer's real income. It may be confusion worse confounded if we, departing from Hicks but following common sense, mark imaginary taxes with negative signs, and imaginary subsidies with positive signs, and yet use both in the explanation of a "positive" income effect. Consistency is hard to restore in this matter and I can do no better than warn the reader about the deceptive signs.

[5] *Op. cit.*, p. 31.

[6] Fritz Machlup, "Professor Hicks' Statics," *Quart. Jour. Econ.*, Feb. 1940, LIV, 280–82.

[7] See footnote 3, above. Samuelson informs me that the method was already used in Slutsky's article, "Sulla teoria del bilancio del consumatore," *Giorn. d. Econ.*, July 1915, LI, 1–26, was then repeatedly described in the index-number literature, and was alluded to by Hicks himself in the Mathematical Appendix to *Value and Capital*, p. 309. An English translation of Slutsky's article is available in *Readings in Price Theory*, G. J. Stigler and K. E. Boulding, ed. (Homewood, 1952).

[8] Hicks probably thinks of his exposition of consumer's surplus, for which he had used the C-method.

[9] J. R. Hicks, "The Four Consumer's Surpluses," *Rev. Econ. Stud.*, 1943–44, XI, 31–41. Hicks gives due credit for "discovering" the mistake to A. M. Henderson, "Consumer's Surplus and the Compensating Variation in Income," *Rev. Econ. Stud.*, 1940–41, VIII, 117–21.

other approach we have to imagine the consumer in a market where goods are rationed out to him, where he may have to pay discriminatory prices for every unit or at least for additional units of the commodity, or where he may be compelled to take certain quantities. The question what is the maximum amount of money the consumer might be willing to pay for a certain quantity can be answered only if we do not permit him to take less than that quantity at that price, as he would if he had his choice. Since consumer's surplus is the excess of this maximum over the actual price paid, its definitions have to provide for some such restraint concerning quantity purchased.

These restraining provisions were made in the descriptions of the four concepts of consumer's surplus included in our catalogue of alternative concepts. And these restraints account also for the size relations between the various income measures. The definition of the compensating consumer's surplus fixes the quantity that was chosen at the changed price and does not permit it to be adjusted when a compensating tax or subsidy reduces or raises the consumer back to the indifference level he had attained before the price change. The definition of the equivalent consumer's surplus freezes the quantity that was chosen before the price change and does not permit it to be adjusted when an equivalent subsidy or tax lifts or depresses the consumer to the indifference level he would attain as a result of the price change. Hence, in the case of a price reduction, the compensating consumer's surplus must be smaller than the compensating variation because a tax in the amount of the latter, with no quantity readjustment permitted, would reduce the consumer below the initial indifference level. (In Figure 5.1, if the consumer were assessed a tax of FH and were compelled to take the quantity OB', he would be worse off than initially.

If he is to stay on the initial indifference level, U_1, he cannot pay more than $BB'' = FS$ as a compensating-surplus tax.) Similarly, the equivalent consumer's surplus must be larger than the equivalent variation because a subsidy in the amount of the latter, with no quantity adjustment permitted, would fail to lift the consumer to the indifference level that the price reduction would afford him. (In Figure 5.1, if the consumer were given a subsidy of only FI and were held to a quantity of OA', he would not reach the indifference level U_3; it would take a subsidy in the amount of $AA'' = \mathrm{FT}$ to get him there.)

C. Arithmetic and Graphical Illustrations

The quantitative relationships expressed here in written language and shown geometrically in an indifference graph may be profitably reviewed by an arithmetic illustration—although to admit the usefulness of such simple devices takes courage in these days of high-powered mathematical techniques. Let us then assume a simple demand schedule with just two prices of a normal good; let us calculate the cost-differences L and P, and let us assign arbitrary but plausible values to the other income variations relevant to movements between these two points of the demand schedule. The demand schedule is reversible and, depending on the direction of the change, each price-quantity pair will in turn constitute the "initial position."

Yet another device will aid in exhibiting the income effects and the substitution effects "operating" upon the quantity of X consumed as a result of the reduction or increase in price. We may draw for the two prices a family of "uncompensated" demand curves, each with income as a parameter. Disregarding the four consumer's surpluses (because they are less helpful in "price-into-quantity analysis") we

DEMAND SCHEDULE FOR GOOD X

	Price 10¢ 9¢	Quantity 1000 1150	Amount Paid $100.00 103.50		
		As price is reduced		*As price is increased*	
Relevant variations		Dollar amount	Fig. 6.1	Dollar amount	Fig. 6.1
Change in expenditure for X		+3.50	MN	−3.50	MN
Cost difference of initial quantity		−10.00	FG	+11.50	FJ
Compensating income variation		−10.50	FH	+11.00	FI
Equivalent income variation		+11.00	FI	−10.50	FH
Compensating consumer's surplus		−10.25	FS	+11.25	FT
Equivalent consumer's surplus		+11.25	FT	−10.25	FS

Note: The inconsistencies in the signs are discussed on p. 83 above. The graph (Figure 5.1) is not drawn to correspond to the dollar amounts used in this illustration.

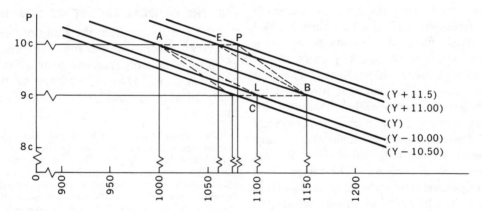

FIGURE 5.2

shall need four demand curves besides the one for the initial income Y: two for incomes after taxes, $(Y - 10.00)$ and $(Y - 10.50)$ and two for incomes after subsidies, $(Y + 11.00)$ and $(Y + 11.50)$, as shown in Figure 5.2. Using the above demand schedule for income Y and connecting the initial positions A (for the price reduction) and B (for the price increase) with the relevant points on the other demand curves, we can identify AC and AL as the two "compensated demand curves" for the price reduction, one after the tax to offset the utility

gain, the other after the tax to offset the cost difference; and BE and BP as the two "compensated demand curves" for the price increase, one after the subsidy to offset the utility loss, the other after the subsidy to offset the cost difference.

We can again trace the effects of the price changes along alternative routes: ACB, ALB, and AEB for the price reduction, BEA, BPA and BCA for the price increase. The alternative substitution and income effects upon the consumption of X can be read off the graph as follows:

Cause	Route	Substitution effect	Income effect	Total
Price reduction from	ACB	$AC = \quad 75$ units	$CB = \quad 75$ units	$AB = \quad 150$ units
10¢ to 9¢	ALB	$AL = \quad 100$ units	$LB = \quad 50$ units	$AB = \quad 150$ units
	AEB	$EB = \quad 90$ units	$AE = \quad 60$ units	$AB = \quad 150$ units
Price increase from	BEA	$BE = -90$ units	$EA = -60$ units	$BA = -150$ units
9¢ to 10¢	BPA	$BP = -70$ units	$PA = -80$ units	$BA = -150$ units
	BCA	$CA = -75$ units	$BC = -75$ units	$BA = -150$ units

D. Marginal Valuation

For the "quantity-into-price" approach we must become better acquainted with "marginal valuation" and the "compensated marginal valuation curve." Hicks had introduced this ingenious device in his 1944 article under the name of "marginal indifference curve." (At that time he used the term "marginal valuation curve" for a curve which is now stowed away in the attic with other old gadgets.) The new marginal valuation curve is presented together with a corresponding average valuation curve. (These curves look exactly like the well-known marginal and average product curves, with which they in fact have much in common.) The compensated marginal valuation curve is designed to show "the amounts of money which the consumer is willing to pay for successive units of the commodity X" provided that he "pays the full marginal valuation of each unit before making his valuation of the next" (p. 86).

What is the difference between the compensated marginal valuation curve and the compensated demand curve? The latter shows the quantities consumed at each price "under the assumption that income is continuously adjusted so as to maintain indifference of the successive positions" (p. 76). The difference is, essentially, that a marginal valuation curve may go up before it goes down, whereas the compensated demand curve can only go down. Any rising part of the marginal valuation curve will not, however, be of practical interest if the consumer can purchase as much as he wants. His demand will be "zero until price falls to his maximum average valuation" (p. 88), and at lower prices the quantities taken will be such as to secure equality between marginal valuation and price.[10]

III. THE GENERAL THEORY OF DEMAND

After graduating from the study of "elementary" theory of demand—"in which the price of no more than one good is liable to change" (p. 47)—we advance to the study of the "general" theory—in which "more than one price-ratio is allowed to

[10] I must briefly report on Hicks' reflections concerning the Giffen case and his discovery of an "anti-Giffen case" (p. 92). Just as the Giffen possibility rests on exceptionally strong income effects upon the *consumption* of exceptionally "strongly inferior" goods, the anti-Giffen possibility rests on exceptionally strong income effects upon the marginal *valuation* of "strongly normal" goods, possibly causing the marginal valuation curve to slope upward for another stretch. But the possibility is only of theoretical interest and of little, if any practical importance. The probability of sufficiently strong income effects is negligible, especially since what counts in practice are not single consumers, but large groups of consumers heterogeneous in tastes as well as incomes (pp. 67-68). But in addition Hicks shows that stretches of Giffen slopes would not provide equilibrium positions and would be quickly passed in swift movements of prices (or of quantities, in the anti-Giffen case). Thus, even if these unlikely situations should exist, they "would not show up," for "All that would be seen . . . would be a fall in price," and "We should not be able to tell that the law of demand was failing to operate, for the effects of that condition would be indistinguishable from the effects of a demand that was extremely inelastic" (p. 94); or especially elastic in the anti-Giffen case.

vary" (p. 107). At the outset Hicks makes us exercise with a "Second Consistency Test," only to conclude that this approach "is not promising" (p. 112). Instead, he puts us to work with so-called "indifference tests." (His penchant for giving a new name to every step in the argument leads to a bewildering proliferation of terms, which few will care to remember even if they should be able to do so.) The "first indifference test" says no more than "that as between two indifferent positions, the compensating variation C is less or equal to the cost-difference P," the Paasche cost-difference; "the second indifference test is expressed by saying that when we are comparing two indifferent positions, C must be greater or equal to L," the Laspeyre cost-difference (p. 116). These are merely new names for old ideas (which I had expressed in my 1940 article). But from these "tests" Hicks is able to deduce that the substitution effect of a price reduction must be positive (or zero, at worst). For, without income effects $P - L = S$, that is, the positive substitution effect is implied in the excess of the Paasche cost-difference over the Laspeyre cost-difference.

Where two or more prices change at the same time, the "Total Substitution Effect" is the sum "of the differences in quantity consumed of each good, each being valued at the corresponding difference in price" (p. 117). If price reductions are "reckoned as positive," and price increases as negative, "the total substitution effect of any price-change, however complex" must always be positive (or zero). This is christened "the First Substitution Theorem"; it contains "the downward slope of the compensated demand curve as a special case" (p. 117). To put it differently, when a compensating variation in income has made two constellations of prices and quantities equally desirable, the price reduction of X times the quantity increase of X, plus the price reduction of Y times the quantity increase of Y, plus etc., can never be negative.

From the "transitivity of indifference" follows "the additivity of compensating variations," as Hicks demonstrates in easy steps. Soon thereafter he makes the non-mathematical readers feel happy by assuring them that they have just been introduced to a statement, in economic terms, of "the fundamental theorem of Riemann integration" (p. 123). Their confidence thus being bolstered up, the readers, determined to hang on for another ride, will be glad to accept the assumption that compensated demand curves can be treated as straight lines, since "any continuous curve, over a sufficiently short stretch, is indistinguishable from a straight line" (p. 125). This will take them to another vista, named "the Reciprocity Theorem."

This theorem, good for comparing three or more price-quantity constellations (with small price differences only) which are made indifferent through compensating income variations, tells us that "the sum of the quantity-changes from (0) to (1) each being valued by the price-change of the same commodity from (0) to (2), equals the sum of the quantity-changes from (0) to (2) each being valued at the corresponding price-change from (0) to (1)" (p. 126). A simple but useful implication of this theorem is that "the cross-effects of price-changes . . . are equal" (p. 127) and hence, "the relation of substitution (and complementarity) is reciprocal" (p. 128). Incidentally, discussions of complementarity are beyond the scope of elementary theory of demand because "in the two-goods case, the relation between the two goods must be that of substitution. . . . Complementarity can only occur when there are other goods outside the group of complements at whose expense the substitution in favour of the group of complements can take place" (p. 129).

Since the designation of the "first" substitution theorem has indicated that there must be more in store, my conscience forbids me to skip the "second substitution theorem." But I shall mention merely that it is chiefly concerned with a "limit on the size of the cross-effect," and provides formal support to the intuitively obvious fact that "*X* and *Y* cannot be highly substitutable for one another unless each has a demand which is highly elastic with respect to its own price." As another boon to the nonmathematical reader, I may quote an aside of the author to the effect that he finds in connection with this theorem an "example of the way in which a blind adherence to standard mathematical methods sometimes produces nonsense results" (p. 134).

While we are on the subject of the cross-effects, it may be worth stressing that all references up to this point have been only to the "cross-substitution effects," isolated by means of compensating income variations. If income is not tampered with, "the equality between the cross-substitution effects may well be masked by inequality between the cross-income effects on income-elasticities" (p. 147). This was clearly set forth by Hicks in his *Value and Capital.*

A. Exceptions to the Law of Demand

Some other consequences of the income effect, however, are either demonstrated in novel ways or newly discovered. The chief question is whether the "Total Income Effect," which is "a combination of the separate income-effects on the separate commodities," may modify the "generalized law of demand." Hicks sees "three possible sorts of exceptions" to the law: "those due to inferior goods, to commodity asymmetry, and to asymmetrical effects of redistribution" (p. 146). The first of these exceptions is of course the "generalization of the Giffen case," in which all or most of the "price-changing goods" are inferior. Since "the share in consumer's expenditure going upon all inferior goods taken together may be much larger than that going upon

any particular inferior good," a large negative income effect has a somewhat better chance of being realized where many prices may change than where only one price changes (p. 139). But it would be a very odd thing indeed if price changes in the same direction happened to be concentrated in the group of inferior goods.

The second exception is "perhaps more interesting." It is conceivable that the income-elasticities of demand for the goods that rise in price are very different from those that fall in price. Imagine sharp price reductions for a group of "necessaries (with income-elasticity zero), and a rise in the prices of a group of luxuries (with high income-elasticity)," with the gains from the price reductions exceeding the losses from the price increases. The freed income would go after the luxuries; if there is no third group of goods, and if the price ratios within the two groups have not changed, the quantities of luxuries consumed may rise despite their higher prices (p. 142). We need not expect this often, if ever, to happen in reality, but it is fun to think about it.[11]

The third exception relates not to the demand of an individual consumer but only to the market demand. In general the "probability of exceptional cases is diminished when we take a large group of heterogeneous consumers together" (p. 144). But there is the possibility of a changed distribution of a constant total income where the gainers and the losers have very different income-elasticities of demand. Thus there is the chance of a "redistribution income-effect," and Hicks can state: "If the price of *X* falls (other prices constant), while the total income of consumers re-

[11] If the luxuries did not rise in price, the demand for them would surely increase by more. Thus the price increases operate in the expected, not exceptional, manner: they reduce the quantities demanded below those that would result from the price fall in necessaries. (This comment is the result of a discussion with William Fellner.)

mains constant, it is always possible that the consumption of X may fall, if income is redistributed from X-likers to X-dislikers" (p. 145). I cannot persuade myself to see this case as an "exception" to the law of demand; the peculiar change in the distribution of income is in no way connected with the change in prices, but is just one of those things that by some queer coincidence may happen and prevent a result of another change that has occurred from being realized. The first two exceptions are due to given conditions and may occur while other things remain unchanged. The "third exception" abrogates the *ceteris paribus* clause and invokes a fortuitous change of other things.

B. Substitutes and Complements

The inversion of "price-into-quantity theory" to "quantity-into-price" theory, which was profitably carried out in "elementary theory," affords no less valuable insights in the general theory. What we have just learned to call the "first substitution theorem" becomes now the "generalized law of Diminishing Marginal Valuation" (p. 153). The main additions to the set of previously formulated propositions on marginal valuation concern the relationships of substitutability and complementarity, and it is on these issues that Hicks proposes some of the most significant revisions of his earlier theory. In part they represent developments of suggestions made since 1939 by Lange, Mosak, and Ichimura.

The most basic revision lies in the recognition of two alternative definitions of substitutability (complementarity), one looking toward the effect of price changes upon quantity with other prices unchanged, the other toward the effect of quantity changes upon valuation with other quantities unchanged. In order to distinguish between the two definitions, Hicks speaks of goods as "*p*-substitutes," "*q*-substi-

tutes," "*p*-complements," and "*q*-complements." Thus, "X and Y are *p*-substitutes when . . . a fall in the price of X [diminishes] the demand for Y, when all *prices* save that of X are fixed, and income is adjusted so as to maintain indifference." And "X and Y are *q*-substitutes when a rise in the quantity of X diminishes the marginal valuation of Y (or the price at which a fixed quantity of Y would be purchased) when the *quantities* of all other commodities than X are fixed, saving the quantity of money, which is adjusted so as to maintain indifference" (p. 156).

Only in the simplest case will *p*-substitutability and *q*-substitutability be exactly equivalent, namely, in the case in which the prices of all other goods than X and Y are fixed. If other prices, say the price of Z, can vary as a result of a price change of X, there may be cross-effects upon the demand for Y which may offset the initial effect of the price change of X; indeed, the cross effect (Z upon Y) may wipe out the initial effect (X upon Y) so that "X and Y would be *q*-substitutes, even though they are *p*-complements" (p. 157). Because of such reactions through third goods the distinction between the two meanings of the relationship is necessary, although the "reciprocity theorem holds for each of the two meanings" (p. 158).

The discussion of related goods in terms of the effects only of price changes had left a bad gap—noted in my 1940 article, identified by Lange,[12] and provisionally filled by Ichimura[13]—in that the effects of other changes, including changes in the system of wants, could not be analyzed with the tools at hand. The "sympathetic" changes in demand of which Lange had spoken in cases of what Hicks now calls

[12] Oskar Lange, "Complementarity and Inter-relations of Shifts in Demand," *Rev. Econ. Stud.,* Oct. 1940, VIII, 58–63.
[13] S. Ichimura, "A Critical Note on the Definition of Related Goods," *Rev. Econ. Stud.,* 1950–51, XVIII, 179–83.

"intrinsic complementarity" (p. 162) can be explained by means of the new set of concepts. It turns out that the marginal valuations of complementary goods may move in different directions while their quantities move together; and that the marginal valuations of close substitutes will move together while their quantities do not. This fits in perfectly with the old insight that "perfect substitutes tend to have constant price-ratios, perfect complements constant quantity-ratios" (p. 165).

Some of the problems of consumer's choice have been unnecessarily clouded by the practice of regarding substitutability (or complementarity) between consumer's goods always as a matter of wants or tastes even when it is a matter of technology. Hicks reminds us of Menger's distinction between "objectives" and "means of reaching" them (p. 166). Consumers may make technical decisions about alternative means of reaching their given objectives. Hence, technical substitutability (or complementarity) is relevant not only in production but also in consumption; not only in the theory of the firm but also in the theory of the household. The brief remarks which Hicks makes on this point may open up good opportunities for enterprising economists, theoretical or empirical, in search of subjects in which to invest their analytical talents.

IV. THE IMPORTANCE OF ALL THAT

Many of the relationships which Hicks "discovers" or elaborates in this book are fascinating to a seasoned teacher of abstract economic theory. Does this make the book and its discoveries "important"? When I tried out some of its arguments on a more worldly economist, his reaction was "So what?". By pragmatic tests, I must admit, we shall hardly be able to claim any importance for Hicks' discoveries. They will in no way affect any recommendations of economic policy, any predictions of future events, any explanations of the past. None of our actions will be different from what it would be if this book had never been written—except perhaps the teaching of some fine points in university courses on pure economic theory (and even here most students may fail to notice the difference).

But is it fair to apply such crudely pragmatic criteria? Judged by such tests most works of art would lack importance, and so would most works in philosophy and logic. Indeed, most improvements of theoretical systems in the empirical sciences would be "unimportant," for as a rule they do not affect the conclusions but merely reduce the number of assumptions from which the results are deduced. The conventions of scientific methodology are quite clear on recognizing the "importance" of reconstructions in which some of the old pillars of a theoretical framework are razed.

I can understand, however, that some discontent with the rule of Occam's Razor may arise if it shaves away some very familiar assumptions and forces us to engage in brain-racking logical exercises in order to deduce our familiar conclusions from fewer (or weaker) hypotheses. This is precisely what Hicks' Revision of Demand Theory does or claims to do. Some very well-known empirical propositions (such as the law of demand) are here deduced, without the use of some very familiar assumptions (such as given systems of utility or indifference), from a smaller number of hypotheses or from less restrictive ones; and this involves heavy demands on the syllogistic agility of the readers. I can hear them say: "Why should we work so hard to obtain our results from three assumptions if we can get them with so much less effort from four or five? After all, hypotheses come quite cheap; why skimp?"

I take it that we must not give in to such lowbrow laziness. Much as we may prefer to economize in mental effort, as gentlemen and scholars we are obliged to economize in hypotheses. "A body of propositions, such as those of pure mathematics or theoretical physics [or, let us add, theoretical economics], can be deduced from a certain apparatus of initial assumptions concerning initial undefined terms. Any reduction in the number of undefined terms and unproved premises is an improvement since it diminishes the range of possible error and provides a smaller assemblage of hostages for the truth of the whole system." This, in Bertrand Russell's words,[14] is the maxim we obey; and under this maxim one may give recognition to the importance of Hicks' work even if one should not be satisfied with the contributions it makes through the theorems which are discussed in the foregoing pages. Whether Hicks' approach is an improvement not only on his earlier presentation but also on the revealed preference approach will probably be debated. The latter uses still fewer assumptions, but Hicks' assumptions are weaker (less restrictive). On different grounds some may claim that revealed preference is superior because of the "empirical meaning" of the fundamental hypothesis. For me it is sufficient that such a hypothesis be "understandable" in the light of my inner experience casually checked against like experiences of others.[15] I find superfluous the polite bows to neopositivism which the revealed preference theorists make. Whether their theory yields conclusions which Hicks' theory cannot yield is another matter, but this is not examined here.

An important book is sometimes enjoyable to read. Unfortunately this cannot be said about this book. Not that higher mathematics or complicated graphs stop the reader's progress. The exposition is non-mathematical; if there are equations and mathematical symbols on many pages of Part III, they are merely abbreviations and are not subjected to algebraic manipulations.[16] Of course, the formally literary exposition is still mathematical in the sense in which all logical reasoning is mathematical. Since the entire book is a tightly knit logical argument, it is not possible for the reader to skim the book with much chance of success; if he attempts to skip a few pages or even paragraphs he is likely to get lost. Indeed, a reader who pauses too long between chapters may have to go back and re-read lest he miss his connections. All this may explain why the book is a difficult one; but it does not explain why it gives little reading pleasure. Does perhaps Hicks' style of writing account for that? It is interesting to speculate how a master of literary exposition—rare indeed among present-day economists—might mould Hicks' material into graceful, enjoyable prose. Hicks is a very serious man and he takes his work very seriously. But could he not, metaphorically speaking, indulge in a smile once in a while? On the rare occasions when he attempts a somewhat humorous touch, the result is not always felicitous. For example, when he announces "there is a dragon waiting at the door who must first be cleared out of the way. It is the old crux of the measurability of utility" (p. 7). To be sure, we have heard of all sorts of creatures being transformed into dragons; but a dragon who is an old crux is even more forbidding than Cardinal Utility.

---

[14] Bertrand Russell, "Philosophical Analysis," *Hibbert Jour.*, July, 1956, LIV, 321.

[15] See Fritz Machlup, "The Problem of Verification in Economics," *South. Econ. Jour.*, July 1955, XXII, 1–21, esp. pp. 16–17.

[16] It is disturbing, though, that Hicks uses dots where in usual practice we would find parentheses; he writes consistently $(p_0 - p_1 \cdot q_1)$ instead of $(p_0 - p_1) q_1$.

The Demand Curve

6. The Marshallian Demand Curve*

MILTON FRIEDMAN[1]

Alfred Marshall's theory of demand strikingly exemplifies his "impatience with rigid definition and an excessive tendency to let the context explain his meaning." [2] The concept of the demand curve as a functional relation between the quantity and the price of a particular commodity is explained repeatedly and explicitly in the *Principles of Economics:* in words in the text, in plane curves in the footnotes, and in symbolic form in the Mathematical Appendix. A complete definition of the demand curve, including, in particular, a statement of the variables that are to be considered the same for all points on the curve and the variables that are to be allowed to vary, is nowhere given explicitly. The reader is left to infer the contents of *ceteris paribus* from general and vague statements, parenthetical remarks, examples that do not purport to be exhaustive, and concise mathematical notes in the Appendix.

In view of the importance of the demand curve in Marshallian analysis, it is natural that other economists should have constructed a rigorous definition to fill the gap that Marshall left. This occurred at an early date, apparently without controversy about the interpretation to be placed on Marshall's comments. The resulting definition of the demand curve is now so much an intrinsic part of current economic theory and is so widely accepted as Marshall's own that the assertion that Marshall himself gave no explicit rigorous definition may shock most readers.

Yet why this particular interpretation evolved and why it gained such unquestioned acceptance are a mystery that requires explanation. The currently accepted interpretation can be read into Marshall only by a liberal—and, I think, strained—reading of his remarks, and its acceptance implicitly convicts him of logical inconsistency and mathematical error at the

* Reprinted from the *Journal of Political Economy* (December 1949) by permission of The University of Chicago Press. Copyright, 1949, pp. 463–74. A brief biographical sketch of the author can be found in the introduction to Reading 2.

[1] I am deeply indebted for helpful criticism and suggestions to A. F. Burns, Aaron Director, C. W. Guillebaud, H. Gregg Lewis, A. R. Prest, D. H. Robertson, G. J. Stigler, and, especially, Jacob Viner, to whose penetrating discussion of the demand curve in his course in economic theory I can trace some of the central ideas and even details of this article. The standard comment that none is to be held responsible for the views expressed herein has particular relevance, since most disagreed with my interpretation of Marshall as presented in an earlier and much briefer draft of this article.

[2] C. W. Guillebaud, "The Evolution of Marshall's *Principles of Economics,*" *Economic Journal,* LII (December, 1942), 333.

very foundation of his theory of demand. More important, the alternative interpretation of the demand curve that is yielded by a literal reading of his remarks not only leaves his original work on the theory of demand free from both logical inconsistency and mathematical error but also is more useful for the analysis of most economic problems.

Section I presents the two interpretations of the demand curve and compares them in some detail; Section II argues that a demand curve constructed on my interpretation is the more useful for the analysis of practical problems, whatever may be the verdict about its validity as an interpretation of Marshall; . . .

I. ALTERNATIVE INTERPRETATIONS OF MARSHALL'S DEMAND CURVE

The demand curve of a particular group (which may, as a special case, consist of a single individual) for a particular commodity shows the quantity (strictly speaking, the maximum quantity) of the commodity that will be purchased by the group per unit of time at each price. So far, no question arises; this part of the definition is explicit in Marshall and is common to both alternatives to be discussed. The problem of interpretation relates to the phrase, "other things the same," ordinarily attached to this definition.

In the first place, it should be noted that "same" in this phrase does not mean "same over time." The points on a demand curve are alternative possibilities, not temporally ordered combinations of quantity and price. "Same" means "same for all points on the demand curve"; the different points are to differ in quantity and price and are not to differ with respect to "other things." [3] In the second place, "all" other

[3] Of course, when correlations among statistical time series are regarded as estimates of demand curves, the hypothesis is that "other things" have

things cannot be supposed to be the same without completely emasculating the concept. For example, if (a) total money expenditure on all commodities, (b) the price of every commodity other than the one in question, and (c) the quantity purchased of every other commodity were supposed to be the same, the amount of money spent on the commodity in question would necessarily be the same at all prices, simply as a matter of arithmetic, and the demand curve would have unit elasticity everywhere.[4] Different specifications of the "other things" will yield different demand curves. For example, one demand curve will be obtained by excluding b from the list of "other things"; another, quite different one, by excluding c.

A. The Current Interpretation

The current interpretation of Marshall's demand curve explicitly includes in the list of "other things" (1) tastes and preferences of the group of purchasers considered, (2) their money income, and (3) the price of every other commodity. The quantities of other commodities are explicitly considered as different at different points on the

been approximately constant over time or that appropriate allowance has been made for changes in them. Similarly, when correlations among cross-section data are regarded as estimates of demand curves, the hypothesis is that "other things" are approximately the same for the units distinguished or that appropriate allowance has been made for differences among them. In both cases the problem of estimation should be clearly distinguished from the theoretical construct to be estimated.

[4] Yet Sidney Weintraub not only suggests that Marshall intended to keep a, b, and c simultaneously the same but goes on to say: "Clearly Marshall's assumption means a unit elasticity of demand in the market reviewed and no ramifications elsewhere; that was why he adopted it" ("The Foundations of the Demand Curve," *American Economic Review*, XXXII [September, 1942], 538–52, quotation from n. 12, p. 541). Weintraub even adds the condition of constant tastes and preferences to a, b, and c, speaking of a change in tastes as shifting the demand curve. Obviously, a, b, and c together leave no room for tastes and preferences or, indeed, for anything except simple arithmetic.

demand curve, and still other variables are ignored.[5]

On this interpretation it is clear that, while money income is the same for different points on the demand curve, real income is not. At the lower of two prices for the commodity in question, more of some commodities can be purchased without reducing the amounts purchased of other commodities. The lower the price, therefore, the higher the real income.

B. An Alternative Interpretation

It seems to me more faithful to both the letter and the spirit of Marshall's writings to include in the list of "other things" (1) tastes and preferences of the group of purchasers considered, (2) their real income, and (3) the price of every closely related commodity.

Two variants of this interpretation can be distinguished, according to the device adopted for keeping real income the same at different points on the demand curve. One variant, which Marshall employed in the text of the *Principles*, is obtained by replacing " (2) their real income" by (2a) their money income and (2b) the "purchasing power of money." Constancy of

[5] Explicit definition of the demand curve in this way by followers of Marshall dates back at least to 1894 (see F. Y. Edgeworth, "Demand Curves" [art.], *Palgrave's Dictionary of Political Economy*, ed. Henry Higgs [rev. ed.; London: Macmillan & Co., 1926]). Edgeworth's article apparently dates from the first edition, which was published in 1894. While Edgeworth does not explicitly attribute this interpretation to Marshall, it is clear from the context that he is talking about a Marshallian demand curve and that he does not regard his statements as inconsistent in any way with Marshall's *Principles*. Though no explicit listing of "other things" is given by J. R. Hicks, *Value and Capital* (Oxford, 1939), the list given above is implicit throughout chaps. i and ii, which are explicitly devoted to elaborating and extending Marshall's analysis of demand. For statements in modern textbooks on advanced economic theory see G. J. Stigler, *The Theory of Price* (New York: Macmillan Co., 1946), pp. 86–90, and Kenneth E. Boulding, *Economic Analysis* (rev. ed.; New York: Harper & Bros., 1948), pp. 134–35.

the "purchasing power of money" for different prices of the commodity in question implies compensating variations in the prices of some or all other commodities. These variations will, indeed, be negligible if the commodity in question accounts for a negligible fraction of total expenditures; but they should not be disregarded, both because empirical considerations must be sharply separated from logical considerations and because the demand curve need not be limited in applicability to such commodities. On this variant all commodities are, in effect, divided into three groups: (a) the commodity in question, (b) closely related commodities, and (c) all other commodities. The absolute price of each commodity in group b is supposed to be the same for different points on the demand curve; only the "average" price, or an index number of prices, is considered for group c; and it is to be supposed to rise or fall with a fall or rise in the price of group a, so as to keep the "purchasing power of money" the same.

The other variant, which Marshall employed in the Mathematical Appendix of the *Principles*, is obtained by retaining " (2) their real income" and adding (4) the average price of all other commodities. Constancy of real income for different prices of the commodity in question then implies compensating variations in money income. As the price of the commodity in question rises or falls, money income is to be supposed to rise or fall so as to keep real income the same.

These two variants are essentially equivalent mathematically,[6] but the assumption

[6] Let x and y be the quantity and price, respectively, of the commodity in question; x' and y', the quantity and price of a composite commodity representing all other commodities; and m, money income. Let

$$x = g(y, y', m, u) \tag{1}$$

be the demand curve for the commodity in question, given a utility function,

$$U = U(x, x', u) \tag{2}$$

of compensating variations in other prices is easier to explain verbally and can be justified as empirically relevant by considerations of monetary theory, which is

where u is a parameter to allow for changes in taste, and subject to the condition

$$xy + x'y' = m \qquad (3)$$

From eq. (3) and the usual utility analysis, it follows that eq. (1), like eq. (3), is a homogeneous function of degree zero in y, y', and m; i.e., that

$$g(\lambda y, \lambda y', \lambda m, u) = g(y, y', m, u) \qquad (4)$$

On the current interpretation, a two-dimensional demand curve is obtained from eq. (1) directly by giving y' (other prices), m (income), and u (tastes) fixed values. A given value of y then implies a given value of x from eq. (1), a given value of x' from eq. (3), and hence a given value of U (i.e., real income) from eq. (2). The value of U will vary with y, being higher, the lower y is.

On my alternative interpretation, u and U are given fixed values and x' is eliminated from eqs. (2) and (3). This gives a pair of equations,

$$x = g(y, y', m, u_0) \qquad (5)$$

$$U_0 = U_0\left(x, \frac{m - xy}{y'}, u_0\right) \qquad (6)$$

where the subscript 0 designates fixed values. The two-dimensional variant involving compensating variations in other prices is obtained by eliminating y' from eqs. (5) and (6) and giving m a fixed value; the variant involving compensating variations in income, by eliminating m from eqs. (5) and (6) and giving y' a fixed value.

The homogeneity of eqs. (5) and (6) in y, y', and m means that x is a function only of ratios among them. Thus eqs. (5) and (6) can be written:

$$x = g(y, y', m, u_0) = g\left(\frac{y}{m}, \frac{y'}{m}, 1, u_0\right)$$

$$= g\left(\frac{y}{y'}, 1, \frac{m}{y'}, u_0\right) \qquad (5')$$

$$U_0 = U_0\left(x, \frac{m - xy}{y'}, u_0\right)$$

$$= U_0\left(x, \frac{1 - x\dfrac{y}{m}}{\dfrac{y'}{m}}, u_0\right) \qquad (6')$$

$$= U_0\left(x, \frac{m}{y'} - x\frac{y}{y'}, u_0\right)$$

The choice of price-compensating variations is equivalent to selecting the forms of these two equations in the next to the last terms of eqs. (5') and (6'); of income-compensating variations, to selecting the forms in the last terms.

presumably why Marshall used this variant in his text. On the other hand, the assumption of compensating variations in income is somewhat more convenient mathematically, which is presumably why Marshall used this variant in his Mathematical Appendix.

On my interpretation, Marshall's demand curve is identical with one of the constructions introduced by Slutsky in his famous paper on the theory of choice, namely, the reaction of quantity demanded to a "compensated variation of price," that is, to a variation in price accompanied by a compensating change in money income.[7] Slutsky expressed the compensating change in money income in terms of observable phenomena, taking it as equal to the change in price *times* the quantity demanded at the initial price. Mosak has shown that, in the limit, the change in income so computed is identical with the change required to keep the individual on the same level of utility (on the same indifference curve).[8] It follows that a similar statement is valid for compensating changes in other prices. In the limit the change in other prices required to keep the individual on the same indifference curve when his money income is unchanged but the price of one commodity varies is identical with the change in other prices required to keep unchanged the total cost of the basket of commodities purchased at the initial prices, that is, to keep unchanged the usual type of cost-of-living index number.

[7] Eugenio Slutsky, "Sulla teoria del bilancio del consumatore," *Giornale degli economisti*, LI (1915), 1–26, esp. sec. 8. [A translation of this article is now available in American Economic Association, *Readings in Price Theory* (Chicago: Richard D. Irwin, Inc., 1952), pp. 27–56.]

[8] Jacob L. Mosak, "On the Interpretation of the Fundamental Equation of Value Theory," in O. Lange, F. McIntyre, and T. O. Yntema (eds.), *Studies in Mathematical Economics and Econometrics* (Chicago: University of Chicago Press, 1942), pp. 69–74, esp. n. 5, pp. 73–74, which contains a rigorous proof of this statement by A. Wald.

C. Comparison
of the Interpretations

The relation between demand curves constructed under the two interpretations is depicted in Figure 6.1. Curve *Cc* repre-

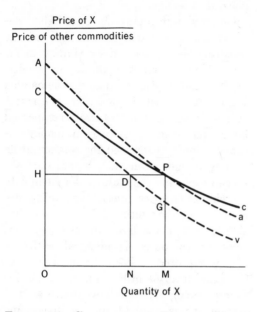

Price of X / Price of other commodities

Quantity of X

FIGURE **6.1** COMPARISON OF DEMAND CURVES CONSTRUCTED UNDER THE TWO INTERPRETATIONS

sents a demand curve of an individual consumer for a commodity *X* drawn on the current interpretation. Money income and the prices of other commodities are supposed the same for all points on it; in consequence, real income is lower at *C* than at *P*, since, if the individual sought to buy *OM* of *X* at a price of *OC*, he would be forced to curtail his purchases of something else. As the curve is drawn, of course, he buys none of *X* at a price of *OC*, spending the sum of *OHPM* on other commodities that his action at a price of *OH* shows him to value less highly than he does *OM* units of *X*. The ordinate is described as the ratio of the price of *X* to the price of other commodities. For the demand curve *Cc* this is a question only of the unit of measure, since other prices are supposed to be the same for all points on it.

From the definition of the demand curve *Cc*, *OC* is obviously the maximum price per unit that an individual would be willing to pay for an infinitesimal initial increment of *X* when his money income and the prices of other commodities have the values assumed in drawing *Cc*. Let us suppose him to purchase this amount at a price of *OC*, determine the maximum price per unit he would be willing to pay for an additional increment, and continue in this fashion, exacting the maximum possible amount for each additional increment. Let these successive maximum prices per unit define the curve *Cv*. The consumer obviously has the same real income at each point on *Cv* as at *C*, since the maximum price has been extracted from him for each successive unit, so that he has gained no utility in the process.

Cv is now a demand curve constructed according to my interpretation of Marshall. If other prices are supposed to be the same, the necessary compensating variations in money income as the price of *X* falls are given by triangular areas exemplified by *HCD* for a price of *OH*: *OH* is the maximum price per unit that the individual will give for an additional infinitesimal increment of *X* when he has spent *OCDN* for *ON* of *X* out of his initial income of, say, *m*; but his situation is exactly the same if, when the price of *X* is *OH*, his income is (*m* − *HCD*) and he spends *OHDN* on *X*; he has the same amount left to spend on all other commodities, their prices are the same, and he has the same amount of *X*; accordingly, his demand price will be the same, and he will buy *ON* of *X* at a price of *OH* and an income of (*m* − *HCD*).[9]

---

[9] In the notation of n. 5, except that *u* is omitted for simplicity, the quantities of *X* and *X'* that will be purchased for any given values of *y* and *y'* and any given real income, U_0, are obtained by solving simultaneously:

$$\frac{U_x}{U_{x'}} = \frac{y}{y'} \tag{1}$$

If compensating variations in other prices rather than in money income are used to keep real income the same, the absolute price of neither X nor other commodities can be read directly from Figure 7.1. For each ratio of the price of X to the price of other commodities, the quantity of X purchased will be that shown on Cv. But the prices of other goods will vary along Cv, rising as the relative price of X falls, so the absolute price of X can no longer be obtained by multiplying the ordinate by a single scale factor.

Figure 7.1 is drawn on the assumption that X is a "normal" commodity, that is, a commodity the consumption of which is higher, the higher the income. This is the reason Cv is drawn to the left of Cc—at every point on Cv other than C, real income is less than at the corresponding point on Cc; hence less X would be consumed.

Curve Aa represents a demand curve on my interpretation of Marshall for a real income the same as at point P on Cc; it is like Cv but for a higher real income. Real income is higher on Aa than on Cc

and

$$U(x, x') = U_0 \qquad (2)$$

where U_x and $U_{x'}$ stand for the partial derivatives of U with respect to x and x', respectively, i.e., for the marginal utility of X and X'. The solution of these equations gives the demand curve on my interpretation of Marshall, using compensating variations in money income.

U_0 $(0, m/y')$ is the utility at C in the diagram. For any given amount of X and given value of y', the amount of X' purchased is obtained by solving

$$U(x, x') = U_0\left(0, \frac{m}{y'}\right) \qquad (3)$$

which is identical with eq. (2). The amount paid for X (the area under Cv) is

$$m - x'y' \qquad (4)$$

The maximum price that will be paid per unit of X is the derivative of eq. (4), or

$$y = -\frac{dx'}{dx} y' = \frac{U_x}{U_{x'}} y' \qquad (5)$$

which is identical with eq. (1). It follows that Cv is a demand curve constructed on my interpretation of Marshall.

for prices above OH, lower for prices below OH, which is the reason Aa is to the right of Cc for prices above OH and to the left of Cc for prices below OH.

D. Why Two Interpretations Are Possible

The possibility of interpreting Marshall in these two quite different ways arises in part from the vagueness of Marshall's exposition, from his failure to give precise and rigorous definitions. A more fundamental reason, however, is the existence of inconsistency in the third and later editions of the *Principles*. In that edition Marshall introduced the celebrated passage bearing on the Giffen phenomenon. This passage and a related sentence added at the same time to the Mathematical Appendix fit the current interpretation better than they fit my interpretation. Although these are the only two items that I have been able to find in any edition of the *Principles* of which this is true, they provide some basis for the current interpretation. . . .

II. THE RELATIVE USEFULNESS OF THE TWO INTERPRETATIONS

The relative usefulness of the two interpretations of the demand curve can be evaluated only in terms of some general conception of the role of economic theory. I shall use the conception that underlies Marshall's work, in which the primary emphasis is on positive economic analysis, on the forging of tools that can be used fairly directly in analyzing practical problems. Economic theory was to him an "engine for the discovery of concrete truth." [10] "Man's powers are limited: almost every one of nature's riddles is complex. He breaks it up, studies one bit at a time, and at last combines his partial solutions with

[10] Alfred Marshall, "The Present Position of Economics" (1885), reprinted in *Memorials of Alfred Marshall*, ed. A. C. Pigou (London: Macmillan & Co., 1925), p. 159.

a supreme effort of his whole small strength into some sort of an attempt at a solution of the whole riddle." [11] The underlying justification for the central role of the concepts of demand and supply in Marshall's entire structure of analysis is the empirical generalization that an enumeration of the forces affecting demand in any problem and of the forces affecting supply will yield two lists that contain few items in common. Demand and supply are to him concepts for organizing materials, labels in an "analytical filing box." The "commodity" for which a demand curve is drawn is another label, not a word for a physical or technical entity to be defined once and for all independently of the problem at hand. Marshall writes:

> The question where the lines of division between different commodities should be drawn must be settled by convenience of the particular discussion. For some purposes it may be best to regard Chinese and Indian teas, or even Souchong and Pekoe teas, as different-commodities; and to have a separate demand schedule for each of them. While for other purposes it may be best to group together commodities as distinct as beef and mutton, or even as tea and coffee, and to have a single list to represent the demand for the two combined. [12]

A. The Distinction between Closely Related and All Other Commodities

A demand function containing as separate variables the prices of a rigidly defined and exhaustive list of commodities, all on the same footing, seems largely foreign to this approach. It may be a useful expository device to bring home the mutual interdependence of economic phenomena; it cannot form part of Marshall's

[11] Alfred Marshall, "Mechanical and Biological Analogies in Economics" (1898), *Ibid.*, p. 314.

[12] Marshall, *Principles of Economics* (8th ed.; London: Macmillan & Co., 1920), p. 100 n. All subsequent page references to the *Principles*, unless otherwise stated, are to the eighth and final edition.

"engine for the discovery of concrete truth." The analyst who attacks a concrete problem can take explicit account of only a limited number of factors; he will inevitably separate commodities that are closely related to the one immediately under study from commodities that are more distantly related. He can pay some attention to each closely related commodity. He cannot handle the more distantly related commodities in this way; he will tend either to ignore them or to consider them as a group. The formally more general demand curve will, in actual use, become the kind of demand curve that is yielded by my interpretation of Marshall.

The part of the Marshallian filing box covered by *ceteris paribus* typically includes three quite different kinds of variables, distinguished by their relation to the variable whose adaptation to some change is directly under investigation (e.g., the price of a commodity): (*a*) variables that are expected both to be materially affected by the variable under study and, in turn, to affect it; (*b*) variables that are expected to be little, if at all, affected by the variable under study but to materially affect it; (*c*) the remaining variables, expected neither to affect significantly the variable under study nor to be significantly affected by it.

In demand analysis the prices of closely related commodities are the variables in group *a*. They are put individually into the pound of *ceteris paribus* to pave the way for further analysis. Holding their prices constant is a provisional step. They must inevitably be affected by anything that affects the commodity in question; and this indirect effect can be analyzed most conveniently by first isolating the direct effect, systematically tracing the repercussions of the direct effect on each closely related commodity, and then tracing the subsequent reflex influences on the commodity in question. Indeed, in many ways, the role of the demand curve itself is as much to provide an orderly means of analyzing these indirect effects as to isolate the direct effect on the commodity in question.

The average price of "all other commodities," income and wealth, and tastes and preferences are the variables in group *b*. These variables are likely to be affected only negligibly by factors affecting primarily the commodity in question. On the other hand, any changes in them would have a significant effect on that commodity. They are put into the pound in order to separate problems, to segregate the particular reactions under study. They are put in individually and explicitly because they are so important that account will have to be taken of them in any application of the analysis.

Price changes within the group of "all other commodities" and an indefinitely long list of other variables are contained in group *c*. These variables are to be ignored. They are too numerous and each too unimportant to permit separate account to be taken of them.

In keeping with the spirit of Marshallian analysis this classification of variables is to be taken as illustrative, not definitive. What particular variables are appropriate for each group is to be determined by the problem in hand, the amount of information available, the detail required in results, and the patience and resources of the analyst.

B. Constancy of Real Income

It has just been argued that any actual analysis of a concrete economic problem with the aid of demand curves will inevitably adopt one feature of my interpretation of Marshall—consideration of a residual list of commodities as a single group. For somewhat subtler reasons this is likely to be true also of the second feature of my interpretation of Marshall—holding real income constant along a demand curve. If an analysis, begun with a demand

curve constructed on the current interpretation, is carried through and made internally consistent, it will be found that the demand curve has been subjected to shifts that, in effect, result from failure to keep real income constant along the demand curve.

An example will show how this occurs. Let us suppose that the government grants to producers of commodity *X* a subsidy of a fixed amount per unit of output, financed by a general income tax, so that money income available for expenditure (i.e., net of tax and gross of subsidy) is unchanged. For simplicity, suppose, first, that no commodities are closely related to *X* either as rivals or as complements, so that interrelations in consumption between *X* and particular other commodities can be neglected; second, that the tax is paid by individuals in about the same income class and with about the same consumption pattern as those who benefit from the subsidy, so that complications arising from changes in the distribution of income can be neglected; and, third, that there are no idle resources. Let *DD* in Figure 6.2 be a de-

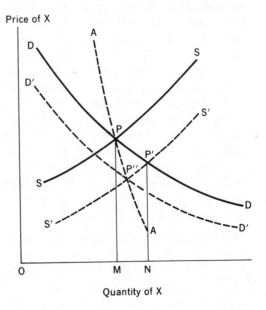

Price of X

Quantity of X

FIGURE 6.2 ILLUSTRATIVE ANALYSIS OF EFFECT OF SUBSIDY

mand curve for commodity X, and SS be the initial supply curve for X, and let the initial position at their intersection, point P, be a position of full equilibrium. The effect of the subsidy is to lower the supply curve to $S'S'$. Since we have ruled out repercussions through consumption relations with other markets and through changes in the level or distribution of money income, it is reasonable to expect that the intersection of this new supply curve and the initial demand curve, point P', will itself be a position of full equilibrium, involving a lower price and larger quantity of X. Yet, if the demand curve is constructed on the current interpretation and if the supply curve is not perfectly inelastic,[13] point P' is not a position of full equilibrium. This can be seen most easily by supposing DD to have unit elasticity, so that the same amount is spent on X at P' as at P. The same amount is then available to spend on all other commodities, and, since their prices are supposed to be the same for all points on DD under the current interpretation, the same quantity of each of them will be demanded. But then where do the resources come from to produce the extra MN units of X? Obviously, our assumptions are not internally consistent. The additional units of X can be produced only by bidding resources away from the production of other commodities, in the process raising their prices and reducing the amount of them produced. The final equilibrium position will therefore involve higher prices and lower quantities of other commodities. But, on the current interpretation, this means a shift in the demand curve for X—say, to $D'D'$—and a final equilibrium position of, say P'."[14]

[13] If it is perfectly inelastic, neither the price nor the quantity of X is changed, so the new position of equilibrium coincides with the old; but the demand curve will pass through the initial position of equilibrium whether constructed on the current interpretation or on mine; hence the two coincide at the one point on them that is relevant.

[14] $D'D'$ will not necessarily be to the left of DD even for a "normal" commodity. The reason is

The assumption that the elasticity of DD is unity is not, of course, essential for this argument. If the elasticity of DD is less than unity, a larger amount than formerly is available to spend on other commodities; at unchanged prices this means a larger quantity demanded. In consequence, while the additional amount of resources required to produce the increased amount of X demanded is smaller when DD is inelastic than when it has unit elasticity, this is counterbalanced by increased pressure for resources to produce other commodities. Similarly, when DD is elastic, the additional amount of resources required to produce the increased quantity of X demanded is larger than when DD has unit elasticity, but some resources are released in the first instance from the production of other commodities.

No such internal inconsistency as that just outlined arises if the demand curve is constructed by keeping real income the same. Curve AA is such a demand curve. At prices of X less than PM, prices of other commodities are supposed to be sufficiently higher than at P to keep real income the same, which involves the release of just enough resources so that the position of final equilibrium, P'', lies on the demand curve so constructed—at least for small changes in the price of X.[15]

———————

that the ordinate of **Fig. 6.2** measures the absolute price of X, so that ordinates of the same height on DD and $D'D'$ represent different ratios of the price of X to the price of other commodities. If the ordinate measured the ratio of the price of X to the price of other commodities, $D'D'$ would always be to the left of DD for "normal" commodities, always to the right for "inferior" commodities.

[15] Let X' be a single composite commodity representing all commodities other than X; x and x', the quantities of X and X'; and y and y', their prices. Let the subscript 1 refer to values at the initial position of equilibrium, P; the subscript 2, to values at the final position, P''. The condition of constant total expenditures means that

$$x_1 y_1 + x_1' y_1' = x_2 y_2 + x_2' y_2' \qquad (1)$$

As was pointed out above (Sec. I, B), in the limit, holding real income constant is equivalent to

The fundamental principle illustrated by this example can be put more generally. The reason why a demand curve constructed under the current interpretation fails to give the correct solution even when all disturbing influences can be neglected is that each point on it implicitly refers to a different productive capacity of the community. A reduction in the price of the commodity in question is to be regarded as enabling the community, if it so wishes, to consume more of some commodities—this commodity or others—without consuming less of any commodity. But the particular change in supply whose consequences we sought to analyze—that arising from a subsidy—does not make available any additional resources to the community; any increase in the consumption of the commodity in question must be at the expense of other commodities. The conditions for which the demand curve is drawn are therefore inconsistent with the conditions postulated on the side of supply. On the other hand, if the demand curve is

---

holding constant the cost of a fixed basket of commodities. Thus, if P'' is considered close to P,

$$x_1y_1 + x_1'y_1' = x_1y_2 + x_1'y_2' \qquad (2)$$

In the neighborhood of P, y_1 can be regarded as the cost per unit of producing X; y_1', as the cost per unit of producing X'. The condition that sufficient resources be released to permit the production of the requisite additional amount of X is therefore

$$(x_2 - x_1)y_1 = -(x_2' - x_1')y_1' \qquad (3)$$

which is equivalent to

$$x_1y_1 + x_1'y_1' = x_2y_1 + x_2'y_1' \qquad (4)$$

But, in the limit, eqs. (1) and (2) imply eq. (4), as can be seen by subtracting eq. (2) from eq. (1) and replacing y_2 and y_2' in the result by $(y_2 - y_1 + y_1)$ and $(y_2' - y_1' + y_1')$, respectively.

More generally, constant real income [with constant total expenditures] involves keeping a price index unchanged; constant use of resources involves keeping a quantity index unchanged; and, in the limit, a constant price index and constant total expenditures imply a constant quantity index.

Note that AA need not be steeper than DD in a graph like **Fig. 6.2**. The point in question is that commented on in n. **14**.

constructed by keeping "real income" the same, no such inconsistency need arise. True, constant "real income" in the sense of "utility" and constant "real income" in the sense of outputs attainable from a fixed total of resources are different concepts, but they converge and can be treated as the same in the neighborhood of a position of equilibrium.

Of course, not all shifts in supply that it is desired to analyze arise in ways that leave the productive capacity of the community unaltered. Many involve a change in productive capacity—for example, changes in supply arising from improvements in technology or the discovery of previously unknown resources. Even in these cases, however, a demand curve constructed on the current interpretation will not serve. There is no reason to expect the differences in productive capacity implicit in constant money income and constant prices of other goods to bear any consistent relation to the change in productive capacity arising on the side of supply.[16] The better plan, in these cases, is to allow separately and directly for the increase in productive capacity by redrawing the demand curves to correspond to an appropriately higher real income and then to use a demand curve on which all points refer to that higher real income.

The main point under discussion can be put still more generally. The opportunities open to a consumer to satisfy his wants depend principally on two factors—the total resources at his disposal and the terms on which he can exchange one commodity for another, that is, on his real income and on relative prices. The form of analysis that is now fashionable distinguishes

---

[16] Note the difference from the previous case of constant productive capacity. As stated above, there is reason to expect constant real income along a demand curve to bear a consistent relation to constant productive capacity in the neighborhood of equilibrium. The reason, in effect, is provided by one of the conditions at equilibrium: the tangency of consumption and production indifference curves.

three effects of changes in his opportunities—the income effect arising from changes in his money income; the income effect arising from changes in the price of a commodity, with unchanged money income and prices of other commodities; and the substitution effect arising from a change in the relative price of a commodity, with unchanged real income.

The distinction between the so-called "substitution" and "income" effects of a change in price is a direct consequence of defining the demand curve according to the current interpretation of Marshall. Its basis is the arithmetic truism that at given prices for all commodities but one, a given money income corresponds to a higher real income, the lower the price of the remaining commodity—at a lower price for it, more of some commodities can be purchased without purchasing less of others. In consequence, a decline in the price of a commodity, all other prices constant, has, it is argued, two effects: first, with an unchanged real income, it would stimulate the substitution of that commodity for others—this is the substitution effect; second, if the money income of the consumers is supposed to be unchanged, the increase in their real income as a result of the decline in price causes a further change in the consumption of that commodity as well as of others—this is the income effect.[17]

The two different kinds of income effects distinguished in this analysis—one arising from a change in money income, the other from a change in the price of one commodity—are really the same thing,

the effect of a change in real income with given relative prices, arising in different ways. It is hard to see any gain from combining the second income effect with the substitution effect; it seems preferable to combine the two income effects and thereby gain a sharp contrast with the substitution effect.

It has often been stated that Marshall "neglected the income effect."[18] On my interpretation of his demand curve, this statement is invalid. One must then say that Marshall recognized the desirability of separating two quite different effects and constructed his demand curve so that it encompassed solely the effect that he wished to isolate for study, namely, the substitution effect. Instead of neglecting the income effect, he "eliminated" it.

The conclusion to which the argument of this section leads is identical with that reached by Frank H. Knight in a recent article, in which he says:

> We have to choose in analysis between holding the prices of all other goods constant and maintaining constant the "real income" of the hypothetical consumer. . . . The treatment of the Slutzky school adopts the assumption that . . . the prices of all other goods (and the consumer's money income) are constant. Hence, real income must change. Of the two alternatives, this seems to be definitely the wrong choice. . . . The simple and obvious alternative is to draw the demand curves in terms of a change in *relative* prices, i.e., to assume that the value of money is held constant, through compensating changes in the prices of other goods, and not that these other prices are held constant.[19]

---

[17] See Slutsky, *op. cit.*; Henry Schultz, *The Theory and Measurement of Demand* (Chicago: University of Chicago Press, 1938), pp. 40–46; J. R. Hicks and R. G. D. Allen, "A Reconsideration of the Theory of Value," *Economica*, XIV (1934), 52–76 and 196–219; Hicks, *op. cit.*, Part I.

[18] Hicks, *op. cit.*, p. 32.
[19] "Realism and Relevance in the Theory of Demand," *Journal of Political Economy*, LII (December, 1944), 289–318, esp. Sec. III, "The Meaning of a Demand Curve," pp. 298–301. Quotation from p. 299.

7. The Marshallian Demand Curve[*]

MARTIN J. BAILEY[1]

Martin J. Bailey (B.A., University of California at Los Angeles, 1951; M.A., Johns Hopkins University, 1953; Ph.D., 1956) was born in Taft, California, in 1927. At present he is on the faculty of the University of Rochester, where he is Associate Dean of the College of Business Administration. From 1955–1965 he was on the faculty of the Department of Economics at the University of Chicago. He then served as a member of the Economic and Political Studies Division of the Institute for Defense Analyses, and as Special Assistant to the Assistant Secretary of Defense for Systems Analysis for Southeast Asia Forces. His research interests are in economic theory and the economics of defense. He is the author of *National Income and the Price Level* and numerous articles in the professional journals.

In an article with the above title, Professor Friedman[2] has urged that a constant-real-income demand curve is a more satisfactory tool for economic analysis than the customary constant-other-prices-and-money-incomes demand curve and that, at least in the first two editions of the *Principles*, this was the type of demand curve which Marshall really had in mind. On the latter, historical question nothing will be said here; but on the former, analytical question I shall contend that Friedman did not make the best choice of a curve as an improvement on the conventional one and that the constant-real-income curve, strictly interpreted, does not on balance possess the superiority he claims for it. Of the various interesting alternative types of demand curve which can be defined, one at least possesses most, if not all, of the advantages which Friedman can claim for any type of constant-real-income demand curve and none of its disadvantages.

In his argument in support of the constant-real-income demand curve Friedman demonstrated that the use of an ordinary demand curve in a demand-supply diagram

* Reprinted from the *Journal of Political Economy* (June 1954) by permission of The University of Chicago Press. (Copyright, 1954), pp. 255–261.

[1] I wish to thank Mr. Amotz Morag and Professors Arnold C. Harberger and Carl F. Christ for their helpful advice and criticisms of early drafts of this note; and I wish to thank Professor Milton Friedman for his advice and criticism at a later stage. Specific acknowledgments to Professor Friedman appear at appropriate points in the text of this note. Responsibility for such errors as remain is, of course, my own.

[2] Milton Friedman, "The Marshallian Demand Curve," *Journal of Political Economy*, LVII (1949), 463–95.

to show the effects of a subsidy on a given commodity fails to take account of the necessary withdrawal of resources from other uses; on the other hand, the constant-real-income demand curve, which in the limit is an approximation of what the community can actually have, allows for this withdrawal of resources and therefore presents a better picture of the final outcome.[3] While Friedman's analysis does not contain any errors, it is liable to serious misinterpretation if its assumptions and their relevance are overlooked; on the other hand, with a different type of demand curve which I shall propose the pitfalls can be avoided, and an analytically superior tool can be had in the bargain.

DEMAND CURVES AND PRODUCTION POSSIBILITIES

Suppose, for simplicity of arrangement, that a fully employed community has the production possibilities between its two competitively produced commodities X and Y as shown by the opportunity-cost curve ST in Figure 7.1(a). Money, different from either commodity, is used as a unit of account only; money incomes are assumed to be spent in full, and the absolute price level to be determined arbitrarily.[4]

From the community indifference curves (for the moment assumed to be defined unambiguously) shown in Figure 7.1(a), we may derive the two demand curves mentioned so far (the constant-real-income and the other-things-equal demand curves) in the customary manner. DD in Figure 7.1(b) is defined by the price-consumption line PC in Figure 7.1(b), and RR is obtained from the equilibrium indifference curve I_1 by noting the quantity of X at which I_1 has any given slope (i.e., mar-

ginal rate of substitution, interpreted as a price ratio, P_x/P_y).

Suppose now that the government pays a subsidy on production of X; the apparent effect after production adjusts itself to the new conditions will be to lower the price of X by some fraction of the amount of the subsidy, changing the price line from $S'T'$ to $S'L$ in Figure 7.1(a), and to leave the price of Y and money income unchanged. Given this apparent opportunity, the community would like to consume to the point C in Figure 7.1(a), that is, to the point W in Figure 7.1(b). However, as Friedman pointed out, this is clearly impossible. Physical supplies are not available, and corresponding to this lack there is an inflationary gap equal to the going amount of the subsidy; also the relative price of Y must fall owing to the shift of production toward more X.

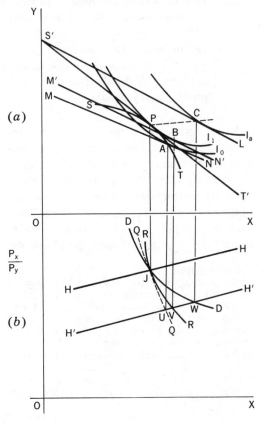

FIGURE 7.1

---

[3] *Ibid.*, pp. 467–74.
[4] Friedman's assumption of a fixed supply of factor services is retained here, since its retention does not cause any loss of generality in the argument.

Hence we must further suppose that the government imposes an income tax always equal to the subsidy. The final equilibrium point is found where a price line which is tangent to an indifference curve where it crosses the production frontier differs in slope from the slope of the production frontier at that point by an amount corresponding to the subsidy. $S'L$ will "shift" to MN, where it is tangent to the indifference curve I_0, lower than I_1, at A. This equilibrium point is only slightly distant from B, the point at which $M'N'$ is tangent to I_1. ($S'L$, $M'N'$, and MN have it in common that each one's slope differs by the rate of subsidy from the slope of the production frontier beneath the point where each one is tangent to an indifference curve.)

It can be seen from this result that neither DD nor RR, in Figure 7.1(b), shows the final outcome correctly. The correct outcome could be obtained only from another type of demand curve, the "production-frontier" demand curve, which would show, for each amount of X, the marginal rate of substitution of the indifference curve which crosses the production frontier at the point where that amount of X is produced. This demand curve is shown as QQ in Figure 7.1(b); if X is not an inferior good, QQ must lie to the left of both RR and DD below J and must lie between them above J (where J in Fig. 7.1(b) corresponds to P in Fig. 7.1(a). Its intersection with $H'H'$ at U, corresponding to A in Figure 7.1(a), shows the true outcome as the result of the imposition of the combination subsidy and income tax.

The production-frontier demand curve is clearly the one hypothetically most desirable for use in the comparative statics of demand analysis, since it shows what in fact the community will take when the repercussions on the production of other commodities are taken into account. Its weakness is that it is defined only for given production conditions. Presumably tastes are relatively constant, whereas real or apparent production conditions are always changing because of fluctuations in weather and crops, changes in government policy, and other factors. Data on market behavior may, to the extent that this is true, be supposed to tell us something about consumer preferences but to tell us little about production conditions. At any moment of time, however, production conditions are in some sense fixed; and for economic analysis it would be desirable to take these conditions into account in analyzing demand. Lacking knowledge of these conditions of the moment, we must adopt some more or less arbitrary method of approximating the effects of a change in policy or the like.

Friedman argues in effect that RR [in Fig. 7.1(b)] is a better approximation to QQ than is DD, since I_1 is tangent to ST at P and so approximates it in the limit, whereas PC has no such limiting property. That is to say, RR is tangent to QQ, but DD is not. This is correct, as long as the community preference field (the function represented by the indifference map) is innocent of any discontinuities in the first and all higher derivatives. Though I suppose there is no reason to doubt its innocence for practical purposes, this qualification should be recognized as relevant. But other arguments developed below substantially weaken the case for the constant-real-income demand curve.

THE CONSTANT-REAL-INCOME CONCEPT

The argument so far has been greatly aided by the use of unexplained community indifference curves. It is now necessary to investigate the meaning of these curves of constant community real income and of the idea of a constant-real-income demand curve. The construction of community indifference curves will not be repeated here; suffice it to say that constant community real income means constant real income for *every individual* in the community.[5] The relevant construction necessarily implies the existence of different distributions of money incomes at different points along a given community indifference curve; the reason for this will become clear in the following discussion.

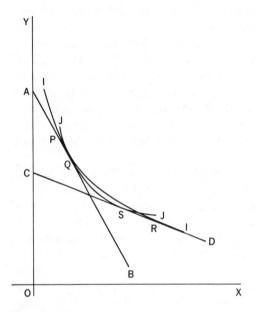

FIGURE 7.2

Consider, in Figure 7.2, the indifference curves of two individuals whose money incomes are equal.[6] When the two indifference maps are superimposed on one another, their opportunity lines will coincide, as, for example, in *AB*. The individual *I* will be in equilibrium at *P*, and the individual *J* will be in equilibrium at *Q*, given

[5] William J. Baumol, "The Community Indifference Map: A Construction," *Review of Economic Studies*, XVII (1949–50), 189–97; and E. J. Mishan, "The Principle of Compensation Reconsidered," *Journal of Political Economy*, LX (1952), 514–17.

[6] For persons with different money incomes, the scales of *X* and *Y* quantities for the person with the larger income may be compressed (in the same proportion) until the two opportunity lines coincide when the indifference maps are superimposed. The argument in the text then applies without change to this case.

the opportunity line *AB*. Now for an arbitrary change in the price of, say, commodity *Y*, what price change of *X* will keep both individuals on the same levels of real income *J* and *I*? It is at once apparent that there need not be *any* price change of *X* which will do the trick. If the price of *Y* should rise until the given money income of each individual could purchase only *OC* of *Y*, then a price of *X* corresponding to the opportunity line *CD* would do it, since *CD* happens to be tangent to both *I* and *J* at *R* and *S*, respectively. But the set of points *C* through which a line can be drawn tangent to both indifference curves is in general a finite set (the principal exception being the case where the two indifference curves coincide) and may be empty, aside from the point *A*. A price compensating constant-real-income demand function for the two individuals must remain undefined except at points such as *C*—that is, we cannot, in general, have a constant-real-income demand "curve" at all, as long as money incomes are held constant.

On the other hand, if money income changes are used—in general, a different change for each individual—then it will always be possible to find an income change for each individual that will just offset any price change (or set of price changes) and permit him to achieve the same indifference curve as before. This, in effect, is what is done in defining community indifference curves.

But if the method of compensating price changes is used, there is no such thing as a constant-real-income demand curve for two individuals taken together. Such a curve can be defined for each one, but the curves cannot be aggregated because the price changes of *Y* offsetting a given price change of *X* would be different for the two individuals. This would be true a fortiori for a larger community; and it would continue to be true whatever the number of commodities.

It should be clear, then, that a constant-real-income demand curve for a community cannot be defined in terms solely of offsetting price movements for all possible price changes of a given commodity unless everybody's tastes are, in effect, identical. In fact, identity of tastes is not sufficient when money incomes are different. What is required is that the indifference curve on which each individual finds himself in equilibrium must be an exact projection of the corresponding indifference curve of every other individual. Unless all indifference systems were homogeneous, identity of tastes would guarantee this coincidence only for an equal distribution of income.

TWO APPROXIMATIONS: CONSTANT APPARENT REAL INCOME AND CONSTANT APPARENT PRODUCTION

The objections against a constant-real-income demand curve, as I have so far defined it, are for any practical purpose overwhelming; recourse may be had, how-

ever, to an approximating concept which avoids these objections.[7] This concept is that of the constant-*apparent*-real-income demand curve, which can be defined for constant-money incomes all around and with no particular knowledge of individual consumer preferences. In Figure 7.3(a) the point P represents, as before, the initial equilibrium point, and $S'T'$ is the equilibrium price line. If the price of X is lowered, the consumers' real income will "apparently" be the same if the price of Y is raised to the point where the consumers are just able to buy the same bill of goods they bought before; that is, the new price line $M''N''$ should pass through P. This, to a first order of approximation, cancels out the income effect to consumers in the aggregate[8] but allows them a small gain in "real income" by substituting X for Y; the new bill of goods they would choose if they had this opportunity would be B', on

[7] In his text Friedman uses the constant-apparent-real-income demand curve (*op. cit.*, pp. 466–67 [p. 92 of the present book]).

[8] If individual incomes are not adjusted, then "income effects" are not removed by this procedure even to a first order of approximation for individuals, since no individual need be consuming the two commodities in the same proportions as they are consumed by the whole community.

However, this consideration may be ignored for the constant-apparent-real-income demand curve, if we like, whereas in the nature of the case it cannot be ignored for the "true" constant-real-income demand curve. Furthermore, if we choose not to ignore it, we need only to know the original quantities bought by each consumer in order to define the constant-apparent-real-income demand curve, whereas for the constant-real-income demand curve one must know the shape and position of each consumer's relevant indifference curve. Similar remarks apply to the constant-apparent-production demand curve discussed below in the text.

So far as I can see, the production-frontier demand curve has the disadvantage that there is no logical way to define it for each individual in the community—it is a purely aggregate function, and any relative income distribution is consistent with its definition. This disadvantage is the antithesis of the disadvantage of the constant-real-income demand curve, which in effect is defined only for the individual.

My earlier omission of the points in this footnote was brought to my attention by Friedman.

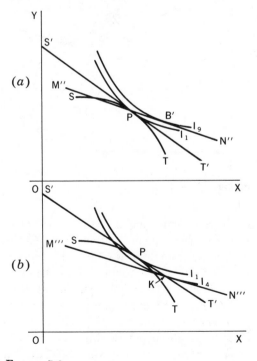

FIGURE 7.3

the community indifference curve I_3, higher than I_1.

The demand curve derived in this way is not the same thing as the true constant-real-income demand curve as previously defined (which depended on the shape of I_1 only), but it can be proved to be a first-order approximation of it,[9] just as the true constant-real-income demand curve is a first-order approximation of the production-frontier demand curve. It follows that the constant-apparent-real-income demand curve is a first-order approximation of the production-frontier demand curve. Furthermore, it does not suffer from the difficulties of definition of the other curve, since it can unambiguously be defined in terms of constant-money incomes for every individual.

In practice, something in the nature of a constant-apparent-real-income demand curve could be derived statistically from ordinary total market data; whereas a true constant-real-income demand curve could not but would require data on every individual. With a statistically derived demand curve in our hands, we would not know what values of the price variables (if any) would give every consumer the same real income (for a constant-money income) as some other set of values of the price variables. However, it would be a simple matter to choose a set of price variables giving the same *apparent* real income (as here defined) to the community as some other set; all that has to be done is to choose a set of prices which keeps a base-weights price index unchanged in value.[10]

However, the possibilities for better practical approximation of the production-frontier demand curve are not yet exhausted. We may with comparable sim-

plicity define a constant-apparent-*production* demand curve; and this will be the best approximation of the lot. In Figure 7.3(b) the line $S'T'$ represents the equilibrium price line as before, and, being tangent to the production frontier ST at P, it represents a local approximation of ST, just as does I_1. A useful demand concept is defined by moving along $S'T'$: for any given price ratio for X and Y, we obtain from the community indifference map that bill of goods among those along $S'T'$ which the community would prefer; that is, we find the community indifference curve I_4, which at its point of crossing of $S'T'$ has the same slope as the given price line, $M'''N'''$.

We may now compare the different conceptions of demand set forth here; the curves are illustrated in Figure 7.4, which

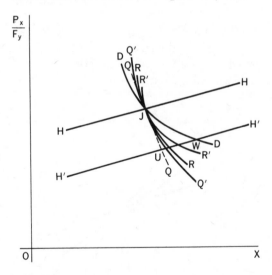

FIGURE 7.4

is derived from Figures 7.1(a), 7.3(a), and 7.3(b) in the same manner as Figure 7.1(b) is derived from Figure 7.1(a). The curves DD, RR, and QQ in Figure 7.4 are the same as in Figure 7.1(a); the new curves $R'R'$ and $Q'Q'$ are the approximations—constant *apparent* real income and production, respectively—discussed in this section.

The curves $R'R'$, RR, and $Q'Q'$ are all

[9] See Jacob L. Mosak, "On the Interpretation of the Fundamental Equation of Value Theory," in O. Lange *et al.* (eds.), *Studies in Mathematical Economics and Econometrics* (Chicago: University of Chicago Press, 1942), p. 73 n.

[10] Friedman, *op. cit.*, p. 467 [p. 92 of the present book].

tangent to QQ at J, a condition which will hold provided the necessary continuity obtains in preference and production; and it can also be seen that $R'R'$, RR, and $Q'Q'$ are successively better approximations in that order to QQ, which represents the demand derived from what the community can actually have. (The relative positions of the various curves depend on the assumption that commodity X is not inferior.) No importance should be attached to the absolute curvatures of the different curves, which depend on the conditions of preference and production; but under the assumed conditions it is necessarily true that QQ, $Q'Q'$, RR, and $R'R'$ are successively more concave upward and that $Q'Q'$ is the best approximation to the shape of QQ.

The constant-apparent-production demand curve can, like the constant-apparent-real-income demand curve, be derived from market data on quantities sold and prices. Just as the constant-apparent-real-income demand curve is obtained from the knowledge of the original equilibrium quantities and of the relevant part of the consumer preference field as revealed in market data, so the constant-apparent-production curve is obtained from a knowledge of the original equilibrium *prices* and of the relevant part of the consumer preference field. The first involves keeping a base-weights price index constant; the second involves keeping a base-weights quantity index constant. Such awkwardness of definition as exists in the constant-apparent-production demand curve disappears if the Continental procedure of expressing prices as a function of quantity is adopted.[11]

The constant-apparent-production curve has the advantage, however, that it represents the true possibilities closer than does the constant-real-income demand curve. *It utilizes information which the latter curve does not use, namely, that the equilibrium*

[11] I am indebted to Friedman for this point.

price ratio is itself an approximation of the alternative bills of goods which the community can in fact have.

There is one other point on which the suggested "improvement" of the conventional demand curve might be rejected: the conventional demand curve is unambiguous about how "other prices" behave, whereas none of the other demand curves is. If there are several commodities, a given change in the price of commodity X may be offset by price changes in other goods in any of a number of different ways still meeting the specifications of the other four types of demand curves. It may make a good deal of difference to the demand for X whether the prices of closely competing or complementary goods are changed a little or a lot to compensate for the change in the price of X. If any demand curve other than the all-other-prices-and-incomes-equal demand curve is used, some arbitrary specification must be made as to how other prices are to change to offset changes in the price of X, such as that all other prices change in the same proportion. It should be recognized that such a solution *is* arbitrary, since whatever choice is made does not necessarily have any connection with the way these prices would really change if, say, a subsidy were imposed on commodity X. The conventional demand curve solves this problem (also arbitrarily, of course) by assuming that other prices do not change at all.

FINAL COMMENT

The conclusion of the above remarks finds me substantially in agreement with Friedman's argument in favor of revising the conventional notion of a demand curve when we desire to analyze the effects of an excise tax or subsidy, although I have come out in favor of even greater revision than he suggested. In the policy problem in question, the community's production opportunities are unaffected, but *apparent* supply conditions are changed. Therefore, it is simplest to use a demand curve along which true supply conditions are (exactly or approximately) unchanged. The conventional demand curve does not meet this specification; consequently, in the problem under consideration one must show a shift in such a demand curve, as well as in the apparent supply curve, as the effect of the policy action.[12] If market data are sufficiently informative, both demand and supply conditions are hypothetically ascertainable, and the production-frontier demand curve may be used. If not, the approximations discussed here may be used, the better of which is the constant-apparent-production demand curve.

The situation is not the same if the problem under consideration involves changes in actual supply conditions such as (*a*) changes in technique, (*b*) crop variations and the like, and (*c*) changes in government activity, altering the availabilities to the private sector of the economy. In any such case the relevant demand curve would change, that is, would "shift." This is true of the production-frontier de-

[12] Friedman, *op. cit.*

mand curve and of all three of its approximations. It is possible that, by coincidence, the new equilibrium might be on the old price-consumption line (*PC* in Fig. 7.1(*a*)); and in this case the conventional demand curve would give the true result without shifting. No such coincidence is possible for the other four demand curves if the new production frontier lies entirely above or below the old one. Beyond this, however, nothing can be said as to whether the outcome of a change in conditions can or cannot be approximated with any single demand curve defined here.

It is therefore evident that the choice of a demand curve for purposes of analysis should depend on the problem in hand; and for some problems no demand curve will perform with the simplicity we might desire. It should therefore also be evident that the use of general equilibrium diagrams such as Figure 7.1(*a*) is an important supplement to clear and accurate analysis. With such diagrams it is still necessary to state the relevant qualifications regarding income distribution, but subject to this the interrelationships between different types of changes in conditions can be shown.

8. Bandwagon, Snob, and Veblen Effects in the Theory of Consumers' Demand*

HARVEY LEIBENSTEIN [1]

Harvey Leibenstein (B.S., Northwestern University, 1945; M.A., 1946; Ph.D., Princeton University, 1951) is Professor of Economics at Harvard University. Until 1967 he was on the faculty of the University of California at Berkeley. He has written widely in the fields of economic theory, economic development and demography; he is the author of *The Theory of Economic-Demographic Development, Economic Backwardness and Economic Growth,* and numerous articles. He has also served as a consultant to the RAND Corporation.

I. THE NATURE OF THE PROBLEM

The desire of some consumers to be "in style," the attempts by others to attain exclusiveness, and the phenomena of "conspicuous consumption," have as yet not been incorporated into the current theory of consumers' demand. My purpose, in this paper, is to take a step or two in that direction.

1. "Non-additivity" in Consumers' Demand Theory

This enquiry was suggested by some provocative observations made by Professor Oskar Morgenstern in his article, "Demand Theory Reconsidered." [2] After examining various aspects of the relation-

* Reprinted by permission of the publishers from Harvey Leibenstein, *The Quarterly Journal of Economics* (May 1950). Cambridge, Mass.: Harvard University Press. Copyright, 1950, by the President and Fellows of Harvard College, pp. 183–207.

[1] The writer wishes to take this opportunity to thank Professor Ansley Coale and Messrs. Carey P. Modlin and Norman B. Ryder for their painstaking criticism of an earlier draft of this paper.

[2] *The Quarterly Journal of Economics,* February 1948, pp. 165–201.

ship between individual demand curves and collective market demand curves Professor Morgenstern points out that in some cases the market demand curve is not the lateral summation of the individual demand curves. The following brief quotation may indicate the nature of what he calls "non-additivity" and give some indication of the problem involved. "Non-additivity in this simple sense is given, for example, in the case of fashions, where one person buys because another is buying the same thing, or vice versa. The collective demand curve of snobs is most likely not additive. But the phenomenon of non-additivity is in fact much deeper; since virtually all collective supply curves are non-additive it follows that the demand of the firms for their labor, raw materials, etc. is also non-additive. This expands the field of non-additivity enormously." [3]

Since the purpose of Professor Morgenstern's article is immanent criticism he does not present solutions to the problems he raises. He does clearly imply, however, that since coalitions are bound to be important in this area only the "Theory of Games" (developed by Von Neumann and Morgenstern) is likely to give an adequate solution to this problem. [4] The present writer is not competent to judge whether this is or is not the case, but he does believe that there are many markets where coalitions among consumers are not widespread or of significance, and hence abstracting from the possibility of such coalitions may not be unreasonable. Should this be the case we may be able to make some headway through the use of conventional analytical methods.

What we shall therefore be concerned with substantially is a reformulation of some aspects of the static theory of consumers' demand while permitting the relaxation of one of the basic implicit assumptions of the current theory—namely, that the consumption behaviour of any in-

dividual is independent of the consumption of others. This will permit us to take account of consumers' motivations not heretofore incorporated into the theory. To be more specific, the proposed analysis is designed to take account of the desire of people to wear, buy, do, consume, and behave like their fellows; the desire to join the crowd, be "one of the boys," etc.—phenomena of mob motivations and mass psychology either in their grosser or more delicate aspects. This is the type of behaviour involved in what we shall call the "bandwagon effect." On the other hand, we shall also attempt to take account of the search for exclusiveness by individuals through the purchase of distinctive clothing, foods, automobiles, houses, or anything else that individuals may believe will in some way set them off from the mass of mankind—or add to their prestige, dignity, and social status. In other words, we shall be concerned with the impact on the theory created by the potential non-functional utilities inherent in many commodities.

2. The Past Literature

The past literature on the interpersonal aspects of utility and demand can be divided into three categories: sociology, welfare economics, and pure theory. The sociological writings deal with the phenomena of fashions and conspicuous consumption and their relationship to social status and human behaviour. This treatment of the subject was made famous by Veblen—although Veblen, contrary to the notions of many, was neither the discoverer nor the first to elaborate upon the theory of conspicuous consumption. John Rae, writing before 1834, has quite an extensive treatment of conspicuous consumption, fashions, and related matters pretty much along Veblenian lines. [5] Rae attri-

[3] *Ibid.*, p. 175 n.
[4] *Ibid.*, p. 201.

[5] John Rae, *The Sociological Theory of Capital* (London: The Macmillan Co., 1905), especially Chap. XIII, "Of Economic Stratification," and Appendix I, "Of Luxury," pp. 218–276.

butes many of these ideas to earlier writers, going so far as to find the notion of conspicuous consumption in the Roman poet Horace; and a clear statement of the "keeping up with the Joneses" idea in the verse of Alexander Pope.[6] An excellent account of how eighteenth and nineteenth century philosophers and economists handled the problem of fashion is given in Norine Foley's article "Fashion."[7] For the most part, these treatments are of a "sociological" nature.

The economist concerned with public policy will probably find the "economic welfare" treatment of the problem most interesting. Here, if we examine the more recent contributions first and then go backward, we find examples of current writers believing they have stumbled upon something new, although they had only rediscovered what had been said many years before. Thus, Professor Melvin Reder in his recent treatment of the theory of welfare economics claims that ". . . there is another type of external repercussion which is rarely, *if ever*, recognized in discussions of welfare economics. It occurs where the utility function of one individual contains, as variables, the quantities of goods consumed by other persons."[8] It can only be lack of awareness of the past literature that causes Reder to imply that this consideration has not been taken up before. Among those who considered the problem earlier are J. E. Meade,[9] A. C. Pigou,[10] Henry Cunynghame,[11] and John Rae.[12]

The similarity in the treatment of this matter by Reder and Rae is at times striking. For example, Reder suggests that legislation forbidding "invidious expenditure" may result in an increase in welfare by freeing resources from "competitive consumption" to other uses.[13] In a similar vein Rae argued that restrictions on the trade of "pure luxuries" can only be a gain to some and a loss to none, in view of the labor saved in avoiding the production of "pure luxuries." It is quite clear from the context that what Rae calls "pure luxuries" is exactly the same as Reder's commodities that enter into "competitive consumption."[14]

One reason why the interpersonal effects on demand have been ignored in current texts may be the fact that Marshall did not consider the matter in his *Principles*. We know, however, from Marshall's correspondence,[15] that he was aware of the problem. Both Cunynghame and Pigou pointed out that Marshall's treatment of consumers' surplus did not take into account interpersonal effects on utility. Marshall seemed to feel that this would make the diagrammatical treatment too complex. Recently, Reder[16] and Samuelson[17] noticed that external economies and diseconomies of consumption may vitiate (or, at best, greatly complicate) their "new" welfare analysis, and hence, in true academic fashion, they assume the problem away. This, however, is not the place to examine the question in detail.

The only attack on the problem from the point of view of pure theory that the writer could find[18] is a short article by

[6] *Ibid.*, pp. 249 and 253.

[7] *Economic Journal*, 1893, pp. 458–474.

[8] *Studies in the Theory of Welfare Economics* (New York: Columbia University Press, 1947), p. 64. Italics mine.

[9] "Mr. Lerner on the Economics of Control," *Economic Journal*, 1945, pp. 51–56.

[10] *The Economics of Welfare* (4th Edition, 1929), pp. 190–192, 225–226, 808.

[11] "Some Improvements in Simple Geometrical Methods of Treating Exchange Value, Monopoly, and Rent," *Economic Journal*, 1892, pp. 35–39.

[12] Rae, *op. cit.*, pp. 277–296.

[13] Reder, *op. cit.*, pp. 65–66.

[14] Rae, *op. cit.*, pp. 282–288.

[15] Pigou, *Memorials of Alfred Marshall*, pp. 433 and 450. These are Marshall's letters to Pigou and Cunynghame which indicate that Marshall had read the articles (*E. J.* 1892, and *E. J.* 1903), where Pigou and Cunynghame consider the matter.

[16] Reder, *op. cit.*, p. 67. "We shall assume, throughout its remainder, that the satisfaction of one individual does not depend on the consumption of another."

[17] *Foundations of Economic Analysis*, p. 224.

[18] James S. Duesenberry, in his recent book, *Income, Saving, and the Theory of Consumer Be-*

Professor Pigou.[19] In this article Pigou sets out to inquire under what circumstances the assumption of the additivity of the individual demand curves "adequately conforms to the facts, and, when it does not so conform, what alternative assumption ought to be substituted for it."[20] It is obvious that the particular choice of alternative assumptions will determine (a) whether a solution can, given the existing analytical tools, be obtained, and (b) whether such a solution is relevant to the real world. Pigou's treatment of the problem is, unfortunately, exceedingly brief. He attempts to deal with non-additivity in both supply and demand curves within the confines of six pages. In examining the additivity assumption he points out that it is warranted when (1) the demand for the commodity is wholly for the direct satisfaction yielded by it or, (2) where disturbances to equilibrium are so small that aggregate output is not greatly changed. After briefly suggesting some of the complexities of non-additivity he concludes that the ". . . problems, for the investigation of which it is necessary to go behind the demand schedule of the market as a whole, are still, theoretically, soluble; there are a sufficient number of equations to determine the unknowns."[21] This last point, which is not demonstrated in Pigou's article, is hardly satisfying since it has been shown that the equality of equations and unknowns is not a sufficient condition for a determinate solution, or indeed for any solution, to exist.[22]

3. The Approach and Limits of the Ensuing Analysis

It should, perhaps, be pointed out at the outset that the ensuing exposition is limited to statics. In all probability, the most interesting parts of the problem, and also those most relevant to real problems, are its dynamic aspects. However, a static analysis is probably necessary, and may be of significance, in order to lay a foundation for a dynamic analysis. In view of the limitations to be set on the following analysis, it becomes necessary to demarcate clearly the conceptual borderline between statics and dynamics.

There are, unfortunately, numerous definitions of statics and there seems to be some confusion on the matter. In view of this it will not be possible to give *the* definition of statics. All that we can hope to do is to choose *a* definition that will be consistent with and useful for our purposes —and also one that at the same time does not stray too far from some of the generally accepted notions about statics. Because of the fact that we live in a dynamic world most definitions of statics will imply a state of affairs that contradicts our general experience. But this is of necessity the case. What we must insist on is internal consistency but we need not, at this stage, require "realism."

Our task, then, is to define a static situation—a situation in which static economics is applicable. Ordinarily, it is thought that statics is in some way "timeless." This need not be the case. For our purposes, a

---

havior (Harvard University Press, 1949), considers problems of a somewhat similar nature but handles them in quite a different manner. Chapter VI on interdependent preferences and the "new" welfare analysis is especially worthy of mention. Duesenberry's treatment of the problem helps considerably to fill an important gap in the current theory. Unfortunately, Mr. Duesenberry's work came to the attention of the writer too late to be given the detailed consideration it deserves.

[19] "The Interdependence of Different Sources of Demand and Supply in a Market," *Economic Journal*, 1913, pp. 18–24.

[20] *Ibid.*, p. 18.

[21] *Ibid.*, p. 24.

[22] On this point cf. Morgenstern, "Professor Hicks on Value and Capital," *Journal of Political Economy*, June 1941, pp. 368–376. See also part of an article by Don Patinkin, "The Indeterminacy of Absolute Prices in Classical Economic Theory," *Econometrica*, January 1949, pp. 310–311, which sets out the conditions under which systems of homogeneous equations will possess no solution.

static situation is not a "timeless" situation, nor is static economics timeless economics. It is, however, "temporally orderless" economics. That is, we shall define a static situation as one in which the order of events is of no significance. We, therefore, abstract from the consequences of the temporal order of events.[23] The above definition is similar to, but perhaps on a slightly higher level of generality than, Hicks's notion that statics deals with "those parts of economic theory where we do not have to trouble about dating." [24]

In order to preserve internal consistency, it is necessary to assume that the period of reference is one in which the consumer's income and expenditure pattern is synchronized. And, we have to assume also that this holds true for all consumers. In other words, we assume that both the income patterns and the expenditure patterns repeat themselves *every* period. There is thus no overlapping of expenditures from one period into the next. This implies, of course, that the demand curve reconstitutes itself every period.[25] The above implies also that only one price can exist during any unit period and that price can change only from period to period. A disequilibrium can, therefore, be corrected only over two or more periods.

II. FUNCTIONAL AND NONFUNCTIONAL DEMAND

At the outset it is probably best to define clearly some of the basic terms we are going to use and to indicate those as-

[23] An excellent discussion of the above problem, the relationship between the notions of time in economics and various definitions of statics and dynamics, can be found in W. C. Hood, "Some Aspects of the Treatment of Time in Economic Theory," *The Canadian Journal of Economics and Political Science,* 1948, pp. 453–468.

[24] *Value and Capital,* p. 115.

[25] The above assumptions are necessary in order to take care of some of the difficulties raised by Professor Morgenstern in "Demand Theory Reconsidered."

pects of demand that we are going to treat. The demand for consumers' goods and services may be classified according to motivation. The following classification, which we shall find useful, is on a level of abstraction which, it is hoped, includes most of the motivations behind consumers' demand.

A. Functional
B. Nonfunctional
   1. External effects on utility
     (a) Bandwagon effect
     (b) Snob effect
     (c) Veblen effect
   2. Speculative
   3. Irrational

By functional demand is meant that part of the demand for a commodity which is due to the qualities inherent in the commodity itself. By nonfunctional demand is meant that portion of the demand for a consumers' good which is due to factors other than the qualities inherent in the commodity. Probably the most important kind of nonfunctional demand is due to external effects on utility. That is, the utility derived from the commodity is enhanced or decreased owing to the fact that others are purchasing and consuming the same commodity, or owing to the fact that the commodity bears a higher rather than a lower price tag. We differentiate this type of demand into what we shall call the "bandwagon" effect, the "snob" effect, and the "Veblen" effect.[26] By the bandwagon effect, we refer to the extent to which the demand for a commodity is *increased* due to the fact that others are also consuming the same commodity. It represents the desire of people to purchase a commodity in order to get into "the swim of things"; in order to conform with the people they wish to be associated with; in

[26] It is assumed from here on that the reader will be aware that these terms will be used in the special sense here defined, and hence the quotation marks will hereafter be deleted.

order to be fashionable or stylish; or, in order to appear to be "one of the boys." By the snob effect we refer to the extent to which the demand for a consumers' good is *decreased* owing to the fact that others are also consuming the same commodity (or that others are increasing their consumption of that commodity). This represents the desire of people to be exclusive; to be different; to dissociate themselves from the "common herd." By the Veblen effect we refer to the phenomenon of conspicuous consumption; to the extent to which the demand for a consumers' good is increased because it bears a higher rather than a lower price. We should perhaps emphasize the distinction made between the snob and the Veblen effect—the former is a function of the consumption of others, the latter is a function of price.[27] This paper will deal almost exclusively with these three types of nonfunctional demand.

For the sake of completeness there should perhaps be some explanation as to what is meant by speculative and irrational demand. Speculative demand refers to the fact that people will often "lay in" a supply of a commodity because they expect its price to rise. Irrational demand is, in a sense, a catchall category. It refers to purchases that are neither planned nor calculated but are due to sudden urges, whims, etc., and that serve no rational purpose but that of satisfying sudden whims and desires.

In the above it was assumed throughout that income is a parameter. If income is not given but allowed to vary, then the income effect on demand may in most cases be the most important effect of all. Also, it may be well to point out that the above

is only one of a large number of possible classifications of the types of consumers' demand—classifications that for some purposes may be superior to the one here employed. We therefore suggest the above classification only for the purposes at hand and make no claims about its desirableness, or effectiveness, in any other use.

III. THE BANDWAGON EFFECT

1. A Conceptual Experiment

Our immediate task is to obtain aggregate demand curves of various kinds in those cases where the individual demand curves are non-additive. First we shall examine the case where the bandwagon effect is important. In its pure form this is the case where an individual will demand more (less) of a commodity at a given price because some or all other individuals in the market also demand more (less) of the commodity.

One of the difficulties in analyzing this type of demand involves the choice of assumptions about the knowledge that each individual possesses. This implies that everyone knows the quantity that will be demanded by every individual separately, or the quantity demanded by all individuals collectively at any given price—after all the reactions and adjustments that individuals make to each other's demand has taken place. On the other hand, if we assume ignorance on the part of consumers about the demand of others, we have to make assumptions as to the nature and extent of the ignorance—ignorance is a relative concept. A third possibility, and the one that will be employed at first, is to devise some mechanism whereby the consumers obtain accurate information.

Another problem involves the choice of assumptions to be made about the demand behaviour of individual consumers. Three possibilities suggest themselves: (1) The demand of consumer *A* (at given prices) may be a function of the total demand of

---

[27] Some writers have not made the above distinction but have combined the two effects into what they termed "snob behaviour" (see Morgenstern, *op. cit.,* p. 190). The above does not imply that our distinction is necessarily the "correct" one, but only that it is found useful in our analysis.

all others in the market collectively. Or, (2) the demand of consumer A may be a function of the demand of all other consumers both separately and collectively. In other words, A's demand may be more influenced by the demand of some than by the demand of others. (3) A third possibility is that A's demand is a function of the number of people that demand the commodity rather than the number of units demanded. More complex demand behaviour patterns that combine some of the elements of the above are conceivable. For present purposes it is best that we assume the simplest one as a first approximation.[28] Initially, therefore, we assume that A's demand is a function of the units demanded by all others collectively. This is the same as saying that A's demand is a function of total market demand at given prices, since A always knows his own demand, and he could always subtract his own demand from the total market demand to get the quantity demanded by all others.

In order to bring out the central principle involved in the ensuing analysis, consider the following *gedankenexperiment*. A known product is to be introduced into a well-defined market at a certain date. The nature of the product is such that its demand depends partially on the functional qualities of the commodity, and partially on whether many or few units are demanded. Our technical problem is to compound the nonadditive individual demand curves into a total market demand curve, given sufficient information about the individual demand functions. Now, suppose that it is possible to obtain an accurate knowledge of the demand function of an

individual through a series of questionnaires. Since an individual's demand is, in part, a function of the total market demand, it is necessary to take care of this difficulty in our questionnaires. We can have a potential consumer fill out the first questionnaire by having him assume that the total market demand, at all prices, is a given very small amount—say 400 units. On the basis of this assumption the consumer would tell us the quantities he demands over a reasonable range of prices. Subjecting every consumer to the same questionnaire, we add the results across and obtain a market demand curve that would reflect the demand situation if every consumer believed the total demand were only 400 units. This, however, is not the real market demand function under the assumption of the possession of accurate market information by consumers, since the total demand (at each price) upon which consumers based their replies was not the actual market demand (at each price) as revealed by the results of the survey. Let us call the results of the first survey "schedule No. 1."

We can now carry out a second survey, that is, subject each consumer to a second questionnaire in which each one is told that schedule No. 1 reflects the total quantities demanded, at each price. Aggregating the replies we obtain schedule No. 2. Schedule No. 1 then becomes a parameter upon which schedule No. 2 is based. In a similar manner we can obtain schedules No. 3, No. 4, . . . , No. n in which each schedule is the result of adding the quantities demanded by each consumer (at each price), *if each consumer believes that the total quantities demanded (at each price) are shown by the previous schedule.* Now, the quantities demanded in schedule No. 2 will be greater than or equal to the quantities demanded in schedule No. 1 for the same prices. Some consumers may increase the quantity they demand when they note that the total quantity demanded, at given

[28] As is customary in economic theory the ensuing analysis is carried out on the basis of a number of simplifying assumptions. The relaxation of some of the simplifying assumptions and the analysis of more complex situations must await some other occasion. The present writer has attempted these with respect to some of the simplifying assumptions but the results cannot be included within the confines of an article of the usual length.

prices, is greater than they thought it would be. As long as some consumers or potential consumers continue to react positively to increases in the total quantity demanded the results of successive surveys will be different. That is, some or all of the quantities demanded in schedule No. 1 will be less than the quantities demanded at the same prices, in schedule No. 2, which in turn will be equal to or less than the quantities demanded, at the same prices, in schedule No. 3, and so on.

At this point it is appropriate to introduce a new principle with the intention of showing that this process cannot go on indefinitely. Sooner or later two successive schedules will be identical. If two successive surveys yield the same market demand schedules, then an equilibrium situation exists since the total quantities demanded, at each price, upon which individual consumers based their demand, turns out to be correct. Thus, if schedule No. n is identical with schedule No. n-1, then schedule No. n is the actual market demand function for the product on the assumption that consumers have accurate information of market conditions.

The question that arises is whether there is any reason to suppose that sooner or later two successive surveys will yield exactly the same result. This would indeed be the case if we could find good reason to posit a principle to the effect that for every individual there is some point at which he will cease to increase the quantities demanded for a commodity, at given prices, in response to incremental increases in total market demand. Such a principle would imply that beyond a point incremental increases in the demand for the commodity by others have a decreasing influence on a consumer's own demand; and, further, that a point is reached at which these increases in demand by others have no influence whatsoever on his own demand. It would, of course, also be necessary to establish that such a principle

holds true for every consumer. It would not be inappropriate to call this the principle of diminishing marginal external consumption effect. Does such a principle really exist? There are some good reasons for believing that it does. First, the reader may note that the principle is analogous to the principle of diminishing marginal utility. As the total market demand grows larger, incremental increases in total demand become smaller and smaller proportions of the demand. It sounds reasonable, and probably appeals to us intuitively that an individual would be less influenced, and indeed take less notice of, a one per cent increase in total demand, than of a ten per cent increase in total demand, though these percentage increases be the same in absolute amount. Second, we can probably appeal effectively to general experience. There are no cases in which an individual's demand for a consumers' good increases endlessly with increases in total demand. If there were two or more such individuals in a market then the demand for the commodity would increase in an endless spiral. Last but not least, the income constraint is sufficient to establish that there must be a point at which increases in a consumer's demand must fail to respond to increases in demand by others. Since every consumer is subject to the income constraint, it must follow that the principle holds for all consumers.[29]

Now, to get back to our conceptual experiment, we would find that after administering a sufficient number of surveys, we would sooner or later get two surveys that yield identical demand schedules. The result of the last survey would then represent the true demand situation that would manifest itself on the market when the commodity was offered for sale. We may

[29] If the reader should object to our dignifying the diminishing marginal external consumption effect by calling it a principle or a law, we could point out that if it is not a "law," then it must be an equilibrium condition.

perhaps justly call such a demand function the equilibrium demand function—or demand curve. The equilibrium demand curve is the curve that exists when the marginal external consumption effect for every consumer, but one,[30] at all alternate prices is equal to zero. All other demand curves may be conceived as disequilibrium curves that can exist only because of temporarily imperfect knowledge by consumers of other people's demand. Once the errors in market information were discovered such a curve would move to a new position.

2. The Bandwagon Effect: Diagrammatical Method

The major purpose of going through the conceptual experiment with its successive surveys was to illustrate the diminishing marginal external consumption effect and to indicate its role in obtaining a determinate demand curve. There is, however, a relatively simple method for obtaining the market demand function in those cases where external consumption effects are significant. This method will allow us to compare some of the properties of the "bandwagon demand curve" with the usual "functional" demand curve; and, it will also allow us to separate the extent to which a change in demand is due to a change in price, and the extent to which it is due to the bandwagon effect.

Given a certain total demand for a commodity as a parameter,[31] every individual

will have a demand function based on this total market demand. Let the alternative total market demands that will serve as parameters for alternate individual demand functions be indicated as superscripts $a, b, \ldots n$ (where $a < b < \ldots < n$). Let the individual demand functions be $d_1, d_2, \ldots d_n$; where every subscript indicates a different consumer. Thus $d_3{}^a$ is the individual demand curve for consumer 3 if the consumer believes that the total market demand is a units. Similarly $d_{500}{}^m$ is the individual demand curve for the 500th consumer if he believes that the total market demand will be m units. We could now add across $d_1{}^a, d_2{}^a, d_3{}^a, \ldots, d_n{}^a$ which will give us the market demand curve D^a, which indicates the quantities demanded at alternate prices if all consumers believed that the total demand was a units. In the same manner we can obtain $D^b, D^c, \ldots, D^n$. These hypothetical market demand curves $D^a, D^b, D^c, \ldots, D^n$ are shown in **Figure 8.1. Now, if we assume that buyers** have accurate knowledge of market conditions (*i.e.*, of the total quantities demanded at every price) then only one point on any of the curves $D^a, D^b, \ldots, D^n$ could be on the real or equilibrium demand curve. These are the points on each curve D^a, $D^b, \ldots, D^n$ that represent the amounts on which the consumers based their individual demand curves; that is, the amounts that consumers expected to be the total market demand. These points are labeled in Figure 8.1 as $E^a, E^b, \ldots, E^n$. **They are** a series of virtual equilibrium points. Given that consumers possess accurate market information, $E^a, E^b, \ldots, E^n$, are the only points that can become actual quantities demanded. The locus of all these points D_B is therefore the actual demand curve for the commodity.

It may be of interest, at this point, to

[30] The fact that the marginal external consumption effect of one consumer is greater than zero can have no effect on the demand schedule since total market demand, at any given price, cannot increase unless there are at least two consumers who would react on each other's demand.

[31] The reader should note that the analysis in the following pages is based on a somewhat different assumption than the *gedankenexperiment*. In the diagrams that follow each demand curve (other than the equilibrium demand curve) is based on the assumption that consumers believe that a fixed amount will be taken off the market at all prices. There is more than one way of deriving the equilibrium demand curve. The earlier method helped to bring out the nature of the

central principle that is involved, while the method which follows will enable us to separate price effects from bandwagon effects and snob effects, etc.

break up changes in the quantity demanded due to changes in price into a price effect and a bandwagon effect; that is, the extent of the change that is due to the change in price, and the extent of the change in demand that is due to consumers adjusting to each other's changed consumption.[32] With an eye on Figure 8.1

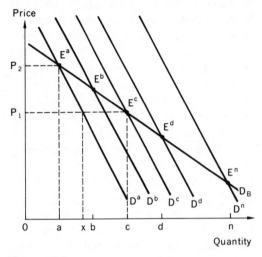

Figure 8.1

consider the effects of a reduction in price from P_2 to P_1. The increase in demand after the change in price is ac. Only part of that increase, however, is due to the reduction in price. To measure the amount due to the reduction in price we go along the demand curve D^a to P_1 which tells us the quantity that would be demanded at P_1 if consumers did not adjust to each other's demand. This would result in an increase in demand of ax. Due to the bandwagon effect, however, an additional number of consumers are induced to enter the market or to increase their demands. There

is now an additional increase in demand of xc after consumers have adjusted to each other's increases in consumption. Exactly the same type of analysis can, of course, be carried out for increases as well as for decreases in price.

We may note another thing from Figure 8.1. The demand curve D_B is more elastic than any of the other demand curves shown in the diagram. This would suggest that, other things being equal, the demand curve will be more elastic if there is a bandwagon effect than if the demand is based only on the functional attributes of the commodity. This, of course, follows from the fact that reactions to price changes are followed by additional reactions, *in the same direction*, to each other's changed consumption.

3. Social Taboos and the Bandwagon Effect

Social taboos, to the extent that they affect consumption, are, in a sense, bandwagon effects in reverse gear. That is to say, some people will not buy and consume certain things because other people are not buying and consuming these things. Thus, there may not be any demand for a commodity even though it has a functional utility, although, apart from the taboo, it would be purchased. Individual A will not buy the commodity because individuals B, C, and D do not, while individuals B, C, and D may refrain from consumption for the same reasons. It is not within the competence of the economist to investigate the psychology of this kind of behaviour. For our purposes we need only note that such behaviour exists and attempt to analyze how such behaviour affects the demand function.

We can proceed as follows. Let d_1^x be the demand curve of the least inhibited individual in the market, where the superscript x is the total quantity demanded in the market upon which he bases his individual demand. Suppose that at market

[32] We are now really in the area of "comparative statics." It may be recalled that we defined statics and our unit period in such a way that only *one* price holds within any unit period. Thus, when we examine the effects of a change in price we are really examining the reasons for the differences in the quantities demanded at one price in one unit period and another price in the succeeding unit period.

demand x consumer 1 will demand at some range of prices one unit of the commodity, but at no price will he demand more. If he believes, however, that the total market demand is less than x units he will refrain from making any purchases. Since, *ex hypothesi*, consumer 1 is the least inhibited consumer, he will, at best, be the only one who will demand one unit of the commodity if consumers expect the total market demand to be x units. It must be clear, then, that x units cannot be a virtual equilibrium point, since only points where the total expected quantity demanded is equal to the actual quantity demanded can be points on the real demand curve, and the quantity x cannot at any price be a point where expected total demand is equal to actual total demand. Now, if the total expected demand were $x + 1$ the actual demand might increase, say, to 2 units. At expected total demands $x + 2$ and $x + 3$, more would enter the market and the actual demand would be still greater since the fear of being different is considerably reduced as the expected demand is increased. With given increases in the expected total demand there must, at some point, be more than equal increases in the actual demand, because, if a real demand curve exists at all, there must be some point where the expected demand is equal to the actual demand. That point may exist, say, at $x + 10$. That is, at an expected total demand of $x + 10$ units a sufficient number of people have overcome their inhibitions to being different so that, at some prices, they will actually demand $x + 10$ units of the commodity. Let us call this point "T"—it is really the "taboo breaking point." The maximum bid (the point T^1 in Figure 8.2) of the marginal unit demanded if the total demand were T units now gives us the first point on the real demand curve (the curve D_B).

How social taboos may effect the demand curve is shown in Figure 8.2. It will be noted that the price axis shows both positive and negative "prices." A negative price may be thought of as the price it would be necessary to *pay* individuals in order to induce them to consume in public a given amount of the commodity; that is, the price that it would be necessary to pay the consumers in order to induce them to disregard their aversion to be looked upon as odd or peculiar.

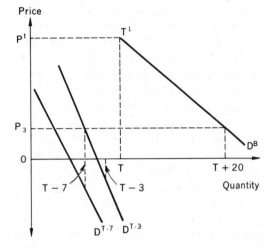

FIGURE **8.2**

As we have already indicated, the point T in Figure **8.2** is the "taboo breaking point." T represents the number of units at which an *expected* total quantity demanded of T units would result in an *actual* quantity demanded of T units at some *real* price. Now, what has to be explained is why an expected demand of less than T units, say $T - 3$ units, would not yield an actual demand of $T - 3$ units at a positive price but only at a "negative price." Let the curve D^{T-3} be the demand curve that would exist if consumers thought the total demand was $T - 3$. Now, at any positive price, say P_3, the amount demanded would be less than $T - 3$, say $T - 7$. The price P_3 can therefore exist only if there is inaccurate information of the total quantity demanded. Once consumers discovered that at P_3 only $T - 7$

was purchased, and believed that this was the demand that would be sustained, their demand would shift to the D^{T-7} curve. At P_3 the amount purchased would now be less than $T-7$ and demand would now shift to a curve to the left of the D^{T-7} curve. This procedure would go on until the demand was zero at P_3. We thus introduce a gap into our demand function and focus attention on an interesting psychological phenomenon that may affect demand. What we are suggesting, essentially, is that given "accurate expectations" of the total quantity demanded on the part of consumers, there is a quantity less than which there will not be any quantity demanded at any real price. In other words, this is a case in which a commodity will either "go over big" or not "go over" at all. It will be noted that at P_3 zero units or $T+20$ units (Figure 8.2) may be taken off the market given "accurate expectations" of the total quantity demanded. It would seem, therefore, that "accurate expectations" of the total quantity demanded at P_3 can have two values depending upon whether people are generally pessimistic or optimistic about other consumers' demands for the commodity in question. If everybody expects that everybody else would not care much for the commodity, then zero units would be the accurate expectation of the total quantity demanded; if everybody, on the other hand, expects others to take up the commodity with some degree of enthusiasm,[33] then $T+20$ units would be the accurate expectation of the total quantity demanded. The factors that would determine one set of expectations rather than the other are matters of empirical investigation in the field of social psychology. The factors involved may be the history of the community, the people's conservatism or lack of conservatism, the

type and quantity of advertising about the commodity under consideration, etc.

The really significant point in Figure 8.2 is T^1, the first point on the real demand curve D_B. As already indicated, it is the point at which the maximum bid of the marginal unit demanded is P_t and the total market demand is T units. If the price were higher than P_t, the Tth unit would not be demanded and all buyers would leave the market because of the effect of the taboo at less than a consumption of T units.[34] By way of summary we might say that the whole point of this section is an attempt to show that in cases where social taboos affect demand the real demand curve may not start at the price-axis but that the smallest possible quantity demanded may be some distance to the right of the price-axis.

IV. THE SNOB EFFECT

Thus far, in our conceptual experiment and diagrammatic analysis, we have considered only the bandwagon effect. We now consider the reverse effect—the demand behaviour for those commodities with regard to which the individual consumer acts like a snob. Here, too, we assume at first that the quantity demanded by a consumer is a function of price and of the total market demand, but that the individual consumer's demand is negatively correlated with the total market demand. In the snob case it is rather obvious that the external consumption effect must reach a limit although the limit may be where one snob constitutes the only buyer. For most commodities and most buyers, however, the motivation for exclusiveness is not that great; hence the marginal external consumption effect reaches zero before that point. If the commodity is to be purchased at all, the external consumption effect must reach a limit, at some price, where the

---

[33] If consumers have accurate expectations of the degree of enthusiasm with which others will take up the product, then they will expect demand to be $T+20$ units.

[34] This is a "pure" case where *all* buyers are governed by taboo considerations.

quantity demanded has a positive value. From this it follows that after a point the principle of the diminishing marginal external consumption effect must manifest itself. We thus have in the snob effect an opposite but completely symmetrical relationship to the bandwagon effect.

The analysis of markets in which all consumers behave as snobs follows along the same lines as our analysis of the bandwagon effect. Because of the similarity we will be able to get through our analysis of the snob effect in short order. We begin, as before, by letting the alternate total market demands that serve as parameters for alternate individual demand curves be indicated by the superscripts $a, b, \ldots, n$ (where $a < b < n$). Let the individual demand functions be $d_1, d_2, \ldots d_n$, where there are n consumers in the market. Again, $d_3{}^a$ signifies the individual demand curve for consumer 3 on the assumption that he expects the total market demand to be "a" units. By adding

$$d_1{}^a + d_2{}^a + \cdots + d_n{}^a = D^a$$
$$d_1{}^b + d_2{}^b + \cdots + d_n{}^b = D^b$$
$$\vdots \qquad \vdots$$
$$d_1{}^n + d_2{}^n + \cdots + d_n{}^n = D^n$$

we obtain the market demand functions on the alternate assumptions of consumers expecting the total market demands to be $a, b, \ldots, n$. Due to snob behaviour the curves $D^a, D^b, \ldots, D^n$ move to the left as the expected total market demand increases. This is shown in Figure 8.3. Using the same procedure as before we obtain the virtual equilibrium points $E^a, E^b, \ldots, E^n$. They represent the only points on the curves $D^a, D^b, \ldots, D^n$ that are consistent with consumers' expectations (and hence with the assumption of accurate information). The locus of these virtual equilibrium points is the demand curve D_S.

Now, given a price change from P_2 to P_1 we can separate the effect of the price change into a price effect and a snob effect.

In Figure 8.3 we see that the net increase in the quantity demanded due to the reduction in price is ab. The price effect, however, is ax. That is, if every consumer expected no increase in the total quantity demanded then the total quantity demanded at P_1 would be Ox. The more extreme snobs will react to this increase in the total quantity demanded and will leave the market.[35] The total quantity demanded will hence be reduced by bx. The net result is therefore an increase in demand of only ab.

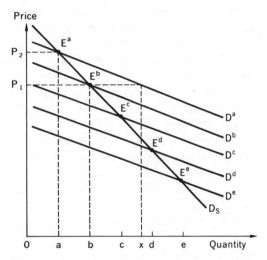

FIGURE 8.3

It may be of interest to examine some of the characteristics of the curves in Figure 8.3. First we may note that all the points on the curves other than D_S (except E^a, $E^b, \ldots, E^n$) are theoretical points that have significance only under conditions of imperfect knowledge. Second, we may note from the diagram that the demand curve for snobs is less elastic than the demand curves where there are no snob effects. The reason for this, of course, is that the increase in demand due to a reduction in price is counterbalanced, in part, by some snobs leaving the market because of the

[35] The other snobs will, of course, reduce their demand but not by an amount large enough to leave the market.

increase in total consumption (*i.e.*, the decrease in the snob value of the commodity). It should be clear, however, that the snob effect, as defined, can never be in excess of the price effect since this would lead to a basic contradiction. If the snob effect were greater than the price effect, then the quantity demanded at a lower price would be less than the quantity demanded at a higher price. This implies that some of the snobs in the market at the higher price leave the market when there is a reduction in the total quantity demanded; which, of course, is patently inconsistent with our definition of snob behaviour. It therefore follows that the snob effect is never greater than the price effect. It follows, also, that D_S is monotonically decreasing if D^a, D^b, ..., D^n are monotonically decreasing.[36]

Finally, it may be interesting to note another difference between the usual functional demand curve and the D_S curve. In the usual demand curve the buyers at higher prices always remain in the market at lower prices. That is, from the price point of view, the bids to buy are cumulative downward. This is clearly not the case in the D_S curve. Such terms as intramarginal buyers may be meaningless in snob markets.

V. THE VEBLEN EFFECT

Although the theory of conspicuous consumption as developed by Veblen and others is quite a complex and subtle sociological construct we can, for our purposes, quite legitimately abstract from the psychological and sociological elements and address our attention exclusively to the effects that conspicuous consumption has on the demand function. The essential economic characteristic with which we are concerned is the fact that the utility derived from a unit of a commodity employed for

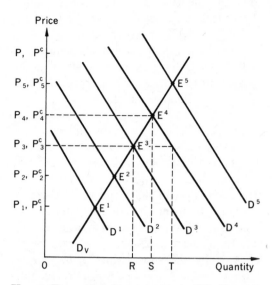

KEY TO FIGURE 8.4. PRICE EFFECT = ST; VEBLEN EFFECT = − TR; NET EFFECT = − SR

FIGURE 8.4

purposes of conspicuous consumption depends not only on the inherent qualities of that unit, but also on the price paid for it. It may, therefore, be helpful to divide the price of a commodity into two categories; the real price and the conspicuous price. By the real price we refer to the price the consumer paid for the commodity in terms of money. The conspicuous price is the price other people think the consumer paid for the commodity[37] and which therefore determines its conspicuous consumption utility. These two prices would probably be identical in highly organized markets where price information is common knowledge. In other markets, where some can get "bargains" or special discounts the real price or conspicuous price need not be identical. In any case, the quantity demanded by a consumer will be a function of both the real price and the conspicuous price.

The market demand curve for commodities subject to conspicuous consumption

---

[36] We shall see below however that the snob effect plus the Veblen effect combined can be greater than the price effect.

[37] More accurately, the conspicuous price should be the price that the consumer thinks other people think he paid for the commodity.

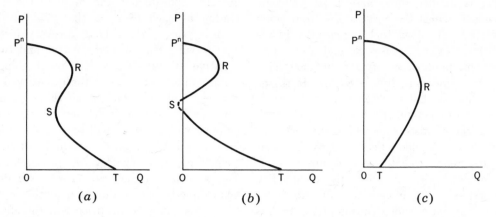

FIGURE **8.5**

can be derived through a similar diagrammatical method (summarized in Figure 8.4). This time we let the superscripts 1, 2, . . . , n stand for the expected conspicuous prices. The real prices are P_1, P_2, . . . , P_n. The individual demand functions are d_1, d_2, . . . , d_n. In this way $d_6{}^3$ stands for the demand curve of consumer number 6 if he expects a conspicuous price of $P_3{}^c$.[38] We can now add across $d_1{}^1$, $d_2{}^1$, . . . , $d_n{}^1$ and get the market demand curve D^1 which indicates the quantities demanded at alternate prices if all consumers expected a conspicuous price of $P_1{}^c$. In a similar manner we obtain D^2, D^3, . . . , D^n. The market demand curves will, of course, up to a point, shift to the right as the expected conspicuous price increases. Now on every curve D^1, D^2, . . . , D^n in Figure 8.4 only one point can be a virtual equilibrium point if we assume that consumers possess accurate market information—the point where the real price is equal to the conspicuous price (that is, where $P_1 = P_1{}^c$, $P_2 = P_2{}^c$, . . . , $P_n = P_n{}^c$). The locus of these virtual equilibrium points E^1, E^2, . . . , E^n gives us the demand curve D_V.

As before, we can separate the effects of

a change in price into two effects—the price effect, and, what we shall call for want of a better term, the Veblen effect. In Figure 8.4 it will be seen that a change in price from P_4 to P_3 will reduce the quantity demanded by RS. The price effect is to increase the quantity demanded by ST; that is, the amount that would be demanded if there were no change in the expected conspicuous price would be OT. However, at the lower price a number of buyers would leave the market because of the reduced utility derived from the commodity at that lower conspicuous price. The Veblen effect is therefore RT.

It should be noted that unlike the D_S curve, the D_V curve can be positively inclined, negatively inclined or a mixture of both. It all depends on whether at alternate price changes the Veblen effect is greater or less than the price effect. It is possible that in one portion of the curve one effect may predominate while in another portion another may predominate. It is to be expected, however, that in most cases, if the curve is not monotonically decreasing it will be shaped like a backward S, as illustrated in Figure 8.5(a). The reasons for this are as follows: First, there must be a price so high that no units of the commodity will be purchased at that price owing to the income constraint (among other reasons). This is the price P^n in Figure 8.5(a),

[38] The expected conspicuous prices are distinguished from the real prices by adding the superscript c to the P's. Thus, to the range of real prices P_1, P_2,. . . . , P_n, we have a corresponding range of conspicuous prices denoted by $P_1{}^c$, $P_2{}^c$, ... $P_n{}^c$.

and it implies that there must be some point at which the curve shifts from being positively inclined to being negatively inclined as price increases. Second, there must be some point of satiety for the good. This is the point T in Figure 8.5(a). It therefore follows that some portion of the curve must be monotonically decreasing to reach T if there exists some minimum price at which the Veblen effect is zero. It is of course reasonable to assume that there is some low price at which the commodity would cease to have any value for purposes of conspicuous consumption. If this last assumption does not hold, which is unlikely, then the curve could have the shape indicated in Figure 8.5(c). Otherwise, it would have the general shape indicated in Figure 8.5(a), or it might be in two segments as illustrated in Figure 8.5(b).

VI. MIXED EFFECTS

Any real market for semidurable or durable goods will most likely contain consumers that are subject to one or a combination of the effects discussed heretofore. Combining these effects presents no new formal difficulties with respect to the determination of the market demand curve, although it complicates the diagrammatic analysis considerably. The major principle, however, still holds. For any price there is a quantity demanded such that the marginal external consumption effect (or the marginal Veblen effect) for all buyers but one, is zero. This implies that for every price change there is a point at which people cease reacting to each other's quantity changes, regardless of the direction of these reactions. If this is so, then for every price there is a determinate quantity demanded, and hence the demand curve is determinate.

Now, for every price change we have distinguished between the price effect and some other, such as the snob, the Veblen, or the bandwagon effect. In markets where all four effects are present we should be able to separate out and indicate the direction of each of them that will result from a price change. That is, every price change will result in two positive and two negative effects—two which, other things being equal, will increase the quantity demanded, and two which, other things being equal, will decrease it. Which effects will be positive and which will be negative will depend on the relative strength of the Veblen effect as against the price effect. The Veblen and the price effects will depend directly on the direction of the price change. An increase in price will therefore result in price and bandwagon effects that are negative, and in Veblen and snob effects that are positive, provided that the price effect is greater than the Veblen effect; that is, if the net result is a decrease in the quantity demanded at the higher price. If, on the other hand, the Veblen effect is more powerful than the price effect, given a price increase, then the bandwagon effect would be positive and the snob effect negative. The reverse would of course be true for price declines.

The market demand curve for a commodity where different consumers are subject to different types of effects can be obtained diagrammatically through employing the methods developed above—although the diagrams would be quite complicated. There is no point in adding still more diagrams to illustrate this. Briefly, the method would be somewhat as follows: (1) Given the demand curves for every individual, in which the expected total quantity demanded is a parameter for each curve, we can add these curves laterally and obtain a map of aggregate demand curves, in which each aggregate curve is based on a given total quantity demanded. (2) The locus of the equilibrium points on each aggregate demand curve (as derived in Figure 8.1) gives us a market demand curve that accounts for both bandwagon and snob effects. This last curve assumes that only one conspicuous price exists. For every conspicuous price there exists a separate map of aggregate demand curves from which different market demand curves are obtained. (3) This procedure yields a map of market demand curves in which each curve is based on a different conspicuous price. Employing the method used in Figure 8.4 we obtain our final market demand curve which accounts for bandwagon, snob, and Veblen effects simultaneously.

VII. CONCLUSION

It is not unusual for a writer in pure theory to end his treatise by pointing out that the science is really very young; that there is a great deal more to be done; that the formulations presented are really of a very tentative nature; and that the best that can be hoped for is that his treatise may in some small way pave the road for future formulations that are more directly applicable to problems in the real world.[39] This is another way of saying that work in pure theory is an investment in the future state of the science where the returns in terms of applications to real problems are really very uncertain. This is probably especially true of value theory where the investment in time and effort is more akin to the purchase of highly speculative stocks rather than the purchase of government bonds. Since this was only a brief essay on one aspect of value theory, the reader will hardly be surprised if the conclusions reached are somewhat less than revolutionary.

Essentially, we have attempted to do two things. First, we have tried to demonstrate that non-additivity is not neces-

[39] See, for example, Samuelson, *Foundations of Economic Analysis,* p. 350, and Joan Robinson, *Economics of Imperfect Competition,* p. 327.

sarily an insurmountable obstacle in effecting a transition from individual to collective demand curves. Second, we attempted to take a step or two in the direction of incorporating various kinds of external consumption effects into the theory of consumers' demand. In order to solve our problem, we have introduced what we have called the principle of the diminishing marginal external consumption effect. We indicated some reasons for believing that for every individual, there is some point at which the marginal external consumption effect is zero. We have attempted to show that if this principle is admitted, then there are various ways of effecting a transition from individual to collective demand curves. The major conclusion reached is that under conditions of perfect knowledge (or accurate expectations) any point on the demand curve, for any given price, will be at that total quantity demanded where the marginal external consumption effect for all consumers but one, is equal to zero.

In comparing the demand curve in those situations where external consumption effects are present with the demand curve as it would be where these external consumption effects are absent, we made three basic points. (1) If the bandwagon effect is the most significant effect, the demand curve is more elastic than it would be if this external consumption effect were absent. (2) If the snob effect is the predominant effect, the demand curve is less elastic than otherwise. (3) If the Veblen effect is the predominant one, the demand curve is less elastic than otherwise, and some portions of it may even be positively inclined; whereas, if the Veblen effect is absent, the curve will be negatively inclined regardless of the importance of the snob effect in the market.

Part IV

SUPPLY

9. The Basis of Some Recent Advances in the Theory of Management of the Firm*

ARMEN A. ALCHIAN

Attacks on the theory of the firm—or more accurately on the theory of behavior of individuals in the firm—have called attention to logical inconsistencies in the profit maximizing criterion and to empirical evidence refuting its implications in a wide class of firms. The empirical evidence seemed overwhelming that individuals working within a firm as managers or employees (and even as employers), pursued policies directed at, for example, increasing sales, gross assets, employees, expenditures for various equipment and facilities beyond those that yield a profit maximum.

Attempts to defend the profit maximizing theory by rigorously treating profits as capital value increments, rather than as current transitory rates of net earnings—so as to avoid the short- and long-run pitfall

* Reprinted from *Journal of Industrial Economics* (November 1965), pp. 30–41, by permission of the publisher. A brief biographical sketch of the author can be found in the introduction to Reading 4.

—removed some conflicting evidence. Similarly a defense asserting that the aberrations are temporary deviations in a search process does eliminate some more of the embarrassing evidence. However, the defense is not adequate; a vast class of behavior conflicting with wealth maximizing remains to be explained.

The observations of behavior that refute the profit or wealth maximizing theory are the 'facts' that some managers incur expenditures apparently in excess of those that would maximize wealth or profits of the owners of the firm. Managers of corporations are observed to emphasize growth of total assets of the firm and of its sales as objectives of managerial actions. Also managers of firms undertake cost reducing, efficiency increasing campaigns when demand falls; under wealth maximization they would already have been doing this. Managerial actions not conducive to the greatest wealth to the stockholders are taken to be well-established facts—and with which there appears to be no quarrel. Baumol emphasizes the managerial objective of sales increases, even to the extent of postulating that sales maximization is an objective. Penrose emphasizes the growth of the asset size of the firms. None of these can be made consistent with stockholder wealth maximization. If one postulates asset growth or sales maximization he will explain some cases but reject a lot of others in which that simply does not hold. Similarly, attempts to posit asset or sales maximization subject to a minimum wealth or profit constraint also runs into the objection that it implies the firm will not make *any* sacrifice in sales no matter how large an increment in wealth would thereby be achievable. Observed behavior simply does not support that attempted revision of the theory. Thus the Baumol type of attempt to modify the theory flounders—which in no way diminishes the importance of the insistence on recognizing inadequacies in the then existing state of theory.

Attacking any theory is easy enough, since none is perfect. But the wide class of empirical observation that *is* explained by economic theory should caution one against sweeping that theory aside and setting up new *ad hoc* theories to explain *only* or *primarily* those events the standard theory will not explain. What is wanted is a generalization of economic theory to obtain an expanded scope of validity without eliminating any (or 'too much') of the class of events for which it already is valid. Too many new theories happen to be *ad hoc* theories, valid only for a smaller class of cases. And among recent attempts to increase the power of the theory of the firm one can find some sparkling examples. Though there is no point in our giving attention to those failures, credit is due them as reminders of the areas in which economic theory awaits valid generalization.

Deserving our attention here are those in which scientific progress toward a more generalized and valid theory is realized.

Two recent works serve as good examples. Especially distinguished is the contribution in Oliver E. Williamson's *The Economics of Discretionary Behavior: Managerial Objective in a Theory of the Firm,* a doctoral thesis (which won a Ford Foundation award) [11]. The other is Robin Marris, *The Economic Theory of Managerial Capitalism* [7]. Now that we have some advances we can look back and determine what prior works served as foundations for the advance. Especially noticeable as pathbreaker was Gary Becker's *Economics of Discrimination* [4], also a doctoral dissertation completed almost ten years ago. From Becker to Marris and Williamson there is worth noting here, the works of Downie [6], Baumol [3], Penrose [9], Simon [10], Averch and Johnson [2], Cyert and March [5].

Perhaps the nature of the advance can be characterized by asserting that the old schizophrenia between consumption and production behavior has been replaced by a consistent, more powerful criterion of utility maximizing. In a sense the utility theory underlying individual behavior in the consumption sphere has swallowed up producer or management theory—with, if we judge the recent literature aright, significant improvements in economic theory. Rather than concentrate on a detailed statement of who said what (and why he should or should not have said it), this paper is an attempt to indicate the nature of that advance—as a sort of survey review of the recent literature.

A means of advance was made explicit by Becker, who insisted that non-pecuniary sources of utility be included in the utility function of an income earner. An owner, manager or employee is prepared to sacrifice some pecuniary income as a source of utility if he is offered enough non-pecuniary goods, which also contribute to utility. Becker concentrated on race, religion and congeniality of colleagues or employees as a source of non-pecuniary utility. He emphasized the production trade-offs or transformation rates between money income and working conditions (including color of colleagues and other non-pecuniary goods) and he pointed out that changes in the trade-off rates would affect the extent to which a person chose non-pecuniary sources (goods) of utility relative to pecuniary income.

There is, of course, nothing novel in this proposition. One can find it in Adam Smith.[1] But with the growth of formalism and rigor of mathematical modes of analysis it seems to have dropped out of the theory. Becker's dissertation stimulated applications of the principle to see if different kinds of institutions implied different trade-off rates between pecuniary and non-pecuniary incomes to managers and employees. Thus, a paper by the present author and R. Kessel [1] applied the analysis to profit limited and regulated businesses—public utilities, for example, and derived the implication that discrimination against racial and religious groups is greater in profit controlled firms. Any firm already earning the maximum *allowable* profit found it almost costless (of profits) to 'buy' that kind of discrimination. Evidence was also presented to corroborate the analysis. Averch and Johnson applied the principle to investment activities of owners of public utilities and derived an implication about the extent to which investment in cost *increasing* activities would be induced.

Marris says the managers will be induced to sacrifice some increment of owner's profits for the sake of the increment of size of firm (and consequent increment of managerial salary). Manager's salaries are larger in larger firms. Therefore they will have an incentive to enlarge the firm beyond the owner's wealth, or profit, maximizing size. Marris makes explicit that stockholders are not blind to this; the costs of their detecting this effect and exerting con-

trols are large enough to make it more economical for stockholders to tolerate the reduced wealth than to incur the costs required to keep the managers more strictly in line with the stockholder's wealth maximizing criterion.

Unfortunately Marris's analysis appears to be slightly marred by a logical confusion between rates of profit *per unit of investment* and absolute growth of wealth (profit) —in view of the fact that the investment is a discretionary *variable*.[2] If I am correct in my understanding, the implication derived by Marris, wherein the manager will seek a growth rate of assets beyond that which maximizes the above mentioned ratio, is completely consistent with simple wealth maximization *to the owners*. Diminishing marginal rate of return on *additional* investment calls for setting that marginal rate of return equal to the rate of interest— maximizing neither the marginal nor the average rate of return per dollar of (variable) investment. However, it would be a simple task to set the analysis aright by formalizing into the manager's opportunity set of choices among wealth to stockholders versus wealth to managers the costs to stockholders of enforcing a stockholders' wealth maximizing criterion on the managers.

Marris says he uses a utility maximizing approach wherein the person has his utility increased not only by higher salaries but also by greater security in his continued incumbency. In a strict sense, this is a wealth maximizing rather than a utility maximizing, approach for the manager. It is that because a greater security is an increase in wealth. If risk of loss of future receipts is reduced, the present value is increased. Hence Marris uses a wealth function in which two components of greater wealth are made explicit—the projected future receipts and the probability of their being realized.

Competing with the utility maximizing

---

[1] Book V, Chapter 1, Article 2 and 3 of his *Wealth of Nations.*

[2] Pp. 254-60.

approach is a wealth or growth of wealth maximizing criterion. Marris devotes most of his book to an exposition of a model in which the growth of the firm is constrained by internal saving out of its business generated income. As it turns out, a wealth growth maximizing criterion is a wealth maximizing criterion. Although Marris offers interesting observations it is his utility maximizing proposition that makes his approach most fruitful—in this reviewer's judgment.

As of the present moment, the best formulation of a theory that seems to be both more general and more valid than the wealth maximizing theory is the utility maximizing approach more fully presented by Williamson. He postulates that the manager can direct the firm's resources to increase his own utility in at least three ways. First, he can get a higher salary by obtaining greater profits for the owners, as in the older profit maximizing model. Second, he can direct the firm's resources so as to increase his salary at the expense of a decrease in profits. In particular, if the manager believes that a large firm is correlated with higher salaries (holding profits constant as a *ceteris paribus*), he will strive more to enlarge the gross asset size of the firm.

Third, the manager can sacrifice some increments to stockholder profits in order to increase expenditures for his own non-pecuniary emoluments within the firm. The extent to which these three avenues are used depends on the costs to the stockholders of detecting and policing the manager's behavior and effectiveness, *i.e.* on the costs, of enforcing contracts. In the modern, large corporation these costs are higher than in the single owner enterprise (and are absent in the owner-operated enterprise).

The third of the avenues listed above is formally admissible if one uses a utility maximizing theory rather than a pecuniary wealth maximizing postulate. By doing so, the manager's behavior is interpreted as choosing among opportunities to obtain increments of non-pecuniary goods in his utility function (*e.g.*, pretty secretaries, thick rugs, friendly colleagues, leisurely work load, executive washrooms, larger work staff, relaxed personnel policies involving job security, time off for statesmanlike community activities, gifts of company funds to colleges, out of town hotel suites, racial and religious discrimination in personnel policy, etc.). The utility maximizing theory is applicable and useful if, and only if, (1) we can identify some of its components (beside direct pecuniary wealth) *and* if (2) we can identify circumstances that involve differences in the costs of each of the various types of managerial non-pecuniary 'goods'. By satisfying these two conditions, we can deduce the relative extent of such activities in each of those circumstances.

One circumstance is the type of ownership of the firm, *e.g.*, corporate ownership, non-profit firm, public utility (with a restricted profit rate), and governmentally owned organizations. In this context, the contributions of the recent literature lie in the clues about the differences in relative costs among various types of organizations.

In conformity with the familiar fundamental theorem of demand, the lower the cost of a good or activity (whether it be a traditional type of economic good or one of a more general class of goods, like pleasant surroundings and those mentioned above) the more it will be demanded. This is all merely standard economic theory applied in a broader nexus of utility affecting components and is in no way an abandonment of the traditional basic theorems.

Williamson and Marris provide advances along the second and third avenues, indicate how to test the theory, and provide examples of tests. Williamson considers emoluments and staff preference as two ways of spending beyond the profit maximizing rate. The preference for larger staffs exists because salaries to a manager are correlated with a larger staff under a manager—a phenomenon best explained, to my knowledge, by Mayer [8].[3]

The approach used by Williamson is expressible as a maximization of the manager's utility, which is a function of several specified variables (*e.g.*, size of staff and profits of the firm). The utility is subject to constraints on the choices he can make about staff and profit. Williamson postulates that profits are affected by the size of the staff (at first profits and staff size are positively related for increasing staff up to level and thereafter negatively related for larger staffs—given the demand environment of the firm). The owners of the firm, by detecting and policing their employees' actions, seek to induce them to select the maximum profit combination, which maximizes owners' utility. Unfortunately for the owners, there are costs of detecting and policing his actions so as to make sure he does select that point. Once these costs are recognized, it is obviously better to avoid some of these costs if the profits saved are less than the costs. Cash registers, sales books and accounting systems are in part devices to enable more efficient detecting and policing of employees' deviations from profit maximization. The greater the costs of this detection and policing, the greater will managers sacrifice profits for the sake of staff size and other means of increasing management utility.

Perhaps Williamson's analysis can be most easily illustrated without doing it too much violence, by his graphic technique. In Figure 9.1, the vertical axis measures profit to the owner-stockholders. The horizontal axis measures staff (or emoluments) to the manager. Curve *AA* is the feasibility curve portraying the opportunity set of combinations of profits and 'staff' open to the man-

ager. The initial positively sloped portion indicates joint increases in staff and profits; the negative portion indicates staff can be larger than the profit maximizing level indicated at the point *K*. One typically shaped utility curve is drawn *UU*. Profits to stockholders enter the manager's utility function in so far as larger profits imply larger salaries to the manager. Similarly, staff enters as an argument in the manager's utility or wealth function in that this too is correlated with salary as well as with emoluments. The familiar conflict of interest between stockholders and manager or between owner and employee, or between taxpayer and government employee is portrayed by the utility curves of the employee-manager's utility function which contains the firm's staff or emolument component whereas only the profit or net value of the firm enters the stockholder's utility function. Point *L* is chosen by the manager.

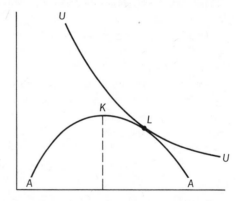

FIGURE **9.1**   STOCKHOLDER PROFITS AND STAFF SIZE AS SOURCES OF UTILITY OR PECUNIARY INCOME TO MANAGER SHIFT EQUILIBRIUM BEYOND MAXIMUM PROFIT SIZE

That point *K* is not chosen reflects the costs that must be borne by stockholders if he tried to detect and prevent *all* deviations from point *K*. The opportunity set bounded by *AA* would be vertically bounded on the right by the dotted line straight down from *K* if, and only if, detection of profit max-

---

[3] Mayer's explanation, in terms of the dependence of marginal product of managers upon the size of assets affected by the managers' decisions, avoids many of the superficial, misleading or downright erroneous explanations relying on convention, prestige, privilege of rank, etc.

imizing actions and the policing were costless.

Any events, circumstances or factors that affect the feasibility curve (taxes, changes in business conditions) can shift the optimum tangency point. (Similarly, anything that shifts the shapes of the utility map will shift the equilibrium position.) Williamson derives the implied effects of corporate tax changes on the position and shape of the opportunity set bounded by AA. He also analyses the effects of a decline in business conditions on the curve AA. Williamson shows that the decrease in demand (and profitability) implies an increased effort to achieve greater *efficiency* in staff size—such as presumably would already have been achieved if the managers were maximizing profits of the stockholder owners. Thus the results differ from those of profit maximization, and they are more like those that seem to be observed in reality.

The significant point is that the equilibrium or solution values involve staff size, corporate expenditures and emoluments beyond the maximum profit combination of profits and staff or emoluments. Thus the owner's profit maximizing hypothesis is apparently replaced with a more general utility maximizing postulate for the manager with the indicated resultant implications. A fixed total tax shifts the AA downward vertically; this leads to a solution with smaller gross size of firm, emoluments and staff. Williamson points out that a firm with several subdivisions could in effect impose a fixed tax on each subdivision—calling it an overhead cost—thereby inducing the subdivision managers to shift their actions more toward profits and less toward staff and gross asset size. The lower the profit to the subdivision the greater the marginal rate of substitution in consumption for managers between profit and other 'goods'. The tax does not change the feasible or opportunity rate of substitution between salary from larger profits and gains from the size and staff, because the slope of the AA curve is unchanged as it is shifted vertically downward. This leads to the leftward revision of the tangency point between the curve AA and the utility line. Marris, as we said, came close to the same result; in fact his book presents a diagram much like Williamson but the axes are different and no utility maximizing approach is involved.

The significance of the utility maximizing approach for the sales maximization approach is rather interesting. Sales maximization, advanced conjecturally by Baumol, is constrained by a 'minimum requisite' profit. Unfortunately, this minimum requisite profit squares neither with the rest of economic theory nor with the facts of life. Managers do not maximize sales regardless of how much they could increase profits if they sacrificed some increment of sales. While sales maximization subject to the postulated constraint gives *some* implications that agree with observed events, it also implies many other things that are refuted by all available evidence. The hypothesis cannot be held out as a serious proposition. Instead, Williamson's model seems to explain the facts that Baumol was seeing and emphasizing. He saw some firm's managers with their eyes on sales—even to the point of increasing sales beyond what everyone would have agreed was the profit maximizing level. Williamson makes this sensible, in that the incentive to increase sales is not treated as a single criterion for maximization, but rather as *a* means of the manager increasing his salary—in much the same fashion as a larger staff under the manager has the same effect. Substitution between these various components (salaries correlated with firm's profits, sales, assets, employees, etc.) affecting the manager's income or utility is the crucial factor, and Williamson emphasizes the factors making the substitution rate non-zero.

Without tarnishing the brilliance of Williamson's work, we can point out a bit of ambiguity. The derivation or basis of his profit-staff feasibility curve AA is not clear. In particular, he does not indicate exactly what is being held constant as a constraint defining the opportunity set. Furthermore, pecuniary and non-pecuniary benefits are mixed together on his emolument and staff division, thus making the utility isoquant an ambiguous concept. However, this can be easily corrected, formally, by adding a new dimension by which he can separate the pecuniary from the non-pecuniary goods to the manager. This would require at least a three dimensional graph and a more detailed mathematical formulation.

One could then include business expenditures designed to increase, not the manager's pecuniary salary, but rather the *non-pecuniary* benefits available within the firm, like those mentioned above in the 'third avenue'. If quantities of these non-pecuniary benefits were explicitly included in the utility function and also indicated along one of the axes of the graph, we could draw iso-utility curves, showing combinations of pecuniary and non-pecuniary goods that yield a constant *utility* to the manager. Then the tangencies of the utility function with the feasibility function (production function of wealth and non-pecuniary benefits) would yield the solution values of profits and types of non-pecuniary managerial benefits for the managers.

If one formulates his analyses in this way, the changes in taxes and especially of changes in ownership structures (which affect the costs for owners to detect and punish non-profit maximizing behavior by their employees) will be reflected in the feasibility set or production function on which the managers can operate. For example, the incentive to achieve maximum feasible profits for any given level of emoluments depends upon the costs of the owners detecting that full realizability and appropriately rewarding or punishing the manager. If a large corporation with many stockholders involves higher detection and policing costs, the inducement for managers

to depart from the objective of their employers is increased. In effect the profit-emolument curve is lowered and made flatter, pushing the manager toward greater emolument and less profit to stockholders.

This model can, and has been, applied to profit-limited public utilities and to non-profit corporations. A lesson to be drawn from these applications is that we can readily improve our analysis of managerial behavior if we first categorize firms according to whether the firm is a public utility (with constraints on the retainable profits) or is a non-profit organization (rather than according to size or simply to corporate versus non-corporate firms). Much loose talk and erroneous blanket generalizations about managerial behavior would be avoided if the differences among *types* of corporate ownership were recognized. Drawing inferences from the behavior of managers of *large* (public utility firms) and applying those inferences to managers of non-public utility firms is not generally justified. What is more viable in one firm is not so viable in another. A further temptation to compare the small manager's behavior with that of a large non-profit or public utility is to confound size with different forms of ownership. Improvements in this direction await merely the application of some routine intellectual toil.

This model certainly can be applied to government ownership, where it may serve to shock some people who think that more government ownership or regulation will solve the problem of making managers conform more to the criteria they are 'told' to seek.

The approach in the literature reviewed here is in stark contrast to that which attempts to use new types of utility functions, such as lexicographic or discrete utility functions. Lexicographic functions rank goods by some criterion and assert that those of a lower rank provide no utility until those of a higher rank achieve some critical amount. For example, there may be no utility of non-pecuniary goods (via prestige, leisure, emoluments, pretty secretaries, etc.) until profits or income achieve some minimum level. Furthermore, increments of the higher ranking goods beyond the critical level have zero utility, so that in effect, substitution among goods is denied. The analyses covered in this review retain the classic utility function but revise the types of constraints on the opportunity set of choices open to the utility maximizer (instead of revising the utility function). It is difficult for this reviewer to place much hope in this lexicographic type of utility function—in view of the clear cut refutation of its implications. The refutation of some of the implications derived with the classic utility functions seem (now that one examines these new analyses) to be the result of the postulated constraint system. By revising the constraints, rather than the utility function, new implications are being derived. Instead of postulating classic constraints of private property with zero costs of detecting and policing employee behavior, a more general theory can be derived from more general or varied types of property constraints. Perhaps unwittingly the literature of managerial behavior is enlarging the realm of formal economic theory to be applicable to more than conventional, individual private property systems.

Another apparent 'casualty' of the utility maximizing approach under the revised constraints is the 'satisficing' or 'aspiration' approaches. The discussion by Marris [10: pp. 266–77] is especially effective in bankrupting 'satisficing', perhaps even more than Marris intended. As he points out, in one sense it amounts to a statement of a constraint, rather than an objective. That is, certain conditions must be satisfied (*i.e.*, losses not incurred). In another sense it indicates a 'maximum'—given the costs of getting more information about the possibility and location of still superior positions. As Marris suggests, the subject faced with a problem involving effort in finding the solution, sets up a tentative solution or target as an aspiration or satisficing level. If he happily succeeds in exceeding that level, he raises his 'aspiration', target or 'satisficing' level. And conversely. In this sense the word is simply a name of the search process for maximizing some criterion—not a replacement or substitute.

There is no sense in trying to summarize a review. Instead a couple of personal impressions are offered. First, and least important, it is embarrassing that some economists feel compelled to preface or defend their work by an attack on the irrelevancy of existing economic theory. Even more embarrassing is their subsequent erroneous use of that theory.

Second, it is a genuine puzzle to me why economics has no 'field' or section (analogous to the 'fields' of money and banking, international trade, public finance, labor, etc.) devoted to 'property rights'. The closest thing to it is the field known as comparative economic systems; yet even there the fundamental role of the particular set of property right, as a specification of the opportunity set of choices about uses of resources, seems inadequately recognized. Especially puzzling is this in view of the fact that Adam Smith's *Wealth of Nations* is heavily concerned with exactly such questions. Perhaps the answer is that the whole of economics is the analysis of property rights in non-free goods. But if that is so, it is puzzling why it has taken so long to bring rigorous analytical techniques to bear on the implications about behavior under different forms of property rights. In any event, a substantial start has now been made—even if it has not been explicitly recognized. Hence one of the major points of this paper has been to try to make explicit and emphasize this basis which, I think, underlies the advances of analyses here reviewed.

REFERENCES

[1] ARMEN A. ALCHIAN and REUBEN A.

KESSEL, 'Competition, Monopoly and the Pursuit of Pecuniary Gain', *Aspects of Labor Economics*, Princeton: National Bureau of Economic Research 1962.

[2] H. AVERCH and L. L. JOHNSON, 'Behavior of the Firm Under Regulatory Constraint'. *American Economic Review*, December 1962, 52, 1052–69.

[3] WILLIAM J. BAUMOL, *Business Behavior, Value and Growth*, Macmillan Co., New York, 1959.

[4] GARY BECKER, *The Economics of Discrimination*, University of Chicago Press, Chicago, 1957.

[5] RICHARD M. CYERT and JAMES G. MARCH, editors, *A Behavioral Theory of the Firm*, Prentice-Hall, Englewood Cliffs, 1963.

[6] JACK DOWNIE, *The Competitive Process*, Gerald Duckworth & Co., London, 1958.

[7] ROBIN MARRIS, *The Economic Theory of 'Managerial' Capitalism*, Free Press of Glencoe, 1964.

[8] THOMAS MAYER, 'The Distribution of Ability and Earnings', *The Review of Economics and Statistics*, May 1960, pp. 189–95.

[9] EDITH T. PENROSE, *The Theory of the Growth of the Firm*, John Wiley and Sons, New York, 1959.

[10] J. G. MARCH and H. A. SIMON, *Organizations*, John Wiley and Sons, New York, 1958.

[11] OLIVER E. WILLIAMSON, *The Economics of Discretionary Behavior: Managerial Objectives in a Theory of the Firm*, Prentice-Hall, Englewood Cliffs, 1964.

10. The Division of Labor Is Limited by the Extent of the Market*

GEORGE J. STIGLER

George J. Stigler (B.B.A., University of Washington, 1931; M.B.A., Northwestern University, 1932; Ph.D., University of Chicago, 1938) was born in Renton, Washington, in 1911. Currently, he is Charles R. Walgreen Distinguished Service Professor of American Social Foundations in the University of Chicago. Before joining the Chicago faculty in 1958, he taught at Iowa State, Minnesota, Brown, and Columbia. He has been on the research staff of the National Bureau of Economic Research since 1947. Stigler is an outstanding authority in the theory of price and the history of economic thought. His publications in these fields include his textbook, *The Theory of Price*, and *Production and Distribution Theories*, and *The Organization of Industry*. He possesses the ability, rare among students of the "dismal science," to combine wit with wisdom, as exemplified by the essays published in his recent book, *The Intellectual and the Market Place*. His chief articles in doctrinal history have been collected in the volume *Essays in the History of Economics*. During 1964 Stigler was President of the American Economic Association.

Economists have long labored with the rate of operation of firm and industry, but they have generally treated as a (technological?) datum the problem of what the firm does—what governs its range of activities or functions. It is the central thesis of this paper that the theorem of Adam Smith which has been appropriated as a title is the core of a theory of the functions of firm and industry, and a good deal more besides. I shall (1) make some brief historical remarks on the theorem, (2) sketch a theory of the functions of a firm, (3)

* Reprinted from the *Journal of Political Economy* (June 1951) by permission of The University of Chicago Press. Copyright, 1951, pp. 185–193.

apply this theory to vertical integration, and (4) suggest broader applications of the theorem.

I. HISTORICAL INTRODUCTION

When Adam Smith advanced his famous theorem that the division of labor is limited by the extent of the market, he created at least a superficial dilemma. If this proposition is generally applicable, should there not be monopolies in most industries? So long as the further division of labor (by which we may understand the further specialization of labor and machines) offers lower costs for larger outputs, entrepreneurs will gain by combining or expanding and driving out rivals. And here was the dilemma: Either the division of labor is limited by the extent of the market, and, characteristically, industries are monopolized; or industries are characteristically competitive, and the theorem is false or of little significance. Neither alternative is inviting. There were and are plenty of important competitive industries; yet Smith's argument that Highlanders would be more efficient if each did not have to do his own baking and brewing also seems convincing and capable of wide generalization.

In the pleasant century that followed on the *Wealth of Nations*, this conflict was temporarily resolved in favor of Smith's theorem by the simple expedient of ignoring the conditions for stable competitive equilibrium. Ricardo, Senior, and J. S. Mill— and their less famous confreres—announced the principle of increasing returns in manufacturing—for Senior it was even an axiom. The exclusion of agriculture was based on the empirical judgment, not that further division of labor was impossible, but that it was a weaker tendency than that of diminishing returns from more intensive cultivation of a relatively fixed supply of land.

This was hardly a satisfactory solution,

and, when Marshall came to reformulate classical economics into a comprehensive and internally consistent system, the dilemma could no longer be ignored. He refused to give up either increasing returns or competition, and he created three theories (of course, not only for this purpose) which insured their compatibility. First, and perhaps most important, he developed the concept of external economies —economies outside the reach of the firm and dependent upon the size of the industry, the region, the economy, or even the whole economic world. Second, he emphasized the mortality of able entrepreneurs and the improbability that a single business would be managed superlatively for any length of time. Third, he argued that each firm might have a partial monopoly—a separate, elastic demand curve for its product—so that, with expansion of its output, the price would usually fall faster than average costs would.

For a time this reconciliation of competition and increasing returns served its purpose, but, as the center of price theory moved toward the firm, Smith's theorem fell into the background. External economies were a rather nebulous category relative to anything so concrete and definite as economists for a time believed the costs of a firm to be. It was pointed out by Professor Knight, moreover, that economies external to one industry may (and perhaps must) be internal to another. The industries in which the economies are internal will tend to monopoly; and, incidentally, it is no longer a foregone conclusion that such economies will be shared with the buyers. Since external economies seemed a refractory material for the popular analytical techniques, they were increasingly neglected.

Marshall's theory of business mortality was also increasingly neglected, with even less explicit consideration. It was not an approach that harmonized well with the economics of a stationary economy, and again the theory was very inconvenient to incorporate into cost and demand curves (especially if one will not use the concept of a representative firm). If the economies of scale within the firm were as strong as Marshall pictured them, moreover, it was not clear that continuously high-quality entrepreneurship was necessary to achieve monopoly. And could the giant firm not grow quickly by merger as well as hesitantly by internal expansion?

Marshall's third theory, of the falling demand curve for the individual firm, lost popularity for a generation because it was incompatible with perfect competition rigorously defined, and this became increasingly the standard model of analysis. And, paradoxically, when the falling demand curve was rediscovered and popularized in the 1930's by the proponents of imperfect and monopolistic competition, they used it not to examine the broad movements of industries and of economies but to focus price theory on the physiology and pathology of the firm.

In 1928, to retrace a step, the neglect of increasing returns had gone so far that Allyn Young felt the need to restore perspective by an emphatic indorsement of the fundamental importance of Smith's theorem: "That theorem, I have always thought, is óne of the most illuminating and fruitful generalizations which can be found anywhere in the whole literature of economics."[1] His position seemed persuasive, but he did not resolve the technical difficulties of incorporating the extent of the market into competitive price theory. Indeed, he openly avoided this problem, asserting that the firm and perhaps also the industry were too small to serve as units of analysis in this area. And so, although Young's and Marshall's and Smith's position is often given lip service to this day, the tributes are tokens of veneration, not

evidences of active partnership with the theory of the firm and the competitive industry.

II. THE FUNCTIONS OF A FIRM

The firm is usually viewed as purchasing a series of inputs, from which it obtains one or more salable products, the quantities of which are related to the quantities of the inputs by a production function. For our purpose it is better to view the firm as engaging in a series of distinct operations: purchasing and storing materials; transforming materials into semifinished products and semifinished products into finished products; storing and selling the outputs; extending credit to buyers; etc. That is, we partition the firm not among the markets in which it buys inputs but among the functions or processes which constitute the scope of its activity.

The costs of these individual functions will be related by technology. The cost of one function may depend upon whether the preceding function took place immediately before or in the immediate vicinity, as when hot ingots are processed with a saving of heat. Or the interrelationships among processes may be remote, as when the entrepreneur must neglect production in order to supervise marketing.

Let us ignore for a moment these interrelationships of costs of various functions, in order to achieve a simple geometrical picture of the firm's costs of production. If the cost of each function depends only on the rate of output of that function, we may draw a unique cost curve for it. Furthermore, if there is a constant proportion between the rate of output of each function and the rate of output of the final product (as when every 100 pounds of cement is bagged), we may draw the cost curves of all functions on one graph, and the (vertical) sum of these costs of various functions will be the conventional average-cost curve of the firm.

[1] "Increasing Returns and Economic Progress," *Economic Journal*, XXXVIII (1928), 529.

We should expect to find many different patterns of average costs of functions: some falling continuously (Y_1); some rising continuously (Y_2); some conventionally U-shaped (Y_3) (see **Figure 10.1**). It is not impossible, of course, that the average cost of some operations first rises and then falls.

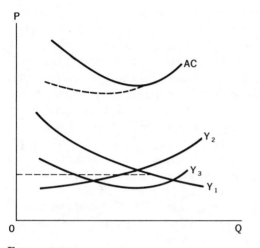

P

AC

Y_2

Y_3

Y_1

O   Q

FIGURE **10.1**

Now consider Smith's theorem. Certain processes are subject to increasing returns; why does the firm not exploit them further and in the process become a monopoly? Because there are other functions subject to diminishing returns, and these are, on balance, at least so costly that average cost of the final product does not diminish with output. Then why does the firm not abandon the functions subject to increasing returns, allowing another firm (and industry) to specialize in them to take full advantage of increasing returns? At a given time these functions may be too small to support a specialized firm or firms. The sales of the product may be too small to support a specialized merchant; the output of a by-product may be too small to support a specialized fabricator; the demand for market information may be too small to support a trade journal. The firm must then perform these functions for itself.

But, with the expansion of the industry, the magnitude of the function subject to increasing returns may become sufficient to permit a firm to specialize in performing it. The firms will then abandon the process (Y_1), and a new firm will take it over. This new firm will be a monopoly, but it will be confronted by elastic demands: it cannot charge a price for the process higher than the average cost of the process to the firms which are abandoning it. With the continued expansion of the industry, the number of firms supplying process Y_1 will increase, so that the new industry becomes competitive and the new industry may, in turn, abandon parts of process Y_1 to a new set of specialists.

The abandonment of function Y_1 by the original industry will alter each firm's cost curves: the curve Y_1 will be replaced by a horizontal line (ignoring quantity discounts) at a level lower than Y_1 in the effective region. The cost curve of the product (drawn with broken lines in Figure 10.1) will be lower, and, on present assumptions, the output at which average costs are a minimum (if only one such output exists) becomes smaller.

Certain functions are also subject to increasing cost; why not abandon or at least restrict the scale of operation of these functions? The foregoing discussion is also applicable here, with one change. When the industry grows, the original firms need not wholly abandon the increasing-cost processes. Part of the required amount of the process (say, engine castings for automobiles) may be made within the firm without high average (or marginal) costs, and the remainder purchased from subsidiary industries.

In order to give a simple geometrical illustration, we have made two assumptions. The first is that the rate of output of the process and the rate of output of the final product are strictly proportional. This will be approximately true of some functions (such as making parts of a single final product), but it will also be untrue of other functions (such as advertising the product). If we drop the assumption, the substance of our argument will not be affected, but our geometrical picture becomes more complicated.[2]

Our second assumption, that the costs of the functions are independent, is more important. Actually, many processes will be rival: the greater the rate of output of one process, the higher the cost of a given rate of output of the other process or processes. Sometimes the rivalry will be technological (as in many multiple-product firms), but almost always it will also be managerial: the wider the range of functions the firm undertakes, the greater the tasks of coordination. Other processes will be complementary: the greater the rate of output of one process, the lower the cost of a given rate of output of the other processes. A most curious example of complementarity is the circular flow of materials within a plant; thus, in the course of making steel, steel plants supply a large part of their requirements for scrap.

If, on balance, the functions are rival, then usually the firm will increase its rate of output of the final product when it abandons a function; and I think that this is generally the case. For example, in the famous study of the Lancashire textile industry by Chapman and Ashton, it was found that firms engaged in both spinning and weaving in 1911 had, on average, 47,634 spindles, while those engaged only in spinning had, on average, 68,055 spindles.[3] But this is not necessary—indeed, they found the converse relationship in number of looms—and the effect of the

range of functions on the size of the firm requires much study before we can reach safe generalizations.

III. VERTICAL INTEGRATION

Many economists believe that, with the growth of firms (and industries?), functions are usually taken over from previous independent industries. For example, United States Steel Corporation now mines its ores, operates its own ore-hauling railroads and ships, and, at the other end, fabricates barrels, oil-field equipment, and houses. (The number of economic views based chiefly on half-a-dozen giant corporations would repay morbid study.)

Broadly viewed, Smith's theorem suggests that vertical disintegration is the typical development in growing industries, vertical integration in declining industries.[4] The significance of the theorem can therefore be tested by an appeal to the facts on vertical integration.

Unfortunately, there are no wholly conclusive data on the trend of vertical integration. The only large-scale quantitative information at hand comes from a comparison of the 1919 study by Willard Thorp with the 1937 study by Walter Crowder of central offices (companies with two or more manufacturing establishments). In 1919, 602 manufacturing companies, or 13.0 per cent of a moderately complete list of 4,635 companies, had two or more establishments making successive products, that is, the product of one establishment was the raw material of another establishment.[5] In 1937, successive

---

[2] We can either draw separate cost curves for the various functions or combine them on one chart, with the scales of the functions chosen so that the optimum amount of each function is shown for the given rate of final output.

[3] S. J. Chapman and T. S. Ashton, "The Sizes of Businesses, Mainly in the Textile Industries," *Journal of the Royal Statistical Society*, LXXVII (1914), 538.

[4] This is not a wholly rigorous implication, however. With the growth of industries, specialism of firms may take the form of dealing with a narrower range of products as well as performing fewer functions on the same range of products.

[5] W. Thorp, *The Integration of Industrial Operation* (Washington, 1924), p. 238. I have omitted railroad repair shops and also the 301 companies having establishments which made successive products, because mining establishments were included.

functions were found in 565 companies (or 10.0 per cent of a more complete list of 5,625 companies).[6] In 1919, successive functions were found in 34.4 per cent of all complex central offices (companies with establishments in two or more industries); in 1937, in only 27.5 per cent. Multiplant companies probably grew in relative importance during this period, so it is possible that a larger share of manufacturing output came from vertically integrated firms. But, so far as these multiplant companies are concerned, there seems to have been a tendency away from vertical integration.[7]

If one considers the full life of industries, the dominance of vertical disintegration is surely to be expected. Young industries are often strangers to the established economic system. They require new kinds or qualities of materials and hence make their own; they must overcome technical problems in the use of their products and cannot wait for potential users to overcome them; they must persuade customers to abandon other commodities and find no specialized merchants to undertake this task. These young industries must design their specialized equipment and often manufacture it, and they must undertake to recruit (historically, often to import) skilled labor. When the industry has attained a certain size and prospects, many of these tasks are sufficiently important to be turned over to specialists. It becomes

profitable for other firms to supply equipment and raw materials, to undertake the marketing of the product and the utilization of by-products, and even to train skilled labor. And, finally, when the industry begins to decline, these subsidiary, auxiliary, and complementary industries begin also to decline, and eventually the surviving firms must begin to reappropriate functions which are no longer carried on at a sufficient rate to support independent firms.

We may illustrate this general development from the cotton textile machinery industry, much of whose history has recently become available.[8] This industry began as a part of the textile industry: each mill built a machine shop to construct and repair its machines. The subsequent history is one of progressive specialism, horizontal as well as vertical: at various times locomotives, machine tools, the designing of cotton mills, and direct selling were abandoned. When the cotton textile market declined in the 1920's, the machinery firms added new products, such as paper machinery, textile machinery for other fabrics, and wholly novel products, such as oil burners and refrigerators. Indeed, one is impressed that even the longer cyclical fluctuations seem to have affected the extent of specialism in much the same way as have the secular trends.

Of course, this is not the whole story of vertical integration, and it may be useful to sketch some of the other forces at work. The most important of these other forces, I believe, is the failure of the price system (because of monopoly or public regulation) to clear markets at prices within the limits of the marginal cost of the product (to the buyer if he makes it) and its marginal-value product (to the seller if he further fabricates it). This phenomenon

[6] W. F. Crowder, *The Integration of Manufacturing Operations* ("T.N.E.C. Monographs," No. 27 [Washington, 1941]), p. 197.

[7] The ratio of "value-added" to value of product is a crude index of the extent of vertical integration *within* establishments. It is interesting to note that in the 17 industries in which this ratio was highest in 1939 in manufacturing, the average number of wage-earners was 16,540. In the 17 industries in which the ratio was lowest, the average number of wage-earners was 44,449. Thus the vertically integrated establishments were in smaller industries than the vertically disintegrated establishments (see National Resources Planning Board, *Industrial Location and National Resources* [Washington, 1943], p. 270).

[8] G. S. Gibb, *The Saco-Lowell Shops* (Cambridge: Harvard University Press, 1950); T. R. Navin, *The Whitin Machine Works since 1831* (Cambridge: Harvard University Press, 1950).

was strikingly illustrated by the spate of vertical mergers in the United States during and immediately after World War II, to circumvent public and private price control and allocations. A regulated price of *OA* was set (Figure 10.2), at which an

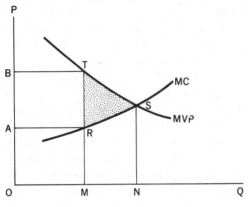

FIGURE 10.2

output of *OM* was produced. This quantity had a marginal value of *OB* to buyers, who were rationed on a nonprice basis. The gain to buyers and sellers combined from a free price of *NS* was the shaded area, *RST*, and vertical integration was the simple way of obtaining this gain. This was the rationale of the integration of radio manufacturers into cabinet manufacture, of steel firms into fabricated products, etc.

Although nonprice rationing provides the most striking examples of this force toward vertical integration, private monopolies normally supply the same incentive. Almost every raw-material cartel has had trouble with customers who wish to integrate backward, in order to negate the cartel prices. Since the cartel members are sharply limited in their output quotas, the discounted future profits of a cartel member need not be high, even with very high prices; so it is profitable for buyers to integrate backward by purchase (as well as by seeking noncartelized supply sources). The Rhenish-Westphalian Coal Cartel, for example, was constantly plagued by this problem:

While a few of the members of the original syndicate agreement of 1893 had been steel companies which produced a part of their own coal and coke requirements, the steel industry, for the most part, had relied upon fuel purchased in the market. The stiffening of prices, coupled with the inelastic terms of sale resulting from the operation of the coal syndicate, now caused the steel companies to seek to free themselves from dependence upon the syndicate.

. . . defensive measures were adopted by all classes of consumers. Some of the large industrial consumers . . . acquired their own mines individually or in groups. Among these were such important companies as the Vereinigte Stahlwerke, Rhenische Stahlwerk-Admiral, Badische Anilin- und Sodafabrik, Norddeutsche Lloyd, Friedrich Krupp, and a number of others representing the electric, gas, railway equipment, rubber and other industries. Also some cities such as Cologne and Frankfurt were among them.[9]

Monopoly is a devious thing, and it leads to vertical integration for other reasons also. A firm cannot practice price discrimination in the stages in which it does not operate; only by fabricating cable could the Aluminum Company of America sell cable at less than the ingot price in competition with copper, while maintaining a higher price on less competitive products.[10] Again, it is possible that vertical integration increases the difficulty of entry by new firms, by increasing the capital and knowledge necessary to conduct several types of operation rather than depend on rivals for supplies or markets.

These remarks are not intended to constitute a theory of vertical integration. There is doubt, indeed, that we want a theory of vertical integration except as part of a theory of the functions of a firm. As soon as one tries to classify the variegated details of production, one finds how artificial and arbitrary "vertical" relation-

[9] A. H. Stockder, *Regulating an Industry* (New York, 1932), pp. 8, 11, and 36.
[10] D. H. Wallace, *Market Control in the Aluminum Industry* (Cambridge: Harvard University Press, 1937), pp. 218–19, 380.

ships are. Whether one wishes to treat vertical relationships separately or as part of a general theory, however, Smith's theorem promises to be a central part of the explanation.

IV. WIDER IMPLICATIONS

If Smith's theorem is less than a complete theory of the division of functions among industries, it is also something more than this: it sheds light on several aspects of the structure and workings of economies. A few of the implications of the principle of increasing specialization will be discussed very tentatively.

One expects to find some relationship between the functional structure of an industry and its geographical structure—after all, reductions of transportation costs are a major way of increasing the extent of the market. (A reminder is hardly necessary that we are dealing with highly interdependent forces and that unilateral causation is implicitly assumed for simplicity and emphasis.) Localization is one method of increasing the economic size of an industry and achieving the gains of specialization. The auxiliary and complementary industries that must operate in intimate co-operation can seldom do so efficiently at a distance. I venture that, within a market area, geographical dispersion is a luxury that can be afforded by industries only after they have grown large (so that even the smaller production centers can reap the major gains of specialization) and that it must be sacrificed for geographical concentration, once the industry begins to shrink in size.

Closely related to this is the influence of localization upon the size of plant. The individual plants can specialize in smaller ranges of products and functions in highly localized industries (the size of the industry in some sense being held constant). In the United States geographically concentrated industries usually have fairly small

plants.[11] There is also some evidence that the plants of an industry are smaller in the larger production centers. For example, in 1937 the average shoe factory in industrial areas had 137 employees, in other areas, 314 employees.[12] The dominance of medium-sized plants in highly localized industries has also been found in England.[13]

During the nineteenth century it was often said that England had the advantage of an "early start"; and this ambiguous statement had an element of truth which Smith's theorem more clearly expresses. As the largest economy in the world, it could carry specialism further than any other country, especially those "general" specialties (like railroads, shipping, banking, etc.) which are not closely attached to any one industry. England's advantage was a big start, as well as an early one.

Those too numerous people who believe that transactions between firms are expensive and those within firms are free will do well to study the organization of England during this period of eminence. In Birmingham, the center of the metal trades, specialism was carried out to an almost unbelievable extent. Consider the small-arms industry in 1860, when Birmingham was still the leading production center of the world:

> Of the 5800 people engaged in this manufacture within the borough's boundaries in 1861 the majority worked within a small district round St Mary's Church. . . . The reason for the high degree of localization is not difficult to discover. The manufacture of guns, as of jewellery, was carried on by a large number of makers who specialized on particular processes, and this method of organization involved the frequent transport of parts from one workshop to another. The master gun-maker—the entrepreneur

[11] National Resources Planning Board, *op. cit.*, pp. 250 ff.
[12] *Ibid.*, p. 257.
[13] P. S. Florence, *Investment, Location, and Size of Plant* (Cambridge, 1948).

—seldom possessed a factory or workshop. . . . Usually he owned merely a warehouse in the gun quarter, and his function was to acquire semi-finished parts and to give these out to specialized craftsmen, who undertook the assembly and finishing of the gun. He purchased materials from the barrel-makers, lock-makers, sight-stampers, trigger-makers, ramrod-forgers, gun-furniture makers, and, if he were engaged in the military branch, from bayonet-forgers. All of these were independent manufacturers executing the orders of several master gun-makers. . . . Once the parts had been purchased from the "material-makers," as they were called, the next task was to hand them out to a long succession of "setters-up," each of whom performed a specific operation in connection with the assembly and finishing of the gun. To name only a few, there were those who prepared the front sight and lump end of the barrels; the jiggers, who attended to the breech end; the stockers, who let in the barrel and lock and shaped the stock; the barrel-strippers, who prepared the gun for rifling and proof; the hardeners, polishers, borers and riflers, engravers, browners, and finally the lock-freers, who adjusted the working parts.[14]

At present there is widespread imitation of American production methods abroad, and "backward" countries are presumably being supplied with our latest machines and methods. By a now overly familiar argument, we shall often be a seriously inappropriate model for industrialization on a small scale. Our processes will be too

specialized to be economical on this basis. The vast network of auxiliary industries which we can take for granted here will not be available in small economies. Their educational institutions will be unable to supply narrowly specialized personnel; they will lack the specialists who can improve raw materials and products. At best, the small economies that imitate us can follow our methods of doing things this year, not our methods of changing things next year; therefore, they will be very rigid. This position has been stated well by one observant citizen of a backward economy, Benjamin Franklin:

> Manufactures, where they are in perfection, are carried on by a multiplicity of hands, each of which is expert only in his own part, no one of them a master of the whole; and if by any means spirited away to a foreign country, he is lost without his fellows. Then it is a matter of extremest difficulty to persuade a complete set of workmen, skilled in all parts of a manufactory, to leave their country together and settle in a foreign land. Some of the idle and drunken may be enticed away, but these only disappoint their employers, and serve to discourage the undertaking. If by royal munificence, and an expense that the profits of the trade alone would not bear, a complete set of good and skilful hands are collected and carried over, they find so much of the system imperfect, so many things wanting to carry on the trade to advantage, so many difficulties to overcome, and the knot of hands so easily broken by death, dissatisfaction, and desertion, that they and their employers are discouraged altogether, and the project vanishes into smoke.[15]

The division of labor is not a quaint practice of eighteenth-century pin factories; it is a fundamental principle of economic organization.

---

[14] G. C. Allen, *The Industrial Development of Birmingham and the Black Country, 1860–1927* (London, 1929), pp. 56–57, 116–17. Commenting on a later period, Allen says: "On the whole, it can be said that specialization was most apparent in the engineering industries in which output was rapidly expanding; while the policy of broadening the basis [product line] was found, mainly, either in the very large concerns, or in industries in which the decline of the older markets had forced manufacturers to turn part of their productive capacity to serve new demands" (*ibid.*, pp. 335–36). The later history of the gun trade, in which American innovations in production techniques were revolutionary, suggest that the organization in Birmingham was defective in its provision for technical experimentation.

[15] "The Interest of Great Britain in America," cited by V. S. Clark, *History of Manufactures in the United States* (New York, 1949), I, 152. Clark adds: "In these words Franklin was but reciting the history of the more important colonial attempts to establish a new industry or to enlarge an old one with which he was personally familiar."

11. The Short Run Revisited*

LOUIS DE ALESSI[1]

Louis De Alessi (B.A. University of California, Los Angeles, 1954; M.A., 1955; Ph.D., 1961) was born in Turin, Italy in 1932. Since 1968 he has been Professor of Economics at George Washington University. He is also a member of the staff of the Natural Resources Policy Center of George Washington University, the Joint Committee on Law and Economics of the American Economic Association, and the Association of American Law Schools. From 1961 to 1968 Professor De Alessi was on the faculty of Duke University. He spent the 1966–1967 academic year with the Institute for Defense Analyses. His primary research interests have been in the fields of price theory, public choice, and the theory of property rights.

The theory of the firm has been the subject of voluminous literature. Nevertheless, some ambiguities and inconsistencies still persist. In particular, the traditional approach to the short run as a period in which the quantities of some inputs cannot be varied [2] requires clarification. The failure to recognize explicitly that the adjustment of a firm to a change in market conditions depends upon the costs and receipts associated with the adjustment leads to a number of ambiguities, including some confusion regarding the regions of the production function that are empirically relevant.

Section I contains a brief statement of the traditional short-run theory of the firm; then, as a first approximation, the main implications regarding the paths of prices and of input proportions in the short run are derived from higher-level economic hypotheses. Section II indicates how the relevant predictions regarding the short-run behavior of the firm may be derived from the wealth-maximizing (stock) approach, avoiding some shortcomings of the traditional profit-maximizing (flow) approach. Section III extends the analysis to the "uneconomic" regions of the production function. Section IV contains a few concluding remarks.

* Reprinted from *American Economic Review* (June 1967) by permission of the publisher, pp. 450–61.

[1] The author . . . acknowledges helpful comments by D. G. Davies, C. E. Ferguson, and J. S. McGee.

[2] For example, see [11, p. 41].

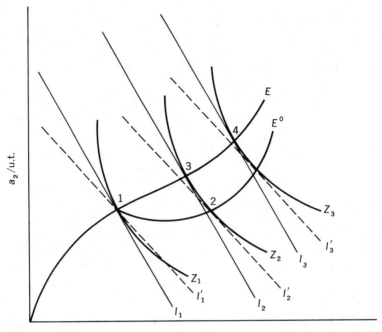

FIGURE 11.1

a_1/u.t.

Consider a competitive firm whose production function[3]

$$Z = f(a_1, a_2) \qquad (1)$$

is hypothesized to be a single-valued, continuous function with continuous first- and second-order partial derivatives; all variables represent flows per unit time.[4] The parameter $Z°$ defines a particular output isoquant, conforming to the usual requirement, with slope at a point equal to $-f_1/f_2$.

Let the firm purchase inputs a_1 and a_2 in perfectly competitive markets at constant prices p_1 and p_2. Total costs of production are given by the linear equation:

$$C = p_1 a_1 + p_2 a_2, \qquad (2)$$

and the parameter $C°$ defines a particular isocost with constant slope equal to $-p_1/p_2$.

Well-known first-order conditions for cost minimization subject to an output constraint require that the input-output combination be on the locus of points (least cost path) where:

$$\frac{f_1}{f_2} = \frac{p_1}{p_2}, \qquad (3)$$

that is, where the ratio of the marginal products of the inputs is equal to the ratio of their prices.[5] In Figure 11.1, the least cost path is shown by OE.

Given the output demand function, the long-run equilibrium conditions for a profit-maximizing firm are easily obtained. Tradi-

---

[3] The following exposition, equations (1) through (3), is standard in the literature. For example, see [6, Ch. 3].

[4] The traditional production function relates rates of input utilization to rates of output. As A. A. Alchian [1] has suggested, however, planned volume (V) of output may be a crucial variable; this point, together with some shortcomings of the flow relative to the stock approach in the analysis of the firm, will be examined in subsequent sections of this paper.

[5] Fulfillment of second-order conditions implies that output isoquants are concave from above over the relevant range [6, p. 51].

tional statements of the theory then turn to the main problem at hand, the response of the individual firm to changes in circumstances (e.g., an increase in the demand for the output of the firm) that disrupt the equilibrium.[6] Let T measure the period from the instant of time some disturbance occurs to the instant of time a given adjustment is completed, where the adjustment may involve a change in input proportions as well as a change in the absolute quantity and in the form of the inputs utilized. The usual procedure is to consider adjustment periods or runs of progressively longer duration, where the longer the run, the more inputs the firm "can" vary and the greater the variation permitted in the quantity of any given input. In the two-input case, one short run may thus be shown by holding a_2 fixed at the initial equilibrium level (e.g., point 1 in Fig. 11.1) and allowing a_1 to vary.

The purpose of distinguishing between runs of different length presumably is to explain the empirical observations that, the shorter the period T, the higher is the cost of the change in output and the fewer the inputs that are varied. It follows that economic theory, *inter alia*, must yield implications consistent with this evidence. By defining the short run as the time period in which some inputs cannot be varied, the desired implications regarding costs are obtained, e.g., [5, pp. 111–15]. This solution, however, avoids a crucial theoretical issue. Implications regarding the proportions in which factors are varied in a given market situation must also be derived from the theory. In particular, the statement that some inputs are held fixed during a given period must be interpreted as a falsifiable

proposition implied by economic theory. The phenomenon in question may be identified (defined) as a short run, but the definition in no sense substitutes for the hypothesis.

All factors of production are variable over any given time interval greater than zero. The rate at which different inputs in fact are varied over time in response to some change in market conditions must depend upon the relative costs and receipts of all the alternative production strategies technologically available to the firm.

As a first approximation, hypothesize that the closer an output program is moved to the present (the shorter the period T) the greater are the costs [1]. Applied to the sellers of the inputs, this proposition implies that as shorter T's are considered the input supply curves decrease (shift to the left) and the greater is the cost to the buyer of varying any given input. That is,

$$p_i = p_i(T), p'_i < 0, \qquad (i = 1, 2); \quad (4)$$

substituting[7] into equation (3) yields:

$$\frac{f_1}{f_2} = \frac{p_1(T)}{p_2(T)}. \quad (5)$$

Equation (4) does not deny that each firm purchases its inputs competitively. The input supply curve facing the individual firm is still hypothesized to be perfectly elastic at the price associated with a particular T; however, the shorter the period the higher is the price intercept.

As shorter periods T are considered, not only do supply functions decrease, but the rates of shifting differ among at least some of the inputs. The ratio $p_1(T)/p_2(T)$ increases, remains the same, or decreases depending upon whether the rate of change in p_1 with respect to T is greater than, equal to, or less than the rate of change in p_2 with respect to T (in all cases, all isocosts

---

[6] For the sake of brevity, the analysis in this paper is usually limited to the consequences associated with an increase in the demand for the output of the firm. The analysis, however, can be easily extended to include the consequences of a decrease in demand, of changes in the input supply function(s), and of changes in the firm's production function due to technological innovations.

[7] Although the analysis developed in this paper is not dependent upon the validity of the following conditions, it may be presumed that eventually $p_i' = 0$, and that $p_i'' > 0$ over at least part of the interval where $p_i' < 0$.

shift to the left as shorter T's are considered).

Each firm is thus hypothesized to consult a family of sets of budget constraints, where each set contains all possible alternative budget constraints of a given slope associated with the particular run contemplated by the firm for the (possibly partial) adjustment. Presumably one family of sets is applicable to expansion and another is applicable to contraction. Given the isoproduct map derived from the traditional production function, a least cost path exists for each input price ratio associated with each adjustment period T. Each short-run least cost path is discontinuous at the original equilibrium point (e.g., $1E°$ in Fig. 11.1), since the firm presumably can continue to produce the current output at the current least cost.

Each short-run least cost path yields a short-run total cost curve. If diminishing returns prevail, the total cost curve (TC) for an increase in output during a particular short run $T°$ would be similar to $TC°$ in Fig. 11.2.[8] The longer the adjustment period T, the closer the short-run total cost curve approaches the long-run TC. Thus, the long-run TC (e.g., TC in Fig. 11.2) is the boundary of all the short-run TC curves.

Economic theory also asserts that the shorter the time interval, the smaller is the price elasticity of the market demand for a commodity. Thus, even in the case of a firm selling its output under purely competitive conditions, different output prices will prevail during at least some of the different adjustment periods considered by the firm. The form of the function relating the demand price per unit of output to T presumably has the same general properties attributed in equation (4) to the input price functions. It follows that a unique total revenue curve and a unique total cost curve may be associated with each run,[9] and the usual criteria may be used to derive the profit-maximizing program for each period.

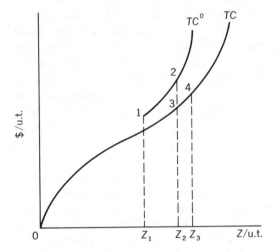

FIGURE 11.2

The analysis developed in this section implies that the firm is induced to seek full adjustment over time rather than instantaneously, and to vary inputs in different proportions as longer T's are considered. In particular, the firm may *choose* to hold one or more inputs fixed during periods of partial adjustment. For example, suppose that a firm initially is producing under conditions of long-run equilibrium (e.g., point 1 in Figs 11.1 and 11.2), and that the demand for its output increases. Given the elasticity of this demand over time and the family of all short-run relative input prices, the

[8] Note that the behavior of the individual firm is at issue. Thus, the *schedule* of input prices (where each price relates to a particular "run") is impounded in *ceteris paribus*. If expansion or contraction of all firms in the industry affects the schedules of input prices (input supply functions facing the industry are not perfectly elastic), then the firm's cost curves will shift accordingly.

The discontinuity in $TC°$ is associated with the approximation developed in this section and the two-dimensional nature of the diagram. A more complete statement of the appropriate cost surface is presented in Section II.

[9] This approach yields the familiar implication that firms will specialize in the speed (time elapsed) of their responses to changes in market conditions.

profit-maximizing program during a particular short run may be that associated with the input price ratio shown by I'_2 (Fig. 11.1), and with point 2 (Figs. 11.1 and 11.2) in particular. In this event, the firm would choose to hold a_2 fixed for a time. The long-run equilibrium output, for an unchanged *schedule* of input prices, would still be along OE (e.g., point 4 in Figs. 11.1 and 11.2). It should be noted that, in the absence of any information regarding the relative costs of varying inputs in different proportions over different time periods, there is no a priori reason for predicting which factor, if any, will be held constant.[10]

It seems generally recognized that adjustment to a change in market conditions is not a free good. So far, the main assertion contained in this paper is that the extent of the adjustment depends upon the relevant costs and receipts. The traditional statement that the quantities of some inputs cannot be varied in the short run implies a denial of the higher-level economic hypotheses that demand curves are negatively sloped (the lower the cost of changing the input mix, *ceteris paribus*, the quicker the full adjustment) and that supply curves are positively sloped (the quicker the full adjustment sought, *ceteris paribus*, the higher the cost of changing the input mix).

Similarity with traditional analysis, however, has been maintained by choosing the particular set of isocosts associated with a particular run, relating the short-run least cost path to the price per unit of output associated with that run, and identifying the profit-maximizing input-output combination.

[10] This conclusion does not seem to be inconsistent with observation. Without allowing empirical evidence to intrude, it might be granted that in some cases the short-run cost of varying the quantity of some types of labor is greater than the cost of varying some types of plants or equipment, while in other cases the opposite cost relationship prevails. For an example of empirical evidence inconsistent with the classical treatment of labor as a purely variable factor, see [9].

The isoquant-based theory of the firm yields decision rules in terms of flows: under long-run competitive equilibrium, at the margin the rate of expenditures on all inputs is equal to the rate of receipts from the sale of the output, where presumably the rates in question remain constant indefinitely. When a disturbance occurs, *ceteris paribus*, the new long-run equilibrium flows may be derived and used to predict the long-run response of the firm. Under these circumstances, the present value of the constant rate of outlay given by each isocost and the present value of the constant rate of receipts associated with each output isoquant will yield present value total cost and total revenue curves with the same shape as the total cost and the total revenue curves given by the profit-maximizing model of traditional theory. Thus application of the usual marginal rules to the stock (wealth) and to the flow (profit) models would yield the same predictions regarding the long-run behavior of the firm. As Alchian and others have emphasized, however, the crucial concept is the *wealth* effect of the alternative strategies considered by the firm; this must be so, since the firm can always alter the time pattern of the flows by either lending or borrowing.

During the process of adjusting to a given disturbance, the pattern of flows for a given firm may be expected to vary from period to period. Predictions regarding the behavior of the firm in the (traditional) short run are usually obtained by examining progressively longer "representative" short runs of unspecified duration. Similarly, the short-run least cost paths derived in the preceding section may be useful pedagogically in deriving implications with respect to the nature of the short-run cost curves, and, in addition, to the short-run changes in input proportions. However, it must be recognized that the decision of the firm to adopt a particular input-output program during a particular time period can only be predicted by discounting to the present the flows associated with the alternative input-output programs for different periods, and then choosing the wealth-maximizing sequence of programs. That is, a rational firm must consider a multiperiod horizon in determining the input-output rates in a specific period; in particular, a firm owning resources must decide the intertemporal allocation of such resources.

A firm responding to a change in market conditions may be viewed as producing the adjustment involved in addition to the other product (Z) under consideration. The present value cost, C_p, of the adjustment may be hypothesized to be a function of (1) x, the rate at which the adjustment is undertaken, (2) V, the total planned adjustment, (3) T^*, the length of the interval between the time when the disturbance occurs and the time when the adjustment is begun, and (4) m, the length of the interval between the time when the adjustment is begun and the time when the adjustment is completed:[11]

$$C_p = f(x, V, m, T^*), \quad C_p \geq 0, \qquad (6)$$

where $f_x > 0$, $f_{xx} > 0$, $f_V > 0$, $f_{VV} < 0$, $f_{zV} < 0, f_{T^*} > 0$ [1]. The total quantity of the adjustment undertaken and its schedule over time would then be determined at the margin in conjunction with the present value of the receipts from the adjustment. In this construct, the long run may be defined as the time period in which deferred changes in the quantity (and form) of each input used by the firm would not lead to a lower input price to the firm in present-value terms.

That is, the individual firm is hypothesized to adjust the quantity and the form of each input it uses until the present value of

the marginal stream of outlays is equal to the present value of the marginal stream of receipts for each input. The firm chooses the least-cost mesh of the alternative input adjustments subject to a set of output constraints related to the elasticity over time of the demand for the firm's output. The wealth-maximizing solution thus yields the total planned change in the quantity and form of each input, the rate at which the change is undertaken, the instant of time when the change is begun, and the time period taken to complete it.[12] *Inter alia*, this approach yields information regarding the time period during which a specific input is held fixed and the schedule at which each input adjustment is phased into the production process.

The procedure outlined in the preceding paragraph would yield one point on the (flow) iso-product map for each period. The input-output program presumably will vary from period to period as the firm completes its adjustment, and may involve holding the rate of utilization of one or more inputs fixed during a given time period.[13]

These comments suggest that a particular input-output combination may appear to be irrational in terms of the flows prevailing in that period, and yet be the rational choice in terms of the wealth-maximizing model. Put more strongly, the flows prevailing in one time period do not provide, by themselves, sufficient information to determine the choice of the output program for that period [1]. Economists have obtained prop-

---

[11] The T^* used in this paper corresponds to the T used by Alchian [1]. Following Alchian, m is a dummy variable whose value is determined by the values assigned to x and to V, where $V = \int_{T^*}^{T^*+m} x(t)dt$ and x may vary over time.

[12] In the case of one type of labor, for example, the present value of the hiring and training costs would be related to the planned number of workers to be added to the labor force, the rate at which such individuals are to be hired and trained, and the instant of time when the hiring and training programs are to begin.

[13] J. Hirshleifer has suggested that a firm may choose to hold some inputs fixed in the short run because of uncertainty regarding the permanence of the initial disturbance [7, p. 250]. The argument developed in this paper, although reinforced by the introduction of uncertainty, suggests that some inputs may be held fixed under conditions of certainty.

ositions regarding the short-run behavior of the firm from a model designed to predict long-run behavior under constant flows, but they have done so only at the cost of ignoring some relevant portions of economic theory.

III

The production function of a firm, according to one definition, ". . . shows the (maximum) quantity of product it [the firm] can produce for given quantities of each of the various factors of production it uses" [5, p. 123]. This definition has been taken to imply that a firm would not use additional quantities of a given input[14] beyond the economic region;[15] that is, out-

put isoquants outside the relevant ridge lines would be straight lines parallel to their respective axes [3, p. 304]. A second definition of the production function rests on the minimum factor quantities necessary for given outputs. On this definition, the segments of the output isoquants outside the ridge lines are taken to vanish [3, p. 304].

Recently, Borts and Mishan have argued for a re-interpretation of the first definition. If a factor is taken to be fixed (and indivisible) during a given time period, and if the firm sells its output under monopolistic conditions, then output isoquants supposedly have meaning in the uneconomic region for the fixed factor and are straight lines parallel to the axis in the uneconomic region for the variable factor.[16] Borts and Mishan conclude that ". . . it is logically inadmissible to construct a diagram in which in

[14] As M. Friedman has pointed out, however, this presumes that the cost of discarding some units of this input is zero [5, pp. 130–131].

[15] The economic region is frequently defined (Rule I) as the range over which the marginal products (MP) of all inputs are greater than zero (and, possibly, equal to zero for some inputs); G. H. Borts and E. J. Mishan do so initially [3, p. 300]. Friedman [5, p. 130] and others, including Borts and Mishan later in the same article [3, p. 305], have noted that the maxim of rational behavior for a firm (Rule II) is to use such a combination of factors that the average product (AP) to each input separately is falling (or at least remains constant).

As Friedman and others recognize, these two rules yield the same answer only if the production function is homogeneous of degree one; then the locus of points (ridge line) where the AP of one input is maximum and the ridge line where the MP of the other input is equal to zero coincide. If the production function is homogeneous of degree less than one, then the ridge lines for AP maximum are outside the ridge lines for $MP = 0$; if the production function is homogeneous of degree greater than one, the order of the ridge lines is reversed.

The two rules, of course, are not mutually exclusive. As Friedman concludes, "The point not to be exceeded is the point of vanishing (marginal) returns; the prudent man will seek to exceed the point of diminishing (average) returns" [5, p. 130].

If production functions are taken to be homogeneous of degree less than one, with degree one as the limit, satisfying the marginal conditions (operating in the range where the output isoquants are concave from above) is sufficient to insure that the AP of each input is either decreasing or constant.

Some economists, e.g., [10, p. 177], have suggested that the derivative of output, dZ (taken

with respect to one of the inputs, when all inputs vary proportionately), first increases (increasing returns to scale) and then decreases (decreasing returns to scale). In the range of increasing returns to scale, application of rules I and II for rational behavior implies that the segments of the negatively sloped output isoquants outside the ridge lines for AP maximum would be in the "uneconomic" region of the production function.

Production functions yielding increasing returns to scale throughout are taken to be empirically irrelevant, since evidence purporting to support such functions has failed to allow for changes in the planned volume of output.

It may be useful to examine the form of the production function implied by Alchian's reformulation of the cost function. If planned volume (V) of output is held constant, the production surface with respect to the rate (x) of output exhibits decreasing returns to scale throughout. If the rate of output is held constant, the production surface with respect to V exhibits increasing returns to scale throughout. If V and x are taken to vary proportionately (the usual case, as suggested by Hirshleifer [7] and apparently accepted by Alchian [2, Ch. 21]), the production envelope at first exhibits increasing returns to scale and then decreasing returns to scale.

[16] Borts and Mishan [3, p. 307] argue that (i) if both factors are indivisible in the short period, the firm is restricted to a point within the economic region; (ii) if both factors are variable during the period in question, all choices must fall within the economic region.

both uneconomic regions the iso-product curves are uniquely determined" [3, p. 307].

If "uneconomic" regions exist,[17] the flow analysis developed in Section I of this paper implies that a firm would not operate within them.[18] Since it has been suggested that a noncompetitive firm using an "indivisible" factor may in fact operate in one of the uneconomic regions in the short run, the point deserves consideration.

The first issue to be examined is that of indivisibility.[19] Why should a factor be indivisible in the short run? To take a standard example, consider a firm using tractors as one of the inputs. Following Friedman [5, pp. 131–32], suppose that tractors come in two sizes, with the tractor of size II being in some relevant sense "twice" the tractor of size I. Tractors presumably come in these two sizes, given the demand function for tractors, due to the lower unit cost associated with producing a larger planned volume of output (V) of each of the fewer models relative to the cost of producing a smaller V of each of a broader range of models [1]. A firm using tractors of size I, following some change such as an increase in the demand for its output, may well prefer to shift to an intermediate-size tractor at an intermediate price.[20] If the cost of an intermediate-size

tractor produced to order is sufficiently high, however, the firm may choose to acquire more of the standard sizes. That is, the choice to acquire some inputs in lumps can be predicted, at least in some relevant cases, by cost considerations alone. It may seem that this argument, if acceptable, applies to "indivisibility in acquisition" and not to "indivisibility in use" [8, pp. 231–33]. But "divisibility" of all inputs in acquisition implies "divisibility" of all inputs in use, since a firm, at some cost, may always choose to modify the structure of its assets or change the form of its inputs.[21] The theory must be capable of predicting the revealed choice of a firm in the short run, under specified circumstances, to vary some inputs in discrete quantities rather than in infinitesimally small quantities; it is not helpful to cloak in the name of indivisibility what is really a plea of ignorance.[22]

The second issue is whether a firm would ever operate in the uneconomic region. The usual argument asserts that a competitive firm ". . . can never produce in the uneconomic region. For if the price falls below the lowest average variable cost (equals highest average return to the variable factor, given the factor price) it will incur

---

[17] This paper is not concerned with the empirical question of whether "uneconomic" regions exist.

[18] As noted earlier, second-order conditions for profit maximization imply that the firm would operate in the range where iso-product curves are concave from above. Moreover, a firm (at least a competitive firm) would operate beyond the region of increasing returns to scale if such a region existed.

[19] The term "indivisibility" has been used to cover a variety of phenomena. For example some economists have used it to describe a factor which cannot be varied during a given interval of time, e.g., [3, p. 304]; some economists have also noted that ". . . indivisibility is necessary for economies of size or scale" [3, p. 305]. This paper is concerned with indivisibility as a short-run phenomenon.

[20] The "half-size man" to drive the "half-size tractor" [5, p. 132] apparently would not be a limit here. In any event I fail to see why, at some suitable price, the "half-size man" (in the tech-

nologically relevant sense) would not be forthcoming.

[21] The distinction between fixed and variable costs is also ambiguous. Whether a firm chooses to vary a particular cost depends upon the relative gains and losses of doing so. At some cost a contract can be broken (as any lawyer will gladly admit), a private radio network substituted for a telephone, and so on.

The only costs which legitimately (i.e., implied by economic theory) cannot be varied are "sunk" costs; such costs, of course, are irrelevant to the decision process.

[22] The preceding statements are not inconsistent with an alternative meaning of indivisibility. As Alchian suggests, the term may be interpreted to cover the phenomenon whereby more durable "dies" result in more than proportional increases in output potential [1, p. 29]. In this sense indivisibility is simply the name given to the sign of certain partial derivatives; it does not explain anything.

negative quasi-rents" [23] [3, p. 305, fn. 2]. A firm facing a negatively sloped demand, however, apparently may do so: "All that is required in order to encompass the uneconomic region . . . is to regard some fixed amount of a factor . . . as being indivisible during the period in question" [3, p. 304].

If the concept of indivisibility is rejected as a short-run crutch, must output programs within the uneconomic region also be rejected? Given the argument developed in Section II, the answer seems to be negative. As the firm considers alternative adjustment periods, the present value cost of varying one input may be sufficiently greater than the present value cost of varying the other input(s) that the firm may choose to operate in one of the uneconomic regions during some limited time period. If wealth, rather than profit, is used as the relevant criterion, a competitive as well as a monopolistic firm may choose to operate for a time in the uneconomic region—particularly if it is granted that uncertainty may exist regarding the permanence of the change in circumstances inducing the adjustment in output. [24]

The preceding comments suggest that, for analytical purposes, it is necessary to show the uniquely determined iso-product curves in each uneconomic region. [25] Whether the firm will operate within any such region during a particular short run can only be determined *after* allowing for the appropriate cost and revenue considerations. Furthermore, although at most one such region would be relevant in the two-input case, $n-1$ regions may be relevant in the n-inputs case.

The concept of a priori fixed, indivisible inputs is misleading. Among other things, such an approach masks the implication that a competitive firm may find it profitable to operate for a time within the uneconomic region. [26]

IV

The traditional approach to the short run as a period in which some inputs cannot be varied is theoretically inadmissible. The substitution of a definition for the corresponding falsifiable hypothesis implied by economic theory masks some empirically relevant issues. In what proportion are inputs to be varied in the short run? Which inputs, if any, are to be held constant? Which regions of the production function are empirically relevant? Why?

The production function must specify which input-output combinations are technologically relevant; cost and revenue information alone can determine which combinations are economically relevant. If it is granted that variation in the input mix is not a free good, then the proportion in which inputs are varied in response to some change in market conditions will depend upon the relative costs and receipts of all the alternative production strategies technologically available to the firm. Moreover, traditional flow analysis yields propositions regarding behavior of the firm in the short run only at the cost of some ambiguities. The wealth-maximizing model suggests that, if "uneconomic" regions exist, they are relevant for competitive as well as for monopolistic firms.

---

[23] It should be noted that Borts and Mishan are working with a linearly homogeneous production function. Their statements would not be necessarily correct, even in the context of flow analysis, if, for example, the production function in question were homogeneous of degree less than one.

[24] R. H. Coase's suggestion that an input be considered ". . . as a right to perform certain (physical) actions" [4, pp. 43–44] is a promising point of departure for further investigations in this area.

[25] E.g., if the present-value cost of not using some resources is zero, the least cost path for these resources outside the relevant ridge lines would then be straight lines parallel to their respective axes.

[26] As Borts and Mishan point out, there is nothing necessarily uneconomic about operating in the uneconomic region.

REFERENCES

1. A. A. ALCHIAN, "Costs and Outputs," in M. Abramovitz and others, *The Allocation of Economic Resources: Essays in Honor of Bernard F. Haley*. Stanford, Calif. 1959.

2. —— AND W. R. ALLEN, *University Economics*, Belmont, Calif. 1964.

3. G. H. BORTS AND E. J. MISHAN, "Exploring the 'Uneconomic Region' of the Production Function," *Rev. Econ. Stud.*, Oct. 1962, *9*, 300–12.

4. R. H. COASE, "The Problem of Social Cost," *Jour. Law and Econ.*, Oct. 1960, *3*, 1–44.

5. M. FRIEDMAN, *Price Theory*, Chicago 1962.

6. J. M. HENDERSON AND R. E. QUANDT, *Microeconomic Theory*. New York 1958.

7. J. HIRSHLEIFER, "The Firm's Cost Function: A Successful Reconstruction?" *Jour. Bus.*, July 1962, *35*, 235–55.

8. F. MACHLUP, *The Economics of Sellers' Competition*. Baltimore 1952.

9. W. Y. OI, "Labor as a Quasi-Fixed Factor," *Jour. Pol. Econ.*, Dec. 1962, *70*, 538–55.

10. W. S. VICKREY, *Microstatics*. New York 1964.

11. A. A. WALTERS, "Production and Cost Functions: An Econometric Survey," *Econometrica*, Jan.–Apr. 1963, *31*, 1–66.

12. Costs and Outputs*

ARMEN A. ALCHIAN[1]

Obscurities, ambiguities, and errors exist in cost and supply analysis despite, or because of, the immense literature on the subject. Especially obscure are the relationships between cost and output, both in the long run and in the short run. Propositions designed to eliminate some of these ambiguities and errors are presented in this paper. More important, these suggested propositions seem to be empirically valid.

COSTS

Costs will be defined initially as the change in equity caused by the performance of some specified operation, where, for simplicity of exposition, the attendant

* Reprinted from *The Allocation of Economic Resources* by Moses Abramovitz and others with permission of the publishers, Stanford University Press. Copyright 1959 by the Board of Trustees of the Leland Stanford Junior University, pp. 23–40. A brief biographical sketch of the author can be found in the introduction to Reading 4.

[1] University of California, Los Angeles, and the RAND Corporation. Indebtedness to William Meckling of the RAND Corporation, who gave many long hours to discussion of the points raised herein, even before the first of several drafts, is very great. Although my egoism prevents sharing the authorship with him, I cannot absolve him from responsibility for any errors that still remain and likewise for any merit the paper may have.

change in income is not included in the computation of the change in equity. Suppose that according to one's balance sheet the present value of his assets were $100, and suppose that at the end of the operation one year later the value of his assets were expected to be $80, not counting the sale value of the product of the operation. The present value of $80 a year hence (at 6 per cent) is $75.47, which yields a cost in present capital value (equity) of $24.53. Because of logical difficulties in converting this present value concept into a satisfactory rate (per unit of time) concept, we defer a discussion of this problem and, for convenience, measure costs in units of present value or equity. Hereafter, the unmodified expression "costs" will always mean the present worth, capital value concept of cost, i.e., the change in equity.

OUTPUT

All the characteristics of a production operation can affect its cost. In this paper we want to direct attention to three characteristics:

1. The rate of output is typically regarded in economic analysis as the crucial feature. But it is only one feature, and

concentration on it alone has led to serious error, as we shall see.

2. Total contemplated volume of output is another characteristic. Is a cumulated output volume of 10,000 or 100 or 1,000,000 units being contemplated? Whatever may be the rate of output, the total volume to be produced is a distinct feature with important effects on cost. Of course, for any rate of output, the larger the total cumulated volume to be produced, the longer the operation will continue. Hence, incorporated in this description of total output is the total time length of the programmed production. Will it span one month or one year, or (at the other extreme) is the contemplated total volume so large that at the rate of output an indefinitely long time is allowed to the production run?

3. The programmed time schedule of availability of output is a further characteristic. For a point output, the programmed date of the output availability is sufficient, but for outputs which continue over time, the time profile (delivery schedule) of the output replaces a single date. We shall call these three distinct aspects the output *rate*, the contemplated *total volume*, and the programmed *delivery dates*.

These three characteristics can be summarized in the following definition, which also defines a fourth characteristic, m, the total length of the programmed schedule of outputs:

$$V = \sum_{T}^{T+m} x(t) \, dt.$$

In this expression V is the total contemplated volume of output, $x(t)$ the output rate at moment t, T the moment at which the first unit of output is to be completed, and m the length of the interval over which the output is made available. Of these four features, only three are independently assignable; the fourth is then constrained.

Unless specific exception is made, in the following we shall always discuss changes in only one of the features, V, $x(t)$, and T, assuming the other two to be constant and letting the full compensatory adjustment be made in m.[2]

PROPOSITIONS ABOUT COSTS AND OUTPUT

Our task is now to make some propositions about the way costs are affected by changes in these variables. Letting C denote costs (i.e., the change in equity), we have

$$C = F(V, x, T, m)$$

subject to the definition of V, which constrains us to three degrees of freedom among the four variables.

PROPOSITION 1

$$\left. \frac{\partial C}{\partial x(t)} \right|_{\substack{T = T_0 \\ V = V_0}} > 0 \qquad (1)$$

The left-hand expression is the derivative of the costs with respect to x, when T and V are held constant, letting m make up the adjustment. It shows the change in costs when the rate of output is increased without increasing V and without changing the delivery date, but with an appropriate reduction of m. Proposition 1 states that the faster the rate at which a given volume of output is produced, the higher its cost. We emphasize that cost means the change in equity, not the *rate* of costs.

PROPOSITION 2

$$\left. \frac{\partial^2 C}{\partial x^2} \right|_{\substack{V = V_0 \\ T = T_0}} > 0 \qquad (2)$$

[2] We note that time or dating enters in a multitude of ways: there is the date at which the delivery of output is to begin; there is the period of time used as a basis for the measure of the rate of output, i.e., so many units per day, per week, or per year; and there is the total time over which the output is to be made available.

The increment in C is an increasing function of the output rate. This is a proposition about increasing marginal cost in present value measure, and is usually derived as an implication of efficient allocation of scarce heterogeneous resources among alternative uses.

Its validity, however, does not depend upon the validity of the premises of the classical model. For example, inventories need not increase in proportion to the rate of output if the variance of random deviations in output rates does not increase more than proportionally to the expected output rate. In this event, a sufficient condition for Proposition 2 as derived by the classical model would be upset. But destruction of sufficient conditions does not eliminate the possibility of all necessary conditions being fulfilled; thus, even if the classical model's assumptions are upset, the proposition could still be true. Whether or not it is, in fact, true cannot be settled by an examination of the model from which it is derived. For present purposes, Proposition 2 can be regarded, if one wishes, as a postulated proposition.[3]

PROPOSITION 3

$$\frac{\partial C}{\partial V}\bigg|_{\substack{x = x_0 \\ T = T_0}} > 0 \qquad (3)$$

C increases with V for given x and date of initial output, T. At a constant output rate, for example, this will require a longer program of production, a larger m.

[3] See T. M. Whitin and M. H. Peston, "Random Variations, Risk and Returns to Scale," *Quarterly Journal of Economics*, LXVIII (November 1954), 603–14, for a longer discussion of some forces that could reverse the inequality of Proposition 2. Some of their suggested forces, e.g., relation between stocks of repairmen and number of machines, are circumvented by the ability to buy services instead of the agents themselves. Another weakness is the association of size of output with the number of independent random forces.

PROPOSITION 4

$$\frac{\partial^2 C}{\partial V^2}\bigg|_{\substack{x = x_0 \\ T = T_0}} < 0 \qquad (4)$$

Increments in C diminish as V increases, for any rate of output, x, and initial output date, T. Thus, for any constant rate of output, as the total planned output is increased by uniform increments, costs (changes in equity) will increase by diminishing increments. The "reasons" for this proposition will be given later.

Proposition 4 also implies decreasing cost *per unit* of total volume, V. We shall state this as a separate proposition.

PROPOSITION 5

$$\frac{\partial C/V}{\partial V}\bigg|_{\substack{x = x_0 \\ T = T_0}} < 0 \qquad (4a)$$

GRAPHIC AND NUMERICAL ILLUSTRATIONS OF PROPOSITIONS 1–5

1. Graphic Illustration

The above properties are shown by the cost surface in Figure 12.1. Proposition 1 describes the slope of a slice on the cost surface where the slice is parallel to the

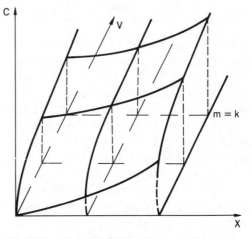

FIGURE 12.1   COST SURFACE AS FUNCTION OF x AND V

Cx plane. Proposition **2** states that the slope of the path of such a slice on the cost surface increases with *x*. Proposition 3 is portrayed by the slope of a slice along the surface parallel to the *CV* plane—going back into the page. The slope of this slice decreases as *V* increases. Proposition 4 describes the decreasing rate at which this surface of costs increases along this slice. Movements in other directions can be visualized. For example, one possible path is to start from the origin and move out some ray. This gives costs as a function of proportional increase in both the rate and the total output for a fixed interval of production, *m*, but the behavior of the cost slope of this slice, except for the fact that it is positive, cannot be derived from these propositions.

2. Tabular, Arithmetic Illustration

TABLE I

Costs, Volume of Output, and Rates of Output

Rate of output, x (per year)	Volume of output			
	1	2	3	4
1	100	180	255	325
2	120	195	265	330
3	145	215	280	340
4	175	240	300	355

For an output rate, *x*, of one per year, beginning at some specified *T*, production must continue for one year to get a total volume, *V*, of 1, for two years to get 2, three years for 3, etc. For a production rate of two per year, production must last one year to get 2 units, two years to get a total of 4, etc. The present value of costs for an output rate, $x(t)$, of two a year for a total *V* of 4 in two years is $330 (which, at 6 per cent, is equal to a two-year annuity of $180 a year).

Proposition 1 is illustrated by the increase in the numbers (costs) in cells down a given column. Proposition 2 is illustrated by the increases in the differences between these cell entries. These differences increase as the rate of output increases, for a given total output. This represents increasing marginal costs (remember that cost is a present value capital concept) for increments in the rate of output. Proposition 3 is illustrated by the behavior of costs along a row (given output rate) as total volume of planned output changes. Proposition 4 states that the increment in *C* is a diminishing increment as one moves across a row, i.e., as total volume of output is larger. For example, in the first row, the output *rate* is one a year. The first cell is therefore an output operation lasting one year, because only one is produced, at the rate of one a year. The total cost is $100. For a total contemplated output of two units, at a rate of one per year, the operation will take two years and the cost is $180. The marginal cost of one more unit of total volume of output—not of one unit higher *rate* of output—is $80. For a total output of three units in three years the cost is $255, an increment of $75, which is less than the previous increment of $80. Here the increments in cost are associated not with increments in rates of output, but with increments in total volume of output. Proposition 5 is illustrated by dividing the cell entries in a row by the output quantities at the head of each column. The quotient, cost per unit of output quantity, decreases as *V* increases.

3. Economic Illustration

A comparison that could be made is the following: Imagine a person to contemplate a total volume of output of one unit at the rate of one a year. But he subsequently revises his plans and produces one more in the next year at the rate of one a year, again planning to produce a total volume of just one unit. Compare the total costs of that operation with an operation in which two units of total output were initially planned at the rate of one a year. Both take two years, but the cost of the latter is $180 while the former's present value is $100 plus $100 discounted back one year at 6 per cent, or a total of $194. Thus it is cheaper to produce from a *plan* for a two-year output of two units at the rate of one a year than to produce two by repetition of methods which contemplate only one total unit of output at the same rate of one a year.

From this example it would appear that a reason for Proposition 4 is that better foresight enables one to see farther into the future and make more accurate forecasts; but this is not the reason, however helpful better foresight may be. A larger planned *V* is produced in a different way from that of a smaller planned *V*. A classic example is the printing press. To get three hundred copies of a letter in one day may be cheaper with mimeograph than with either typewriter or offset printing. The mimeograph method may be so much superior that, even if the rate of output were stepped up to 300 in an hour (instead of in a day), mimeographing might still be cheaper than typing. This does not deny that higher rates of output imply higher costs, as for example that 300 in an hour will cost more than 300 in two hours. The method of production is a function of the volume of output, especially when output is produced from basic dies—and there are few, if any, methods of production that do not involve "dies." Why increased expenditures on more durable dies should result in more than proportional increase of output potential is a question that cannot be answered, except to say that the physical principles of the world are not all linear (which may or may not be the same thing as "indivisible").[4] Different methods of

[4] Could it be that the term "indivisibility" has been meant to cover this phenomenon? A yes or no answer to that question is impossible because of the extreme vagueness and ambiguity with which the term has been used. Furthermore, the question is probably of little, if any, significance.

tooling, parts design, and assembly is the usual explanation given in the production engineering literature.

Proposition 4 seems not to be part of current economic principles. Yet it may be the key to seeing the error in some attempts to refute Proposition 2, which applies to increased *rates* of output for constant total volume of output (or, as we shall see later, for perpetuity durations of output). Propositions 2 and 4 refer to two counterforces, rate of output and total planned volume of output. What would be the net effect of increases in both cannot be deduced from the present propositions. All that can be said is that if the rate of output is increased for a given total contemplated volume of output, the increment in cost will be an increasing function of the rate of output. Proposition 4, on the other hand, implies diminishing increments as *V* increases, and it implies a lower per-unit cost for a larger total volume of output. Thus, we have the possibility that higher rates of production might be available at lower unit costs if they are associated with a larger volume of output, because this latter factor may be sufficient to overcome the effects of the higher output rate.

A larger volume of output could, of course, be obtained by both longer time and faster rates of production, but the relationship between time and volume should not be allowed to mask the fact that it is total contemplated volume of output—not the longer duration of output—that is here asserted (maybe erroneously) to be the factor at work in Propositions 3 and 4.

If both the *volume* and the *rate* of output change in the same direction, the two effects on costs are not in the same direction, and neither the net effect on the rate of change of *increments* in the cost nor even the effect on the costs per unit of total volume of output is implied by these or any other accepted postulates. It has been said, for example, that if some automobile manufacturer were to cut V, the volume of cars produced of a given year's model, from one million to a half-million, costs per car would increase. This statement could refer either to a reduction in V achieved by producing for half the number of months at an unchanged monthly rate of output or to a simultaneous and parallel reduction in both V, the volume, and x, the monthly rate of output. If it refers to the former, it is a restatement of Proposition 5; if it refers to the latter, it is a statement that cannot be deduced from our propositions, which imply merely that costs would be lower if both V and x were reduced than if V alone were lowered.

Even returns to scale seem to have been confused with the effect of size of output. It is conjectured that a substantial portion of the alleged cases of increasing returns to scale in industries or firms is the result of ignoring the relation of costs to volume (rather than to rate) of output. The earlier discussions of automobile production and printing costs are simple illustrations of how this confusion can occur.

How many of the cases of alleged decreasing costs to *rates* of output are really decreasing costs to *volume* of output is an open question. Is it too much to expect that all of them can be so explained? Or that the realm of such cases can be greatly reduced by allowing for V, instead of letting x be the only variable? But that dirty empirical task is left for later and more ambitious efforts.

The observed concentration on a standardized model, e.g., four or five different sizes of tractors as distinct from a much greater possible range, is explained by the effect of volume of output on cost. Although an infinite range is possible, the concentration on a smaller set of fewer alternatives is more economical for most problems. The only way economic theory heretofore could explain this apparent anomaly was to invoke a falling cost curve for small output rates, in turn dependent

upon some kind of unidentified indivisibility or returns to scale. Now the explanation may be contained in Propositions 4 and 9.

MORE PROPOSITIONS

Four more propositions remain. Proposition 6 is given in a footnote because its implications will not be suggested in this paper.[5] Propositions 7 and 8 concern the

[5] PROPOSITION 6

$$\left. \frac{\partial^2 C}{\partial x \partial V} \right|_{T = T_0} < 0 \qquad (5)$$

This says that the marginal present value-cost with respect to increased rates of output decreases as the total contemplated output increases. This can be regarded as a conjectural proposition, whose implications will not be developed in this paper. And the same proposition can be re-expressed as

$$\left. \frac{\partial^2 C}{\partial V \partial x} \right|_{T = T_0} < 0 \qquad (6)$$

This states that marginal present-value costs of increased quantity of output decrease as the rate of output increases.

Of interest is the relationship between these postulates and the implied shape of the production possibility function, where the rate and the volume of output are the two output alternatives. The cost isoquant with x and V as the arguments can be convex or concave. Usually a concave function is implied when rates of output of two different products are the arguments. However, J. Hirshleifer, "Quality vs. Quantity: Cost Isoquant and Equilibrium," *Quarterly Journal of Economics*, LXIV (November 1955), 596–606, has pointed out that convex production possibilities are implicit in many engineering cost functions when quality and quantity are the alternative outputs. Hirshleifer, as it seems from his context, is really discussing cases where his quantity variable refers to volume and not to rate of output. Had he really meant rate of output rather than volume, his results might not have been so "reasonable." The convexity or concavity of the cost isoquant, it may be recalled, is given by the sign of

$$\frac{d^2 x}{dV^2} = \frac{F_{xx} F_y{}^2 - 2 F_{xv} F_x F_v + F_{vv} F_x{}^2}{F_v{}^3}$$

Substituting our postulated conditions shows that the expression may be of any sign, hence the indeterminacy of the concavity or convexity prop-

effects of changes in T, the time between the decision to produce and the delivery of output.

PROPOSITION 7

$$\left. \frac{\partial C}{\partial T} \right]_{\substack{x = x_0 \\ V = V_0}} < 0 \qquad (7)$$

This is not shown in the graph or in the table, but it says that the longer the time between decision to produce and delivery of output, the less the cost.

If we think of a single output point, then T is relatively unambiguous. If the output is to be made available over a period of time, then T could be defined as the beginning moment of output. But many different output programs are possible, even when they all extend over the same interval. One might be tempted to use some sort of average T, say, the date of output weighted by the rate of output. However, such an average T cannot be used for our purposes, because any particular value of T can be identified with an infinite variety of output patterns. Since we are talking about partial derivatives, the whole problem is easily avoided. All we need do is to state that, if one moves any output program or schedule closer to the present (or farther into the future) by a simple time shift, T will have decreased (or increased). Whatever the shape of the output schedule, a reduction of the interval between the present moment and the beginning of the output date (a sort of uniform time-wise shifting) will increase cost. A more deferred output schedule (whatever its unchanged shape) will mean a lower cost.

Proposition 7 is really a corollary of Proposition 2. The slower the rate at which inputs are purchased, the lower their price

erty. However, concavity of the cost isoquant where the two arguments are rates of production for two different products is still implied.

because the lower are the costs to the seller, when Proposition 2 is applied to the seller.

Not only do the supply curves of inputs fall (or shift to the right) as more time is allowed, but the rates of shifting differ among inputs. The supply curves of some inputs are more elastic than those of others; and the rate at which the price elasticity of supply increases with T differs among inputs. Thus, while in an immediate period the price elasticity of supply of input x may be low relative to that of input y (and it may always be lower than that of y), the *ratio* of the costs of increments in y to the costs of increments in x may change with deferred purchase. If the ratio decreases, deferred purchases of y relative to purchases of x will be economical. In other words, it is not merely the slope of the supply curve or the price elasticity of supply that determines which inputs are going to be increased earliest. Rather, it is the rate at which these price elasticities *change* with deferred purchase that is critical. Thus, as stated earlier, the input x with a very low price elasticity of supply will vary more in the immediate period than the input of y with a higher price elasticity if the deferment of purchases by, say, a month would lower the cost of y more than that of x. As an extreme, if the supply curves of two inputs, x and y, were both horizontal, the input of one of them would be increased less if with deferred purchase the price or supply curve would become lower—though still horizontal. That input whose price would become lower with a deferred purchase would be increased in quantity later, with the relatively heavy present increase concentrated on that input whose deferred purchase price would not be as much lower.

PROPOSITION 8

All the derivatives in Propositions 1–5 are diminishing functions of T, but not all diminish at the same rate. This proposition asserts a difference in the extent to which inputs will be varied in the immediate, the short, and the longer period.

Short and long run Statements to the effect that certain inputs are fixed in the short run are frequent and characteristic. In fact, there is no such fixed factor in any interval other than the immediate moment *when all are fixed*. Such statements may represent a confusion between revealed choice and technological constraints. There are no technological or legal restraints preventing one from varying any of his inputs. Even in Viner's classic statement of the short- and long-run cost curves, the short run is defined in terms of some *fixed* inputs and other inputs which can be varied as desired.[6] He stated that the long run is the situation in which all the inputs are "freely" variable. One need only ask, "What do the desires to adjust depend upon in the short run?" and, "What does 'freely' variable mean?" The first is answered by "costs" and potential receipts of the variations, and the second by noting that "freely" does not mean that costs of changes are zero. The fact is that the costs of varying the inputs differ among inputs, and the ratios of these costs vary with the time interval within which the variation is to be made. At any *calendar* moment, T, the producer will choose which input to vary according to *economic costs* and not because of technical or legal fixities that prevent the changing of some inputs.[7]

Debate over definitions or postulates is pertinent only in the light of their purpose. The purpose of the short- and long-run distinction is, presumably, to explain the path of prices or output (x or V?) over time in response to some change in demand

or supply. The postulate of fixed inputs, and others more variable with the passing of time, does imply a pattern of responses that seems to be verified by observable evidence. On that count, the falsity of the postulate is immaterial. But if there are other implications of such a postulate that are invalidated by observable evidence, the postulate becomes costly. The question arises, therefore, whether it is more convenient and useful to replace the fixity postulate by a more general one that yields all the valid implications that the former one did and more besides, while at the same time avoiding the empirically false implications. It appears that the proposed alternative is cheaper in terms of logical convenience, more general, and more valid in its implications. But that is a judgment which is perhaps best left to the reader.

The differences between a short-run (near T) and a long-run (distant T) operation imply differences in costs, and these costs are pertinent to an explanation of the path of prices or costs over time in response to a lasting change in demand or factor availabilities. For example, for a lasting increase in demand, the output made available at more distant dates is produceable at a lower cost; this means that the supply at a given cost will be larger and the price lower in the more distant future as the longer-run operations begin to yield their output. These outputs, having been planned for a later T date, are lower in cost. Output will be larger for a given price, thus reducing price in the market. This longer-run lower cost is the phenomenon whose explanation has usually been sought by resort to fixity of some particular inputs in the short run. The above argument suggests that this phenomenon can be explained without the fixity assumption that in turn leads to other, empirically wrong, implications.

The implication of our proposition is worth emphasizing here. It is that we define a "short run" and a "long run" not as

[6] J. Viner, "Cost Curves and Supply Curves," *Zeitschrift fur Nationalökonomie*, III (1931), No. 1, 23–46.

[7] The nearest, but still different, presentation of the immediate, short run, and long run found by the author is that contained in Friedman's unpublished lecture notes. Other statements may exist; an exhausting search of the literature failed to clarify exactly what is meant by the long run and short run.

differing in the fixity of some inputs; instead, we use T as the length of the run, and then from Proposition 8 derive the implications that were sought by the fixity assumption.

Most important, however, Proposition 8 makes it clear that there is not both a "long-run" and "short-run" cost for any given output program. For any given output program there is only *one* pertinent cost, *not* two. Unambiguous specification of the output or action to be costed makes the cost definition unambiguous and destroys the illusion that there are two costs to consider, a short- and a long-run cost for any given output. There is only one, and that is the *cheapest* cost of doing whatever the operation is specified to be. To produce a house in three months is one thing, to produce it in a year is something else. By uniquely identifying the operation to be charged there results one cost, not a range of costs from immediate to short- to longer-run costs. There is a range of operations to be considered, but to each there is only *one* cost. The question is not, "What are the long-run or short-run costs of some operation?" but instead, "How do total, average, and marginal costs vary as the T of the operation is changed?" Answer: "They decrease as T increases, according to Propositions 7 and 8."

The significance of this should be evident in the debate about marginal cost pricing policies for "optimal" output. Also the use of short-run and long-run costs as alternatives in public utility pricing appears to be a ripe area for clarification of concepts.

What the relationship is between the presently suggested effects of T, which we have just called a short- or long-run effect, and the common short run or long run in the standard literature is not entirely clear. Rather vague and imprecise implications about short and long run are available. Hence, rather than assert that the T effect

is here being proposed as a substitute for the standard short-run analysis, the reader is left free to supply his own interpretation of the conventional "run" and to supplement or replace it, however he chooses, with the present proposition.

PROPOSITION 9

The preceding propositions refer to costs of outputs for a given distribution of knowledge, F, at the present moment, to situations where technology is held constant.[8]

Proposition 9 is "As the total quantity of units produced increases, the cost of *future* output declines." The cost per unit may be either the average cost of a given number of incremental units of output or the cost of a specific unit. This is not identical with the earlier Proposition 4 referring to the effects of the larger planned V. There the effect was a result of varying *techniques* of production, not of changes in technology. Here we are asserting that knowledge increases as a result of production—that the cost function is lowered. It is not simply a matter of a larger V, but rather a lower cost for any subsequent V, consequent to improved knowledge. This distinction should not be attributed necessarily to all the explanations of the learning curve. Some describers of the learning curve bring in the effect of different techniques consequent to different-sized V. Others also mention that, as output is produced and experience acquired, improved knowledge is acquired. Thus, even if one continually planned to produce small batches of output, so the V was constant but repeated, the costs would nevertheless be falling. In the present presentation we have chosen to separate these two effects in logic and principle, attributing the first effect, that of technique, to changes in

[8] Technology, the state of distribution of knowledge, is different from techniques of production, which can be changed at any time, even with a constant technology.

planned *V* but with a given state of knowledge (as in Proposition 4), while the second effect, that of increased knowledge consequent to accumulated production experience, is isolated in Proposition 9. A review of industrial and production management literature will show that both effects are adduced and incorporated in the learning curve discussion, contrary to our decision to separate them. This proposition about the rate of change in technology is accepted in industrial engineering. Usually the proposition is known as the "learning curve" or "progress curve." [9]

Several factors have been advanced as a rationale for this proposition: job familiarization, general improvement in coordination, shop organization and engineering liaison, more efficient subassembly production, and more efficient tools. An extensive literature on this proposition has been developed, but it seems to have escaped integration with the rest of cost theory in economics. [10]

Nevertheless, the proposition is a well-validated proposition and is widely used in industrial engineering. The significant implication of this proposition is that, in addition to rate of output, an important variable in determining total costs is the total planned output, for two reasons: first, because of changes in technique via **Proposition 4**, and, second, because the larger is the planned and ultimately realized output, the greater is the accumulated experi-

ence (technology) and knowledge at any point in the future via **Proposition 9**. Thus, the average cost per unit of output will be lower, the greater is the planned and ultimately experienced output. A more complete discussion of the evidence for this proposition would require a separate paper.

ON THE ADVANTAGES OF THE CAPITAL VALUE MEASURE

Use of capital values enables one to avoid misleading statements like "We are going to operate at a loss in the near future, but operations will be profitable later," "In the short run the firm may operate at a loss so long as receipts exceed variable costs," "A firm operates with long-run rather than short-run objectives." All of these statements are incorrect if liabilities or assets (other than money) are owned by the enterprise. What seems to be meant when a person talks about expecting to have losses for a while before getting profits is that cash flows will be negative for a while, but it is difficult to see how this is in any relevant sense a situation of losses. And, similarly, when a person talks about expecting losses it appears that he means he expects future events to occur which are unfavorable; and in this case the change belief about the future is immediately reflected in current values if not in current money flows —as many a stockholder has learned. Any periods during which expectation about future events becomes more favorable are periods of increasing equity (i.e., of profits), even though the period in which the more favorable events will occur is in the future. When a firm reports that it operated during the past quarter at a loss, it means simply that the net present value of assets decreased during that period, even though the future cash receipts and outlays have not yet been realized. The profits are in the present moment—the increase in equity—as some stockholders have joy-

---

[9] Sometimes the curve is called an 80 per cent progress curve, because it is sometimes asserted that the cost of the 2*n*th item is 80 per cent of the cost of the *n*th item. Thus the fortieth plane would involve only 80 per cent of the direct man hours and materials that the twentieth plane did.

[10] See W. Hirsch, "Manufacturing Progress Functions," *Review of Economics and Statistics,* XXXIV (May 1952), 143–55. A less accessible, but more complete, reference to the published material is given in H. Asher, *Cost-Quantity Relationship in the Airframe Industry* (The RAND Corporation, Santa Monica, California), July 1956. But see P. A. Samuelson, *Economics* (McGraw-Hill, New York, 1948), p. 473, where it is mentioned but left unincorporated.

ously learned. The presently anticipated increase in *future* receipts relative to future outlays means an increase in *present* equity values, profits.

Statements to the effect that a firm would willingly and knowingly operate at a loss in the short run are consistent only with an identification of costs with money flows, and are certainly inconsistent with the postulates of seeking increased wealth (or utility) as a goal or survival attribute. Such identification of costs with money flows eliminates capital theory from the theory of the firm and from much of price theory. There is no cause to pay this price since it is just as easy not to abandon capital theory, and if one retains it more useful implications will be derived.

Yet, in economic texts costs are almost always measured as *time-rates*, and only rarely as capital values. At first blush this would seem to be an irrelevant or trivial distinction, since capital values are merely the present values of *receipt* or *outlay* streams. But what about going from capital values to time rates of *cost* streams? New problems arise in this effort. Suppose that the outlay stream for some operation is used as the basis for cost calculations. If, and only if, *no* other assets or liabilities are involved can money flows be identified with costs; otherwise they represent, in part, accumulations of assets or liabilities. As soon as assets and liabilities are admitted, money flows are not synonymous with costs, and changes in values of assets or liabilities must now be included. With the break between money outlays and costs, the measure of costs becomes the change in present value of net equity consequent to some action (ignoring receipts, for present purposes).

If a firm signed a contract and committed itself to produce some quantity of output, then the cost it has incurred in signing the contract and obligating itself to produce the output is its decrease in equity, say $E_a - E_b$. At moment a, prior

to the contract, the equity or net wealth of the firm is E_a. At this moment the firm considers entering into some production plan. If it does so, what will happen to its equity at the end of the plan, or how will the equity change over that interval? If, for the moment, we ignore the receipts or income from that plan, the decrease of equity by moment b would be the measure of cost of the output operation which it is obligated to perform. The difference, $E_a - E_b$, between the equity (E_a) at the beginning and the *present* value (E_b) of the equity (E_t) at the end of the operation, is the total cost, C, of the operation.

The *time-rate* of costs (of change in equity) is given by dE/dt, the slope of the line from E_a to E_t, which is quite different from C. The former, dE/dt, is a derivative, a time rate of change. The latter, C, is the integral of the former. It is a finite difference, $E_a - E_t$, obtained from two different points on the E curve, while the former is the slope of the E curve and can be obtained only after an E curve is obtained. What is the meaning of the E *curve* in such a case? Presumably it means that, if the firm decided at any moment to stop further output, under this contract it would find itself with an equity indicated by the height of the line E_aE_t. Ignoring the contractual liability for obligation to produce according to the contract, the equity declines along the E line; but if one does regard the contract performance liability, the equity does not change as output is produced because there is an exactly offsetting reduction in contractual liability as output is produced. The equity of the firm stays constant over the interval if the outlays and asset values initially forecast were forecast correctly.

If the *rate* of cost, dE/dt, or if the E curve is plotted not against time, but against the *output rate*, we do not get a curve similar in interpretation to the usual total cost curve in standard cost curve analysis. The *rate* of cost, dE/dt can be converted to average cost per unit of rate of output by dividing the rate of cost, dE/dt, by the associated rate of output at that moment, and the marginal time-rate of cost is obtained by asking how the slope of the equity curve dE/dt is affected by changes in x, i.e., $(d^2E/dt\ dx)$.

The difference between this curve, where dE/dt is plotted against x, and the usual time rate of cost curve analysis is that our current analysis is based on a larger set of variables, $x(t)$ and V, and hence dE/dt cannot be drawn uniquely merely against the rate of output, $x(t)$. A new curve must be drawn for each output operation contemplated; even worse, there is no assurance that such a curve of dE/dt drawn against the rate of output on the horizontal axis would have only one vertical height for each output rate. The curve might fold back on itself and be multivalued because one value of dE/dt might be associated with a particular rate of output early in the operation and another different value later in the operation, even though at both moments the output rate were the same.

The number of cost curves that could be drawn is greater by at least an extra factor, V. In fact, we have at least two families of curves, one for different values of V and one for different time profiles of $x(t)$, and it is not clear what is usually assumed about these in the standard cost curve analysis. One possibility is to assume that the length of the production run, m, or the contemplated total output, V, does not affect the rate at which equity changes for any given output rate. The difficulty with this position is not merely that it is logically wrong but that it leads to implications that are refuted by everyday events.

A kind of average or marginal cost can be defined on the basis of the approach suggested earlier. For any given contemplated operation, the change in equity implied can be computed and evaluated in present worths. If this cost is divided by the total contemplated volume of output, V, the result is present value cost per unit of product (not time rate per unit *rate* of output). If the same total output were to be produced at a higher output rate, x, and thus within a shorter time interval m, the total cost (change in equity) would be greater, and so the cost per unit of total volume of output would be higher. As noted in the first part of this paper, the increase in total present value cost, $\partial C/x$ (not $d^2E/dt\ dx$), is the marginal cost, consequent to an increased rate of output. By varying the contemplated rates of output x for any given total output plan (V and T), one can get different total capital costs. These changes in total capital costs can be called the marginal capital costs. But it is important to note again that there are as many such marginal capital value cost functions as there are different possible total output patterns that can be contemplated, and these marginal capital costs are not time rates of costs.

CONCLUSION

Four features have been emphasized in the foregoing pages. First, the distinction between rate and quantity of output; second, changes in technology as distinct from changes in technique; third, the use of calendar time dates of output instead of technical fixity for distinguishing output operations; fourth, the use of capital value concepts instead of rates of costs.

The first and second features (and the ones that are emphasized in this paper) enable us to capture within our theory the lower costs attendant on larger quantities of output—not rates of output. Everyday experience where large rates of output are available at lower prices could be explained as a movement down the buyer's demand curve as the seller, in order to sell a larger amount, lowers price. But this seems to be incapable of explaining all such situations. Another explanation usually advanced is the economies of scale, where scale is related to *rate* of output. However, an alternative explanation suggested here is the lower cost resulting, not from higher *rates* of output per unit time, but from larger planned volume of total output quantities. An examination of the production management and engineering literature reveals much greater emphasis on batch or lot size as contrasted to the rate of output. Frequently the latter is not much of a variable in each particular firm's decision. This means that the extent to which rate of output *is* varied may be slight—not that it can't be varied or that its significance is slight. That there has been confusion between the rate of output and the batch size or quantity planned is sure. How much cannot be known.

The third feature—that of identifying each output operation with a calendar date and then postulating that the more distant the date the smaller the change in equity (the smaller the cost)—provides a way to escape the unnecessary bind imposed by the definition of short-run costs as that which results from fixed inputs. The ambiguous idea of two different costs, a short-run and a long-run cost for a given output, disappears and is replaced by one cost for each different program of output.

What must have been assumed in our present literature about the factors mentioned here? Was the rate of output profile assumed to be a constant rate extending into perpetuity? The answer could not be ascertained from an exhausting reading of the literature nor from analogically implied conditions. Certainly the standard cost curve analysis does not envisage a perpetuity output at some given rate, nor does it seem to specify the effects of shorter-length runs at any output. For example, Stigler, in his well-known paper on the effects of planning for variations in the rate of output, imagines one to be moving along a given cost curve appropriate to the case in which output varies. This desirable attempt to modify the cost curve analysis would have been more successful if the output had been further specified or identified in terms of V and T. Then the conventional curves would have disappeared, and many logical inconsistencies and ambiguities could have been removed from the standard analysis. But merely drawing the curve flatter and higher does not avoid the problems of appropriate interpretation of costs for unspecified values of the pertinent variables.

Finally, introduction of a new variable, V, complicates the equilibrium of demand and supply, for now there must be a similar element in demand which will determine the equilibrium size of V, if such there be. Suffice it to say here that even though consumers may not act or plan consciously in terms of V, their actions can be interpreted in terms of a resultant aggregative V. Producers, in contemplating the demand for their products, will be required to think of capital value or present value of income with the rate of output integrated into a V—possibly a break-even V—on the basis of which they may make production plans. A simple rate of output, price relationships, will not be sufficient. But this remains to be developed later, only if the present propositions prove valid and useful.

13. Mathematical, or "Linear," Programming: A Nonmathematical Exposition*

ROBERT DORFMAN

Robert Dorfman (B.A., Columbia University, 1936; M.A., 1937; Ph.D., University of California at Berkeley, 1950) was born in New York City in 1916. From 1950 to 1955 he was on the faculty of the University of California (Berkeley) and since that time he has been Professor of Economics at Harvard. He is noted for his work in operations research, economic statistics, economic theory, and, in particular, as coauthor of *Linear Programming* and *Economic Analysis* (with Paul A. Samuelson and Robert M. Solow). He is a consultant to the RAND Corporation and during the academic year 1960–1961 was a Fellow of the Center for Advanced Study in the Behavioral Sciences at Stanford. Dorfman is also a Fellow of the Econometric Society.

This paper is intended to set forth the leading ideas of mathematical programming[1] purged of the algebraic apparatus which has impeded their general acceptance and appreciation. This will be done by concentrating on the graphical representation of the method. While it is not possible, in general, to portray mathematical programming problems in two-dimensional graphs, the conclusions which we shall draw from the graphs will be of general validity and, of course, the graphic representation of multidimensional problems has a time-honored place in economics.

The central formal problem of economics is the problem of allocating scarce resources so as to maximize the attainment

* Reprinted from the *American Economic Review* (December 1953) by permission of the publisher, pp. 797–825.

[1] The terminology of the techniques which we are discussing is in an unsatisfactory state. Most frequently they are called "linear programming" although the relationships involved are not always linear. Sometimes they are called "activities analysis," but this is not a very suggestive name. The distinguishing feature of the techniques is that they are concerned with programming rather than with analysis, and, at any rate, "activities analysis" has not caught on. We now try out "mathematical programming"; perhaps it will suit.

of some predetermined objective. The standard formulation of this problem—the so-called marginal analysis—has led to conclusions of great importance for the understanding of many questions of social and economic policy. But it is a fact of common knowledge that this mode of analysis has not recommended itself to men of affairs for the practical solution of their economic and business problems. Mathematical programming is based on a restatement of this same formal problem in a form which is designed to be useful in making practical decisions in business and economic affairs. That mathematical programming is nothing but a reformulation of the standard economic problem and its solution is the main thesis of this exposition.

The motivating idea of mathematical programming is the idea of a "process" or "activity." A process is a specific method for performing an economic task. For example, the manufacture of soap by a specified formula is a process. So also is the weaving of a specific quality of cotton gray goods on a specific type of loom. The conventional production function can be thought of as the formula relating the inputs and outputs of all the processes by which a given task can be accomplished.

For some tasks, *e.g.*, soap production, there are an infinite number of processes available. For others, *e.g.*, weaving, only a finite number of processes exist. In some cases, a plant or industry may have only a single process available.

In terms of processes, choices in the productive sphere are simply decisions as to which processes are to be used and the extent to which each is to be employed. Economists are accustomed to thinking in terms of decisions as to the quantities of various productive factors to be employed. But an industry or firm cannot substitute Factor A for Factor B unless it does some of its work in a different way, that is, unless it substitutes a process which uses A

in relatively high proportions for one which uses B. Inputs, therefore, cannot be changed without a change in the way of doing things, and often a fundamental change. Mathematical programming focusses on this aspect of economic choice.

The objective of mathematical programming is to determine the optimal levels of productive processes in given circumstances. This requires a restatement of productive relationships in terms of processes and a reconsideration of the effect of factor scarcities on production choices. As a prelude to this theoretical discussion, however, it will be helpful to consider a simplified production problem from a common-sense point of view.

I. AN EXAMPLE OF MATHEMATICAL PROGRAMMING

Let us consider an hypothetical automobile company equipped for the production of both automobiles and trucks. This company, then, can perform two economic tasks, and we assume that it has a single process for accomplishing each. These two tasks, the manufacture of automobiles and that of trucks, compete for the use of the firm's facilities. Let us assume that the company's plant is organized into four departments: (1) sheet metal stamping, (2) engine assembly, (3) automobile final assembly, and (4) truck final assembly—raw materials, labor, and all other components being available in virtually unlimited amounts at constant prices in the open market.

The capacity of each department of the plant is, of course, limited. We assume that the metal stamping department can turn out sufficient stampings for 25,000 automobiles or 35,000 trucks per month. We can then calculate the combinations of automobile and truck stampings which this department can produce. Since the department can accommodate 25,000 automobiles per month, each automobile requires 1/25,000 or 0.004 per cent of monthly capacity. Similarly each truck requires 0.00286 per cent of monthly capacity. If, for example, 15,000 automobiles were manufactured they would require 60 per cent of metal stamping capacity and the remaining 40 per cent would be sufficient to produce stampings for 14,000 trucks. Then 15,000 automobiles and 14,000 trucks could be produced by this department at full operation. This is, of course, not the only combination of automobiles and trucks which could be produced by the stamping department at full operation. In Figure 13.1, the line labeled "Metal Stamping" represents all such combinations.

Similarly we assume that the engine assembly department has monthly capacity for 33,333 automobile engines or 16,667 truck engines or, again, some combination of fewer automobile and truck engines. The combinations which would absorb the full capacity of the engine assembly department are shown by the "Engine As-

sembly" line in Figure 13.1 We assume also that the automobile assembly department can accommodate 22,500 automobiles per month and the truck assembly department 15,000 trucks. These limitations are also represented in Figure 13.1.

We regard this set of assumptions as defining two processes: the production of automobiles and the production of trucks. The process of producing an automobile yields, as an output, one automobile and absorbs, as inputs, 0.004 per cent of metal stamping capacity, 0.003 per cent of engine assembly capacity, and 0.00444 per cent of automobile assembly capacity. Similarly the process of producing a truck yields, as an output, one truck and absorbs, as inputs, 0.00286 per cent of metal stamping capacity, 0.006 per cent of engine assembly capacity, and 0.00667 per cent of truck assembly capacity.

The economic choice facing this firm is the selection of the numbers of automobiles and trucks to be produced each month,

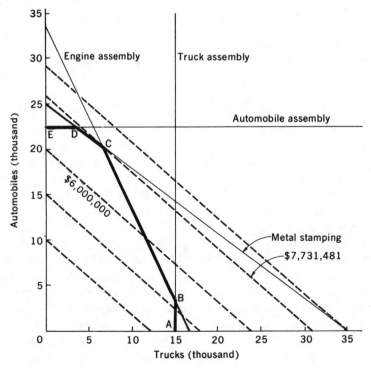

FIGURE 13.1   CHOICES OPEN TO AN AUTOMOBILE FIRM

subject to the restriction that no more than 100 per cent of the capacity of any department can be used. Or, in more technical phraseology, the choice consists in deciding at what level to employ each of the two available processes. Clearly, if automobiles alone are produced, at most 22,500 units per month can be made, automobile assembly being the effective limitation. If only trucks are produced, a maximum of 15,000 units per month can be made because of the limitation on truck assembly. Which of these alternatives should be adopted, or whether some combination of trucks and automobiles should be produced depends on the relative profitability of manufacturing trucks and automobiles. Let us assume, to be concrete, that the sales value of an automobile is $300 greater than the total cost of purchased materials, labor, and other direct costs attributable to its manufacture. And, similarly, that the sale value of a truck is $250 more than the direct cost of manufacturing it. Then the net revenue of the plant for any month is 300 times the number of automobiles produced plus 250 times the number of trucks. For example, 15,000 automobiles and 6,000 trucks would yield a net revenue of $6,000,000. There are many combinations of automobiles and trucks which would yield this same net revenue; 10,000 automobiles and 12,000 trucks is another one. In terms of Figure 13.1, all combinations with a net revenue of $6,000,000 lie on a straight line, to be specific, the line labelled $6,000,000 in the figure.

A line analogous to the one which we have just described corresponds to each possible net revenue. All these lines are parallel, since their slope depends only on the relative profitability of the two activities. The greater the net revenue, of course, the higher the line. A few of the net revenue lines are shown in the figure by the dashed parallel lines.

Each conceivable number of automobiles and trucks produced corresponds to a point on the diagram, and through each point there passes one member of the family of net revenue lines. Net revenue is maximized when the point corresponding to the number of automobiles and trucks produced lies on the highest possible net revenue line. Now the effect of the capacity restrictions is to limit the range of choice to outputs which correspond to points lying inside the area bounded by the axes and by the broken line ABCDE. Since net revenue increases as points move out from the origin, only points which lie on the broken line need be considered. Beginning then with Point A and moving along the broken line we see that the boundary of the accessible region intersects higher and higher net revenue lines until point C is reached. From there on, the boundary slides down the scale of net revenue lines. Point C therefore corresponds to the highest attainable net revenue. At point C the output is 20,370 automobiles and 6,481 trucks, yielding a net revenue of $7,731,481 per month.

The reader has very likely noticed that this diagram is by no means novel. The broken line, ABCDE, tells the maximum number of automobiles which can be produced in conjunction with any given number of trucks. It is therefore, apart from its angularity, a production opportunity curve or transformation curve of the sort made familiar by Irving Fisher, and the slope of the curve at any point where it has a slope is the ratio of substitution in production between automobiles and trucks. The novel feature is that the production opportunity curve shown here has no defined slope at five points and that one of these five is the critical point. The dashed lines in the diagram are equivalent to conventional price lines.

The standard theory of production teaches that profits are maximized at a point where a price line is tangent to the production opportunity curve. But, as we have just noted, there are five points where our production opportunity curve has no tangent. The tangency criterion therefore fails. Instead we find that profits are maximized at a corner where the slope of the price line is neither less than the slope of the opportunity curve to the left of the corner nor greater than the slope of the opportunity curve to the right.

Diagrammatically, then, mathematical programming uses angles where standard economics uses curves. In economic terms, where does the novelty lie? In standard economic analysis we visualize production relationships in which, if there are two products, one may be substituted for the other with gradually increasing difficulty. In mathematical programming we visualize a regime of production in which, for any output, certain factors will be effectively limiting but other factors will be in ample supply. Thus, in Figure 13.1, the factors which effectively limit production at each point can be identified by noticing on which limitation lines the point lies. The rate of substitution between products is determined by the limiting factors alone and changes only when the designation of the limiting factors changes. In the diagram a change in the designation of the limiting factors is represented by turning a corner on the production opportunity curve.

We shall come back to this example later, for we have not exhausted its significance. But now we are in a position to develop with more generality some of the concepts used in mathematical programming.

II. THE MODEL OF PRODUCTION IN MATHEMATICAL PROGRAMMING

A classical problem in economics is the optimal utilization of two factors of production, conveniently called capital and labor. In the usual analysis, the problem is formulated by conceiving of the two factors as cooperating with each other in accordance with a production function which states the maximum quantity of a product which can be obtained by the use of stated quantities of the two factors. One convenient means of representing such a production function is an "isoquant diagram," as in Figure 13.2. In this familiar

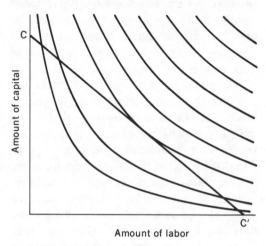

FIGURE 13.2   AN ISOQUANT DIAGRAM

figure, quantities of labor are plotted along the horizontal axis and quantities of capital along the vertical. Each of the arcs in the body of the diagram corresponds to a definite quantity of output, higher arcs corresponding to greater quantities.

If the prices per unit of capital and labor are known, the combinations of labor and capital which can be purchased for a fixed total expenditure can be shown by a sloping straight line like CC' in the figure, the slope depending only on the relative prices. Two interpretations follow immediately. First, the minimum unit cost of producing the output represented by any isoquant can be achieved by using the combination of labor and capital which corresponds to the point where that isoquant is tangent to a price line. Second, the greatest output attainable with any given expenditure is represented by the isoquant which is tangent to the price line corresponding to that expenditure.

This diagram and its analysis rest upon the assumption that the two factors are continuously substitutable for each other in such wise that if the amount of labor employed be reduced by a small amount it will be possible to maintain the quantity of output by a *small* increase in the amount of capital employed. Moreover, this analysis assumes that each successive unit decrement in the amount of labor will require a slightly larger increment in the amount of capital if output is to remain constant. Otherwise the isoquants will not have the necessary shape.

All this is familiar. We call it to mind only because we are about to develop an analogous diagram which is fundamental to mathematical programming. First, however, let us see why a new diagram and a new approach are felt to be necessary.

The model of production which we have just briefly sketched very likely is valid for some kinds of production. But for most manufacturing industries, and indeed all production where elaborate machinery is used, it is open to serious objection. It is characteristic of most modern machinery that each kind of machine operates efficiently only over a narrow range of speeds and that the quantities of labor, power, materials and other factors which cooperate with the machine are dictated rather inflexibly by the machine's built-in characteristics. Furthermore, at any time there is available only a small number of different kinds of machinery for accomplishing a given task. A few examples may make these considerations more concrete. Earth may be moved by hand shovels, by steam or diesel shovels, or by bulldozers. Power shovels and bulldozers are built in only a small variety of models, each with inherent characteristics as to fuel consumption per hour, number of operators and assistants required, cubic feet of earth moved per hour, etc. Printing type may be set by using hand-fonts, linotype machines or monotype machines. Again, each machine is available in only a few models and each has its own pace of operation, power and space requirements, and other essentially

unalterable characteristics. A moment's reflection will bring to mind dozens of other illustrations: printing presses, power looms, railroad and highway haulage, statistical and accounting calculation, metallic ore reduction, metal fabrication, etc. For many economic tasks the number of processes available is finite, and each process can be regarded as inflexible with regard to the ratios among factor inputs and process outputs. Factors cannot be substituted for each other except by changing the levels at which entire technical processes are used, because each process uses factors in fixed characteristic ratios. In mathematical programming, accordingly, process substitution plays a rôle analogous to that of factor substitution in conventional analysis.

We now develop an apparatus for the analysis of process substitution. For convenience we shall limit our discussion to processes which consume two factors, to be called capital and labor, and produce a single output. Figure 13.3 represents such

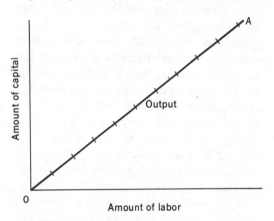

FIGURE 13.3 A PROCESS

a process. As in Figure 13.2, the horizontal axis is scaled in units of labor and the vertical axis in units of capital. The process is represented by the ray, OA, which is scaled in units of output. To each output there corresponds a labor requirement found by locating the appropriate mark on the process ray and reading straight down.

The capital requirement is found in the same manner by reading straight across from the mark on the process line. Similarly, to each amount of labor there corresponds a quantity of output, found by reading straight up, and a quantity of capital, found by reading straight across from the output mark.

It should be noted that the quantity of capital in this diagram is the quantity used in a process rather than the quantity owned by an economic unit; it is capital-service rather than capital itself. Thus, though more or less labor may be combined with a given machine—by using it more or fewer hours—the ratio of capital to labor inputs, that is, the ratio of machine-hours to labor hours—is regarded as technologically fixed.

Figure 13.3 incorporates two important assumptions. The fact that the line OA is straight implies that the ratio between the capital input and the labor input is the same for all levels of output and is given, indeed, by the slope of the line. The fact that the marks on the output line are evenly spaced indicates that there are neither economies nor diseconomies of scale in the use of the process, *i.e.*, that there will be strict proportionality between the quantity of output and the quality of either input. These assumptions are justified rather simply on the basis of the notion of a process. If a process can be used once, it can be used twice or as many times as the supplies of factors permit. Two linotype machines with equally skilled operators can turn out just twice as much type per hour as one. Two identical mills can turn out just twice as many yards of cotton per month as one. So long as factors are available, a process can be duplicated. Whether it will be economical to do so is, of course, another matter.

If there is only one process available for a given task there is not much scope for economic choice. Frequently, however, there will be several processes. Figure 13.4

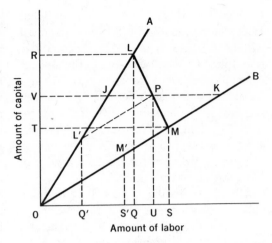

FIGURE 13.4 TWO PROCESSES

represents a situation in which two procedures are available, Process A indicated by the line OA and Process B indicated by OB. We have already seen how to interpret points on the lines OA and OB. The scales by which output is measured on the two rays are not necessarily the same. The scale on each ray reflects the productivity of the factors when used in the process represented by that ray and has no connection with the output scale on any other process ray. Now suppose that points L and M represent production of the same output by the two processes. Then LM, the straight line between them, will represent an isoquant and each point on this line will correspond to a combination of Processes A and B which produces the same output as OL units of Process A or OM units of Process B.

To see this, consider any point P on the line LM and draw a line through P parallel to OB. Let L' be the point where this line intersects OA. Finally mark the point M' on OB such that OM' = L'P. Now consider the production plan which consists of using Process A at level OL' and Process B at level OM'.[2] It is easy to show that this

---

[2] An alternative construction would be to draw a line through point P parallel to OA. It would intersect OB at M'. Then we could lay off OL'

production plan uses OU units of labor, where U is the labor coordinate of point P, and OV units of capital, where V is the capital coordinate of point P.[3]

Since the coordinates of point P correspond to the quantities of factors consumed by OL' units of Process A and OM' units of Process B, we interpret P as representing the combined production plan made up of the specified levels of the two processes. This interpretation implies an important economic assumption, namely, that if the two processes are used simultaneously they will neither interfere with nor enhance each other so that the inputs and outputs resulting from simultaneous use of two processes at any levels can be found by adding the inputs and outputs of the individual processes.

In order to show that P lies on the isoquant through points L and M it remains only to show that the sum of the outputs corresponding to points L' and M' is the same as the output corresponding to point L or point M. This follows at once from the facts that the output corresponding to any point on a process ray is directly proportional to the length of the ray up to that point and that the triangles LL'P and LOM in Figure 13.4 are similar.[4] Thus if

we have two process lines like OA and OB and find points L and M on them which represent producing the same output by means of the two processes then the line segment connecting the two equal-output points will be an isoquant.

We can now draw the mathematical programming analog of the familiar isoquant diagram. Figure 13.5 is such a dia-

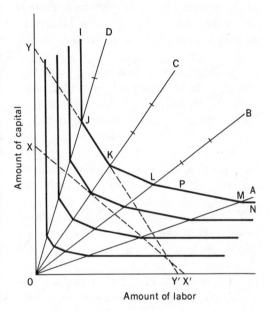

FIGURE **13.5** FOUR PROCESSES

equal to M'P on OA. This would lead to exactly the same results as the construction used in the text. The situation is analogous to the "parallelogram of forces" in physics.

[3] Proof: Process A at level OL' uses OQ' units of labor, Process B at level OM' uses OS' units of labor, together they use OQ' + OS' units of labor. But, by construction, L'P is equal and parallel to OM'. So Q'U = OS'. Therefore, OQ' + OS' = OQ' + Q'U = OU units of labor. The argument with respect to capital is similar.

[4] Proof: Let Output (X) denote the output corresponding to any point, X, on the diagram. Then Output (M')/Output (M) = OM'/OM and Output (L')/Output (L) = OL'/OL. By assumption: Output (L) = Output (M). So Output (M')/Output (L) = OM'/OM. Adding, we have:

$$\frac{\text{Output (M')} + \text{Output (L')}}{\text{Output (L)}}$$

$$= \frac{\text{OM'}}{\text{OM}} + \frac{\text{OL'}}{\text{OL}} = \frac{\text{L'P}}{\text{OM}} + \frac{\text{OL'}}{\text{OL}} = \frac{\text{L'L}}{\text{OL}} + \frac{\text{OL'}}{\text{OL}} = 1.$$

gram with four process lines shown. Point M represents a particular output by use of Process A and points L, K, J represent that same output by means of Processes B, C, D, respectively. The succession of line segments connecting these four points is the isoquant for that same output. It is easy to see that any other succession of line segments respectively parallel to those of MLKJ is also an isoquant. Three such are shown in the figure. It is instructive to compare Figure 13.5 with Figure 13.2 and note the strong resemblance in appearance as well as in interpretation.

We may draw price lines on Figure 13.5, just as on the conventional kind of isoquant diagram. The dashed lines XX' and YY' represent two possible price l:nes. Consider XX' first. As that line is drawn, the maximum output for a given expenditure can be obtained by use of Process C alone, and, conversely, the minimum cost for a given output is also obtained by using Process C alone. Thus, for the relative price regime represented by XX', Process C is optimal. The price line YY' is drawn parallel to the isoquant segment JK. In this case Process C is still optimal, but Process D is also optimal and so is any combination of the two.

It is evident from considering these two price lines, and as many others as the reader wishes to visualize, that an optimal production program can always be achieved by means of a single process, which process depending, of course, on the slope of the price line. It should be noted, however, that the conventional tangency criterion is no longer applicable.

We found in Figure 13.5 that an optimal economic plan need never use more than a single process for each of its outputs.[5] That conclusion is valid for the situation depicted, which assumed that the services of the two factors could be procured in any amounts desired at constant relative prices. This assumption is not applicable to many economic problems, nor is it used much in mathematical programming. We must now, therefore, take factor supply conditions into account.

III. FACTOR SUPPLIES AND COSTS

In mathematical programming it is usual to divide all factors of production into two classes: unlimited factors, which are available in any amount desired at constant unit cost, and limited or scarce factors, which are obtainable at constant unit cost up to a fixed maximum quantity

and thereafter not at all. The automobile example illustrates this classification. There the four types of capacity were treated as fixed factors available at zero variable cost; all other factors were grouped under direct costs which were considered as constant per unit of output.

The automobile example showed that this classification of factors is adequate for expressing the maximization problem of a firm dealing in competitive markets. In the last section we saw that when all factors are unlimited, this formulation can be used to find a minimum average cost point.

Both of these applications invoked restrictive assumptions and, furthermore, assumptions which conflict with those conventionally made in studying resource allocation. In conventional analysis we conceive that as the level of production of a firm, industry or economy rises, average unit costs rise also after some point. The increase in average costs is attributable in part to the working of the law of variable proportions,[6] which operates when the inputs of some but not all factors of production are increased. As far as the consequences of increasing some but not all inputs are concerned, the contrast between mathematical programming and the marginal analysis is more verbal than substantive. A reference to Figure 13.4 will show how such changes are handled in mathematical programming. Point J in Figure 13.4 represents the production of a certain output by the use of Process A alone. If it is desired to increase output without increasing the use of capital, this can be done by moving to the right along the dotted line JK, since this line cuts successively higher isoquants. Such a movement would correspond to using increasingly more of Process B and increasingly less of Process

---

[5] Recall, however, that we have not taken joint production into account nor have we considered the effects of considerations from the demand side.

[6] *Cf.* J. M. Cassels, "On the Law of Variable Proportions," in W. Fellner and B. F. Haley, eds., *Readings in the Theory of Income Distribution* (Philadelphia, 1946), pp. 103–18.

A and thus, indirectly, to substituting labor for capital. If, further, we assume that unit cost of production is lower for Process A than for Process B this movement would also correspond to increasing average cost of production. Thus both marginal analysis and mathematical programming lead to the same conclusion when factor proportions are changed: if the change starts from a minimum cost point the substitution will lead to gradually increasing unit costs.

But changing input proportions is only one part of the story according to the conventional type of analysis. If output is to be increased, any of three things may happen. First, it may be possible to increase the consumption of all inputs without incurring a change in their unit prices. In this case both mathematical programming and marginal analysis agree that output will be expanded without changing the ratios among the input quantities and average cost of production will not increase.[7] Second, it may not be possible to increase the use of some of the inputs. This is the case we have just analyzed. According to both modes of analysis the input ratios will change in this case and average unit costs will increase. The only difference between the two approaches is that if average cost is to be plotted against output, the marginal analyst will show a picture with a smoothly rising curve while the mathematical programmer will show a broken line made up of increasingly steep line segments. Third, it may be possible to increase the quantities of all inputs but only at the penalty of increasing unit prices or some kind of diseconomies of scale. This third case occurs in the marginal analysis, indeed it is the case which gives long-run cost curves their familiar shape, but mathematical programming has no counterpart for it.

[7] *Cf.* F. H. Knight, *Risk, Uncertainty and Profit* (Boston, 1921), p. 98.

The essential substantive difference we have arrived at is that the marginal analysis conceives of pecuniary and technical diseconomies associated with changes in scale while mathematical programming does not.[8] There are many important economic problems in which factor prices and productivities do not change in response to changes in scale or in which such variations can be disregarded. Most investigations of industrial capacity, for example, are of this nature. In such studies we seek the maximum output of an industry, regarding its inventory of physical equipment as given and assuming that the auxiliary factors needed to cooperate with the equipment can be obtained in the quantities dictated by the characteristics of the equipment. Manpower requirement studies are of the same nature. In such studies we take both output and equipment as given and calculate the manpower needed to operate the equipment at the level which will yield the desired output. Studies of full employment output fall into the same format. In such studies we determine in advance the quantity of each factor which is to be regarded as full employment of that factor. Then we calculate the optimum output obtainable by the use of the factors in those quantities.

These illustrations should suffice to show that the assumptions made in mathematical programming can comprehend a wide variety of important economic problems. The most useful applications of mathematical programming are probably to problems of the types just described, that is, to problems concerned with finding

[8] Even within the framework of the marginal analysis the concept of diseconomies of scale has been challenged on both theoretical and empirical grounds. For examples of empirical criticism see Committee on Price Determination, Conference on Price Research, *Cost Behavior and Price Policy* (New York, 1943). The most searching theoretical criticism is in Piero Sraffa, "The Laws of Returns under Competitive Conditions," *Econ. Jour.*, Dec. 1926, XXXVI, 535–50.

optimum production plans using specified quantities of some or all of the resources involved.

IV. ANALYSIS OF PRODUCTION WITH LIMITED FACTORS

The diagrams which we have developed are readily adaptable to the analysis of the consequences of limits on the factor supplies. Such limits are, of course, the heart of Figure 13.1 where the four principal lines represent limitations on the process levels which result from limits on the four factor quantities considered. But Figure 13.1 cannot be used when more than two processes have to be considered. For such problems diagrams like Figures 13.3, 13.4, and 13.5 have to be used.

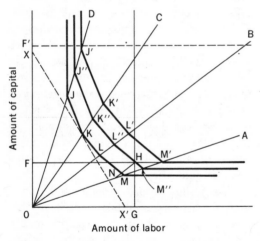

FIGURE 13.6 FOUR PROCESSES, WITH LIMITATIONS

Figure 13.6 reproduces the situation portrayed in Figure 13.5 with some additional data to be explained below. Let OF represent the maximum amount of capital which can be used and thus show a factor limitation. The horizontal line through F divides the diagram into two sections: all points above the line correspond to programs which require more capital than is available; points on and below the line

represent programs which do not have excessive capital requirements. This horizontal line will be called the capital limitation line. Points on or below it are called "feasible," points above it are called "infeasible."

The economic unit portrayed in Figure 13.6 has the choice of operating at any feasible point. If maximum output is its objective, it will choose a point which lies on the highest possible isoquant, *i.e.*, the highest isoquant which touches the capital limitation line. This is the one labelled J'K'L'M', and the highest possible output is attained by using Process A.

Of course, maximum output may not be the objective. The objective may be, for example, to maximize the excess of the value of output over labor costs. We shall refer to such an excess as a "net value." The same kind of diagram can be used to solve for a net value provided that the value of each unit of output is independent of the number of units produced [9] and that the cost of each unit of labor is similarly constant. If these provisos are met, each point on a process ray will correspond to a certain physical output but also to a certain value of output, cost of labor, and net value of output. Further, along any process ray the net value of output will equal the physical output times the net value per unit and will therefore be proportional to the physical output. We may thus use a diagram similar to Figure 13.6 except that we think of net value instead of physical output as measured along the process rays and we show isovalue line instead of isoquants. This has been done on Figure 13.7, in which the maximum net value attainable is the one which corresponds to the isovalue contour through point P, and is attained by using Process C.

It should be noted in both Figures 13.6

[9] This is a particularly uncomfortable assumption. We use it here to explain the method in its least complicated form.

and **13.7** that the optimal program consisted of a single process, that shifts in the quantity of capital available would not affect the designation of the optimal process though they would change its level, and that the price lines, which were crucial in Figure 13.5, played no rôle.

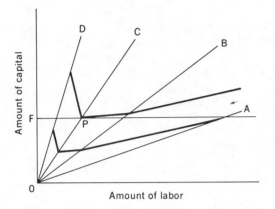

FIGURE **13.7** FOUR PROCESSES WITH ISOVALUE LINES

The next complication, and the last one we shall be able to consider, is to assume that both factors are in limited supply. This situation is portrayed in Figure 13.6 by adding the vertical line through point G to represent a labor limitation. The available quantity of labor is shown, of course, by the length OG. Then the points inside the rectangle OFHG represent programs which can be implemented in the sense that they do not require more than the available supplies of either factor. This is the rectangle of feasible programs. The greatest achievable output is the one which corresponds to the highest isoquant which touches the rectangle of feasible programs. This is the isoquant J″K″L″M″, and furthermore, since the maximum isoquant touches the rectangle at H, H represents the program by which the maximum output can be produced.

This solution differs from the previous ones in that the solution-point does not lie on any process ray but between the rays

for Processes A and B. We have already seen that a point like H represents using Process A at level ON and Process B at level NH.

Two remarks are relevant to this solution. First: with the factor limitation lines as drawn, the maximum output requires two processes. If the factor limitation lines had been drawn so that they intersected exactly on one of the process rays, only one process would have been required. If the factor limitation lines had crossed to the left of Process D or to the right of Process A, the maximizing production plan would require only one process. But, no matter how the limitation lines be drawn, at most two processes are required to maximize output. We are led to an important generalization: maximum output may always be obtained by using a number of processes which does not exceed the number of factors in limited supply, if this number is greater than zero. The conclusions we drew from Figures 13.6 and 13.7 both conform to this rule, and it is one of the basic theorems of mathematical programming.

Second: although at most two processes are required to obtain the maximum output, which two depends on the location of the factor limits. As shown, the processes used for maximum output were Processes A and B. If somewhat more capital, represented by the amount OF′, were available, the maximizing processes would have been Processes C and D. If two factors are limited, it is the ratio between their supplies rather than the absolute supplies of either which determines the processes in the optimum program. This contrasts with the case in which only one factor is limited. Just as the considerations which determine the optimum set of processes are more complicated when two factors are limited than when only one is, so with three or more limited factors the optimum conditions become more complicated still and soon pass the reach of intuition. This,

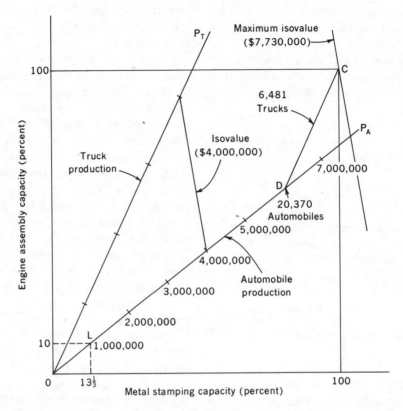

FIGURE **13.8**   AUTOMOBILE EXAMPLE, OPTIMAL PLAN

indeed, is the *raison d'être* of the formidable apparatus of mathematical programming.

We can make these considerations more concrete by applying them to the automobile example. Referring to Figure 13.1, we note that the optimum production point, C, lay on the limitation lines for engine assembly and metal stamping, but well below the limits for automobile and truck assembly. The limitations on automobile and truck assembly capacity are, therefore, ineffective and can be disregarded. The situation in terms of the two effectively limiting types of capacity is shown in Figure 13.8.

In Figure 13.8 the ray P_A represents the process of producing automobiles and P_T the process of producing trucks. These two processes can be operated at any combination of levels which does not require the use of more than 100 per cent of either metal stamping or engine assembly capacity. Thus the rectangle in the diagram is the region of feasible production programs. The optimal production program is the one in the feasible region which corresponds to the highest possible net revenue.[10] Thus it will be helpful to construct isorevenue lines, as we did in Figure 13.7. To do this, consider automobile production first. Each point on P_A corresponds to the production of a certain number of automobiles per month. Suppose, for example, that the scale is such that point L represents the production of 3,333 automobiles per month. It will be recalled that each automobile

[10] Since the objective of the firm is, by assumption, to maximize revenue rather than physical output, we may consider automobile and truck production as two alternative processes for producing revenue instead of as two processes with disparate outputs.

yields a net revenue of $300. Therefore, 3,333 automobiles yield a revenue of $1,000,000. Point L, then, corresponds to a net revenue of $1,000,000 as well as to an output of 3,333 automobiles per month. Since (see Figure 13.1), 3,333 automobiles require $13\frac{1}{3}$ per cent of metal stamping capacity and 10 per cent of engine assembly capacity, the coordinates of the $1,000,000 net revenue point on P_A are established at once. By a similar argument, the point whose coordinates are $26\frac{2}{3}$ per cent of metal stamping capacity and 20 per cent of engine capacity is the $2,000,000 net revenue point on P_A. In the same manner, the whole ray can be drawn and scaled off in terms of net revenue, and so can P_T, the process ray for truck production. The diagram is completed by connecting the $4,000,000 points on the two process lines in order to show the direction of the isorevenue lines.

The optimum program is at point C, where the two capacity limits intersect, because C lies on the highest isorevenue line which touches the feasible region. Through point C we have drawn a line parallel to the truck production line and meeting the automobile production line at D. By our previous argument, the length OD represents the net revenue from automobile production in the optimal program and the length DC represents the net revenue from trucks. If these lengths be scaled off, the result, of course, will be the same as the solution found previously.

V. IMPUTATION OF FACTOR VALUES

We have just noted that the major field of application of mathematical programming is to problems where the supply of one or more factors of production is absolutely limited. Such scarcities are the genesis of value in ordinary analysis, and they generate values in mathematical programming too. In fact, in ordinary analysis the determination of outputs and the determination of prices are but two aspects of the same problem, the optimal allocation of scarce resources. The same is true in mathematical programming.

Heretofore we have encountered prices only as data for determining the direct costs of processes and the net value of output. But of course the limiting factors of production also have value although we have not assigned prices to them up to now. In this section we shall see that the solution of a mathematical programming problem implicitly assigns values to the limiting factors of production. Furthermore, the implicit pricing problem can be solved directly and, when so solved, constitutes a solution to the optimal allocation problem.

Consider the automobile example and ask: how much is a unit (1 per cent) of each of the types of capacity worth to the firm? The approach to this question is similar in spirit to the familiar marginal analysis. With respect to each type of capacity we calculate how much the maximum revenue would increase if one more unit were added, or how much revenue would decrease if one unit were taken away. Since there is a surplus of automobile assembly capacity, neither the addition nor the subtraction of one unit of this type would affect the optimum program or the maximum net revenue. Hence the value of this type of capacity is nil. The analysis and result for truck assembly are the same.

We find, then, that these two types of capacity are free goods. This does not imply that an automobile assembly line is not worth having, any more than, to take a classic example, the fact that air is a free good means that it can be dispensed with. It means that it would not be worth while to increase this type of capacity at any positive price and that some units of these types could be disposed of without loss.

The valuation of the other types of capacity is not so trivial. In Figure 13.9 possible values per per cent of engine assembly capacity are scaled along the horizontal axis and values per per cent of metal stamping capacity are scaled along the vertical axis. Now consider any possible pair of values, say engine assembly capacity worth $20,000 per unit and metal stamping worth $40,000. This is represented by point A on the figure. Applying these values to the data on pages 174–175, the values of capacity required for producing an automobile is found to be: $(0.004 \times \$40,000) + (0.003 \times \$20,000) = \$220$ which is well under the value of producing an automobile, or $300.[11] In the same way, if engine assembly capacity is worth $60,000 per per cent of capacity and metal stamping capacity is valued at $30,000 per unit (point B), the cost of scarce resources required to produce an automobile will be exactly equal to the value of the product. This is clearly not the only combination of resource values which will precisely absorb the value of output when the resources are used to produce automobiles. The automobile production line in the figure, which passes through point B, is the locus of all such value combinations. A similar line has been drawn for truck production to represent those combinations of resource values for which the total value of resources used in producing trucks is equal to the value of output. The intersection of these two lines is obviously the only pair of resource values for which the marginal resource cost of producing an additional automobile is equal to the net value of an automobile and the same is true with respect to trucks. The pair can be found by plotting or, with more precision, by algebra. It is found that 1 per cent of engine assembly capacity is worth $9,259 and 1 per cent of metal stamping capacity is worth $68,056.

To each pair of values for the two types of capacity, there corresponds a value for the entire plant. Thus to the pair of values represented by point A there corresponds the plant value of $(100 \times \$20,000) +$

[11] These unit values are also marginal values since costs of production are constant.

$(100 \times \$40,000) = \$6,000,000$. This is not the only pair of resource values which give an aggregate plant value of $6,000,000. Indeed, any pair of resource values on the dotted line through A corresponds to the same aggregate plant value. (By this stage, Figure 13.9 should become strongly reminiscent of Figure 13.1.) We have drawn a number of dotted lines parallel to the one just described, each corresponding to a specific aggregate plant value. The dotted line which passes through the intersection of the two production lines is of particular interest. By measurement or otherwise this line can be found to correspond to a plant value of $7,731,500 which, we recall, was found to be the maximum attainable net revenue.

Let us consider the implications of assigning values to the two limiting factors from a slightly different angle. We have seen that as soon as unit values have been assigned to the factors an aggregate value is assigned to the plant. We can make the aggregate plant value as low as we please, simply by assigning sufficiently low values to the various factors. But if the values assigned are too low, we have the unsatisfactory consequence that some of the processes will give rise to unimputed surpluses. We may, therefore, seek the lowest aggregate plant value which can be assigned and still have no process yield an unimputed surplus. In the automobile case, that value is $7,731,500. In the course of finding the lowest acceptable plant value we find specific unit values to be assigned to each of the resources.

In this example there are two processes and four limited resources. It turns out that only two of the resources were effectively limiting, the others being in relatively ample supply. In general, the characteristics of the solution to a programming problem depend on the relationship between the number of limited resources and the number of processes taken into consideration. If, as in the present instance, the number

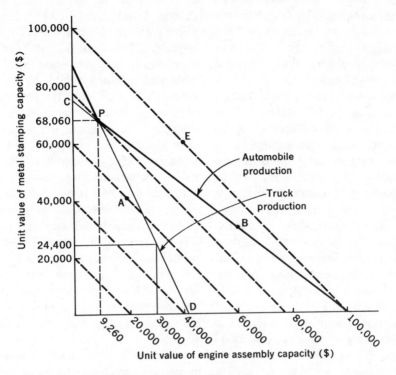

FIGURE **13.9**   AUTOMOBILE EXAMPLE, IMPLICIT VALUE

of limited resources exceeds the number of processes it will usually turn out that some of the resources will have imputed values of zero and that the number of resources with positive imputed values will be equal to the number of processes.[12] If the number of limited resources equals the number of processes all resources will have positive imputed values. If, finally, the number of processes exceeds the number of limited resources, some of the processes will not be used in the optimal program. This situation, which is the usual one, was illustrated in Figure 13.6. In this case the total imputed value of resources absorbed will equal net revenue for some processes and will exceed it for others. The number of processes for which the imputed value of resources absorbed equals the net revenue

will be just equal to the number of limited resources and the processes for which the equality holds are the ones which will appear at positive levels in the optimal program. In brief, the determination of the minimum acceptable plant value amounts to the same thing as the determination of the optimal production program. The programming problem and the valuation problem are not only closely related, they are basically the same.

This can be seen graphically by comparing Figures 13.1 and 13.9. Each figure contains two axes and two diagonal boundary lines. But the boundary lines in Figure 13.9 refer to the same processes as the axes in Figure 13.1, and the axes in Figure 13.9 refer to the same resources as the diagonal boundary lines in Figure 13.1. Furthermore, in using Figure 13.1 we sought the net revenue corresponding to the highest dashed line touched by the boundary; in using Figure 13.9 we sought the aggregate

[12] We say "usually" in this sentence because in some special circumstances the number of resources with positive imputed values may exceed the number of processes.

value corresponding to the lowest dashed line which has any points on or outside the boundary; and the two results turned out to be the same. Formally stated, these two figures and the problems they represent are *duals* of each other.

The dualism feature is a very useful property in the solution of mathematical programming problems. The simplest way to see this is to note that when confronting a mathematical programming problem we have the choice of solving the problem or its dual, whichever is easier. Either way we can get the same results. We can use this feature now to generalize our discussion somewhat. Up to now when dealing with more than two processes we have had to use relatively complicated diagrams like Figure 13.6 because straightforward diagrams like Figure 13.1 did not contain enough axes to represent the levels of the processes. Now we can use diagrams modeled on Figure 13.9 to depict problems with any number of processes so long as they do not involve more than two scarce factors. Figure 13.10 illustrates a diagram for four processes and is, indeed, derived from Figure 13.6. In Figure 13.10 line A repre-

sents all pairs of factor values such that Process A would yield neither a profit nor a loss. Lines B, C, and D are similarly interpreted. The dashed line T is a locus along which the aggregate value of the labor and capital available to the firm (or industry) is constant. Its position is not relevant to the analysis; its slope, which is simply the ratio of the quantity of available labor to that of capital, is all that is significant. The broken line JKLMN divides the graph into two regions. All points on or above it represent pairs of resource values such that no process gives rise to an unimputed surplus. Let us call this the acceptable region. For each point below that broken line there is at least one process which does have an unimputed surplus. This is the unacceptable region. We then seek for that point in the acceptable region which corresponds to the lowest aggregate plant value. This point will, of course, give the set of resource values which makes the accounting profit of the firm as great as possible without giving rise to any unimputed income. The point which meets these requirements is K, and a dotted line parallel to T has been drawn through it to

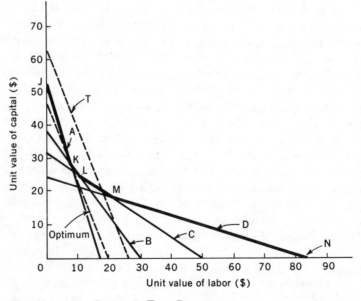

FIGURE 13.10   THE VALUATION PROBLEM, FOUR PROCESSES

indicate the minimum acceptable aggregate plant value.

At point K Processes A and B yield zero profits, and Processes C and D yield losses. Hence Processes A and B are the ones which should be used, exactly as we found in Figure 13.6. To be sure, this diagram does not tell the levels at which A and B should be used, any more than Figure 13.6 tells the valuations to be placed on the two resources. But finding the levels after the processes have been selected is a comparatively trivial matter. All that is necessary is to find the levels which will fully utilize the resources which are not free goods. This may be done algebraically or by means of a diagram like Figure 13.8.

VI. APPLICATIONS

In the first section we asserted that the principal motivation of mathematical programming was the need for a method of analysis which lent itself to the practical solution of the day-to-day problems of business and the economy in general. Immediately after making that claim we introduced a highly artificial problem followed by a rather extended discussion of abstract and formal relationships. The time has now come to indicate the basis for saying that mathematical programming is a practical method of analysis.

The essential simplification achieved in mathematical programming is the replacement of the notion of the production function by the notion of the process. The process is a highly observable unit of activity and the empirical constants which characterize it can be estimated without elaborate analysis. Furthermore in many industries the structure of production corresponds to operating a succession of processes, as we have conceived them. Many industrial decisions, like shutting down a bank of machines or operating an extra shift, correspond naturally to our concept of choosing the level of operation of a process. In brief, mathematical programming is modelled after the actual structure of production in the hope that thereby it will involve only observable constants and directly controllable variables.

Has this hope been justified? The literature already contains a report of a successful application to petroleum refining.[13] I have made a similar application which, perhaps, will bear description. The application was to a moderate-sized refinery which produces premium and regular grades of automotive gasoline. The essential operation studied was blending. In blending, ten chemically distinct kinds of semirefined oil, called blending stocks, are mixed together. The result is a saleable gasoline whose characteristics are approximately the weighted average of the characteristics of the blending stocks. For example, if 500 gallons of a stock with octane rating of 80 are blended with 1,000 gallons of a stock with octane rating of 86 the result will be $500 + 1,000 = 1,500$ gallons of product with octane rating of $(\frac{1}{3} \times 80) + (\frac{2}{3} \times 86) = 84$.

The significant aspect of gasoline blending for our present purposes is that the major characteristics of the blend—its knock rating, its vapor pressure, its sulphur content, etc.—can be expressed as linear functions of the quantities of the various blending stocks used. So also can the cost of the blend if each of the blending stocks has a definite price per gallon. Thus the problem of finding the minimum cost blend which will meet given quality specifications is a problem in mathematical programming.

Furthermore, in this refinery the quantities of some of the blending stocks are definitely limited by contracts and by refining capacity. The problem then arises: what are the most profitable quantities of output

[13] A. Charnes, W. W. Cooper, and B. Mellon, "Blending Aviation Gasolines," *Econometrica*, Apr. 1952, XX, 135–59.

of regular and premium gasoline, and how much of each blending stock should be used for each final product. This problem is analogous to the artificial automobile example, with the added complication of the quality specifications. The problem is too complicated for graphic analysis but was solved easily by arithmetical procedures. As far as is known, mathematical programming provides the only way for solving such problems. Charnes and Cooper have recently published the solution to a similar problem which arose in the operations of a metal-working firm.[14]

An entirely different kind of problem, also amenable to mathematical programming, arises in newsprint production. Freight is a major element in the cost of newsprint. One large newsprint company has six mills, widely scattered in Canada, and some two hundred customers, widely scattered in the United States. Its problem is to decide how much newsprint to ship from each mill to each customer so as, first, to meet the contract requirements of each customer, second, to stay within the capacity limits of each mill, and third, to keep the aggregate freight bill as small as possible. This problem involves 1,200 variables (6 mills × 200 customers), in contrast to the two or four variable problems we have been discussing. In the final solution most of these variables will turn out to be zero —the question is which ones. This problem is solved by mathematical programming and, though formidable, is not really as formidable as the count of variables might indicate.

These few illustrations should suffice to indicate that mathematical programming is a practical tool for business planning. They show, also, that it is a flexible tool because both examples deviated from the

format of the example used in our exposition. The petroleum application had the added feature of quality specification. In the newsprint application there were limits on the quantity of output as well as on the quantities of the inputs. Nevertheless mathematical programming handled them both easily.

On the other hand, it should be noted that both of these were small-scale applications, dealing with a single phase of the operation of a single firm. I believe that this has been true of all successful applications to date. Mathematical programmers are still a long way from solving the broad planning problem of entire industries or an entire economy. But many such broad problems are only enlarged versions of problems which have been met and solved in the context of the single firm. It is no longer premature to say that mathematical programming has proved its worth as a practical tool for finding optimal economic programs.

VII. CONCLUSION

Our objective has been only to introduce the basic notions of mathematical programming and to invest them with plausibility and meaning. The reader who would learn to solve a programming problem—even the simplest—will have to look elsewhere,[15] though this paper may serve as a useful background.

Although methods of solution have been omitted from this exposition, we must emphasize that these methods are fundamental to the whole concept of mathematical programming. Some eighty years ago Walras conceived of production in very much the

---

[14] A. Charnes, W. W. Cooper, and Donald Farr and Staff, "Linear Programming and Profit Preference Scheduling for a Manufacturing Firm," *Jour. Operations Research Society of America*, May 1953, I, 114–129.

[15] The standard reference is T. C. Koopmans, ed., *Activity Analysis of Production and Allocation* (New York, 1951). Less advanced treatments may be found in A. Charnes, W. W. Cooper, and A. Henderson, *An Introduction to Linear Programming* (New York, 1953); and my own *Application of Linear Programming to the Theory of the Firm* (Berkeley, 1951).

same manner as mathematical programmers, and more recently A. Wald and J. von Neumann used this view of production and methods closely allied to those of mathematical programming to analyze the conditions of general economic equilibrium.[16] These developments, however, must be regarded merely as precursors of mathematical programming. Programming had no independent existence as a mode of economic analysis until 1947 when G. B. Dantzig announced the "simplex method" of solution which made practical application feasible.[17] The existence of a method whereby economic optima could be explicitly calculated stimulated research into the economic interpretation of mathematical programming and led also to the development of alternative methods of solution. The fact that economic and business problems when formulated in terms of mathematical programming can be solved numerically is the basis of the importance of the method. The omission of methods of solution from this discussion should not, therefore, be taken to indicate that they are of secondary interest.

We have considered only a few of the concepts used in mathematical programming and have dealt with only a single type of programming problem. The few notions we have considered, however, are the basic ones; all the rest of mathematical programming is elaboration and extension of them. It seems advisable to mention two

directions of elaboration, for they remove or weaken two of the most restrictive assumptions which have here been imposed.

The first of these extensions is the introduction of time into the analysis. The present treatment has dealt with a single production period in isolation. But in many cases, successive production periods are interrelated. This is so, for example, in the case of a vertically integrated firm where the operation of some processes in one period is limited by the levels of operation in the preceding period of the processes which supply their raw materials. Efficient methods for analyzing such "dynamic" problems are being investigated, particularly by George Dantzig.[18] Although the present discussion has been static, the method of analysis can be applied to problems with a time dimension.

The second of these extensions is the allowance for changes in the prices of factors and final products. In our discussion we regarded all prices as unalterable and independent of the actions of the economic unit under consideration. Constant prices are, undeniably, a great convenience to the analyst, but the method can transcend this assumption when necessary. The general mathematical theory of dealing with variable prices has been investigated [19] and practical methods of solution have been developed for problems where the demand and supply curves are linear.[20] The assumption of constant prices, perhaps the most restrictive assumption we have made, is adopted for convenience rather than from necessity.

[16] Walras' formulation is in *Éléments d'économie politique pure ou théorie de la richesse sociale,* 2d ed. (Lausanne, 1889), 20ᵉ Leçon. The contributions of A. Wald and J. von Neumann appeared originally in *Ergebnisse eines mathematischen Kolloquiums,* Nos. 6, 7, 8. Wald's least technical paper appeared in *Zeitschrift für Nationalökonomie,* VII (1936) and has been translated as "On some Systems of Equations of Mathematical Economics," *Econometrica,* Oct. 1951, XIX, 368–403. Von Neumann's basic paper appeared in translation as "A Model of General Economic Equilibrium," *Rev. Econ. Stud.,* 1945–46, XIII, 1–9.

[17] G. B. Dantzig, "Maximization of a Linear Function of Variables Subject to Linear Inequalities," T. C. Koopmans, ed., *op. cit.,* pp. 339–47.

[18] "A Note on a Dynamic Leontief Model with Substitution" (abstract), *Econometrica,* Jan. 1953, XXI, 179.

[19] See H. W. Kuhn and A. W. Tucker, "Non-Linear Programming," in J. Neyman, ed., *Proceedings of the Second Berkeley Symposium on Mathematical Statistics and Probability* (Berkeley, 1951), pp. 481–92.

[20] I reported one solution of this problem to a seminar at the Massachusetts Institute of Technology in September 1952. Other solutions may be known.

Mathematical programming has been developed as a tool for economic and business planning and not primarily for the descriptive, and therefore predictive, purposes which gave rise to the marginal analysis. Nevertheless it does have predictive implications. In so far as firms operate under the conditions assumed in mathematical programming it would be unreasonable to assume that they acted as if they operated under the conditions assumed by the marginal analysis. Consider, for example, the automobile firm portrayed in Figure 13.1. How would it respond if the price of automobiles were to fall, say by $50 a unit? In that case the net revenue per automobile would be $250, the same as the net revenue per truck. Diagrammatically, the result would be to rotate the lines of equal revenue until their slope was 45 degrees. After this rotation, point C would still be optimum and this change in prices would cause no change in optimum output. Mathematical programming gives rise, thus, to a kinked supply curve.

On the other hand, suppose that the price of automobiles were to rise by $50. Diagrammatically this price change would decrease the steepness of the equal revenue lines until they were just parallel to the metal stamping line. The firm would then be in a position like that illustrated by the YY′ line in Figure 13.5. The production plans corresponding to points on the line segment DC in Figure 13.1 would all yield the same net revenue and all would be optimal. If the prices of automobiles were to rise by more than $50 or if a $50 increase in the price of automobiles were accompanied by any decrease in the price of trucks, the point of optimal production would jump abruptly from point C to point D.

Thus mathematical programming indicates that firms whose choices are limited to distinct processes will respond discontinuously to price variations: they will be insensitive to price changes over a certain range and will change their levels of output sharply as soon as that range is passed. This theoretical deduction surely has real counterparts.

The relationship between mathematical programming and welfare economics is especially close. Welfare economics studies the optimal organization of economic effort; so does mathematical programming. This relationship has been investigated especially by Koopmans and Samuelson.[21] The finding, generally stated, is that the equilibrium position of a perfectly competitive economy is the same as the optimal solution to the mathematical programming problem embodying the same data.

Mathematical programming is closely allied mathematically to the methods of input-output analysis or interindustry analysis developed largely by W. W. Leontief.[22] The two methods were developed independently, however, and it is important to distinguish them conceptually. Input-output analysis finds its application almost exclusively in the study of general economic equilibrium. It conceives of an economy as divided into a number of industrial sectors each of which is analogous to a process as the term is used in mathematical programming. It then takes either of two forms. In "open models" an input-output analysis starts with some specified final demand for the products of each of the sectors and calculates the level at which each of the sector-processes must operate in order to meet this schedule of final demands. In "closed models" final demand does not appear but attention is concentrated on the fact that the inputs required by each sector-process must be supplied as outputs by some other sector-processes. Input-output analysis then calculates a mutually compatible set of

[21] T. C. Koopmans, "Analysis of Production as an Efficient Combination of Activities," in T. C. Koopmans, ed., *op. cit.*, pp. 33–97; P. A. Samuelson, "Market Mechanisms and Maximization" (a paper prepared for the Rand Corp., 1949).
[22] W. W. Leontief, *The Structure of American Economy 1919–1939*, 2nd. ed. (New York, 1951).

output levels for the various sectors. By contrast with mathematical programming the conditions imposed in input-output analysis are sufficient to determine the levels of the processes and there is no scope for finding an optimal solution or a set of "best" levels. To be sure, input-output analysis can be regarded as a special case of mathematical programming in which the number of products is equal to the number of processes. On the other hand, the limitations on the supplies of resources which play so important a rôle in mathematical programming are not dealt with explicitly in input-output analysis. On the whole it seems best to regard these two techniques as allied but distinct methods of analysis addressed to different problems.

Mathematical programming, then, is of significance for economic thinking and theory as well as for business and economic planning. We have been able only to allude to this significance. Indeed, apart from the exploration of welfare implications, very little thought has been given to the consequences for economics of mathematical programming because most effort has been devoted to solving the numerous practical problems to which it gives rise. The outlook is for fruitful researches into both the implications and applications of mathematical programming.

Part V

MARKET STRUCTURES

The Polar Cases
of Competition and Monopoly

14. What Is
Perfect Competition?*

JOAN ROBINSON

Joan Robinson, Reader of Economics in Girton College, Cambridge, was born in 1903 and educated at Cambridge University. She is among the most distinguished economic theorists of our time. Her publications include *The Economics of Imperfect Competition, Essays in the Theory of Employment, Introduction to the Theory of Employment, Essay on Marxian Economics, The Accumulation of Capital, Collected Economic Papers,* and *Economic Philosophy.* Joan Robinson's pathbreaking work on imperfect competition, in which she developed many of the most important instruments in the economist's "kit of tools," will assure her a lasting place in economic history. She has, through her work on capital accumulation, contributed to the revival of interest in the problems of classical economics.

What do we mean by "perfect competition"? The phrase is made to cover so many separable ideas, and is used in so many distinct senses, that it has become almost valueless as a means of communication. It seems best therefore to begin with a definition. By perfect competition I propose to mean a state of affairs in which the demand for the output of an individual seller is perfectly elastic.

This is a far more restricted definition than that which is to be found in many modern writings. To Professor Knight, for instance, perfect competition entails rational conduct on the part of buyers and sellers, full knowledge, absence of frictions, perfect mobility and perfect divisibility of factors of production, and completely static conditions.[1] This definition is unusually wide. More commonly these various strands of thought are separated from each other and the term "perfect competition" applied only to some of them. There are, however, two notions which seem to be very closely linked in many minds and lumped together as "perfect competition." These are, first, a situation in which a single seller cannot influence price (that is perfect competition in my terminology) and second, a situation in which a single seller cannot make more than normal profits. Leaving all the rest on one side I wish to

* Reprinted by permission of the publishers from Joan Robinson, *The Quarterly Journal of Economics* (November 1934). Cambridge, Mass.: Harvard University Press. Copyright, 1934, by the President and Fellows of Harvard College, pp. 104–120.

[1] *Risk, Uncertainty, and Profit,* pp. 76–80.

confine myself to discussing only these two meanings of the phrase "perfect competition."

Mr. Sraffa, whose article[2] of 1926 took such an important part in the work of emancipating economic analysis from the tyranny of the assumption of perfect competition, was not himself completely aware of the freedom that he was winning for us. He was content to say that when competition is imperfect there is no need to consider the problem of normal profits and the entry of new firms into an industry, since the entry of new firms into an imperfect market must necessarily be difficult.[3] But it is a simple step to carry Mr. Sraffa's own argument to its logical conclusion. He had shown that in the real world almost every market is imperfect, and it would be impossible to contend that in the real world new firms hardly ever enter any industry. In 1930 Mr. Shove[4] was still adopting a somewhat ambiguous attitude to the question and failed to snap completely the connection between the notion of perfect competition and the notion of free entry into an industry.

Professor Chamberlin in 1933 performed a useful service in categorically separating the two ideas. He distinguishes between "pure competition" and "perfect competition."[5] *Pure* competition is a state of affairs in which the demand for the output of each firm is perfectly elastic[6] while *perfect*

competition may be conceived to require the further conditions of "an ideal fluidity or mobility of factors," "absence of uncertainty,"[7] or "such further 'perfection' as the particular theorist finds convenient and useful to his problem." Here the issue is clearly stated. But Professor Chamberlin's terminology is somewhat misleading, and pays a verbal tribute to the old confusion. It seems better boldly to define *perfect* competition in the terms which he confines to *pure* competition and so to force the particular theorist to state specifically what further conditions he finds it useful to assume for the purposes of each problem.

In his article on "Doctrines of Imperfect Competition"[8] Mr. Harrod appears at first sight to follow this procedure, and his definition of "perfect competition" is the same as my own. But in the course of his argument it becomes clear that even for him "perfect competition" implies free entry.[9] It therefore seems desirable, before discussing the conception of a perfectly elastic demand, for the output of an individual seller to say something about the other strand of thought which has been entangled with it—the notion of normal profits.

The idea of normal profits in its most naïve form is the idea of a single general level of profits. Profits in any one industry, on this view, are normal when they are the same as profits in the generality of other industries. But there is obviously no more reason to expect a uniform level of profit for enterprise than there is to expect a uniform level of rent for land. In the world depicted in the well-known beginners' question, in which all land is alike in respect of fertility and site value, there is a uniform rate of rent per acre in the long period.

---

[2] "The Laws of Returns under Competitive Conditions," *Economic Journal*, December 1926.
[3] *Ibid.*, p. 549.
[4] "Symposium on Increasing Returns and the Representative Firm," *Economic Journal*, March 1930.
[5] *The Theory of Monopolistic Competition*, p. 6.
[6] Professor Chamberlin does not give quite this account of "pure competition." He says, "Purity requires only the absence of monopoly, which is realized when there are many buyers and sellers of the *same* (perfectly standardized) product" (*op. cit.*, p. 25). These conditions, as we shall find, are unnecessarily severe, but by "absence of monopoly" he appears to mean a state of affairs in which no one firm can raise its price without

sacrificing the whole of its sales, and this is the essential point.
[7] Professor Chamberlin is here referring to Professor Knight, *loc. cit.*
[8] In this Journal, May 1934, p. 443.
[9] *Loc. cit.*, p. 460.

In a world in which all entrepreneurs are alike there would be a uniform rate of profit in all industries in the long period. In the real world entrepreneurship is no more homogeneous than land in the real world. This view of uniform normal profits may therefore be dismissed as a beginner's simplification. The idea that there is one level of profits which obtains in competitive industries, and that when competition is not perfect profits must exceed this level, is clearly untenable.

Indeed, this is one of those problems in which the main difficulty is to see what the difficulty is. Normal profits are simply the supply price of entrepreneurship to a particular industry. The essence of the notion of normal profits is that when profits are more than normal, new firms will enter the trade, and normal profits are simply the profits which prevail when there is no tendency for the number of firms to alter. It is possible, of course, that the number of firms may be arbitrarily restricted. The firms may require a license from some controlling authority, or the existing firms may be so strong that they are able to fend off fresh competition by the threat of a price war. They may even resort to violence to prevent fresh rivals from appearing on the scene. In such cases no level of profits, however high, will be great enough to tempt new firms into the trade, and the supply of enterprise to that trade is perfectly inelastic at the existing amount. For such an industry any level of profits is normal, and the term ceases to have a useful application.

In all less extreme cases there will be some elasticity of supply of new enterprise, which may be small or great according to the circumstances of the trade. The normal level of profits will be different in different industries and different at different scales of the same industry, and the level of normal profits will depend upon the conditions of supply of enterprise. Trades which require unusual personal ability or special qualifications, such as the power to command a large amount of capital for the initial investment, will tend to have a high level of normal profits; trades which are easy to enter will have a lower level.

Now there is nothing in all this which is connected with the notion of perfect competition, in the sense in which I use that phrase. It is true that a high level of normal profits will often be found where competition is imperfect. The fact that an old-established firm enjoys "good will" has the effect both of giving it a hold upon the market which enables it to influence the price of the commodity which it sells and of increasing the cost of entry to new rivals. And the powerful firm which uses the methods of "unfair competition" to strangle rivals is highly unlikely to be selling in a perfect market. But this association of high normal profits (not abnormally high profits) with imperfect competition is a purely empirical one. The two conceptions are analytically quite distinct, and we shall have made a considerable advance towards clear analysis when we have learned habitually to distinguish them.

But quite apart from this gratuitous confusion the whole notion of normal profits is beset with difficulties. Mr. Shove[10] has pointed out that there is not one level of normal profits, but two. The level of profits which will attract new enterprise into an industry is usually higher than the level which is just sufficient to retain existing enterprise. Entry into a trade is likely to involve considerable initial expense, and often involves, as Marshall was fond of pointing out, a lean period of low profits before the name of the firm becomes known. To move out of this trade into another would involve fresh sacrifice. "When you are in you are in" and if demand falls after you are established you will prefer to stay where you are at a level of reward that would not have tempted you to enter the trade if you had the choice still to make.

[10] *Economic Journal,* March 1933, pp. 119–121.

This notion of a gap between the two levels of normal profits is associated by Mr. Harrod with imperfect competition.[11] And it must be conceded that a gap is likely to occur wherever good will is important, so that in fact the phenomenon is likely to be found in many industries where the market is imperfect. But it is important to realize that there is no necessary connection between the two ideas. The existence of the gap depends upon costs of movement from one industry to another, and these may very well occur when competition is perfect. Moreover, competition may be imperfect, for instance from differential transport charges, when there are no costs of movement. A gap between the upper level of reward, necessary to tempt new resources into an industry, and the lower level, necessary to drive old resources out, will exist wherever there is cost of movement between one trade and another, and the double level of normal profits is merely one example of a phenomenon which may affect every factor of production equally.

A general discussion of the phenomenon of the gap would lead us far afield, and in the present paper I propose only to inquire whether the existence of the gap destroys the usefulness of the notion of normal profits. Before tackling this question it is necessary to make a digression upon the manner in which equilibrium is attained. When we are considering discontinuous changes in the number of firms in an industry the existence of the gap between the two levels of profits is a very serious matter. When profits are more than normal in a certain industry a number of fresh entrepreneurs (each in ignorance of the others' action) come into the trade. With this new competition actual profits are depressed much below the level that tempted

[11] See Harrod, *Economic Journal*, June 1933, p. 337 and this Journal, May 1934, p. 457. In the latter article Mr. Harrod, if I understand him aright, uses the phrase "excess profit" to describe any surplus above the lower normal level.

in the new entrepreneurs, but they are not perhaps low enough to drive out any existing firms. The industry will continue at this swollen size, and it will be in equilibrium in the sense that no new enterprise tends to enter it or old enterprise to leave it. Yet the actual size of the industry, the price of the commodity, and the level of profits ruling, are determined by the number of firms, which is determined by the excessive optimism of the latest entrants. In such a case the supply price of any amount of output depends to a large extent upon the immediate past history of the industry. If fewer firms had happened to enter in the period of high profits the present price of a given output would have been higher; if more had entered it would have been lower. The whole notion of a unique long-period supply curve breaks down, and with the notion of a supply curve the notion of normal profits goes by the board.

In order therefore to justify the notion of a supply curve at all we must make the artificial assumption that equilibrium is attained by a gradual and continuous movement. When profits are more than normal a few firms enter. Profits decline; if they are still more than normal a new firm comes in, and another, and another, until profits are just reduced to the upper normal level and there is no incentive for one fresh firm to enter. Equilibrium is thus reached without oscillation. Similarly, when profits fall below the lower normal level first one then another decides to abandon the struggle, and profits for those that remain are gradually raised till each of the remaining firms is contented with its lot, and no more find it worth while to leave.

This account of the matter is obviously extremely unrealistic if we have to do with large erratic movements of demand. But if demand is expanding or contracting continuously it is plausible to suppose that firms enter or leave the industry one by one. I think, therefore, that in order to retain the idea of a long-period supply curve we may permit ourselves to take this view of the process of reaching equilibrium. And then the existence of two levels of profits introduces only a minor complication into the analysis.

There are two supply curves, one above the other. The upper one applies only to expansions of the industry, and the lower one applies only to contractions.

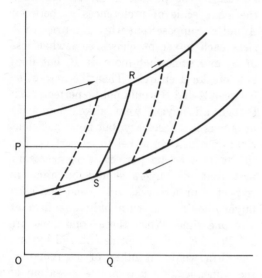

FIGURE 14.1

Each point on the upper curve is joined to that point on the lower curve at which the number of firms is the same by what I call a "quasi-long-period supply curve" [12]—the supply curve of a fixed number of firms. This is determined under perfect competition by the marginal cost curves of the given number of firms. Suppose we are considering an expansion of demand, and we start from a position in which price is *OP* and output *OQ*. Then as demand is raised supply price climbs up the quasi-long-period supply curve to *R*, and then proceeds (for further increases of demand) along the upper long-period supply curve to the right. Now suppose that we start from the same point and consider a contraction

[12] *Economics of Imperfect Competition*, p. 47.

of demand. Then supply price slides down the quasi-long-period curve to *S* and for further contractions of demand supply price follows the lower long-period curve to the left.

The quasi-long-period position does of course depend upon past history. There is a continuous series of quasi-long-period curves, and which curve we are on at any moment depends upon the number of firms in existence at that moment, just as the familiar short-period curve depends upon the amount of fixed plant that there happens to be in the industry. But the pair of long-period curves is as much uniquely determined as the old-style single long-period curve ever was.[13] By making an admittedly unrealistic assumption about the way in which equilibrium is attained we can rescue the long-period supply curve from the perils of the gap between the upper and lower levels of normal profits.

So much for normal profits. Leaving all this on one side let us return to the main question. What is perfect competition? Let us take our stand boldly on the formal definition and see what it requires of us.

Competition is perfect when the demand for the output of any one firm individually is perfectly elastic. In what conditions can this be true? We are accustomed to say that there are two conditions:

1. That the market must be perfect.
2. That the number of firms must be large.

Let us examine these two conditions in turn.

The first condition, that the market must be perfect, was dealt with by Mr. Sraffa. Marshall writes, "The more nearly perfect

[13] The width of the gap depends upon the length of the period in respect to which the curves are drawn. For some industries, in a sufficiently long period, there will be no gap at all; for others a considerable gap would be found even if an indefinitely long period were taken into account. The familiar short-period supply curve bridges the gap at its widest point.

a market is, the stronger is the tendency for the same price to be paid for the same thing at the same time in all parts of the market; but of course if the market is large, allowance must be made for the expense of delivering the goods to different purchasers." [14] Mr. Sraffa pointed out[15] that absence of frictions is not sufficient to make a market perfect, since buyers may have good and permanent reasons for preferring the output of one firm to that of another, while the presence of differential transport costs may be sufficient by itself to make the market imperfect. Moreover, he showed that the condition that the same price shall rule throughout the market is not adequate to define perfection, for if all the firms in an industry are alike in respect both to the costs and the conditions of demand, the same price will rule throughout the market no matter how imperfect it may be.

Professor Chamberlin's attitude to the perfection of the market is not quite clear. He seems to associate imperfection simply with differentiation of the product.[16] But the relationship between differentiation of the commodity and imperfection of the market is somewhat complicated. Physical differentiation is not a *necessary* condition for market imperfection. Two commodities may be alike in every respect except the names of the firms producing them, and yet the market in which they are sold will be imperfect if different buyers have different scales of preference as between the two firms. Nor is differentiation a *sufficient* condition for market imperfection. Two firms may be producing two distinct commodities and yet these two commodities may be sold against each other in a perfect market. Suppose that every individual buyer will pay 6*d*. more for *A* than for *B*, and that everyone buys either *A* or *B*, never some of each. Then when *B* is selling

at 1/– the smallest rise in the price of *A* above 1/6 will cause every buyer to transfer his custom to *B*, and the sales of *A* will cease; and the smallest fall in the price of *A* below 1/6 will increase its sales by an amount equal to the whole output of *B*. The demand for either *A* or *B*, given the price of the other, is perfectly elastic, although they are two distinct commodities.

On the other hand the market will not necessarily be perfect if all buyers have the same scale of preferences as between *A* and *B*. Suppose that when the price of *A* rises each buyer purchases somewhat less of *A*, and somewhat more of *B*, but does not forsake *A* entirely. Then the market as between *A* and *B* would not be perfect, even though all buyers were alike. Similarity of buyers is a necessary, but not a sufficient condition for the market to be perfect. For the market to be perfect it is necessary first that all buyers should be alike in respect to preferences, and second that each buyer should deal with only one firm at any one time. When these conditions are fulfilled a rise in the price charged by any one firm would, if other prices remained the same, lead to a complete cessation of its sales. And this is the criterion of a perfect market.

The definition of a commodity is completely arbitrary, and the definition of a market depends upon the definition of a commodity. Suppose that we start with a single quality of a certain perfectly homogeneous product, offered for sale by a firm at a single place and time, and group with it all other products which satisfy the condition of market perfection. In most cases we shall reach the boundary of the perfect market even before we have reached the boundary of the output of a single firm. Now let us agree upon a certain degree of imperfection in the market and group together all products in respect to which the imperfection has less than the agreed value. This group of products may be described as a single commodity. Often we

[14] *Principles of Economics,* p. 325.
[15] *Loc. cit.,* p. 542.
[16] *Op. cit.,* Chapter IV. Mr. Harrod adopts the same view, in this Journal, May 1934, p. 445.

can fix a convenient boundary by obvious natural landmarks, so that within it we have products which are all obviously in an everyday sense a single commodity (steam-coal, or chewing-gum) and all products outside the boundary are other commodities. But at best there must be some arbitrary element in drawing the boundary, and all products must be regarded as a continuous series in more or less close rivalry with each other. Thus the first prerequisite of perfect competition is a "commodity" clearly demarcated from others by a boundary of natural gaps in the chain of substitutes, within which the market is perfect.

The second condition required for perfect competition is that the number of firms selling within the market is such that when any one firm alters its price there is no consequent alteration in the prices charged by the others. It is this condition that we must now examine.

First it is necessary to stop up a blind alley that might lead us astray. It is sometimes supposed that for competition to be perfect it is necessary that the number of buyers should be large.[17] But this is the reverse of the truth. If there is only one buyer the market for each firm must be perfect, since a relative lowering of the price by any firm would cause the single buyer to prefer its output to that of the others. And if there is more than one buyer it is necessary for perfection of the market that the buyers should all be exactly alike in respect of their preferences. The larger the number of buyers who are potential customers of any one firm the more likely is the market to be imperfect, since the more likely are differences of preference to occur.[18]

To return to the main argument—the number of sellers necessary to secure perfect competition in a perfect market. On this point there seems to be a considerable amount of confusion. Cournot stated [19] that competition will be perfect if each seller provides so small a part of the total output of a commodity that his removal from production would make no appreciable difference to price. On this view the number of firms required for even approximately perfect competition must be extremely great. Now there is nothing unrealistic in the notion of a firm so small that its total disappearance would leave price unaffected. A certain farmer may very well root up his three acres of strawberries without producing any effect upon the price of strawberries in Covent Garden market. But is this not because, in the real world, demand curves always contain small but perceptible discontinuities? Until amount is reduced enough to put say a halfpenny on to price no one will notice that anything has happened. But if we assume (as we must do at this level of abstraction) a perfectly continuous demand curve, the conception of a number of firms so great that each produces a negligibly small proportion of the output of an industry, is a somewhat uncomfortable one. But it is clear that Cournot's condition is much too severe.

More commonly it is said to be sufficient for perfect competition that an increase in

---

[17] E.g., Chamberlin, see above, p. 105, note 6.

[18] Similarly, the larger the number of sellers supplying any one buyer the more likely is the market to be imperfect from the point of view of buyers. The fact that the market must be perfect, from the point of view of sellers, if there is only one buyer, and is likely to be imperfect from

the point of view of a buyer if there are many sellers, throws some light upon the question of "bargaining strength" between employers and workers. In the ordinary case a single buyer, that is, one employer, will be buying from a fairly large number of sellers—the workers. Thus the workers are necessarily in the weak position of selling in a perfect market, whereas the employer is very likely to be in the strong position of buying in an imperfect market. For the employer there will be some element of what I call "monopsony" in the situation, whereas for unorganized workers there is no element of monopoly. Cf. Harrod, *loc. cit.*, p. 460.

[19] *Mathematical Principles of the Theory of Wealth* (Bacon's translation), p. 90.

the output of any one firm should produce a negligible effect upon price. But this way of stating the matter is extremely unsatisfactory. How exactly does the number of firms come into the picture? Is the individual firm conceived to increase its output by a certain definite amount (one ton of coal)? In that case the effect upon price (given the elasticity of the total demand curve) depends upon the ratio of this amount (one ton) to the total output of the industry and the number of firms has nothing to do with the case. Or is the firm conceived to increase its output by a certain proportion, say 5 per cent? Then certainly the smaller is the share of this firm in the total output, the less will be the effect upon price; but why should we be concerned with a *proportionate* change in the output of a firm? The apparent simple statement dissolves into a haze of ambiguities as soon as it is closely examined.

From this fog we emerge when the condition is stated in a third way. A small increase in output made by a single firm, the output of other firms remaining the same, will produce a perceptible effect upon the price of the commodity. But if the total output of the firm is sufficiently small, the price cut upon its whole output, when a unit is added to the output of the industry, will be negligible. Marginal revenue is equal to price *minus* the fall in value of the old output when output is increased by one unit. If the output of the firm is very small the difference between marginal revenue and price will be very small. Marginal revenue will be almost equal to price and the demand curve for the firm will have an elasticity sufficiently near to infinity for us to say that competition is almost perfect. The point is, not that the change in price due to a change in output is negligible when the number of firms is large, but the effect of the change of price upon any one firm is negligible. Competition will be more perfect the smaller is the ratio of the output of one firm to the out-

put of the industry, and more perfect the greater is the elasticity of the total demand curve. At first sight it may appear strange that the degree of competition *within* an industry should be affected by the elasticity of the total demand curve. But after all it is natural that this should be so. For the form of the demand curve represents the degree of competition between the product of this industry and other commodities. The stronger the competition from substitutes for this commodity the smaller the degree of competition within the industry necessary to secure any given elasticity of demand for each separate producer.

This third statement appears to give a far more reasonable account of the matter than the account given in the first two statements. It was at this stage I had arrived when I wrote my book on the *Economics of Imperfect Competition*. I was then too much under the influence of tradition to imagine that there was anything more to be said about the matter, but I now feel that the argument must be pushed a stage further.

The difficulty lies in the assumption that when one firm in a competitive industry adds a unit to output the output of the other firms remains unchanged. Clearly if we take the continuity of the demand curve and of the marginal cost curves seriously this assumption is unwarranted. A small increase in the output of the industry will produce a small but perceptible fall in price. The fall in price will lead all other firms to reduce output by some fraction of a unit, since each equates marginal cost to price. We thus reach the conclusion that an increase in the output of one firm by one unit will *not* increase the output of the industry by a whole unit, but by something less. If competition is absolutely perfectly perfect an increase in the output of one firm by one unit would leave the output of the industry unchanged and there would be no change in price at all. Competition will be near enough to perfection for practical purposes if an increase in the output of one firm by one unit increases the output of the industry by so much less than one unit that the effect upon price is negligible.

This argument is different from the argument of the third stage. At the third stage we said that an increase in the output of a firm by one unit *would* produce a perceptible effect upon price, but the share of the firm in the loss due to the price cut would be so small as not to affect its conduct. At the stage where I now stand we say that a unit increase in the output of one firm will not produce a perceptible effect upon price at all.

If we adopt this position it remains to inquire what effect will be produced upon the output of the other firms when one firm increases its output. This will clearly depend upon the slopes of the marginal cost curves of the other firms. The proposition to which my lengthy preamble leads up is this—it is impossible to discuss the number of firms required to ensure perfect competition without discussing the marginal cost curves of the firms composing the industry.[20]

First consider the case in which the firms have falling marginal costs for all outputs. Then so long as the market is perfect it is impossible for two firms to survive in the industry. If there are two firms each will be anxious to increase its output at the expense of the other and any cut in price made by one of them will be answered by an equal cut by the other. Price will be driven down to the point at which one or other of the firms is forced out of the industry, and when only one firm is left in possession of the field it is impossible that competition should be perfect. Of course both firms may survive if each is afraid to begin the war. The price may then be at any level, but the situation cannot be re-

[20] Cf. Harrod, *Economic Journal,* December 1933, p. 664.

garded as an equilibrium position, since any accidental increase in output by either firm would precipitate price cutting.

Next consider the case in which marginal costs are constant. Then if there are two firms competition will be perfect. Either by lowering its price to a level infinitesimally less than the marginal cost of the other can drive it from the field, and either by raising its price infinitesimally above the marginal cost of the other will lose its whole market. Here then we have perfect competition. But this situation cannot persist in the long period. For a firm with constant marginal costs long-period average costs must be falling, since there must always be some fixed element in the cost of a firm, if only the minimum income of the entrepreneur. Thus when price is equal to marginal cost it is less than average cost and one or other of the firms must ultimately disappear.

We are brought back therefore to the familiar conclusion that marginal costs must be rising if more than one firm is to survive in a perfect market. Consider, then, an industry consisting of several firms for each of which marginal costs are rising. For each firm marginal cost will be equal to price. Suppose that one of these firms makes a unit increase in output. In the first instance the price of the commodity will fall to an extent depending upon the slope of the total demand curve. This fall in price will lead the remaining firms to contract output to an extent determined by the slope of their marginal cost curves. In the new position the output of one firm is greater by a unit, the output of each other firm is less by a fraction of a unit, and the price is lower than before. It follows that the cut in price associated with a unit increase in the output of one firm will be smaller, given the number of firms, the less is the slope of the marginal cost curves of the other firms. And it will be smaller, given the slopes of the marginal cost curves, the greater is the number of firms. Competition can only be absolutely perfect, given rising marginal costs, if the number of firms is infinite. Absolute perfection of competition is therefore an impossibility. Let us agree to call competition perfect if the price cut associated with a unit increase of output by one firm is less than a certain small finite value. Then for any given slope of the marginal cost curves there is a certain number of firms which will make competition perfect. This number will be smaller the smaller the slope of the marginal cost curves, and greater the greater the slope of the marginal cost curves.

In the limiting case, where the marginal cost curves are rising vertically, we revert to our third account of the matter in which it was assumed that the output of the other firms was fixed. We are thus led to the conclusion that when supply for each firm is completely inelastic the number of firms required to give even a reasonable approximation to perfect competition must be indefinitely great.

At first sight this conclusion appears rather strange. If we are really required to believe that in the well-known case of the fish market on Saturday night there is not quite perfect competition, must we conclude that the competitive output is not sold? That some of the fish is always allowed to rot? This would certainly be hard to accept. But here another proposition comes to our rescue. When supply is perfectly inelastic it makes no difference whether competition is perfect or not. Marginal revenue is equal to marginal cost at the same output as price is equal to marginal cost, provided that the elasticity of the individual demand curve is greater than unity. Therefore price and output are the same whatever the individual elasticity of demand. Thus, although there is not, strictly speaking, perfect competition among the fishmongers on Saturday night, yet the competitive output will be sold at the competitive price unless the demand curve for fish is highly inelastic.[21]

We have thus reached the conclusion that there is not one universal value for the "large number of firms" which ensures perfect competition.[22] In each particular case, with given slopes of the marginal cost curves, there is a certain definite number of firms which will produce competition of an agreed degree of perfection, and this number, in some cases, may be quite small.

[21] The elasticity of the demand for one seller will be less than unity if the elasticity of the total demand falls short of unity to a sufficient extent.

[22] Professor Chamberlin (*op. cit.*, p. 49) rather weakly suggests that 100 would be a "large number," though in the particular case that he is considering two would have been enough.

15. The Concept of Monopoly and the Measurement of Monopoly Power*

ABBA P. LERNER [1]

Abba P. Lerner [B.Sc. (Econ.), London, 1932; Ph.D., 1943] was born in Bessarabia, Russia, in 1903 and grew up in London, England. He is now Professor of Economics at the University of California (Berkeley) and, before this, he taught at the London School of Economics, the University of Virginia, the University of Kansas City, Amherst College, the New School for Social Research, Roosevelt University, and Michigan State University. Lerner's major works include *The Economics of Control, The Economics of Employment, Essays in Economic Analysis,* and *Everybody's Business.* He has written widely in many areas of economic theory, including welfare economics, capital theory, employment theory, and the theory of socialistic economics. Early in his career Lerner was a founder of *The Review of Economic Studies* and was its managing editor from 1933 to 1937. From 1953 to 1956 he was Economic Advisor to the government of Israel. He is a Fellow of the Econometric Society and in 1966 was made a Distinguished Fellow of the American Economic Association. Lerner's rare abilities as a teacher and scholar are attested to by Milton Friedman in his review of *The Economics of Control,* which refers to Lerner's skill and patience in exposition, his flexibility of mind, his profound interest in social welfare, and his willingness to accept and courage to state what seems to him right social policy, regardless of precedent or accepted opinion.

I

Monopoly, says the dictionary, is the exclusive right of a person, corporation or state to sell a particular commodity. Economic science, investigating the economic

* Reprinted from the *Review of Economic Studies* (June 1943) by permission of the publisher, pp. 157–175.

[1] The great advances made in the subject of this article since the major part of it was written —particularly in the work of Mr. Chamberlin and Mrs. Robinson—have rendered many parts of it out of date. In preparing it for publication, while

aspects of this legal right, found that they all resolved themselves into the implications of the power of the monopolist—as distinguished from a seller in a competitive market—arbitrarily to decide the price of the commodity, leaving it to the buyers to decide how much they will buy at that price, or, alternatively, to decide the quantity he will sell, by so fixing the price as to induce buyers to purchase just this quantity. Technically this is expressed by saying that the monopolist is confronted with a falling demand curve for his product or that the elasticity of demand for his product is less than infinity, while the seller in a purely[2] competitive market has a horizontal demand curve or the elasticity of demand for his product is equal to infinity.

The monopolist is normally assumed to tend to fix the price at the level at which he makes the greatest profit or "monopoly revenue." This monopoly revenue constitutes a levy upon the consumers that the monopolist is able to appropriate for himself purely in virtue of his restrictive powers *qua* monopolist, and it is the consumers' objection to paying this levy that lies at the base of popular feeling against the monopolist.

In addition to this it is claimed that monopoly is harmful in a more objective sense. A levy which involves a mere transference from buyer to monopolist cannot be said to be harmful from a social point of view unless it can be shown that the monopolist is less deserving of the levy than the people who have to pay it; either because he is in general a less deserving kind of person, or because the transference

will increase the evils of inequality of incomes. But the levy is not a mere transference. The method of raising it, namely, by increasing the price of the monopolised commodity, causes buyers to divert their expenditure to other, less satisfactory, purchases. This constitutes a loss to the consumer which is not balanced by any gain reaped by the monopolist, so that there is a net social loss.

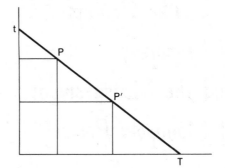

FIGURE 15.1

The nature of the loss here loosely expressed seems to have defied attempts at more exact exposition, the difficulties encountered on these attempts having even induced some to declare that this commonsense view of a social loss is an illusion, while more careful sceptics prefer to say that nothing "scientific" can be said about it. The account given above clearly will not do as a general and accurate description of the nature of the social loss. Where a consumer spends as much as before on the monopolised commodity when the price is raised, he cannot be said to divert expenditure to other and less satisfactory channels, and where he spends more[3] upon

---

cutting out some of these parts, I have been so much under the influence of this recent work that I cannot say how much of what is here published is really my own.

[2] "Pure" competition is different from "perfect" competition. The former implies perfection of competition only in respect of the complete absence of monopoly and abstracts from other aspects of perfection in competition. This useful distinction is suggested by Chamberlin. See his *Theory of Monopolistic Competition*, p. 6.

[3] Where as much or more is spent on a commodity when the price is raised the elasticity of demand is equal to or less than unity. This may appear incompatible with the condition of monopolistic equilibrium that elasticity of demand shall be greater than unity (as long as marginal cost is positive). There is, however, no incompatibility, for the two elasticities of demand are different things. The elasticity that has to be greater than unity for monopolistic equilibrium is the elasticity at the *point* on the demand curve corresponding to the position of monopolistic

the commodity than at the lower competitive price it might even be argued that there is a net social gain in so far as the consumer is induced to spend more on the commodity which is more urgently needed and less on other commodities! There seems little to choose between this argument and the counter-argument, that as long as the elasticity is greater than zero some consumer (or unit of consumption) is induced to change the direction of his expenditure so that he suffers the uncompensated inconvenience which constitutes the net social loss. Does this mean that if a man's demand is completely inelastic (so that the increased price brings no diminution in the amount of the monopolised commodity consumed and the whole of the levy is sacrificed ultimately in the form of other commodities) the expenditure of the income, as diminished by the amount of the levy, is not interfered with by the existence of the monopoly?—i.e. that if he had paid the levy in cash and prices were not affected he would have reduced his consumption of other commodities in the same way? Or is it more reasonable to suppose that a rise in a particular price

will always tend to diminish purchases of the dearer commodity, where a cash levy (prices remaining unchanged) would diminish all expenditures in the same proportion so that if the same amount of the monopolised commodity is bought at the higher price, a cash diminution in income of the size of the levy would have *increased* the demand for that commodity? The problems do not seem to be amenable to treatment on these lines.[4]

The commonsense attitude is, however, not easily balked. Another attempt was made to deal with the problem by Marshall, by means of the apparatus of consumers' surplus. If it is assumed that the marginal utility of money is unchanged, or that the change is so small that it may legitimately be neglected, it can be shown that the money value of the consumers' surplus lost is greater than the monopoly revenue gained, so that we have a theoretical measure of the net social loss due to the monopoly. There are, of course, many important weaknesses in this treatment, and some ways of applying it are completely wrong. The marginal utility of money can be considered unchanged only if we are considering a small change in the price of only one commodity. This makes it impossible to add the consumers' surplus obtained by an individual from different goods. Quite wrong is any attempt to speak of the consumers' surplus of a community and to derive it from the communal demand curve. And there are other traps to be avoided in this connection which are quite well known. But the exclusive preoccupa-

---

equilibrium. The elasticity that is equal to or less than unity when the amount spent on the commodity remains unchanged or increases as the price is raised, is the elasticity over the *arc* of the demand curve from the point of competitive equilibrium to the point of monopolistic equilibrium. The arc elasticity in this sense will normally be less than the point elasticity, as will appear from the diagram. If tT is the demand curve (here drawn a straight line), P' the point of competitive equilibrium, and P the point of monopolistic equilibrium, then the *point* elasticity at the monopoly equilibrium will be $\dfrac{PT}{Pt}$ while the arc elasticity will be $\dfrac{P'T}{Pt}$, which is smaller. The arc elasticity must be smaller unless the demand curve is so concave (upwards) that it shows a constant or increasing point elasticity as price is lowered. The point elasticity at the competitive position will, of course, be $\dfrac{P'T}{P't}$. For the explanation of this definition of "arc elasticity," see my note on "The Diagrammatical Representation of Elasticity of Demand," in No. 1 of the REVIEW.

[4] In the last few months Dr. J. R. Hicks and Mr. R. G. D. Allen have been making investigations on these lines and have demonstrated by means of the indifference curve apparatus that, with continuous indifference curves, an absolutely inelastic demand curve must be accompanied by a negatively sloping expenditure curve. This means that a change in income (prices remain unchanged) would bring about a change *in inverse direction* of the amount of the commodity bought. They have not been interested, however, in the problems dealt with in this article.

tion of teachers of economics with putting their pupils on their guard against these insufficiencies and dangers has tended to make them deny the problem with which the concept of consumers' surplus was intended to deal—the net social loss and its nature. It is not intended here to deny or even to belittle the dangers and confusions attendant on the use of the concept of consumers' surplus, but it does seem that some light can be thrown on the problem by its use.

From the consumers' surplus approach there has emerged a clarification of the rent element in monopoly revenue. It is only in the case of constant or decreasing average cost that the amount of monopoly revenue is necessarily less than the loss of consumers' surplus. The monopoly revenue will be greater if the average cost curve rises steeply enough. This gave the impression that the monopolistic restriction brought about a net social gain so that the competitive output was too great and it would be beneficial to tax industries which were "subject to diminishing returns." In correcting this view it was shown that against the monopoly revenue was to be reckoned not only the loss of consumers' surplus, but also the reduction in rents as compared with those receivable under competition. If the reductions of rent is not allowed for, the diminution of costs of the marginal units, as output is restricted, is attributed to all the *infra*-marginal costs where there has been no reduction in social costs, but only a transference of income from the receivers of rent. In the accompanying Figure 15.2 *AR* is the average revenue or demand curve (which, to avoid the quarrels over consumers' surplus, we can consider as the sum of a number of identical demand curves of similar individuals), *MR* is the marginal revenue curve, *AC* is average costs, and *MC* is marginal costs. *P'* will be the competitive point where output is *OM'* and price is *M'P'*, and *P*, which is perpendicularly

above *A*, where *MR* and *MC* cut, will be the monopoly point where output is *OM* and price is *MP*. Consumers' surplus lost is equal to *SPP'T*, while monopoly revenue is *SPQR*, which may be greater. But against this must be reckoned the loss in rents, *RQP'T*, so that there is a net social loss of *PQP'*.

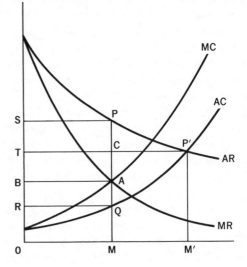

FIGURE 15.2

One is tempted to divide the monopoly revenue *SPQR* into two parts, *SPCT* and *RQCT*, and to say that the former is the monopoly revenue extracted from consumers while the latter is the monopoly revenue extracted from receivers of rent or producers' surplus. It is exactly parallel to the extraction of monopoly revenue from the receivers of consumers' surplus, but is obtained in virtue of the monopolist being confronted with a rising supply curve instead of with a falling demand curve. It is a gain obtained by a "single" buyer instead of a gain obtained by a "single" seller. The appropriate parallel name for it would be *Monopsony Revenue*.[5] This dichotomy of the monopoly revenue is based on a comparison of the monopoly

[5] Joan Robinson, in *The Economics of Imperfect Competition*, introduces the word Monopsony, but does not speak of Monopsony Revenue.

position with the competitive position.[6] *PC* is the rise in price and *QC* is the fall in average cost, so that these quantities multiplied by the monopolistic output give the monopoly revenue and the monopsony revenue respectively.

It will, however, not do to compare the monopoly position with the competitive position for the purpose of making the dichotomy, for by this procedure it is made to depend upon the shape of the curves for outputs between the monopolistic output *OM* and the competitive output *OM'*, which may be a long way from it. It does not seem reasonable that the degree of monopsony or monopoly at output *OM* should be dependent upon what happens to demand or cost curves in the vicinity of output *OM'*. And apart from this the taking of the competitive output and price as a base from which everything is to be measured leads to more concrete inconsistencies. Thus we may attempt to find the amount of monopoly revenue (in the more exact sense, that is, not including monopsony revenue), by considering what it would be if the average cost were constant at the competitive level so that there was no monopsony. *AC* and *MC* would then coincide with *TP'*, and the monopoly revenue would not be *SPCT* but some other larger amount, for the output could not be *OM* but some other amount. If we reverse this process, assuming that the demand curve and the *MR* curve are horizontal,

we again find that the monopsony revenue is not *RQCT* but some other larger amount, and the output is not *OM* but, again, some other amount.[7]

The direct comparison of monopolistic with competitive equilibrium further assumes that cost conditions are the same and that demand conditions are the same. Neither of these is likely, and the combination of both is much less likely.

A more reasonable procedure for the allocation of the gains as between monopoly and monopsony revenue is to take as a basis not the price which would obtain if there were neither monopoly nor monopsony, but instead of that the actual conditions of the monopoly-monopsony equilibrium. With the given demand curve pure[8] monopoly output could only be *OM* if the horizontal *AC* curve were coincident with *AB*, in which case the monopoly revenue would be equal to *SPAB*. With the

---

[6] By monopoly position is meant a position in which the demand curve does not appear horizontal to all the firms in the industry. The simplest case of this is when there is only one firm which coincides with the whole industry, and that is what is shown in Fig. 15.2 at the monopoly position *P*. Monopoly is essentially a property of *firms* and by a monopolistic industry is meant nothing more than an industry in which *firms* have downward sloping demand curves. And, of course, only a firm is interested in maximising monopoly revenue. If the demand curve for the whole industry is horizontal, the industry is in a competitive condition, but that is only because in this case every firm in the industry must also have a horizontal demand curve—even if there is only one firm.

[7] In Fig. 15.2, where both *AR* and *AC* are concave upwards, the output under monopoly without monopsony would be less than *OM*, and the output under monopsony without monopoly would be greater than *OM*. The outputs are given by the abscissae of the points where *TP'* is cut by *MR* and *MC* respectively. If *AR* and *AC* are convex, the outputs would move in the opposite direction. If they are straight lines, or if the convexity of one is just offset by the concavity of the other, the output will be the same as when the monopoly and monopsony are found in combination. If the elimination of monopsony changes the output in one direction, the elimination of monopoly would change output in the other direction, and *vice versa*.

[8] By *pure monopoly* is meant a case where one is confronted with a falling demand curve for the commodity one sells, but with a horizontal supply curve for the factors one has to buy for the production of the commodity; so that one sells as a monopolist but buys in a perfect market. Similarly, *pure monopsony* stands for perfect competition in the market where one sells, but monopsony in the market where one buys—being confronted with a horizontal demand curve but a rising supply curve. *Pure monopoly* is monopoly free from all elements of monopsony. *Pure monopsony* is monopsony free from all elements of monopoly. *Pure competition* stands for freedom from all elements of both monopoly and monopsony. The *purity* of monopoly or of monopsony has nothing to do with the *degree* of monopoly or monopsony.

given *AC* curve the pure monopsony output could only be *OM* if the horizontal demand curve is coincident with *AB*, in which case the monopsony revenue would be equal to *RQAB*, and *RQAB* and *SPAB* do add up to the monopoly-monopsony revenue *SPQR*.

From this it appears that the monopoly revenue per unit of output, *AP*, is the excess of price over marginal cost, so that the mark of the absence of monopoly is the equality of price or *average* receipts to *marginal* cost, and the mark of the absence of monopsony is the equality of *average* cost to *marginal* receipts.[9]

The test more usually accepted is the equality of average costs to price or average receipts. It is this equation which is regularly given as the definition of "competitive" position,[10] and a suggestion like the one here given is likely to meet with a lecture on the impropriety of comparing averages with marginal values. It would seem, however, that the orthodox point of view is not only based upon too great a readiness to consider perfect competition

as the ideal type of economic phenomena towards which all things tend, but are deterred more or less only by "frictions" (for in perfect competition all these equations become identical), but is in some measure induced by the habit of using straight lines in diagrams dealing with monopoly, and thus missing the problem. For in this case, *AB* of **Figure 15.2** would coincide with *P'T*, and the two dichotomies of the monopoly-cum-monopsony revenue are identical.

The point at issue is not merely a verbal one of definition—a quibble as to what it is better to call the "competitive" position. The importance of the competitive position lies in its implications of being a position which in some way or another is better than other positions. It is the position in which the "Invisible Hand" has exerted its beneficial influences to the utmost. It has become the symbol for the social optimum. Its importance for us here is in giving us a basis against which we can compare the effect of monopoly in order to see the social loss, if any, that the existence of a monopoly brings about. Is the social optimum that position at which prices are equal to average cost, or that at which price equals marginal cost and average cost equals marginal revenue?

The social optimum relative to any distribution of resources (or income) between different individuals (and we cannot here go into the problems connected with optimum distribution) will be reached only if the resources which are to be devoted to satisfying the wants of each individual are so allocated between the different things he wants, that his total satisfaction would not be increased by any transference of resources from the provision of any one of the things he gets to any other thing he wants. This would show itself in the impossibility of any individual being put in a preferred position without putting another individual in a worse position. We may adopt this as our criterion or test of

---

[9] *Marginal* cost and *marginal* receipts are, of course, always equal to each other in any equilibrium, whether monopolistic or monopsonistic, or both or neither. It is, therefore, possible to express the same relationships in terms of the equality of price or average receipts to marginal receipts and the equality of average costs to marginal costs. But this procedure rules out conditions of disequilibrium together with monopoly or monopsony, so that to affirm this would be merely to say in other words that the demand or supply curve is horizontal, so that by definition there is no monopoly or monopsony. The relationships given in the text are not the merely mathematical relationships between an average and its corresponding marginal curve, but between real conditions of costs on the one hand and of receipts on the other. It will be seen below that these relationships will not always coincide with the tautologous alternatives suggested in this footnote.

[10] Even Mrs. Robinson defines "competitive output" and "competitive price" as that output or price at which $AC = AR$ or price (*op. cit.*, p. 160), although she demonstrates most clearly in other parts of the book how this condition ($AC = AR$) is also reached in monopolistic or imperfectly competitive equilibrium.

the achievement of the relative optimum. If in any set of circumstances it is possible to move one individual into a preferred position without moving another individual into a worse position (i.e. such that the original position is preferred to it by the individual affected), we may say that the relative optimum is not reached; but if such a movement is impossible, we may say that the relative optimum has been attained. The conditions which must be satisfied if the optimum is attained can be formulated quite simply.

Any change in the position of any individual means a change in the quantity of goods (and services) he consumes. For any such a change to take place it is necessary that there shall be either (a) a *similar* change in the total quantity of goods produced or (b) an *opposite* change in the total quantity of goods consumed by others, or (c) some combination of (a) and (b). In the case of (a), consumption by other people need not be interfered with by the change, the whole change in the consumption by one individual being covered by changes in production. In the case of (b), there need be no change in production, any increase in the consumption of particular goods by one individual be provided by decreases in their consumption by others, and any decreases in the consumption of other goods by one individual being covered by increases in their consumption by others. In case (c) both kinds of compensating movements take place, but these can be separated and dealt with as cases of (a) and (b) so that no special treatment is necessary.

If a change in the consumption of various goods by one individual which improves his position is compensated solely by a movement of type (a), consumption by all other individuals need not be affected. This means that the effect of the movement from the previous position was to make one individual better off without making any other individual worse off. The

previous position could not, therefore, have been an optimum position. One condition, then, of the optimum position is that any change in the quantity of goods consumed by any individual which improves his position cannot be compensated by a movement of type (a).

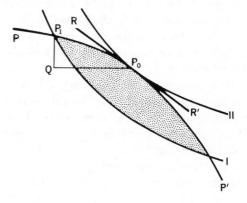

FIGURE 15.3

This is illustrated in Figure 15.3,[11] PP' is a section of the displacement cost curve (or productive indifference curve) of the whole community. I and II are consumption indifference curves of one individual. The indifference curves are superimposed upon the displacement cost curve, so that the point on the indifference map which represents the quantities of the commodities X (measured horizontally) and Y (measured vertically), consumed by the individual in the initial position, coincides with the point on the communal displacement cost curve which represents the total amount of the commodities (X and Y) produced in the whole community in the initial position. If P_1 is this position, a movement from P_1 to any point above I represents a movement favourable to one individual. Compensating movements of type (a) from P_1 are, however, limited to points below PP'. The shaded area in the diagram represents positions to which

[11] I am indebted to Mr. V. Edelberg for the suggestion of the application of the indifference curve apparatus to the problem in this manner.

movements from P_1 are favourable to one individual and can be compensated by movements of type (*a*). Thus a movement from P_1 to P_0 represents a diminution in the production of Y by an amount P_1Q and an increase in the production of X by an amount QP_0,[12] accompanied by a similar change in one individual's consumption which moves him on to the higher indifference curve II; while the quantities of goods remaining to be consumed by other people are unaffected.

It is, of course, not necessary that any improvement should go up to the highest possible point—here P_0. A movement from P_1 to any other point in the shaded area indicates an improvement, but leaves room for still further improvement.

Such a movement is possible as long as the indifference curve cuts the displacement cost curve, giving an overlapping (shaded) area. Our first condition for the optimum position can be expressed by saying that these curves must not cut.

If the curves are smooth this will mean that they are tangential as at P_0, but our condition is satisfied without the tangency of the curves, if either (or both) of the curves changes directions suddenly at the point where the curves meet or that it forms an angle. What is necessary is merely

[12] It is not necessary that all or any of the identical units of factors set free from the production of Y should be used in the production of X. They, or a part of them, may go to the production of a third commodity Z, as substitutes for other factors which are released to produce the additional X; and there may be any number of such steps. This, of course, does not mean that every commodity is a *direct* displacement cost for every other commodity at the margin (in the sense that factors can move directly from one to the other without economic loss), as would be the case if each factor had the same marginal productivity in all uses—universal substitutability of factors at the margin. It only means that there is some path, however indirect, whereby a diminution in the production of one commodity permits an increase in the production of any other commodity, leaving the quantity of the rest of the commodities unaffected. That is what is meant by drawing a displacement cost curve for any two commodities.

that the curves shall meet at P_0 without cutting. This condition must be fulfilled for every individual in the community.

The movement of one individual to a preferred position, may, however, be covered by opposite changes in the consumption of others. This, too, can be examined in the same diagram. Let I and II represent the same indifference curves as before, but let PP' represent now not the displacement cost curve, but the indifference curve of any other individual, turned through $180°$ around the common point which shows the combinations of goods consumed by the individual. If the indifference curves cut, as they do in our diagram if P_1 is the common point, there is an overlapping area, shaded in the diagram, showing the possibility of improving the position of one without worsening the position of the other. A movement from P_1 to P_0 improves the position of *one* individual and leaves the other at another point on the same indifference curve PP', and, therefore, not worse off. Movements from P_1 to any intermediate point in the shaded area would make both individuals better off. In order to satisfy the condition of the optimum it is therefore again necessary that there should be no gap between the curves, i.e. that they should not cut. If they are smooth, it means that they are tangential, and that the slopes of the indifference curves of both individuals were parallel in the initial position, since the turning of a curve through $180°$ does not change any slopes.

The diagrammatical treatment restricts one to the consideration of only two commodities. This does not matter for the present purpose, since the relationships described have to obtain for every pair of all the commodities in the economy. This is because the failure of the conditions to be satisfied for *any* pair of commodities shows a possibility for improvement which is incompatible with an optimum position.

If both of these conditions are satisfied,

as between each individual's indifference curves and the communal displacement costs curve on the one hand, and as between each individual's indifference curves and every other individual's (inverted) indifference curves, on the other hand, it is impossible to improve the position of any individual without worsening the position of some other individual. The optimum position, relative to the distribution of income between individuals, is attained.

Can we make any use of such a complicated set of conditions? If it were necessary to investigate separately the slopes of the indifference curves of all individuals for all pairs of commodities in order to discover whether the conditions are satisfied, it would be most profitable to discontinue this analysis at once. But there is no need for all this. We need merely assume that some of the indifference curves are smooth at the positions representing the amounts consumed by the individuals, and that each individual, in buying goods for his own consumption, considers the price as given. Under these conditions the relative prices of each pair of goods in the market will accurately reflect the slopes of the indifference curves where these are smooth; and for those cases, where an indifference curve forms an angle, the ratio between the prices will give a line (RR' in Figure 17.3) of such slope that the indifference curve will lie wholly *above* it, meeting it but not cutting it if it is superimposed on the consumption point P_0. The mere existence of a free market in consumption goods thus satisfies the second of our two conditions.

The first condition is satisfied if the price ratio on the market, represented by the slope of the line RR', is such that the displacement curve lies wholly *below* it, meeting it at the production-consumption point P_0, but not cutting it. If the displacement cost curve is smooth and, therefore, tangential to RR', this will mean that the price ratio is proportional to the marginal

displacement costs, which condition is satisfied if *price is equal to marginal cost.*

From this analysis we see that the optimum is reached when the price reflects the alternatives given up at the margin, whether this alternative is considered in physical terms of some other commodity or whether we go direct to the satisfactions that the physical alternatives represent. The loss involved in monopoly can be seen in the divergence between price and this marginal cost. The loss involved in monopsony is of exactly the same nature, and a parallel analysis is rendered unnecessary if we translate the rising supply curve that is seen by the monopsonist into a falling demand curve by considering the purchase of A for B as the sale of B for A. This loss is avoided only if price to the consumer (AR) is equal to marginal cost (MC), and if the wages of labour (AC) are equal to its marginal product ($=MR$). If we prefer we may put the latter statement in the form of demand. The price of leisure demanded by labourers (AR) (which is his wage) must be equal to the marginal cost of his leisure (MC) (which is equal to the marginal product of the labour withdrawn).

II

In considering the degree of monopoly in a particular field one's first inclination seems to be to hark back to the etymological meaning of the word and to see how close the situation is to the conditions which accompany a "single seller." On this line one would say that there is complete monopoly if there is actually only one seller, and that the monopoly element diminishes as the number of sellers increases. One could construct some kind of index of the degree of monopoly, such as the inverse of the number of sellers, which would give values ranging from unity in the case of this kind of "complete" monopoly to zero in the case of an infinite number of sellers.

The most obvious of the many reasons why this will not do is that there may be a very high degree of monopoly (in any sense other than that of the formula for such an index), even where there are many sellers, if one or two sellers control a sufficiently large proportion of the total supply. For this reason one turns instead to discover how great a proportion of the total supply is controlled by one or a few individuals or organisations. The same information may also be sought more indirectly by inquiries into the size of firms.

This procedure, however, is still quite inappropriate for measuring the degree of monopoly if we are interested in its economic and social implications of control over price and social loss as discussed in the first part of this paper. This is seen most clearly when we observe that control by a single firm of 100 per cent. of the supply of a commodity for which the demand is infinitely elastic (which will always be the case if there is some equally satisfactory substitute available at a constant price) is absolutely unimportant and has no economic significance, while a "partial" monopoly of a commodity for which the demand is inelastic may be able to raise price by reducing output and is clearly a much more effective case of monopoly.

The statistical method of measuring monopoly, besides missing the main issue in this way, encounters enormous practical difficulties in which investigators can hardly hope to avoid getting entangled. The problems of allowing for changes in taste and technique, in transport and in business organisation, of dealing with firms making many products and of discovering the degree to which different firms compete with one another or mitigate the competition by Gentlemen's Agreements, trade conventions, business alliances, and so on, are just a few worth mentioning, but there is one that interests us particularly here, and that is the relatively simple one of defining the commodity.

A man may have a considerable degree of monopolistic power although he is in control of only a very small part of the supply of a commodity if he is afforded some protection from the competition of the rest of the supply by the cost of transporting other supplies to his market. Under these conditions the price of the commodity will be different in different places. The best way of dealing with this is to declare that objects having the same physical characteristics are not the same goods if they are at different places. Location is an essential and distinguishing characteristic of economic goods, and the only relationship between the prices of similar goods in different places is that which results from the possibilities of transforming the one good into the other by transporting it from the one place to the other.

And location is not the only variant of this kind, but rather the simplest species of a large genus, and is useful for a simplified exposition of the problems involved. Every specialised gradation of every particular quality of every "commodity" may be treated as "distance," and the cost of changing the quality to a particular grade as the cost of "transport." Some of these problems are dealt with by Hotelling in his article, "Stability in Competition," *Economic Journal*, 1929, p. 41, where he gives examples ranging from the sweetness of cider to the service of churches.

To these variants must be added also all fictitious variations, such as are successfully imposed upon the minds of buyers by skilful advertising, as well as the tendencies of customers to buy from one seller rather than from another by sheer force of habit. Here the "distance" is the fictitious difference in quality or the goodwill of the customer, while the "transport costs" are the costs involved in overcoming the "goodwill" whether by reducing price or by counter-advertisement.

This splitting up of the conception of a commodity of course multiplies the number of commodities indefinitely, and seems to create monopolies in the most unexpected places. Carried to its logical extreme, every firm now becomes a monopoly, since it is impossible for more than one unit of product to be in the same place. But even without going to such extremes it becomes impossible to apply the simple measures of monopoly that we are criticising. Further difficulties are yet to arise.

While the idea of considering the same things at different places as different goods seems to have spread considerably, the full revolutionary implications of this step forward in the picturing of the equilibrial forces do not seem to have been quite realised.

In calling the same thing at different places different commodities, we have rejected the criterion of physical similarity as a basis for the recognition or classification of commodities and have put in its place the principle of substitutability at the margin.

If the same thing at a different place is not the same commodity it is only because the difference in its location prevents it from being substituted for, or used in the same way as, the same thing here. But this principle can be applied in the converse form too. With substitutability as the principle it is no longer necessary for different units of the same commodity to have the same physical characteristics as long as they are substitutable at the margin for the purpose that the buyer wants them. This means that if one pound of coal gives me the same heating power as four pounds of wood, that both of these items cost the same on the market, and I am indifferent as to which I have, then one pound of coal and four pounds of wood represent the same number of units of the same commodity. It means, further, that if I am indifferent as to whether I have one hundredweight of coal every week during the winter, or an overcoat to keep me warm, then a winter's coal and an overcoat are equal quantities of the same commodity. Further still, if I am indifferent as to whether I have a wireless set for £10 or whether I have the satisfaction of saving ten Chinese children from starvation, the wireless set in London is the same quantity of the same commodity as £10 worth of rice in China; while if I get the same satisfaction from a £100 motorcar here and now as I could from a Mediterranean cruise next year, which costs £100 plus the accumulated interest on the money, then the motor-car here and now and the Mediterranean cruise next year are equal quantities of the same commodity. Physical qualities, spacial and temporal position are irrelevant now that we have the ultimate criterion of substitutability at the margin. If any quantity or complex of goods and services can be substituted at the margin for any other quantity of goods and services (and therefore have the same market value), then they are both equal quantities of the same commodity. It would perhaps be best to give terminological recognition to such a break with traditional usage by speaking of "units of accommodation" instead of units of commodities.

If this way of looking at things seems paradoxical, it is only because we have not yet completely freed ourselves from the crudely materialistic conception of goods with which the Physiocrats and Adam Smith were the first to wrestle. The inadequacy of a purely physical criterion of commodities is obvious when we consider the enormous physical difference which we neglect if they do not affect the qualities in which we are interested (that is which affect our satisfactions), of which we are often completely unconscious, but which are of so much importance to Mr. Sherlock Holmes. Physically there are no two similar articles even apart from location. If two objects are considered to be items of the same good, it is only because they are "good for" the same purpose—always, ultimately, the satisfaction of a want. It is futile to say that the motor-car and the Mediterranean cruise satisfy different wants until we are able to define "similar" wants otherwise than as wants that are satisfied by physically similar objects. There is no *qualitative* criterion of wants. Wants can only be considered as similar when the person who feels them displays equal concern for their satisfaction and thus shows them to be equal in *quantity*. To follow any other course is to sacrifice the logic of the science to the irrelevant convenience of the shopkeeper.

It may be objected that this concept of commodity is so abstract and elusive as to be unusable. That is perfectly correct. But therein lies a great part of its advantages. It cannot be used like the more material conception to drown the theory in irrelevant statistics. It puts an end to attempts, here, to find a measure of monopoly in terms of the proportion of the supply of a commodity under single control and clears the way to a better understanding.

Another line of approach that suggests itself is to compare the amount of monopoly revenue with the total receipts, and to take this ratio as a measure of the degree of monopoly power. Allowance is thus made for the size of the industry or the firm. We will obtain values ranging from 0 in the case of perfect competition to 1 where the whole of receipts is monopoly revenue, and at first glance all seems well.

This procedure will, however, not do, for what we want in the measure of monopoly is not the amount of tribute individuals can obtain for themselves from the rest of the community, by being in an advantageous monopolistic position, but the divergence of the system from the social optimum that is reached in perfect competition. From this point of view the monopolist gains are not to be distinguished from rents of scarce property that he owns, or any other source of individual income.

The independence of the monopolist gain from the social loss can perhaps most clearly be brought out by a consideration of how far they can vary independently. The limiting case is seen where the demand curve for the product of a monopolist coincides over considerable range with his average cost curve. Here the monopoly revenue is zero wherever the monopolist produces within this range, yet he has control over price, and the social loss will be different according to what output the monopolist decides to produce. It clearly will not do to say that the degree of monopoly power in such a case is zero.

If the average cost curve is horizontal such a divergence cannot occur. The firm can only change output while keeping monopoly revenue zero if the demand curve is also horizontal, and that means perfect competition in either case and no social loss. But in such a case we are comparing not merely monopoly revenue with total receipts, which is the same as the ratio between average receipts minus costs and average receipts (and which is also seen in the ratio between average costs and average receipts), but also *marginal costs* with *average receipts*, and it is in divergence between these, as we have seen above, that the essence of monopoly is to be found.

In such cases (where the cost curve is horizontal) the ratio of monopoly revenue to total receipts coincides exactly with the ratio of the divergence of price from marginal cost to price, and it is this latter formula that I wish to put forward as the measure of monopoly power. If $P = $ price and $C = $ marginal cost, then the index of the degree of monopoly power is $\dfrac{P-C}{P}$.

It will be observed that this formula looks like the inverse of the formula for the elasticity of demand. It differs from it only in that the item marginal cost replaces the item marginal receipts. In equilibrium as normally conceived marginal costs coincide with marginal receipts so that our formula becomes identical with the inverse of the elasticity of demand. It will be best to consider this as a special case.

In this special case we can find the degree of monopoly power via the elasticity of demand. The determination of this elasticity of demand is not to be confused with that of Pigou and Schultz in finding the elasticity of demand (as part of the demand function) for a materially (physically) defined commodity on a market. What we want here is the elasticity of demand for the product of a particular firm. This is much easier to obtain, for it is only when he knows the shape of the demand curve for his product that any entrepreneur can obtain his maximum profit; and he is, therefore, always applying himself energetically to obtaining as accurate an estimate as possible of this elasticity. This does not mean that the entrepreneur will be able to fill in the elasticity of demand on a questionnaire form. He will rarely know what the term means. But his unfamiliarity with the technical jargon of economists must not be held to show an ignorance of so primary a principle for intelligent business management as the urgency of knowing the effect of price changes on sales. His behaviour in running the business for maximum profit will enable any student to deduce the (estimated) elasticity of demand from the firm's cost curve and the selling price. From the average cost curve the marginal cost curve can be derived. The marginal cost is equal to the marginal receipt, output being adjusted so as to make them equal if profit is maximised. The elasticity of demand is equal to the price divided by the difference between price and marginal cost—it is the inverse of our formula for the measurement of the degree of monopoly power.

In finding the degree of monopoly in this special case "via the elasticity of demand" we found that the easiest way of finding the elasticity of demand was via

the degree of monopoly. We may, therefore, leave out the elasticity of demand altogether and just keep to our formula all the time. In the special case both come to the same thing, but we must use the new formula and not the inverse of the elasticity of demand whenever we consider cases where the maximum monopoly revenue is not obtained in practice.

This may be accidental, as when the monopolist does not know the shape of his demand curve and his estimate of the elasticity of demand at the actual output is erroneous; or it may be intentional. The price and output may intentionally be fixed in a manner which does not give the maximum monopoly revenue:

1. When the monopolist is not working on purely business principles, but for social, philanthropic or conventional reasons sells *below* this price commodities which it is considered socially desirable to cheapen —as when a public authority supplies cheap transport facilities—or sells *above* this price commodities which are considered socially harmful—as may be done by a State liquor monopoly.

2. When the monopolist is working on purely business principles, but keeps the price and his profits lower than they might be so as to avoid political opposition or the entry of new competitors. The second could, perhaps, better be considered as a case where the demand is more elastic in the long period, taking into account the contingent competition, than in the short period, and where the monopolist takes a long period view.

In all such cases our formula is not equal to the inverse of the elasticity of demand; but wherever there appears a divergence between the two it is our formula and not the inverse of the elasticity of demand which gives the measure of what we want. In the first case—where the monopolist's estimate of the elasticity of demand is erroneous—the consumers will in every way be in exactly the same position as if the elasticity were what the monopolist thinks it is. If he over-estimates the elasticity of demand he will sell a larger amount at a lower price. If he thinks the elasticity is infinite—i.e. that if he produced less he would not be able to get a better price—he will make price equal to marginal cost, and the effect on consumers will be the same as if there were perfect competition.[13] The unused monopoly power will be there, but being unknown and unused it is, economically, as if it were not there. For practical purposes we must read monopoly power not as *potential* monopoly, but as monopoly *in force*.

If the monopolist underestimates the elasticity of demand he will sell a smaller quantity and at a higher price than at the point of maximum monopoly revenue. The only difference between this and the previous case is that the monopolist's error brings a loss to consumers instead of a gain. The monopolist himself, of course, loses by the error in either case. The consumer here has to pay a higher price or else do without. It is again just as if the elasticity of demand were what the monopolist thinks it is. This may sound as if the monopoly *in force* is here greater than the *potential* monopoly power, but the inverse of the elasticity of demand at the maximum revenue point does not really give the potential monopoly power. It gives just that degree of monopoly power which it is necessary to put into force in order to obtain the maximum revenue and which is in force where the maximum revenue is being obtained. The monopolist always has power in excess of this; but as the employment of it can only bring him a loss, he normally does not

[13] Mrs. Robinson has pointed out to me that the delusion that elasticity is infinite would persist only if *MC* happened to equal price already. This is the easiest case for the correction of a mistaken estimate in the process of adjustment to it. The same possibility exists with any estimated elasticity of demand as long as the marginal cost and the estimated marginal receipts do not coincide and so preclude any adjustments.

use it intentionally. If he chooses to use it he can, of course, for the exercise of this power consists of diminishing the amount he produces. Potential monopoly power is only used to its maximum when the monopolist stops all production. What our formula gives is the degree of monopoly power in force.

The same arguments apply to cases where the maximum monopoly revenue is not obtained for social, philanthropic or conventional reasons or for the purpose of avoiding political opposition or contingent competition. In the last case, our procedure saves us all further investigation into the complications involved in considering the length of the period upon which the demand curve is based. The appropriate costs to be reckoned are those of the present, or rather of the immediate future, so as to enable us to measure temporary monopolies. The degree of monopoly over a long period is perhaps best expressed in an average of the short-period monopolies over the period.

The primary unit to which our measure of monopoly applies is the firm in the very shortest period. In order to get a measure of monopoly over a period we had to take an average of such coefficients of monopoly. In order to get a measure of monopoly over an industry we have to follow the same procedure and find an average of monopoly of the separate firms included in the industry. The "industry" is to be considered as a group of firms, chosen for the purpose of the special investigation. It is quite unnecessary, for this purpose, to say anything at all about the "commodity" which the "industry" produces, nor is there any need to be able to draw demand or supply curves for the industry. All the difficulties of definition of "commodity" or "industry" are completely avoided.

More strictly a simple average of the degrees of monopoly in firms may be used to indicate the degree of monopoly in an industry only in the very limited sense of the degree of monopoly *at that stage*. It is not a measure of the degree to which the application of the resources of the community to the production of the products of the "industry" diverges from the social optimum. That depends upon two other sets of conditions in addition to this *local* element of monopoly.

The first of these is the degree of monopoly in the firms (or "industries") producing the raw materials for all the previous stages in the production of the products. The restriction of productions in any stage has its effects in all the succeeding stages. The final degree of reduction of product will depend upon the degree of monopoly in all the preceding stages. These have to be aggregated so as to give the tendency to divergence from the social optimum in the whole series of the production stages of the product; this phenomenon may be called the transitiveness of monopoly.

Theoretically, this can be done quite simply. What we want is the divergence between the price of the product and its marginal *social* cost. If in all the previous stages price is equal to marginal cost, the marginal cost to the firm is also the marginal social cost. If in any stage there is a divergence, price being above marginal cost, that divergence is a gap in the social cost. The social cost can then be calculated by multiplying the price by a factor for each stage in production, each factor being the ratio of the marginal cost to the price in the corresponding stage. Thus, if there are five stages and in each stage the degree of monopoly is $\frac{1}{5}$, marginal cost over price in each stage is $\frac{4}{5}$, the social cost is $(\frac{4}{5})^5$ of the price of the final product, and by our formula the "social" degree of monopoly is $I - (\frac{4}{5})^5$.

Practical difficulties that arise in attempts to measure the "social" degree of monopoly, or different products may be attacked by any of the tricks of the trade of mathematical statistics. It may be necessary to assume average degrees of monopoly in separate stages and to calculate

"social" degree of monopoly by the number of stages, and so on; but it is not intended here to discuss anything but the simplest theoretical implications.

The second set of complicating considerations arise when we ask the even more ambitious question: What is the (social) degree of monopoly in the society as a whole? From this general point of view the conditions for that optimum distribution of resources between different commodities that we designate the absence of monopoly are satisfied if prices are all *proportional* to social marginal cost. If the "social" degree of monopoly is the same for *all* final products (including leisure) there is no monopolistic alteration from the optimum at all. The absolute height of "social" degrees of monopoly becomes completely unimportant.

This is because if the "social" degree of monopoly is the same for all products it *must* be equal to zero in real terms. For from the social point of view, the marginal cost of any product is always some other product. If the "social" degree of monopoly for product A is positive, this means that the price of A is greater than the price of some other product B which is the alternative foregone. The price of B cannot then be greater than the price of A. If both degrees of monopoly are equal they must both be zero.

What is important is the deviations between the degrees of monopoly; and it is this which must be measured in order to answer our question. A suitable measure for this is the standard deviation of the "social" degrees of monopoly of all final products in the society.

Another complication arises in the growingly important cases where it is found to be profitable to extend or maintain the amount sold, not by reducing price but by expenditure on advertising, salesmanship, gifts, coupons and beautiful wrappings—all of which can be subsumed under the heading of "marketing costs." In such cases what becomes of the elasticity of demand?

In the recent cost controversy, "marketing costs" were eagerly seized upon in attempts at a conciliation between decreasing costs and competitive equilibrium.[14] Such arguments may be described with some justification as contriving to exhibit decreasing costs at peace with competitive equilibrium by the device of leaving out of account the marketing element in the costs which is increasing so rapidly that *total costs* are not decreasing at all; the contradiction being hidden by a separation of "productive" from "marketing" costs.

This solution of the problem cannot, however, be dismissed as mere word-jugglery. It does show the actual working of the forces involved, and it is only the terminology that is unfortunate. What we have here is not perfect competition but *monopolistic* or *imperfect* competition. Chamberlin and Robinson have developed a more satisfactory line of attack on these problems, but how are we to find the falling demand curve which will entitle us to put these cases into this category and enable us to deal with them in the same way?

In order to obtain this it is essential to separate productive from marketing costs. The marketing costs involved in selling a given quantity of product must be subtracted from the gross receipts, just as if they were all direct or indirect reductions in price, leaving a definite total and average net receipts. For each quantity produced different prices may be charged and different marketing costs incurred. For each output some combination of prices charged and marketing costs incurred will leave a maximum average (and total) residue after subtracting the average (or total) marketing costs, and this maximum is the relevant Average Net Receipts for that output. The locus of such points will be the Average Net Receipts curve for the firm, and this is the "demand curve" which we need. This aver-

age net receipts curve and the corresponding marginal net receipts curve have to be used in conjunction with the "productive" cost curves which we may call "net" cost curves.

If the average net receipts curve is negatively inclined, one proceeds just as in the simple analysis of imperfect competition where there are no selling costs. The firm equates its marginal net cost to its marginal net receipts, and the degree of monopoly is equal to average net receipts over average net receipts minus marginal net costs, and the divergence of the position from the social optimum is illustrated by the fact that production is not carried on at the minimum average cost, but the firm produces less than this optimum output, stopping at a point where the average net cost curve is tangential to the average net receipts curve. The social loss, if any, due to the expenditure of resources on advertising is *not* taken into account in the measurement of monopoly. The measure will be the same whether the marketing costs are large or small, and whether they are given to the consumer in forms corresponding to cash, or whether they have important influences on his tastes for good or for bad. The social effects of different kinds of advertising constitute a quite separate problem.

If the average net receipts curve is horizontal where the marginal net costs curve cuts it, there is no monopoly. The existence of marketing costs is quite another matter.

But there is no reason why the average net receipts curve should not slope upwards! It may well be that a larger quantity can be sold at a higher price at the same or a smaller *average* cost of marketing, and there is no ground for considering such a combination of circumstances as in any way exceptional. We must apply the same analysis here and not be deterred if the results at first appear a little strange.

If the firm with a rising average net revenue curve has a constant cost curve, or can acquire more of the product from other

<hr>

[14] As by R. Harrod in his article on "The Law of Decreasing Costs," *Economic Journal*, Dec. 1931.

firms without affecting its marketing possibilities, we have another form of the paradox of the incompatibility of equilibrium with a horizontal demand curve and a falling average cost curve below it. The marginal revenue and the marginal cost curves cannot meet until the conditions are changed. Either the receipts curves must begin to fall or the cost curves must rise.

The interesting case—the one which can remain in equilibrium in these conditions—is the case where the average costs of the firm rise after a time as output increases, and where it cannot obtain more from other firms at the same price, either because the other firms' costs rise or because to do this would interfere with the reputation of the firm and upset its marketing possibilities.

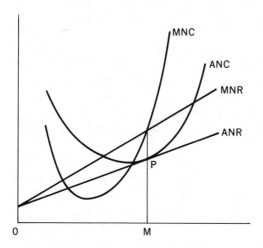

FIGURE 15.4

This is shown in Figure 15.4, where the firm is in equilibrium producing an output *OM*.

Average net receipts (*ANR*) are equal to average net costs (*ANC*), and marginal net receipts (*MNR*) are equal to marginal net costs (*MNC*). The degree of monopoly is here *negative* since marginal cost is greater than average receipts. This may appear surprising, but it merely means that the divergence from the social optimum is in the direction opposite to that usually

brought about by monopolies. Instead of the firm producing *less* than it should, it is producing *more;* the same kind of social harm is done, and it is reflected in the same way by the excess of the average cost over the minimum.

In finding an average degree of monopoly in an "industry," positive and negative monopolies may cancel out in whole or in part. Does this harm our apparatus?

I do not think it does this at all. It rather brings out the true nature of our measure as an index of *divergence* from an optimum. In any group of firms taken together to make an "industry," divergences may, and should, be expected to some extent to cancel out. For we are now considering the application of resources to this "industry" as against the rest of the economy. If of two firms within the "industry," one is producing too much and the other too little from the point of view of the economy as a whole; the industry may not be producing either too much or too little. The maladjustment becomes a local affair which we must neglect in this larger consideration.

When our "industry" becomes the whole society, there cannot be too much or too little resources used, and as we have seen above, all the individual positive and negative monopolies must cancel out. This does not mean that society as a whole must always be in an optimum position, nor does it take any meaning away from the concept. It only means that the larger the fraction of the whole society one wishes to examine, the less legitimate is it to use particular analysis. In applying the particular mechanism to the whole economy we get the appropriate *reductio ad absurdum.* What is relevant for general analysis is not the *sum* of individual degrees of monopoly but their *deviations.* The standard deviations as suggested above may perhaps be used one day to give an estimate of the divergence of society from the social optimum of production relative to a given distribution of income.

IMPERFECT COMPETITION

16. Excess Capacity and Monopolistic Competition*

JOHN M. CASSELS

John M. Cassels (B.A., the University of Alberta, 1924; B.A., Oxford University, Rhodes Scholar, 1927; Ph.D., Harvard University, 1934) was born in Scotland in 1901. He has taught at Alberta, Harvard, and Stephens College, and is now at the University of Colorado. Cassels is best known for a number of classic articles that he has contributed to economic theory. In addition to the following selection, these include his essay "On the Law of Variable Proportions," which is reprinted in The American Economic Association's *Readings in the Theory of Income Distribution*. Cassels has had wide experience in government and business, in the course of which he has been concerned with problems of consumer economics, economic aid, international trade, and the defense program.

The term excess capacity which has featured so prominently in economic discussions of recent date has a dangerously deceptive appearance of simplicity and definiteness. As a matter of fact, altho the basic idea of the concept is clearly enough suggested by the term, the variety of particular meanings that may be attached to it is so great that unless it is used and interpreted with the greatest of care it is likely to result in serious confusion of thought. The difficulties involved are especially great when the term is used, as it has been by Professor Chamberlin and others, in their analyses of the effects of monopolistic competition on the character of industrial organization. An attempt will be made in the present paper to clear up some of the misunderstandings that have arisen with respect to the conclusions which follow from Chamberlin's theory and to push the analysis of these particular problems a small step further.[1]

The central idea in the concept of excess capacity can best be brought out by means of an exceptionally simple illustrative case. Suppose that during a certain part

* Reprinted by permission of the publishers from John M. Cassels, *The Quarterly Journal of Economics* (May 1937). Cambridge, Mass.: Harvard University Press. Copyright, 1937, by the President and Fellows of Harvard College, pp. 426–443.

[1] Although the scope of this paper has not been extended to include any specific discussion of the important empirical studies that have recently been made of excess capacity in the United States it is, of course, related to them indirectly. See E. G. Nourse and associates, *America's Capacity to Produce*, published by the Brookings Institution, 1934; and Harold Loeb and associates, *A Chart of Plenty*, 1935.

of every year a town is dependent for its water supply on the contents of a natural reservoir which is replenished annually during the rainy season. Then if this reservoir held twice as much water as the people of the town had any use for when it was supplied to them free of charge, we should naturally say that it had an excess capacity of one hundred per cent; and in this case there could be little ambiguity about the statement. If the needs of the consumers varied from year to year we would have to specify whether we were measuring excess above normal needs or excess above maximum needs but the actual quantities concerned would be definitely determined by the physical measurements of the reservoir and the satiation points of the consumers' desires for water. Excess capacity is the difference between the output that the productive agent in question is capable of producing and the output it is actually called on to produce. This seems to be the basic idea of the concept wherever it is used, though in most cases the problem of giving precision to its meaning is rendered extremely difficult by the fact that neither the output obtainable nor the output called for is entirely determined by physical conditions or by unrestricted consumption requirements. Both are capable, as a rule, of wide variations according to the economic circumstances laid down as the conditions of the case, particularly the prices of the products and the cost-rates of the factors of production.

EXCESS CAPACITY
OF FIXED FACTORS

As a first step in our analysis of the difficulties thus created we must recognize that the term excess capacity is sometimes used with reference to the *fixed* factors of a firm, an industry, or a community, while at other times it is used with reference to *all* the factors involved in the functioning of the economic unit concerned. If because a pig-iron producer is using only half his blast furnaces we say that there is one hundred per cent excess capacity in his business it is evident that we can be referring only to the fixed factors in the business. The output of pig-iron could be doubled without increasing the number of furnaces, but it could not be doubled without increasing the amounts of coal and iron ore and labor that are used. On the other hand if we say in a time of depression, when production has fallen off to two-thirds of its normal level, that the community has an excess capacity of fifty per cent we must clearly be referring to the whole complex of productive agents taken together.

The excess capacity referred to by Chamberlin is an excess of all the factors in an industry, but in order to provide a sound basis for the discussion of this concept which follows, it is necessary first to consider briefly some of the difficulties involved in formulating, even in purely theoretical terms, a quantitatively exact definition of what is meant by the more elementary concept of excess capacity of fixed factors in an individual firm. It is with reference to fixed factors that the idea of excess capacity is most familiar to economists as well as to business men and it is this form of excess capacity which is so frequently called to attention by its obvious physical manifestations—mills standing idle, factories working shortened shifts, buildings unoccupied, ships laid up in dock, and so on. Evidently the importance of any given percentage of excess capacity (in this sense) in a firm or an industry will depend on the relative proportions in which the fixed and variable factors have to be combined to produce the product economically. The greater the part played by fixed factors the more important will be the problem of excess capacity.[2]

[2] It should be noted in this connection that the excess capacity of fixed factors in an industry means in most cases something different from the sum of the excess capacities of the firms in the

This type of excess capacity is naturally related to the short-run cost curves of the individual firms. It is generally agreed that, since the absolute technical upper limit of the output obtainable from the fixed factors is likely to lie far beyond the realm of practical economic operations, their capacity output should be taken as that at which the average full costs of production are at their minimum. Even if this is accepted, however, we are still left without any definite basis of measurement. The shapes of the cost curves and the outputs at which the full costs per unit will be minimized will depend on the cost-rates applied to the inputs of all the factors concerned. The optimum volume of output will vary directly with the valuation placed on the fixed factors and inversely with the prices at which the variable factors are charged. It is commonly said that from a short-run point of view the overhead costs should be treated as zero, in which case the optimum output would be at the minimum point on the curve of average variable costs. But such an output would obviously have no significance for our purpose. On the other hand we should get an equally meaningless result if we accepted a valuation of the factors which included the capitalized gains from some source of monopoly power. We are concerned not with the fixed overhead charges of the firm as such but with the economic values of the fixed factors of production used by it.

The problem of finding a satisfactory method of valuation is by no means an easy one. Different methods will be appropriate in different cases depending on the nature

of the conditions under consideration and the immediate purpose for which the analysis is being undertaken and in each case the exact meaning of the term excess capacity will vary according to the particular method that is chosen. Without attempting here to give an exhaustive enumeration of the methods that might conceivably be employed, it will be useful to distinguish briefly between certain important general types of methods. We may begin by making a distinction between those cases in which the valuation of a factor is dependent on its earning power in some specialized use to which it is irrevocably committed and those cases in which some sort of general market valuation can be used. When valuations of the former kind are involved any computation of costs becomes, in a sense, tautological yet they are probably to be preferred to zero valuations when these are the only alternatives from which to choose. Among the cases in which more general market valuations can be applied a further distinction may be made between valuations that are made for practical purposes and valuations that are to be assumed for theoretical purposes. For practical purposes the fixed factors might be valued at original cost less depreciation, replacement cost less depreciation, or at some arbitrary value thought reasonable by appraisers. Variable factors might be valued at their current prices or at the prices prevailing for them in some selected base period or at some other prices regarded as representative of their average or normal values. Since the economically optimal outputs conditioned by these different valuations may vary widely, it is important to bear in mind that from the purely practical point of view as well as from the theoretical, there is no unique and unconditional measure of capacity.

In the present paper we are more directly concerned with the valuations that may be chosen for purposes of theoretical analysis. The variety of methods from which it is

---

industry since there are some factors, such as labor, which, though variable from the point of view of the firm, may, if specialized or localized, be fixed from the point of view of the industry. It should also be recognized that even from the point of view of the individual firm the factors which have to be regarded as fixed will depend to some extent on the period of time under consideration and the magnitude of the output variations in question.

possible to choose may be illustrated simply by reference to four which seem to be particularly significant in connection with the analysis that is to follow. One method is to use the long-run equilibrium price that would tend to be established in actual markets as they exist. A second is to work with prices which would tend to be established in the long run under assumed conditions of perfect competition. A third is to use the long-run equilibrium prices that would tend to be established under some definitely specified conditions of monopolistic competition. And finally, a fourth method is to take the long-run equilibrium prices under the particular set of assumed conditions which would (in some sense) maximize the national dividend. The importance of recognizing the distinction between these will become more apparent at a later stage in the discussion.

In a similar way the question would arise as to whether excess capacity should be measured from the output actually being produced at the prevailing prices, say in a depression period, or from the output that would be sold in "normal" times at "normal prices" or from some other output theoretically determined by the particular conditions laid down, as for example under some given type of monopolistic competition. The choice depends entirely on the purpose for which the concept is being used.

EXCESS CAPACITY OF ALL FACTORS

When we turn from these considerations relating to the excess capacity of the fixed factors used by individual firms to deal with the sort of excess capacity to which Chamberlin refers we are confronted with still another set of problems. Since his analysis (in this part of the book) is based on long-run cost curves the reasoning applicable to the short-run curves is inapplicable here. Yet, because of the similarity in the shapes of the two sets of curves, as

he draws them,[3] the danger of misinterpretation is considerable. When we see from the relation of the sloping demand curve to the U-shaped cost curve in some of his familiar diagrams that the equilibrium output must of necessity be less than that for which the costs would be at a minimum it is not unnatural to think of the difference between these outputs as an indication of the extent to which the fixed factors are under-utilized. The tendency to make this mistake is increased by the convenient way in which such an interpretation seems to connect up with current observations of reality. Business men and economists alike are agreed that in certain industries the amount of physical plant and equipment is in excess of reasonable requirements. It happens that in many of these industries conditions of monopolistic competition prevail and at first glance it appears that an explanation of this excess physical capacity is to be found in the diagrams referred to. This, however, is seen to be a complete mistake when we recall that from the long-run point of view there are no fixed factors at all. Although the long-run curve of average full costs has the same general shape as the corresponding short-run curve, its significance is entirely different. The cost associated with each output is the minimum at which it could be produced in the given state of the arts and with given cost-rates when *all* the factors are combined together in the most appropriate forms and proportions.

As the scale of operations of a firm is increased it becomes possible to make a finer adjustment of the proportions in which any given factors of production are combined with one another. It also becomes possible

[3] Chamberlin calls attention to this similarity in the shapes of the curves on p. 139 where he cautions the reader that they must be interpreted according to the nature of the particular problem under consideration. The character which they have in the part of his discussion relating to excess capacity is stated on pp. 20–21 and is more fully explained in Appendix B.

to use larger machines wherever they have a technical superiority over smaller ones, to use more highly specialized machines, and to apply further than could be done in a smaller business the principle of division of labor among its employees. For these reasons the long-run cost curve will have a tendency to fall as output is increased, at least until a certain volume has been attained. There are, however, increasing difficulties to be encountered in the coördination of the work of all the different factors as the size of the business is enlarged as a consequence of which, after a certain volume of output has been attained, the economies of large-scale production are outweighed by the diseconomies and the cost curve begins to rise. According to Chamberlin's view further opportunities for improvements in the character and combination of the factors continue to be presented indefinitely as the output is increased. This accounts for the U-shaped character of the curves he draws. On the basis of this reasoning the curve (when minor irregularities have been smoothed out) must slope downwards continuously to the point where the economies are just offset by the diseconomies and it must slope upwards continuously thereafter. This explanation, as will be seen at once, is entirely different from the one which accounts for the U-shaped character of the short-run cost curve.

It is true that at any output less than that which would minimize long-run costs there will be present of necessity some small amount of excess capacity in the fixed factors such as was discussed above, but it is important to remember that no indication whatever of this amount is to be obtained from a comparison of the given output with the optimum that is indicated by the long-run curve. The reason that some excess capacity of this sort is bound to be present in this case is that for any output at which the long-run cost curve is negatively inclined, so also must be the short-run curve. Since the long-run curve represents the lowest cost for which each output could be produced, no point on any short-run curve can lie below it. This means that no short-run curve can cut it and therefore all common points must be points of tangency. At points of tangency the curves must have the same slope and consequently wherever the long-run costs are declining so also must be the short-run costs.[4] But the short-run curve may turn up immediately this point is passed while the long-run curve continues to descend for an indefinite distance beyond it.

When the term excess capacity is used in connection with an analysis based on long-run cost curves, it clearly cannot be meant to refer to this excess of the fixed factors but must refer in some sense to an excess capacity of *all* the factors employed by an industry. What is actually meant by Chamberlin is the presence in an industry of an amount of general productive resources which if they were more efficiently employed could produce an output that would add more to the national dividend.[5] It should be noted here that whenever there is present in the community a desire for differentiation of sellers the method of utilizing the given factors of production which will contribute most to the national dividend, and may therefore be regarded as the optimum, will not be that which would be most appropriate under conditions of pure competition. More will be said of this later. For the present we must simply rec-

[4] This is well explained by R. F. Harrod in his article on "Doctrines of Imperfect Competition," in the *Quarterly Journal of Economics,* May, 1934.

[5] It is recognized, of course, that an entirely satisfactory measure of the quantity of general productive resources invested in an industry is perhaps impossible to find, but for many purposes, unless the industry is a very large one or uses a very large proportion of some particular unique resource, the displacement value or opportunity cost of the factors may be accepted as a fair approximation to the measure that we want. With respect to the measurement of the national dividend we should simply follow Professor Pigou.

ognize that the appropriate measure of this type of excess capacity would be the difference between the actual contribution to the national dividend and that which could be obtained from the same resources if they were combined together in the most efficient way (i.e. most efficient with reference to the selected definition of maximum national dividend). It will be observed that excess capacity of this sort cannot exist for any one firm which is in long-run equilibrium, since at any point on its long-run cost curve all the factors employed by it are, by definition, combined in the way most appropriate to that output. It is a concept which can apply only to the industry as a whole.[6]

CHAMBERLIN'S ANALYSIS

With these basic concepts in mind we are now in a position to understand more easily the particular use made of the term excess capacity in Chamberlin's analysis. His book is specifically intended to deal with cases in which both monopoly and competitive elements are present. He begins by distinguishing between those monopoly elements that are due to the fewness of the sellers and those which are due to the differentiation of the product dealt in.[7] Since cases in which two or some other given small number of sellers were supposed to be selling a strictly standardized product had been dealt with before by other economists, he naturally begins by refining the analysis based on these particular assumptions in his chapter on "duopoly and oligopoly." Then he proceeds to his pathbreaking analysis of cases in which the product is differentiated. All cases of this sort are included under the general heading of "monopolistic competition." His analysis is developed systematically by the consideration successively of four distinct cases in which different basic assumptions are made. He would admit that these assumptions are not always as explicitly stated nor as clearly explained in advance as they might be. The difficulties of his readers have consequently been increased but the logic of his own analysis is unimpaired.

In the following summary some liberties have been taken in matters of arrangement and phraseology, but the ideas are strictly those of the text. In the first case it is assumed [8]: (i) that there are many sellers, (ii) that entry into the industry is free, (iii) that the effects of individual actions are completely diffused, and (iv) that the individuals are aggressive in their price policies. What is meant by the effects of individual actions being completely diffused is that "any adjustment of price or product by a single producer spreads its influence over so many of his competitors that the impact felt by any one is negligible and does not lead him to any readjustment of his own situation." [9] What is meant by the individuals being aggressive in their price policies is that there is nothing in their psychological make-ups, or their bookkeeping methods, or their ideas of business ethics, or their institutional arrangements, which will prevent them cutting price when the competitive situation calls for price cutting. In the second case it is assumed [10]: (i) that instead of many sellers there are only a few, and (ii) that no new competitors are free to enter the industry. (This second assumption seems to be carried over from the older theories of duopoly.) From these two assumptions it follows (iii) that competitors are conscious of the effects of one another's acts and, consequently, (iv) price policies are likely to be to some extent non-aggressive. In the third case it is as-

[6] It is recognized that difficulties, perhaps in some cases insurmountable, are involved in the retention of the concept of an industry under conditions of product differentiation, but the discussion of that issue is beyond the scope of the present paper.

[7] See p. 8.

[8] Pp. 71–100.

[9] P. 83.

[10] Pp. 100–102.

sumed [11]: (i) that there are many sellers and (ii) there is free entry into the industry, but (iii) that the effects of individual actions instead of being diffused are quite strongly felt by a relatively small group of *close* competitors and, consequently, (iv) price policies will tend to be non-aggressive. In the fourth case it is assumed [12]: (i) that the numbers are large and (ii) that entry is free, but that, although (iii) the effects of individual actions may be widely diffused, (iv) the price policies of the sellers are, nevertheless, for one reason or another, non-aggressive.

It is particularly important for our present purpose to distinguish clearly between these different cases because it is one of Chamberlin's most significant, although most imperfectly understood conclusions, that excess capacity (of all factors) can never be brought into existence by monopolistic competition of the first type. Contrary to a widely accepted interpretation of his analysis the existence of a sloping individual demand curve, with its point of tangency to the left of the minimum point on the long-run cost curve, is not taken by him as evidence that excess capacity will exist in the industry under equilibrium conditions. The logic of his position is stated in the text as follows:

> We may regard the elasticity of dd′ as a rough index of buyers' preferences for the "product" of one seller over that of another. The equilibrium adjustment therefore becomes *a sort of ideal*. With fewer establishments, larger scales of production, and lower prices it would always be true that buyers would be willing to pay more than it would cost to give them a greater diversity of product; and conversely, with more producers and smaller scales of production, the higher prices they would pay would be more than such gains were worth.[13]

The differentness of the sellers (including differentness of location) may be regarded as a quality of the "product" which is appreciated by consumers in the same way as color or shape or flavor is appreciated; and there is no reason to treat the costs involved in providing this quality as being essentially different from the costs of giving the products any other qualities.

As has been already pointed out there are very serious difficulties involved in the determination of any kind of optimum output. While there are certain specific difficulties to be encountered in dealing with this particular one, there can be little doubt that when a desire for differentiation of sellers is present in the community under consideration (as it is under Chamberlin's first set of assumptions) his "sort of ideal" is more significant in this connection than the optimum appropriate to conditions of pure competition determined simply by the minimum points on the long-run cost curves of the producers. Against it, however, two types of objection may be raised.

In the first place it may be objected that, in spite of what Chamberlin has said about consumers getting just the amount of differentiation they are willing to pay for, there is no guarantee that the marginal social costs of these products will be exactly equal to their prices as they should be if the national dividend is to be maximized. From the social point of view each individual producer of a differentiated product is in the position occupied in Pigou's analysis of welfare economics by a one-firm industry operating under conditions of decreasing supply price.[14] If all other production was being carried on under conditions of constant costs and perfect competition the marginal social cost of a differentiated product would be somewhat less than the corresponding marginal social net product and a fairly definite idea of the error in our measure could be obtained. It must be remembered, however, that even under these conditions the increase of output from these

---

[11] Pp. 102–105.
[12] Pp. 105–109.
[13] Pp. 93–94. The italics are mine.

[14] *Economics of Welfare* (4th ed.), Appendix iii.

producers which would be necessary in order to equalize the marginal social net products of resources throughout the economic system would not necessarily carry them anywhere near to the output that would minimize their long-run average production costs per unit. Moreover if the assumption that all other production is carried on under constant costs and perfect competition is withdrawn, it is no longer certain that the defect of the particular producers under consideration is on the side of underproduction. In other words Chamberlin's "sort of ideal" corresponds only approximately to the output which would be necessary to maximize the national dividend and the error involved in any particular case may be that either too much or too little of the differentiated product in question is produced. Of this he himself seems to have been more or less clearly aware from the start. It is evident from his language that, although he perceived the logical deficiencies of the generally accepted concept of a purely competitive optimum and the necessity of rejecting it for the purposes of his analysis, he had no intention of insisting that he had found a perfectly satisfactory substitute. Subsequent work by Mr. R. F. Kahn[15] has shown how this line of analysis may be more fully developed and in any discussion of the problems involved it may be assumed that Chamberlin's treatment of excess capacity could be further refined, wherever necessary, by the use of Kahn's "ideal" in place of his own "sort of ideal."

The second type of objection is of a rather different character. It rests upon a recognition of the fact that consumers do not always know how much differentiation would be beneficial for them. Nor can they control very accurately through their market responses the amount of differentiation that is actually given them. These are undoubtedly valid criticisms of our existing

economic system and the agreement would be almost unanimous that certain extreme cases of artificial differentiation are distinctly wasteful from the social point of view. But it must be recognized that in the formulation of such judgments we are led almost inevitably to introduce considerations which, according to usual distinctions, are non-economic in character. If we question the social desirability of having half a dozen competing brands of cigarettes, must we not also be prepared to question in a similar way the desirability of having cigarettes at all, or at least of having them in the quantity that we do have them? Such questions have to be dealt with in the development of social policies and it is by no means the intention of the present writer to argue that economists should refrain from any consideration of them. But it must be admitted that the method adopted by Chamberlin, of working out first an analysis in which ethical considerations are passed over, is one in favor of which very strong arguments have been adduced. It is on the basis of this analysis that he concludes that monopolistic competition of his first type would have no tendency to produce excess capacity.

Excess capacity in Chamberlin's sense might be present in any of the other three cases because of the fact that, for one reason or another, price policies are likely to be non-aggressive. As he points out quite clearly in the text,[16] the presence of differentiation will in actual practice result very commonly in the fulfilment of the conditions of his third case because of the "closeness" of some particular competitors. Nevertheless it is important for the logic of the analysis to recognize that differentiation does not of itself account for the development of excess capacity.[17] Actually

[15] "Notes on the Ideal Output," *Economic Journal,* March 1935.

[16] Pp. 103–104.
[17] Unfortunately the widely read interpretation of Chamberlin given by Mr. N. Kaldor in his article on "Market Imperfections and Excess Capacity" (*Economica*, February 1935), makes it appear as if he did attribute excess capacity di-

it is only in connection with his third and fourth cases that Chamberlin makes any reference to excess capacity. In his second case, although it might be in existence, the fact that the number of competitors in the industry is taken as given precludes the possibility of any discussion of the process by which it was brought into being. In discussing his third and fourth cases[18] he explains how, when the price policies are non-aggressive and entry into the industry is free, each individual producer may find himself under equilibrium conditions producing at an output smaller and a cost higher than would have been determined by the sloping demand curve for his particular product under conditions of aggressive price competition.[19]

EXCESS CAPACITY AND OVERINVESTMENT

Before leaving this subject it will be well to make a clear distinction between *excess capacity* and *overinvestment* in an industry. Overinvestment relates to the question of the ideal distribution of resources between all the different industries contributing to the national dividend. The distribution which would tend to maximize the

national dividend is generally accepted as the ideal, and the quantity of resources which should be put into any particular industry to attain this end is regarded as the ideal investment for that industry. Overinvestment would therefore be measured by the extent to which the resources actually put into any industry exceed this ideal amount. This is clearly a different thing from excess capacity, although they may very readily become confused. Without attempting to reach any final decision as to what the ideal investment would actually be, let us consider the relative quantities of resources likely to be invested in an industry under conditions of pure competition, monopolistic competition with aggressive price policies, and monopolistic competition with non-aggressive price policies. It does not seem possible to reach any definite conclusions about this in cases where the entry into the industry is not free (as in Chamberlin's third case) but in other cases where the entry is assumed to be free, the matter turns out to be more simple than it would at first sight appear to be. It follows from the assumption of free entry into the industry that (in equilibrium) profits will be at the competitive level. These necessary profits are included in the cost curves with which we are working, and the entrepreneurial services for which they are the necessary compensation are among the general productive resources utilized in the industry. Therefore the total amount paid by buyers for the output of the industry is equal to the total value of the general productive resources used to produce it[20] (accepting market valuations of the factors as reasonably satisfactory measures for the present purpose).

rectly to the differentiation of the product and that he would measure it by comparing the monopolistic output with the purely competitive optimum. Mr. Kaldor seems to have overlooked the change in assumptions between the first case and the fourth and has treated the conclusions reached at the end of the chapter as if they followed from the conditions laid down at the beginning of it.

[18] See particularly the discussion on p. 105. It should be noted in this connection that certain difficulties are raised if the assumption of similarity in the cost function of all producers is given up. Without denying the importance of these difficulties it seems best in the present paper to pass them over without any detailed discussion.

[19] On p. 171 he says, "Whenever price competition fails to function, whether because each seller is in close competition with only a few others or for any other reason, the result is not merely higher prices, but also excess capacity as a permanent and normal characteristic of the equilibrium adjustment."

[20] It must be remembered, of course, that demand curves and cost curves represent quantities that will be bought or produced in some particular period of time (a day or a week or a year, or any other period). In the present discussion of the investment of resources in an industry, we must take the period within which all the factors that are fixed from the short-run point of view would be completely worn out.

It follows from this that the amount of resources used in the industry when equilibrium is established under the different sets of conditions assumed will depend on the elasticity of the demand curve in the general market for the product of the industry. Admittedly this concept of a general market demand curve loses much of its precision when product differentiation is present but it seems permissible here to follow Chamberlin in using it for the sake of simplifying the exposition. If the elasticity of demand is unity throughout the relevant range, the investments under conditions of pure competition, monopolistic competition with aggressive price policies, and monopolistic competition with non-aggressive price policies will all be the same. If the demand is inelastic, the investment under monopolistic competition with aggressive price policies will be greater than under pure competition, and under monopolistic competition with non-aggressive price policies it would be still greater. If the demand were elastic, the investment under monopolistic competition with aggressive price policies would be less than under pure competition, and under monopolistic competition with non-aggressive price policies it would be still less. The importance of distinguishing clearly between *"excess capacity"* and *"overinvestment"* can now be made more apparent. This is strikingly brought out by the example of monopolistic competition with non-aggressive price policies in a market where the demand is elastic; because in this case there will be excess capacity in the industry, while there will almost certainly be underinvestment compared either with Pigou's ideal for purely competitive conditions, or Chamberlin's "sort of ideal" for conditions of monopolistic competition, or Kahn's ideal for monopolistic competition.

It may be noted in passing that even in cases where the investment of resources is less, the number of producers will always be greater under monopolistic competition

with aggressive price policies than under pure competition, and still greater under monopolistic competition with non-aggressive price policies. This follows from the fact that within the relevant range of production, the *arc* elasticity of demand, between the prices corresponding to any of our ideal investments and any other price that is higher, must always be less than the *arc* elasticity of the representative individual long-run average cost curve between the costs equal to these prices. This is equivalent to pointing out on Chamberlin's Figure 14 (p. 91) that the individual demand curve DD′ lies above the average cost curve as far to the left of R as production could rationally be carried on.

This whole matter may perhaps be made more clear by a simple arithmetical example. Suppose that under conditions of pure competition, equilibrium would be established with the price at $1.00 and with 100 firms each producing 1,000 units of product. The total amount paid for this output would be $100,000 and this would also be the value of the resources used. Suppose then that differentiation is introduced and that the new equilibrium price is $1.05 and the output per producer at this cost is 800 units. The 100 original producers could now supply the market with 80,000 units but because of the relations noted above between the elasticities of the demand curve and the cost curve, it follows that buyers are willing at a price of $1.05 to take more than this amount. Suppose, the demand being elastic, they would take 88,000 units, then we know that equilibrium must have been established by the entry of ten new producers into the industry. This is consistent with what Chamberlin has said. Although he has made no statement about the quantity of resources, there is a danger that readers may jump to the conclusion that since the number of producers must always be greater, the total resources used in the industry must also be greater than under pure competition. From the example here considered, it can be seen that this is not the case when the demand is elastic. The resources under pure competition had a value of $100,000, while under monopolistic competition of the first type the total resources used were worth only $92,400 ($1.05 × 88,000). The same relations would hold if the comparison were made between monopolistic competition with aggressive and non-aggressive price policies.

CONCLUSION

The most important conclusion emerging from the foregoing discussion is that the term excess capacity must be used and interpreted with the greatest of care if serious misunderstandings and errors in logic are to be avoided. The central idea in the concept is the difference between actual output and potential output. Potential output is conditioned in most cases by economic circumstances and must be interpreted as being the optimum output from the economic point of view. We have seen that this will be different according to the periods of time that are allowed for adjustments in the scale of output. Careful distinction must always be made between the excess capacity of *fixed* factors which exists for the short run and the excess capacity of *all* factors which may be present over the long run; and it must be recognized that in both cases the amount of excess capacity present will depend to some extent on the valuations placed on the various factors of production that are employed in the industry under consideration.

17. Advertising Expenditures: A Suggested Treatment*

NORMAN S. BUCHANAN[1]

Norman S. Buchanan (B.A., University of Toronto, 1927; M.A., Cornell University, 1929, Ph.D., 1931) was born in 1905 and died in 1958. At the time of his death he was Director of Social Sciences for the Rockefeller Foundation. Buchanan is the author of a number of books, including *International Investment and Domestic Welfare* and *Approaches to Economic Development* (with H. S. Ellis).

The general theory of selling costs, which received its initial statement of any length at the hands of Professor Chamberlin, has been subsequently re-examined by several writers with illuminating results.[2] Not all authors have used precisely the same assumptions, nor have they in every case been concerned with the problem in quite the form in which Professor Chamberlin originally raised the issue. A solution to the theoretical problem of selling expenditures is here offered which, the writer believes, is both simpler and more flexible

* Reprinted from the *Journal of Political Economy* (August 1942) by permission of The University of Chicago Press. Copyright, 1942, pp. 537–557.

[1] The writer is indebted to the Social Science Research Council for a fellowship, when the present paper was partially developed.

[2] An extensive bibliography of the literature on selling costs up to 1936 will be found in E. H. Chamberlin, *The Theory of Monopolistic Competition* (2d ed.; Cambridge, Mass., 1936), p. 217. The theoretical problems raised by selling expenditures have' been analyzed especially in the following: *ibid.*, chap. vii; T. O. Yntema, summary of a paper read before the American Economic Association, December, 1933, in *American Economic Review, Supplement*, XXIV (1934), 21–23; H. Smith, "Advertising Costs and Equilib-rium," *Review of Economic Studies*, II (1933), 62–65; Robert M. Shone, "Selling Costs," *Review of Economic Studies*, II (1933), 225–31; R. D. Soucey, "Group Equilibrium with Selling Costs Variable," *Review of Economic Studies*, VI (1939), 222–25; E. K. Zingler, "Advertising Costs and the Maximization of Profit," *Economica*, VII (new ser., 1940), 318–21. Some discussion of the special problems of advertising and duopoly will be found in George J. Stigler, "Notes on the Theory of Duopoly," *Journal of Political Economy*, XLVIII (1940), 521–41, at 537–39.

than any of those hitherto available; but it is conceded that the differences in substantive conclusions are not great.

I

Professor Chamberlin's[3] theory of selling costs is based on the reasonable assumption that selling costs yield, first, increasing returns but subsequently decreasing returns. In the complete case, selling costs, the product offered for sale, and prices are all variable simultaneously. But Chamberlin finds it convenient to develop his theory through three partial cases, taking one variable at a time, while the other two are set at rest. For example, by taking price and product as given, it is possible to indicate the optimum selling-cost outlay; or, again, by assuming total selling cost and product as given, one can indicate the optimum price. The complete case in which all three variables are dealt with simultaneously is treated only summarily by indicating the general characteristics of the equilibrium adjustment.[4]

This technique is theoretically unobjectionable, but it is cumbersome in comparison with the neatness and simplicity of the treatment elsewhere in the theory of monopolistic competition. The theory cannot be expounded diagrammatically without the use of numerous figures, and only by visual comparison can one indicate the optimum combination of price, product, and selling expenditure.[5] Moreover, there is perhaps the added disadvantage that the problem is not formulated in a manner analogous to that in which it would present itself to an entrepreneur in the real world. Typically, the latter would doubtless proceed on the assumption that there would be some demand for his product,

even with zero selling-cost outlays. What the entrepreneur would consider important is the increment in sales receipts accompanying increments in selling expenditures. He would ask: "How much more can I sell and at what prices if I make selling outlays of differing amounts, and will my net returns be greater or less than if I make no selling expenditures whatsoever?" [6] The typical retail merchant, for example, would assume that he would have some sales from merely displaying his merchandise, even if he did not advertise at all.[7] His problem is: "How much will advertising increase the demand for my product under given conditions, and what is the maximum advertising outlay it will pay me to undertake?"

The exposition that follows attempts to combine at the same time varying advertising expenditures and varying prices (and quantities) and to indicate what combination thereof will maximize returns to the enterprise. Instead of dealing with one variable at a time, the method to be described allows one to deal with price and advertising expenditures as simultaneous variables. The problem of product differentiation, however, is not dealt with except in so far as advertising expenditures inevitably change the buyers' estimation of the worth of the commodity. From the point of view of the producer at least, the product is assumed to be given in the sense that the same production function governs its output throughout the whole

---

[3] *Op. cit.,* chap. vii.

[4] *Ibid.,* pp. 147–49.

[5] See, e.g., *ibid.,* pp. 147–49 and 167–69, where the solution is briefly sketched. A diagram showing the accomplished equilibrium adjustment, but not the process, appears on p. 148.

[6] Smith (*op. cit.,* p. 63) poses the problem in precisely this fashion.

[7] Zingler (*op. cit.,* p. 318) suggests that advertising may be divided into two parts, "one of which is referred to as quantity-increasing—the assumption is that its purpose is to sell a greater quantity of a commodity at the same price— and the other is referred to as price-increasing— the assumption is that its purpose is to sell the same quantity of the commodity in question at a higher price." Such a distinction serves no very useful purpose, since the firm is concerned to maximize returns by whatever means available, i.e., by varying both quantity and price if necessary.

analysis.[8] Our treatment is graphical rather than algebraic.

Instead of speaking of "selling costs" in what follows, we speak of "advertising outlays" or "expenditures." Although the latter term is not unambiguous, it is perhaps less imprecise and offers fewer problems of definition than does the broader term "selling costs." [9] While the following discussion is directed to what is ordinarily understood by "advertising expenditures," it will for the most part be equally valid when applied to the broader category of expenditures known as "selling costs."

II

In Figure 17.1 we make the case very simple by assuming that production costs are zero and that the only relevant consideration is advertising cost. Let DD_1 be the demand curve confronting the firm, independent of any advertising outlays: it indicates the amount the firm would sell at all various prices if it did *not* advertise. If MR_1 is the marginal revenue curve appropriate to DD_1, the firm will maximize its net returns by fixing a price of P_1, at which the quantity sold is Q_1, since only when marginal revenue is zero will total gross receipts be a maximum. Let us now assume that the entrepreneur contemplates advertising outlays. Let us assume, as seems reasonable, that some minimum advertising expenditure, A, must be incurred

before the effect upon the demand schedule becomes perceptible, and let DD_a be the new demand curve resulting from it.[10] With aggregate advertising expenditure, A, the curve of average advertising cost will be a rectangular hyperbola, S_a. The horizontal distance between DD_1 and DD_a indicates the increase in the quantities that can be sold at each respective price as a consequence of spending an aggregate amount A on advertising. The effect upon sales may

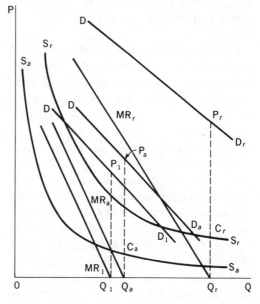

FIGURE 17.1

be marked at some prices but negligible at others, depending upon a variety of factors: DD_a need not parallel DD_1. With MR_a the marginal revenue curve corresponding to the average revenue curve DD_a, the optimum price is P_a, at which the quantity sold is Q_a. Aggregate excess of receipts over expenses is indicated by the rectangle having OQ_a as its base and P_aC_a as its altitude. As drawn in the figure, it is clear that, with aggregate advertising expenses of an amount A, net receipts are

---

[8] On the cost side, with given prices of input factors, we operate with one production-cost schedule all the way through. In Chamberlin's analysis each product differentiation is associated with a unique cost schedule, which presumably is assumed to be an inevitable accompaniment of differentiating the product. While this way of treating product differentiation is in the writer's opinion not wholly satisfactory, the difficulties involved do not affect the present argument and need not be considered here. The initial stages of our own analysis employ the simplifying assumption that production costs are zero.

[9] As is common knowledge, the demarcation in many cases between production costs and selling costs is shadowy rather than sharp.

[10] In Fig. 17.1, DD_a is more than a "perceptible" distance from DD_1. But this is only to facilitate the reading of the diagram by visual inspection. It is logically incorrect.

smaller than those to be had without advertising.

There will be a whole family of demand curves from the right and upward from DD_a, corresponding to advertising outlays of $A + 1$, $A + 2$, $A + 3$, ... R . . . . N. . . . . Similarly, there will be a family of S curves (one for each aggregate amount of advertising expenditure), each of which indicates the range of average advertising costs at different rates of sales. The curve S_{a+1}, slightly to the right of S_a, will be relevant to the demand curve DD_{a+1}, and so forth.

The position of each demand curve being determined in the manner just described, the optimum rate of sale for each demand curve will be where its respective marginal revenue curve intersects the quantity axis.[11] The price will be that indicated by erecting a perpendicular from that point to the appropriate demand curve. But the intersection of this perpendicular with the curve of average advertising costs calling the particular demand curve into existence shows how much advertising costs will average per unit of sales. Hence, the series of points C_a, ... , C_r show, by their vertical distance from the base, average advertising costs for each optimum rate of sales; and the series of points P_1, P_a, ... , P_r, indicate optimum selling prices.

Figure 17.2 is based directly on Figure 17.1. If we connect all the optimum selling prices on the different demand curves, we obtain a curve LAR, the locus of optimum average revenues. Similarly, by connecting all the average advertising costs we secure a curve LAS, the locus of average advertising costs. Every point on LAR is a point on a particular demand curve: that point at which aggregate gross receipts are a maximum, i.e., if production costs are zero, the point at which marginal revenue becomes zero. Every point on LAS indicates average advertising cost when average

[11] Let it be recalled that we are so far assuming zero production costs.

revenue is equivalent to the point on LAR exactly above it (or below it).[12]

In Figure 17.2, if we operate with the LAS curve, we can read off the results in terms of gross income of advertising outlays of different amounts by raising a perpendicular to LAR. On the other hand, if we operate with the LAR curve, we can deduce the advertising outlays required to produce a given total gross income (for a particular demand curve) by dropping

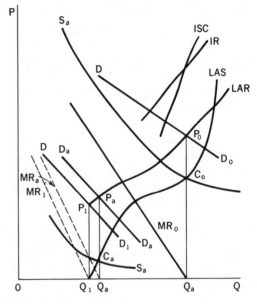

FIGURE 17.2

a perpendicular to LAS. For any point on the abscissa the difference between the area of the rectangle indicating gross receipts and that indicating total advertising expenditure is, of course, the net gain. But what constitutes the *optimum* advertising expenditure?

If curves such as LAR and LAS are continuous, each of them has a marginal or incremental curve appropriate to it. Let

[12] Since there are doubtless diminishing returns from expenditure on advertising, average advertising costs may exceed average revenue. In Fig. 17.2, it will be observed, LAS is below LAR through most of its length, but it crosses LAR high up and to the right and then subsequently lies above it.

such incremental curves be IR and ISC, respectively.[13] The intersection of these two incremental curves must determine the optimum advertising expenditure. In other words, the rectangle indicating profits will be the largest possible at that point on the abscissa which lies directly below the point of intersection of ISC and IR. In Figure 17.2 this optimum is indicated by S_o, which creates the demand curve DD_o. The marginal revenue curve relevant thereto is, of course, MR_o, and the price is P_oQ_o, while the quantity sold is Q_o. Average advertising cost per unit of output is C_oQ_o. The points P_o, C_o, and Q_o lie directly below the point of intersection of IR and ISC, which fixes their position.

III

It is worth speculating upon the different shapes and positions that LAR and LAS might conceivably assume. Advertising may have more effect upon the demand at high than at low prices. If this be true, then the quantities sold after advertising is first undertaken may be smaller and the price higher than when no selling outlays at all were made. In terms of the courses traced by LAR and LAS this means that they may be "backward rising" over a certain range before they commence moving upward and to the right.[14] If, on the other hand, advertising primarily increases

demand in the lower price ranges, LAR and LAS would move more rapidly to the right and less quickly upward than we have drawn them in Figure 17.2.

In general, it seems reasonable to assume that, after a certain initial stage, advertising by any given firm will at first yield increasing returns but then subsequently decreasing returns. In other words, demand curves will at first shift upward and to the right more rapidly than the rectangular hyperbolas representing the larger advertising outlays which "create" the demand. Consequently, the vertical distance between LAR and LAS will tend to widen as they move to the right. Subsequently, however, it becomes more and more difficult to attract customers from competing firms or to alter buyers' preferences for this type of product as opposed to others. As a result, LAS begins to rise more rapidly than LAR: the vertical distance between them narrows, until in due course LAS cuts LAR from below and ultimately lies above it. Beyond the point of intersection, of course, average advertising expense is greater than average receipts.

It is not inconceivable that there might be more than one point of intersection of LAR and LAS. This could be the case, for example, if, as total advertising expenditures increased, one gradually moved over to an entirely different type of advertising which permitted access to markets not previously available at all. For instance, if a firm is shifting from a local market to country-wide distribution and is planning a national advertising program through the popular magazines and the radio, it will probably have to spend some large sum as a minimum or not try to tap the national market at all.[15] Consequently, the distance between LAR and LAS as we move to the right in Figure 17.2 may nar-

---

[13] In Fig. 17.2 both IR and ISC are not drawn throughout their whole length but only in the neighborhood of their point of intersection. This is done deliberately for two reasons: first, the diagram would be unnecessarily complicated and, second, ISC (and possibly IR, too) would probably describe a quasi-parabola in its early stages. Since ISC is "marginal" to LAS, this is very likely if LAS typically has the shape we have given it. However, it should be emphasized that in any case ISC has its origin at Q_1, while IR has its origin at P_1.

[14] While it is possible that IR could be negative over a certain range, the same is not true of ISC because the assumption is that the increment in advertising expenditures is always positive from an outlay of A on upward.

[15] This is analogous to the point previously made, viz., that it will not be worth advertising at all unless one is willing to spend some minimum sum.

row but subsequently widen out again. As total advertising expenditures are increased, the resulting demand curves for the product may become more or less elastic. The more elastic they become, the flatter will *LAR* tend to be. And it is not inconceivable that *LAR* might dip below the horizontal for some small range, although this seems unlikely. In this instance advertising could be said to have reduced the price of the product—an advantage often claimed on its behalf. In any case *LAR* would not continue to fall indefinitely, because the limit to gradually increasing elasticity is a horizontal demand curve.

If one is concerned with "long-run" solutions as contrasted with optimum short-run adjustments, it is necessary to recognize that what one firm can do under conditions of monopolistic competition is also open to other enterprises. No one firm can long retain any advantage it has gained. If one admits the possibility of excess returns tending to disappearance under conditions of monopolistic competition, leaving only "normal" returns (in some sense), then the additional gains from advertising expenditures would also disappear. One would obtain a "tangency" solution with respect to advertising that was parallel to that obtained by Chamberlin in his case of group equilibrium.[16] Diagrammatically, the group equilibrium case would be roughly as follows: In Figure 17.2, *LAS*, except at its very beginning, would lie above *LAR* throughout its whole range, but they would be tangent to each other at some one point upward and to the right of the origin. Only one combination of advertising expenditure and resulting demand curve would allow an equality between average revenue and average advertising cost. In one respect, however, such a solution contradicts one basic assumption with which we have chosen to operate thus far. We have assumed that, even without advertising, a

[16] *Op. cit.*, p. 92.

demand for the product would still exist. Consequently, as long as we retain this assumption there would be no necessity for the entrepreneur to accept the tangency adjustment, since he could always retreat to the position of zero advertising-cost outlays and obtain a return over the going rate.[17] The case can be modified, however, to make it realistic easily enough by assuming that no demand for the product would exist without advertising.[18] In this instance *LAR* as well as *LAS* would commence on the abscissa. For the tangency case of group equilibrium *LAR* would lie below *LAS* throughout its whole range except for the point of tangency. Only one advertising outlay would permit the firm to obtain a normal rate of return.

Since advertising can take such a wide variety of forms on short notice, however, it is doubtful if group equilibrium in the usual sense is more than a theoretical possibility. In the writer's opinion it is improbable that a group equilibrium embracing a tangency solution has any counterpart in the real world. It may be approached at times, but it is unlikely ever to be attained. What is more probable is that the range over which *LAR* lies above *LAS* in Figure 17.2 is considerably smaller than we have drawn it. It is often said, for example, that much competitive advertising "cancels out" or that, where all the firms in an industry advertise, no one firm can afford not to advertise on about the average scale without reducing its profits. In terms of Figure 17.2 such commonplace expressions are nothing more than a way of saying that LAS lies above LAR for all

[17] Once we admit production costs, of course, this difficulty disappears.
[18] This case is perhaps not quite so fantastic as it might first appear. Many pleasure resorts in the mountains and beaches now in existence have their expenses almost entirely made up of selling costs in the economic sense. What people come to enjoy is the air or the view. What they pay for as an admission charge is mostly the cost of having the existence of "the view" brought to their attention.

but a small portion of its length. Some considerable advertising outlay is necessary to avoid losses, simply because other firms advertise. From the point of view of the consumer the price of the product is probably higher and the quantity sold smaller than would be the case if all firms cut their advertising expenditures by the same percentage.

IV

The argument so far has been formulated on the simplifying assumption that production costs are nonexistent, but the method already outlined can be applied to the case of positive production costs with only minor modifications.

If conditions of constant cost prevail, then, of course, the intersections of all the many marginal revenue curves with the horizontal marginal cost curve will determine the optimum prices and quantities for the many demand curves resulting from advertising in different amounts. Rather than the optimum prices and quantities being determined (as in Figures 17.1 and 17.2) by the intersections of the marginal revenue curves with the abscissa, they will be fixed, instead, by the points of intersection of the different marginal revenue curves with the horizontal straight line indicating marginal cost of production. For the same series of demand curves as in Figure 17.2 the optimum prices will in every case be higher and the quantities sold smaller as a consequence of introducing production costs which are constant per unit of output. The locus of average combined cost, which we could call $LACC$, would commence, not on the abscissa, as in Figure 17.2, but at some point above and to the left of the position it occupies in the figure.[19] LAR, similarly, would commence in the same vertical plane as $LACC$ but would be above and to the left of its

position in Figure 17.2. The origin of LAR might be either above or below the origin of $LACC$, though both are in the same vertical plane, according to whether the firm is able to show an excess of average receipts over average costs with zero outlays for advertising. If average receipts at the optimum point on DD_1 exceed average costs, then the origin of LAR will lie above the origin of $LACC$ and vice versa.[20]

The case where production costs are not constant per unit of output can be dealt with similarly by means of the apparatus in Figures 17.3 and 17.4. In Figure 17.3 let

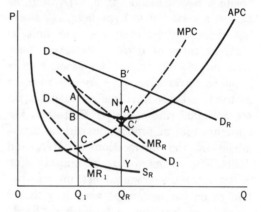

FIGURE 17.3

DD_1, as before, represent the demand conditions for the product prior to any expenditures for advertising. MR_1 is the marginal revenue curve appropriate to DD_1. Let APC and MPC be, respectively, the curves of average and marginal production costs per unit of output. With advertising outlays of zero the firm will maximize its returns by producing at the rate of Q_1 sold at the price Q_1B, since at this rate marginal cost is equal to marginal revenue. Actually, the firm suffers losses under these conditions, since average cost

[19] No curve with the notation $LACC$, of course, appears in Fig. 17.2.

[20] DD_1 is the demand curve for the product before any selling expenditures are undertaken. With production costs of zero LAS must always begin on the abscissa. LAR will always lie above it in the same vertical plane as long as there is some demand for the product even without advertising outlays.

of production is greater than average revenue: the former being AQ_1, while the latter is only BQ_1. Losses are AB per unit of output or, in the aggregate, $(AB)(OQ_1)$. Nevertheless, if DD_1 is the demand curve and APC the cost function, the firm can only worsen its position by shifting to any other price and output.[21]

Let us now suppose that the firm attempts to improve its position by advertising. As before, we may assume that a minimum amount A must be spent on advertising before there is any perceptible change in the demand curve. This will create a new demand curve, DD_a, and, as before, a rectangular hyperbola, S_a, showing average advertising cost per unit at different rates of output. However, since DD_a is possible only if an amount A is spent on advertising, we may regard A as a "fixed" expense having no influence upon the optimum rate of output.[22] Rather, the optimum rate of production will be determined by the intersection of MR_a and MPC. The optimum rate of output being so determined, average advertising cost per unit of output is derived according to the usual procedure for determining "fixed" costs per unit of production. Total average costs per unit of output is simply the summation of average production costs and average advertising costs.

Since DD_a would lie very close to DD_1 in the diagram, it is not shown in Figure 17.3. Similarly, MR_a and S_a are not shown either. However, let DD_r represent the demand curve corresponding to advertising outlays of an amount R so that DD_r is upward and to the right of DD_a. In other words, R is some advertising expenditure of greater total amount than A. The argument of the preceding paragraph applies without alteration except for the change of lettering. The optimum rate of output is Q_r. Average cost of production per unit of output is $A'Q_r$. Average advertising cost per unit is YQ_r. Total average cost (production and advertising cost) is NQ_r, where NA' equals YQ_r. The intersection of MPC and MR_r at C' determines the optimum rate of output.

It is clear at once that B and B' are only two optimum points on two different demand curves where the optima are determined in the manner already described. But between DD_1 and DD_r there are theoretically a great number of demand curves, each the consequence of a particular outlay on advertising. DD_1 is the demand curve before any advertising; DD_r the demand curve when advertising outlays are R.[23] Between them is a demand curve corresponding to every advertising outlay greater than zero but less than R. And beyond DD_r there will be similar demand curves corresponding to various advertising outlays greater than R.

In the same manner there will be a whole series of points like point N, lying between A and N, indicating average total costs when price and output have been determined by the intersection of MPC and the many marginal revenue curves corresponding to the different demand curves.[24] Each and every demand curve, except

---

[21] Conceivably, the firm might be better off by not producing at all than by producing OQ_1.

[22] The sequence of argument here is that advertising in the amount A determines the demand curve DD_a; given DD_a, the intersection of MR_a and MPC determines the optimum rate of output. S_a, the rectangular hyperbola indicating average advertising costs per unit output, has no bearing upon the determination of the optimum rate of output. Once the demand curve is given, this is entirely a matter of marginal costs of production and the marginal revenue curve relative to the given demand curve.

[23] Once it is decided to make advertising outlays of an amount R, the rectangular hyperbola S_r has no effect on marginal cost and hence no effect on output. The only effect S_r has in determining output is to call DD_r into existence.

[24] At point A in Fig. 17.3 average total cost is production cost only, since by assumption DD_1 is the demand for the product when outlays for advertising are zero.

DD_1, will have a related rectangular hyperbola like S_r, which, in a sense, calls it into existence.

The net consequence is that we have a whole series of points like B and B', which may be connected into a line to yield a curve which is the locus of average revenue; each point on the locus curve is an optimum in the sense already indicated. In the same manner we have a whole series of points like A and N representing average total costs. These can likewise be connected into a locus curve. Let us now turn to Figure 17.4.

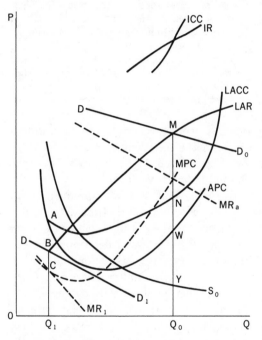

FIGURE **17.4**

Figure 17.4 is nothing more than the extension of Figure 17.3 to its logical conclusion. APC and MPC are, respectively, the curve of average production costs and the curve of marginal production costs. As before, DD_1 and MR_1 are the average and marginal revenue curves, portraying the demand conditions for the product *before any selling outlays are undertaken*. LAR

is the locus of the optimum average revenues determined in the manner previously indicated,[25] while $LACC$ is the locus of average combined (production and advertising) cost. $LACC$ and LAR have incremental curves correlative to them—ICC and IR, respectively—which are only sketched in part in order not to complicate the diagram unduly. Where these two incremental curves intersect must determine the optimum rate of production, the optimum advertising expenditure, and the optimum price. For the sake of completeness these are all shown in **Figure 17.4**. The optimum advertising-cost outlays are an amount O, and per unit of output they are indicated by the rectangular hyperbola S_o. When advertising is of a total sum O, the demand curve is DD_o, whose marginal revenue curve is MR_o. But with a given demand curve DD_o, the optimum price is MQ_o, at which the quantity sold is Q_o. Average production cost per unit of output is WQ_o, average advertising cost is YQ_o, and average combined cost is NQ_o. YQ_o is, of course, equal to NW. MN is average profit per unit of production and sale, while $(MN)(OQ_o)$ is the aggregate profit. This is the largest total gain which the firm is able to obtain, given the original demand for its product, DD_1, the cost function, APC, and the effect of advertising upon the demand for its product.

The shape and position of $LACC$ and LAR (and hence ICC and IR) are determined by two factors: first, the effect of advertising upon the original demand for the product, whether it becomes more or less elastic, etc.; second, the behavior of APC as the firm increases its output beyond Q_1. For the advertising outlays prescribe the demand curve for the product, while the optimum rate of production and sale is determined by the intersection of the marginal production cost and the marginal

[25] That is, by joining all points such as B, B', etc., in **Fig. 17.3** into a curve.

revenue curve appropriate to the given demand curve. *LACC* and *LAR* are a function of two variables, not one.

V

As far as the writer can discover, the only diagrammatic solution to the problem of advertising outlays at all similar to the one described in the previous section is one put forward originally by H. Smith and then adapted to a diagram in three dimensions by Robert M. Shone.[26] Smith's technique is to take any price on the demand curve before advertising is undertaken and determine the optimum adver-

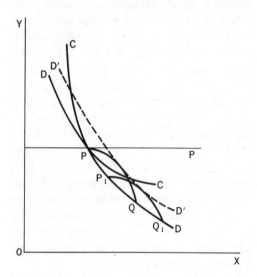

Figure 17.5

tising expenditure for that particular price. He then takes various prices in sequence and determines in a similar manner the optimum advertising outlay for each price. This yields a series of appropriate (i.e., most profitable) advertising expenditures relevant to the various prices. In order to simplify the ensuing commentary on Smith's technique his diagram is reproduced in Figure 17.5 with its original letter-

[26] Smith, *op. cit.*, p. 62; Shone, *op. cit.*, p. 225. Smith states in a footnote that "the diagram owes its present shape to Mr. A. P. Lerner."

ing.[27] In Figure 17.5, *DD* is the demand curve for the product in the absence of advertising. The firm is assumed to be in equilibrium, with no unnecessary profits being earned, at a price *P* on *DD*, at which *CC*, the production-cost curve, is tangent to the demand curve. To consider the effect of advertising:

> Draw the line *PQ* from the point *P* so that the vertical distance between any point on *PP* (the price line) represents the average cost per unit of selling the quantity indicated at the price *P*. *PQ* is thus the net average receipts curve, after deducting the cost of advertising, at the price *P*. Thus, at the price *P*, the firm can now make a profit: this profit shall be at its maximum, for that price, at the point at which it is possible to describe the largest rectangle from *OY* with the top of the right-hand upright at a point on *PQ* and its bottom at a point on *CC*.[28]

In other words, wherever the largest rectangle of the sort defined can be drawn in the area inclosed by *CC* and *PQ*, we have the optimum advertising outlay ·for the price *P*: per unit of salable product it will be the vertical distance from *PQ* to *PP*. But, if we can draw a line such as *PQ* from the price *P* on *DD* and determine the optimum advertising outlay for that price, we can also draw similar lines, e.g., P_1Q_1, from all other points on *DD* and determine similar optima. Hence, for every price we have a curve such as *PQ*, or P_1Q_1, and each such curve has an optimum point.[29] By drawing an envelope curve to all such optimum points on the *PQ* curves, we get

[27] See *op. cit.*, p. 62. A more satisfactory rendition of Smith's figure appears in his article "Discontinuous Demand Curves and Monopolistic Competition," *Quarterly Journal of Economics*, XLIX (1935), 542–50 (cf. Diagram I, p. 544).
[28] Smith, "Advertising Costs and Equilibrium," pp. 62–63.
[29] It should be observed in passing that *PQ* curves which lie below *CC* throughout their whole length necessarily involve the firm in losses rather than profits through advertising. The curve P_1Q_1, for example, in Smith's diagram is such a curve.

the curve labeled $D'D'$ in **Figure 17.5.**[30] Having determined $D'D'$, we have then only to compare it with CC in order to discover the maximum-profit position. Some one price and advertising outlay, presumably, will yield a larger aggregate net profit than any other combination of price and advertising expenditure, i.e., the largest rectangle having an altitude extending vertically from CC to $D'D'$ and a base from that point on CC to OY.[31] It should be observed that the selling price will be higher than the point on $D'D'$ where this rectangle is inscribed.[32] For instance, the tangency point of PQ and $D'D'$ is the optimum advertising outlay for the price PP.[33]

One comment to be made on this solution relates to the probable shape which $D'D'$ might assume. Let us recall that $D'D'$ is an envelope curve tangential to all curves such as PQ at the point indicating the maximum profit possibilities for various prices when advertising outlays are incurred. Each point on $D'D'$, therefore, lies directly below a particular point on some demand curve called into existence when

the optimum advertising expenditure for a particular price is incurred. For example, at the price PP an advertising expenditure per unit in the amount shown by the vertical distance downward from PP to the tangency point of PQ, and $D'D'$ calls into existence some demand curve which passes through that point on PP. But if we take a price $P + \Delta P$, there is no assurance that the corresponding point on a line similar to PP will lie on the *same* demand curve as that created by making the optimum advertising expenditure at the price P. In other words, at prices P and $P + \Delta P$ the respective optimum advertising expenditures may well be different, so that P and $P + \Delta P$ lie on two different demand curves. Unless the optimum advertising expenditures are identical at P and $P + \Delta P$, the demand curves *must* be different. But if this is true, $D'D'$ need not have any such regular shape as has been assigned to it in Figure 17.5. It would be continuous, but it might have sudden changes of direction, depending upon how effective were advertising outlays at different prices.[34] Since $D'D'$ is formed by taking the optimum advertising expenditure for each price, there is no reason to suppose that its shape is predictable on a priori grounds. In any case it is not obvious that its form would approximate that assigned to it in Figure 17.5. And if $D'D'$ might assume a variety of shapes for the reasons already suggested, no one combination of price and advertising expenditure necessarily exists which is a *maximum maximorum*.[35]

Our other comment on Smith's technique

[30] That is, $D'D'$ is tangent to all the PQ curves at their respective optimum points. Smith calls it the average net receipts curve ("Advertising Costs and Equilibrium," p. 63).

[31] "The absolute maximum profit position is that at which it is possible to describe the largest rectangle from OY with the top of its right-hand upright at a point on *any* of the PQ curves and with the bottom at a point on CC. As $D'D'$ is the envelope of all PQ curves, this is also the largest rectangle with its right-hand upright limited by $D'D'$ and CC" (*ibid.*, p. 64).

[32] In his article, "Discontinuous Demand Curves and Monopolistic Competition," p. 544, Smith draws a curve connecting all such prices and writes: "The locus of all such points is $A'R'$, the 'demand' curve for the product when all the resources of publicity are fully exploited by the producer" (p. 545).

[33] It should be pointed out that only that portion of the PQ curves, of which there is a whole family, lying above CC is relevant to the discussion of positive returns from advertising. P_1Q_1, for example, shows negative returns from advertising. Smith does not indicate this restriction in his discussion.

[34] If a firm makes any given advertising expenditure, the shift in the demand curve at all prices will probably not be equal; at least there is no reason to suppose this would be true. However, this is not Smith's technique at all. He derives $D'D'$ from a schedule showing the optimum sum to be spent on advertising at each and every price. Hence, theoretically, every optimum outlay for advertising might call forth a different demand curve. This point has been alluded to by Yntema (*op. cit.*, p. 22).

[35] Cf. above, p. 271.

is simply that in the typical case an entrepreneur would not approach the problem of advertising by the steps just described. Surely, the entrepreneur would be more likely to visualize the problem directly in terms of increments of advertising expense compared to increments of profits than first to calculate the optimum outlays at all various prices and then select that one which is superior to all others. It is submitted that the method described in the earlier portions of the present paper is to be preferred, if for no other reason, because as an approach in terms of marginal increments it is symmetrical with the strategy commonly employed in attacking similar problems.

One further comment on Smith's analysis. He starts his analysis from a "long-run" equilibrium adjustment for the particular firm: average cost is equal to average revenue. Is it equally applicable to the case of a firm in short-run equilibrium, i.e., where marginal cost is equal to marginal revenue but average revenue is in excess of average cost? Perhaps the same technique can be employed. But the diagram will be so much more complex and difficult to interpret than Figure 17.5 that its expository usefulness would be greatly diminished.[36]

VI

As remarked earlier, any conclusions on the effects of advertising reached by the application of the technique here suggested probably will not differ greatly from those derived by other methods. The often raised question as to whether advertising in-

creases the price of the product cannot be answered in unequivocal terms. It will depend upon the shape and position of $LACC$ relative to LAR in Figure 17.4. The number of possible shapes which these curves might assume with reference to each other is legion. A few generalizations concerning the determinants, however, are perhaps worth mentioning. First, the more advertising increases the price elasticity of demand for the product as the curve shifts to the right, the less, *ceteris paribus*, will be the rise in price. If the increase in elasticity is very great, advertising might even lower the price below what it would be in the absence of advertising. Second, the more nearly the firm is operating under conditions of falling average cost before advertising is undertaken, the greater the likelihood, *ceteris paribus*, that average combined costs—production and selling—will be as low as or lower than production costs alone before advertising was undertaken. In other words, NQ_o in Figure 17.4 *might* be less than BQ_1. The chances of this possibility's being realized in practice seem rather remote. It seems reasonable to suppose, however, that the range over which $LACC$ lies below LAR for the typical enterprise is rather smaller than we have drawn it in Figure 17.4. Also, from what empirical studies are available, probably APC is more nearly horizontal over the relevant range than we have sketched it. There would appear to be some substantial reasons for believing that the origin of $LACC$ is typically above the origin of LAR in the case of business enterprises in the real world. Probably most firms would operate at a loss if they did not advertise: if their more immediate competitors do advertise, the demand curve for their particular product without advertising would lie below their cost curve. Advertising puts them in the range of profitable operations. But a simultaneous cut in advertising by all firms in the industry might lower the price and increase profits just because so

---

[36] If we are concerned with only short-run equilibrium, where it suffices if marginal cost equals marginal revenue, CC (**Fig. 17.5**) will lie below DD over much of its range; curves like PQ will cut DD and terminate on CC wherever CC lies below DD. If $D'D'$ is an envelope curve as in Fig. 17.5, it may be above or below DD and may even intersect it. Our earlier suggestion about possible irregularities in the shape of $D'D'$ is doubly reinforced in this case (see above, pp. 245f.).

much advertising simply "cancels out" between firms in the same general industry.[37] Finally, *LACC* in Figure 17.4 probably cuts *LAR* from below before very high rates of production are attained, because of the rapidly diminishing returns from advertising. While the familiar "tangency" solution of a long-run equilibrium in monopolistic competition is probably never attained in the real world, nevertheless, the area inclosed by *LACC* and *LAR* in Figure 17.4 is, perhaps characteristically, considerably smaller than we have portrayed it.

The foregoing analysis has been carried through on the purely theoretical level and, as such, encounters the familiar difficulties when applied to the vastly more complicated real world in which we live. Two limitations of this sort are particularly worth mentioning in any discussion of advertising. First, there is undoubtedly a time lag between expenditure on advertising and the resulting shift in the demand curve for the product. How long this interval will be will depend upon a variety of factors: the advertising media adopted, the form of competitors' advertising, how firmly fixed are buyers' buying habits, etc.; second, the analysis has assumed throughout that the firm knows how effective advertising expenditure is in shifting the demand for its product. In fact, business enterprises are usually far from certain of the effects of advertising upon the demand for their wares and spend a good deal of money trying to find out by devious subterfuges.[38] In other words, real-world business enterprises do not know precisely how much advertising increases the demand for their product or prevents it from declining. Yet this difficulty is present wherever in partial equilibrium analysis one assumes that the firm knows the demand schedule for its salable product. It is probably no more damaging in dealing with the problem of advertising expenditures than elsewhere.

[37] Cf. above, p. 240.

[38] For an interesting discussion of the uncertainty surrounding the effectiveness of advertising see H. Smith, "The Imputation of Advertising Costs," *Economic Journal*, XLV (1935), 682–99.

18. The Plateau Demand Curve and Utility Theory[*]

G. WARREN NUTTER[1]

G. Warren Nutter (A.B., University of Chicago, 1944; A.M., 1948; Ph.D., 1949) was born in Topeka, Kansas, in 1923. At present he is Assistant Secretary of Defense for International Security Affairs in the Department of Defense. He is on leave from the University of Virginia, where he is Paul G. McIntire Professor of Economics and Director of the Thomas Jefferson Center for Studies in Political Economy. He has also taught at Lawrence College and Yale University. Since 1955 he has been a member of the research staff of the National Bureau of Economic Research. His published works include *The Extent of Enterprise Monopoly in the United States* and *The Growth of Industrial Production in the Soviet Union*. Nutter is a noted authority in the areas of price theory, the economics of the Soviet Union, comparative economic systems, and industrial organization. During World War II he served in the infantry and was awarded a Bronze Star. In 1964, he was economic advisor to the Republican nominee for the presidency, Senator Barry Goldwater.

It is interesting how many "new" ideas in economics turn out to have been carefully worked out some time ago. This is certainly true of the basic notions behind the so-called "new competition," which were fully explored at a very early stage in the discussion of monopolistic competition. An example is the argument that only a portion of a firm's demand curve needs to be completely elastic to induce competitive behavior, or marginal-cost pricing. One finds on reviewing the literature that this point was made twenty years ago by A. J. Nichol,[2] who argued that product differentiation is quite consistent with competitive behavior if there is a sizable group of "marginal buyers" who do not care which differentiated product they buy at going prices. In the normal case, he went on to argue, there will be such a group.

[*] Reprinted from the *Journal of Political Economy* (December 1955) by permission of The University of Chicago Press. Copyright, 1955, pp. 525–528.

[1] I am very grateful to A. M. Okun, J. Tobin, and J. H. Young for their searching review of earlier drafts of this paper.

[2] "The Influence of Marginal Buyers on Monopolistic Competition," *Quarterly Journal of Economics*, XLIX (1934–35), 121–35.

It is a little puzzling that this point did not catch on widely with economists, since it is not obviously refuted by evidence, though clearly subject to refutation. In particular, an outstanding implication of this hypothesis is that relative prices of products in the same differentiated group should not be significantly affected by a change in cost conditions alone—for instance, by a change in excise-tax rates. All changes in relative prices should be traceable to changes on the demand side, such as those caused by advertising campaigns and other "differentiations" of products. Relatively little effort would be needed to carry out a careful empirical study that would more or less settle the matter, but a broad study of this nature has never been undertaken. One reason may be that economists view "marginal buying" by individuals as inconsistent with established utility theory. Buyers who behave this way apparently cannot exist in a world where marginal rates of substitution diminish in all directions. Failing a convincing rationalization for "marginal buying," theorists may have been inclined to rule it out as highly unlikely. The modest purpose of this note is to suggest that "marginal buying" can in fact be rationalized without distorting established utility theory.

Let us start by examining a bit more carefully what Nichol's hypothesis says. The firm's demand curve under monopolistic competition is taken to be defined when the prices of all closely related products, including those in the differentiated group, are held constant.[3] The curve may be described in two ways, both of which come down to the same thing. We may say, first of all, that the firm can sell "daily" any amount between OA and OB when it charges the price OC (Figure 18.1). That

is to say, it may vary its rate of selling between OA and OB without causing any noticeable change in the price it can charge. Looked at another way, any price perceptibly above OC would lower the rate of selling below OA, while any price perceptibly below OC would raise the rate of selling above OB. If the range of output AB

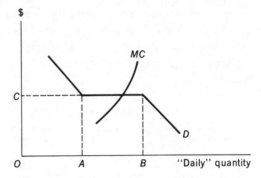

FIGURE **18.1**

is "large" in relation to the output likely to be produced by the firm, its demand curve will have a significant discontinuity or, stated in other terms, a completely elastic plateau. Such a demand curve will lead to competitive pricing if the firm's long-run marginal costs rise up to meet this plateau, as shown in Figure 18.1.

This plateau demand curve says that there are "marginal buyers" who do not care, when relative prices are at the level determined by OC, whether they buy this product or others in the differentiated group. At the proper relative prices they will treat the differentiated varieties as if they were the same product, and they will move with indifference among them, choosing what they consume on the basis of "easy availability" or some equally trivial consideration.[4] Each marginal buyer will presuma-

[3] There is no need to enter an extended discussion of other conditions held constant. It is convenient and relevant to hold some concept of real income constant, that is, to assume that there are no "income" effects from price changes that occur solely within the differentiated group.

[4] Product differentiation should be understood to include, by analogy, differences in location of sellers relative to buyers. Two-dimensioned space or nonuniform distribution of sellers relative to buyers is enough to give "marginal buyers" to a firm selling an otherwise undifferentiated product. This is, in fact, the case Nichol focused on.

bly consume a determinate amount of all products in the group taken together, but the consumption mix will be indeterminate. The analogy with so-called "pure" competition is quite straightforward: the (marginal) buyers are not concerned with who sells the product, since all sellers (varieties) are viewed as identical. As in the case of pure competition, there must be a large number of actual or potential sellers (varieties); otherwise it does not make sense to hold prices of other varieties constant in defining a particular firm's demand curve.

This view of "marginal buying" is not consistent with the postulate that marginal rates of substitution diminish in all directions. Put in the familiar terms of indifference curves, the curves relating any two varieties of a differentiated product (consumption elsewhere the same) are pictured as convex downward for every consumer. This implies that, at every price ratio, the consumer purchases either only one of the varieties or a determinate mix of both. For "marginal buying" to occur, the indifference curves must be straight lines. That is to say, the marginal rate of substitution of one variety for another must be constant. Does the established theory of consumer choice have a place for constant marginal rates of substitution?

It clearly has. A constant marginal rate of substitution between two products says nothing more than that they are viewed by the consumer as "perfect substitutes" for each other. This case is recognized in the standard works of recent times on the theory of choice, but it does not get much attention.[5] Perfect substitutes are appar-

ently taken to be merely samples of a "homogeneous" product, and the theory of choice sets out to discuss relations among, not within, "homogeneous" products. Unfortunately, the matter is not so simple.

It all comes down to the frustrating problem of defining products. This problem is, for understandable reasons, typically begged in works on the theory of choice, where definitions are circular and implicit: a "product" is a thing that has a diminishing marginal rate of substitution for all other "products."[6] This will plainly not do. Even though it may ultimately be necessary to admit that there is no simple way to define products outside the structure of theory itself, the problem must be carefully explored; for the usable content of theory is much affected if what are taken there as separate products turn out in the world about us not to be separate in the same sense.

Perhaps the best way to get at what is in question is to face up first to the problem of defining a "homogeneous" product. It would be nice if we could end the matter by saying that a product is homogeneous if all samples of it are physically identical; but this definition will not stand examination. No two grains of sand are completely identical; homogeneity in this sense is reserved for the imaginary world of quanta of energy. This observation is painfully trite and puristic, and yet it is pertinent. The obvious point is that we mean by "homogeneity" something much less than physical identity. We mean, in fact, nothing more than identity in the mind of the consumer: such differences as there are among samples of the product are of no concern to him; every unit in every sample is considered the same from the point of view of want satisfaction—the marginal

[5] Hicks includes the case of perfect substitutes (*Value and Capital* [2d ed.; London: Oxford University Press, 1948], p. 49) but says little about it and apparently does not see that it contradicts his "stability conditions" for demand (*ibid.*, p. 306). This contradiction is pointed out in an article by Edwin B. Wilson, which gives the formal mathematics for the case ("Hicks on Perfect Substitutes," *Quarterly Journal of Economics,* LIX [1944–45], 134–40).

[6] For example, Samuelson says: "For present purposes each good and service is taken as clearly defined, homogeneous, divisible, etc." (*Foundations of Economic Analysis* [Cambridge: Harvard University Press, 1948], p. 96). This would certainly seem to be a question-begging definition.

rate of substitution between samples is constant and unitary. This comes down to saying that different things belong to the same "homogeneous" product if the consumer thinks they do. And, even though this is an uncomfortable place to end up, it is the best we can do on a formal level of analysis.

This line of reasoning inevitably leads us to extend the notion of constant marginal rates of substitution beyond the region of "homogeneous" products. Let us proceed by way of a homely example. The picky housewife to the side, a shopper will ordinarily view any one pound of new Maine potatoes as the same as any other in the same display; and the indifference curves relating any two batches will have a constant slope of unity. Now what about old as opposed to new, or Idaho as opposed to Maine, potatoes? Or, to put the point more strongly, what about one brand of cigarettes as opposed to another? It would seem that the difference in treatment of "homogeneous" and "differentiated" products is essentially one of degree, not of kind. To be more explicit, the marginal rate of substitution between two varieties of a differentiated product may not be unitary, but it may normally be expected to be constant. The varieties are "pure" substitutes for each other even though they may not be "perfect" substitutes.[7] This is an extreme simplification, but for the moment let it stand.

[7] This distinction is formally meaningless in that the units of measurement for the varieties can always be defined so that the rate of substitution is unity. Hence the varieties are always "perfect" substitutes if they are "pure" substitutes. The distinction has meaning nonetheless when we confine our thinking to the units in which varieties are conventionally expressed. Thus one standard-sized can of Brand X peas might be considered equivalent to two standard-sized cans of Brand Y peas. The two brands would then be "pure" substitutes. To convert them to "perfect" substitutes, X would have to be measured in units of one can and Y in units of two cans, and their prices would have to be expressed accordingly.

In the case of the simplest types of "quality" differentiation, there is no difficulty in seeing this point. Consider, for example, two different light bulbs alike in all respects except that one lasts twice as long as the other. The longer-lasting bulb is worth two of the other, no matter in what proportions they may be consumed.

The point is not so obvious for more complex differentiation, where diverse mixtures of services are involved in the varieties of product. If the services can be bought separately, there is no real problem. Thus a box of breakfast cereal with a toy in it is equivalent to one without, plus a toy. Such cases are far from exceptional; many products are nothing more than linear combinations of other products. We recognize this on the productive-factor side when we talk about capital, but we seem to ignore it on the product side.

The real trouble comes when the "extra" services are inseparable from the product itself. Although aspirin is aspirin and every brand (given the sampling variation) has the same antiheadache properties, some may go to work faster than others. There is no way to buy the fast-action property and add it to the slow-acting brand. Similarly, either the washing machine works automatically, or it does not. Here it would seem that each variety is really a different product, in the sense that the marginal rate of substitution between varieties will vary with the proportions in which they are consumed.

But we must be careful not to leap to that conclusion, for the problem typically facing the consumer is one of balancing a set of "extras" for this variety against another set for that one. It is too much to expect that the representative consumer's mind contains a multidimensioned calculus, by means of which he carefully notes and makes account for every difference in the complex of services provided by each variety of a differentiated product. This certainly seems unlikely for items purchased only infrequently—the whole category of consumer durables, for one thing. The consumer normally approaches the purchase of an automobile, for example, as something not to be repeated soon. Hence, in a rapidly changing world, he does not anticipate facing again the same set of alternatives with the same indifference map. After looking over the various makes and balancing out their differing features, he undoubtedly establishes a rough linear scale of preferences for them. By comparing this scale with going prices, he makes his pick.

The problem here is one of treading a fine line of distinction, of determining when differences in grades or qualities of the same product become actual differences in products. Here, as in all things, "nature makes no leap"; the one kind of distinction gradually and imperceptibly shades into the other. But though "nature makes no leap," the human mind must if it is to grapple with nature; and so we may be sure that definite lines are drawn between products and that similar things on either side of the lines are treated as varying grades of products. The evidence is nowhere plainer than in everyday speech, where we classify products into categories and subcategories. Thus we may speak of tea or black tea alone; of aspirin or Bayer's aspirin; of low-priced automobiles or Chevrolets; and so on. In each of these cases, we have in mind, first, a distinct kind of basic service (product) and, second, a specific grade of that service. We are really saying that the grades are purely substitute ways of getting the service, even though better or worse ways. Mixing the grades together is not usually thought of as producing a superior service: more pleasure in smoking does not typically come from using several brands of cigarettes. This

view of the making of choices seems to accord well enough with much of our behavior. Many decisions are figuratively made by the flip of a coin: we often decide to "go out" for the evening before deciding where to go. On a more concrete level, brand allegiance, when it exists, is a partial thing: the man who insists on his favorite cigar does not pay the slightest heed to the brand of matches handed him.

Of course, even if the substitution rates between varieties of a differentiated product are, in the majority of cases, viewed as being constant by most consumers, this is not sufficient to bring about plateau demand curves. In addition, a significant fraction of consumers must agree on a consistent pattern of substitution rates.[8] That is to say, there must be a "homogeneity of tastes" on the part of a sizable minority of consumers. Fads and styles demonstrate this homogeneity in extreme form, while the use in mass advertising of a limited line of appeal attests to its generality.[9] But there is no sense speculating at length on these matters when the proof of the pudding is in the eating. The assumptions required for the plateau demand curve are reasonable if the curve itself withstands empirical testing. Still, we do require that the most fundamental assumptions make introspective sense. Hence this note, which may or may not have met its purpose.

[8] The substitution rates for any one consumer depend on, among other things, his real income. Hence "income" effects of price changes, if significant, might rule out the possibility of a plateau demand curve even if all other conditions were met.

[9] Advertising does, of course, have a place in a world of plateau demand curves. The aim in such a world is to shift the plateau, both upward and to the right, if possible. That is to say, advertising would aim at changing the slope of consumers' indifference curves.

19. The Nature of Equilibrium in Monopolistic Competition*

HAROLD DEMSETZ[1]

Harold Demsetz (B.S., University of Illinois, 1953; M.A., and M.B.A., Northwestern University, 1953; Ph.D., 1959) was born in Chicago, Illinois in 1930. He is now Professor of Economics at the Graduate School of Business and the Law School of the University of Chicago. Professor Demsetz, whose major teaching and research interests are in the fields of microeconomic theory and market organization, has also taught at the University of Michigan and the University of California at Los Angeles. In addition, he has been active in the research community, having served with both the RAND Corporation and the Center for Naval Analyses. He has published widely in professional journals, with many articles on the nature of costs and equilibrium in alternative market contexts, particularly in monopolistic competition. He has also written several recent articles on the characteristics and implications of property rights.

Since its publication in 1933, Chamberlin's *The Theory of Monopolistic Competition* has provided the rationale for the belief that product differentiation will result in "excess" capacity once equilibrium has been established in an industry. The purpose of this paper is twofold: first, to show briefly that Chamberlin did not develop the nature of equilibrium in monopolistic competition in a manner that permits judgments about efficiency and, second, to re-examine Chamberlin's equilibrium to permit certain statements about efficiency to be made. This re-examination shows that excess capacity is not a necessary implication of the assumptions underlying Chamberlin's model.

To these ends, I proceed first with a summary restatement of Chamberlin's equilibrium and its inability to answer questions about efficiency. The next section develops some tools whose use permits a more meaningful analysis of equilibrium in monopolistic competition. The third section discusses

* Reprinted from *Journal of Political Economy* (February 1953), by permission of The University of Chicago Press. Copyright, 1953, pp. 21–30.

[1] I should like to thank Professors R. B. Heflebower, R. H. Strotz, R. W. Clower, and F. M. Westfield and Mr. R. Piron, all of Northwestern University, for their helpful comments.

the nature of this equilibrium and the possibilities for "efficient" production. Throughout this paper the discussion is carried on within a purely static framework.

In his consideration of the large-numbers case, Chamberlin shows the adaptation of price, selling expenditure, and product quality to the equilibrium of, first, the firm and, second, the industry (or, in Chamberlin's terminology, the "group"). I shall drop product quality from this list of controllable parameters. This will shorten the paper and will not invalidate the argument. Chamberlin first determines the selling cost associated with selling various quantities of a firm's product at a given price. He assumes first increasing, then decreasing, returns so that average selling cost exhibits the usual ∪ shape. The price, assumed as given, may be at any level whatever, and thus it may or may not be high enough to cover selling plus production costs at any particular level of output. However, there is a level of output and associated selling outlay that either maximizes profits or minimizes losses for the given price. These selling costs are added to production costs, and, at the given price, the best combination of production and selling cost is determined by the intersection of marginal cost and price.

Chamberlin then holds selling costs fixed and determines the best combination of price and cost, given the demand curve resulting from the fixed selling cost. If we let the product be of variable quality, we would go through the same procedure, varying the production costs associated with different product qualities while keeping selling cost and price fixed. Chamberlin then goes on to say:

> Finally, when product, price, and selling expenses are all three subject to variation, the solution may be reached by an extension of the same method. Let the procedure of the last case, giving the most advantageous

price and selling outlay for a given "product," be repeated for all possible "products," and that one chosen which affords the largest profit of all. Or let the procedure for the discovery of the best combination of product and price be repeated for all possible selling outlays. It matters not in what order the parts are assembled. Together they compose and illustrate the very general proposition that (all circumstances with regard to competing substitutes being given) the entrepreneur will select that combination of product, price, and selling expenditure for which his total profits are a maximum.[2]

If this combination results in abnormally high profits, entry will take place until a zero-profit equilibrium is reached. Chamberlin's zero-profit group equilibrium is illustrated in Figure 19.1. That this is an equilibrium, Chamberlin shows as follows: Let the firm keep its price constant and optimally vary selling cost so as to sell rates of output different from Q'. The combined average selling and production cost curve so obtained is indicated cc' (where APC is the average production cost).

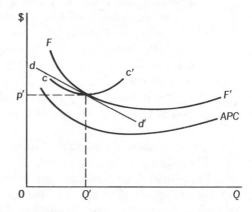

FIGURE 19.1

Clearly, every quantity other than Q' results in losses if a variation in output is sought by this means. Suppose the firm keeps selling costs constant as typified by

[2] Edward Chamberlin, *The Theory of Monopolistic Competition* (6th ed.; Cambridge, Mass.: Harvard University Press, 1950), p. 147.

curve FF' and considers selling other quantities by changing price. With selling cost constant, the price-quantity relation is given by the demand curve dd', which everywhere lies beneath the combined cost curve, FF'. Since the firm cannot improve its position by varying either price or selling cost, it is in equilibrium, as is the industry if all firms have the same cost and demand curves.

However, none of the curves FF', cc', or dd' provides any criteria by which to judge the "efficiency" of the industry equilibrium.[3] Since the firm is free to vary price and selling cost simultaneously, neither FF' nor cc' presents a cost expansion path that is relevant for outputs different from Q', nor does dd' present a relevant sales expansion path for selling quantities other than Q'. This deficiency in Chamberlin's geometric presentation has allowed erroneous opinions to arise that misinterpret the equilibrium as being to the left of the low point of some relevant combined selling and production average cost curve. Undoubtedly, this is a result of forgetting that Chamberlin's FF' and dd' curves are drawn strictly on the assumption that selling cost is fixed. Before any judgment can be made about the nature of the Chamberlinian equilibrium, it is necessary to allow the firm to expand output by optimally varying price and selling cost and then to examine the equilibrium price and quantity in relation to the cost structure so derived. The next section deals with the derivation of cost and revenue curves that are relevant for price and output decisions under monopolistically competitive conditions.

II

To begin with, consider a particular rate of output, say, Q_1, and with each different possible price of Q_1 associate the minimum selling expenses required to sell Q_1. As the price under consideration gets higher, so does the required selling expense. At first, a small increase in selling expense would probably allow the seller to raise price considerably and still sell all of Q_1. Later, as more and more selling expense is incurred, selling activities become less efficient as a substitute for price decreases, so that small increases in price require large additions to selling expense if Q_1 is to be sold. This is illustrated by the isoquant Q_1 in Figure 19.2. Two additional isoquants, Q_0 and Q_2, are also shown.[4] The order of the subscripts of the isoquants corresponds to the order of quantity. Thus, as we move from right to left, quantity increases. The point at which a particular isoquant touches the price axis indicates the maximum price at which that quantity can be sold if no selling expenses are incurred.

For each quantity, as price is increased, the seller earns a larger total revenue. The increase in total revenue is proportional to price, the exact proportionality depending upon the quantity under consideration. If from the total revenue curve associated with each quantity the cost of producing that quantity is deducted, the optimal price–selling-cost combination for each quantity will be given by that point for which total revenue (net of production cost) minus selling cost is greatest. This is done graphically in Figure 19.2. For example, consider Q_1. At a price $P = 0$, zero total revenue is

[4] Isoquants of this type can be found in K. E. Boulding, *Economic Analysis* (3d ed.; New York: Harper & Bros., 1955), p. 777. See also Norman S. Buchanan, "Advertising Expenditures: A Suggested Treatment," *Journal of Political Economy,* August, 1942, pp. 537–57. (Reprinted supra, pp. 237.) Buchanan develops an analysis of selling expenditures similar to that presented here in that price and quantity produced are allowed to vary simultaneously with selling cost. Instead of using isoquants, Buchanan arrives at a best selling cost-price-quantity combination by shifting the conventional demand curve as selling cost changes. However, he does not examine the probable shape of the locus of best selling cost-price combinations, nor does he consider the implications for equilibrium under monopolistically competitive conditions.

[3] By "efficiency," I refer only to the level of average cost.

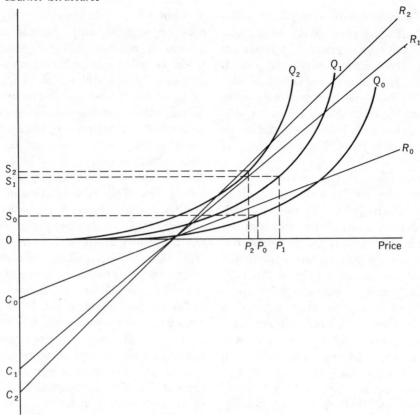

FIGURE 19.2   VERTICAL AXIS: SELLING COST, REVENUE NET OF PRODUCTION COST

earned, and, when production costs are deducted, they result in a net loss. This net loss is indicated by Q_1 on the vertical axis. As price is increased, total revenue is increased, resulting in revenue curve R_1. Up to the point representing the maximum price at which Q_1 can be sold with no selling cost, only the cost of production need be deducted from total revenue to determine profit; after this price is reached, selling cost must also be deducted.

The optimal price–selling-cost combination is located where the vertical difference between R_1 and the isoquant Q_1 is greatest (or smallest in the case of minimum losses). If this combination involves positive selling cost, it will be determined by the equality between the slope of R_1 and that of isoquant Q_1. The slope of R_1 is equal to Q_1; the slope of the isoquant Q_1 is given by the

marginal rate of substitution between selling cost and price. If the optimal combination does not involve selling cost, it is determined by the price at which Q_1 meets the price axis. The optimal combination in the case of isoquant Q_1 is P_1 and S_1.

In considering the revenue curves for Q_0 and Q_2, we must keep two differences in mind. First, since Q_0 is less and Q_2 more than Q_1, the production cost of Q_0 is less and of Q_2 more than that of Q_1. This is taken into consideration in Figure 19.2 by having the vertical intercepts of R_0 and R_2, respectively, higher and lower than the intercept of R_1. Second, R_2 must increase at a faster rate and R_0 at a slower rate than R_1, because the quantities are, respectively, more and less than Q_1.

The process shown in Figure 19.2 can be repeated for all possible quantities. For each quantity an optimal price–selling-cost combination will be determined. From this isoquant map, we can determine the type of average revenue curve necessary for the seller to make decisions rationally. I call this curve a *mutatis mutandis* average revenue curve (*MAR*), since it allows selling cost to vary so as to manipulate consumer preferences optimally. The isoquant map also determines the appropriate cost structure associated with each point on the *MAR* curve, and it is this curve that presents meaningful alternatives to the seller. The shape attributed to the *MAR* curve is of crucial significance. If we hold with Chamberlin that selling expenses go through the stages of first increasing and then decreasing effectiveness, the shape of the *MAR* curve is typified by the solid lines in Figure 19.3. The *MAR* curve first increases and then decreases, and associated with it is an appropriate *mutatis mutandis* marginal revenue curve (*MMR*).

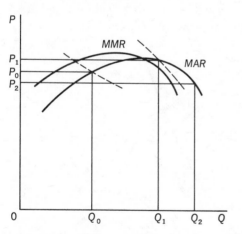

FIGURE **19.3**

This *MAR* curve reflects the seller's ability to increase the quantity sold at the same time that he is increasing the price at which it sells, because selling expenditures are, at first, a very good substitute for price decreases. By increasing his selling cost, the seller is able to take advantage of first local and then national selling media (he may

also, for example, be able to use a higher quality of selling personnel). Therefore, it is not implausible that the *MAR* curve may at first increase. However, as selling expenditures increase further, they become a poorer substitute for a price decrease if sales are to be expanded in the most profitable manner possible, and the *MAR* curve levels off and decreases.

The shape of the *MAR* curve shown in Figure 19.3 is based on the isoquants and revenue curves of Figure 19.2. It represents the most profitable way to expand sales if both price and selling expenditure are variable. The existence of a maximum in Figure 19.3 is reflected in Figure 19.2 by the high rate of increase of R_1 compared with R_0. This high rate of increase is due to the assumption that for any given price the first increases in selling expenditure increase the quantity that can be sold very significantly, and it is this resulting quantity that determines the slope of R_1. Additional increases in selling expenditures increase the quantity sold at any given price much less spectacularly. Hence the slope of R_2 is only a little steeper than that of R_1. Selling expenditures go through this same pattern along any particular isoquant in Figure 19.2, which is the reason for their marked upward concavity. However, it does not pay to increase selling expenditures along any particular isoquant, say, Q_0, to the same extent that it does when moving from isoquant to isoquant, since it would be ridiculous to advertise nationally if Q_0 were so small a quantity that it would be exhausted by sales to local buyers.

The assumption of these increasing and then decreasing stages of effectiveness for selling expenditure is partly justifiable on the same technological grounds as the ∪-shaped average cost of production curve. But additional reasons may be present in the reaction of potential buyers to increasing amounts of promotional effort. Potential buyers may not respond so readily when the number of television commercials is increased from eleven to twelve a day as they did when the number went from zero to one a day.

It must be kept clearly in mind that the *MAR* curve of Figure 19.3 represents the most profitable sales expansion path. Through each point on this modified revenue curve there passes a conventional demand curve (two of which are shown by the dotted lines in Fig. 19.3). However, the *MAR* curve is drawn in a manner that makes it the locus of price–selling-cost combinations that are superior, for their respective outputs, to any other point on the conventional average revenue curves.

Each point on the *MAR* curve has associated with it a cost of production, determined by the quantity of output, and a selling cost for which this point is the best. The combined production and selling cost associated with each point is equal to the vertical distance between the vertical intercept of the revenue curve and the optimum selling cost as determined in Figure 19.2. Therefore, if a vertical line is drawn

through each point on the *MAR* curve, it passes through a well-defined average cost of producing and selling the quantity associated with that point. This is done in Figure 19.4. In this figure the *MAR* curve is superimposed on a cost structure composed of these production and selling costs. The *APC* curve is the usual average production cost curve, to it are added the appropriate average selling costs of Figure 19.2 as determined by the quantities with which they are associated. The combined average cost curve is the average total cost curve (*ATC*) of Figure 19.4, and the point where it meets the *APC* curve is that point to the left of which quantities can be sold most profitably if no selling costs are incurred.

With the *ATC* curve is associated a marginal cost curve which intersects the *MMR* curve at the most profitable combination of price, production and selling cost, and quantity sold. This equilibrium position is stable so long as the *MC* curve intersects the *MMR* curve from below. The *MAR* curve of Figures 19.3 and 19.4 presents the

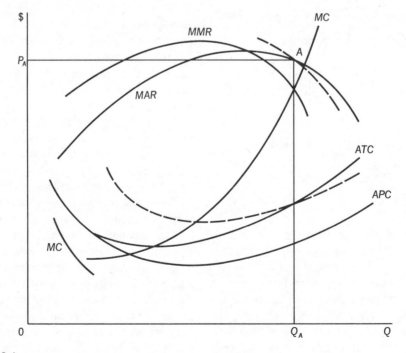

Figure 19.4

relevant alternatives facing the seller. The ATC and MAR curves can now be used to examine the nature of equilibrium in monopolistic competition.

III

In Figure 19.4 the initial equilibrium of the firm is denoted by A. If the seller were to consider selling a slightly smaller quantity of output, he would not move up the conventional average revenue curve (indicated by the dotted line through A), since it requires that selling expenses be held fixed at the level they were when he sold Q_A; this would raise the ATC curve to the left of Q_A sufficiently to make any point on the conventional average revenue curve to the left of A inferior to the corresponding point on the MAR curve. The same reasoning holds for movements down the conventional curve; in this case, the reduction in price required by the conventional curve would result in a revenue loss too great to be made up by holding selling costs constant. The cost curve that would result from movements along the conventional demand curve is indicated by the lower dotted line. These alternatives must be inferior to points on the MAR curve, because the latter were derived so as to be the best possible combinations of the variables under the seller's control.

If we assume, as in Figure 19.4, that excess profits are being earned, new firms will enter the industry and force the existing sellers to re-evaluate the MAR curve. This can be done only by reconstructing Figure 19.2, since it may involve both a shift in the MAR curve and a change in the cost structure. The pattern of readjustment that results depends on the effect that entry has on the shape and position of the isoquants of Figure 19.2.

Entry can be viewed as displacing the isoquants to the left so that for any given amount of selling cost the firm can now sell the same amount only by offering it at a

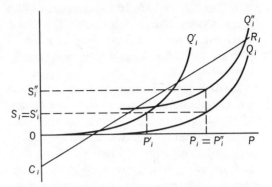

FIGURE 19.5   VERTICAL AXIS: SELLING COST, REVENUE NET OF PRODUCTION COST

lower price. The position of the revenue curves remains the same, but the points on the isoquants that have the same slope as the revenue curves move to the left. If the shape of the isoquants remains the same, the new best combinations will involve the same selling cost but lower prices. This is indicated by the shift from isoquant Q_i to Q'_i in Figure 19.5. This means that the resulting MAR curve will define a new locus of best combinations at which each quantity is sold at a lower price, but with the same cost structure. This is the type of adjustment assumed in the remainder of this paper and is shown by the dotted MAR curve of Figure 19.6.

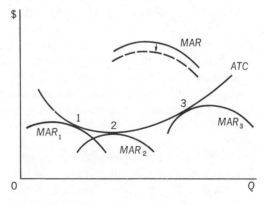

FIGURE 19.6

A second possible type of effect of entry is a vertical displacement of the isoquants. This is shown by the shift from isoquant Q_i

to Q''_i in Figure 19.5. In this case, since the optimal price remains the same, the *MAR* curve would not shift, but selling cost would increase until an equilibrium was established.

A third general type of effect would be a change in both the shape and the position of the isoquants. This would be the most probably change and would carry an isoquant in a northwesterly direction such that each quantity could then be sold optimally only if price were lowered and selling costs increased.

Any of these three cases could be used with equal validity in the following argument; I use the first, since it does not require the redrawing of cost curves and since it most resembles the development of equilibrium commonly used to rationalize excess capacity.

As long as excess profits are being earned, entry will continue, and the *MAR* curve will continue to shift downward. This process will go on until the *MAR* curve becomes tangent to the *ATC* curve. When this takes place, excess profits will be eliminated, and entry will cease.

Three possible equilibrium positions now confront us. They are shown in Figure 19.6. These equilibriums are identical to the possible Chamberlinian solutions, but they do not lead to the misinterpretation that arises from Chamberlin's presentation. If excess profits are eliminated as in equilibrium *2*, the firm is producing a differentiated product at the lowest average total cost. The possibility of this equilibrium is sufficient to invalidate the necessity of excess capacity in the Chamberlinian large-numbers case.

If excess profits are eliminated as in equilibrium *1*, it may pay for one seller to buy out another (or, perhaps, to sell to a private labeler). This could enable him to increase his sales by increasing his selling expense (for example, taking over the other seller's selling expense), but it would involve a less than proportionate increase in

average total cost, since he is operating on the declining portion of his cost curve.[5] This action would prove profitable for all members of the industry until equilibrium position *2* is reached.

If excess profits are eliminated, as in equilibrium *3*, it might pay for a seller to operate a larger number of plants so that the same quantity could be sold with the same selling cost and a lower average production cost. This action would prove profitable for all members of the industry until excess profits were eliminated by entry and position *2* was reached.

The preceding arguments for rationalization of the industry to equilibrium *2* depend on assumptions that should be made explicit. The movement from position *1* to position *2* may not be wholly possible if the differentiated products are not identically produced. The production of two products in a plant may involve costs that are not incurred by the production of a single product (for example, it might be necessary to clean equipment before the second product could be produced). Similarly, there may be extra costs in advertising two differentiated brands of the same basic product. Thus the cost curve pictured in Figure 19.6 may exaggerate the savings that could be had by rationalization through buying out and producing another seller's product. These savings may be either partially or wholly offset by the additional cost involved in producing a second differentiated product. Rationalization, given freedom of contract, will proceed only up to the point where the advantages are just offset by the additional cost, and, although there is pressure to move toward position *2*, only a partial movement may occur.

Likewise, the rationalization from posi-

[5] See Donald Dewey, "Imperfect Competition No Bar to Efficient Production," *Journal of Political Economy*, LXVI (February, 1958), 24–33. In this article Dewey makes this rationalization argument, but he deals only with a completely homogeneous product and fails to take up some crucial assumptions which are mentioned above.

tion *3* to position *2* requires that there be no diseconomies of firm size (in contrast to plant size). To the extent that such diseconomies exist rationalization may be only partly undertaken. In any case, the equilibrium may be at position *2*, or, if it is elsewhere, there will be a tendency to approximate position *2* as closely as diseconomies of firm size and required production techniques will allow. In the long run, when the cost of adjusting plant capacity is not prohibitive, these same pressures will work toward the lowest point on the long-run cost curve. Indeed, the lowest point on the long-run curve will be approximated better than in the short run if some of the possible diseconomies of firm size and production techniques can be avoided by a full adjustment of all factors of production.

Of course, if I retain the assumption that it is profitable to differentiate a product, as I must if the discussion is to be conducted on Chamberlin's terms, even equilibrium position *2* involves resources devoted to selling effort. Whether or not this is efficient cannot be answered until welfare economists devise a method for separating socially desirable from undesirable selling expenditures.

Even if equilibrium *2* should be achieved, it would be doubly fortuitous if, at the equilibrium output, both the average selling cost curve and the average production cost curve should be at their respective low points. If they are not, the equilibrium output represents a sort of compromise in which average selling cost is lowest to the left (or right) of the minimum average total cost and average production cost is lowest to the right (or left). It appears that, to achieve the lowest possible cost, firms would need to pool their selling activities through some intermediary, or buy each other out, to a different degree than is required if only production costs are to be optimally rationalized.

The argument made above for the possibility of efficient production in the face of product differentiation was based on a *MAR* curve that had the shape of an inverted ∪. The curve may or may not actually take this shape, although the increasing and decreasing stages of selling effectiveness that guarantee it seem a reasonable assumption. The fact that the *MAR* curve may take this shape is sufficient to prove there is nothing inherent in monopolistic competition that necessarily implies excess capacity.

Nonetheless, the *MAR* curve may not have the shape I have given to it, and its shape may vary from industry to industry. It seems worthwhile to point out that there are other shapes which just as effectively tend to bring production to the point of lowest average cost. The *MAR* curve might be horizontal throughout most of its length. The interval during which selling efforts are just able to substitute profitably for a price change may be considerably wider than I have drawn it. A third shape that serves equally well is that which would be obtained by eliminating the portion of the *MAR* curve to the left (or to the right) of its maximum, that is, by doing away with the stage during which selling expenses become more effective (or less effective). So long as the maximum height of the *MAR* curve is such that it is tangent to a horizontal line, it does not matter whether this maximum is located on the left, on the right, or in between the extremities. The case I have illustrated will hold so long as a horizontal tangency is possible. It may well be that in some industries the *MAR* curve does not have such a maximum but instead is negatively inclined throughout its length. In such a case, excess capacity will be a condition of industry equilibrium in the purely static case of monopolistic competition.

20. Multiple-Plant Firms, Cartels, and Imperfect Competition*

DON PATINKIN [1]

Don Patinkin (B.A., the University of Chicago, 1943; M.A., 1945; Ph.D., 1947) is Professor of Economics in the Eliezer Kaplan School of Economics and the Social Sciences of the Hebrew University of Jerusalem and Director of the Falk Project for Economic Research in Israel. He was born in Chicago in 1922 and later emigrated to Israel after completing his formal education. Patinkin has also taught at the University of Chicago and the University of Illinois and was on the staff of the Cowles Commission for Economic Research. His research has primarily been in the microeconomic theory of money; he is, without question, among the most renowned of monetary theorists. Many recent students of economics have learned general equilibrium theory from his *Money Interest and Prices*, and from his classic articles, "Price Flexibility and Full Employment" and "Keynesian Economics and the Quantity Theory." Patinkin is a Fellow of the Econometric Society.

Although theories of imperfect competition have long since found a recognized

* Reprinted by permission of the publishers from Don Patinkin, *The Quarterly Journal of Economics* (February 1947). Cambridge, Mass.: Harvard University Press. Copyright, 1947, by the President and Fellows of Harvard College, pp. 173–205.

[1] I cannot overemphasize my debt to Professor Henry C. Simons, on whose Economics 201 Syllabus (mimeographed, University of Chicago Bookstore) this article is so largely based. Although Professor Simons did not see the manuscript before his untimely death, I discussed with him several of the points involved. I am also indebted to Bert Hoselitz, H. Gregg Lewis, and William H. Nicholls (all of the University of

place in textbooks, varying degrees of dissatisfaction with them have persisted due to their restrictive assumptions. To a very considerable extent this situation must continue until we have many more detailed studies of specific firms and industries and their methods of operation. The difficulty is, of course, the procuring of information. Even if many corporations overcame their reluctance to open their books to economists, those fundamental and intimate de-

Chicago), who read an earlier draft of this article and offered valuable criticisms and suggestions.

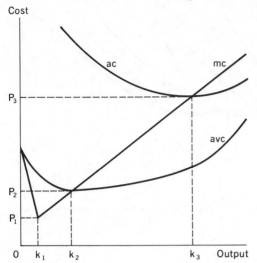

FIGURE 20.1

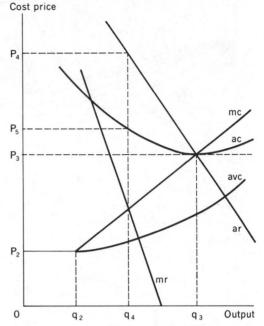

FIGURE 20.2

tails of corporate policy formation which are not translatable into bookkeeping entries would still be lacking. To some extent, however, the empirical evidence already available to us provides a basis for significant improvement in the theory. Accordingly, I plan in this article (1) to extend the analysis to deal with multiple-plant firms[2] and (2) to present a generalized oligopoly solution which can be employed as a frame of reference in empirical studies.

I

To illustrate the problem of multiple-plant firms, I shall first consider a case of perfect monopoly. For simplicity assume a linear demand curve remaining constant throughout the discussion, completely unspecialized factors of production (precluding any monopsony power), and a single product. Assume that the monopoly firm consists of 100 individual (and identical) plants, each of the long-run optimum size

[2] The usual one-firm-one-plant analysis is completely unrealistic. Thus, in 1937 the 50 largest manufacturing corporations owned 2869 plants, or an average of 57.4 per firm. No firm owned less than seven plants, while one owned 497. (TNEC, Monograph No. 27, The Structure of Industry, pp. 675–714.)

and with cost curves indicated in Figure 20.1, where ac, mc, and avc represent average, marginal, and average variable costs, respectively. For convenience we have assumed that the plant marginal cost curve is composed of two linear sections.

We turn now to the problem of constructing the monopolist's short-run marginal cost curve (Figure 20.2), noting that in the short-run (by definition) the monopolist cannot change the number of plants in existence. Consider a given output q_i;[3] the question is, how will the monopolist allocate this output among the different plants in order to minimize costs? The answer falls into two parts, according as q_i is greater or less than $q_2 = 100k_2$. In the former case the optimum allocation would be to have the output equally distributed among the plants. This readily follows from Figure 20.1. If one plant is producing more than another, its marginal cost will be higher; consequently, a reduc-

[3] The units of the abscissa of Figure 20.2 are related to those of Figure 20.1 by the equation $k_j = q_j/100$ for any j.

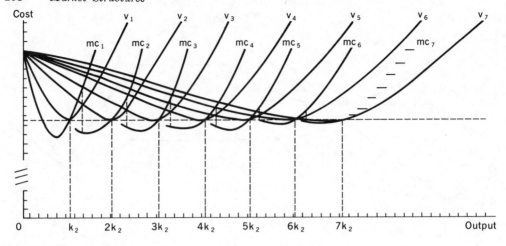

FIGURE **20.3**

tion in total cost can be effected by shifting the output from the former to the latter.[4] This process will continue until all plants are producing the same amount. We thus get the right-hand part of the marginal cost curve in Figure 20.2. To construct the marginal cost curve for outputs less than q_2 we note that no plant *in operation* will produce less than k_2; any desired output $q_i < q_2$ will be produced by having x plants produce k_2 units apiece (where k_2 is the output corresponding to minimum average variable costs for the plant—cf. Figure 20.1), with the remaining $100-x$ plants left idle. (x is obviously determined by the relationship $xk_2 = q_i$.) This may be proved as follows. In the short run the monopolist must bear the fixed expenses of the 100 plants. Therefore he will minimize total expenses for any given output by minimizing total variable expenses. Consider now the given output $q_i < q_2$. If this output were equally allocated among all plants, each plant would produce $k_i < k_2$ at an average variable cost of $p_i > p_2$. Then the total variable costs would be $100k_ip_i$. However, the total variable costs, if x plants were to produce k_2 apiece, would be xk_2p_2. But $100k_ip_i > xk_2p_2$, since $100k_i = xk_2 = q_i$ and

$p_i > p_2$. This is perfectly general and holds for any $q_i < q_2$ and $k_i < k_2$. In this range the monopolist would operate keeping some plants idle. The average variable cost would be $xk_2p_2/xk_2 = p_2$. Therefore, until q_2, the average variable cost curve is a horizontal line at a height p_2. By definition, the marginal cost curve, in this range, coincides with it.[5]

Strictly speaking the linear shape of the marginal cost curve is only an approximation which is approached as the number of plants increases. The actual shape is pictured in Figure 20.3; this may be considered as a "blowup" of Figure 20.2 (note the break in the vertical axis). For convenience, however, we have considered a firm consisting of only seven plants, each of the type described in Figure 20.1. v_i is the average variable cost of the firm, if i plants (neither more nor *less*) are used to produce a given output in the cheapest way possible. The v_i have a common origin, since one unit of output will always be produced by one plant producing one unit, regardless of the number of plants. As i increases, v_i tends to flatten out, since any given in-

---

[4] This holds for the cost curves usually dealt with, but is not general. Cf. Section II below.

[5] The position of the marginal cost curve in this range can also be established by noting that it can never be less than p_2, for the total expenses can always be reduced by at least p_2 per unit simply by closing down a plant.

crease in output will increase the output per plant less the more plants there are. From our previous discussion we know that v_i will reach its minimum at an output of ik_2 and a height of $p_2 (i = 1, 2 \ldots 7)$; that is, the minimum points are equidistant and at the same height.[6] The intersection of v_i and v_{i+1} indicates where it would be profitable to employ an additional plant. The heavy kinked [7] curve is thus the relevant average variable cost curve of the firm. It is tangent to the horizontal line (p_2 units high) at the outputs $nk_2 (n = 1, 2 \ldots 7)$. Similarly, we construct a marginal cost curve mc_i for each v_i. For higher values of i, mc_i will approach closer to v_i since the latter tends to flatten out. It is possible that ranges may exist for which mc_i becomes a step function. This is especially true for the rising part, where the assumption that output will be equally allocated is more probable; mc_7 is drawn on this assumption. Then an output of $7k_2 + 1$ is produced, with six plants producing k_2 and one producing $k_2 + 1$; an output of $7k_2 + i$ ($i = 2, 3 \ldots 7$) is produced by having $7 - i$ plants produce k_2 apiece, and i produce $k_2 + 1$—so that the marginal cost for all these outputs is the same. Thus, for outputs greater than $7k_2$, mc_7 is a rising step function, with steps seven units wide. On corresponding assumptions, in Figure 20.2 the marginal cost curve for outputs greater than q_2 is a step function with steps 100 units wide. As long as the width of the step is small relative to the scale of Figure 20.2,

we can approximate the rising part of the curve by a straight line.

In fact, due to the decreasing portions of the v_i and mc_i curves, we cannot construct these curves by allocating the output equally among the i plants. There do not seem to be any short-cut rules to follow, and the curves can be constructed only by trial and error allocations of the given output in different ways among the i plants and noting which way minimizes total variable cost. Similarly, it is impossible to determine by any simple rule when v_i and v_{i+1} will intersect—that is, when a new plant will be brought into operation. There might even be multiple intersection of v_i and v_{i+1}. For differently shaped plant cost curves we get entirely different results. Thus, for example, in the case of two plants we can construct cost curves such that the total variable cost is minimized by having one plant produce on the *rising* part of its marginal cost curve, and the other on the *falling* part (see Section II of this article).

Since the allocation of any given output is now determined, we can construct the other costs curves in Figure 20.2 making use of the data in Figure 20.1. For the demand curve ar the optimum output is at q_4, and the per-unit monopoly profit is $p_4 - p_5$. The usual textbook analysis stops at this point, with the implication that the monopolist is not producing at the point of minimum average cost (q_3) and should make no attempt to do so if he is to maximize profits. This certainly holds for the short run, but in the long run the monopolist can change his position by adjusting the number of plants through investment and disinvestment.

The problem is then one of determining the long-run cost curves of the monopolist (cf. Figure 20.4). The fundamental fact which must be noted here is that even in the long run the monopoly will not proceed to build different sized plants; investment and disinvestment in the firm will take

---

[6] These results are given more generally with the aid of some very neat mathematics in M. F. W. Joseph, "A Discontinuous Cost Curve and the Tendency to Increasing Returns," *Economic Journal*, Vol. 43 (1933), pp. 390–393. However, the exposition there is impaired by the unwarranted assumption that any output is equally allocated among plants. Cf. Section II of this article.

[7] That is, a *continuous* curve with *discontinuous* derivatives at certain points. Curves of this type have been erroneously referred to in the literature as "discontinuous."

place only by changing the number of plants. This follows from our assumption that the existing plants are of the long-run optimum size.

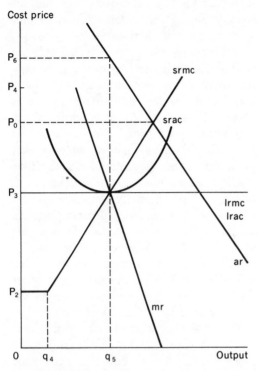

FIGURE 20.4

The construction of the monopolist's long-run average cost curve is analogous to the construction of the short-run average variable cost curve for outputs less than q_2. The process is identical if we note that in the long run (by definition) all costs are variable costs. We need only to observe that in the argument p_2 is replaced by p_3 and q_2 becomes infinitely large. In the long run the monopolist will minimize the cost of producing any output q_j by arranging his investment and disinvestment policies so that he will have exactly y plants, each producing k_3 (cf. Figure 20.1), where y is determined by the relation $y = q_j/k_3$. In other words, the optimum method of producing any given output is to have each plant producing at its minimum average

cost point, and adjusting the number of plants (by investment and disinvestment) so that the desired output can be produced. The total cost of *any* output q_j will then be yk_3p_3 and the average cost p_3, so that the long-run average cost curve (*lrac*) will be a horizontal line at the height p_3; the long-run marginal cost curve (*lrmc*) will coincide with it.[8]

The long-run equilibrium price and output in Figure 20.4 (assuming ar to remain constant) are p_6 and q_5, respectively. The long-run price and monopoly profits are each greater than in the short run. Once the optimum long-run output q_5 is determined, the optimum number of plants in the long run—$m = q_5/k_3$—is simultaneously determined. Thus, in the long run the monopolist will have m plants and the short-run average and marginal cost curves *srac* and *srmc* (Figure 20.4). *srac* will obviously have its minimum point at the output q_5, since for that output each of the m plants will be producing at its own minimum point k_3. Since $m < 100$, the marginal cost curve for the firm with m plants remains horizontal at p_2 over a shorter interval than when the firm consists of 100 plants. Specifically, for the case of m plants, mc remains constant only until $q_6 = mk_2 < q_2 = 100k_2$. It is interesting to note that in the long run the monopolist will *of necessity* be producing at the minimum point of his short-run average cost curve. We must now determine what particular assumption we have made that has led to this unusual result.

First let us distinguish between intra-plant and interplant economies and diseconomies. Intraplant economies are what we usually have in mind when we speak of economies of large-scale production. These are derived from increases in the size of

[8] We must make reservations here analogous to those made above concerning the shape of the average variable cost curve for outputs less than q_2.

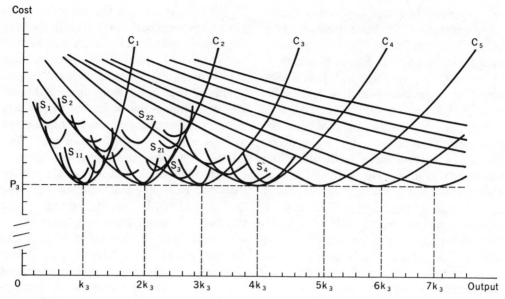

FIGURE **20.5**

plant which enable use of more specialized and efficient machinery, develops skills in performing specialized tasks, eliminates movements of workers, and so on. Interplant economies are reductions in (social) cost following from the fact that two or more plants operate under a common management, instead of being separately owned. These take the form of economies in purchases and sales of materials, research, flexibility, "scientific management," risk-bearing, financing, integration, etc. Diseconomies of both types are due to increasing difficulties of coördination, bureaucratic inefficiency, etc. That there are substantial and continuing intraplant economies has been shown to be true in many industries;[9] but on the question of interplant economies very little empirical evidence is available. Similarly, we have little information about the diseconomies.

Let us now consider the long-run average

[9] J. M. Blair, "The Relation between Size and Efficiency of Business," *Review of Economic Statistics*, Vol. 24, pp. 125–135 (1942); Joseph Steindl, *Small and Big Business*, Oxford University Institute of Statistics, Monograph No. 1 (1945).

cost curve (Figure 20.5).[10] The curve c_1 is the traditional Harrod-Viner envelope of the family of one-plant short-run cost curves, s_1. The specific s_1 (say s_{11}) which is tangent to c_1 at the latter's minimum point is (by assumption) our curve of **Figure 20.1**. Consider now any specific curve of the s_2 family—say s_{21}. This curve is constructed by allocating a given output in the best way possible among two plants of *arbitrary size*. We construct an s_2 curve for every possible combination of different size plants. We then construct the c_2 curve by marking off for any given output an ordinate equal to that of the lowest point on any member of the family of curves s_2 for that given output. Strictly speaking, c_2 is not an envelope curve, since there can obviously be members of s_2 which do not touch it: for example, s_{22} in Figure 20.5. From our previous exposition we know that the s_2 curve tangent to c_2 at the latter's minimum point is that formed from two identical plants each of the size indicated in Figure 20.1. A similar interpretation holds for the other s_{jr}

[10] Figure 20.5 may be considered as a blowup of Figure 20.4; note the break in the vertical axis.

and c_i curves. The latter will tend to flatten out as i increases. We know from our preceding discussion that c_i will reach its minimum for an output of $k_3 i$ at a height of $p_3 (i = 1, 2, \ldots \infty)$; that is, the minimum points are equidistant and at the same height.[11] The intersection of c_j and c_{j+1} indicates where it would be profitable for the monopolist to build a $(j + 1)$-st plant. The heavy kinked curve is therefore the long-run average cost curve. In the case of other indivisibilities, the c_i curves would also be kinked, resulting in the long-run average cost curve having still more kinks than pictured here. The long-run marginal cost curve is discontinuous and of the same general shape of that in Figure 20.3 (for outputs less than $7k_1$), except that it extends indefinitely out, approaching more and more to the horizontal line at p_3. In order not to make Figure 20.5 too cumbersome, this curve has not been included.

The declining portion of c_1 measures the extent of intraplant economies: the greater k_3 the greater their importance. The importance of interplant economies is measured by the relative positions of the successive minimum points of the long-run average cost curve. There are four major possibilities. (1) They may lie on a horizontal line; this is the situation depicted in Figure 20.5. It implies that there are no interplant economies or diseconomies, or that they offset each other identically for every output. (2) They may lie on a curve which remains a horizontal line for a significant distance and then begin to rise; here there are only interplant diseconomies. (3) The curve declines and then becomes horizontal; here there are only interplant economies. (4) The curve has the traditional U-shape pattern.

We see now that the previous unusual results for the monopoly case follow from our assuming situation (1) to hold; otherwise, there is no *necessity* for the monopo-

list to be operating at the minimum point of his short-run cost curve even in the long run. But it is essential to note that even in the traditional case (4), where from a purely probability viewpoint there is least likelihood that in the long run he will operate at the minimum point, the *probability* is greater than usually realized that his cost will be close to the minimum cost. This follows from the construction of the cost curves, which makes it impossible for the long-run *multiple*-plant cost curve (even if U-shaped) to be less flat-bottomed than the long-run *single*-plant cost curve.[12]

Formulation of the problem in this way focuses attention on the central policy problem of monopoly: optimum size of firm. Dissolution as the answer to monopoly is subject to two fundamental criticisms. (a) If firms are to be of optimum size, there might not be enough independent firms resulting from the dissolution to make the operation of competition possible. In other words, we will replace monopoly with some oligopoly situation, and it is quite possible that we would be as badly off as under monopoly. We shall deal more fully with this in Section III. (b) Even if there are originally enough independent firms for competition to work, the situation might be unstable and develop into oligopoly.

Thus situation (1) is very favorable as far as (a) is concerned, depending only on the size of k_3 relative to market output. But the independent firms would then be in the familiar unstable situation of a long-run constant cost curve, and there would be no *economic* limit to their possible growth. The dissolution provisions would also have to define optimum firm and prevent firms from growing any larger.[13] Situ-

[11] Cf. note 6 above.

[12] Though we have developed the theory of multiple-plant cost curves for monopoly only, it is clear that the construction of the cost curves is perfectly general and will hold in any of the cases of imperfect competition. These cases should be modified accordingly.

[13] In the event that dissolution succeeded in placing each plant under separate ownership and

ation (2) is most favorable for a policy of dissolution, since it has the advantage over (1) that there is an economic limit to the growth of the independent firms. The case for dissolution is weakest under (3). Here again it depends on where the curve straightens out. Even if it is at a relatively small output (say $3k_3$, so that each competitive firm would consist of 3 plants), there would still be the problem of preventing indefinite growth. This problem would not be so bad under (4), but in either (3) or (4), if we insisted on making each plant a separate firm, we could do so only at the expense of efficiency in production. The cost would, of course, vary with the shape of the curve formed from the successive minimum points.

II

Our purpose in this section is to deal more mathematically with the short-run situation and show under what conditions equalization of marginal costs by equalizing outputs of the plants will not minimize costs to the firm.[14] We shall deal primarily

<hr />

making perfect competition work, in our preceding example we would have short-run equilibrium established at a price of p_0 (cf. Figure 20.4). This follows from our assumption that the ingredients are completely unspecialized, so that the supply curve for the competitive industry coincides with the marginal cost curve of the monopolist. This supply curve intersects the industry demand curve at the price p_0, thus establishing the short-run price for the competitive industry. Since this price exceeds minimum average cost (p_2) the industry is not in long-run equilibrium: firms will flow into the industry and the supply curve will shift over to the right until a price p_3 is established (again employing the assumption of a constant costs industry). This will be the case when there are 100 firms (with one plant each) in the industry (cf. Figure 20.2). Thus, in Cassels' terminology, for the monopoly we have no long-run excess capacity (in situation (1)), though there is underinvestment if we accept perfect competition as a criterion. (J. M. Cassels, "Excess Capacity and Monopolistic Competition," this JOURNAL, Vol. 51 (1936–37), pp. 440–443.) (Reprinted supra, pp. 224–234.)

[14] This section may be omitted without disturbing the continuity between Sections I and III.

with the case of a two-plant firm and offer (a) a geometric proof and then (b) a more general algebraic proof.

(*a*) Assume for convenience that each plant (*A* and *B*) has the same marginal cost curve reaching its minimum at *b*. For total outputs $x < 2b$ it is well known that equalization of marginal cost does not minimize cost (cf. (*b*) below). It is also obvious that in the case of a symmetric marginal cost curve an output of $2b$ can be produced either with each plant producing *b* or with one producing $b + d$ and the other $b - d$, where *d* is any positive constant less than or equal to *b*. We shall ignore these more trivial cases and consider $x = 2(b + 1)$, which could be produced with each plant producing $b + 1$. In order that it should be produced, instead, with *A* producing *a* and *B* producing $2(b + 1) - a$, and *that this should be the only possible way of minimizing cost*, we have the follow-

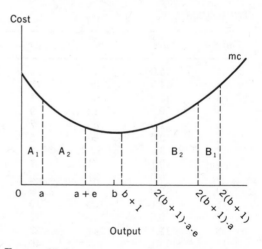

FIGURE 20.6

ing necessary and sufficient conditions (cf. Figure 20.6):

1. $A_1 < B_1$—otherwise the entire output would be produced in *B*. This condition insures that *at least a* will be produced in *A*.

2. For any $0 < e \leqslant b + 1 - a$ it is true that $A_2 > B_2$. The most important value of $e = b + 1 - a$; for this insures that, even

though we equalize the marginal costs by equalizing outputs of the two operating plants, we are not minimizing costs. The statement must hold for the other values of e to insure that no other point on the falling part of the marginal cost curve is the minimizing one.

These two conditions are very general and impose no restrictions inconsistent with the generally accepted U-shaped marginal cost curve. In general the class of cost curves meeting these conditions will have the following characteristics: (a) sharply falling initial stages, (b) flattening out for a short interval, then (c) rising even more sharply. (c) brings about condition (1); (a) and (b) together tend to bring about condition (2). To prove the first statement in this paragraph, we offer the following actual example.

Let A and B each have the cost curves described in Table 20.1. We must now con-

TABLE 20.1

Output	avc	tvc	mc
1	15.0	15	15
2	14.0	28	13
3	13.0	39	11
4	12.0	48	9
5	11.0	55	7
6	10.0	60	5
7	9.4	66	6
8	9.1	73	7
9	9.0	81	8
10	9.0	90	9
11	9.1	100	10
12	9.8	117	17
13	11.1	144	27
14	13.1	184	40
15	15.9	239	55

struct the v_1 and v_2 curves (cf. Figure 20.3). The v_1 curve is, of course, represented by Table 20.1. The v_2 curve is constructed in Table 20.2. From a comparison of Tables 20.1 and 20.2 we see that v_2 intersects v_1 between outputs 11 and 12, so that the v_2 curve for an output of 12 is the relevant one. Yet this output, which could

be produced by each plant producing at its minimum marginal cost output, is produced with one plant on the rising part of its marginal cost curve and the other on the falling.

(b) Consider again the case of a 2-plant firm.[15] Consider the plants as separate factors of production, and let $c(x_1)$ and $c(x_2)$ be the total variable cost curves of A and B, respectively, where x_1 is the output of A and x_2 of B. Then for any fixed output k the monopolist will seek to minimize

$$C = c(x_1) + c(x_2)$$

subject to the side condition

$$x_1 + x_2 = k$$

We employ the Lagrange multiplier and form

$$F = c(x_1) + c(x_2) - \lambda(x_1 + x_2 - k)$$

Minimizing F with respect to x_1 and then x_2 and eliminating λ we get as our first order conditions the familiar results

$$\partial c/\partial x_1 = \partial c/\partial x_2$$

In order that F should be a minimum, we need the second order conditions fulfilled.[16]

$$D = \begin{vmatrix} 0 & \dfrac{\partial c}{\partial x_1} & \dfrac{\partial c}{\partial x_2} \\ \dfrac{\partial c}{\partial x_1} & \dfrac{\partial^2 c}{\partial x_1{}^2} & 0 \\ \dfrac{\partial c}{\partial x_2} & 0 & \dfrac{\partial^2 c}{\partial x_2{}^2} \end{vmatrix}$$

$$= -\left(\dfrac{\partial c}{\partial x_1}\right)^2 \left(\dfrac{\partial^2 c}{\partial x_2{}^2}\right) - \left(\dfrac{\partial c}{\partial x_2}\right)^2 \left(\dfrac{\partial^2 c}{\partial x_1{}^2}\right) < 0$$

Noting that $\left(\dfrac{\partial c}{\partial x_i}\right)^2$ is identically > 0, and that $\dfrac{\partial^2 c}{\partial x_i{}^2} \begin{smallmatrix} < \\ > \end{smallmatrix} 0$ $(i = 1, 2)$ according as marginal cost is falling, at a minimum, or

[15] I wish to express my appreciation to Trygve Haavelmo (University of Chicago) for his assistance in formulating the results of this paragraph.

[16] Cf. J. R. Hicks, *Value and Capital* (1939), pp. 305 ff.

TABLE 20.2

| Output | Plant A | | Plant B | | TVC |
	Output	tvc(A)	Output	tvc(B)	tvc(A) + tvc(B)
1	1	15	0	0	15
2	1	15	1	15	30
3	2	28	1	15	43
4	3	39	1	15	54
5	4	48	1	15	63
6	5	55	1	15	70
7	6	60	1	15	75
8	7	66	1	15	81
9	8	73	1	15	88
10	9	81	1	15	96
11	10	90	1	15	105
12	11	100	1	15	115
13	7	66	6	60	126
14	7	66	7	66	132
15	8	73	7	66	139

rising, we can formulate the following results:

1. For outputs $x = x_1 + x_2 < b$ (where b is the output for plant minimum marginal cost), each plant will of necessity be producing on the falling part of the curve. Therefore $D > 0$ and equalizing marginal cost by equalizing outputs will *maximize* total costs. Minimum costs are achieved by having one plant produce the entire output.

2. If $x_1 = x_2 = b$, then $D = 0$ and this allocation may be neither a minimum nor a maximum.

3. If $x = x_1 + x_2 > 2b$ and we equalize marginal costs by equalizing outputs, then each plant is producing on the rising part of the marginal cost curve and $D < 0$. This assures us that this allocation will minimize costs *relative to* all alternative allocations such that each plant is producing on the rising part of the marginal cost curve; that is, this allocation is the optimum one within a neighborhood such that every point is on the rising part of the curve. However, if we permit allocations such that one plant is producing on the falling part and one on its rising part, then for this allocation we may have $D > 0$; thus the allocation achieved by equalizing marginal

costs may be neither a minimum nor a maximum relative to the whole extent of the marginal cost curve.

These results can be represented graphically with the aid of Figure 20.7. From the

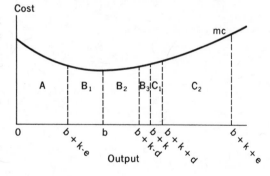

FIGURE 20.7

shape of the marginal cost curve (which reaches its minimum as the output b) we know, for an output of $2(b + k)$, $C_1 > B_3$ as long as $d < k$. Therefore the total variable costs are less when the allocation is $b + k$ to each one than any other allocation $b + k + d$, $b + k - d$ (where $d < k$). Analogous results hold when total output is less than b: then from the shape of the curve we see that equalizing marginal cost will bring about a greater total variable cost than any other allocation. When, however, we permit the possibility of the allocation being $b + k - e$, $b + k + e$ (where $e > k$) we are no longer sure that $b + k$, $b + k$ will yield a smaller total variable cost than the former allocation. Specifically, the former allocation will be less when

$$2A + B + C < 2(A + B)$$

where $B = B_1 + B_2 + B_3$; $C = C_1 + C_2$

This reduces to

$$C < B \text{ or } B_1 > C - (B_2 + B_3) > 0$$

Obviously by increasing the absolute value of the slope of the falling part of the marginal cost curve in the neighborhood of the minimum point, we can make B_1 as large as desired, while keeping the right side of this last inequality constant. Thus a marginal cost curve satisfying this inequality can easily be constructed.

These results can readily be generalized to the case of n plants, each with its own total variable cost curve $c_i(x_i)$, where the c_i are not necessarily the same. Our first and second order conditions are shown below.

These results leave us with the conclusion that it is impossible to formulate any general rules to determine how many plants (in the short run) will be used to produce a given output, except the one proved in the section above, namely, with k plants, each with minimum average variable cost at $x_i = g$, outputs of $ng (n = 1, 2, \ldots k)$ will be produced by having n plants each produce g. Furthermore, it is theoretically possible that $x = x_1$ will be produced with j plants, $x = x_1 + d$ with $j + 1$ plants, and $x = x_1 + d + e$ with j plants again. Consequently our Figure 20.3 should allow for the possibility of multiple intersection of the v_i curves.[17]

Finally, we should note that these problems do not arise under perfect competition, which may well explain why they have so long been neglected. In imperfect competi-

[17] In a comment on this article, Wassily Leontief showed that at most one plant would be operated on the decreasing part of its marginal cost curve. See W. W. Leontief, "Multiple-Plant Firms: Comment," *Quarterly Journal of Economics*, LXI (1947), pp. 650–651.—D. P.

$$\frac{\partial c_1}{\partial x_1} = \frac{\partial c_2}{\partial x_2} = \cdots = \frac{\partial c_n}{\partial x_n}$$

$$\begin{vmatrix} 0 & \dfrac{\partial c_1}{\partial x_1} & \dfrac{\partial c_2}{\partial x_2} \\[2mm] \dfrac{\partial c_1}{\partial x_1} & \dfrac{\partial^2 c_1}{\partial x_1{}^2} & 0 \\[2mm] \dfrac{\partial c_2}{\partial x_2} & 0 & \dfrac{\partial^2 c_2}{\partial x_2{}^2} \end{vmatrix} < 0$$

$$\begin{vmatrix} 0 & \dfrac{\partial c_1}{\partial x_1} & \dfrac{\partial c_2}{\partial x_2} & \dfrac{\partial c_3}{\partial x_3} \\[2mm] \dfrac{\partial c_1}{\partial x_1} & \dfrac{\partial^2 c_1}{\partial x_1{}^2} & 0 & 0 \\[2mm] \dfrac{\partial c_2}{\partial x_2} & 0 & \dfrac{\partial^2 c_2}{\partial x_2{}^2} & 0 \\[2mm] \dfrac{\partial c_3}{\partial x_3} & 0 & 0 & \dfrac{\partial^2 c_3}{\partial x_3{}^2} \end{vmatrix} < 0$$

$$\cdots \begin{vmatrix} 0 & \dfrac{\partial c_1}{\partial x_1} & \dfrac{\partial c_2}{\partial x_2} & \cdots & \dfrac{\partial c_n}{\partial x_n} \\[2mm] \dfrac{\partial c_1}{\partial x_1} & \dfrac{\partial^2 c_1}{\partial x_1{}^2} & 0 & \cdots & 0 \\[2mm] \dfrac{\partial c_2}{\partial x_2} & 0 & \dfrac{\partial^2 c_2}{\partial x_2{}^2} & \cdots & 0 \\ \cdot & \cdot & \cdot & \cdots & \\ \cdot & \cdot & \cdot & \cdot & \\ \cdot & \cdot & \cdot & \cdots & \\[2mm] \dfrac{\partial c_n}{\partial x_n} & 0 & 0 & \cdot & \dfrac{\partial^2 c_n}{\partial x_n{}^2} \end{vmatrix} < 0$$

tion there is only a demand curve for the firm as a whole, and not for any individual plant. Therefore, before we can discuss equilibrium for the firm we must construct the aggregate cost curve for the firm as a whole. However, under perfect competition there exists a separate demand curve for each plant, namely, an infinitely elastic curve at the level of the market price. Consequently we can determine the equilibrium output of each plant independently of what takes place in other plants. In other words, the fact of the unlimited market which is present under perfect competition enables us to consider each plant separately.

Analytically this can be shown as follows. Consider a firm with n plants; the amount x_i is produced by the i-th plant, which has the total cost curve $g_i(x_i)$ $(i = 1, 2, \ldots n)$. Let p = price of the product sold by the firm. By our assumption of perfect competition p is considered by the firm as given. Then the firm maximizes its profit

$$\pi = px - \sum_{i=1}^{n} g_i(x_i)$$

subject to

$$x = \sum_{i=1}^{n} x_i.$$

Substituting we have

$$\pi = p \sum_{i=1}^{n} x_i - \sum_{i=1}^{n} g_i(x_i)$$

from which follow our familiar maximizing conditions

$$\partial \pi / \partial x_i = p - \frac{\partial g_i(x_i)}{\partial x_i} = 0 \ (i = 1, 2, \cdots n)$$

that is, the marginal cost of each plant must equal the market price, our usual condition for equilibrium under perfect competition.

III

In this section I shall assume that the monopoly has been dissolved and replaced by one hundred independent firms, and then consider the arrangements that might grow up between them in the absence of perfect competition. This failure of competition to develop may be due either to active desire to achieve monopoly gains, or to passive acceptance of noncompetitive arrangements due to interdependence and indeterminacy which make it impossible to adopt the rules of perfect competition.

We must recognize at the outset that in any realistic approach to the problem of monopoly and oligopoly we cannot deal in purely economic terms, but must introduce concepts and motivations which more closely approximate international power politics. On the one hand, corporation leaders have "corporationistic" feelings, together with a desire for power that is inherent in large size. On the other, corporations frequently undertake expansion programs for defensive purposes as well as for aggressive: vertical integration must be undertaken to assure strategic raw materials and market outlets—the corporation cannot allow itself to become dependent on other firms for these essentials. (The analogy to protectionism and war is complete.) In democratic societies the freedom of individuals becomes the ultimate limit to this integrative process; these societies prevent the corporation from achieving complete security by restricting its control over the factor of production labor, with its right to strike, and freedom of contract. Similarly, horizontal integration must be adopted, if the firm is to retain its position in the industry. The firm must accumulate large reserves, for in the event of a price war, victory is not to the most efficient but to the one with the largest reserves. In each case, it is the fear of imperfect competition which makes the corporation adopt methods of imperfect competition itself. This is what makes the oligopoly problem so difficult: it cannot be solved piecemeal. This vicious circle will continue until economists provide rules for the social control of oligopolies that will both protect the public and be workable: indeterminacy must be removed without leaving the door open to collusive exploitation. In brief, some criteria must be provided to distinguish "good" imperfect competition from "bad." It is quite likely that the controls devised will involve a much greater degree of direct government intervention than we have known heretofore.

Despite these qualifications, I now proceed to examine the workings of a market-sharing oligopoly arrangement among the newly independent firms. I shall attempt to show that this cartel arrangement (as we shall refer to it) should be used as a general model for practical studies of imperfect competition. This is not to say that as it stands it is realistic; in fact, its assumptions will prove to be quite arbitrary. However, it does provide a convenient "jumping-off" point from which modifications can be made to deal with actual cases.

Assume that the one hundred independent firms set up a central office which decides on a common price and output policy for the industry. The cartel allocates quotas among the different firms in such a way as to minimize the costs of any given output. We no longer continue with our unrealistic (monopoly) assumption that the cartel can control entry into the industry. In fact, and this is the distinguishing feature, we assume that, as a result of anti-monopoly laws or the pressure of public opinion, there is free entry. Specifically, we assume that the anti-monopoly laws prevent single ownership of the industry and restrictions on entry, but permit agreements (either tacit or explicit) among the supposely competitive firms. The cartel must thus permit any firm which wishes to do so to enter the industry and become a member of the cartel. In order to determine the short-run and long-run equilibria of the cartel, we must first construct its cost curves.[18]

[18] The reader should make modifications to the shape and construction of these curves analogous to those pointed out for the curves in the preceding section. Since I have already dealt at length with this problem, it will be omitted here.

Let us first consider the short-run marginal cost curve. For outputs greater than q_2 (Figures 20.8 and 20.2) the cartel will minimize costs by equalizing marginal costs among all firms and having each produce an equal amount. For outputs less than q_2 the cartel will follow exactly the same procedure as the monopoly in allocating production: x firms will produce k_2 units apiece, where x is determined by the equation $xq_2 = q_i$, where q_i is any output less than or equal to q_2. The short-run cartel situation is thus identical with short-run monopoly (Figure 20.2). Each firm will produce k_4 to give a total output for the industry of q_4 and a price of p_4. The firms will share according to their quotas (and therefore equally) the cartel profits, which are equal to the area of the rectangle $p_4 r_1 s_1 p_{12}$.

In the long run the existence of these cartel profits will attract new firms into the industry.[19] Assume that these too become part of the cartel. We must now consider what happens to the short-run cost curves of the cartel as new firms enter. By assumption the existing plant is the optimum one; therefore, assuming no changes in technology or prices of factors, the new firms will build plants of exactly the same size. Assume also that one firm continues to operate only one plant.

As in the case of short-run monopoly, marginal cost can never fall below p_2. But in the long run, as new firms enter, the point corresponding to q_2 in Figure 20.2 moves over further to the right (cf. Figure 20.8). Specifically, for any number of plants

[19] New investment might of course also come from the old firms' expanding in order to increase their quotas and relative standing in the industry. Or they might wait until a new firm establishes itself, and then buy it up along with its quota. This last was the pattern of the German potash cartel and is also characteristic of the American meat packing industry. Cf. George W. Stocking, *The Potash Industry* (1931); Wm. H. Nicholls, "Market-Sharing in the Packing Industry," *Journal of Farm Economics*, Vol. 22 (1940), pp. 225–240.

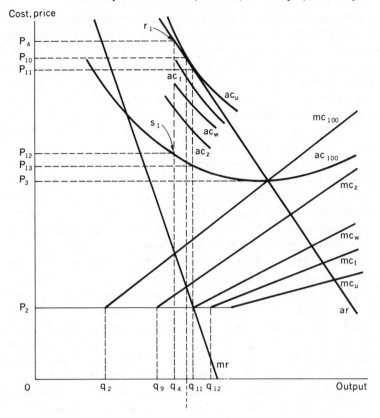

FIGURE **20.8**

$z > 100$, the marginal cost curve (mc_z) will be a horizontal line at the level p_2 until the point $q_9 = zk_2$. Outputs up to this point will be produced by keeping some plants idle and the remaining plants each producing k_2. For outputs greater than q_9 (with z firms), the cartel will allocate quotas equally among the firms and the marginal cost curve will rise. The marginal cost curve for z firms not only is horizontal for a longer stretch than that for 100 firms, but the slope of its rising part is smaller; therefore it will always lie below the marginal cost curve for 100 firms. This is true because for any given increase in output the increase in marginal cost for z firms is less than that for 100 firms, since the increased output can be shared among a greater number of firms. For example, for a given increase in the cartel output, with only 100 firms each one might have to increase out-

put from k_1 to k_3; while for z firms, each one might only have to increase from k_1 to k_2, with a corresponding smaller increase in marginal costs (cf. Figure 20.1). Another way of looking at this is to note that the "steps" in the rising part of the curve become wider as more firms enter (cf. above, p. 265).

So much for the marginal cost curve. As more firms enter, the total fixed cost, and therefore the average fixed cost curve, will rise uniformly. But the average variable cost for the cartel with any number of plants $z > 100$ will be less than, or equal to, the average variable costs with 100 firms. Until q_2 the curves will coincide as horizontal straight lines at the level p_2. For outputs from q_2 to q_9 the z curve will continue horizontally, while the other curve will begin to rise. For outputs greater than q_9 the average variable cost for z firms

(avc_z) will also begin to rise, always remaining, of course, below its marginal cost curve. It will also lie below avc_{100}, since for any output $q_i > q_9$ each firm will produce a smaller output and will thus have lower average variable costs (cf. Figure 20.1). Consequently there is no definite relationship between the average cost curve for z firms and that for 100 firms: it might be higher in some intervals and lower in others. For example, if the cartel output were such that with 100 firms each firm were producing k_3 or less (Figure 20.1), an increasing number of firms would reduce (for the fixed cartel output) the output per firm and drive each firm to the left and higher on its average cost curve. Therefore, the cartel average cost for this output would be greater with z firms than with 100. If, on the other hand, cartel output were such that with 100 firms each one were producing immediately to the right of k_3, then for a slight increase in the number of firms the cartel average cost for that output would be decreased, as each plant was pushed down to its minimum point k_3; while for larger increases in the number of plants each one would be pushed up on the falling part of the average cost curve until the cartel average cost was higher than with 100 firms. If, finally, with 100 firms the output is such that each plant is far to the right on its average cost curve, then even for large increases in the number of firms, cartel average cost would be reduced. However, for the output q_3 with 100 firms, each firm is producing at its minimum average cost. We have thus the first situation described here, and therefore for any given output $q_j < q_3$ the cartel average cost with a greater number of firms will be greater than with a smaller number. For outputs greater than q_3 the other two situations will hold.

From our previous discussion we see that, as new firms enter, the marginal cost curve is pushed uniformly to the right. Since we have assumed that the average revenue

(and therefore the marginal revenue) curve remains constant, this means that in the long run cartel price will fall and output increase. Thus, for z firms we have equilibrium with output $q_{10} > q_4$ and price $p_{10} < p_4$.

Let us suppose that even with z firms there are still cartel profits; then new firms will continue to enter. Assume that the number of firms increases to w where $w = q_{11}/k_2$. The same relationships hold between the cost curves of the cartel with w firms and the cartel with z firms as between z firms and 100 firms. The equilibrium output will be $q_{11} > q_{10}$ and the price $p_{11} < p_{10}$. Assume, now, that even with w firms profits are still being made. Let the new number of firms be t, where $t = q_{12}/k_2$. Let us examine the effect of this new inflow of firms on the equilibrium situation.

The marginal cost curve (mc_t) is changed as indicated in Figure 20.8. The first significant point is that *the equilibrium output has not changed* and is still at q_{11}. Furthermore, the output q_{11} will be produced in exactly the same way as with w firms: w plants will produce k_2 each to yield a total output of $k_2w = q_{11}$. The remaining $t - w$ plants will remain idle and be paid their fixed costs and aliquot share of the cartel profits.[20] The other significant point is that average costs for an output q_{11} with t firms *will definitely be greater* than for w firms. This follows because average variable cost is the same in both cases ($= p_2$), while average fixed cost is greater in the former due to the additional fixed costs of the $t - w$ new firms. Thus per-unit profit is definitely smaller. If there are still profits, new firms will continue to enter, driving up the average cost curve for the output q_{11} until it is tangent to the demand curve at that output. At this point price will equal average expense and there will be no profits and no further inducements to enter. The

[20] Theoretically, at this point a new firm could obtain its share of cartel profits by merely *threatening* to build a new plant.

industry will then be in long-run equilibrium.[21] It can be shown, however, that both in theory and in practice this equilibrium is a very unstable one.

The long-run equilibrium number of firms in the industry, u, can be determined as follows. Total profits P, when there are w firms, are

$$P = p_{11}q_{11} - (q_{11}p_2 + wf)$$

where f is the total fixed cost per plant and p_2 the average variable cost. Then

$$u = w + \frac{P}{f}.$$

That is, the number of new firms above w is limited by the amount of cartel profits available to pay them their fixed expenses in order to keep them idle.[22]

The long-run equilibrium is thus one of both excess capacity (in the sense that the cartel is operating below its long-run minimum cost point) and overinvestment.[23] If we measure excess capacity in terms of the output that could be yielded if output were at a point where marginal cost equals price, the results are equally impressive. Although there are more plants in the cartel than under long-run competitive equilibrium, the industry output is less and the cost and price higher, with a very low (normal) rate of profit.[24]

Such long-run equilibria are highly unstable. This is clearly shown in our model by the discrepancy between the marginal revenue of the *firm* (which approximately equals price on the assumption of non-retaliation) and its own very low marginal cost. Each individual firm realizes the ease and profit with which it could sell additional units beyond its quota. Thus the temptation to "bootlegging," smuggling, and "chiseling" is strong. As cartel profits decrease with the influx of new firms, this pressure becomes irresistible, especially for the low-cost firms, and the eventual breakdown of cartel discipline is inevitable. The pernicious (for the cartel) fact remains that it is to the *maximum advantage* of each firm to stay out of the cartel and sell in unlimited quantities at the cartel price (or just below it), while all other firms remain members of the cartel and by their common restrictive policies hold up the price. This has been the pattern of breakdown of many cartels, with rubber (the Stevenson Plan) as the classic example.[25]

---

[21] The classic case of a cartel in such a long-run equilibrium is the German potash cartel, which in 1928 operated only 60 of 229 plants. B. R. Wallace and L. R. Edminster, *International Control of Raw Materials* (1930), Chap. 4.

[22] It is interesting to note that the graphic equilibrium obtained here is similar to that of the familiar Chamberlin product differentiation case. But here the curves refer to the *industry* as a whole, not to the individual firm. Also, here the equilibrium is obtained solely by shifts in the cost curves, while there the main shift takes place through the demand curve (for the individual firm).

[23] Whereas under monopoly there was no excess capacity and underinvestment. This last pernicious and wasteful effect of the cartel is what makes many economists believe that a situation of out-and-out monopoly is preferable to a cartel. Cf. above, p. 268–269, note 13.

[24] Excess capacity is here presented as the outcome of cartel operations, and the cartel itself is

depicted as beginning from a situation of perfect competition. As is well known, however, excess capacity frequently first arises through shifts in demand or technological changes, precipitates a disastrous period of "cutthroat competition," which is finally ended by setting up a cartel arrangement. This pattern has been especially important among products with low income elasticities of demand—the so-called primary products (e.g. the rubber, coffee, and wheat cartels). Thus excess capacity is itself a *cause* of the cartel. Cf. J. W. F. Rowe, *Markets and Men* (1936); Wallace and Edminster, op. cit., W. Y. Eliott et al., *International Control in the Non-Ferrous Metals* (1937).

[25] Cf. Rowe, op. cit.; K. E. Knorr, *World Rubber and Its Regulation* (1945); Rowe, "Studies in the Artificial Control of Raw Material Supplies: No. 2, Rubber," London and Cambridge Economic Service, Special Memorandum No. 34 (1931); C. R. Whittlesey, Governmental Control of Crude Rubber (1931). The last two are excellent critical studies of the Stevenson Plan.

That the same pattern was at work in the U. S. copper export cartel after the first World War is evident from the following testimony of C. F. Kelley (president of Anaconda Copper Mining Co.) before the TNEC (Hearings, Vol. 25, pp. 13164–13165):

"The Copper Export Association finally broke

Another cause of instability lies in a fact from which our model abstracts by its assumption of uniform cost curves for all firms. There is a fundamental conflict of interest (within the cartel) between the low-cost and high-cost firms, with the latter insisting on high enough prices to cover their costs as the condition of their remaining in the cartel. There is also the very difficult problem of allocating quotas among the firms, which always creates much dissension and bickering. The forces described in this and the preceding paragraph go a long way in explaining the breakdown of many of our cartels. The cartel is in the unenviable position of having to satisfy everyone, for one dissatisfied producer can bring about the feared price competition and the disintegration of the cartel. Thus the successful cartel must follow a policy of continuous compromise.

In view of the difficulties of maintaining cartel discipline, it is not surprising that successful cartels have resorted to one or more of the following practices: (*a*) invoked government aid to compel membership and enforce cartel decisions (quotas and prices)—especially true of Europe; (*b*) controlled entry into, and operation within, the industry through patents—a frequent practice in the chemical industries; (*c*) controlled entry into, and operation within, the industry by ownership over the scarce raw material cartelized, e.g. tin, potash, lead; (*d*) compelled membership or prevented insubordination by dumping at (temporarily) greatly reduced prices in the market area of the non-coöperating producer. The cartel is frequently prevented

from following this last practice by force of law (especially anti-dumping tariffs) or public opinion.

IV

In the United States open cartel arrangements of the type analyzed here are not frequent, since they are strongly discouraged by antitrust law—even more so than outright merger. Nevertheless, I shall show that many of the (tacit) arrangements which do evolve in our economy have striking similarities to our cartel model. An unfortunate result of the classification of imperfect competition into several types is the failure to recognize that in actual life these types are inextricably mixed. Insofar as our economy can be characterized by a single pattern, I think it is one in which the given industry produces differentiated products and consists of a few (say three or four) very large firms doing the bulk of the business, plus many smaller "independents." The large firms act more or less as leaders for the industry in setting price policy, and so on. Some form of tacit or explicit market sharing arrangement (by percentages, market areas, recognized customers, etc.) exists to modify (if not remove) competition between the large firms. They might also proceed on the assumption that the other dominant firms will follow their prices both upwards and downwards. This gives results identical with our cartel model. The industry also has a trade association to help in maintaining discipline and implementing the price policies of the leading dominant firms.

The steel, petroleum, agricultural implements, anthracite coal, light bulb, cigarette, meat packing, and many other industries all fall within this general pattern.[26] In all these industries there has also been a decided tendency for the (original) dominant firms to decline in relative importance over

---

up due to two causes. One was the withdrawal of certain members, led by the Miami Copper Co. . . . There was an increase in competition from nonmembers abroad. There was a constant undercutting of price, and certain members felt *that they were holding the umbrella,* and it was more desirable to have freedom, and so gradually by withdrawals it lost its importance." (Italics mine.)

[26] Cf. A. R. Burns, *The Decline of Competition* (1936), especially Chap. 3 and pp. 140–145.

the years. In some cases, this has been serious (steel, petroleum, meat packing); in others, relatively mild (anthracite coal, light bulb, cigarette). The decline has not taken place in absolute size; rather, the several industries have grown, but the dominant firms have grown at a slower rate. The dominant firms have apparently also attempted to pursue a policy of price stabilization, and have succeeded in varying degrees.

If we now interpret these facts in terms of our cartel model, we get very fruitful results. We must first consider the dominant firms as taking the place of the cartel "central office" and setting policies for the whole industry. They will discourage price-cutting by exhortation, "social" pressure, repeated stressing of the disaster which faces the industry as a result of price-cutting, and threats (explicit or implied) of underselling non-coöperating firms in their markets, if they persist. United States Steel and Standard Oil were, in their early years, notorious examples of this last practice. Through these methods the dominant firms are more or less able to maintain discipline within the industry and agreement on a common price. Even if the dominant firms are low-cost firms, they still may set a higher price than they themselves would prefer, in order to satisfy the other (high-cost) producers and prevent them from price cutting. As a rule, the dominant firms try to follow a policy of price stabilization. This may be due to the simplicity of the rule, or it may reflect the fear that arises every time the price is changed: whether the lead will be followed. In brief, the relationship between leaders and followers may be so delicate that the leaders take every care to prevent subjecting it to stress.

The decline in the relative position of the leader is readily explained as the familiar cartel phenomenon of the inflow of new firms and the expansion of old ones. The dominant firms themselves may not expand at the same rate as the industry, since they tend to be near their maximum size, and further expansion might involve them in many of the inefficiencies of large-scale operation. It is also possible that the dominant firms are high-cost producers and that the price set by them, though yielding relatively small profits in their case, would enable the other (low-cost) firms to earn much higher profits, thus increasing their incentive to enter the industry and expand. Finally, it should be noted that the decline in relative position may be due to weakness in the control exercised by the dominant firms. During periods of declining demand the "independents" will indulge in much more price cutting in order to increase their sales. It is quite possible (and seems to have been the case in steel and copper, for example) that the dominant firm will continue with its stabilized higher price and not retaliate for a time; that is, it expects it will still profit by this policy, although it is in the position of "holding the umbrella" for the other firms and restricting its own output relatively more than theirs.[27]

Finally, it is very instructive to examine those industries in which the dominant firms have declined relatively little. The results are what we might have expected from our cartel model (cf. above, p. 278). General Electric has been able to maintain its position because it could control entry into the light bulb industry through ownership of vital patents. The dominant anthracite coal companies have control of most of the anthracite reserves. The "Big Four" in cigarettes have prevented entry by establishing monopoly through advertising. The depression, however, partly broke down this last monopoly by allowing the cheaper brands to establish themselves; and in recent years Philip Morris has established itself, in its turn, by a vigorous advertising campaign.[28]

[27] Cf. Burns, op. cit., pp. 140 ff.
[28] Cf. A. A. Bright and W. R. Maclaurin, "Economic Factors Influencing the Development and Introduction of the Fluorescent Lamp," *Journal*

The preceding paragraphs, though necessarily quite sketchy, provide a rough outline of the thesis I have tried to present in this section: that the cartel model is the most fruitful approach to economic analysis of our real world, focusing attention on the significant points of the problem. This general statement will now be amplified by applying the thesis to a specific industry and noting the particular ways in which the cartel features appear. The example I have chosen is the milk distributing industry, whose striking resemblance to our cartel model makes it truly a "textbook case." [29]

Due to the perishability and high transportation costs of their product, milkshed coöperatives, made up of thousands of members, are able to operate more or less within a closed market. The coöperative bargains collectively with the distributors and sets a price on fluid (Class I) milk. It cannot, however, control the output of its members, and therefore all milk not used in fluid form is sold as surplus (Class II) milk at prices near competitive levels. This is used for butter, cream, condensed milk, and other processed dairy products. The individual producer is either allotted a quota on which he can receive the Class I price (receiving the Class II price on everything above this quota) or he receives the Class I price on a percentage of his sales equal to the percentage of the total coöperative sales which was used for Class I purposes. Over a period of time expansion takes place as (1) new producers are attracted into the dairy industry within the existing milkshed, (2) the individual members expand their production, and (3) the higher price set by the coöperative itself extends the geographical area of the milkshed.

As the size and output of the milkshed increase, the proportion of surplus milk increases still faster. This brings down the average price received by the producer. If there were completely free entry, the *average* price would tend to fall to the competitive level, with two possible results.

1. At any time of the coöperative's existence, it is to the advantage of any individual producer to stay out of the coöperative and sell to non-participating dealers who sell primarily fluid milk. They will thus obtain a higher price than the average obtainable within the coöperative, but lower than the bargained Class I price. Note that this is also to the advantage of the non-participating distributor, since it (a) enables him to obtain Class I milk at a lower price than his competitor (participating) distributors and (b) throws a greater burden of surplus milk on them. Thus it is to the common interest of producers' and distributors' organizations to prevent free entry at both levels. When increasing amounts of surplus milk continuously lower the average price and increase the discrepancy between it and the Class I price, this unremitting pressure becomes overwhelming and, if not counteracted, causes the disintegration of the coöperative long before the "competitive" price is reached.

2. But, of course, counter measures will be put into effect before this danger point is reached. Government assistance will be called in—health ordinances will be used to restrict the area of the milkshed and discipline recalcitrant producers. (The Rhode Island ordinance requiring milk from outside the state to be colored pink is classic.) Where this does not suffice, force can also be used (milk-dumping, for example). Action will also be directed at the non-participating distributors, for without these as an outlet the non-coöperating producer would be lost, unless he could do his own distributing. The producers' and distributors' organizations will thus try to

---

of Political Economy, Vol. 51 (1943), pp. 429–450; Burns, op. cit., p. 123.

[29] For the following account I have drawn heavily on John M. Cassels, *A Study of Fluid Milk Prices* (Harvard Economic Studies No. 54) (1937), Chaps. 5–6 and Appendix A; and Wm. H. Nicholls, Imperfect Competition within Agricultural Industries (1941), Chaps. 10–11.

eliminate them, either with government assistance (again via health ordinances) or pure coercion (their bottles broken or held back at the bottle-exchange, their workers beaten, and so on). Finally the government itself is called in to fix and enforce the price, usually by arbitrating or participating in the bargaining between coöperatives and distributors and giving these results legal sanction.[30]

V

In conclusion it should be noted that to a large extent the general imperfect competition case described above can be dealt with by a market-sharing solution from the viewpoint of a single firm whose individual demand curve shifts to the left as new firms enter. For the following reasons, however, I believe that the cartel model is a more satisfactory analytical tool for revealing certain of the forces at work and should therefore be used in addition to the market-sharing analysis.

1. There are some cases for which the cartel model is an exact, and not merely an approximate, description, in the sense that there is an actual body making and enforcing decisions from the viewpoint of the industry as a whole. The market-sharing analysis, with its emphasis on the individual firm, is obviously inapplicable here. In

our own economy we have the examples of the milk industry, bituminous coal (Guffey Coal Act), oil (state proration laws and the Connally Act), and industries with strong trade associations. When we extend our view to the international scene, the examples become much more numerous: rubber, tin, wheat, sugar, coffee, etc. None of these can be satisfactorily analyzed from a market-sharing point of view.

2. Even when the industry has not set up any official central office, our previous analysis has shown that through the interaction of dominant and independent firms we get approximate cartel results. Here, too, the dominant firms will make some decisions from the viewpoint of the industry. For example, they may not maximize short-run profits, in order not to attract new firms. But if we look at it from the viewpoint of each firm, the latter would not gain by foregoing its profit while the other firms retained theirs. The cartel model is necessary to bring out the nature of these industry decisions.

3. The cartel model shows with graphic clarity the development of long-run excess capacity and overinvestment.

4. Obviously, from a firm analysis we could not obtain the results of having new firms entering the industry and remaining idle.

5. The cartel model reveals more precisely the inner mechanisms, forces, and conflicts leading to the disintegration of industry agreements and explains the resort to extra-economic methods of maintaining them.

[30] Cf. TNEC Monograph No. 32, *Economic Standards of Government Price Control*, Part II, "Public Pricing of Milk" for government regulation of fluid milk marketing in Oregon, California, Indiana, Wisconsin, and New York. Federal price fixing is also discussed (pp. 57–229).

21. Stackelberg's Indifference Maps: Extension of the Analysis to Related Market Structures*

WILLIAM FELLNER

William Fellner (B.S. Luros Federal Institute of Technology, Hungary, 1927; Ph.D. University of Berlin, 1929) was born in Budapest, Hungary in 1905 and came to the United States in 1939. Professor Fellner, at present, is Sterling Professor of Economics at Yale University, where he has been on the faculty since 1952. From 1939 through 1952 he was on the faculty of the University of California at Berkeley. He has also held visiting appointments at Columbia, Harvard, and Oxford Universities. One of the most versatile of modern economists, Professor Fellner has broken new ground in many fields of economic theory, including the theory of oligopoly, the history of economic thought, macroeconomic theory and policy, the theory of technological change and of economic growth, and the theory of behavior under uncertainty. He has published numerous articles and books, including *Monetary Policies and Full Employment, Competition Among the Few* (from which the selection reprinted is taken), *Trends and Cycles in Economic Activity, The Emergence and Content of Modern Economic Analysis*, and *Probability and Profit*. His most recent research has focused on technological change, economic growth, and behavior under conditions of uncertainty. During 1969 Professor Fellner was president of the American Economic Association.

This chapter contains a discussion of Heinrich von Stackelberg's oligopoly analysis, as developed in his *Marktform und*

* Reprinted from William Fellner, *Competition Among the Few*, Augustus M. Kelley, Publishers, 1949. Chapter III, pp. 98–119. Copyright 1949 by William Fellner.

Gleichgewicht. Stackelberg was particularly successful in linking the oligopoly problem to that of a family of related market structures. Any oligopoly theory should be capable of developing these links because the type of analysis applying to oligopoly is suitable for examining a whole family of market structures. Stackelberg's theory brought this out very clearly. However, the specific oligopoly theory he developed is not the kind of qualified joint-maximization theory we outlined in Chapter I.[1] It is a sophisticated version of the kind of theory we attempted to appraise in Chapter II [2] and *from which* we shall subsequently develop a transition toward qualified joint maximization. In connection with a discussion of Stackelberg's theory we may therefore show what emerges for the family of related market structures (not merely for oligopoly itself) from the classical type of theory considered in Chapter II; and we may construct the bridge toward joint maximization for these structures, too.

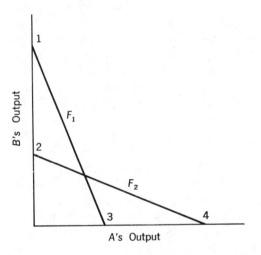

FIGURE 21.1

GENERAL CHARACTERISTICS

Stackelberg operates with reaction functions which—just like the F functions of

[1] Editors' Note: The theory outlined in Chapter I of *Competition Among the Few* attributes the observed deviations of oligopolistic from monopolistic behavior to the inability of oligopolists to agree on the distribution of the obtainable joint profit under conditions typically involving a substantial degree of uncertainty.

[2] Editors' Note: Chapter II contains a discussion of the Cournot-type and the Bertrand-type oligopoly theories. See also the next footnote.

Figure 21.1 [3]—express each producer's individual profit maximization for given values of the rival's variables. These reaction functions are derived from the profit-indifference maps of the individual participants as drawn against axes along which the value of the producer's own variable and that of his rival's variable are measured. In other words, the profit-indifference map of a producer shows those combinations of the value of his own variable and of that of his rival's which give the producer in question identical aggregate profits. From these indifference maps it is possible to indicate how a producer maximizes his profits, given the value of his rival's variable. The model includes as possibilities the Cournot type of intersection-point equilibria, the corresponding leadership equilibria,[4] and the disequilibrium developing if both parties strive for leadership. Moreover, since the reaction functions are derived from the underlying indifference map, it is possible to indicate which of these possibilities is likely to materialize. We can find out at what point of his profit-indifference map a producer arrives if he adjusts the value of his own variable to given values of his rivals variable, and where he arrives if he is successful in inducing his rival to adjust. The intersection-point equilibrium *à la* Cournot tends to be established if, in view of the individual indifference maps, both firms find followership (that is, the leadership of the rival) preferable to leadership. This is

[3] Editors' Note: Figure 21.1 is a portrayal of the Cournot theory for undifferentiated duopoly, a portrayal involving linearity assumptions, and F_1 is A's reaction function showing A's output for alternative outputs of B, while F_2 is B's reaction function showing B's output for alternative outputs of A. We should add also that the intercepts 1 and 4 measure the competitive output in the market as a whole, while the intercepts 2 and 3 measure the monopoly output, and that the intersection of the two reaction functions marks the Cournot duopoly equilibrium.

[4] I.e., the equilibria characterized by the fact that one firm selects the (from its point of view) optimal point along the reaction function of the other.

the case if the leadership point of the rival lies at a higher profit-indifference level for both firms than does the "own" leadership point. In this case both firms will adjust to the given value of the leader's variable and by so doing they will gradually move into the intersection point of the reaction functions. This is because each firm takes the value of his rival's variable as given. Leadership equilibrium materializes if leadership is more favorable than followership to the firm in question, while followership is more favorable to the other firm. However, if the indifference maps are such that leadership would be preferable to both firms, then both will be striving for leadership equilibrium, but the two firms will, of course, be striving for different equilibria. Each will select the (from its point of view) optimal point along the reaction function of the other; yet "the other" will not in reality be moving along its own reaction function but will also be trying to select the (from its own point of view) optimal point along the reaction function of its rival. This struggle may last any length of time, or it may end by the submission of one party into followership. Stackelberg discussed the outcome on many alternative assumptions and he found that mutual striving for leadership is likely to develop in a disconcertingly large number of possible cases.[5] We shall call such an outcome "Stackelberg disequilibrium." At the time when he published his book (1934) he seems to have felt that the likelihood of such disequilibrium on a great many markets provided justification for the corporate state. This idea is expressed in a separate brief section at the end of the book.

THE SCOPE OF THE THEORY

(1) *With respect to the variables included:* The theory is based on reaction functions expressing individual profit max-

imization for given values of the rival's variable. In the initial definition of the concepts, no limitation is introduced on *what* the variables are. In the detailed analysis of the problem, the technique is handled in such a way that quantity of output *or* price may be "the" variable. Undifferentiated duopoly and undifferentiated duopsony are exceptions. In these cases "the" variable is *unequivocally* the quantity of output. Interpreting the variable as the price would here lead into the straight (unmodified) Bertrand problem which Stackelberg does not consider a legitimate problem. For undifferentiated duopoly and duopsony, he rejects the assumption that the firms may believe that their rival's price is given regardless of what price *they* set because it must be obvious to both firms that the two prices must be the same if both firms are to be on the market simultaneously. Under all other market structures, where the products are not identical, it is conceivable that one firm should set its price on the assumption that the price of the other firm is given. This is, in fact, the follower's attitude, with price as the relevant variable, and it is analogous to the attitude of output followers in the framework of the Cournot-type model (where output is the relevant variable). Thus, follower's policies on the part of both firms result in an equilibrium corresponding to the intersection point of the two reaction functions, while leadership policies of one firm coupled with follower's policies of the other result in leadership equilibrium,[6] and leadership policies on the part of both firms result in Stackelberg disequilibrium. In the cases examined by Stackelberg, the profit-indifference maps are analyzed for output as the relevant variable, for price as

---

[5] For an analogous problem, described by Professor Bowley in a framework where reaction func-

tions are defined with conjectural variation, cf. footnote 14, Chapter II, *Competition Among the Few.*

[6] That is to say, in an equilibrium marked by that point along the follower's reaction function which is optimal from the leader's point of view.

the relevant variable, and for the possibility that "the" variable means output for the one firm and price for the other.[7] The attempt is made to read from the indifference maps whether the two firms, respectively, are likely to strive for (price or output) leadership or for (price or output) followership. The conclusion is that, in most cases examined, both firms are likely to strive for leadership. Sales expenditures and the product itself are not treated as further variables.

(2) *With respect to the number of firms:* The graphic method, which is supplemented by mathematics in the appendix of *Marktform und Gleichgewicht,* lends itself to the analysis of duopoly and duopsony but not to that of oligopoly and oligopsony. Consequently, the theory is developed for two-firm markets, with occasional hints at the extension of the conclusions to markets with more firms. There is a presumption that the addition of more firms increases the likelihood of Stackelberg disequilibrium. For, whenever duopoly or duopsony result in Stackelberg disequilibrium, the addition of further firms cannot produce equilibrium: the striving of two firms for leadership is sufficient to exclude equilibrium, and there is no reason to assume that the addition of other firms will typically induce either of the two original firms (which were striving for leadership) now to strive for followership. And when duopoly or duopsony result in intersection-point equilibrium, or in leadership equilibrium, the addition of further firms may very easily produce Stackelberg disequilibrium. Given the general premises of his theory, Stackelberg's conclusions would seem to hold *a fortiori* under oligopoly and oligopsony. But technically the theory is developed only for two-firm markets.

(3) *With respect to market structures:* From our standpoint, the most significant

feature of the theory is its broad scope with respect to market structures. It includes several market relationships which in one form or another give rise to the *kind* of difficulty with which we are faced in duopoly theory. In addition to undifferentiated duopoly and duopsony, the following market structures are included: two firms producing substitutes (differentiated duopoly), two firms producing complementary goods, two firms buying substitutes (differentiated duopsony), two firms buying complementary goods, and two firms, one of which sells to the same competitive industry from which the other firm buys. Some relationship of this general character is very much more common than duopoly or duopsony in the narrower sense, but a significant problem of the kind here considered arises only if the relationship between the products in question is sufficiently close to be taken into account in policy formation.

STACKELBERG'S TYPES

If along the abscissa we measure the value assumed by the variable of firm A (for example, A's output), and along the ordinate we measure the value assumed by the variable of firm B, then we can draw a profit-indifference map for firm A, letting the indifference levels rise or fall as we move upward from the abscissa; and we can draw a profit-indifference map for firm B, letting the indifference levels rise or fall as we move to the right from the ordinate. The indifference curves of which these maps consist connect pairs of values (of the two variables, respectively) such that along an indifference curve the aggregate profit of a firm remains the same.

The indifference curves may be *concave* viewed from the axis to which they are drawn;[8] and the maximum point of the successive curves may lie increasingly *toward the other axis* as we move upward from the

---

[7] Except that undifferentiated duopoly and undifferentiated duopsony are analyzed only for output as the relevant variable.

[8] I.e., viewed from the abscissa for firm A, and from the ordinate for firm B.

axis to which they are drawn (cf. Figure 21.2). If both these conditions are met, the map is said to be "Type *α*." Secondly, the curves may be *concave* but the maximum point may lie increasingly *away from the other axis*, as we move upward. This characterizes Type *β* (cf. Figure 21.3). We have Type *γ* if the curves are *convex* and the minimum points lie successively *toward the other axis* as we move upward from the axis to which the curves are drawn (cf. Figure 21.4). Type *δ* is characterized by *convexity* plus the condition that the minimum points lie increasingly *away from the other* axis, as we move up (cf. Figure 21.5).

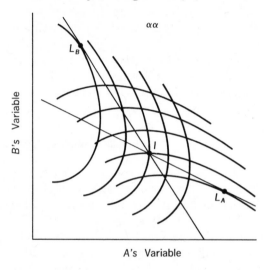

FIGURE 21.2

The meaning of concavity (viewed from the axis to which the curves are drawn[9]) is that the firm in question suffers if the rival raises the value of *his* variable. The meaning of convexity is that the firm in question benefits from this circumstance. This can be seen by the following consideration. Draw a straight line parallel to the axis to which the indifference map is drawn,[10] that is, perpendicular to the axis along which the variable of the rival is measured. The

[9] I.e., viewed from the abscissa for firm *A*, and from the ordinate for firm *B*.
[10] I.e., parallel to the abscissa for *A*, or to the ordinate for *B*.

straight line expresses a given value of the rival's variable, and it becomes tangent to an indifference curve at some point. It is well known that such a point of tangency expresses maximum profitability for a given value of the rival's variable only if the indifference curves are concave and the indifference levels *fall* as we move away from the axis *to which* they are concave; or if the indifference curves are convex and the indifference levels *rise*. Otherwise these tangencies are minima and no maximum is discernible. If these points of tangency express minimum (rather than maximum) profitability,[11] the economically insignificant cases develop in which for a given value of the rival's variable profits rise monotonically and indefinitely as the firm in question moves from the point of tangency toward infinite output (or prices) on the one hand, and toward zero output (or prices)[12] on the other. Barring this assumption, that is, for the economically significant cases, *concavity (α or β) means that "own" profits fall, and convexity (γ or δ) means that they rise, as the rival increases the value of his variable*.[13] This is required for the establishment of maximum profit values for given values of the rival's variable.

We have seen that for Types *α* and *γ* the points of tangency (with lines perpendicular to the axis of the rival) lie increasingly close to the axis of the rival as we move upward from the axis to which the indifference map is drawn. The contrary is true of

[11] And if, therefore, the area lying outside an indifference curve marks higher profits than the area encompassed by the same indifference curve.
[12] Generally speaking, toward infinite and zero value of the variable which is measured along the axis of the firm in question.
[13] The argument implies that an indifference curve is concave or convex throughout its course. Conditions are conceivable in which the indifference curves turn from convex or concave and *vice versa* as we move along them. In this case some points of tangency might mark minimum profits and others maximum profits. But even in this case, economic analysis must be focussed on the areas in which maximization takes place, and for these areas the argument of the text is valid.

Types β and δ. This means that *in Types α and γ an increase in the value of the rival's variable induces the firm in question to select a smaller value for its own variable, while the contrary is true in Types β and δ.* The points of tangency with lines perpendicular to the axis of the rival are, of course, the maximum points of concave indifference curves and the minimum points of convex indifference curves. In both cases they are maximum-profit points for given values of the rival's variable. The reaction function of a firm is the locus of these points. The leadership point of a firm is found by identifying that point of the *rival's* (follower's) reaction function where it becomes tangent to an indifference curve *of the firm in question* (the leader). The followership point is the same as the rival's leadership point, and it is found by the analogous procedure. If both indifference maps are known, it is possible to say whether both firms will be striving for leadership (Stackelberg disequilibrium) or for followership (which leads to the intersection-point equilibrium), or whether the one will be striving for leadership and the other for followership (leadership equilibrium).

with sixteen combinations. Using his symbols, the type to which firm A belongs is written first and the type to which firm B belongs second. For example, $\alpha\alpha$ means that both belong to Type α, while $\alpha\gamma$ means that A belongs to Type α and B to Type γ. For discussion of the economically significant cases it is not necessary to examine all sixteen combinations in detail. We shall limit ourselves here to representing graphically the combinations $\alpha\alpha$, $\beta\beta$, $\gamma\gamma$, $\delta\delta$, $\delta\alpha$, and $\delta\beta$.

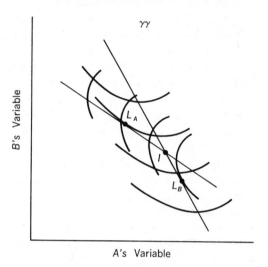

FIGURE **21.4**

These play the most important role in Stackelberg's analysis, although complete reproduction of the analysis would require examining more than these six combinations.

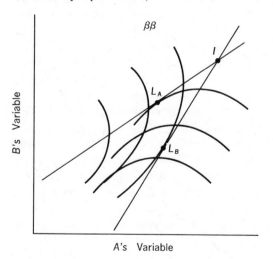

FIGURE **21.3**

Stackelberg distinguishes four types (α, β, γ, and δ), and consequently he is faced

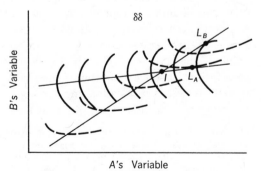

FIGURE **21.5**

In the following diagrams the intersection point of the reaction functions is marked I, the leadership point of firm A (which lies on the reaction function of B) is marked L_A, and the leadership point of firm B (which lies on the reaction function of A) is marked L_B.

THE SPECIFIC MARKET STRUCTURES

Cases 1 and 2. Undifferentiated Duopoly and Undifferentiated Duopsony On normal assumptions about demand and cost functions these are $\alpha\alpha$ cases. As was pointed out, the variable of both firms is interpreted here unequivocally as output. Each firm suffers by a rise in the output of its rival (hence *either α or β*), and the profit-maximizing output *falls* for each firm if the rival's output, which is taken for given, *rises* (hence α). This follows from the italicized passages on pages **68–70** (of original text). Stackelberg mentions β as an exceptional possibility, without discussing the nature of the exceptional assumptions which would have to be made. These assumptions would certainly have to be very peculiar, and we are not quite satisfied that they are consistent with the usual definition of these market structures. It seems obvious, by inspection of Figure 21.1, that under $\alpha\alpha$ each firm will be striving for leadership. Hence, Stackelberg disequilibrium.

Case 3. Two Firms Producing Rival Goods (duopoly with product differentiation)[14] If "the" variable is interpreted as quantity of output, the relevant combination is $\alpha\alpha$. For each firm suffers from a rise in the value of the rival's variable, and normally each firm will reduce its output if the rival's output (to which it is "adjusting") rises. If the variable is interpreted as price, the

relevant combination is $\delta\delta$. For each duopolist will gain by a rise in the value of the rival's variable, and each firm will raise its price if the rival's price (which is taken for granted) increases. Stackelberg disequilibrium arises from $\alpha\alpha$, while $\delta\delta$ produces *either* intersection-point equilibrium *or* leadership equilibrium.[15] Are the conclusions derived from $\alpha\alpha$ or those derived from $\delta\delta$ relevant? In cases of this kind Stackelberg applies the following technique to find out whether the ultimate outcome is likely to be such as in combination $\alpha\alpha$ or such as in combination $\delta\delta$. For the sake of an "experiment" he interprets A's variable as quantity of output and B's variable as price, and he examines the combination $\delta\alpha$, from A's point of view (cf. Figure 21.6). In the combination $\delta\alpha$ the leadership point of B means *price* followership for A because this point is B's optimal point along the *price* reaction function (δ-type reaction function) of A. The leadership point of A is a *quantity* leadership point because it is A's optimal point along the quantity reaction function (α-type reaction function) of B. Examination of $\delta\alpha$ establishes that quantity leadership is superior to price followership, from A's point of veiw (because L_B must lie southwest of the intersection point of the reaction functions, while L_A must lie northwest of the same point and consequently north of L_B). The same statement may be made for B, after exchanging their roles in the foregoing analysis. Hence, $\alpha\alpha$ is the relevant combination, and Stackelberg disequilibrium may be expected. Intersection-point equilibrium of the $\delta\delta$ variety assumes that each firm strives for price followership, with the other firm operating along a δ map, while $\delta\delta$ leadership equilib-

---

[14] Duopoly with product differentiation is really a special subcase of Case 3 characterized by very high cross-elasticities. Case 3 merely requires positive cross-elasticities. Cf. footnote 16, p. 287 of this text, and also the Appendix to Chapter 1 of *Competition Among the Few*.

[15] It produces intersection-point equilibrium if L_B lies higher than L_A in A's indifference map and also L_A lies higher than L_B in B's map (so that both strive for followership); it produces leadership equilibrium if either L_A or L_B lies higher in both maps. But inspection of the combination shows that if L_A lies above L_B in A's map, L_B cannot lie above L_A in B's map. This excludes Stackelberg's disequilibrium.

rium assumes that one firm strives for price followership with the other firm operating along a δ map. Analysis of the δα combination excludes these equilibria because it establishes the proposition that firms strive for quantity leadership rather than for price followership if their rivals operate along δ maps. Furthermore, the δα leadership equilibrium is excluded because both firms strive for leadership in the δα combination just as in the αα combination.

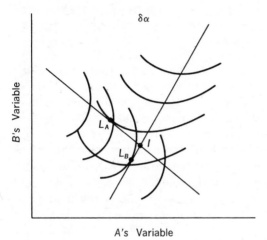

$\delta\alpha$

B's Variable

A's Variable

FIGURE **21.6**

Case 4. Two Firms Producing Complementary Goods[16] If the variable is interpreted as

[16] Complementarity may here be interpreted to mean that two goods are in such a relation that the demand for one rises if the supply of the other rises. If the demand for a good falls with a rise in the supply of the other then they are rival goods, as in Cases 3 and 5. These rival goods are sometimes called "substitute goods." To call them rival goods is preferable because the contrary relationship (complementarity) does not imply that the elasticity of substitution between the goods is zero. In other words, complementarity does not imply fixed proportions, or *perfect* complementarity. Cournot discussed conditions under perfect complementarity, and he showed that if one firm produces the one and the other produces the other good, and if *A* believes that the price charged by *B* remains unaffected by what *A* is doing, and *B* believes that the price charged by *A* remains unaffected by what *B* is doing, then a determinate equilibrium will be established (cf. *Mathematical Researches*, ch. ix). This, of course, is the same kind of intersection-point equilibrium which Cour-

quantity of output, the combination δδ is established. The argument is analogous to those by which the relevant combinations were established for Cases 1, 2, and 3.

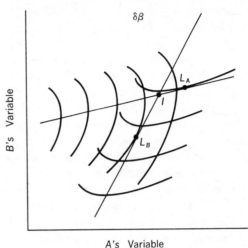

$\delta\beta$

B's Variable

A's Variable

FIGURE **21.7**

Again by analogous reasoning, αα is established for price as "the" variable; and examination of the combination δα establishes the likelihood that both firms will seek price leadership. In other words, the outcome is likely to be the same as in the combination αα—Stackelberg disequilibrium.

Case 5. Two Firms Buying Rival Goods[17] (duopsony with product differentiation) If the variable is interpreted as quantity of output,

not had established in his Chapter VII for undifferentiated duopoly, except that it applies to two producers supplying perfectly complementary goods (rather than perfect substitutes) and except that price rather than output is treated as the relevant variable. In other words, while Cournot did not extend his analysis from undifferentiated duopoly to the whole family of related market structures, he did extend it to one, rather narrowly defined, member of that family. In comparing the results he also showed that while on his assumptions the undifferentiated duopoly price was always lower than the monopoly price, the prices charged by the two producers of perfectly complementary goods were higher than those which would be established if the two producers formed a monopoly.

[17] Cf. footnotes 14 and 16, pp. 288 and 289 of this text.

the familiar kind of reasoning establishes the combination $\alpha\alpha$ (with possible but unlikely exceptions). If the variable is price, $\beta\beta$ is established. Examination of the combination $\alpha\beta$ leads to the conclusion that the outcome will be the same as in $\alpha\alpha$—Stackelberg disequilibrium.[18]

Case 6. Two Firms Buying Complementary Goods If quantity is "the" variable, the combination $\delta\delta$ is established; if price is "the" variable, $\gamma\gamma$. Examination of $\delta\gamma$ leads to the conclusion that the outcome is likely to be the same as in $\gamma\gamma$, where for each firm its own leadership point is superior (resulting here in an attempt, by both, to establish *price* leadership).[19]

Case 7. One Firm Selling to a Competitive Industry from Which the Other Buys (indirect bilateral monopoly) If quantity is "the" variable, $\delta\delta$ is established, while interpretation of the variable as price leads to $\delta\beta$. In the combination $\delta\delta$ both firms strive for followership (intersection-point equilibrium), or one firm for leadership and the other for followership,[20] while in $\delta\beta$ both strive for leadership. Examination of the relevant hybrid combinations leads to a presumption that the ultimate outcome is likely to be the same as in $\delta\beta$, not as in $\delta\delta$.

In summary, it may be repeated that Stackelberg disequilibrium is the most typical outcome. And, given the framework in which the reasoning is carried out, disequilibrium is even more likely than would appear at first sight. For, while Stackelberg does establish a presumption for his kind of disequilibrium in many cases, he does not prove the existence of a *stable* intersection point (in the first quadrant) in the cases where the tendency might be toward intersection-point equilibrium.[21] This, however, is of no great significance because the outcome almost always is Stackelberg disequilibrium. In fact, in the brief summary here given this was consistently the outcome. In one or two cases, exceptional possibilities were mentioned even in this brief summary. It is not easy to interpret these. Some of the exceptional possibilities of Stackelberg's schemes were not pointed out explicitly in our account. In some of these cases one is led to expect intersection-point equilibrium.[22]

CRITICISM OF CLASSICAL OLIGOPOLY THEORY EXTENDED

The type of oligopoly analysis in which Stackelberg's system belongs is technically characterized by the use of reaction functions expressing individual profit maximization for given values of the rival's variable. Limiting the approach to reaction functions of this sort stems from the desire to exclude collusion and spontaneous co-ordination and thereby to separate the problem at hand from the monopoly problem. It seems more promising to look elsewhere for the distinctive features of the oligopoly problem and of the problem of related market structures. Co-ordination under oligopoly is typically limited or incomplete and the distinctive features of oligopolistic markets reflect themselves in these limitations.

The attempt to exclude the problem of collusion by the quasi-mechanistic use of reaction functions has not only led to unrealistic results but has proved rather unsuccessful even on its own grounds. Leadership equilibria can scarcely be said to exclude quasi-agreement. Under leadership, the policies of any one firm are based on the *correct* assumption that the other firm is acting in a specific way, and the other firm would have no reason to act in this fashion if *it* did not *correctly* assume that the first

---

[18] We have not drawn $\alpha\beta$.

[19] We have not drawn $\delta\gamma$.

[20] Cf. footnote 15, p. 288 of this text.

[21] The first quadrant is of course the only economically meaningful quadrant.

[22] As Stackelberg points out, his kind of disequilibrium becomes even more likely for oligopoly than for duopoly because equilibrium requires that *all* oligopolists (or *all* oligopolists *except one*) be striving for followership.

firm acts in a specific way. Yet, while leadership equilibria may be said to contain an element of collusion or of spontaneous co-ordination, they represent an arbitrary and unintelligent form of co-ordination if leadership expresses itself in selecting a point along a reaction function of the traditional kind (which expresses follower's individual profit maximization for given values of the leader's variable). Such leadership equilibria stand in no meaningful relationship to joint-profit maximization. The value of the market variables at which industry profits are maximized is quite different from the values established if one firm maximizes its profits on the assumption that the values of the rival's variables are given and the other firm sets the (from its point of view) optimal values on the understanding that the first firm behaves as just described. Yet, given the relative strength of the rival firms, each firm earns higher profits if joint profits *are* maximized. It is true that, on realistic assumptions, unlimited (or complete) oligopolistic co-ordination should not typically be expected. The reasons are connected with the fact that, in the passage of time, the relative strength of the rival firms changes in an unpredictable way, and with the fact that sometimes the relative strength of the firms is insufficiently known even "as of now." Consequently, the prevailing forms of co-ordination are incomplete forms; they contain "outlets." This gives rise to the most important specific problems in oligopoly theory. But it is impossible to interpret the leadership equilibria (along the traditional reaction functions) as resulting from co-operative arrangements with *meaningful* outlets. These equilibria, while "collusive" in a sense, deviate from the maximization of the industry profit *blindly,* that is to say, not in a meaningful manner.

It might be objected that the intersection-point equilibria are not collusive in the foregoing sense, and that therefore they are at least consistent with the postulate that collusion should be excluded from the analysis of the problem. This is true but the objection does not establish the usefulness of the equilibrium concept in question. For these "equilibria" rest on arbitrary and incorrect notions regarding rival behavior.[23] It is quite arbitrary to assume that just these notions will be formed, or that, if formed, they will never be tested for validity. Along Stackelberg's line of reasoning this becomes particularly apparent. Intersection-point equilibria are said to result from a mutual attempt at followership, that is, at the rival's leadership. However, what is accomplished is not the rival's leadership but something different. Each firm assumes that the other firm will select a point along a reaction function which in reality plays no part whatsoever in shaping the policies of the other firm. Therefore, the function has no *raison d'être* for the analysis of the problem under consideration, unless it is maintained that a very special kind of incorrect assumption is made about what the rival is trying to do and that the individual firms are incapable of interpreting their experience which shows clearly enough that their assumptions are incorrect.

The foregoing criticism applies to an entire stage of development of oligopoly theory from which Stackelberg's system emerged as its most mature product. The concept of the Stackelberg disequilibrium (stemming from a mutual attempt at leadership) does not call for qualifying this appraisal. Stackelberg disequilibrium may either be interpreted as resulting from the arbitrary and incorrect assumption, mutually held, that the rival moves along a reaction function which in reality is nonexistent for the rival; or it may be interpreted as resulting from an attempt to force the rival into reacting along such a function and thereby to force him into accepting

---

[23] The arbitrary and incorrect notions derive from the assumption that the value of the rival's variable is given regardless of one's own moves.

the role of the follower. But if one firm has the power to force the other firm into anything, why would it not prefer to force its rival into something more favorable for the powerful firm, and possibly also for the weaker firm? These objections uniformly point to the likelihood of attempts at joint-profit maximization, with qualifications (or deviations) which must be subject to reasonable interpretation.[24] This is true

of oligopoly as well as of the family of related market structures. For all these market structures it seems reasonable to assume ability to agree on relative strength on the basis of factors (a) through (d) of Chapter I (pages 24–9 of *Competition Among the Few*; and to assume a tendency toward joint maximization. It then becomes necessary, however, to examine separately the specific circumstances which produce deviations from the maximization of the joint profit. In other words, the effective limits of oligopolistic co-ordination must be examined.

---

[24] When considering Stackelberg's system the most mature product growing out of the preceding stages of development, we imply that reaction functions with conjectural variation have proved a blind alley. Stackelberg takes no cognizance of them and in fact none of the difficulties here discussed could be solved by introducing them. Reaction functions with conjectural variation are necessarily based on arbitrary and incorrect notions regarding rival behavior. At the intersection point these assumptions happen to be quasi-correct in the sense that each firm lends its variable the value which the other firm expects. This cannot be true at any other point because wherever it is true the functions must coincide. But if this is true only in the intersection point, then even in the intersec-

tion point each firm "maximizes its profits" in a nonsensical way. They maximize their profits on the assumption that the reaction functions, which intersect at that point, are valid; and that, therefore, if either firm moved out of the intersection point, the other would react in a definite fashion. But the functions are not valid, and each firm can convince itself easily enough that, if it moved out of the intersection point, the other firm would not react along its alleged reaction function.

22. Potential Entry
into Oligopoly*

DOUGLAS NEEDHAM

Douglas Needham (B.S. First Class Honours, London University, 1961; M.A., Princeton University, 1963; Ph.D., 1965) was born in Leeds, England in 1940. He is now on the faculty of the State University of New York at Brockport, having taught previously at Princeton and the London School of Economics. Professor Needham, whose primary fields of interest are industrial structure and economic theory, has also been a consultant to the British Ministry of Defence. He is the author of *Economic Analysis and Industrial Structure* and the editor of *Readings in the Economics of Industrial Organization*.

The term entry barriers refers to obstacles preventing new firms from engaging in the production of a particular category of output. Conventional price theory concludes that the price charged for the product of an industry characterized by perfectly easy entry cannot, in the long run, exceed average cost of production. Perfect ease of entry is said to exist if there are no barriers to entry into the industry concerned. If any entry barriers exist, price cannot in the long run exceed cost by more than the "height" of such barriers, it is argued. More recently, some economists have argued that the threat of potential entry may affect the price charged by firms already established in an industry and preserve the aforementioned relationship even in the short run, and despite the absence of actual entry If valid, this line of reasoning elevates entry barriers, and in particular their height, to a position of great importance in determining price and output patterns in the economy as a whole.

We turn now to examine the role of entry barriers as a regulator of price, focusing particular attention upon the behavioral assumptions required to validate the above propositions.

ALTERNATIVE REACTIONS TO ENTRY

Entry into an industry shall be defined as the production, by a firm new to the industry, of a product that is a perfect substitute, in the minds of buyers, for the prod-

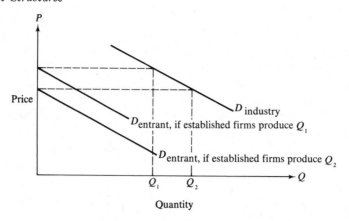

FIGURE **22.1**   THE DEMAND CURVE FACING A POTENTIAL ENTRANT

uct of firms already established in the industry. This definition is quite consistent with variety in the physical and other characteristics of the products of different firms in a given industry. It must also be emphasized that entry as defined is not accomplished if a firm previously outside an industry simply acquires the plant of an already established firm and operates it; that is, the mere change of ownership of existing plant capacity does not constitute entry. On the other hand, entry by a firm new to the industry need not necessarily involve the creation of a new firm; a firm already established in a particular industry may enter another industry if it builds capacity and adds an additional product to its product line.

Whether a decision maker will enter a particular industry or not depends upon the anticipated profitability of such a course of action. The profits anticipated by a potential entrant as a result of producing the product in question depend upon his cost conditions and upon the post-entry demand conditions anticipated by the firm for its product. These demand conditions, and therefore the profits anticipated by a potential entrant, depend upon the anticipated reaction of existing producers in the industry to entry. The greater the post-entry quantity of output produced by established firms, for example, the lower the

price obtainable for any given quantity of the entrant's output. The many alternative reactions that are possible can each be viewed as a quantity of output which the existing firms can elect to produce after entry while reducing the price, or accepting reductions, to the extent required to enforce such an output policy. Diagrammatically, the potential entrant will then be confronted by a sloping demand curve which is the segment of the industry demand curve to the right of the *post-entry* quantity which the potential entrant expects existing firms to select, as shown in Figure 22.1.

SYLOS POSTULATE

Much of the existing theory of entry is based upon the implicit or explicit assumption, sometimes referred to as the Sylos postulate, that potential entrants behave as though they expected existing producers in an industry to maintain their output at the pre-entry level in the face of entry, and that established firms do in fact behave in this manner if entry occurs.

Given the Sylos postulate, the potential entrant is confronted by a sloping demand curve which is the segment of the industry demand curve to the right of the *pre-entry* quantity produced by existing firms. The potential entrant will decide whether or not to enter the industry by comparing this demand curve with his own cost conditions.

The entrant's costs must include the opportunity cost of the profit which can be earned in other industries; only if a firm can earn more profits in the industry being considered than can be earned elsewhere will the firm enter that industry.

Three main types of barrier to entry are customarily distinguished. First, preferences of buyers for the products of established firms as compared to those of new entrants. Such preferences can, however, always be overcome if the new entrant invests sufficiently in sales promotion activities, and the essence of preferences as a barrier to entry is that to secure comparably favorable price for any given quantity of output, the entrant would have to incur sales promotion costs per unit of output which are greater than those of established firms. In view of the definition of entry given earlier, preference barriers, if they exist, will emerge as a difference in the unit costs of established and potential entrant firms respectively. For this reason, preference barriers will be grouped for purposes of this analysis with the second major category of entry barrier, absolute cost advantages. Absolute cost advantages exist if the costs of established firms, at any comparable scale of output, are lower than those of potential entrants. Such advantages may result from the need of new entrants to overcome accumulated buyer preference for the product of established firms, or from other factors such as lower prices paid by established firms for inputs

or investment funds. The third major type of entry barrier is economies of scale, resulting in a declining long-run average cost curve for the product in question. Some economists list legal barriers as a fourth type of entry barrier, while others would not distinguish them as a separate type of barrier, preferring instead to include the various types of legal barrier under the three main categories of barrier already listed. For example, patents giving established firms exclusive rights over strategic productive techniques or product designs may place potential entrants at a disadvantage in cost if they must use more costly techniques or must pay royalties for use of the patented technique or product. Such legal barriers may therefore be included with absolute cost barriers. Other legal barriers, however, such as laws prohibiting entry absolutely, or requiring operators to obtain government granted licenses, may not be reflected in costs, and must be listed as a separate category of entry barrier. The succeeding analysis confines itself to the three main categories of barrier already listed.

The presence of absolute cost differences, or scale economies, is not by itself sufficient to guarantee a barrier to entry—entry will occur despite such factors, provided that the entrant's anticipated demand conditions result in a situation in which the entrant expects to be able to make a profit. This is the case, for example, in both situations shown in Figure 22.2. The curves labeled

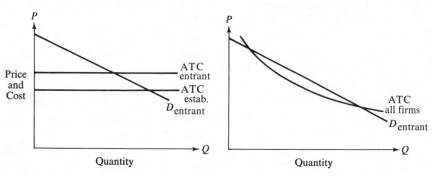

FIGURE 22.2 ENTRY DESPITE ABSOLUTE COST DIFFERENCES AND SCALE ECONOMIES

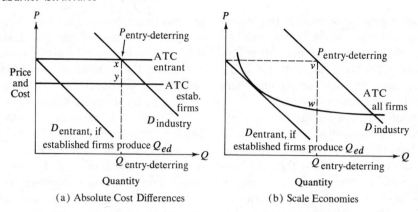

FIGURE **22.3** MAXIMUM PRICE-COST DIFFERENCES UNDER THE SYLOS POSTULATE

ATC entrant and ATC established depict, respectively, the average cost curves of a potential entrant and an established firm.

Given the Sylos postulate, the position of the demand curve confronting a potential entrant is determined by the pre-entry price and output of established firms. Where absolute cost differences exist, if the pre-entry price exceeds the average cost in established firms by more than the difference in average cost between potential entrant and established firms, the entrant's demand curve will be above his cost curve (in view of the assumed constancy of established firms' output at the pre-entry level) and entry will occur since the entrant expects to make a profit. Entry will lower market price if established firms do in fact behave in the expected manner and attempt to maintain output at the pre-entry level. Entry will not occur if the pre-entry price exceeds cost in established firms by less than the difference in average cost between potential entrant and established firms, for in such circumstances, given the Sylos postulate, the entrant's anticipated demand curve will be below his cost curve. The greater the difference in absolute costs of established firms and potential entrant the greater the amount by which industry price can exceed cost of established firms without inducing entry. If the extent to which industry price can exceed average cost in established firms

is used as a measure of the height of entry barriers, the height of absolute cost entry barriers, given the Sylos postulate, is measured by the distance xy in Figure 22.3(a). The distance equals precisely the absolute cost difference between established firms and potential entrants.

If scale economies exist, the maximum amount by which price can exceed average cost without inducing entry, given the Sylos postulate, is determined by the size of the market, the elasticity of market demand at any price, the scale at which economies of scale are exhausted and the rate at which average cost declines. The height of the scale economies barrier to entry is measured by the distance vw in Figure 22.3(b).

If both types of entry barrier exist, the maximum amount by which price can exceed average cost without inducing entry, given the Sylos postulate, will be determined by the height of the larger of the two barriers.

The following propositions are valid if firms behave in accordance with the Sylos postulate:

1. Entry will occur if price exceeds average cost of the marginal, or least efficient, established firm by more than an amount that is directly related to the magnitude of scale economies and absolute cost differences between established firms and new

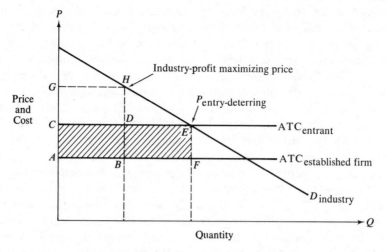

FIGURE 22.4 PRICING TO DETER ENTRY UNDER THE SYLOS POSTULATE

entrant, and price cannot exceed cost by more than this amount in the long run, though it may do so in the short run, that is, until entry has occurred.

2. If existing producers in an industry try to deter potential entrants, this relationship between price and cost will be preserved even in the short run. That is, in order to deter entry, existing producers must charge a price which does not exceed average cost by more than the height of scale economy or absolute cost entry barriers. Only if such a price is set will entry seem unprofitable to potential entrants, provided that they expect existing firms to keep their output levels constant in the face of entry.

Whether producers will attempt to deter potential entrants depends upon the relative profitability of charging a short-run profit-maximizing price, and pricing to deter entry. The relative profitability of the two courses of action depends primarily on the anticipated lapse of time before entry will occur in response to existing firms charging a price higher than the entry-deterring price. This proposition can be demonstrated with the aid of Figure 22.4. Diagrammatically, assuming the existence of absolute cost barriers and ignoring dis-

counting of more distant profits, the choice is between profits equal to area *ACEF*, obtained by pricing to deter entry, and profits equal to

$$\frac{\text{area } ABHG \times \binom{\text{period before}}{\text{entry occurs}} + \text{area } ABDC \times \binom{\text{period after}}{\text{entry occurs}}}{\text{total period to which the industry demand curve applies}}$$

If entry in response to a price higher than the entry-deterring price is instantaneous, for example, profits from charging a price higher than the entry-deterring price are equal to area *ABDC*, and producers will adopt the alternative course of action, and price to deter entry. At the other extreme, if entry does not occur before the end of the period to which the industry demand curve applies, profits from charging a short-run profit maximizing price are area *ABHG*, and existing firms in the industry will not price to deter entry.

CONSEQUENCES OF ALTERNATIVE REACTIONS

The propositions in the preceding section cease to be valid if potential entrants do not assume that established firms will maintain their output at the pre-entry level. It is the *post-entry* output of existing firms anticipated by potential entrants that determines the anticipated price at which the entrant can sell any given output level. *Pre-entry* price and quantity sold are themselves generally irrelevant as far as the potential entrant is concerned, and only become relevant to the entry decision in special cases in which entrants assume that the post-entry quantity supplied by established firms will equal the pre-entry quantity. It is not true, as is often stated in elementary price theory texts, that the relevant question for a new entrant is whether existing firms are charging prices at which the new entrant can make above normal profits. Rather, it is whether the reaction of established firms to entry will result in a *post-entry* price which permits the entrant to make above normal profits.

The post-entry quantity supplied by existing firms which will deter entrants (since it will imply a post-entry market price which will not enable the entrant to cover costs at any level of output), and the entry-deterring price, are uniquely determined by long-run demand and cost functions of the industry, as explained in the previous section. However, entry will not necessarily occur if pre-entry price exceeds the entry-deterring price so determined. If, for example, the potential entrant expects established firms to produce a post-entry quantity which will not permit the entrant to cover his costs, entry will not occur irrespective of the pre-entry price that is being charged by established firms. The size of absolute cost differences and scale economies relative to the size of total market demand no longer place a limit on the amount by which price can permanently exceed unit cost in the established firms, even in the long run.

Moreover, if the pre-entry price charged by established firms has no influence on the entrant's decision, it follows that charging a price lower than the industry profit-maxi-

mizing price, in order to deter entry, cannot possibly be an optimal strategy from the point of view of established firms with profit-maximizing objectives. This conclusion is obvious in the example quoted in the preceding paragraph in which entry does not take place, for in this event the established firms are forgoing profits if they charge a price other than the price which maximizes industry profit. It is perhaps less obvious, but equally true, even if potential entrants decide to enter the industry because they expect the reaction of existing producers to entry will be such as to permit the entrant to earn a profit. If entry is independent of pre-entry price charged by existing firms, the post-entry profits of existing firms will be the same whether or not those firms charged a pre-entry price that maximizes industry profits in the pre-entry period; therefore, pricing to deter entry and earning pre-entry profits below the maximum possible level must lower the total profits of firms practicing such a policy relative to the profits that can be earned if potential entry is ignored. Limit pricing will not be the most profitable course of action for existing producers unless they believe that potential entrants expect established firms to attempt to maintain their output at the pre-entry level in the face of entry.

The question remains, what grounds are there for assuming that potential entrants expect established firms to attempt to maintain output at the pre-entry level, or that established firms expect them to behave in this way? Some economists have suggested that this is the policy that is most unfavorable to new entrants. In the absence of some constraint which prevents established firms from increasing the level of their output in response to entry, however, this conclusion is not warranted. (Such a constraint could be provided, for example, by an antitrust policy which would regard increases in output by established firms in response to entry as a restrictive practice.) If existing firms increase their output after entry has occurred, the price which the entrant can obtain for any given quantity of output is lower than if existing firms maintained their output at the pre-entry level. Thus, by increasing output after entry has occurred, established firms can force losses upon the entrant firm. There is no such thing as the most unfavorable policy for entrants, short of driving price down to zero. From the point of view of potential entrants, the most unfavorable policy which established firms are likely to consider adopting is surely the policy of trying to deter entrant firms by supplying a post-entry quantity which drives market price down below the entrant firm's costs. There is, however, no more reason why potential entrants should expect established firms to react in this way in all circumstances than there is reason to believe that they will attempt to maintain output constant in all circumstances, as the Sylos postulate assumes. In atomistic market structures, to be sure, the behavior of potential entrants will very likely correspond to the Sylos postulate. Under pure competition or monopolistic competition, for example, no individual established seller will take account of entry, any more than it will take account of the behavior of its existing rivals. By definition, in such markets the actions of any individual seller, whether established firm or new entrant, will have no noticeable effect upon other sellers, and will not, therefore, provoke any reaction. Therefore, the Sylos postulate is a valid description of the behavior of potential entrants considering entering an atomistic industry. The situation is different in oligopolistic industries. In such industries, individual established firms are by definition affected by and aware of the actions of other firms, whether established firms or new entrants, and may be expected to react by potential entrants. The exact nature of the reaction, however, cannot be determined by a priori reasoning. In the final analysis, how potential entrants

actually behave, or how established firms believe them to behave, is a matter for empirical investigation.

Before we leave the subject of the determinants of potential entrants' behavior, it is necessary to mention briefly one other possible barrier to entry. Thus far it has been pointed out that if the entrant's anticipated demand and cost conditions indicate that a profit can be made, entry will occur. In order to enter, however, the firm must, in addition, have sufficient money capital to purchase the inputs required to produce the level of output which it expects to be able to sell at a profit. If the cost of investment funds is higher for a potential entrant than for established firms, this will be reflected as an absolute cost difference and will therefore be covered by the analysis of absolute cost barriers. If, however, a potential entrant is unable to obtain funds at any price, the capital requirements barrier will not be reflected in the entrant's cost curves and must therefore be treated as a separate category of entry barrier. The belief is widely held that the requirement of a large amount of liquid funds for investment by an entrant firm constitutes some sort of barrier to its entry. While the argument the potential entrants simply cannot raise enough money (presumably at any price) to finance entry, or that established firms can raise money more easily and cheaply than potential entrants, is plausible if the new entrant is a new firm setting up business for the first time, it is less so if one considers the possible entry of a large going business concern into a new industry.

ACTUAL ENTRY AND LEVEL OF INDUSTRY PRICE AND OUTPUT

Although the height of entry barriers will not place a limit on the amount by which price can exceed average cost, even in the long run, if potential entrants expect entry-

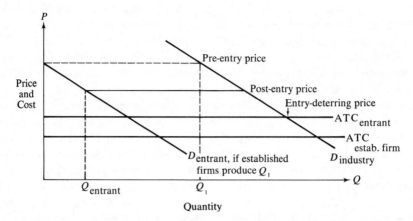

FIGURE 22.5   THE EFFECTS OF ACTUAL ENTRY ON INDUSTRY PRICE AND OUTPUT

deterring behavior by established firms after entry has occurred, entry will occur whenever potential entrants expect the reaction of established firms will permit entrants to make profits. The question remains, will *actual* entry itself lower market price and place a limit on the amount by which price can exceed average cost in the long run?

The answer to this question depends on how established firms and new entrants behave after entry has taken place. If established firms attempt to maintain their output at the pre-entry level, entry will drive down the market price, but the resulting market price may continue to exceed average cost by more than the height of absolute cost and scale economy entry barriers, as Figure 22.5 demonstrates.

Only if additional entry occurs will market price be driven down further, and this depends on whether new potential entrants expect the established firms to continue to react to entry by attempting to maintain output at the pre-entry level.

If, contrary to the expectations of new entrants, established firms try to deter entry by increasing output, market price will be driven down at least until it exceeds cost by no more than the height of entry barriers until the entrant has been eliminated, but can then be raised again unless and until entry occurs again. It can hardly be argued that further entry will prevent price being raised again, unless entrants ignore the previous behavior of established firms in response to entry.

The third possibility is that existing firms may reduce their output in the face of entry, and that industry price continues to exceed cost by more than the height of entry barriers, perhaps even remaining unchanged despite the occurrence of entry and despite the absence of any collusion between firms in the industry. This possibility can be illustrated by the following example employing the extreme assumption that there are no scale economy or absolute cost barriers to entry into a particular industry. If each firm in an industry assumes that any price it charges will be matched by all other firms in the industry, each firm's demand curve will be a fraction of the industry demand curve, the size of the fraction determined by the anticipated share of market demand accruing to the firm if all firms charge the same price for the same product. Figure 22.6 illustrates this proposition in the case of a linear market demand curve.

Increases in the number of firms in the industry will cause the subjective demand curve assuming price matching of each established firm to pivot down without

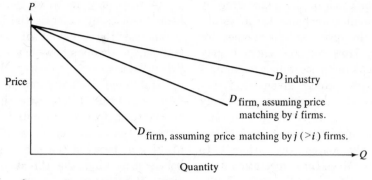

FIGURE 22.6   ENTRY WITH PRICE MATCHING

changing the intercept of that curve. Since, by definition, there are no economies of scale and no absolute cost differences, the cost curves of established and newly entered firms will be identical, and marginal cost of production and distribution will be constant.

With linear cost and demand functions, the price which maximizes a firm's profits depends only on the intercept of the demand curve and on marginal cost of production and distribution.[1] In the absence of scale economies, marginal cost is by definition constant; further, the entry of an additional firm leaves the intercept of an established firm's demand curve assuming price matching unchanged. Therefore, if the industry demand curve is linear (and firms expect rivals to behave as postulated), it follows that entry will leave the profit-

---

[1] For example, with the demand function $p = a - bq$ and the total cost function $C = cq + K$

$$\text{Profit} = aq - bq^2 - cq - K$$

For maximum profit, $\dfrac{dP}{dq} = 0$

Therefore, $a - 2bq - c = 0,$ or $q = \dfrac{a-c}{2b}$

Substituting the profit-maximizing quantity into the demand function we obtain the profit-maximizing price as a function of its determinants, as follows:

$$p = a - b\frac{(a-c)}{2b} = \frac{2a - a + c}{2} = \frac{a+c}{2}$$

Thus, the profit-maximizing price depends solely on c, the marginal cost of production, and a, the y intercept of the demand curve.

maximizing price of each established firm unchanged. Finally, since the new entrant's cost conditions are identical with those of established firms, and its demand curve is linear with the same intercept as the demand curve of established firms, the profit maximizing new entrant will charge the same price as established firms. In these circumstances, entry does not change industry price and output, but merely changes the number of firms producing that output —an output which maximizes industry profits.

The preceding example emphasizes that the relationship between industry price and unit cost depends upon the behavior of individual firms established in the industry, and that this behavior can take a number of different forms. Even in the absence of entry barriers, actual entry into the industry will not necessarily drive price down to equality with unit cost unless firms in the industry ignore each others' behavior in deciding upon their individual policies. The example also shows that the number of firms in an industry is only relevant to explaining industry behavior insofar as it influences expectations about rivals' behavior.

If entry barriers exist, it is still possible for industry price to remain unchanged despite the entry of additional firms into the industry. For example, with absolute cost barriers added to the previous example, although the price which maximizes profits, given the assumption of price matching by all firms, remains unchanged for established firms, this price will be higher for new entrants. However, the entrant **may** passively accept the price which maximizes established firms' profits, given entry, believing that established firms are unlikely to match a higher price set by the entrant, although believing that established firms will very likely match any attempt to undercut them. Given this expectation, passive acceptance of the price set by established firms may be the most profitable course of action for an entrant.

THEORY OF ENTRY AS AN EXTENSION OF OLIGOPOLY THEORY

Two main points emerge from the preceding discussion. First, whether entry into an industry will occur depends upon the post-entry behavior of established firms anticipated by potential entrants. Such behavior can take various alternative forms, each of which implies a different anticipated level of profits accruing to the entrant and which need not necessarily correspond to the pre-entry behavior of established firms. Second, the effect of entry on industry price and output depends upon the actual post-entry behavior of firms in the industry including any new entrants, and varies with the assumptions regarding rivals' reactions made by the individual firms in the industry after entry has occurred.

In each case, the analogy between the theory of entry and the oligopoly situation of traditional price theory should be apparent to the reader. Oligopoly theory deals with firms' behavior, taking into account the firms' expectations regarding the behavior of other firms *already producing the product*. As for the effect of potential entry on the behavior of established firms, entry theory merely extends the number of firms considered by established firms in their policy making, to firms *not already in the*

group who may react to the established firms' policies by entering the industry.

Whereas the behavior of potential entrants depends upon how they expect established firms to react to entry, the behavior of established firms depends upon how established firms *think* potential entrants expect them to react to entry. It must be stressed that in order to establish any a priori link between the behavior of established firms and the threat of potential entry, it is necessary to show that established firms believe potential entrants to be influenced by the *pre-entry* behavior of established firms. Since the profitability of entry depends upon the *post-entry* behavior of established firms anticipated by potential entrants, this virtually amounts to a need to show that potential entrants expect the pre-entry and post-entry behavior of established firms to be the same. Theories which attempt to show that behavior of established firms is influenced by the threat of potential entry stand or fall according to whether established firms believe that the Sylos postulate is an accurate description of potential entrants' behavior.

MEASURING ENTRY BARRIERS

The height of entry barriers into an industry will be reflected by the extent to which price can exceed average cost in established firms without inducing entry. In the section of this chapter entitled Sylos Postulate, it was demonstrated that, given the Sylos postulate, price could not, in the long run, exceed average cost by more than an amount which is directly related to scale economies and absolute cost differences between established firms and potential entrants. In these circumstances information concerning scale economies and absolute cost differences alone would enable one to rank industries in terms of the height of entry barriers. If, however, potential entrant firms' behavior does not correspond to the Sylos postulate, the amount by which price can exceed cost without inducing entry bears no direct relationship to scale economies and absolute cost differences. If potential entrants anticipate entry-deterring behavior by established firms, price may exceed average cost in established firms by much more than absolute cost differences or scale economies alone would suggest. It follows that one can then no longer judge the height of entry barriers merely by reference to scale economies and absolute cost differences. In addition, since the height of the barrier to entry is also a function of the conjectures of potential entrants concerning the reactions of established firms to their entry, some kind of index is required which would indicate the reaction to entry anticipated by potential entrants.

Even without such an index, however, there are certain other features of an industry which indicate the ease or difficulty of entry, for example the extent to which industry demand is increasing over time. In general, entry will be easier if industry demand is increasing, for a potential entrant will be able to enter the industry without encroaching upon the markets of existing firms, and without necessitating a decline in the profitability of pre-entry levels of output produced by existing firms.

Finally, our discussion of entry barriers has been conducted on the assumption of a fixed and unchanging technology. If the cost curves of potential entrant and established firms differed, it was because of higher prices paid for inputs, or less efficient inputs, used by the potential entrant. In a world of changing technology, entry into an industry may of course be gained through the use of some new technology. There is no a priori reason why established firms in an industry should have a monopoly of the rate of change of technological knowledge applicable to the industry. If, as a result of their own technological

efforts, potential entrants obtain an absolute cost advantage over established firms, entry will probably occur irrespective of the anticipated reaction of established firms.

RECOMMENDED READINGS

1. Bain, J. S., "A Note on Pricing in Monopoly and Oligopoly," *American Economic Review*, March 1949.
2. ———, "Conditions of Entry and the Emergence of Monopoly," in E. H. Chamberlin (ed.) *Monopoly and Competition and Their Regulation* (London: Macmillan & Co., Ltd., 1954) pp. 215–241.
3. ———, *Barriers to New Competition* (Cambridge, Mass.: Harvard University Press, 1956).
4. Comanor, W. S., and T. A. Wilson, "Advertising, Market Structure and Performance," *Review of Economics and Statistics*, November 1967.
5. Hines, H., "Effectiveness of 'Entry' by Already Established Firms," *Quarterly Journal of Economics*, February 1957.
6. Johns, B. L., "Barriers to Entry in a Dynamic Setting," *Journal of Industrial Economics*, November 1962.
7. Mann, H. M., "Seller Concentration, Barriers to Entry, and Rates of Return in Thirty Industries, 1950–1960," *Review of Economics and Statistics*, August 1966.
8. Modigliani, F., "New Developments on the Oligopoly Front," *Journal of Political Economy*, June 1958.
9. Osborne, D. K., "The Role of Entry in Oligopoly Theory," *Journal of Political Economy*, August 1964.
10. Sylos-Labini, P., *Oligopoly and Technical Progress* (Cambridge, Mass.: Harvard University Press, 1962).
11. Wenders, J. T., "Entry and Monopoly Pricing," *Journal of Political Economy*, October 1967.

Part VI

APPLICATIONS
TO PROBLEMS
OF RESOURCE
ALLOCATION

23. On the Economics
of Transfer Pricing*

JACK HIRSHLEIFER[1]

Jack Hirshleifer (S.B., Harvard 1945; Ph.D., 1950) is Professor of Economics at University of California, Los Angeles. He was born in Brooklyn, New York, in 1925. An economist with The RAND Corporation until 1955, he has also taught at the Graduate School of Business of the University of Chicago. He has written numerous articles on various aspects of price theory and applications thereof, and also in the area of investment and capital theory. He is co-author of *Water Supply: Economics, Technology, and Policy,* and author of *Investment, Interest, and Capital.*

In order to achieve the benefits of decentralization in decision-making, many corporations have developed divisional organizations in which some or all of the separate divisions are virtually autonomous "profit centers." This paper is concerned with the problem of pricing the goods and services that are exchanged between such divisions within a firm and with how these prices should be set in order to induce each division to act so as to maximize the profit of the firm as a whole. The problem is an important one, because the prices which are set on internal transfers affect the level of activity within divisions, the rate of return on investment by which each division is judged, and the total profit that is achieved by the firm as a whole.

Two recent papers which have drawn attention to the crucial importance of transfer-price policies have also discussed alternative approaches to the problem.[2] The paper by Cook recommends the use of market-based prices, at least as an ideal, while Dean favors "negotiated competitive prices." Such brief description does not, of course, do justice to either of the articles, both of which were more concerned with drawing attention to the importance of decentralization and transfer pricing than with rigorous determination of optimal

* Reprinted from *Journal of Business* (July 1956), by permission of The University of Chicago Press. Copyright, 1956, pp. 172–184.

[1] The author would like to thank Milton Friedman for his criticisms and suggestions.

[2] Paul W. Cook, Jr., "Decentralization and the Transfer-Price Problem," *Journal of Business,* XXVIII (April, 1955), 87–94; and Joel Dean, "Decentralization and Intra-company Pricing," *Harvard Business Review,* XXXIII (July–August, 1955), 65–74.

transfer-price rules. The argument made in the present paper is that market price is the correct transfer price only where the commodity being transferred is produced in a competitive market, that is, competitive in the theoretical sense that no single producer considers himself large enough to influence price by his own output decision. If the market is imperfectly competitive, or where no market for the transferred commodity exists, the correct procedure is to transfer at marginal cost (given certain simplifying conditions) or at some price between marginal cost and market price in the most general case.[3]

A. CONDITIONS OF THE ANALYSIS

For the sake of precision, we shall somewhat more formally restate the problem under investigation. A firm sets up two or more internal profit centers. Each of these is to maximize its own separate profits, possibly subject to restraints or rules imposed by over-all management. Exchanges of goods may take place between two such centers. At what price should the unit of commodity be valued for the purpose of computing the "profits" of the selling and buying centers? The goal, for the present theoretical analysis, will be to establish that mode of pricing which leads the autonomous profit centers to make decisions yielding the largest aggregate profit for the firm as a whole.

As a concrete case, let us take a firm with two such centers: a manufacturing unit (the seller division) and a distribution unit (the buyer division). The commodity exchanged—called the "intermediate product"—is the commodity as it leaves the manufacturing unit. There is also a final

[3] This statement is itself an oversimplification, since pricing at marginal cost is a necessary but not a sufficient condition. What is involved is a whole mode of procedure, described below, for finding the optimum price from the point of view of the over-all interests of the firm.

product to be sold by the distribution unit.

Unless stated otherwise, we shall assume that both *technological independence* and *demand independence* apply between the operations of the two divisions. Technological independence means that the operating costs of each division are independent of the level of operations being carried on by the other. Demand independence means that an additional external sale by either division does not reduce the external demand for the products of the other. Demand independence is a more special assumption than technological independence. The latter, we might expect, would apply at least approximately to a wide variety of practical situations. In general, however, we would expect there to be at least some demand dependence—for example, additional sales of the final product by the distribution division would tend to reduce external demand for the intermediate product. This point will be discussed in more detail later.

B. TRANSFER PRICE FOR BEST JOINT LEVEL OF OUTPUT

Suppose that a single joint level of output is to be determined for the two divisions; the distribution division will handle exactly as much product as the manufacturing division will turn out. A common level of output might rationally be required by central management under either of two different sets of circumstances: (1) there might be no market for the intermediate product at all, in which case there is no way for the manufacturing division to dispose of a surplus or for the distribution division to make up a deficiency, or (2) there might be a strong relation of technological dependence between the operations of the two divisions, such that marginal costs for either division jump sharply in shifting to dealings with the outside market. For example, imagine an integrated steel mill, with two divisions exchanging molten iron. Shipping excess iron out of the mill could

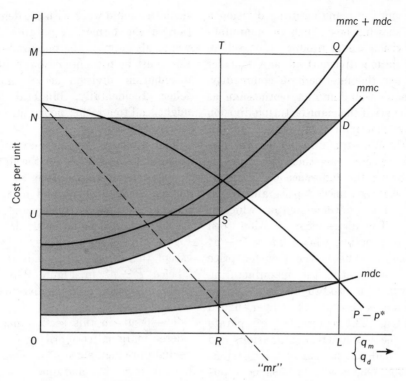

FIGURE 23.1   DETERMINATION OF BEST JOINT LEVEL OF OUTPUT

involve high handling costs to the selling division, and purchasing iron outside could involve high reheating costs to the buying division so that trading on the external market might rationally occur only under very unusual conditions. (This point will be alluded to again in Section F, which discusses technological dependence.)

The determination of the best joint level of output is shown in Figure 23.1. In this diagram quantity of output is measured along the horizontal axis for both divisions, q_m representing output of the manufacturing division and q_d of the distribution division. (We assume that the units of the intermediate and the final commodities are commesurate. In some cases there will be an obvious natural unit: e.g., pairs of shoes exchanged between a shoe-manufacturing and a shoe-retailing division. Sometimes, as when the intermediate product is copper and the final product copper wire, it may be necessary to express the quantities of the latter in terms of some transformed unit

like pounds of copper contained.) Prices and costs per unit of output are measured vertically. The curves labeled mmc and mdc represent the marginal manufacturing cost and the marginal distribution cost, respectively, each as a function of output.

Assuming that there is a competitive market for the final product, the distribution division will face a ruling price P. The best solution for the firm as a whole is to set the joint level of q_m and q_d at the output such that $mmc + mdc = P$ —that is, where the over-all marginal cost equals the price of the final product. If P equals the vertical distance OM in Figure 23.1, the optimum output is OL.

Such an output would be established by central management by adding the mdc and mmc curves of the separate divisions. It is simple, however, to devise a transfer-price rule which will lead the divisions autonomously to the same solution. Suppose that the distribution division calls for and secures from the manufacturing division a schedule showing how much the manufacturing division would produce (i.e., sell to the distribution division) at any transfer price p^* for the intermediate commodity. This schedule would, in fact, be the same as the mmc curve if the manufacturing division rationally determines its output to set $mmc = p^*$.[4] With this information, the distribution division can then determine a curve showing the difference or "margin" $(P - p^*)$ between market price and transfer price for any level of output which it might set. The distribution division then finds its own output where $mdc = P - p^*$ at OL and establishes the transfer price $LD = ON$. Evidently, the manufacturing division will then also produce at OL, since that is where $mmc = p^*$. The upper shaded area in Figure 23.1 represents the separate profit of the manufacturing division, and the lower shaded area that of the distribution division. One condition must be stipulated: the distribution division must not be permitted to increase its separate profit by finding a quasi-marginal revenue curve *marginal* to $P - p^*$ (the one labeled "mr") and establishing an output of OR and a transfer price of $RS = OU$. This would amount to the distribution division's exploiting the manufacturing division by acting as a monopolistic buyer of the latter's product, in which case the gain to the former would be more than offset by the loss to the latter, and so the firm as a whole would lose thereby. The net loss is evident from the fact that firm output would be set at OR rather than at the optimal level of OL.

In the current discussion the distribution division has been given the dominant role in decision-making. This could be reversed without any essential change; instead of the distribution division working with the supply function of the manufacturing division,

the latter could work with the demand function of the former. A parallel stipulation would also apply: the manufacturing division must be prevented from exploiting the distribution division as a monopolistic seller. Incidentally, bilateral bargaining might lead to a rather poor solution in these circumstances.

The solution remains essentially unchanged if the market for the final product is not perfectly competitive. In that case, a sloping demand curve and marginal revenue curve could be constructed instead of the horizontal demand curve MTQ used in Figure 23.1. The process is exactly as before, except that what corresponds to the curve labeled $P - p^*$ in Figure 23.1 would be $MR - p^*$, where MR is marginal revenue for the final product.

The result in this section may be considered marginal cost pricing for the intermediate product, since $p^* = mmc$. We shall find, in fact, that marginal cost pricing in this sense is a quite general answer for transfer pricing under conditions of demand independence. It is, however, marginal cost pricing only in a special sense, where the rules of procedure described above are set up. These rules are designed so as to correspond to the solution that a centralized management would arrive at with full information—namely, to set the sum of the divisional marginal costs equal to price (in the perfectly competitive case) or marginal revenue (in the imperfectly competitive case) in the final market.

C. TRANSFER PRICE WITH COMPETITIVE INTERMEDIATE MARKET

We shall now drop the assumption that a single joint level of output must be established for the two divisions together. Instead, each division is assumed to be free to determine its own output, with the manufacturing division selling its excess production, if any, on the intermediate market, and the distribution division similarly

---

[4] Technically, this statement is correct only over the range where mmc exceeds average variable cost.

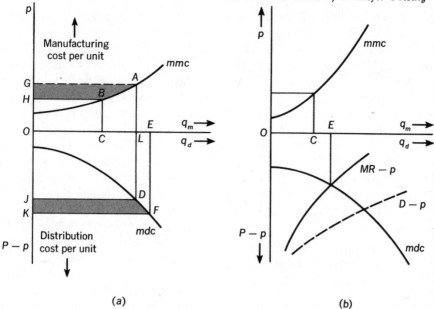

FIGURE 23.2   BEST DIVISIONAL LEVELS OF OUTPUT, COMPETITIVE INTERMEDIATE MARKET

calling on this market to supply any excess of the quantity it desires to handle over that available from the manufacturing division. For the present, we assume that the intermediate market is competitive, so that a price p for the intermediate commodity exists. The final market is also assumed to be competitive. It then follows from the assumption of technological independence that each of the divisions is indifferent between trading the intermediate commodity within or outside the firm.

In Figure 23.2(a), manufacturing cost per unit is measured *upward* along the vertical axis, and distribution cost per unit is measured *downward*. If $p = OH = BC$, then the manufacturing division should produce the output OC. If $P - p = EF$, the distribution division should handle the output OE. If both are required to set a best joint level of output, however, that output is OL, which is where $mmc + mdc = P$. Here P is measured by the vertical distance AD, which is constructed so as to equal $BC + EF$ (i.e., $p + [P - p]$). Evidently, the requirement of a single joint level of output led to the manufacturing division's

producing too much and the distribution division too little. The net increase in profit over that solution is measured by the excess of the area $JKFD$ over the area $BHGA$ in Figure 23.2(a). Since $GH = JK$, it is evident from the geometry that the excess must be positive. This argument assumes technological independence.

If a transfer price p^* is to be established in this case, clearly it should be equal to p, because at any other p^* one of the two divisions will refuse to trade. Actually, under our assumptions there is no particular need for internal trading at all, since the divisions are effectively independent firms with common ownership. On the other hand, there is no objection to internal trading, and this can only take place if $p^* = p$.

The assumption of a competitive market for the *final* commodity is not essential for this result. If we assume that the distribution division faces a sloping demand curve as in Figure 23.2(b),[5] we merely substitute

[5] The demand curve is labeled $D - p$, representing the quantity demanded in terms of the netback to the distribution division after subtracting the transfer outlay of p.

marginal revenue MR for P in making our output decision. In Figure 23.2(b) the distribution division produces at OE where $mdc = MR - p$. The correct transfer price remains $p^* = p$.

In general, then, if the intermediate market is competitive, the transfer price should be the market price irrespective of the competitiveness of the market for the final product. For this case, however, p also equals mmc, so our earlier contention that marginal-cost pricing is the more general solution is not refuted by this result.

D. TRANSFER PRICE WITH IMPERFECTLY COMPETITIVE INTERMEDIATE MARKET

We now turn to the substantially more difficult case where the market for the intermediate product is not perfectly competitive, so that—setting aside the demand of the distribution division itself—the external market for the intermediate product facing the manufacturing division has a sloped demand curve. However, we assume demand independence, that is, sales made by the manufacturing division in the intermediate market do not reduce the demand for the final product sold by the distribution division, and, conversely, internal sales to the distribution division do not reduce external demand. In general, we would expect some demand dependence. For example, if the manufacturing division sells shoes both internally and externally, one would expect that each additional sale to the distribution division would reduce the final market demand for shoes sold to independent distributors, and this demand reduction would soon be reflected in the intermediate market demand for external sales of the manufacturing division. Nevertheless, we can imagine reasonable cases where the internal and external sales would have substantially independent demands. For example, our shoe firm could distribute its manufactured products solely through independent distributors

in the domestic market, its own distribution division being limited to sales in the foreign market. Or a copper concern might use some of its copper internally only for a wire-fabricating division, while selling externally only to producers who make pots and pans or any copper products other than wire.

Under these conditions the firm is in a position akin to that of a discriminating monopolist; it sells the output of its manufacturing division in one market and of its distribution division in another.[6] We shall first derive the over-all solution for the firm and then find that mode of transfer pricing which will permit autonomous realization of this solution. The over-all solution is to equate the joint marginal cost of production with the net marginal revenue in each separate market. The word "net" means that we must adjust the market marginal revenue by the incremental cost of delivering to the market concerned.[7] In this case, we assume no delivery cost to the market for the intermediate product, so the relevant marginal revenue is simply that derived from the external demand for the intermediate product. In the case of the distribution division, however, marginal distribution cost must be subtracted from market marginal revenue to derive net marginal revenue for the firm's output of the final commodity.

The solution is illustrated in Figure 23.3. Figure 23.3(a) shows the demand curve d and the marginal revenue curve mr for the intermediate product. Figure 23.3(b) shows the demand curve D and the marginal revenue curve MR facing the distribution division in the final product market. The mdc curve is as before, and the net marginal revenue curve nMR is the vertical difference between MR and mdc. In Figure

---

[6] The firm need only have the power to separate its markets and to face imperfect competition in the intermediate market. The final market may be perfectly competitive.

[7] This point is neglected in standard economic textbooks but usually is of great importance in applied economic problems.

23.3(c) the two curves mr and nMR are plotted, together with their horizontal sum mr_t. The maximum profit solution is to establish the output q_m of the manufacturing division by the intersection of the mmc and mr_t curves at Q.[8] The amount sold on the intermediate market is OM (shown also in Fig. 23.3(a)), and the amount sold by the distribution division is OD (shown also in Fig. 23.3(b)).

The solution just discussed would be arrived at directly by a central decision agency with the appropriate information. We have not yet discussed the pattern of transfer pricing which would lead to the optimal result, given autonomous decision-making by one or both divisions. It can be seen immediately, however, that the correct transfer price to achieve the maximum-profit result is $p^* = OA = mmc$. In Figure 23.3(b) setting p^* equal to OA would lead the distribution division to handle the correct amount OD. It would arrive at this by setting p^* equal to nMR, which is equivalent to setting $mmc + mdc$ equal to MR. This suggests the rule that marginal-cost pricing (i.e., setting the transfer price equal to mmc) be adopted for the conditions examined here. However, we do not know quite enough to assert this yet, because the level of mmc is a function of q_m, and q_m itself is dependent upon q_d. This difficulty, however, is not hard to resolve. All that is required is that the distribution division indicate to the manufacturing division its demand for the intermediate product as a function of p^*—namely, the curve nMR. The manufacturing division, incidentally, must be instructed to accept this curve as a marginal revenue curve to be added to mr to get mr_t. This stipulation, analogous to those made in Section B, is necessary, because there might otherwise be an incentive for the manufacturing division to treat the

[8] An explanation of this standard solution is given in economic texts (see, e.g., G. J. Stigler, *The Theory of Price* [rev. ed.; New York: Macmillan Co., 1952], p. 217).

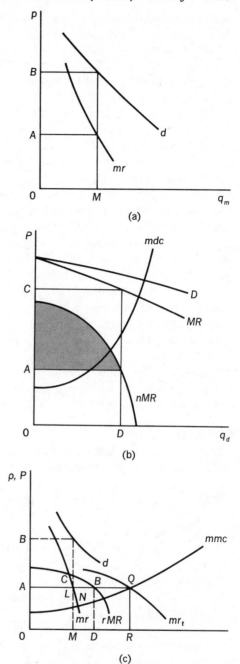

FIGURE 23.3 SOLUTION FOR IMPERFECTLY COMPETITIVE INTERMEDIATE MARKET

demand curve of its affiliate on the same par as an external demand curve, which would lead to constructing a curve *marginal* to nMR for adding to mr to get mr_t, with a view to charging the affiliate a transfer price higher than *mmc*. This would be equivalent to using the monopoly power of the manufacturing division to exploit the internal as well as the external market for the intermediate commodity; the effect of doing so would be to increase the apparent profit of the manufacturing division separately but to depart from the over-all optimum for the firm by imposing a greater loss of profit upon the distribution division.

Our transfer-price rule, then, for the case where demand independence and technological independence apply, with the market for the intermediate commodity imperfectly competitive (the market for the final product may be perfectly or imperfectly competitive), is to establish the price at marginal manufacturing cost—or, more generally, at the marginal producing cost of the seller division. This is to be understood, however, as a shorthand statement for following the rules indicated in the previous paragraph, which we may state more formally as follows:

Distribution division:

1. Determine the *nMR* curve and convey the information to the manufacturing division.

2. Given the transfer price p^*, produce where $p^* = nMR$.

Manufacturing division:

1. Determine *mr* and sum *mr* and *nMR* to get mr_t.

2. Produce where $mmc = mr_t$.

3. Establish p^* at the *mmc* determined by (2)—*OA* in Figure 23.3(c).

4. Establish *p* at the price along the demand curve *d* corresponding to the output reserved to outsiders—in Figure 23.3(c) *OM* is sold to outsiders at the price *OB*. Evidently, *p* always exceeds p^*.

One defect of this analysis is that the divisional "profits" determined by the transfer price established as here advocated do not provide an unequivocal answer as to

whether or not to abandon a subsidiary. (This was also true in the analysis of Sec. B.) Turning again to Figure 23.3(b), the shaded area represents the profit of the distribution division before allowing for any separable fixed costs of that division. Suppose that the separable distribution fixed costs are such as to exactly equal the shaded area and that it is possible to avoid these costs by abandoning the distribution operation. The implication, then, is that we are indifferent as to having the distribution subsidiary. In fact, however, we are not, because, with the *mmc* curve as drawn, the distribution division is being charged a transfer price p^* which is contributing to the "profit" of the manufacturing division. In Figure 23.3(c) the quantity *OM* is sold directly by the manufacturing division, and the quantity *OD* = *CQ* is transferred to the distribution division. The total manufacturing cost for the items transferred is *MLQR*, while the aggregate transfer payments are *MCQR*. The incremental advantage to the manufacturing division of the internal market is the area *LCQ* less the small triangular area *CLN*, the latter representing the additional profit on external sales of the intermediate commodity which would have been made had there been no transfers to the distribution division.

Unfortunately, the true profitability to the firm of having a distributing division is not always greater than the profitability of that division alone. A differently shaped *mmc* curve yielding the same marginal solution—in particular, a ∪-shaped curve with most of the area above *OA*—can lead to the distribution division's being, on balance, a negative contributor to the profits of the manufacturing division. We may summarize the present point by saying that the transfer-price policy indicated gives the correct solution for firm operations in terms of autonomous determination of marginal levels of operations. For non-marginal adjustments like abandoning a subsidiary, the autonomous calculations based on the transfer-price rule discussed will not generally be correct, and a correct decision requires an over-all examination of the cost and revenue functions of the firm as a whole.

E. DEMAND DEPENDENCE

The analysis to this point has assumed demand independence—that the markets for the intermediate commodity and for the final commodity are entirely independent. Generally speaking, the firm's two markets will be connected in that an additional internal sale to a distributing subsidiary would be expected to lead to some reduction of external demand on the part of purchasers of the intermediate commodity who compete with the distributing subsidiary in the market for the final good. However, demand dependence is a matter of degree. For the instance already cited of a firm making an internal transfer of copper to be used only for wire, and external sales of copper to be used only for pots and pans, our demand independence model of Section D would apply in all substantial respects. If, however, both the internal and the external demands were for copper to be used for wire, demand dependence would probably be too strong to be ignored.

For analytical purposes it is convenient to define a category of "perfect demand dependence," which is a situation in which customers in the final product market are perfectly indifferent between purchasing the product of the distributing subsidiary or of its competitors, perfect competition being assumed, and where all the competitors as well as the distributing subsidiary secure the intermediate product solely from the manufacturing subsidiary of the firm studied. For this case, the following points briefly summarize the results of a somewhat complex analysis which is not reproduced here.

1. In long-run equilibrium, as defined in economic theory, enough firms enter any industry so as to eliminate economic profit in that industry; that is, what is eliminated is any economic surplus over and beyond the normal return to factors employed in the industry, plus rents accruing to unique factors (such as unusually favorable location) responsible for reducing the cost functions of particular firms below the general level of the industry. Under these conditions, and assuming that there are no unusual features about the cost function of the distributing subsidiary which distinguish it from the outside competitors, there is no advantage to be gained by granting the distributing subsidiary any lower price for the transferred commodity than the price charged to outsiders. The manufacturing unit can, by its monopolistic situation, essentially secure all the surplus available to the industry, and so there is no point in attempting to get more by artificially expanding the output of the distributing subsidiary—in fact, this can lead only to a net loss for the firm as a whole.[9]

2. In the short run, however, all the economic profit in the industry may not have been eliminated by changes of scale of plants or entry of new competitors. In these circumstances the monopolist of the intermediate product can capture some of this economic surplus by selling at a subsidized price to a subsidiary operating in the final product market. It follows from the above that, if a monopolist in the intermediate market does not have such a subsidiary, he will in general be able to gain by buying out an independent distributor at the value of the latter's economic surplus—which will be less than the net advantage of the subsidiary to the manufacturing unit.

The case for a subsidized price can be illustrated in terms of a numerical example. Suppose that there are a hundred firms in the final product market, that Q_e is the quantity being distributed by outsiders, q_d is the quantity distributed by the sub-

---

[9] This result was pointed out to the author by Milton Friedman.

sidiary in the final product market, and P is the price of the final product.

Let the demand for the product be given by the equation

$$P = 100 - \tfrac{1}{100}(Q_e + q_d),$$

let the marginal manufacturing cost be given by $mmc = 0$,[10] and let the marginal distribution cost be given by $mdc = 20 + 2q_d$ for each of the independent distributors as well as the distributing subsidiary.

Given these relations, it can be shown that the optimal market price p (assuming no subsidy) is equal to 40. However, if a subsidy is permitted, it can be shown that the optimal transfer price p^* is approximately $13\tfrac{1}{3}$. Since mmc is zero throughout, this result for the optimal transfer price falls between the market pricing of Section C and the marginal-cost pricing of Sections B and D. While this is a special case, it reveals the nature of the general solution.

3. The analysis of this section has, up to this point, assumed perfect demand dependence. More generally speaking, a degree of demand dependence may exist somewhere between perfect dependence and absolute independence. Perhaps the most likely situation is that in which the product of the distributing subsidiary is differentiated, to some degree, from that of its competitors. Still, there may be some demand dependence in that additional sales of the distributing subsidiary would have some adverse effect on outside sales. Partial demand dependence might also occur if the firm we are considering is not a sole monopolist in the intermediate market but shares the market as an oligopolist with one or a few other firms. In this case an additional sale of the

distributing subsidiary might lead to losses of sales for all the oligopolists together, but the manufacturing branch of the firm subsidizing its subsidiary might not bear the full impact of the loss. (This argument assumes that the oligopolists in the intermediate market jointly establish the optimum monopoly price for the group, each taking a certain fraction of the market.) In general, the solution for partial demand dependence will lie somewhere between the solutions discussed in Section D and in the earlier paragraphs of this section.

F. TECHNOLOGICAL DEPENDENCE —SOME COMMENTS

Technological dependence may affect, in more or less complicated ways, the indicated optimum output for the firm as a whole and therefore the transfer-price rule which determines the optimum output for the divisions operating separately. The level of operations in Division A may raise or lower the marginal cost function of Division B, and vice versa.

We shall not attempt an analytical solution of the over-all problem here. A formal solution for optimum behavior of the firm would run in terms of the economic theory of multiple products, but this would only be a first step to the solution in terms of transfer price. We shall, instead, make only some general comments.

1. In the typical firm producing more than one product, it seems likely that additional production in any one line will tend to reduce the average and the marginal costs of producing the other. The existence of such complementarities in production (i.e., the ability to produce the products jointly more cheaply than if they were produced separately) is a common reason for producing a secondary product, and, even if a secondary product were produced for

---

[10] This assumption is made only to simplify the analysis. It could occur in a real situation if, for example, the branch of the firm here called the "manufacturing division" (but actually simply the selling division in an internal exchange) was engaged solely in licensing use of a patent in exchange for a royalty on each unit of output produced by the licensee.

other reasons, it would be unlikely to be retained by a firm if its adverse effect on the other products were serious.

2. It appears that a beginning approach to the problem of transfer pricing under conditions of technological dependence would involve establishment of an internal "tax" or "subsidy" to make the autonomous calculations of the separate division take into account the effects on the margin of impaired or enhanced productivity in the other divisions.

3. Fairly frequently, a vertically integrated firm will not trade outside the firm on an intermediate market at all but will instead establish a level of joint output at which the selling division and the buying division will both produce. Under technological independence, such behavior is difficult to explain (see Sec. C above). With technological dependence under conditions of complementarity, however, such behavior becomes more understandable. When any division produces beyond the level which keeps it in step with the other vertically integrated divisions, the excess units are more costly to produce than if all the divisions had increased output together.

G. CONCLUSIONS

1. If a single joint level of output is to be determined (because no market for the intermediate commodity exists, or for any other reason), this output should be such that the sum of the divisional marginal costs equals the marginal revenue in the final market. To achieve this result by internal pricing, the transfer price must equal the marginal costs of the seller division. This is only a necessary condition, however, and not a sufficient one. The full solution involves one of the divisions presenting to the other its supply schedule (or demand schedule, as the case may be) as a function of the transfer price. The second division then establishes its output and the transfer

price by a rule which leads to the optimum solution specified above for the firm as a whole.

2. Given technological independence and demand independence, if a perfectly competitive market for the intermediate commodity exists, transfer price should be market price. If the market for the intermediate commodity is imperfectly competitive, transfer price should be at the marginal costs of the selling division. The latter is the more general solution. In the general case of imperfect competition, the price of the intermediate commodity will exceed the marginal cost of the seller division. Transfer pricing at the market will then lead to excessive output by the seller division and insufficient output by the buyer division—in comparison with the optimum solution.

3. Where technological dependence exists, the situation is so complex that we have not been able to indicate even the nature of the general solution. We suspect that the prospects for divisional autonomy may be poor under these conditions.

4. Where demand dependence exists, the analysis is rather complex. Generally speaking, the solution falls between market price and marginal cost.

5. Even under the assumptions of demand independence and technological independence, the optimal rule for transfer price leads to correct output adjustments only on the margin. It does not follow that, if an autonomous division is apparently losing money at the established transfer price, the firm would really increase its profits by abandoning the operation concerned.

We may close with some remarks about the practical implications of the foregoing analysis. Most commonly, divisional autonomy is probably desired not so much to rationalize interdivisional trading as to create incentives for the separate "profit centers" which will lead to improved internal efficiency within each. Nevertheless, cases may arise in which the former objective is the dominant one, and even where the latter is dominant some of the potential gains may be lost by an improper transfer-price rule or policy. In practice, the rule of pricing at the market is apparently the one most frequently adopted, and there are circumstances in which that rule is appropriate. Where it is not, however, the consequences of adopting it may be serious. Perhaps even more serious are the possible consequences of the error warned of in paragraph 5 above—evaluating the over-all operations of a division (with a view toward either expanding or abandoning it) on the basis of its separate "profit" calculated from the established transfer price, whether correct or incorrect. When non-marginal decisions like abandoning a subsidiary are under consideration, a calculation of the incremental revenues and costs of the operation as a whole to the firm should be undertaken.

24. The Factor Proportions Problem in Underdeveloped Areas*

RICHARD S. ECKAUS[1]

Richard S. Eckaus (B.S., Iowa State University, 1946; A.M., Washington University, St. Louis, 1948; Ph.D., Massachusetts Institute of Technology, 1954) was born in Kansas City, Missouri, in 1926. Before assuming his present position at MIT in 1962 he was on the faculty of Brandeis University. His primary fields of interest are economic theory and economic development, and his publications include a book entitled *Planning for Growth: Multisectoral, Intertemporal Models Applied to India* (with Kirit S. Parikh).

The concepts "structural disequilibrium," "overpopulation," "technological unemployment" and "underemployment" appear frequently in the literature on underdeveloped areas and there is considerable discussion of the comparative desirability for use in such areas of relatively labor-intensive or capital-intensive techniques. This paper is intended to help clarify some of the underlying issues and to begin to provide a theoretical basis for their analysis.

Many of the underdeveloped areas of the world have large agrarian populations in which there is either persistent open unemployment or in which the marginal productivity of the working force is so low that it is commonly believed that withdrawal of a sizable fraction would not significantly affect output. This seems to be the case to varying degrees for much of Asia and the Middle East. Other countries, such as Italy, show persistent urban as well as rural unemployment or underemployment. It is a common feature of the unemployment in these countries that it fails to respond to fiscal policy measures designed to increase employment by stimulating effective demand. Use of conventional income-generating techniques appears in fact to create inflationary pressures and balance-of-payments difficulties long before full employment is approached.

This interpretation of the condition of many underdeveloped areas has led to the

* Reprinted from the *American Economic Review* (September 1955) by permission of the publisher, pp. 539–565.

[1] The author wishes to express his gratitude to the Center for International Studies, under whose auspices he did the work upon which this paper is based, to the seminar group of the Center for criticism and encouragement and especially to F. M. Bator and P. N. Rosenstein-Rodan. He is also indebted to P. A. Samuelson and to R. Solow for their interest.

formulation of a number of alternative explanatory hypotheses which are presented in Section I. One of these hypotheses appears, at this stage of investigation, to be particularly fruitful in casting light on some of the outstanding characteristics of underdeveloped areas and is elaborated in Section II. Two approaches to the problems of empirical testing of the hypotheses are outlined in Section III.

The hypotheses presented below suggest that the unemployment difficulties of underdeveloped areas are not basically due to lack of effective demand but stem from "market imperfections," limited opportunities for technical substitution of factors and inappropriate factor endowments.[2] The techniques of analysis of factor market imperfections are well known.[3] The implications of limited technical substitutability of factors were first analyzed by Abraham Wald [4] and more recently by the linear programming techniques.[5] Further development of the theoretical analysis in this paper consists mainly of an elaboration of geometrical techniques, which are used to apply the theory specifically to the problems of underdeveloped areas.

I. THE FACTOR PROPORTIONS HYPOTHESES

The analysis which follows has grown out of the suggestion by C. P. Kindleberger that underdeveloped areas such as

Italy are characterized by "structural disequilibrium at the factor level." This concept, formulated by Kindleberger and E. Despres, is identified as follows:

> Disequilibrium at the factor level may arise either because a single factor receives different returns in different uses or because the price relationships among factors are out of line with factor availabilities.[6]

This suggestion has been the starting point for two types of explanation of unemployment or underemployment in underdeveloped areas. The first type assumes that available technology would permit full use of the working force at some set of relative prices and finds the source of unemployment in various types of "imperfections" in the price system. The second type suggests that there are limitations in the existing technology or the structure of demand which lead to a redundancy of labor in densely populated, underdeveloped areas. The two types of hypotheses are combined in Section II to obtain a more general analysis.

A. The Market Imperfections Hypotheses

In the accompanying figure the vertical axis represents the rate of real wages and the horizontal axis the amount of labor. The curves DD' and SS' represent the aggregate supply and demand relations for a typical industry if factor markets are competitive. Under competitive conditions the wage rate would settle at E.[7]

Suppose, however, that trade union pressures, immobility of labor, government social legislation or other factor-market imperfections maintain the wage rate at W rather than allowing it to fall to E. The effective labor supply curve would be WS'.

---

[2] The hypotheses and analysis have come to be known at the Center for International Studies, M.I.T., as the "factor proportions" problem.

[3] *E.g.*, Joan Robinson, *Essays in the Theory of Employment,* 2nd ed. (Oxford, 1947), Ch. 2.

[4] A. Wald, "Über einige Gleichungssysteme der mathematischen Okonomie," *Zeitschr. f. Nationalökon.,* Dec. 1936, VII, 636–70; *cf.* also, W. L. Valk, *Production, Pricing and Employment in the Static State* (London, 1937), p. 58.

[5] *E.g.*, R. Dorfman, *Application of Linear Programming to the Theory of the Firm* (Berkeley, 1951). In an as yet unpublished paper ("Full Employment and Fixed Coefficients of Production") M. Fukuoka also related the assumption of fixed coefficients in production to the problem of unemployment.

[6] C. P. Kindleberger and E. Despres, "The Mechanism for Adjustment in International Payments—The Lessons of Postwar Experience," *Am. Econ. Rev.,* Proceedings, May 1952, XLII, 338.

[7] Fixed supply and demand curves such as those in Figure 24.1, suppose, of course, constant resources, technology and consumer tastes.

At the higher wage rate the demand for labor would not absorb all the labor available and it could be said, as Kindleberger does, that, *ceteris paribus*, the wage rate does not represent factor endowments.

To isolate the influence of various types of imperfections let us now consider a case in which factor mobility, or lack of it, is not important and continue to confine the analysis to a closed economy. If the system had become adjusted to a particular complex of rigidities there would be no need for factor mobility in the absence of changes in techniques or tastes.[8]

The comparative use of the factors of production, depending as it does on the factor-price ratios and technology, would, however, reflect the "true availability" of labor only if wages were kept at E in Figure 24.1. If wages are kept at W there is an

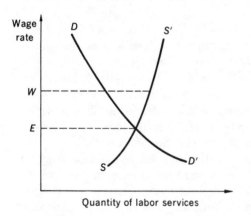

FIGURE 24.1

"artifically" high ratio of the price of labor to the price of capital. Since we are explicitly assuming that factor substitution is, in fact, possible, a structure of production may result with a higher capital-labor ratio than otherwise. If the diagram were representative of large parts of an economy, as

[8] "If effective demand always moved up and down in the same well-worn channels, a supply of each type of labor would always be ready waiting to meet demand for it, when effective demand expanded, and the question of mobility would not arise." Joan Robinson, *op. cit.*, p. 30.

output increased full employment of the given labor force would require the use of more capital than if the structure of production were adjusted to a lower labor-capital price ratio, unless the substitution effects were offset by increasing returns to scale. In a country in which capital was scarce and unemployment of considerable magnitude, the attempt to achieve full employment by use of relatively capital-intensive investment would be more likely to lead to inflation and balance-of-payments difficulties, short of full employment, than if more labor-intensive techniques were used.

The development of social policy in economically underdeveloped areas frequently proceeds more rapidly than economic growth. Imitation of the techniques of more advanced countries is not confined to technology. Elaborate social security legislation and aggressive government-encouraged union movements are often found in densely populated, low per capita income countries which are just on the threshold of economic advancement. There is little or no scope for such devices for raising wages except in the relatively more advanced and well-organized sectors. Therefore, new industrial projects may face the prospect of wage rates quite different from those prevailing in the handicraft and agrarian sectors and thus may be compelled to use different factor proportions. These considerations suggest that the foregoing analysis may be quite relevant for underdeveloped areas.

The next step in the analysis is to abandon the assumptions of constant technology and consumer tastes and to investigate the effects of changes in the composition of demand for goods and factors due to such influences as changes in methods of production or in the directions or levels of demand as a result of changes in tastes or foreign competition. In this second case, as the level of aggregate effective demand rises, goods will be demanded in different proportions than formerly and the location and magnitudes of the demand for factors of production will shift. If labor is not mobile, or if it takes considerable wage increases to shift it, then factor disequilibrium such as depicted in Figure 24.1 for the preceding case of constant tastes and technology would develop in certain industries. An increase in the level of effective demand would push other industries to the limits of capacity relatively quickly in this second case. Money wages and prices would begin to rise, not uniformly but in the "bottleneck" sectors, prior to the achievement of general full employment. New investment in these sections would tend to increase still further the substitution of capital for labor while offsetting tendencies in the relatively stagnant sectors would work slowly, if at all. The balance of payments under the pressure of growing domestic inflationary pressures and increased demand for capital imports would tend also to develop deficits at an earlier stage in the expansion of national income. This could all be superimposed upon and could aggravate the "factor disequilibrium" previously discussed. It would be distinguishable, however, as there would be evidence of excess capacity and stranded capital-goods resources indicating an original misallocation or a structural shift.

There is at least superficial evidence to suggest that the factors stressed in this hypothesis may be operative in some underdeveloped countries. For example, although Italy has a persistent unemployment of about 2 million in a population of around 47 million, there are also some sectors of the Italian economy, such as shipbuilding, in which there is persistent unused physical capital plant and equipment. Moreover, we would expect that in underdeveloped areas the working force would be even more bound by tradition, reluctance to change location and barriers to social as well as physical movement than is the case in more advanced, industrialized

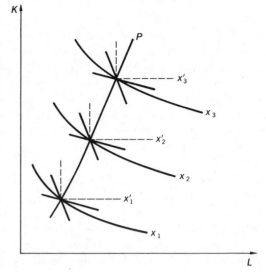

FIGURE 24.2

countries; this would also contribute to the problems created by structural change.

Closely related to this second hypothesis is an explanation which locates the source of factor disequilibrium in barriers to the entry of new firms into profitable industries whose expansion is limited by various types of monopolistic restrictions. This and the other types of "imperfections" could aggravate the "factor disequilibrium."

One further related hypothesis remains to be considered here.[9] Suppose that, whatever the actual characteristics of the production function and degree of technical substitutability of factors, businessmen believe that they face a production function with constant coefficients, *i.e.*, no factor substitution is possible. Indian businessmen, for example, may believe that the "American way" of producing is the best and only way and that this always involves high ratios of capital to labor. Plant engineers accustomed to emulating "Western" technology may not be sensitive to the range of choice actually available in manufacturing processes and may impose unnec-

[9] I am indebted to F. M. Bator for the suggestion of this case.

essary technical constraints on managers in underdeveloped countries. Thus in Figure 24.2, although the solid lines, x_1, x_2 . . . may represent the real contours of the production function, businessmen may regard the dashed lines x_1', x_2' . . . as the ones along which they must move.

In this case the expansion path P would be independent of the factor-price ratios, and, therefore, of the supply curve of labor such as indicated in Figure 24.1. Expansion of effective demand would tend to run into the limits imposed by capital capacity prior to the achievement of full employment with consequent inflationary tendencies and balance-of-payments difficulties. This could take place even if Figure 24.2 were not characteristic of all sectors of industry.

B. The Technological Restraints Hypothesis

It is fairly common for observers to report finding modern, capital-intensive equipment and techniques used in underdeveloped areas where relative factor prices would suggest the use of more labor-intensive techniques. I should now like to suggest that the use of the "modern" techniques is not necessarily irrational emulation but the result of real limitations in the technological choices available, and that this, in turn, is a major source of labor employment problems in underdeveloped areas. At this point the exposition will be oversimplified to indicate in stark outline the nature of the argument. In the next section the hypothesis will be combined with some of the market imperfections hypotheses in an attempt to describe some of the major characteristics of underdeveloped and overpopulated areas by the use of a relatively simple theoretical framework.

The basic assumptions of the following analysis are: (1) in large sectors of an economy there are only a few alternative processes which can be utilized; (2) these

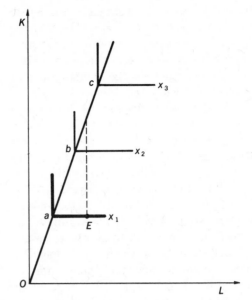

FIGURE 24.3

processes are relatively capital-intensive.[10] There have been frequent comments which describe certain features of underdeveloped and overpopulated areas as essentially the result of limited variability in the coefficients of production. An example of this kind of comment is the frequently observed "underemployment" in agriculture, where this is taken to mean that, with agricultural techniques remaining unchanged, withdrawal of farm labor would not reduce output.

The Case of One Good, Two Factors and One Process In the first, most simple case to be considered, suppose that only one good is produced in the economy, national product, which requires two factors, capital and labor.[11] Assume also that only one process can be used to produce national product, *i.e.*, that the factors must be used in fixed proportions. This situation is represented in

[10] A production "process" is a way of combining different factors of production whose *proportions* are determined by technology, although the *scale* of production and thus the absolute quantities of the factors used may be freely variable.

[11] Confining the analysis to only two factors is not essential but highly convenient for geometrical demonstrations.

Figure 24.3, where the heavy black line represents national output, x_1 of 1 unit; the lighter lines represent higher outputs. Quite irrespective of relative factor prices points *a, b, c*, etc., represent the combinations of factors which will be used to produce output and the slope of the line joining these points is equal to the constant, capital-labor ratio.

Only when the factors of production are actually available in proportions equal to the fixed capital-labor ratio is there the possibility that both can simultaneously be fully utilized. If the actual factor endowment is off the line *oabc*, for example, at point *E*, there must inevitably be some unemployment of labor which is not amenable to any fiscal or monetary policy for its alleviation. Labor is a redundant factor and only by increasing capital stock in the amount indicated by the length of the dashed line can the unemployment be eliminated.[12] Conventional compensatory fiscal policy would, in this case, only result in inflationary pressures. The persistent open and "disguised" unemployment in underdeveloped countries may be at least partially of this kind.

Two or More Processes Suppose now that a second and a third relatively more labor-intensive process is developed for the production of the same good, national output, so that three processes are now available. This is represented in Figure 24.4 by the existence of two more right-angled constant-product lines for a unit of output and two additional expansion paths, *ocd* and *oef*.

In addition to the alternative combinations of factors which may be used to produce a unit of output represented by points *a* and *c* and *e* the lines *ac* and *ce* also represent combinations of factors which will

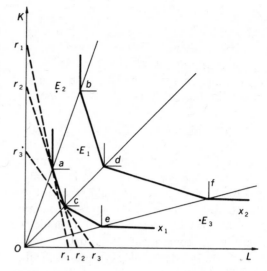

Figure 24.4

yield a unit of output. It is possible to be between *a* and *c* on line *ac* for example, by using the first process and the second process in different combinations. If the resources are taken away from the first process, output would fall. But if these resources are then used in the second process, output would rise. It can be shown rigorously[13] and may be appreciated intuitively that there is some withdrawal of factors from process 1 and subsequent use in process 2 which will restore output to the unit level. Correspondingly the line *bd* represents combinations of process 1 and process 2 and of the two factors capital and labor which are optimal for the production of the x_2 level of output.[14]

In this second case where several processes are available the proportions in which the two factors can be used are not confined to either the expansion path of the first process or the expansion path of the second process, or both, but may be any place within the area bounded by *oab* and

---

[12] I recognize that it is stretching a definition considerably to call redundant factors "unemployed." However, since it is specifically the hypothesis of this paper that the labor called "unemployed" or "underemployed" in underdeveloped areas is redundant, I shall with this warning, use the terms interchangeably.

[13] *Cf.* Dorfman, *op. cit.*, pp. 39–41.

[14] It can be seen by drawing a line from *a* to *e* that, for any output, any combination involving processes 1 and 3 would require more of at least one factor than a combination of processes 2 and 3.

oef. Thus the factor endowment E_1, while inevitably implying some unemployment of labor when only the first process was available, can now be fully utilized by using the first process on a smaller scale and switching some of the capital to the second process. If, however, the factor endowment should be outside the area bounded by the two expansion paths, at E_2 or E_3, for example, structural unemployment of capital capacity or of labor would ensue in exactly the same manner as in the preceding case of one process, regardless of factor-price ratios or fiscal policy.

If more than two processes are available to the economy, full employment of all factors will be *possible* at a nonzero wage so long as the proportions in which factors are endowed fall on or within the limits set by the processes with the most extreme factor-use ratios. This suggests an observation which is, by now, almost trite: reduction of underemployment in overpopulated areas requires the addition of scarce factors. This may, however, be accomplished in a variety of ways, such as the use of dry farming methods and drought- and heat-resistant hybrids which increase the land available for farming.

In the case in which just one process is available, changes in relative factor prices can not affect the proportions in which factors are used. This is not true when there are two or more processes available. In this case factor proportions employed will, in competitive markets, vary with factor prices and the achievement of full employment, if technologically possible with the given factor endowment, will depend on factor prices. In Figure 24.4, r_1, r_2, and r_3 are constant-expenditure lines illustrating three possible sets of factor prices. The line r_2 has the special feature that its slope is equal to that of the constant-product curve between points a and c.[15]

If the price ratio of factors were of the r_1 or r_3 types only one process and one ratio of factors would be used. To employ completely each of the factors in an endowment like E_1, the very special factor-price ratio r_2 would be necessary. A factor-price ratio slightly different from r_2 would be sufficient to move factor use ratios away from E_1 to one of the isoquant vertices. Moreover, having reached a vertex of an isoquant it would be possible for large changes in relative factor prices to occur without leading to factor substitution.

Two Goods and Two Factors An interesting question is whether the restriction of the analysis to only a single good is responsible for the character of the conclusion. By use of an Edgeworth-Bowley type box diagram we can continue to have the advantage of graphic techniques without loss of simplicity and extend the analysis to the case of two goods.

Let us now assume that we have two goods x_1 and x_2, each of which can be produced by two, fixed-proportions processes, and that constant returns to scale prevail;[16] only two factors, capital, K, and labor, L, are used. Figure 24.5(a) shows a few of the infinity of equal-product lines which could be drawn for different outputs of the two goods. The solid lines refer to product 1, the dashed lines to product 2. In Figure 24.5(b), these isoquants are used to construct a box diagram. The dimensions of each side of the box represent the total amount of factors available. Any point within the box simultaneously represents four quantities: the amount of capital and the amount of labor used in producing x_1 which is determined by measurement from the lower left-hand corner, and the amount of capital and the amount of

---

[15] Constant expenditure lines r_4 and r_5 could be drawn analogously to r_2 and r_1, with a slope equal to that of ce, and less than that of ce, respectively.

[16] The assumption of constant returns to scale is, of course, maintained not because it is considered the best description of reality but for its analytical convenience. Some comments on the effects on the analysis of dropping this assumption are made below.

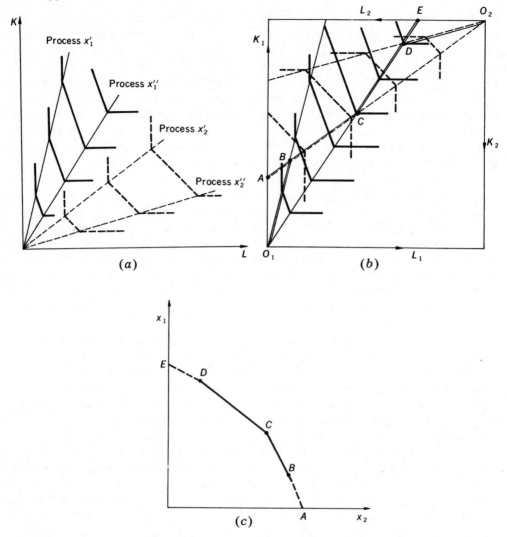

(a)

(b)

(c)

FIGURE 24.5

labor used in the x_2 industry, measured from upper righthand corner.

Figure 24.5(*b*) provides the basis for the derivation of the "efficiency locus" for the two goods x_1 and x_2. If production takes place at any point off this locus, it is possible by recombination of factors to produce more of one good without diminishing the output of the other. If along the efficiency locus corresponding amounts of the two goods are read off and plotted on a chart as in Figure 24.5(*c*), the trans-

formation or production-possibility curve between x_1 and x_2 is obtained.

To locate a point on the efficiency locus we must specify a particular amount of x_1 to be produced and find the maximum of x_2 which can simultaneously be produced. Graphically, we must move along the specified x_1 isoquant crossing x_2 equal-product lines until we reach the highest x_2 isoquant obtainable. The optimum positions achieved will thus be located at tangencies of the x_1 and x_2 equal-product lines where the lines just touch without crossing. Since, in the present case, each equal-product line is made up of segments of straight lines, the optimal positions will be corner tangencies. By repetition of this maximizing process for a series of points the entire efficiency locus can be determined.

Since in the present case the efficiency locus for the two goods is a rather complicated succession of line segments we shall trace it out carefully. Starting at O_1, zero output of x_1, the maximum output of x_2 obtainable is indicated at point A and could be computed by dividing O_2A by the scale factor applicable to process x_2'. If output of x_1 is now increased relative to x_2, it will be most efficient, at first, to use process x_1' and for x_2 to be produced with process x_2'; production of x_1 would then move along the expansion path O_1B and x_2 should decrease along the expansion path x_2' to point B. In this first stage capital is a redundant factor and labor is relatively scarce. The economic system adjusts to this condition by directing the use of the most capital-intensive processes to be used for the production of both goods.

As production of x_1 is expanded beyond point B it would be best now to use both process x_1' and process x_1'' in combinations indicated by the intersection of O_2A with the constant-product lines for commodity x_1 as long as these intersections lie between the expansion paths of x_1' and x_1''; production of x_2 should continue to be by means of process x_2' alone, however. This second stage is indicated by the points on the segment BC which belong to both the combination of x_1' and x_1'' and process x_2'. By tracing along an x_1 isoquant between B and C it can be seen that shifting to the expansion path O_2A makes possible a larger production of x_2 for the particular output of x_1 than if we had remained on the path O_1B. As production of x_1 is expanded in this stage and production of x_2 is decreased, capital becomes more scarce relative to

labor due to the relatively high labor-capital ratio of the resources released by the decrease in production of x_2.

In the third stage, as output of x_1 is farther increased, it is most efficient to use only process x_1''. But now for any given output of x_1, the maximum amount of x_2 can be obtained by use of the more labor-intensive process x_2'' in combination with process x_2'. The third stage on the efficiency locus is indicated by line CD.

Finally, still further expansion of production x_1 continues to be best done along the expansion path of process x_1'' until, at point E, x_1 is being produced to the complete exclusion of x_2. In this fourth and final stage the output of x_2 should be produced only by process x_2''.

Only in the fourth stage and the first stage of the efficiency locus would optimum allocation imply some unemployment of one of the factors. In the first stage the unemployment of capital for different outputs of x_1 and x_2 is indicated by the vertical distance between lines AB and O_1B. In the final stage the unemployment of labor is measured by the horizontal distance between lines DE and DO_2.

Actually the occurrence and qualitative significance of any of the stages depends on both technology and factor endowments. If process x_1'' were relatively more labor-intensive than is shown, its expansion path would pivot to the right and stage 2 in Figure 24.5(b) would be prolonged. As common sense would suggest, development of a sufficiently labor-intensive process for x_1 could cause stages three and four to disappear entirely and with them the possibility that there could be an "optimal" configuration which involved unemployment of labor. A similar effect would result from a decrease in the amount of labor endowment. This could be depicted by squeezing together the left- and right-hand sides of the box in Figure 24.5(b). Increasing the labor supply would mean stretching the box horizontally. This would not only increase the range of outputs associated with stage 4 but also, if pushed far enough, first eliminate stage 1, the capital unemployment stage and then stage 2.

The points $ABCDE$ on the technical transformation curve in Figure 24.5(c) correspond to the similarly lettered points on the efficiency locus in Figure 24.5(b).[17] At first when only a little x_1 is produced and, relatively, a lot of x_2, we should move along the segment AB using process x_1' and x_2'. Unemployment of capital associated with this segment on Figure 24.5(b) will be reduced as we approach B. Relative labor scarcity is limiting along this segment and the slope of the line segment AB will depend on the ratio of the labor inputs of output of x_2 to x_1. The relative labor intensity of process x_2' compared to process x_1' as drawn on Figure 24.5(a) accounts for the steepness of the segment.

The line segment ED on Figure 24.5(c) has an exactly analogous justification to that for the segment AB. Labor unemployment will be reduced as D is approached from point E. Capital is the only scarce factor and the relative capital intensity of process x_1'' as compared to process x_2'' accounts for the flatness of ED.

Point C is located conveniently relative to points B and D. More of x_1 is produced at C than at B, though not so much more as produced at point D. Likewise less x_2 is produced at C than at B though not as much less at D. The segments BC and CD will be straight lines as can be verified by noting in Figure 24.5(b) that, due to the assumption of constant returns to scale in all processes, there must be a constant ratio between changes in output of x_2 along the

line O_2A between C and B, for example, and changes in output of x_1.

It was pointed out with regard to the efficiency locus in Figure 24.5(b) that changes in factor endowment and technology could shorten, extend or even completely eliminate various stages of the efficiency locus. This applies also to the separate segments of the technical transformation curve. The technical transformation curve of Figure 24.5(c) illustrates all the possible stages which could be produced by this simple case, from unemployment of capital to unemployment of labor. It should not be presumed that this range of possibilities will actually exist in a particular system at any one time. Rather, it is the hypothesis of this paper that technology and factor endowments in underdeveloped areas are such that a segment like DE, in which labor is redundant, is important in their transformation curves.

To demonstrate the importance of demand conditions for employment when the conditions assumed in the present hypothesis exist, we shall draw a transformation curve in Figure 24.6 consisting only of

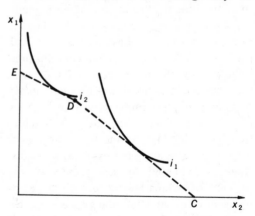

FIGURE 24.6

[17] In the constant-returns-to-scale case, only relative factor endowments are important in determining the *shape* of the transformation curve. If the absolute factor endowments were changed while relative factor endowments remain constant, it would amount to sliding the northeast and southwest vertices of the box on the connecting diagonal.

stage CD, along which there is full employment of both capital and labor, and the labor-redundant stage DE. This can be envisaged as the result of a high rate of population growth which has stretched the labor axis very far. We can now see that actual achievement of full employment depends on the relative demands for the two goods. Market baskets whose composition falls along *CD* will allow full employment; along *DE* labor will be redundant. A geometrical demonstration which is suggestive, though lacking in rigor can be given. Suppose that the lines i_1 and i_2 represent two different possibilities for the community's indifference curve for the two goods. Only in the case in which the indifference curve is tangent along *CD* will optimal output imply full employment. The community must face a conflict in goals between full employment and maximum value of output if i_2 is in fact its indifference curve.[18] Extending the analysis to include many goods would widen the range within which factor endowments could vary without unemployment of one or more factors resulting. There would, however, still be no guarantee that the composition of goods demanded would always hit on a full-employment point.

It may also be observed that if it is possible to buy and sell in foreign trade at price ratios between the slopes of *CD* and *DE*, full employment would again be possible though not necessary. To determine whether or not it would result, it would be necessary to know the reciprocal demands for exports and imports.

It would be possible to elaborate this model now by investigating the implications for the analysis of market imperfections such as were considered in the previous section. This extension will be postponed to the following section, however, and applied to a model of underdeveloped areas designed to be somewhat more realistic. As it stands the present analysis gives us, I believe, important insight into the problems of underdeveloped areas. It presents a hypothesis which helps account for the inflationary tendencies of underdeveloped areas under the impact of programs designed to raise effective demand, and for the stubbornness of unemployment in such areas.

The analysis of this section also provides a more precise definition for the "technological unemployment" mentioned in *Measures for the Economic Development of Underdeveloped Countries*.[19] Technological unemployment may be a real problem for underdeveloped areas if it is defined, as in this section, as redundant labor arising from resource and technological restraints and the structure of demand.

II. A MODEL OF UNDERDEVELOPED AND OVERPOPULATED AREAS [20]

Though the analysis of the previous section is suggestive, it is hard to believe that all of the unemployment and underemployment in underdeveloped areas represents literally useless labor. Moreover, the assumption of only a few alternative processes and a quite limited range for substitution of factors does not seem to fit well the technological characteristics of a number of important industries, as, for example, agriculture. I shall attempt therefore to move toward greater realism by use of a two-sector model (one section with fixed, and one with variable coefficients of production), and investigation of the effects of market imperfections in such a

---

[18] A major qualification to this analysis, still on the static level, is the possibility that the shape and position of the community indifference curves might not be independent of the particular processes or combinations of processes which are used. To handle this difficulty it would be necessary to determine the shifts in income distribution which result from changes in factor prices and to explore the differentials in tastes of the recipients of the different types of income.

[19] United Nations, Department of Economic Affairs (New York, 1951).

[20] I am particularly indebted to P. N. Rosenstein-Rodan for discussion of the issues raised in this section.

system. To the assumption of limited opportunities for substitution in some industries is added the hypothesis that in many other industries there is a considerable range of variability in the proportions in which factors can be used.

It will be useful to initiate the discussion under the assumption that each of the two sectors produce the same product. Suppose that in Figure 24.7 the constant-prod-

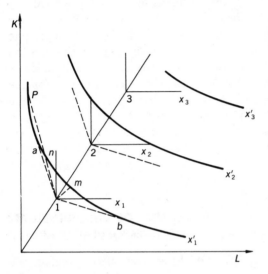

FIGURE 24.7

uct lines of the fixed-coefficient industry are represented by the lines x_1, x_2, ...[21] and the constant-product lines of the variable coefficient industry by the lines x_1', x_2'. . . .

The output x_1 could be produced by the factor combination and technique represented by point 1 or any of the factor combinations using the variable proportions technique represented by the line x_1'. Moreover, following the reasoning on page 200 above, it is also possible to produce x_1 by simultaneously using both the fixed-coefficients and variable coefficients tech-

niques. All of the lines which could be drawn from point 1 to line x_1' represent a *combination* of methods which would produce output x_1; all such lines fall between the lines $1a$ and $1b$ which are drawn from point 1 just tangent to line x_1'.[22] The "efficiency locus" for specified outputs can be traced out by determining, for given amounts of one of the factors, the minimum amount of the other factor necessary to produce the output. If this is done for output x_1 when very little labor is available it is best to produce by the use of the variable coefficients process alone; a representative factor use for this case is at point p. As more labor becomes available the minimum amount of capital required to produce x_1 is found by sliding down the variable coefficients constant-product line to point a. Line $a1$ represents different combinations of the variable-coefficients technique located at a and the fixed-coefficient process. When the labor available is further increased, the minimum amounts of capital necessary to produce x_1 are found by moving along line $a1$. As labor available is still further increased the line $1b$ is the next segment of the efficiency locus used, for reasons analogous to those given for the use of segment $a1$. Finally, when labor is increased beyond the amount available at point b, again only the variable coefficients method should be used to produce x_1.

Output x_1 could also be produced by process combinations and amounts of factors which do not lie on the efficiency locus, of course. Line $p1$ represents a series of such combinations, using in varying proportions the variable coefficients techniques located at p or n and the fixed-coefficient process located at point 1. Any combination of methods along $pn1$, however, would result in higher costs for x_1 than a method found on the efficiency locus; methods along $pn1$ could also be used to produce

---

[21] Although the constant-product lines for the fixed-coefficients sector are drawn in Figure 24.7 as if only one process is available, the demonstration is perfectly general and its implications are applicable when more than one process is available for the fixed-coefficient industry.

[22] I am indebted to R. Solow for the criticism of a previous paper which led to this formulation.

larger amounts than x_1. Of course, many lines like $pn1$ could be drawn between $a1$ and the vertical portion of the fixed-coefficient x_1 isoproduct line and, analogously, between $1b$ and the horizontal portion of the fixed-coefficient isoproduct line. Lines like $1m$, of which many could also be drawn, represent combinations of methods which would also produce x^1, but require more of *both* labor and capital than points on the efficiency locus. The boundaries of lines such as $1m$ are the vertical and horizontal portions of the fixed-coefficients x_1 isoproduct line.

Figure 24.7 embodies the constant-returns-to-scale assumption for both the fixed-coefficients and variable-coefficients method. This is not necessarily the most realistic or relevant assumption, however, nor does the relative position of the two types of curves, or the shape of the variable-coefficients isoquants necessarily correspond closely to reality. It is useful to recognize other, special cases which may have important empirical significance. In Figure 24.7, for example, only the extremes of the isoproduct curves of the variable-coefficients technique were a part of the efficiency locus for any particular output, and, as drawn, relatively little substitution was possible at such extremes. It would, of course, be possible to draw figures in which the "efficient" isoproduct ridge lines follow the variable-coefficients lines so as to allow substitution of factors over a considerable range.

The effect of divergent rates of return to scale on the shape and slope of the constant-product ridge lines is illustrated in Figure 24.8 for one possible set of relations. In the fixed-coefficients process it is assumed that there are increasing returns to scale (shown by decreasing distances between x_1, x_2, x_3, along any ray from the origin). In the variable-coefficients method constant returns to scale are the rule (shown by constant distances between x_1', x_2', x_3', along a ray from the origin). In

this example, the efficient isoproduct lines change their shape as output is increased. For output x_1 only the variable-coefficients constant-product line is relevant. For output x_2 the "efficient" isoproduct ridge line involves use of both the fixed and variable-coefficient techniques. Finally, for output x_3, only the fixed-coefficient technique is "efficient" and the ridge lines involving the variable-coefficient method necessarily have a positive slope.

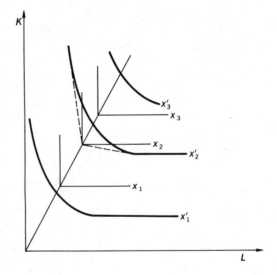

FIGURE 24.8

Figure 24.8 provides the formal basis for some useful deductions. Changes in factor prices which might at one scale of output induce shifts in the proportions in which factors are used, may not induce such shifts at another scale of output or may only produce smaller shifts. Likewise techniques of production not feasible at one scale of production may become mandatory for efficiency at another scale.

In Figures 24.6, 24.7 and 24.8 it is particularly clear that in order for the system to travel along its most efficient production isoquant it is necessary that factor prices be flexible. Factor price rigidities would make parts of the efficient constant-product lines unattainable for profit-maximizing businessmen.

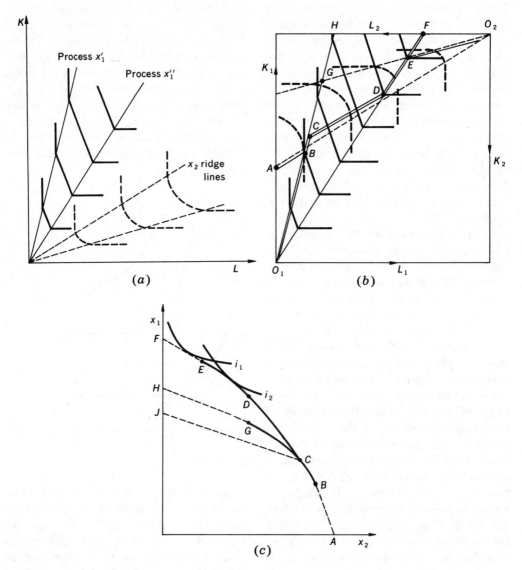

FIGURE 24.9

We can now go rapidly through an analysis of the two-sector model hypothesis assuming that each sector produces a different commodity. The geometrical representation of this, using the box diagram technique introduced in the previous section, is provided by Figure 24.9(a). The assumption that for x_1 only two alternative processes are available is maintained for convenience; the resulting production-possibility curves for x_1 are shown by the solid lines. The assumption of variable-coefficients in the production of x_2 is limited to the sector between its ridge lines because at these ridge lines the marginal productivity of one of the factors becomes zero and further input of this factor would have no effect on output.[23]

The production functions for x_1 and x_2

[23] It is assumed that there is no disposal problem and, thus, that the production isoquants do not bend back on themselves.

are reproduced in the box diagram in Figure 24.9(b): the dimensions of the box are determined by the factor endowments.[24] Using this box diagram we can trace out the efficiency locus for the two products by repeatedly asking the question, "For a given amount of x_1 what is the maximum amount of x_2 which can be produced?" In the process of tracing out the efficiency locus, the transformation curve can be drawn for the two goods.

Starting at O_1, zero output of x_1, the maximum amount of x_2 producible is given by O_2A. If the output of x_1 is increased relative to x_2, it would be most efficient at first to use process x_1' for x_1 and to produce x_2 by traveling along its most capital-intensive ridge line, O_2A. This represents optimal behavior up to point B. In this stage although both products are being produced capital is a redundant factor. This results in spite of the variability of coefficients in production of x_2 because outside the upper ridge line of x_2 capital has zero marginal productivity. Stage 1 is represented on the transformation curve in Figure 24.9(c) as segment AB.

The efficiency locus from B to C is traced out by finding the succession of points at which the x_1 constant-product curves touch the highest x_2 constant-product curves. In this stage process x_1' will be used for x_1 and a varying combination of factors for x_2. The segment of the transformation curve for this stage, BC, will be curved as equal increases in production of x_1 along x_1' will not result in constant changes in output of x_2. Only along rays from the origin O_2 will equal distances imply equal differences in output of x_2. BC will be concave to the origin as is "normal" for transformation curves; graphically it can be seen that smaller and smaller changes along x_1' are needed in order to move across equal changes in output of x_2. As produc-

tion moves from B to C the points at which x_1' corners touch the x_2 isoquants will be characterized by smaller and smaller slopes on the x_2 isoquants, corresponding to the decreasing capital-labor ratio used in the production of x_2. At some point, C, the capital-labor ratio in x_2 will become equal to the capital-labor ratio represented by the negatively slanting portion of the x_1 isoquants. A ray from the origin O_2 to point C will intersect every x_2 isoquant at a point with identical slopes. Thus CD, the third stage of the efficiency locus and the transformation curve, will be the series of tangencies of the negatively slanting portion of the x_1 isoquants, representing combinations of processes x_1' and x_1'' and the x_2 isoquants along the ray O_2C. The segment of the transformation curve corresponding to CD lies on a ray from O_2 and thus the equal jumps across the x_1 isoquants will mark out constant changes in production of x_2.

At point D and for further increases in output of x_1 relative to x_2 it would be best to use only process x_1'' for production of x_1. The segment of the transformation curve, DE, corresponding to DE on the efficiency locus, is curved for reasons similar to those which created the curvature of segment BC.

The final stage of the efficiency locus is the labor unemployment stage. The marginal productivity of labor has fallen to zero in the x_2 sector and in a perfect factor market wages would fall to zero. EF represents this final stage on the transformation curve in Figure 24.9(c).

$ABCDEF$ in Figure 24.9(c) is the full transformation curve for this case. There are now curved as well as straight-line segments, and the kinks characteristic of the previous transformation curves have disappeared.[25]

In Figure 24.9(b), as in Figure 24.5(b),

---

[24] Again only the ratio of the factor endowments is important as long as constant returns to scale is assumed.

[25] Being off the efficiency curve, it may be noted is like being on an isoquant $1m$ in the single-good case. *Cf.* Figure 24.7 above.

it is possible to visualize the effects of structural changes by altering the shape and position of the production isoquants for each product and the dimensions of the box.

The box diagram approach helps to clarify the implication of the differences in substitutability in the fixed-coefficient and variable-coefficient sectors. It is clear that the outputs at which one or another factor becomes redundant will be determined by the limits of substitution in the variable-coefficients sector and the most extreme labor- and capital-intensive processes in the fixed-coefficient sector, not by the discontinuities of the latter sector. These have other important effects, however.

Suppose that the respective demands for output are such that a large part of the available capital is drawn into the capital-intensive and fixed-coefficient sector. The amount of labor which can be absorbed in these sectors is dependent on the amount of capital available. Since capital is a scarce factor, labor employment opportunities in this sector are limited by its availability rather than by demand for output. The relatively plentiful labor supply is then pushed into the variable-coefficient sector and absorbed there as long as the marginal value productivity of labor is higher than the wages it receives.

In this case, as in the models of the preceding sections, unemployment is not due to lack of effective demand and as a result cannot be relieved by conventional contra-cyclical economic policy designed to stimulate spending. If employment opportunities in the fixed-coefficient sectors were limited by capital scarcity or some other resource bottleneck, an increase in demand rather than stimulating additional output would only create inflationary pressures. Likewise, in the variable-coefficient sectors if the marginal productivity of labor were zero, the first effects of an increase in demand for output would be an increase in prices without an increase in production.

If more of the scarce factors were made available to the fixed-coefficient sectors, more labor could then be employed and would be used, if there were an effective demand for its output. Additional amounts of the scarce factors in the variable-coefficients sector would also increase labor productivity and output if demand were adequate.

It is possible in this case of two sectors, one of fixed and one of variable coefficients, for a divergence to exist between the full-employment output and the output with maximum value, just as in the case of fixed-coefficient processes for each of two goods, as depicted in Figure 24.6 above. This could result even if there were no market imperfections. If, in Figure 24.9(c), the community indifference curves were like i_1 rather than i_2 so that the tangency occurred in the capital-scarcity, labor-surplus stage, the divergence could exist. On the other hand, community indifference curves shaped like i_2 would mean that it would be possible for full-employment output and maximum-value output to be identical. This demonstration is subject to the same qualifications applied to the one-good case.

Without empirical knowledge, it is not possible to evaluate certainly the relative importance of each of the stages of the transformation curve 24.9(c). However, according to the hypothesis advanced here the transformation curve for underdeveloped areas would consist mainly of the high labor-intensity and labor-unemployment segments such as *DE* and *EF*.

We have thus far in this section assumed the existence of competitive markets and profit-maximizing entrepreneurs. We have shown that, even under such assumptions, technology, factor endowments and final demands may combine in ways which make it very difficult for underdeveloped areas to solve their problems of unemployment and underemployment. It is possible now to broaden the analysis by combining it with the analysis of the effects of market imperfections discussed in Section I to determine what further problems are created when some of the assumptions of competition are dropped.

Behind the transformation curve lie many fine adjustments as factors are shifted from one industry to another and recombined in varying proportions to obtain the maximum output from one industry for given outputs of the other industry. It has been assumed in deriving the transformation curve that the necessary adjustments would be accomplished as they would be in a perfect factor market. But flexibility within wide limits is required to achieve every possible position on a transformation locus such as that in Figure 24.9(c). When imperfections and rigidities of various types obstruct the movements of factors and prices, the system will not be able to achieve its optimum transformation curve but will instead do no better than to move along some other, less than optimal curve. Limited factor-price flexibility may be quite serious when at least one good is produced with fixed-coefficient processes. If rigid factor prices render a relatively labor-intensive process unprofitable, the only alternative process may involve a big jump to a quite capital-intensive process as well as a drastic obstacle to substitution in the variable-coefficients process.

Since we are interested in the effect of imperfections in the factor markets, it will be useful to distinguish transformation curves which assume perfect adjustments in the factor markets; these will be called "technical transformation curves." Transformation curves which take into account market imperfections will be different from the technical transformation curves; these latter relations will be designated "market transformation curves." [26] Different types

of market imperfections will create different types of shifts away from the technical transformation curve, so there is not one market transformation curve for each technical transformation curve but many.

It may help to approximate reality to assume that factor-price ratios in the variable-coefficients sector are relatively more flexible than those in the fixed-coefficients sector. This might result from differential strength of union organization or susceptibility to government wage controls. Suppose, for example, that by means of union pressures or minimum wage legislation real wages of labor were maintained so that in the fixed coefficients sector the labor-capital price ratio was set above that represented by the slope of the constant product curve combining processes x_1' and x_1'' in Figure 24.9(b); the factor-price ratio in the variable coefficients sector may still be assumed to vary freely. The cost-minimizing combination of factors is determined for any particular output at the point at which the production-possibility schedule for that output touches the lowest expenditure line. If the production-possibility schedule has any slope at this point, it is a condition of equilibrium that this slope be equal to the factor-price ratio which determines the slope of the expenditure line. As a result under the present assumptions process x_1'' would never be used. It would always be more profitable to use process x_1' alone in producing x_1. The transformation curve would be $ABCGH$ in Figure 24.9(c); this is below the technical transformation curve and has a much longer range of unemployment. If both sectors were characterized by such high, inflexible factor-price ratios, the economy's

[26] The effect of factor-market imperfections in shifting the market transformation curve inside the technical transformation curve has been

pointed out and analyzed for international trade by G. Haberler, "Some Problems in the Pure Theory of International Trade," *Econ. Jour.*, June 1950, LX, 223–40 and by P. Samuelson, "Evaluation of Real National Income," *Oxford Econ. Papers*, Jan. 1950, II (N.S.), 18–19 for welfare economics; others have probably also noted the effect.

transformation curve would approach *ABCJ*.[27]

Barriers to the movement of factors would have the effect of moving the market transformation curve even further inside the technical transformation curve and increasing the range over which a factor is redundant.

Thus imperfections in factor markets have several undesirable effects. They reduce the amount of goods available and create a wider range of combinations of goods over which labor may become unemployed, depending on the structure of final demand.

Although the effects of rigid wages on the transformation curve of the economy are clear, welfare judgments as to the results of removal of the factor-price rigidities are subject to the same qualifications as in the previous case. Much depends on the effects of a change in methods on the income distribution and, via income distribution, on community preferences.

III. EMPIRICAL VERIFICATION

The analysis above is based on hypotheses which can be tested empirically and which deserve to be given factual content. Empirical testing requires measurement of the proportions in which productive factors can be and are actually used. Essentially the objective of such research would be an investigation of production functions.

Although the concept of the production function has been familiar for some time, its empirical investigation has, as is common, been neglected with important noteworthy exceptions. In this connection it should be noted that even though it is sometimes presented as an analysis of productive processes and its terminology is taken

from the theory of production, input-output analysis, as it now stands, does not reveal the technologies actually in use in an economy. For this purpose a much higher degree of disaggregation would be necessary than is currently practiced or appears feasible. Interindustry flows may strongly reflect historical incidents by which certain technical processes are concentrated in a particular sector which subcontracts for other sectors. Or, if similar technical processes are widely used, the interindustry flows in a particular year may reflect different cyclical patterns in industry; one industry producing at its capacity may subcontract to another industry which has equipment capable of performing the necessary operations and is cyclically depressed.[28] Studies of capital coefficients made for input-output tables do indicate, however, a method which can be used for a factor proportions study.[29]

The objective of the process analysis approach newly developed at the RAND Corporation is exactly the empirical determination of production functions. The emphasis of the process analysis approach in establishing all the alternatives on a production-possibility schedule, which is essential for programming, is somewhat different from a factor proportions study. For the latter study not only the range of possibilities but the relative frequencies of their use and dynamic considerations involved in choice are important. The methods of process analysis can also be used for a factor proportions study, however.

For the study of factor proportions two general approaches seem to be available. The first, suggested by input-output studies of capital coefficients and which will be

---

[27] Barriers to capital movement created by monopoly may create situations analogous to those described above resulting from labor-market imperfections.

[28] This point is made with force by H. Markowitz in *Process Analysis of the Metal Working Industries*, The RAND Corporation (Santa Monica, 1953), pp. 7–8.

[29] Esp. the studies made by the Inter-Industry Analysis Branch of the Office of Chief Economist, Bureau of Mines, U. S. Department of Interior.

called the "product analysis" method, involves a census in each plant studied of the amounts of each type of factor of production used in the expansion of the output of a particular product. The second method, based on classifications of technical processes, requires the determination of the combinations of factors actually used by firms to perform certain standardized "tasks."

These approaches to the factor proportions study are not necessarily logically separate, nor should they always be completely different in application. The great advantage of process analysis in precise identification of outputs can compensate for the weakness of product analysis where multiproduct plants are involved. The advantage of product analysis in inclusion of all contributing inputs can be important when using the process analysis approach where it is difficult to isolate the contributions of all inputs. Thus, it is important in particular cases to have in mind a method combining both the product and process analyses.

The application of product analysis can be made in two ways: (1) By abstracting the data required from the engineering plans which are prepared when a new investment is undertaken and which list the construction, equipment, labor and materials required for the operation of the plant. Accounting records of new investment expenses could also supply part of the necessary information. (2) By means of "factor inventories" of existing plants to provide for these plants the information which the investment plan analysis provides for new expansions. No easy and automatic application of product analysis techniques is possible in the face of problems such as those raised by multiproduct firms and the measurement of the expansion of capacity. These problems can often be overcome, I believe, to make this a fruitful method.

Process analysis is based on the conception that all productive activity can be divided into separate technical processes with similar outputs whose inputs can be identified and compared. Process analysis thus provides another logically satisfactory approach to study of factor proportions. The process analysis approach can moreover provide the basis for a comparison of factor proportions by final products, and thus for an independent check of factor proportions computed by the product analysis method. This could be achieved by determining the appropriate physical processes and levels of activity necessary for the output of a particular final product and aggregating their factor inputs. The procedure just described is, in fact, that actually used in modern engineering practice in plant and equipment design and layout.

The disadvantage of the process analysis approach, however, stemming from the kinds of information which would be generally available, I believe, occurs precisely. where the product analysis method is strong. The information for the process analysis approach must come from the records of inputs to particular processes and these records, because of the purposes for which they are kept, will seldom be sufficiently detailed and comprehensive as to the inputs involved in a process. As a result it will often be necessary in using the process analysis approach to estimate the contributions of "indirect" inputs to the processes studied.

A major source of information for the application of the process analysis approach may be the time cards kept by many firms. These cards list for each worker the time which he takes at each type of machine which he uses to perform the operations on the particular piece. These cards would have the labor inputs and machines specified for particular tasks and often contain other useful data as well. The job sheets which accompany production orders are also sources of information as they list the time per unit and in total required by each type of machine and process to finish a particular item.

IV. CONCLUSIONS

In this paper a number of different hypotheses have been developed and combined for the purpose of explaining outstanding features of some underdeveloped areas: the persistence of unemployment and underemployment, the coexistence of "modern" capital-intensive techniques and methods using a great deal of labor and little capital, and large differentials in factor returns in different sectors. I have suggested that to a considerable degree these conditions may be the result of a few characteristic conditions: factor-market imperfections, and limited technical substitutability of factors, with divergences between the proportions in which goods are demanded and in which they can be supplied with full use of available factors.

Factor-market imperfections which limit factor mobility create employment problems in underemployed areas with low per capita incomes and limited capital resources which are not different in kind but are much different in degree from those existing in the more advanced countries.

When the proportions in which factors can be combined are variable without limit, *i.e.*, with decreasing but always positive marginal returns to labor, additional labor can always produce additional output. If the technical substitutability of factors is limited, as is suggested here, the possibility of labor redundancy arises. Even if there are some sectors in which labor always has a positive marginal product there may be a divergence between maximum value output and full employment output if there is insufficient demand for the output of these sectors. These possibilities are again more important for the underdeveloped areas whose resource endowments are often not suited to the factor proportions dictated by the technological leadership of advanced countries. Differences in income distribution and the range of products may also make limited technical substitutability a more pressing problem in underdeveloped than in advanced areas.

25. Crime and Punishment: An Economic Approach*

GARY S. BECKER [1]

Gary S. Becker (A.B., Princeton University, 1951; A.M., University of Chicago, 1953; Ph.D., 1955) was born in Pottsville, Pennsylvania in 1930. Formerly in the economics department at Columbia, he is now at the University of Chicago, where he is University Professor in the Department of Economics, and is also a member of the Senior Research Staff of the National Bureau of Economic Research. Perhaps the best known of his numerous publications are *The Economics of Discrimination* and *Human Capital*. His brilliance as a research scholar was given formal recognition in 1966 when the American Economic Association awarded him its John Bates Clark medal, an honor given every other year "to that economist under the age of forty who is adjudged to have made a significant contribution to economic thought and knowledge." The citation conferring this honor upon him noted that "Gary Becker's versatility and imagination have enlarged the scope and power of our science. In his skillful hands, economic analysis illuminates basic aspects of human beings in society: the importance of investment to augment their productive capacity, the allocation of their time, the growth of their numbers, their crimes and punishments, their racial prejudices. Throughout his work he displays a rare combination of rigor and relevance." Becker, perhaps more than any other author, has clarified the role that price theory can play in understanding human behavior.

I. INTRODUCTION

Since the turn of the century, legislation in Western countries has expanded rapidly to reverse the brief dominance of laissez

* Reprinted from *Journal of Political Economy* (March–April 1968), by permission of The University of Chicago Press. Copyright, 1968, pp. 169–217 (deleting mathematical appendix, pp. 209–215).

[1] I would like to thank the Lilly Endowment for financing a very productive summer in 1965 at the University of California at Los Angeles. While there I received very helpful comments on an earlier draft from, among others, Armen Alchian, Roland McKean, Harold Demsetz, Jack Hirshliefer, William Meckling, Gordon Tullock, and Oliver Williamson. I have also benefited from comments received at seminars at the University of Chicago, Hebrew University, RAND Corporation, and several times at the Labor Workshop of Columbia; assistance and suggestions from Isaac Ehrlich and Robert Michael; and suggestions from the editor of this journal.

faire during the nineteenth century. The state no longer merely protects against violations of person and property through murder, rape, or burglary but also restricts "discrimination" against certain minorities, collusive business arrangements, "jaywalking," travel, the materials used in construction, and thousands of other activities. The activities restricted not only are numerous but also range widely, affecting persons in very different pursuits and of diverse social backgrounds, education levels, ages, races, etc. Moreover, the likelihood that an offender will be discovered and convicted and the nature and extent of punishments differ greatly from person to person and activity to activity. Yet, in spite of such diversity, some common properties are shared by practically all legislation, and these properties form the subject matter of this essay.

In the first place, obedience to law is not taken for granted, and public and private resources are generally spent in order both to prevent offenses and to apprehend offenders. In the second place, conviction is not generally considered sufficient punishment in itself; additional and sometimes severe punishments are meted out to those convicted. What determines the amount and type of resources and punishments used to enforce a piece of legislation? In particular, why does enforcement differ so greatly among different kinds of legislation?

The main purpose of this essay is to answer normative versions of these questions, namely, how many resources and how much punishment *should* be used to enforce different kinds of legislation? Put equivalently, although more strangely, how many offenses *should* be permitted and how many offenders *should* go unpunished? The method used formulates a measure of the social loss from offenses and finds those expenditures of resources and punishments that minimize this loss. The general criterion of social loss is shown to incorporate as special cases, valid under special assumptions, the criteria of vengeance, deter-

rence, compensation, and rehabilitation, that historically have figured so prominently in practice and criminological literature.

The optimal amount of enforcement is shown to depend on, among other things, the cost of catching and convicting offenders, the nature of punishments—for example, whether they are fines or prison terms—and the responses of offenders to changes in enforcement. The discussion, therefore, inevitably enters into issues in penology and theories of criminal behavior. A second, although because of lack of space subsidiary, aim of this essay is to see what insights into these questions are provided by our "economic" approach. It is suggested, for example, that a useful theory of criminal behavior can dispense with special theories of anomie, psychological inadequacies, or inheritance of special traits and simply extend the economist's usual analysis of choice.

II. BASIC ANALYSIS

A. The Cost of Crime

Although the word "crime" is used in the title to minimize terminological innovations, the analysis is intended to be sufficiently general to cover all violations, not just felonies—like murder, robbery, and assault, which receive so much newspaper coverage —but also tax evasion, the so-called white-collar crimes, and traffic and other violations. Looked at this broadly, "crime" is an economically important activity or "industry," notwithstanding the almost total neglect by economists.[2] Some relevant evi-

[2] This neglect probably resulted from an attitude that illegal activity is too immoral to merit any systematic scientific attention. The influence of moral attitudes on a scientific analysis is seen most clearly in a discussion by Alfred Marshall. After arguing that even fair gambling is an "economic blunder" because of diminishing marginal utility, he says, "It is true that this loss of probable happiness need not be greater than the pleasure derived from the excitement of gambling, and we are then thrown back upon the induction [*sic*]

dence recently put together by the President's Commission on Law Enforcement and Administration of Justice (the "Crime Commission") is reproduced in Table 25.1.

TABLE 25.1

Economic Costs of Crimes

Type	Costs (Millions of Dollars)
Crimes against persons	815
Crimes against property	3,932
Illegal goods and services	8,075
Some other crimes	2,036
Total	14,858
Public expenditures on police, prosecution, and courts	3,178
Corrections	1,034
Some private costs of combatting crime	1,910
Over-all total	20,980

Source: President's Commission (1967d, p. 44).

Public expenditures in 1965 at the federal, state, and local levels on police, criminal courts and counsel, and "corrections" amounted to over $4 billion, while private outlays on burglar alarms, guards, counsel, and some other forms of protection were about $2 billion. Unquestionably, public and especially private expenditures are significantly understated, since expenditures by many public agencies in the course of enforcing particular pieces of legislation, such as state fair-employment laws,[3] are not included, and a myriad of private precautions against crime, ranging from suburban living to taxis, are also excluded.

that pleasures of gambling are in Bentham's phrase 'impure'; since experience shows that they are likely to engender a restless, feverish character, unsuited for steady work as well as for the higher and more solid pleasures of life" (Marshall, 1961, Note X, Mathematical Appendix).

[3] Expenditures by the thirteen states with such legislation in 1959 totaled almost $2 million (see Landes, 1966).

Table 25.1 also lists the Crime Commission's estimates of the direct costs of various crimes. The gross income from expenditures on various kinds of illegal consumption, including narcotics, prostitution, and mainly gambling, amounted to over $8 billion. The value of crimes against property, including fraud, vandalism, and theft, amounted to almost $4 billion,[4] while about $3 billion worth resulted from the loss of earnings due to homicide, assault, or other crimes. All the costs listed in the table total about $21 billion, which is almost 4 per cent of reported national income in 1965. If the sizeable omissions were included, the percentage might be considerably higher.

Crime has probably become more important during the last forty years. The Crime Commission presents no evidence on trends in costs but does present evidence suggesting that the number of major felonies per capita has grown since the early thirties (President's Commission, 1967a, pp. 22–31). Moreover, with the large growth of tax and other legislation, tax evasion and other kinds of white-collar crime have presumably grown much more rapidly than felonies. One piece of indirect evidence on the growth of crime is the large increase in the amount of currency in circulation since 1929. For sixty years prior to that date, the ratio of currency either to all money or to consumer expenditures had declined very substantially. Since then, in spite of further urbanization and income growth and the spread of credit cards and other kinds of

[4] Superficially, frauds, thefts, etc., do not involve true social costs but are simply transfers, with the loss to victims being compensated by equal gains to criminals. While these are transfers, their market value is, nevertheless, a first approximation to the direct social cost. If the theft or fraud industry is "competitive," the sum of the value of the criminals' time input—including the time of "fences" and prospective time in prison—plus the value of capital input, compensation for risk, etc., would approximately equal the market value of the loss to victims. Consequently, aside from the input of intermediate products, losses can be taken as a measure of the value of the labor and capital input into these crimes, which are true social costs.

credit,[5] both ratios have increased sizeably. This reversal can be explained by an unusual increase in illegal activity, since currency has obvious advantages over checks in illegal transactions (the opposite is true for legal transactions) because no record of a transaction remains.[7]

B. The Model

It is useful in determining how to combat crime in an optimal fashion to develop a model to incorporate the behavioral relations behind the costs listed in Table 25.1. These can be divided into five categories: the relations between (1) the number of crimes, called "offenses" in this essay, and the cost of offenses, (2) the number of offenses and the punishments meted out, (3) the number of offenses, arrests, and convictions and the public expenditures on police and courts, (4) the number of convictions and the costs of imprisonments or other kinds of punishments, and (5) the number of offenses and the private expenditures on protection and apprehension. The first four are discussed in turn, while the fifth is postponed until a later section.

1. Damages   Usually a belief that other members of society are harmed is the motivation behind outlawing or otherwise restricting an activity. The amount of harm would tend to increase with the activity level, as in the relation

$$H_i = H_i(O_i),$$

with

$$H'_i = \frac{dH_i}{dO_i} > 0,$$

(1)

where H_i is the harm from the ith activity

and O_i is the activity level.[8] The concept of harm and the function relating its amount to the activity level are familiar to economists from their many discussions of activities causing external diseconomies. From this perspective, criminal activities are an important subset of the class of activities that cause diseconomies, with the level of criminal activities measured by the number of offenses.

The social value of the gain to offenders presumably also tends to increase with the number of offenses, as in

$$G = G(O),$$

with

$$G' = \frac{dG}{dO} > 0.$$

(2)

The net cost or damage to society is simply the difference between the harm and gain and can be written as

$$D(O) = H(O) - G(O).$$

(3)

If, as seems plausible, offenders usually eventually receive diminishing marginal gains and cause increasing marginal harm from additional offenses, $G'' < 0$, $H'' > 0$, and

$$D'' = H'' - G'' > 0,$$

(4)

which is an important condition used later in the analysis of optimality positions [see, for example, the Mathematical Appendix (omitted here)]. Since both H' and $G' > 0$, the sign of D' depends on their relative magnitudes. It follows from (4), however, that

$$D'(O) > 0 \text{ for all } O > O_a \text{ if } D'(O_a) \geq 0. \quad (5)$$

Until Section V the discussion is restricted to the region where $D' > 0$, the region providing the strongest justification for outlawing an activity. In that section the general problem of external diseconomies is reconsidered from our viewpoint, and there $D' < 0$ is also permitted.

---

[5] For an analysis of the secular decline to 1929 that stresses urbanization and the growth in incomes, see Cagan (1965, chap. iv).

[6] In 1965, the ratio of currency outstanding to consumer expenditures was 0.08, compared to only 0.05 in 1929. In 1965, currency outstanding per family was a whopping $738.

[7] Cagan (1965, chap. iv) attributes much of the increase in currency holdings between 1929 and 1960 to increased tax evasion resulting from the increase in tax rates.

[8] The ith subscript will be suppressed whenever it is to be understood that only one activity is being discussed.

The top part of Table 25.1 lists costs of various crimes, which have been interpreted by us as estimates of the value of resources used up in these crimes. These values are important components of, but are not identical to, the net damages to society. For example, the cost of murder is measured by the loss in earnings of victims and excludes, among other things, the value placed by society on life itself; the cost of gambling excludes both the utility to those gambling and the "external" disutility to some clergy and others; the cost of "transfers" like burglary and embezzlement excludes social attitudes toward forced wealth redistributions and also the effects on capital accumulation of the possibility of theft. Consequently, the $15 billion estimate for the cost of crime in Table 25.1 may be a significant understatement of the net damages to society, not only because the costs of many white-collar crimes are omitted, but also because much of the damage is omitted even for the crimes covered.

2. The Cost of Apprehension and Conviction
The more that is spent on policemen, court personnel, and specialized equipment, the easier it is to discover offenses and convict offenders. One can postulate a relation between the output of police and court "activity" and various inputs of manpower, materials, and capital, as in $A = f(m, r, c)$, where f is a production function summarizing the "state of the arts." Given f and input prices, increased "activity" would be more costly, as summarized by the relation

$$C = C(A)$$

and

$$C' = \frac{dC}{dA} > 0. \tag{6}$$

It would be cheaper to achieve any given level of activity the cheaper were policemen,[9] judges, counsel, and juries and the

more highly developed the state of the arts, as determined by technologies like fingerprinting, wire-tapping, computer control, and lie-detecting.[10]

One approximation to an empirical measure of "activity" is the number of offenses cleared by conviction. It can be written as

$$A \cong pO, \tag{7}$$

where p, the ratio of offenses cleared by convictions to all offenses, is the over-all probability that an offense is cleared by conviction. By substituting (7) into (6) and differentiating, one has

$$C_p = \frac{\partial C(pO)}{\partial p} = C'O > 0$$

and $\tag{8}$

$$C_o = C'p > 0$$

if $pO \neq 0$. An increase in either the probability of conviction or the number of offenses would increase total costs. If the marginal cost of increased "activity" were rising, further implications would be that

$$C_{pp} = C''O^2 > 0,$$
$$C_{oo} = C''p^2 > 0,$$

and $\tag{9}$

$$C_{po} = C_{op} = C''pO + C' > 0.$$

A more sophisticated and realistic approach drops the implication of (7) that convictions alone measure "activity," or even that p and O have identical elasticities, and introduces the more general relation

$$A = h(p, O, a). \tag{10}$$

The variable a stands for arrests and other determinants of "activity," and there is no presumption that the elasticity of h with respect to p equals that with respect to O. Substitution yields the cost function $C = C(p, O, a)$. If, as is extremely likely, h_p, h_o, and h_a are all greater than zero, then

[9] According to the Crime Commission, 85–90 per cent of all police costs consist of wages and salaries (President's Commission, 1967a, p. 35).

[10] A task-force report by the Crime Commission deals with suggestions for greater and more efficient usage of advanced technologies (President's Commission, 1967e).

clearly C_p, C_o, and C_a are all greater than zero.

In order to insure that optimality positions do not lie at "corners," it is necessary to place some restrictions on the second derivatives of the cost function. Combined with some other assumptions, it is *sufficient* that

$$C_{pp} \geq 0,$$
$$C_{oo} \geq 0,$$
$$\text{(11)}$$
and
$$C_{po} \cong 0$$

(see the Mathematical Appendix [omitted here]). The first two restrictions are rather plausible, the third much less so.[11]

Table 25.1 indicates that in 1965 public expenditures in the United States on police and courts totaled more than $3 billion, by no means a minor item. Separate estimates were prepared for each of seven major felonies.[12] Expenditures on them averaged about $500 per offense (reported) and about $2,000 per person arrested, with almost $1,000 being spent per murder (President's Commission, 1967a, pp. 264–65); $500 is an estimate of the average cost

$$AC = \frac{C(p, O, a)}{O}$$

of these felonies and would presumably be a larger figure if the number of either arrests or convictions were greater. Marginal costs (C_o) would be at least $500 if condition (11), $C_{oo} \geq 0$, were assumed to hold throughout.

3. The Supply of Offenses   Theories about the determinants of the number of offenses differ greatly, from emphasis on skull types and biological inheritance to family up-

bringing and disenchantment with society. Practically all the diverse theories agree, however, that when other variables are held constant, an increase in a person's probability of conviction or punishment if convicted would generally decrease, perhaps substantially, perhaps negligibly, the number of offenses he commits. In addition, a common generalization by persons with judicial experience is that a change in the probability has a greater effect on the number of offenses than a change in the punishment,[13] although, as far as I can tell, none of the prominent theories shed any light on this relation.

The approach taken here follows the economists' usual analysis of choice and assumes that a person commits an offense if the expected utility to him exceeds the utility he could get by using his time and other resources at other activities. Some persons become "criminals," therefore, not because their basic motivation differs from that of other persons, but because their benefits and costs differ. I cannot pause to discuss the many general implications of this approach,[14] except to remark that criminal behavior becomes part of a much more general theory and does not require ad hoc concepts of differential association, anomie,· and the like,[15] nor does it assume perfect knowledge, lightning-fast calculation, or any of the other caricatures of economic theory.

This approach implies that there is a function relating the number of offenses by any person to his probability of conviction, to his punishment if convicted, and to other

[11] Differentiating the cost function yields $C_{pp} = C''(h_p)^2 + C'h_{pp}$; $C_{oo} = C''(h_o)^2 + C'h_{oo}$; $C_{po} = C''h_o h_p + C'h_{po}$. If marginal costs were rising, C_{pp} or C_{oo} could be negative only if h_{pp} or h_{oo} were sufficiently negative, which is not very likely. However, C_{po} would be approximately zero only if h_{po} were sufficiently negative, which is also unlikely. Note that if "activity" is measured by convictions alone, $h_{pp} = h_{oo} = 0$, and $h_{po} > 0$.

[12] They are willful homicide, forcible rape, robbery, aggravated assault, burglary, larceny, and auto theft.

[13] For example, Lord Shawness (1965) said, "Some judges preoccupy themselves with methods of punishment. This is their job. But in preventing crime it is of less significance than they like to think. Certainty of detection is far more important than severity of punishment." Also see the discussion of the ideas of C. B. Beccaria, an insightful eighteenth-century Italian economist and criminologist, in Radzinowicz (1948, I, 282).

[14] See, however, the discussions in Smigel (1965) and Ehrlich (1967).

[15] For a discussion of these concepts, see Sutherland (1960).

variables, such as the income available to him in legal and other illegal activities, the frequency of nuisance arrests, and his willingness to commit an illegal act. This can be represented as

$$O_j = O_j(p_j, f_j, u_j), \qquad (12)$$

where O_j is the number of offenses he would commit during a particular period, p_j his probability of conviction per offense, f_j his punishment per offense, and u_j a portmanteau variable representing all these other influences.[16]

Since only convicted offenders are punished, in effect there is "price discrimination" and uncertainty: if convicted, he pays f_j per convicted offense, while otherwise he does not. An increase in either p_j or f_j would reduce the utility expected from an offense and thus would tend to reduce the number of offenses because either the probability of "paying" the higher "price" or the "price" itself would increase.[17] That is,

$$O_{pj} = \frac{\partial O_j}{\partial p_j} < 0$$

and $\qquad\qquad\qquad\qquad (13)$

$$O_{fj} = \frac{\partial O_j}{\partial f_j} < 0.$$

which are the generally accepted restrictions mentioned above. The effect of changes in some components of u_j could also be anticipated. For example, a rise in the income available in legal activities or an increase in law-abidingness due, say, to "education" would reduce the incentive to enter illegal activities and thus would reduce the number of offenses. Or a shift in the form of the punishment, say, from a fine to imprisonment, would tend to reduce the number of offenses, at least temporarily, because they cannot be committed while in prison.

This approach also has an interesting interpretation of the presumed greater response to a change in the probability than in the punishment. An increase in p_j "compensated" by an equal percentage reduction in f_j would not change the expected income from an offense[18] but could change the expected utility, because the amount of risk would change. It is easily shown that an increase in p_j would reduce the expected utility, and thus the number of offenses, more than an equal percentage increase in f_j[19] if j has preference for risk; the increase in f_j would have the greater effect if he has aversion to risk; and they would have the same effect if he is risk neutral.[20] The widespread generalization that offenders are

---

[16] Both p_j and f_j might be considered distributions that depend on the judge, jury, prosecutor, etc., that j happens to receive. Among other things, u_j depends on the p's and f's meted out for other competing offenses. For evidence indicating that offenders do substitute among offenses, see Smigel (1965).

[17] The utility expected from committing an offense is defined as

$$EU_j = p_j U_j(Y_j - f_j) + (1 - p_j)U_j(Y_j),$$

where Y_j is his income, monetary plus psychic, from an offense; U_j is his utility function; and f_j is to be interpreted as the monetary equivalent of the punishment. Then

$$\frac{\partial EU_j}{\partial p_j} = U_j(Y_j - f_j) - U_j(Y_j) < 0$$

and

$$\frac{\partial EU_j}{\partial f_j} = -p_j U'_j(Y_j - f_j) < 0$$

as long as the marginal utility of income is positive. One could expand the analysis by incorporating the costs and probabilities of arrests, detentions, and trials that do not result in conviction.

[18] $EY_j = p_j(Y_j - f_j) + (1 - p_j)Y_j = Y_j - p_j f_j.$

[19] This means that an increase in p_j "compensated" by a reduction in f_j would reduce utility and offenses.

[20] From n. 17

$$-\frac{\partial EU_j}{\partial p_j} \frac{p_j}{U_j}$$

$$= [U_j(Y) - U_j(_jY - f_j)] \frac{p_j}{U_j} \gtrless -\frac{\partial EU_j}{\partial f_j} \frac{f_j}{U_j}$$

$$= p_j U'_j(Y_j - f_j) \frac{f_j}{U_j}$$

as

$$\frac{U_j(Y_j) - U_j(Y_j - f_j)}{f_j} \gtrless U'_j(Y_j - f_j).$$

The term on the left is the average change in utility between $Y_j - f_j$ and Y_j. It would be greater than, equal to, or less than $U'_j(Y_j - f_j)$ as $U''_j \gtrless 0$. But risk preference is defined by $U''_j > 0$, neutrality by $U''_j = 0$, and aversion by $U''_j < 0$.

more deterred by the probability of conviction than by the punishment when convicted turns out to imply in the expected-utility approach that offenders are risk preferrers, at least in the relevant region of punishments.

The total number of offenses is the sum of all the O_j and would depend on the set of p_j, f_j, and u_j. Although these variables are likely to differ significantly between persons because of differences in intelligence, age, education, previous offense history, wealth, family upbringing, etc., for simplicity I now consider only their average values, p, f, and u,[21] and write the market offense function as

$$O = O(p, f, u). \qquad (14)$$

This function is assumed to have the same kinds of properties as the individual functions, in particular, to be negatively related to p and f and to be more responsive to the former than the latter if, and only if, offenders on balance have risk preference. Smigel (1965) and Ehrlich (1967) estimate functions like (14) for seven felonies reported by the Federal Bureau of Investigation using state data as the basic unit of observation. They find that the relations are quite stable, as evidenced by high correlation coefficients; that there are significant negative effects on O of p and f; and that usually the effect of p exceeds that of f, indicating preference for risk in the region of observation.

A well-known result states that, in equilibrium, the real incomes of persons in risky activities are, at the margin, relatively high or low as persons are generally risk avoiders or preferrers. If offenders were risk preferrers, this implies that the real income of offenders would be lower, at the margin, than the incomes they could receive in less

[21] p can be defined as a weighted average of the p_j, as

$$p = \sum_{j=1}^{n} \frac{O_j p_j}{\sum_{i=1}^{n} O_j},$$

and similar definitions hold for f and u.

risky legal activities, and conversely if they were risk avoiders. Whether "crime pays" is then an implication of the attitudes offenders have toward risk and is not directly related to the efficiency of the police or the amount spent on combatting crime. If, however, risk were preferred at some values of p and f and disliked at others, public policy could influence whether "crime pays" by its choice of p and f. Indeed, it is shown later that the social loss from illegal activities is usually minimized by selecting p and f in regions where risk is preferred, that is, in regions where "crime does not pay."

4. Punishments　Mankind has invented a variety of ingenious punishments to inflict on convicted offenders: death, torture, branding, fines, imprisonment, banishment, restrictions on movement and occupation, and loss of citizenship are just the more common ones. In the United States, less serious offenses are punished primarily by fines, supplemented occasionally by probation, petty restrictions like temporary suspension of one's driver's license, and imprisonment. The more serious offenses are punished by a combination of probation, imprisonment, parole, fines, and various restrictions on choice of occupation. A recent survey estimated for an average day in 1965 the number of persons who were either on probation, parole, or institutionalized in a jail or juvenile home (President's Commission 1967b). The total number of persons in one of these categories came to about 1,300,-000, which is about 2 per cent of the labor force. About one-half were on probation, one-third were institutionalized, and the remaining one-sixth were on parole.

The cost of different punishments to an offender can be made comparable by converting them into their monetary equivalent or worth, which, of course, is directly measured only for fines. For example, the cost of an imprisonment is the discounted sum of the earnings foregone and the value placed on the restrictions in consumption and freedom. Since the earnings foregone and the value placed on prison restrictions vary from person to person, the cost even of a prison sentence of given duration is not a unique quantity but is generally greater, for example, to offenders who could earn more outside of prison.[22] The cost to each offender would be greater the longer the prison sentence, since both foregone earnings and foregone consumption are positively related to the length of sentences.

Punishments affect not only offenders but also other members of society. Aside from collection costs, fines paid by offenders are received as revenue by others. Most punishments, however, hurt other members as well as offenders: for example, imprisonment requires expenditures on guards, supervisory personnel, buildings, food, etc. Currently about $1 billion is being spent each year in the United States on probation, parole, and institutionalization alone, with the daily cost per case varying tremendously from a low of $0.38 for adults on probation to a high of $11.00 for juveniles in detention institutions (President's Commission, 1967*b*, pp. 193–94).

The total social cost of punishments is the cost to offenders plus the cost or minus the gain to others. Fines produce a gain to the latter that equals the cost to offenders, aside from collection costs, and so the social cost of fines is about zero, as befits a transfer payment. The social cost of probation, imprisonment, and other punishments, however, generally exceeds that to offenders, because others are also hurt. The derivation of optimality conditions in the next section is made more convenient if social costs are written in terms of offender costs as

$$f' \equiv bf, \qquad (15)$$

where f' is the social cost and b is a coefficient that transforms f into f'. The size of b

[22] In this respect, imprisonment is a special case of "waiting time" pricing that is also exemplified by queuing (see Becker, 1965, esp. pp. 515–16, and Kleinman, 1967).

varies greatly between different kinds of punishments: $b \cong 0$ for fines, while $b > 1$ for torture, probation, parole, imprisonment, and most other punishments. It is especially large for juveniles in detention homes or for adults in prisons and is rather close to unity for torture or for adults on parole.

III. OPTIMALITY CONDITIONS

The relevant parameters and behavioral functions have been introduced, and the stage is set for a discussion of social policy. If the aim simply were deterrence, the probability of conviction, p, could be raised close to 1, and punishments, f, could be made to exceed the gain: in this way the number of offenses, O, could be reduced almost at will. However, an increase in p increases the social cost of offenses through its effect on the cost of combatting offenses, C, as does an increase in f if $b > 0$ through the effect on the cost of punishments, bf. At relatively modest values of p and f, these effects might outweigh the social gain from increased deterrence. Similarly, if the aim simply were to make "the punishment fit the crime," p could be set close to 1, and f could be equated to the harm imposed on the rest of society. Again, however, such a policy ignores the social cost of increases in p and f.

What is needed is a criterion that goes beyond catchy phrases and gives due weight to the damages from offenses, the costs of apprehending and convicting offenders, and the social cost of punishments. The social-welfare function of modern welfare economics is such a criterion, and one might assume that society has a function that measures the social loss from offenses. If

$$L = L(D, C, bf, O) \qquad (16)$$

is the function measuring social loss, with presumably

$$\frac{\partial L}{\partial D} > 0, \qquad \frac{\partial L}{\partial C} > 0, \qquad \frac{\partial L}{\partial bf} > 0, \quad (17)$$

the aim would be to select values of f, C, and possibly b that minimizes L.

It is more convenient and transparent, however, to develop the discussion at this point in terms of a less general formulation, namely, to assume that the loss function is identical with the total social loss in real income from offenses, convictions, and punishments, as in

$$L = D(O) + C(p, O) + bpfO. \quad (18)$$

The term $bpfO$ is the total social loss from punishments, since bf is the loss per offense punished and pO is the number of offenses punished (if there are a fairly large number of independent offenses). The variables directly subject to social control are the amounts spent in combatting offenses, C; the punishment per offense for those convicted, f; and the form of punishments, summarized by b. Once chosen, these variables, via the D, C, and O functions, indirectly determine p, O, D, and ultimately the loss L.

Analytical convenience suggests that p rather than C be considered a decision variable. Also, the coefficient b is assumed in this section to be a given constant greater than zero. Then p and f are the only decision variables, and their optimal values are found by differentiating L to find the two first-order optimality conditions,[23]

$$\frac{\partial L}{\partial f} = D'O_f + C'O_f + bpfO_f + bpO = 0 \quad (19)$$

and

$$\frac{\partial L}{\partial p} = D'O_p + C'O_p + C_p \\ + bpfO_p + bfO = 0. \quad (20)$$

If O_f and O_p are not equal to zero, one can divide through by them, and recombine terms, to get the more interesting expressions

$$D' + C' = -bpf\left(1 - \frac{1}{\epsilon_f}\right) \quad (21)$$

and

$$D' + C' + C_p\frac{1}{O_p} = -bpf\left(1 - \frac{1}{\epsilon_p}\right), \quad (22)$$

where

$$\epsilon_f = -\frac{f}{O}O_f$$

and $\quad\quad\quad\quad\quad\quad\quad\quad\quad (23)$

$$\epsilon_p = -\frac{p}{O}O_p.$$

The term on the left of each equation gives the marginal cost of increasing the number of offenses, O: in equation (21) through a reduction in f and in (22) through a reduction in p. Since $C' > 0$ and O is assumed to be in a region where $D' > 0$, the marginal cost of increasing O through f must be positive. A reduction in p partly reduces the cost of combatting offenses, and, therefore, the marginal cost of increasing O must be less when p rather than when f is reduced (see Fig. 25.1); the former could even be negative if C_p were sufficiently large. Average "revenue," given by $-bpf$, is negative, but marginal revenue, given by the right-hand side of equations (21) and (22), is not necessarily negative and would be positive if the elasticities ϵ_p and ϵ_f were less than unity. Since the loss is minimized when marginal revenue equals marginal cost (see Fig. 25.1), the optimal value of ϵ_f must be less than unity, and that of ϵ_p could only exceed unity if C_p were sufficiently large. This is a reversal of the usual equilibrium condition for an income-maximizing firm, which is that the elasticity of demand must exceed unity, because in the usual case average revenue is assumed to be positive.[24]

Since the marginal cost of changing O through a change in p is less than that of changing O through f, the equilibrium marginal revenue from p must also be less than that from f. But equations (21) and (22) indicate that the marginal revenue from p can be less if, and only if, $\epsilon_p > \epsilon_f$. As pointed

---

[23] The Mathematical Appendix (not reprinted here) discusses second-order conditions.

[24] Thus if $b < 0$, average revenue would be positive and the optimal value of ϵ_f would be greater than 1, and that of ϵ_p could be less than 1 only if C_p were sufficiently large.

out earlier, however, this is precisely the condition indicating that offenders have preference for risk and thus that "crime does not pay." Consequently, the loss from offenses is minimized if p and f are selected from those regions where offenders are, on balance, risk preferrers. Although only the attitudes offenders have toward risk can directly determine whether "crime pays," rational public policy indirectly insures that "crime does not pay" through its choice of p and f.[25]

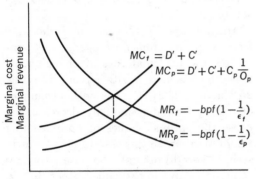

$$MC_f = D' + C'$$
$$MC_p = D' + C' + C_p \frac{1}{O_p}$$
$$MR_f = -bpf\left(1 - \frac{1}{\epsilon_f}\right)$$
$$MR_p = -bpf\left(1 - \frac{1}{\epsilon_p}\right)$$

Number of offenses

FIGURE 25.1

I indicated earlier that the actual p's and f's for major felonies in the United States generally seem to be in regions where the effect (measured by elasticity) of p on offenses exceeds that of f, that is, where offenders are risk preferrers and "crime does not pay" (Smigel, 1965; Ehrlich, 1967). Moreover, both elasticities are generally less than unity. In both respects, therefore, actual public policy is consistent with the implications of the optimality analysis.

If the supply of offenses depended only on pf—offenders were risk neutral—a reduction in p "compensated" by an equal percentage increase in f would leave unchanged pf, O, $D(O)$, and $bpfO$ but would reduce the loss, because the costs of appre-

hension and conviction would be lowered by the reduction in p. The loss would be minimized, therefore, by lowering p arbitrarily close to zero and raising f sufficiently high so that the product pf would induce the optimal number of offenses.[26] A fortiori, if offenders were risk avoiders, the loss would be minimized by setting p arbitrarily close to zero, for a "compensated" reduction in p reduces not only C but also O and thus D and $bpfO$.[27]

There was a tendency during the eighteenth and nineteenth centuries in Anglo-Saxon countries, and even today in many Communist and underdeveloped countries, to punish those convicted of criminal offenses rather severely, at the same time that the probability of capture and conviction was set at rather low values.[28] A promising explanation of this tendency is that an increased probability of conviction obviously absorbs public and private resources in the form of more policemen, judges, juries, and so forth. Consequently, a "compensated" reduction in this probability obviously reduces expenditures on combatting crime, and, since the expected punishment is unchanged, there is no "obvious" offsetting increase in either the amount of

[25] If $b < 0$, the optimality condition is that $\epsilon_p < \epsilon_f$, or that offenders are risk avoiders. Optimal social policy would then be to select p and f in regions where "crime does pay."

[26] Since $\epsilon_f = \epsilon_p = \epsilon$ if O depends only on pf, and $C = 0$ if $p = 0$, the two equilibrium conditions given by eqs. (21) and (22) reduce to the single condition

$$D' = -bpf\left(1 - \frac{1}{\epsilon}\right).$$

From this condition and the relation $O = O(pf)$, the equilibrium values of O and pf could be determined.

[27] If $b < 0$, the optimal solution is p about zero and f arbitrarily high if offenders are either risk neutral or risk preferrers.

[28] For a discussion of English criminal law in the eighteenth and nineteenth centuries, see Radzinowicz (1948, Vol. I). Punishments were severe then, even though the death penalty, while legislated, was seldom implemented for less serious criminal offenses.

Recently South Vietnam executed a prominent businessman allegedly for "speculative" dealings in rice, while in recent years a number of persons in the Soviet Union have either been executed or given severe prison sentences for economic crimes.

damages or the cost of punishments. The result can easily be continuous political pressure to keep police and other expenditures relatively low and to compensate by meting out strong punishments to those convicted.

Of course, if offenders are risk preferrers, the loss in income from offenses is generally minimized by selecting positive and finite values of p and f, even though there is no "obvious" offset to a compensated reduction in p. One possible offset already hinted at in footnote 28 is that judges or juries may be unwilling to convict offenders if punishments are set very high. Formally, this means that the cost of apprehension and conviction, C, would depend not only on p and O but also on f.[29] If C were more responsive to f than p, at least in some regions,[30] the loss in income could be minimized at finite values of p and f even if offenders were risk avoiders. For then a compensated reduction in p could raise, rather than lower, C and thus contribute to an increase in the loss.

Risk avoidance might also be consistent with optimal behavior if the loss function were not simply equal to the reduction in income. For example, suppose that the loss were increased by an increase in the ex post "price discrimination" between offenses that are not and those that are cleared by punishment. Then a "compensated" reduction in p would increase the "price discrimination," and the increased loss from this could more than offset the reductions in C, D, and $bpfO$.[31]

---

[29] I owe the emphasis on this point to Evsey Domar.

[30] This is probably more likely for higher values of f and lower values of p.

[31] If p is the probability that an offense would be cleared with the punishment f, then $1 - p$ is the probability of no punishment. The expected punishment would be $\mu = pf$, the variance $\sigma^2 = p(1 - p)f^2$, and the coefficient of variation

$$\nu = \frac{\sigma}{\mu} = \sqrt{\frac{1 - p}{p}};$$

v increases monotonically from a low of zero when

IV. SHIFTS IN THE BEHAVIORAL RELATIONS

This section analyzes the effects of shifts in the basic behavioral relations—the damage, cost, and supply-of-offenses functions —on the optimal values of p and f. Since rigorous proofs can be found in the Mathematical Appendix (not reprinted here), here the implications are stressed, and only intuitive proofs are given. The results are used to explain, among other things, why more damaging offenses are punished more severely and more impulsive offenders less severely.

An increase in the marginal damages from a given number of offenses, D', increases the marginal cost of changing offenses by a change in either p or f (see Fig. 25.2(a) and 25.2(b)). The optimal number of offenses would necessarily decrease, because the optimal values of both p and f would increase. In this case (and, as shortly seen, in several others), the optimal values of p and f move in the same, rather than in opposite, directions.[32]

$p = 1$ to an infinitely high value when $p = 0$.

If the loss function equaled

$$L' = L + \psi(\nu), \qquad \psi' > 0,$$

the optimality conditions would become

$$D' + C' = -bpf\left(1 - \frac{1}{\epsilon_f}\right) \qquad (21)$$

and

$$D' + C' + C_p\frac{1}{O_p} + \psi'\frac{d\nu}{dp}\frac{1}{O_p}$$
$$= -bpf\left(1 - \frac{1}{\epsilon_p}\right). \qquad (22)$$

Since the term $\psi'(d\nu/dp)(1/O_p)$ is positive, it could more than offset the negative term $C_p(1/O_p)$.

[32] I stress this primarily because of Bentham's famous and seemingly plausible dictum that "the more deficient in certainty a punishment is, the severer it should be" (1931, chap. ii of section entitled "Of Punishment," second rule). The dictum would be correct if p (or f) were exogenously determined and if L were minimized with respect to f (or p) alone, for then the optimal value of f (or p) would be inversely related to the given value of p (or f) (see the Mathematical Appendix [omitted here]). If, however, L is minimized with respect to both, then frequently they move in the same direction.

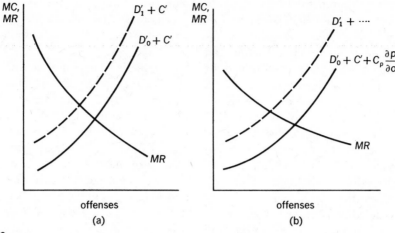

FIGURE 25.2

An interesting application of these con- clusions is to different kinds of offenses. Although there are few objective measures of the damages done by most offenses, it does not take much imagination to conclude that offenses like murder or rape generally

TABLE 25.2

PROBABILITY OF CONVICTION AND AVERAGE PRISON TERM FOR SEVERAL MAJOR FELONIES, 1960

	Murder and Non-negligent Man-slaughter	Forcible Rape	Robbery	Aggra-vated Assault	Burglary	Larceny	Auto Theft	All These Felonies Combined
1. Average time served (months) before first release:								
a) Federal civil institutions	111.0	63.6	56.1	27.1	26.2	16.2	20.6	18.8
b) State institutions	121.4	44.8	42.4	25.0	24.6	19.8	21.3	28.4
2. Probabilities of apprehension and conviction (per cent):								
a) Those found guilty of offenses known	57.9	37.7	25.1	27.3	13.0	10.7	13.7	15.1
b) Those found guilty of offenses charged	40.7	26.9	17.8	16.1	10.2	9.8	11.5	15.0
c) Those entering federal and state prisons (excludes many juveniles)	39.8	22.7	8.4	3.0	2.4	2.2	2.1	2.8

Source: 1, Bureau of Prisons (1960, Table 3); 2 (*a*) and (*b*), Federal Bureau of Investigation (1960, Table 10); 2 (*c*), Federal Bureau of Investigation (1961, Table 2), Bureau of Prisons (n.d., Table A1; 1961, Table 8).

do more damage than petty larceny or auto theft. If the other components of the loss in income were the same, the optimal probability of apprehension and conviction and the punishment when convicted would be greater for the more serious offenses.

Table 25.2 presents some evidence on the actual probabilities and punishments in the United States for seven felonies. The punishments are simply the average prison sentences served, while the probabilities are ratios of the estimated number of convictions to the estimated number of offenses and unquestionably contain a large error (see the discussions in Smigel, 1965, and Ehrlich, 1967). If other components of the loss function are ignored, and if actual and optimal probabilities and punishments are positively related, one should find that the more serious felonies have higher probabilities and longer prison terms. And one does: in the table, which lists the felonies in decreasing order of presumed seriousness, both the actual probabilities and the prison terms are positively related to seriousness.

Since an increase in the marginal cost of apprehension and conviction for a given number of offenses, C', has identical effects as an increase in marginal damages, it must also reduce the optimal number of offenses and increase the optimal values of p and f. On the other hand, an increase in the other component of the cost of apprehension and conviction, C_p, has no direct effect on the marginal cost of changing offenses with f and *reduces* the cost of changing offenses with p (see Fig. 25.3). It therefore reduces the optimal value of p and only partially compensates with an increase in f, so that the optimal number of offenses increases. Accordingly, an increase in both C' and C_p must increase the optimal f but can either increase or decrease the optimal p and optimal number of offenses, depending on the relative importance of the changes in C' and C_p.

The cost of apprehending and convicting

offenders is affected by a variety of forces. An increase in the salaries of policemen increases both C' and C_p, while improved police technology in the form of fingerprinting, ballistic techniques, computer control, and chemical analysis, or police and court "reform" with an emphasis on professionalism and merit, would tend to reduce both, not necessarily by the same extent. Our analysis implies, therefore, that although an improvement in technology and reform may or may not increase the optimal p and reduce the optimal number of offenses, it does reduce the optimal f and thus the need to rely on severe punishments for those convicted. Possibly this explains why the secular improvement in police technology and reform has gone hand in hand with a secular decline in punishments.

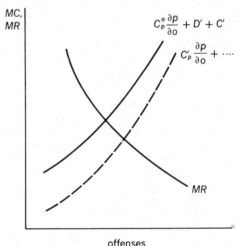

$$C_p^o \frac{\partial p}{\partial o} + D' + C'$$

$$C_p' \frac{\partial p}{\partial o} + \cdots$$

FIGURE 25.3

C_p, and to a lesser extent C', differ significantly between different kinds of offenses. It is easier, for example, to solve a rape or armed robbery than a burglary or auto theft, because the evidence of personal identification is often available in the former and not in the latter offenses.[33] This

[33] "If a suspect is neither known to the victim nor arrested at the scene of the crime, the chances of ever arresting him are very slim" (President's Commission, 1967e, p. 8). This conclusion is based on a study of crimes in parts of Los Angeles during January, 1966.

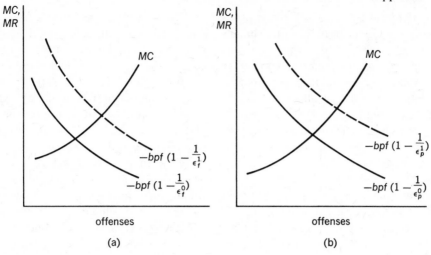

FIGURE 25.4

might tempt one to argue that the p's decline significantly as one moves across Table 25.2 (left to right) primarily because the C_p's are significantly lower for the "personal" felonies listed to the left than for the "impersonal" felonies listed to the right. But this implies that the f's would increase as one moved across the table, which is patently false. Consequently, the positive correlation between p, f, and the severity of offenses observed in the table cannot be explained by a negative correlation between C_p (or C') and severity.

If $b > 0$, a reduction in the elasticity of offenses with respect to f increases the marginal revenue of changing offenses by changing f (see Fig. 25.4(a)). The result is an increase in the optimal number of offenses and a decrease in the optimal f that is partially compensated by an increase in the optimal p. Similarly, a reduction in the elasticity of offenses with respect to p also increases the optimal number of offenses (see Fig. 25.4(b)), decreases the optimal p, and partially compensates by an increase in f. An equal percentage reduction in both elasticities a fortiori increases the optimal number of offenses and also tends to reduce both p and f. If $b = 0$, both marginal revenue functions lie along

the horizontal axis, and changes in these elasticities have no effect on the optimal values of p and f.

The income of a firm would usually be larger if it could separate, at little cost, its total market into submarkets that have substantially different elasticities of demand: higher prices would be charged in the submarkets having lower elasticities. Similarly, if the total "market" for offenses could be separated into submarkets that differ significantly in the elasticities of supply of offenses, the results above imply that if $b > 0$ the total loss would be reduced by "charging" *lower* "prices"—that is, lower p's and f's—in markets with *lower* elasticities.

Sometimes it is possible to separate persons committing the same offense into groups that have different responses to punishments. For example, unpremeditated murderers or robbers are supposed to act impulsively and, therefore, to be relatively unresponsive to the size of punishments; likewise, the insane or the young are probably less affected than other offenders by future consequences and, therefore,[34] prob-

[34] But see Becker (1962) for an analysis indicating that impulsive and other "irrational" persons may be as deterred from purchasing a commodity whose price has risen as more "rational" persons.

ably less deterred by increases in the probability of conviction or in the punishment when convicted. The trend during the twentieth century toward relatively smaller prison terms and greater use of probation and therapy for such groups and, more generally, the trend away from the doctrine of "a given punishment for a given crime" is apparently at least broadly consistent with the implications of the optimality analysis.

An increase in b increases the marginal revenue from changing the number of offenses by changing p or f and thereby increases the optimal number of offenses, reduces the optimal value of f, and increases the optimal value of p. Some evidence presented in Section II indicates that b is especially large for juveniles in detention homes or adults in prison and is small for fines or adults on parole. The analysis implies, therefore, that other things the same, the optimal f's would be smaller and the optimal p's larger if punishment were by one of the former rather than one of the latter methods.

V. FINES

A. Welfare Theorems and Transferable Pricing

The usual optimality conditions in welfare economics depend only on the levels and not on the slopes of marginal cost and average revenue functions, as in the well-known condition that marginal costs equal prices. The social loss from offenses was explicitly introduced as an application of the approach used in welfare economics, and yet slopes as incorporated into elasticities of supply do significantly affect the optimality conditions. Why this difference? The primary explanation would appear to be that it is almost always implicitly assumed that prices paid by consumers are fully transferred to firms and governments, so that there is no social loss from payment.

If there were no social loss from punishments, as with fines, b would equal zero, and the elasticity of supply would drop out of the optimality condition given by equation (21).[35] If $b > 0$, as with imprisonment, some of the payment "by" offenders would not be received by the rest of society, and a net social loss would result. The elasticity of the supply of offenses then becomes an important determinant of the optimality conditions, because it determines the change in social costs caused by a change in punishments.

Although transferable monetary pricing is the most common kind today, the other is not unimportant, especially in underdeveloped and Communist countries. Examples in addition to imprisonment and many other punishments are the draft, payments in kind, and queues and other waiting-time forms of rationing that result from legal restrictions on pricing (see Becker, 1965) and from random variations in demand and supply conditions. It is interesting, and deserves further exploration, that the optimality conditions are so significantly affected by a change in the assumptions about the transferability of pricing.

B. Optimality Conditions

If $b = 0$, say, because punishment was by fine, and if the cost of apprehending and convicting offenders were also zero, the two optimality conditions (21) and (22) would reduce to the same simple condition

$$D'(O) = 0. \qquad (24)$$

Economists generally conclude that activities causing "external" harm, such as factories that pollute the air or lumber operations that strip the land, should be taxed or otherwise restricted in level until the marginal external harm equalled the marginal

---

[35] It remains in eq. (22), through the slope O_p, because ordinarily prices do not affect marginal costs, while they do here through the influence of p on C.

private gain, that is, until marginal net damages equalled zero, which is what equation (24) says. If marginal harm always exceeded marginal gain, the optimum level would be presumed to be zero, and that would also be the implication of (24) when suitable inequality conditions were brought in. In other words, if the costs of apprehending, convicting, and punishing offenders were nil and if each offense caused more external harm than private gain, the social loss from offenses would be minimized by setting punishments high enough to eliminate all offenses. Minimizing the social loss would become identical with the criterion of minimizing crime by setting penalties sufficiently high.[36]

Equation (24) determines the optimal number of offenses, $\hat{O}$, and the fine and probability of conviction must be set at levels that induce offenders to commit just $\hat{O}$ offenses. If the economists' usual theory of choice is applied to illegal activities (see Sec. II), the marginal value of these penalties has to equal the marginal private gain:

$$V = G'(\hat{O}), \qquad (25)$$

where $G'(\hat{O})$ is the marginal private gain at $\hat{O}$ and V is the monetary value of the marginal penalties. Since by equations (3) and (24), $D'(\hat{O}) = H'(\hat{O}) - G'(\hat{O}) = 0$, one has by substitution in (25)

$$V = H'(\hat{O}). \qquad (26)$$

The monetary value of the penalties would equal the marginal harm caused by offenses.

Since the cost of apprehension and conviction is assumed equal to zero, the probability of apprehension and conviction could be set equal to unity without cost. The monetary value of penalties would then simply equal the fines imposed, and equation (26) would become

$$f = H'(\hat{O}). \qquad (27)$$

Since fines are paid by offenders to the rest of society, a fine determined by (27) would exactly compensate the latter for the marginal harm suffered, and the criterion of minimizing the social loss would be identical, at the margin, with the criterion of compensating "victims."[37] If the harm to victims always exceeded the gain to offenders, both criteria would reduce in turn to eliminating all offenses.

If the cost of apprehension and conviction were not zero, the optimality condition would have to incorporate marginal costs as well as marginal damages and would become, if the probability of conviction were still assumed to equal unity,

$$D'(\hat{O}) + C'(\hat{O}, 1) = 0. \qquad (28)$$

Since $C' > 0$, (28) requires that $D' < 0$ or that the marginal private gain exceed the marginal external harm, which generally means a smaller number of offenses than when $D' = 0$.[38] It is easy to show that equation (28) would be satisfied if the fine equalled the sum of marginal harm and marginal costs:

$$f = H'(\hat{O}) + C'(\hat{O}, 1).[39] \qquad (29)$$

In other words, offenders have to compensate for the cost of catching them as well as for the harm they directly do, which is a natural generalization of the usual externality analysis.

The optimality condition

$$D'(\hat{O}) + C'(\hat{O}, \hat{p}) + C_p(\hat{O}, \hat{p}) \frac{1}{O_p} = 0 \qquad (30)$$

would replace equation (28) if the fine rather than the probability of conviction

---

[36] "The evil of the punishment must be made to exceed the advantage of the offense" (Bentham, 1931, first rule).

[37] By "victims" is meant the rest of society and not just the persons actually harmed.

[38] This result can also be derived as a special case of the results in the Mathematical Appendix [omitted here] on the effects of increases in C'.

[39] Since equilibrium requires that $f = G'(\hat{O})$, and since from (28)

$$D'(\hat{O}) = H'(\hat{O}) - G'(\hat{O}) = -C'(\hat{O}, 1),$$

then (29) follows directly by substitution.

were fixed. Equation (30) would usually imply that $D'(\hat{O}) > 0$,[40] and thus that the number of offenses would exceed the optimal number when costs were zero. Whether costs of apprehension and conviction increase or decrease the optimal number of offenses largely depends, therefore, on whether penalties are changed by a change in the fine or in the probability of conviction. Of course, if both are subject to control, the optimal probability of conviction would be arbitrarily close to zero, unless the social loss function differed from equation (18) (see the discussion in Sec. III).

C. The Case for Fines

Just as the probability of conviction and the severity of punishment are subject to control by society, so too is the form of punishment: legislation usually specifies whether an offense is punishable by fines, probation, institutionalization, or some combination. Is it merely an accident, or have optimality considerations determined that today, in most countries, fines are the predominant form of punishment, with institutionalization reserved for the more serious offenses? This section presents several arguments which imply that social welfare is increased if fines are used *whenever feasible*.

In the first place, probation and institutionalization use up social resources, and fines do not, since the latter are basically just transfer payments, while the former use resources in the form of guards, supervisory personnel, probation officers, and the offenders' own time.[41] Table 25.1 indicates that the cost is not minor either: in the United States in 1965, about $1 billion was spent on "correction," and this estimate excludes, of course, the value of the loss in offenders' time.[42]

Moreover, the determination of the optimal number of offenses and severity of punishments is somewhat simplified by the use of fines. A wise use of fines requires knowledge of marginal gains and harm and of marginal apprehension and conviction costs; admittedly, such knowledge is not easily acquired. A wise use of imprisonment and other punishments must know this too, however, and, in addition, must know about the elasticities of response of offenses to changes in punishments. As the bitter controversies over the abolition of capital punishment suggest, it has been difficult to learn about these elasticities.

I suggested earlier that premeditation, sanity, and age can enter into the determination of punishments as proxies for the elasticities of response. These characteristics may not have to be considered in levying fines, because the optimal fines, as determined, say, by equations (27) or (29), do not depend on elasticities. Perhaps this partly explains why economists discussing externalities almost never mention motivation or intent, while sociologists and lawyers discussing criminal behavior invariably do. The former assume that punishment is by a monetary tax or fine, while the latter assume that non-monetary punishments are used.

Fines provide compensation to victims,

---

[40] That is, if, as seems plausible,

$$\frac{dC}{dp} = C'\frac{\partial O}{\partial p} + C_p > 0,$$

then

$$C' + C_p \frac{1}{\partial O/\partial p} < 0,$$

and

$$D'(\hat{O}) = -\left(C' + C_p \frac{1}{\partial O/\partial p}\right) > 0.$$

[41] Several early writers on criminology recognized this advantage of fines. For example, "Pecuniary punishments are highly economical, since all the evil felt by him who pays turns into an advantage for him who receives" (Bentham, 1931, chap. vi), and "Imprisonment would have been regarded in these old times [*ca.* tenth century] as a useless punishment; it does not satisfy revenge, it keeps the criminal idle, and do what we may, *it is costly*" (Pollock and Maitland, 1952, p. 516; my italics).

[42] On the other hand, some transfer payments in the form of food, clothing, and shelter are included.

and optimal fines at the margin fully compensate victims and restore the status quo ante, so that they are no worse off than if offenses were not committed.[43] Not only do other punishments fail to compensate, but they also require "victims" to spend additional resources in carrying out the punishment. It is not surprising, therefore, that the anger and fear felt toward ex-convicts who in fact have *not* "paid their debt to society" have resulted in additional punishments,[44] including legal restrictions on their political and economic opportunities[45] and informal restrictions on their social acceptance. Moreover, the absence of compensation encourages efforts to change and otherwise "rehabilitate" offenders through psychiatric counseling, therapy, and other programs. Since fines do compensate and do not create much additional cost, anger toward and fear of appropriately fined persons do not easily develop. As a result, additional punishments are not usually levied against "ex-finees," nor are strong efforts made to "rehabilitate" them.

One argument made against fines is that they are immoral because, in effect, they permit offenses to be bought for a price in the same way that bread or other goods are bought for a price.[46] A fine *can* be consid-

ered the price of an offense, but so too can any other form of punishment; for example, the "price" of stealing a car might be six months in jail. The only difference is in the units of measurement: fines are prices measured in monetary units, imprisonments are prices measured in time units, etc. If anything, monetary units are to be preferred here as they are generally preferred in pricing and accounting.

Optimal fines determined from equation (29) depend only on the marginal harm and cost and not at all on the economic positions of offenders. This has been criticized as unfair, and fines proportional to the incomes of offenders have been suggested.[47] If the goal is to minimize the social loss in income from offenses, and not to take vengeance or to inflict harm on offenders, then fines should depend on the total harm done by offenders, and not directly on their income, race, sex, etc. In the same way, the monetary value of optimal prison sentences and other punishments depends on the harm, costs, and elasticities of response, but not directly on an offender's income. Indeed, if the monetary value of the punishment by, say, imprisonment were independent of income, the length of the sentence would be *inversely* related to income, because the value placed on a given sentence is positively related to income.

We might detour briefly to point out some interesting implications for the probability of conviction of the fact that the

---

[43] Bentham recognized this and said, "To furnish an indemnity to the injured party is another useful quality in a punishment. It is a means of accomplishing two objects at once—punishing an offense and repairing it: removing the evil of the first order, and putting a stop to alarm. This is a characteristic advantage of pecuniary punishments" (1931, chap. vi).

[44] In the same way, the guilt felt by society in using the draft, a forced transfer *to* society, has led to additional payments to veterans in the form of education benefits, bonuses, hospitalization rights, etc.

[45] See Sutherland (1960, pp. 267–68) for a list of some of these.

[46] The very early English law relied heavily on monetary fines, even for murder, and it has been said that "every kind of blow or wound given to every kind of person had its price, and much of the jurisprudence of the time must have consisted of a knowledge of these preappointed prices" (Pollock and Maitland, 1952, p. 451).

The same idea was put amusingly in a recent

Mutt and Jeff cartoon which showed a police car carrying a sign that read: "Speed limit 30 M per H —$5 fine every mile over speed limit—pick out speed you can afford."

[47] For example, Bentham said, "A pecuniary punishment, if the sum is fixed, is in the highest degree unequal. . . . Fines have been determined without regard to the profit of the offense, to its evil, or to the wealth of the offender. . . . Pecuniary punishments should always be regulated by the fortune of the offender. The relative amount of the fine should be fixed, not its absolute amount; for such an offense, such a part of the offender's fortune" (1931, chap. ix). Note that optimal fines, as determined by eq. (29), do depend on "the profit of the offense" and on "its evil."

monetary value of a given fine is obviously the same for all offenders, while the monetary equivalent or "value" of a given prison sentence or probation period is generally positively related to an offender's income. The discussion in Section II suggested that actual probabilities of conviction are not fixed to all offenders but usually vary with their age, sex, race, and, in particular, income. Offenders with higher earnings have an incentive to spend more on planning their offenses, on good lawyers, on legal appeals, and even on bribery to reduce the probability of apprehension and conviction for offenses punishable by, say, a given prison term, because the cost to them of conviction is relatively large compared to the cost of these expenditures. Similarly, however, poorer offenders have an incentive to use more of their time in planning their offenses, in court appearances, and the like to reduce the probability of conviction for offenses punishable by a given fine, because the cost to them of conviction is relatively large compared to the value of their time.[48] The implication is that the probability of conviction would be systematically related to the earnings of offenders: negatively for offenses punishable by imprisonment and positively for those punishable by fines. Although a negative relation for felonies and other offenses punishable by imprisonment has been frequently observed and deplored (see President's Commission, 1967c, pp. 139–53), I do not know of any studies of the relation for fines or of any recognition that the observed negative relation may be more a consequence of the nature of the punishment than of the influence of wealth.

Another argument made against fines is that certain crimes, like murder or rape,

are so heinous that no amount of money could compensate for the harm inflicted. This argument has obvious merit and is a special case of the more general principle that fines cannot be relied on exclusively whenever the harm exceeds the resources of offenders. For then victims could not be fully compensated by offenders, and fines would have to be supplemented with prison terms or other punishments in order to discourage offenses optimally. This explains why imprisonments, probation, and parole are major punishments for the more serious felonies; considerable harm is inflicted, and felonious offenders lack sufficient resources to compensate. Since fines are preferable, it also suggests the need for a flexible system of instalment fines to enable offenders to pay fines more readily and thus avoid other punishments.

This analysis implies that if some offenders could pay the fine for a given offense and others could not,[49] the former should be punished solely by fine and the latter partly by other methods. In essence, therefore, these methods become a vehicle for punishing "debtors" to society. Before the cry is raised that the system is unfair, especially to poor offenders, consider the following.

Those punished would be debtors in "transactions" that were never agreed to by their "creditors," not in voluntary transactions, such as loans,[50] for which suitable precautions could be taken in advance by creditors. Moreover, punishment in any economic system based on voluntary market transactions inevitably must distinguish between such "debtors" and others. If a rich man purchases a car and a poor man steals one, the former is congratulated, while the latter is often sent to prison when apprehended. Yet the rich man's purchase is equivalent to a "theft" subsequently com-

---

[48] Note that the incentive to use time to reduce the probability of a given prison sentence is unrelated to earnings, because the punishment is fixed in time, not monetary, units; likewise, the incentive to use money to reduce the probability of a given fine is also unrelated to earnings, because the punishment is fixed in monetary, not time, units.

[49] In one study, about half of those convicted of misdemeanors could not pay the fines (see President's Commission, 1967c, p. 148).

[50] The "debtor prisons" of earlier centuries generally housed persons who could not repay loans.

pensated by a "fine" equal to the price of the car, while the poor man, in effect, goes to prison because he cannot pay this "fine."

Whether a punishment like imprisonment in lieu of a full fine for offenders lacking sufficient resources is "fair" depends, of course, on the length of the prison term compared to the fine.[51] For example, a prison term of one week in lieu of a $10,000 fine would, if anything, be "unfair" to wealthy offenders paying the fine. Since imprisonment is a more costly punishment to society than fines, the loss from offenses would be reduced by a policy of leniency toward persons who are imprisoned because they cannot pay fines. Consequently, optimal prison terms for "debtors" would not be "unfair" to them in the sense that the monetary equivalent to them of the prison terms would be less than the value of optimal fines, which in turn would equal the harm caused or the "debt."[52]

[51] Yet without any discussion of the actual alternatives offered, the statement is made that "the money judgment assessed the punitive damages defendant hardly seems comparable in effect to the criminal sanctions of death, imprisonment, and stigmatization" ("Criminal Safeguards . . . ," 1967).

[52] A formal proof is straightforward if for simplicity the probability of conviction is taken as equal to unity. For then the sole optimality condition is

$$D' + C' = -bf\left(1 - \frac{1}{\epsilon_f}\right). \tag{1'}$$

Since $D' = H' - G'$, by substitution one has

$$G' = H' + C' + bf\left(1 - \frac{1}{\epsilon_f}\right), \tag{2'}$$

and since equilibrium requires that $G' = f$,

$$f = H' + C' + bf\left(1 - \frac{1}{\epsilon_f}\right), \tag{3'}$$

or

$$f = \frac{H' + C'}{1 - b(1 - 1/\epsilon_f)}. \tag{4'}$$

If $b > 0$, $\epsilon_f < 1$ (see Sec. III), and hence by eq. (4'),

$$f < H' + C', \tag{5'}$$

where the term on the right is the full marginal harm. If p as well as f is free to vary, the analysis becomes more complicated, but the conclusion about the relative monetary values of optimal imprisonments and fines remains the same (see the Mathematical Appendix [not included here]).

It appears, however, that "debtors" are often imprisoned at rates of exchange with fines that place a low value on time in prison. Although I have not seen systematic evidence on the different punishments actually offered convicted offenders, and the choices they made, many statutes in the United States do permit fines and imprisonment that place a low value on time in prison. For example, in New York State, Class A Misdemeanors can be punished by a prison term as long as one year or a fine no larger than $1,000 and Class B Misdemeanors, by a term as long as three months or a fine no larger than $500 (*Laws of New York*, 1965, chap. 1030, Arts. 70 and 80).[53] According to my analysis, these statutes permit excessive prison sentences relative to the fines, which may explain why imprisonment in lieu of fines is considered unfair to poor offenders, who often must "choose" the prison alternative.

D. Compensation and the Criminal Law

Actual criminal proceedings in the United States appear to seek a mixture of deterrence, compensation, and vengeance. I have already indicated that these goals are somewhat contradictory and cannot generally be simultaneously achieved; for example, if punishment were by fine, minimizing the social loss from offenses would be equivalent to compensating "victims" fully, and deterrence or vengeance could only be partially pursued. Therefore, if the case for fines were accepted, and punishment by optimal fines became the norm, the traditional approach to criminal law would have to be significantly modified.

First and foremost, the primary aim of

[53] "Violations," however, can only be punished by prison terms as long as fifteen days or fines no larger than $250. Since these are maximum punishments, the actual ones imposed by the courts can, and often are, considerably less. Note, too, that the courts can punish by imprisonment, by fine, or by both (*Laws of New York*, 1965, chap. 1030, Art. 60).

all legal proceedings would become the same: not punishment or deterrence, but simply the assessment of the "harm" done by defendants. Much of traditional criminal law would become a branch of the law of torts,[54] say "social torts," in which the public would collectively sue for "public" harm. A "criminal" action would be defined fundamentally not by the nature of the action[55] but by the inability of a person to compensate for the "harm" that he caused. Thus an action would be "criminal" precisely because it results in uncompensated "harm" to others. Criminal law would cover all such actions, while tort law would cover all other (civil) actions.

As a practical example of the fundamental changes that would be wrought, consider the antitrust field. Inspired in part by the economist's classic demonstration that monopolies distort the allocation of resources and reduce economic welfare, the United States has outlawed conspiracies and other constraints of trade. In practice, defendants are often simply required to cease the objectionable activity, although sometimes they are also fined, become subject to damage suits, or are jailed.

If compensation were stressed, the main purpose of legal proceedings would be to levy fines equal to[56] the harm inflicted on society by constraints of trade. There would be no point to cease and desist orders, imprisonment, ridicule, or dissolution of companies. If the economist's theory about monopoly is correct, and if optimal fines were levied, firms would automatically cease any constraints of trade, because the gain to

them would be less than the harm they cause and thus less than the fines expected. On the other hand, if Schumpeter and other critics are correct, and certain constraints of trade raise the level of economic welfare, fines could fully compensate society for the harm done, and yet some constraints would not cease, because the gain to participants would exceed the harm to others.[57]

One unexpected advantage, therefore, from stressing compensation and fines rather than punishment and deterrence is that the validity of the classical position need not be judged a priori. If valid, compensating fines would discourage all constraints of trade and would achieve the classical aims. If not, such fines would permit the socially desirable constraints to continue and, at the same time, would compensate society for the harm done.

Of course, as participants in triple-damage suits are well aware, the harm done is not easily measured, and serious mistakes would be inevitable. However, it is also extremely difficult to measure the harm in many civil suits,[58] yet these continue to function, probably reasonably well on the whole. Moreover, as experience accumulated, the margin of error would decline, and rules of thumb would develop. Finally, one must realize that difficult judgments are also required by the present antitrust

---

[54] "The cardinal principle of damages in Anglo-American law [of torts] is that of *compensation* for the injury caused to plaintiff by defendant's breach of duty" (Harper and James, 1956, p. 1299).

[55] Of course, many traditional criminal actions like murder or rape would still usually be criminal under this approach too.

[56] Actually, fines should exceed the harm done if the probability of conviction were less than unity. The possibility of avoiding conviction is the intellectual justification for punitive, such as triple, damages against those convicted.

[57] The classical view is that $D'(M)$ always is greater than zero, where M measures the different constraints of trade and D' measures the marginal damage; the critic's view is that for some M, $D'(M) < 0$. It has been shown above that if D' always is greater than zero, compensating fines would discourage all offenses, in this case constraints of trade, while if D' sometimes is less than zero, some offenses would remain (unless $C'[M]$, the marginal cost of detecting and convicting offenders, were sufficiently large relative to D').

[58] Harper and James said, "Sometimes [compensation] can be accomplished with a fair degree of accuracy. But obviously it cannot be done in anything but a figurative and essentially speculative way for many of the consequences of personal injury. Yet it is the aim of the law to attain at least a rough correspondence between the amount awarded as damages and the extent of the suffering" (1956, p. 1301).

policy, such as deciding that certain industries are "workably" competitive or that certain mergers reduce competition. An emphasis on fines and compensation would at least help avoid irrelevant issues by focusing attention on the information most needed for intelligent social policy.

VI. PRIVATE EXPENDITURES AGAINST CRIME

A variety of private as well as public actions also attempt to reduce the number and incidence of crimes: guards, doormen, and accountants are employed, locks and alarms installed, insurance coverage extended, parks and neighborhoods avoided, taxis used in place of walking or subways, and so on. Table 25.1 lists close to $2 billion of such expenditures in 1965, and this undoubtedly is a gross underestimate of the total. The need for private action is especially great in highly interdependent modern economies, where frequently a person must trust his resources, including his person, to the "care" of employees, employers, customers, or sellers.

If each person tries to minimize his expected loss in income from crimes, optimal private decisions can be easily derived from the previous discussion of optimal public ones. For each person there is a loss function similar to that given by equation (18):

$$L_j = H_j(O_j) + C_j(p_j, O_j, C, C_k) + b_j p_j f_j O_j. \quad (31)$$

The term H_j represents the harm to j from the O_j offenses committed against j, while C_j represents his cost of achieving a probability of conviction of p_j for offenses committed against him. Note that C_j not only is positively related to O_j but also is negatively related to C, public expenditures on crime, and to C_k, the set of private expenditures by other persons.[59]

The term $b_j p_j f_j O_j$ measures the ex-

[59] An increase in C_k—O_j and C held constant—presumably helps solve offenses against j, because more of those against k would be solved.

pected [60] loss to j from punishment of offenders committing any of the O_j. Whereas most punishments result in a net loss to society as a whole, they often produce a gain for the actual victims. For example, punishment by fines given to the actual victims is just a transfer payment for society but is a clear gain to victims; similarly, punishment by imprisonment is a net loss to society but is a negligible loss to victims, since they usually pay a negligible part of imprisonment costs. This is why b_j is often less than or equal to zero, at the same time that b, the coefficient of social loss, is greater than or equal to zero.

Since b_j and f_j are determined primarily by public policy on punishments, the main decision variable directly controlled by j is p_j. If he chooses a p_j that minimizes L_j, the optimality condition analogous to equation (22) is

$$H'_j + C'_j + C_{jp_i} \frac{\partial p_j}{\partial O_j}$$
$$= -b_j p_j f_j \left(1 - \frac{1}{\epsilon j p_j}\right). [61] \quad (32)$$

[60] The expected private loss, unlike the expected social loss, is apt to have considerable variance because of the small number of independent offenses committed against any single person. If j were not risk neutral, therefore, L would have to be modified to include a term that depended on the distribution of $b_j p_j f_j O_j$.

[61] I have assumed that

$$\frac{\partial C}{\partial p_i} = \frac{\partial C_k}{\partial p_i} = 0,$$

in other words, that j is too "unimportant" to influence other expenditures. Although usually reasonable, this does suggest a modification to the optimality conditions given by eqs. (21) and (22). Since the effects of public expenditures depend on the level of private ones, and since the public is sufficiently "important" to influence private actions, eq. (22) has to be modified to

$$D' + C' + C_p \frac{\partial p}{\partial O} + \sum_{i=1}^{n} \frac{dC}{dC_i} \frac{dC_i}{dp} \frac{\partial p}{\partial O}$$
$$= -bpf \left(1 + \frac{1}{\epsilon_p}\right), \quad (22')$$

and similarly for eq. (21). "The" probability p is, of course, a weighted average of the p_j. Eq. (22') incorporates the presumption that an increase in public expenditures would be partially thwarted by an induced decrease in private ones.

The elasticity ϵ_{jp_j} measures the effect of a change in p_j on the number of offenses committed against j. If $b_j < 0$, and if the left-hand side of equation (32), the marginal cost of changing O_j, were greater than zero, then (32) implies that $\epsilon_{jp_j} > 1$. Since offenders can substitute among victims, ϵ_{jp_j} is probably much larger than ϵ_p, the response of the total number of offenses to a change in the average probability, p. There is no inconsistency, therefore, between a requirement from the optimality condition given by (22) that $\epsilon_p < 1$ and a requirement from (32) that $\epsilon_{jp_j} > 1$.

VII. SOME APPLICATIONS

A. Optimal Benefits

Our analysis of crime is a generalization of the economist's analysis of external harm or diseconomies. Analytically, the generalization consists in introducing costs of apprehension and conviction, which make the probability of apprehension and conviction an important decision variable, and in treating punishment by imprisonment and other methods as well as by monetary payments. A crime is apparently not so different analytically from any other activity that produces external harm and when crimes are punishable by fines, the analytical differences virtually vanish.

Discussions of external economies or advantages are usually perfectly symmetrical to those of diseconomies, yet one searches in vain for analogues to the law of torts and criminality. Generally, compensation cannot be collected for the external advantages as opposed to harm caused, and no public officials comparable to policemen and district attorneys apprehend and "convict" benefactors rather than offenders. Of course, there is public interest in benefactors: medals, prizes, titles, and other privileges have been awarded to military heroes, government officials, scientists, scholars, artists, and businessmen by public and private bodies. Among the most famous are Nobel Prizes, Lenin Prizes, the Congressional Medal of Honor, knighthood, and patent rights. But these are piecemeal efforts that touch a tiny fraction of the population and lack the guidance of any body of law that codifies and analyzes different kinds of advantages.

Possibly the explanation for this lacuna is that criminal and tort law developed at the time when external harm was more common than advantages, or possibly the latter have been difficult to measure and thus considered too prone to favoritism. In any case, it is clear that the asymmetry in the law does not result from any analytical asymmetry, for a formal analysis of advantages, benefits, and benefactors can be developed that is quite symmetrical to the analysis of damages, offenses, and offenders. A function $A(B)$, for example, can give the net social advantages from B benefits in the same way that $D(O)$ gives the net damages from O offenses. Likewise, $K(B, p_1)$ can give the cost of apprehending and rewarding benefactors, where p_1 is the probability of so doing, with K' and $K_p > 0$; $B(p_1, a, v)$ can give the supply of benefits, where a is the award per benefit and v represents other determinants, with $\partial B/\partial p_1$ and $\partial B/\partial a > 0$; and b_1 can be the fraction of a that is a net loss to society. Instead of a loss function showing the decrease in social income from offenses, there can be a profit function showing the increase in income from benefits:

$$\Pi = A(B) - K(B, p_1) - b_1 p_1 aB. \quad (33)$$

If Π is maximized by choosing appropriate values of p_1 and a, the optimality conditions analogous to equations (21) and (22) are

$$A' - K' = b_1 p_1 a \left(1 + \frac{1}{e_a}\right) \quad (34)$$

and

$$A' - K' - K_p \frac{\partial p_1}{\partial B} = b_1 p_1 a \left(1 + \frac{1}{e_p}\right), \quad (35)$$

where

$$e_a = \frac{\partial B}{\partial a} \frac{a}{B}$$

and

$$e_p = \frac{\partial B}{\partial p_1} \frac{p_1}{B}$$

are both greater than zero. The implications of these equations are related to and yet differ in some important respects from those discussed earlier for (21) and (22).

For example, if $b_1 > 0$, which means that a is not a pure transfer but costs society resources, clearly (34) and (35) imply that $e_p > e_a$, since both $K_p > 0$ and $\partial p_1/\partial B > 0$. This is analogous to the implication of (21) and (22) that $\epsilon_p > \epsilon_f$, but, while the latter implies that, at the margin, offenders are risk *preferrers*, the former implies that, at the margin, benefactors are risk *avoiders*.[62] Thus, while the optimal values of p and f would be in a region where "crime does not pay"—in the sense that the marginal income of criminals would be less than that available to them in less risky legal activities—the optimal values of p_1 and a would be where "benefits do pay"—in the same sense that the marginal income of benefactors would exceed that available to them in less risky activities. In this sense it "pays" to do "good" and does not "pay" to do "bad."

As an illustration of the analysis, consider the problem of rewarding inventors

[62] The relation $e_p > e_a$ holds if, and only if,

$$\frac{\partial EU}{\partial p_1} \frac{p_1}{U} > \frac{\partial EU}{\partial a} \frac{a}{U}, \qquad (1')$$

where

$$EU = p_1 U(Y + a) + (1 - p_1)U(Y) \qquad (2')$$

(see the discussion on pp. 345–346). By differentiating eq. (2'), one can write (1') as

$$p_1[U(Y + a) - U(Y)] > p_1 a U'(Y + a), \qquad (3')$$

or

$$\frac{U(Y + a) - U(Y)}{a} > U'(Y + a). \qquad (4')$$

But (4') holds if everywhere $U'' < 0$ and does not hold if everywhere $U'' \geq 0$, which was to be proved.

for their inventions. The function $A(B)$ gives the total social value of B inventions, and A' gives the marginal value of an additional one. The function $K(B, p_1)$ gives the cost of finding and rewarding inventors; if a patent system is used, it measures the cost of a patent office, of preparing applications, and of the lawyers, judges, and others involved in patent litigation.[63] The elasticities e_p and e_a measure the response of inventors to changes in the probability and magnitude of awards, while b_1 measures the social cost of the method used to award inventors. With a patent system, the cost consists in a less extensive use of an invention than would otherwise occur, and in any monopoly power so created.

Equations (34) and (35) imply that with any system having $b_1 > 0$, the smaller the elasticities of response of inventors, the smaller should be the probability and magnitude of awards. (The value of a patent can be changed, for example, by changing its life.) This shows the relevance of the controversy between those who maintain that most inventions stem from a basic desire "to know" and those who maintain that most stem from the prospects of financial awards, especially today with the emphasis on systematic investment in research and development. The former quite consistently usually advocate a weak patent system, while the latter equally consistently advocate its strengthening.

Even if A', the marginal value of an invention, were "sizeable," the optimal decision would be to abolish property rights in an invention, that is, to set $p_1 = 0$, if b_1 and K [64] were sufficiently large and/or the elasticities e_p and e_a sufficiently small. In-

[63] These costs are not entirely trivial: for example, in 1966 the U.S. Patent Office alone spent $34 million (see Bureau of the Budget, 1967), and much more was probably spent in preparing applications and in litigation.

[64] Presumably one reason patents are not permitted on basic research is the difficulty (that is, cost) of discovering the ownership of new concepts and theorems.

deed, practically all arguments to eliminate or greatly alter the patent system have been based either on its alleged costliness, large K or b_1, or lack of effectiveness, low e_p or e_a (see, for example, Plant, 1934, or Arrow, 1962).

If a patent system were replaced by a system of cash prizes, the elasticities of response would become irrelevant for the determination of optimal policies, because b_1 would then be approximately zero.[65] A system of prizes would, moreover, have many of the same other advantages that fines have in punishing offenders (see the discussion in Sec. V). One significant advantage of a patent system, however, is that it automatically "meters" A', that is, provides an award that is automatically positively related to A', while a system of prizes (or of fines and imprisonment) has to estimate A' (or D') independently and often somewhat arbitrarily.

B. The Effectiveness of Public Policy

The anticipation of conviction and punishment reduces the loss from offenses and thus increases social welfare by discouraging some offenders. What determines the increase in welfare, that is "effectiveness," of public efforts to discourage offenses? The model developed in Section III can be used to answer this question if social welfare is measured by income and if "effectiveness" is defined as a ratio of the maximum feasible increase in income to the increase if all offenses causing net damages were abolished by fiat. The maximum feasible increase is achieved by choosing optimal values of the probability of apprehension and conviction, p, and the size of punishments, f (assuming that the coefficient of social loss from punishment, b, is given).[66]

Effectiveness so defined can vary between zero and unity and depends essentially on two behavioral relations: the costs of apprehension and conviction and the elasticities of response of offenses to changes in p and f. The smaller these costs or the greater these elasticities, the smaller the cost of achieving any given reduction in offenses and thus the greater the effectiveness. The elasticities may well differ considerably among different kinds of offenses. For example, crimes of passion, like murder or rape, or crimes of youth, like auto theft, are often said to be less responsive to changes in p and f than are more calculating crimes by adults, like embezzlement, antitrust violation, or bank robbery. The elasticities estimated by Smigel (1965) and Ehrlich (1967) for seven major felonies do differ considerably but are not clearly smaller for murder, rape, auto theft, and assault than for robbery, burglary, and larceny.[67]

Probably effectiveness differs among offenses more because of differences in the costs of apprehension and conviction than in the elasticities of response. An important determinant of these costs, and one that varies greatly, is the time between commission and detection of an offense.[68] For the

---

[65] The right side of both (34) and (35) would vanish, and the optimality conditions would be

$$A' - K' = 0 \qquad (34')$$

and

$$A' - K' - K_p \frac{\partial p_1}{\partial B} = 0. \qquad (35')$$

Since these equations are not satisfied by any finite values of p_1 and a, there is a difficulty in allocating the incentives between p_1 and a (see the similar discussion for fines in Sec. V).

[66] In symbols, effectiveness is defined as

$$E = \frac{D(O_1) - [D(\hat{O}) + C(\hat{p}, \hat{O}) + b\hat{p}\hat{f}\hat{O}]}{D(O_1) - D(O_2)},$$

where $\hat{p}$, $\hat{f}$, and $\hat{O}$ are optimal values, O_1 offenses would occur if $p = f = 0$, and O_2 is the value of O that minimizes D.

[67] A theoretical argument that also casts doubt on the assertion that less "calculating" offenders are less responsive to changes in p and f can be found in Becker (1962).

[68] A study of crimes in parts of Los Angeles during January, 1966, found that "more than half the arrests were made within 8 hours of the crime, and almost two-thirds were made within the first week" (President's Commission 1967e, p. 8).

earlier an offense is detected, the earlier the police can be brought in and the more likely that the victim is able personally to identify the offender. This suggests that effectiveness is greater for robbery than for a related felony like burglary, or for minimum-wage and fair-employment legislation than for other white-collar legislation like antitrust and public-utility regulation.[69]

C. A Theory of Collusion

The theory developed in this essay can be applied to any effort to preclude certain kinds of behavior, regardless of whether the behavior is "unlawful." As an example, consider efforts by competing firms to collude in order to obtain monopoly profits. Economists lack a satisfactory theory of the determinants of price and output policies by firms in an industry, a theory that could predict under what conditions perfectly competitive, monopolistic, or various intermediate kinds of behavior would emerge. One by-product of our approach to crime and punishment is a theory of collusion that appears to fill a good part of this lacuna.[70]

The gain to firms from colluding is positively related to the elasticity of their marginal cost curves and is inversely related to the elasticity of their collective demand curve. A firm that violates a collusive arrangement by pricing below or producing more than is specified can be said to commit an "offense" against the collusion. The resulting harm to the collusion would depend on the number of violations and on the elasticities of demand and marginal cost curves, since the gain from colluding depends on these elasticities.

If violations could be eliminated without cost, the optimal solution would obviously be to eliminate all of them and to engage

in pure monopoly pricing. In general, however, as with other kinds of offenses, there are two costs of eliminating violations. There is first of all the cost of discovering violations and of "apprehending" violators. This cost is greater the greater the desired probability of detection and the greater the number of violations. Other things the same, the latter is usually positively related to the number of firms in an industry, which partly explains why economists typically relate monopoly power to concentration. The cost of achieving a given probability of detection also depends on the number of firms, on the number of customers, on the stability of customer buying patterns, and on government policies toward collusive arrangements (see Stigler, 1964).

Second, there is the cost to the collusion of punishing violators. The most favorable situation is one in which fines could be levied against violators and collected by the collusion. If fines and other legal recourse are ruled out, methods like predatory price-cutting or violence have to be used, and they hurt the collusion as well as violators.

Firms in a collusion are assumed to choose probabilities of detection, punishments to violators, and prices and outputs that minimize their loss from violations, which would at the same time maximize their gain from colluding. Optimal prices and outputs would be closer to the competitive position the more elastic demand curves were, the greater the number of sellers and buyers, the less transferable punishments were, and the more hostile to collusion governments were. Note that misallocation of resources could not be measured simply by the deviation of actual from competitive outputs but would depend also on the cost of enforcing collusions. Note further, and more importantly, that this theory, unlike most theories of pricing, provides for continuous variation, from purely competitive through intermediate situations to purely monopolistic pricing. These situations differ primarily because of differences

---

[69] Evidence relating to the effectiveness of actual, which are not necessarily optimal, penalties for these white-collar crimes can be found in Stigler (1962, 1966), Landes (1966), and Johnson (1967).

[70] Jacob Mincer first suggested this application to me.

in the "optimal" number of violations, which in turn are related to differences in the elasticities, concentrations, legislation, etc., already mentioned.

These ideas appear to be helpful in understanding the relative success of collusions in illegal industries themselves! Just as firms in legal industries have an incentive to collude to raise prices and profits, so too do firms producing illegal products, such as narcotics, gambling, prostitution, and abortion. The "syndicate" is an example of a presumably highly successful collusion that covers several illegal products.[71] In a country like the United States that prohibits collusions, those in illegal industries would seem to have an advantage, because force and other illegal methods could be used against violators without the latter having much legal recourse. On the other hand, in countries like prewar Germany that legalized collusions, those in legal industries would have an advantage, because violators could often be legally prosecuted. One would predict, therefore, from this consideration alone, relatively more successful collusions in illegal industries in the United States, and in legal ones in prewar Germany.

VIII. SUMMARY AND CONCLUDING REMARKS

This essay uses economic analysis to develop optimal public and private policies to combat illegal behavior. The public's decision variables are its expenditures on police, courts, etc., which help determine the probability (p) that an offense is discovered and the offender apprehended and convicted, the size of the punishment for those convicted (f), and the form of the punishment: imprisonment, probation, fine, etc. Optimal values of these variables can be chosen subject to, among other things,

[71] An interpretation of the syndicate along these lines is also found in Schilling (1967).

the constraints imposed by three behavioral relations. One shows the damages caused by a given p, and the third the effect of changes offenses (O), another the cost of achieving a given number of illegal actions, called in p and f on O.

"Optimal" decisions are interpreted to mean decisions that minimize the social loss in income from offenses. This loss is the sum of damages, costs of apprehension and conviction, and costs of carrying out the punishments imposed, and can be minimized simultaneously with respect to p, f, and the form of f unless one or more of these variables is constrained by "outside" considerations. The optimality conditions derived from the minimization have numerous interesting implications that can be illustrated by a few examples.

If carrying out the punishment were costly, as it is with probation, imprisonment, or parole, the elasticity of response of offenses with respect to a change in p would generally, in equilibrium, have to exceed its response to a change in f. This implies, if entry into illegal activities can be explained by the same model of choice that economists use to explain entry into legal activities, that offenders are (at the margin) "risk preferrers." Consequently, illegal activities "would not pay" (at the margin) in the sense that the real income received would be less than what could be received in less risky legal activities. The conclusion that "crime would not pay" is an optimality condition and not an implication about the efficiency of the police or courts; indeed, it holds for any level of efficiency, as long as optimal values of p and f appropriate to each level are chosen.

If costs were the same, the optimal values of both p and f would be greater, the greater the damage caused by an offense. Therefore, offenses like murder and rape should be solved more frequently and punished more severely than milder offenses like auto theft and petty larceny. Evidence on actual probabilities and punishments in the United

States is strongly consistent with this implication of the optimality analysis.

Fines have several advantages over other punishments: for example, they conserve resources, compensate society as well as punish offenders, and simplify the determination of optimal p's and f's. Not surprisingly, fines are the most common punishment and have grown in importance over time. Offenders who cannot pay fines have to be punished in other ways, but the optimality analysis implies that the monetary value to them of these punishments should generally be less than the fines.

Vengeance, deterrence, safety, rehabilitation, and compensation are perhaps the most important of the many desiderata proposed throughout history. Next to these, minimizing the social loss in income may seem narrow, bland, and even quaint. Unquestionably, the income criterion can be usefully generalized in several directions, and a few have already been suggested in the essay. Yet one should not lose sight of the fact that it is more general and powerful than it may seem and actually includes more dramatic desiderata as special cases. For example, if punishment were by an optimal fine, minimizing the loss in income would be equivalent to compensating "victims" fully and would eliminate the "alarm" that so worried Bentham; or it would be equivalent to deterring all offenses causing great damage if the cost of apprehending, convicting, and punishing these offenders were relatively small. Since the same could also be demonstrated for vengeance or rehabilitation, the moral should be clear: minimizing the loss in income is actually very general and thus is *more useful* than these catchy and dramatic but inflexible desiderata.

This essay concentrates almost entirely on determining optimal policies to combat illegal behavior and pays little attention to actual policies. The small amount of evidence on actual policies that I have examined certainly suggests a positive correspon-dence with optimal policies. For example, it is found for seven major felonies in the United States that more damaging ones are penalized more severely, that the elasticity of response of offenses to changes in p exceeds the response to f, and that both are usually less than unity, all as predicted by the optimality analysis. There are, however, some discrepancies too: for example, the actual tradeoff between imprisonment and fines in different statutes is frequently less, rather than the predicted more, favorable to those imprisoned. Although many more studies of actual policies are needed, they are seriously hampered on the empirical side by grave limitations in the quantity and quality of data on offenses, convictions, costs, etc., and on the analytical side by the absence of a reliable theory of political decision-making.

Reasonable men will often differ on the amount of damages or benefits caused by different activities. To some, any wage rates set by competitive labor markets are permissible, while to others, rates below a certain minimum are violations of basic rights; to some, gambling, prostitution, and even abortion should be freely available to anyone willing to pay the market price, while to others, gambling is sinful and abortion is murder. These differences are basic to the development and implementation of public policy but have been excluded from my inquiry. I assume consensus on damages and benefits and simply try to work out rules for an optimal implementation of this consensus.

The main contribution of this essay, as I see it, is to demonstrate that optimal policies to combat illegal behavior are part of an optimal allocation of resources. Since economics has been developed to handle resource allocation, an "economic" framework becomes applicable to, and helps enrich, the analysis of illegal behavior. At the same time, certain unique aspects of the latter enrich economic analysis: some punishments, such as imprisonments, are necessarily non-monetary and are a cost to society as well as to offenders; the degree of uncertainty is a decision variable that enters both the revenue and cost functions; etc.

Lest the reader be repelled by the apparent novelty of an "economic" framework for illegal behavior, let him recall that two important contributors to criminology during the eighteenth and nineteenth centuries, Beccaria and Bentham, explicitly applied an economic calculus. Unfortunately, such an approach has lost favor during the last hundred years, and my efforts can be viewed as a resurrection, modernization, and thereby I hope improvement on these much earlier pioneering studies.

REFERENCES

Arrow, Kenneth J. "Economic Welfare and Allocation of Resources for Invention," in National Bureau Committee for Economic Research. *The Rate and Direction of Inventive Activity: Economic and Social Factors.* Princeton, N.J.: Princeton Univ. Press (for the Nat. Bureau of Econ. Res.), 1962.

Becker, Gary S. "Irrational Behavior and Economic Theory," *J.P.E.,* Vol. LXX (February, 1962).

———. "A Theory of the Allocation of Time," *Econ. J.,* Vol. LXXV (September, 1965).

Bentham, Jeremy. *Theory of Legislation.* New York: Harcourt Brace Co., 1931.

Bureau of the Budget. *The Budget of United States Government, 1968, Appendix.* Washington: U.S. Government Printing Office, 1967.

Bureau of Prisons. *Prisoners Released from State and Federal Institutions.* ("National Prisoner Statistics.") Washington: U.S. Dept. of Justice, 1960.

———. *Characteristics of State Prisoners, 1960.* ("National Prisoner Statistics.") U.S. Dept. of Justice, n.d.

———. *Federal Prisons, 1960.* Washington: U.S. Dept. of Justice, 1961.

Cagan, Phillip. *Determinants and Effects of Changes in the Stock of Money, 1875–1960.* New York: Columbia Univ. Press (for the Nat. Bureau of Econ. Res.), 1965.

"Criminal Safeguards and the Punitive Damages Defendant," *Univ. Chicago Law Rev.,* Vol. XXXIV (Winter, 1967).

Ehrlich, Isaac. "The Supply of Illegitimate Activities." Unpublished manuscript, Columbia Univ., New York, 1967.

Federal Bureau of Investigation. *Uniform Crime Reports for the United States.* Washington: U.S. Dept. of Justice, 1960.

———. *Ibid.,* 1961.

Harper, F. V., and James, F. *The Law of Torts,* Vol. II. Boston: Little-Brown & Co., 1956.

Johnson, Thomas. "The Effects of the Minimum Wage Law." Unpublished Ph.D. dissertation, Columbia Univ., New York, 1967.

Kleinman, E. "The Choice between Two 'Bads'—Some Economic Aspects of Criminal Sentencing." Unpublished manuscript, Hebrew Univ., Jerusalem, 1967.

Landes, William. "The Effect of State Fair Employment Legislation on the Economic Position of Nonwhite Males." Unpublished Ph.D. dissertation, Columbia Univ., New York, 1966.

Laws of New York, Vol. II (1965).

Marshall, Alfred. *Principles of Economics.* 8th ed. New York: Macmillan Co., 1961.

Plant, A. "The Economic Theory concerning Patents for Inventions," *Economica,* Vol. I (February, 1934).

Pollock, F., and Maitland, F. W. *The History of English Law.* Vol. II. 2d ed. Cambridge: Cambridge Univ. Press, 1952.

President's Commission on Law Enforcement and Administration of Justice. *The Challenge of Crime in a Free Society.* Washington: U.S. Government Printing Office, 1967 (a).

———. *Corrections.* ("Task Force Reports.") Washington: U.S. Government Printing Office, 1967 (b).

————. *The Courts.* ("Task Force Reports.") Washington: U.S. Government Printing Office, 1967(c).

————. *Crime and Its Impact—an Assessment.* ("Task Force Reports.") Washington: U.S. Government Printing Office, 1967(d).

————. *Science and Technology.* ("Task Force Reports.") Washington: U.S. Government Printing Office, 1967(e).

Radzinowicz, L. *A History of English Criminal Law and Its Administration from 1750.* Vol. I. London: Stevens & Sons, 1948.

Schilling, T. C. "Economic Analysis of Organized Crime," in President's Commission on Law Enforcement and Administration of Justice. *Organized Crime.*

("Task Force Reports.") Washington: U.S. Government Printing Office, 1967.

Shawness, Lord. "Crime *Does* Pay because We Do Not Back Up the Police," *New York Times Magazine*, June 13, 1965.

Smigel, Arleen. "Crime and Punishment: An Economic Analysis." Unpublished M.A. thesis, Columbia Univ., New York, 1965.

Stigler, George J. "What Can Regulators Regulate? The Case of Electricity," *J. Law and Econ.*, Vol. V (October, 1962).

————. "A Theory of Oligopoly," *J.P.E.*, Vol. LXXII (February, 1964).

————. "The Economic Effects of the Antitrust Laws," *J. Law and Econ.*, Vol. IX (October, 1966).

Sutherland, E. H. *Principles of Criminology*, 6th ed. Philadelphia: J. B. Lippincott Co., 1960.

26. Price Discrimination in Medicine*

REUBEN A. KESSEL[1]

Reuben A. Kessel (M.B.A., Chicago, 1948; Ph.D., 1954) was born in Chicago, Illinois, in 1923. He spent several years with the RAND Corporation. In 1956 he returned to the University of Chicago, where he is now Professor of Business Economics. His special fields of interest include monetary theory, finance, and industrial organization. Kessel's study on *The Cyclical Behavior of the Term Structure of Interest Rates* has been published by the National Bureau of Economic Research and he has contributed many articles to the major professional journals.

Many distinguished economists have argued that the medical profession constitutes a monopoly, and some have produced evidence of the size of the monopoly gains that accrue to the members of this profession.[2] Price discrimination by doctors, i.e., scaling fees to the income of patients, has been explained as the behavior of a discriminating monopolist.[3] Indeed this has become the standard textbook example of discriminating monopoly.[4] However this explanation of price discrimination has

* Reprinted from the *Journal of Law and Economics* (October 1958) by permission of the publisher, pp. 20–53.

[1] The author is indebted to A. A. Alchian, W. Meckling, A. Enthoven, and W. Taylor of the RAND Corporation, W. Gorter, A. Nicols, and J. F. Weston of UCLA, H. G. Lewis and A. Rees of the University of Chicago, and Gary Becker of Columbia University for assistance.

[2] M. Friedman and S. Kuznets, *Income from Independent Professional Practice* (1945); M. Friedman in *Impact of the Trade Union*, p. 211, edited by D. M. Wright (1951); Also K. E. Boulding, *Conference on the Utilization of Scientific and Professional Manpower*, p. 23 (1944).

The results of the Friedman-Kuznets study, at p. 133, using pre-war data, indicate that the costs of producing doctors are seventeen per cent greater than the costs of producing dentists, while the average income of doctors is thirty-two per cent greater.

[3] J. Robinson, *Economics of Imperfect Competition*, p. 180 (1933). For example, the world famed Mayo Clinic discriminates in pricing. Albert Deutsch, The Mayo Clinic, 22 Consumer Reports 37, 40 (Jan. 1957). A finance department makes inquiries into the patient's economic status and scales the bills accordingly. Fees are not discussed in advance.

[4] E. A. G. Robinson, *Monopoly*, p. 77 (1941); C. E. Daugherty and M. Daugherty, *Principles of Political Economy*, p. 591 (1950); T. Scitovsky, *Welfare and Competition*, p. 408 (1941); K. E. Boulding, *Economic Analysis*, p. 662 (1955); S. Enke, *Intermediate Economic Theory*, p. 42 (1950); G. Stigler, *The Theory of Price*, p. 219 (1952).

been incomplete. Economists who have sub-scribed to this hypothesis have never in-dicated why competition among doctors failed to establish uniform prices for iden-tical services. For any individual doctor, given the existing pattern of price discrimi-nation, income from professional services would be maximized if rates were lowered for affluent patients and increased for poor patients. However, if many doctors en-gaged in such price policies, a pattern of prices for medical services would be estab-lished that would be independent of the incomes of patients. Yet despite this incon-sistency between private interests and the existing pattern or structure of prices based on income differences, this price structure has survived. Is this a contradiction of the law of markets? Why is it possible to ob-serve in a single market the same service sold at different prices?

The primary objective of this paper, which is an essay in positive economics, is to show by empirical evidence that the standard textbook rationalization of what appears to be a contradiction of the law of markets is correct. It will be argued that the discriminating monopoly model is valid for understanding the pricing of medical services, and that each individual buyer of medical services that are produced jointly with hospital care constitutes a unique, separable market. In the process of pre-senting evidence supporting this thesis, other closely related phenomena will be considered. These are (1), why the AMA favors medical insurance prepayment plans that provide money to be used to buy med-ical services, but bitterly opposes compara-ble plans that provide instead of money, the service itself and (2), why the AMA has opposed free medical care by the Vet-erans Administration for veterans despite the enormous increase in the quantity of medical services demanded that would re-sult from the reduction to zero of the pri-vate costs of medical care for such a large group.

The second half of this paper represents an attempt, by means of an application of the discriminating monopoly model, to fur-ther our understanding of many unique characteristics of the medical profession. If the medical profession constitutes a dis-criminating monopoly, what inferences can be drawn concerning the relationship be-tween this monopoly and other economic, sociological and political aspects of the medical profession? In particular, does the discriminating monopoly model shed any light upon, (1) why a higher percentage of doctors belong to professional organiza-tions than is true of other professions, (2) why doctors treat one another and their families free of charge, (3) why doctors, compared with any other professional group, are extremely reluctant to criticize one another before the public, (4) why specialists are over-represented among the hierarchy of organized medicine, (5) why a transfer of membership in good standing from one county society to a second some-times requires serving a term as a proba-tionary member, (6) why advertising that redounds to the interest of the medical pro-fession as a whole is approved whereas ad-vertising that is designed to benefit par-ticular individuals or groups is strongly opposed, (7) why malpractice insurance is less expensive for members of organized medicine than it is for non-members, or finally (8) why minority groups, particu-larly Jews, have been discriminated against in admission to medical schools? [5]

The body of this paper is divided into five sections. These are, in order of presen-tation, a hypothesis alternative to the price discrimination hypothesis, a history of the

[5] It is worth noting that there is no inconsist-ency between the validity of the explanation to be presented and the inability of any or all mem-bers of the medical profession, past, present or future, to understand the economic arguments that follow. All that is required of doctors is the ability to engage in adaptive behavior of a very rudimentary character. Consult A. A. Al-chian, Uncertainty, Evolution, and Economic Theory, 58 *J. Pol. Econ.* 211 (1950).

development of the powers that enable organized medicine to organize effectively a discriminating monopoly, evidence supporting the validity of the discriminating monopoly model for understanding the pricing of medical services, and lastly an application of the discriminating monopoly model to rationalize many characteristics of the medical profession that have been hitherto thought of as either anomalies or behavior that could best be explained as non-economic phenomena.

I. A HYPOTHESIS ALTERNATIVE TO THE DISCRIMINATING MONOPOLY MODEL

The standard position of the medical profession on price discrimination is in conflict with what might be regarded as the standard position of the economics profession. Economists argue that price discrimination by doctors represents the profit maximizing behavior of a discriminating monopolist; the medical profession takes the contrary position that price discrimination exists because doctors represent a collection agency for medical charities.[6] The income of these charities is derived from a loading charge imposed upon well-to-do patients. This income is used to finance the costs of hiring doctors to provide medical care for the poor who are sick. The doctor who is hired by the medical charity and the medical charity itself are typically the same person. Since the loading charge that is imposed upon non-charity patients to support the activities of medical charities is proportional to income or wealth, discriminatory prices result. The following quotation from an unnamed but highly re-

spected surgeon presents the position of the medical profession.

> I don't feel that I am robbing the rich because I charge them more when I know they can well afford it; the sliding scale is just as democratic as the income tax. I operated today upon two people for the same surgical condition—one a widow whom I charged $50, the other a banker whom I charged $250. I let the widow set her own fee. I charged the banker an amount which he probably carries around in his wallet to entertain his business friends.[7]

It is relevant to inquire, why have we had the development of charities operated by a substantial fraction of the non-salaried practitioners of a profession in medicine alone? Why hasn't a parallel development occurred for such closely related services as nursing and dental care? Why is it possible to observe discrimination by the Mayo Clinic but not the A and P? Clearly food is as much of a "necessity" as medical care. The intellectual foundation for the existence of price discrimination and the operation of medical charities by doctors appears to rest upon the postulate that medicine is in some sense unlike any other commodity or service. More specifically, the state is willing to provide food, clothing, and shelter for the indigent but not medical care.[8] Since medical care is so

---

[6] However, there is not a unanimity of views either among economists or medical men. Means, a retired professor of clinical medicine at Harvard and a former president of the American College of Surgeons, takes the point of view of the economists. He describes this price policy as charging what the traffic will bear. J. H. Means, *Doctors, People and Government*, p. 66 (1953).

[7] Seham, "Who Pays the Doctor?," 135 *New Republic* 10, 11 (July 9, 1956). Those who favor price discrimination for this reason ought to be in favor of a single price plan with a system of subsidies and taxes. Such a scheme, in principle, could improve the welfare of both the poor and the well-to-do relative to what it was under price discrimination.

The equity of a tax that is imposed upon the sick who are well-to-do as contrasted with a tax upon the well-to-do generally has not troubled the proponents of this method of taxation.

[8] H. Cabot contends that the community is unwilling to provide for the medical care of the indigent. Therefore the system of a sliding scale of fees has evolved; pp. 123, 266 ff. He estimates that the more opulent members of the community pay ". . . from five to thirty times the average fee . . ." p. 270, *The Doctors Bill* (1935). Robinson has defended discriminatory pricing of medical services in sparsely populated areas

important, doctors do not refuse to accept patients if they are unable to pay. As a consequence, discrimination in pricing medical services is almost inevitable if doctors themselves are not to finance the costs of operating medical charities.

The foregoing argument in defense of price discrimination in medicine implies that a competitive market for the sale of medical services is inconsistent with the provision of free services to the indigent. This implication is not supported by what can be observed elsewhere in our economy. Clearly there exist a number of competitive markets in which individual practitioners provide free goods or services and price discrimination is absent. Merchants, in their capacity of merchants, give resources to charities yet do not discriminate in pricing their services. Similarly many businesses give huge sums for educational purposes. Charity is consistent with non-discriminatory pricing because the costs of charity can be and are paid for out of the receipts of the donors without recourse to price discrimination.

However the fact that non-discriminatory pricing is consistent with charity work by doctors doesn't imply that discriminatory pricing of medical services is inconsistent with the charity hypothesis. Clearly what can be done without discrimination can, *a fortiori*, be done with discrimination. Therefore, it is pertinent to ask, is there any evidence that bears directly on the validity of the charity interpretation of price discrimination? The maximizing hypothesis of economics implies that differences in fees can be explained by differences in demand. The charity hypothesis propounded by the medical profession implies that differences in fees result from

income differences. The pricing of medical services to those who have medical insurance provides that what might be regarded as a crucial experiment for discriminating between these hypotheses. Whether or not one has medical insurance affects the demand for medical service but does not affect personal income. Consequently if the charity hypothesis is correct, then there should be no difference in fees, for specified services, for those who do and those who do not have medical insurance. On the other hand, if the maximizing hypothesis of economics is correct, then fees for those who have medical insurance ought to be higher than for those who do not have such insurance. Existing evidence indicates that if income and wealth differences are held constant, people who have medical insurance pay more for the same service than people who do not have such insurance. Union leaders have found that the fees charged have risen as a result of the acquisition of medical insurance by their members; fees, particularly for surgery, are higher than they would otherwise be if the union member were not insured.[9] Members of the insurance industry have found that ". . . the greater the benefit provided the higher the surgical bill. . . ."[10] This suggests that the principle used for the determinations of fees is, as Means pointed out, what the traffic will bear. Obviously fees determined by this principle will be highly correlated with income, although income will have no independent predictive

by using an argument based on indivisibilities. "A Fundamental Objection to Laissez-Faire," 45 *Economic Journal* 580 (1935). For a refutation of this position, see Hutt, "Discriminating Monopoly and the Consumer," 46 *Economic Journal* 61, 74 (1936).

[9] E. A. Schuler, R. J. Mowitz, and A. J. Mayer, *Medical Public Relations* (1952), report the attitude of lay leaders of the community towards the medical profession. For the attitudes of union leaders and why they have these attitudes, see p. 97 ff.

[10] Lorber in "Hearings Before the House Committee on Interstate and Foreign Commerce on Health Inquiry," 83d Cong. 2d Sess. pt. 7, p. 1954 (1954); Also Joanis, "Hospital and Medical Costs," *Proceedings of the Fourth Annual Group Meeting of the Health and Accident Underwriters Conference*, p. 18 (Feb. 19–20, 1952).

content for fees if the correlation between income and what the traffic will bear is abstracted.[11]

Other departures from the implications of the hypothesis that price discrimination results from the desires of the medical profession to finance the costs of medical care for the indigent exist. These are: (1) Doctors typically do not charge each other for medical care when clearly inter-physician fees ought to be relatively high since doctors have relatively high incomes. (2) The volume of free medical care, particularly in surgery, has declined as a result of the rise in real per capita income in this country in the last twenty years. Yet there has been no change in the extent of price discrimination. As real per capita income rises, price discrimination ought to fade away. There is no evidence that this has been the case.[12] (3) There exists no machinery for matching the receipts and disbursements of medical charities operated by individual doctors. There are no audits of the receipts and the expenditures of medical charities and well-to-do patients are not informed of the magnitude of the loading charges imposed. Moreover one study of medical care and the family budget reported ". . . no relation in the case of the individual doctor between the free services actually rendered and this recoupment, the whole system is haphazard any way you look at it." [13]

---

[11] The principle of what the traffic will bear and the indemnity principle of insurance are fundamentally incompatible and in principle make medical care uninsurable. This has been a real problem for the insurance industry and in part accounts for the relative absence from the market of major medical insurance plans. See the unpublished doctoral dissertation of A. Yousri, *Prepayment of Medical and Surgical Care in Wisconsin*, p. 438, University of Wisconsin Library (1956).

[12] Berger, "Are Surgical Fees Too High?," 32 *Medical Economics* 97, p. 100 ff. (June 1955).

[13] Deardorff and Clark, op. cit. supra note 10, pt. 6, p. 1646.

II. HISTORY OF THE DEVELOPMENT OF THE MEDICAL MONOPOLY

A necessary condition for maintaining a structure of prices that is inconsistent with the maximization by doctors of individual income is the availability and willingness to use powerful sanctions against potential price cutters. When one examines the problems that have been encountered in maintaining prices that are against the interests of individual members of a cartel composed of less than fifteen members, one cannot help being impressed with the magnitude of the problem confronting a monopoly composed of hundreds of thousands of independent producers. Yet despite the fact that medicine constitutes an industry with an extraordinarily large number of producers, the structure of prices for a large number of medical services nevertheless reflects the existence of discrimination based on income. This implies that very strong sanctions must be available to those empowered to enforce price discipline. Indeed, *a priori* reasoning suggests that these sanctions must be of an order of magnitude more powerful than anything we have hitherto encountered in industrial cartels. What are the nature of these sanctions? How are they employed? In order to appreciate fully the magnitude of the coercive measures available to organized medicine, it is relevant to examine the history of medicine to understand how these sanctions were acquired.

Medicine, like the profession of economics today, was until the founding of the AMA a relatively competitive industry. With very few exceptions, anyone who wanted to practice was free to hang out a shingle and declare himself available. Medical schools were easy to start, easy to get into, and provided, as might be expected in a free market, a varied menu of medical training that covered the complete quality spectrum. Many medical schools of this time were organized as profit-making institutions and had stock outstanding. Some schools were owned by the faculty.

In 1847, the American Medical Association was founded and this organization immediately committed itself to two propositions that were to lead to sharp restrictions upon the freedom of would-be doctors to enter the medical profession and the freedom of patients to choose doctors whom the AMA felt were not adequately qualified to practice medicine. These propositions were (1) that medical students should have acquired a "suitable preliminary education" and (2) that a "uniform elevated standard of requirements for the degree of M.D. should be adopted by all medical schools in the United States.[14]

These objectives were achieved in two stages. During the first stage, the primary concern of the AMA was licensure. In the second, it was accrediting schools of medicine. During the first stage, which began with the founding of the AMA and lasted until the turn of the century, organized medicine was able by lobbying before state legislatures to persuade legislators to license the practice of medicine. Consequently the various states set up boards of medical examiners to administer examinations to determine whether or not applicants were qualified to practice medicine and to grant licenses to those the State Board deemed qualified to practice. Generally speaking, organized medicine was very successful in its campaign to induce states to license physicians. However, the position of organized medicine was by no means unopposed. William James, in testimony offered before the State House in Boston in 1898 when legislation concerned with licensing of non-medically trained therapists was being considered, adopted a nineteenth century liberal position. To quote from this testimony:

One would suppose that any set of sane persons interested in the growth of medical truth would rejoice if other persons were found willing to push out their experience in the mental healing direction, and to provide a mass of material out of which the conditions and limits of such therapeutic methods may at last become clear. One would suppose that our orthodox medical brethren might so rejoice; but instead of rejoicing they adopt the fiercely partisan attitude of a powerful trade union, they demand legislation against the competition of the "scabs.". . . The mind-curers and their public return the scorn of the regular profession with an equal scorn, and will never come up for the examination. Their movement is a religious or quasi-religious movement; personality is one condition of success there, and impressions and intuitions seem to accomplish more than chemical, anatomical or physiological information. . . . Pray, do not fail, Mr. Chairman, to catch my point. You are not to ask yourselves whether these mind-curers do really achieve the successes that are claimed. It is enough for you as legislators to ascertain that a large number of our citizens, persons whose number seems daily to increase, are convinced that they do achieve them, are persuaded that a valuable new department of medical experience is by them opening up. Here is a purely medical question, regarding which our General Court, not being a wellspring and source of medical virtue, not having any private test of therapeutic truth, must remain strictly neutral under penalty of making the confusion worse. . . . Above all things, Mr. Chairman, let us not be infected with the Gallic spirit of regulation and regimentation for their own abstract sakes. Let us not grow hysterical about law-making. Let us not fall in love with enactments and penalties because they are so logical and sound so pretty, and look so nice on paper.[15]

[14] A. Flexner, "Medical Education in the U.S. and Canada," Bull. No. 4, *Carnegie Foundation for the Advancement of Teaching,* p. 10 (1910).

[15] 2 *Letters of W. James,* pp. 66–72 (edited H. James, 1920). Dollard reports that James took this position at the risk of being drummed out of the ranks of medicine. Dollard, "Monopoly and Medicine," speech delivered at Medical Center, UCLA, to be published by the University of California Press as one of a series of papers presented in

However, it was not until the second stage that economically effective power over entry was acquired by organized medicine. This stage began with the founding in 1904 of the Council on Medical Education of the AMA. This group dedicated itself to the task of improving the quality of medical education offered by the medical schools of the day. In 1906, this committee undertook an inspection of the 160 medical schools then in existence and fully approved of the training in only 82 schools. Thirty-two were deemed to be completely unacceptable. As might be expected, considerable resentment developed in the medical colleges and elsewhere as a result of this inspection. Consequently the council withheld publication of its findings, although the various colleges were informed of their grades.[16] In order to gain wider acceptance of the results of this study, the Council solicited the aid of the Carnegie Foundation. "If we could obtain the publication and approval of our work by the Carnegie Foundation for the Advancement of Teaching, it would assist materially in securing the results we were attempting to bring about."[17] Subsequently Abraham Flexner, representing the Carnegie Foundation, with the aid of N. P. Colwell, secretary of the Council on Medical Education, repeated the AMA's inspection and grading of medical schools. In 1910, the results of the labors of Flexner and Colwell were published.[18] This report, known as the Flexner report, recommended that a substantial fraction of the existing medical schools be closed, standards be raised in the re-

mainder, and admissions sharply curtailed. Flexner forcefully argued that the country was suffering from an overproduction of doctors and that it was in the public interest to have fewer doctors who were better trained. In effect, Flexner argued that the public should be protected against the consequences of buying medical services from inadequately trained doctors by legislating poor medical schools out of business.[19]

If impact on public policy is the criterion of importance, the Flexner report must be regarded as one of the most important reports ever written. It convinced legislators that only the graduates of first class medical schools ought to be permitted to practice medicine and led to the delegation to the AMA of the task of determining what was and what was not a first class medical school. As a result, standards of acceptability for winning a license to practice medicine were set by statute or by formal rule or informal policy of state medical examining boards, and these statutes or rules provided that boards consider only graduates of schools approved by the AMA and/or the American Association of Medical Colleges whose lists are identical.[20]

The Flexner report ushered in an era, which lasted until 1944, during which a large number of medical schools were shut down. With its new found power, the AMA

---

celebration of Robert Gordon Sproul's 25th anniversary as President of the University of California. The significance of consumers' sovereignty has been recognized by at least one other maverick doctor. Means, op. cit. supra note 6, at p. 72.

[16] Johnson in Fishbein, *A History of the American Medical Association*, p. 887 ff. (1947).

[17] Bevan, "Cooperation in Medical Education and Medical Service," 90 *Journal of the American Medical Association* 1175 (1928).

[18] Flexner, op. cit. supra note 14.

[19] Flexner, op. cit. supra note 14, at p. 14. Two errors in economic reasoning are crucial in helping Flexner establish his conclusions. One is an erroneous interpretation of Gresham's Law. This law is used to justify legislation to keep low quality doctors out of the medical care market by interpreting it to mean that second-class doctors will drive first-class doctors out of business. The other is that raising the standards of medical education is necessarily in the public interest. Flexner fails to recognize that raising standards implies higher costs of medical care. This argument is on a par with arguing that we should keep all cars of a quality below Cadillacs, Chryslers, and Lincolns off the automobile market.

[20] Hyde and Wolff, "The American Medical Association: Power, Purpose, and Politics in Organized Medicine," 63 *Yale Law Journal* 969 (1954).

vigorously attacked the problem of certification of medical schools. By exercising its power to certify, the AMA reduced the number of medical schools in the United States from 162 in 1906 to 85 in 1920, 76 in 1930 and 69 in 1944.[21] As a result of the regulation of medical schools, the number of medical students in school in the United States today is 28,500, merely 5,200 more than in 1910 when Flexner published his report.[22]

The AMA, by means of its power to certify what is and what is not a class A medical school, has substantial control over both the number of medical schools in the United States and the rate of production of doctors.[23] While the control by the AMA over such first class schools as, say, Johns Hopkins is relatively weak because it would be ludicrous not to classify this institution as a class A school, nevertheless control over the aggregate production rate of doctors is great because of its more substantial power over the output of less distinguished medical schools.

The delegation by the state legislatures to the AMA of the power to regulate the medical industry in the public interest is on a par with giving the American Iron and Steel Institute the power to determine the output of steel. This delegation of power by the states to the AMA, which was actively sought and solicited, placed this organization in a position of having to serve two masters who in part have conflicting interests. On the one hand, the AMA was given the task of providing an adequate supply of properly qualified doctors. On the other hand, the decision with respect to what is adequate training and an adequate number of doctors affects the pocketbooks of those who do the regulating as well as their closest business and personal associates. It is this power that has been given to the AMA that is the cornerstone of the monopoly power that has been imputed by economists to organized medicine.[24]

III. EVIDENCE SUPPORTING THE DISCRIMINATING MONOPOLY MODEL

The preceding analysis tells us nothing about the mechanism for controlling the price policies of individual doctors; it only implies that the rate of return on capital invested in medical training will be greater than the rate of return on capital invested

[21] These figures are from R. M. Allen, *Medical Education and the Changing Order*, p. 16 (1946). Allen imputes this decline in the number of medical schools to a previous error in estimating the demand for doctors. The decline in the number of schools in existence represented an adjustment to more correctly perceived demand conditions for medical care.

[22] Dollard, op. cit. supra note 15. This result was far from unanticipated. Bevan, the head of the AMA's Council on Medical Education, clearly anticipated a decline in both medical students and schools. "In this rapid elevation of the standard of medical education with the increase in preliminary requirements and greater length of course, and with the reduction of the number of medical schools from 160 to 80, there occurred a marked reduction in the number of medical students and medical graduates. We had anticipated this and felt that this was a desirable thing. We had an over-supply of poor mediocre practitioners." Bevan, op. cit. supra note 17, at p. 1176. Friedman and Kuznets state, "Initially, this decline in the number of physicians relative to total population was an unplanned by-product of the intensive drive for higher standards of medical education." Op. cit. supra note 5 at pp. 10–11. It may have been a by-product, and there are some grounds for doubts on this count, but it surely was not unanticipated.

[23] Dr. Spahr contends that there is a ". . . widespread but erroneous belief that the AMA governs the profession directly and determines who may practice medicine." "Medicine's Neglected Control Lever," 40 *Yale Rev.* 25 (1950). She correctly contends that this power belongs to the state but fails to recognize that it has been delegated to the AMA by the state. Mayer on the other hand recognizes both the power in the hands of the AMA and its source. He argues

that the AMA has life and death powers over both medical schools and hospitals, 180 *Harpers* 27 (Dec. 1939).

[24] Dollard, op. cit. supra note 22, concedes that medicine is a monopoly but argues that the AMA has used its power, by and large, in the public interest. Therefore, he implies that the monopoly power of the AMA has been unexploited, and the profession has acted against its own self interest.

in other classes of professional training. This difference in returns is imputable as a rent on the power of the AMA to control admissions to the profession by means of control over medical education. Here it will be argued that control over the pricing policies of doctors is directly and immediately related to AMA control of medical education. The relationship is that control over medical education is the primary instrumentality for control over individual price policies. More specifically, control over post-graduate medical training—internship and residency, and control over admission to specialty board examinations —is the source of the power over the members of the medical profession by organized medicine.

A. The Control Mechanism

Part of nearly every doctor's medical education consists of internship and for many also a period of hospital service known as residency. Internship is a necessary condition for licensure in most states. This training is administered by hospitals. However, hospitals must be approved by the AMA for intern and residency training, and most non-proprietary, i.e., nonprofit, hospitals in this country are in fact approved for at least intern training. Each approved hospital is allocated a quota of positions that can be filled by interns as part of their training. Hospitals value highly participation in internship and residency training programs. These programs are valued highly because at the prevailing wage for intern services, it is possible to produce hospital care more cheaply with interns than without them. Interns to hospitals are like coke to the steel industry: in both cases, it is perfectly possible to produce the final product without these raw materials; in both cases, the final product can be produced more cheaply by using these particular raw materials.

There exist some grounds for suspecting that the wages of interns are maintained at an artificially low level, i.e., that interns receive compensation that is less than the value of their marginal product: (1) Hospitals are reporting that there is a "shortage" of interns and have been known to send representatives to Europe and Asia to invite doctors to serve as interns.[25] (2) University hospitals are more aggressive bidders for intern services than non-university hospitals. The fraction of the available intern positions that are filled by university hospitals is greater than by non-university hospitals.[26] If controls are exercised over what hospitals can offer in wages to interns, university hospitals are apt to be less vulnerable to the threat of loss of their class A hospital ratings than non-university hospitals. This would be true for the same reason that Johns Hopkins would have a freer hand in determining the size of its freshman class. The status of university hospitals is stronger because these hospitals are likely to be among the better hospitals in the country. Therefore, if controls over intern wages exist then it seems reasonable to suspect they would be relatively weaker over the wages of interns in university hospitals. For this reason, one would expect university hospitals to be more aggressive in bidding for interns.

However, whether or not interns are underpaid, the AMA has control over the supply of a vital, in an economic sense, agent of production for producing hospital care. Revocation of a hospital's Class A rating implies the loss of interns. In turn, the loss of interns implies higher costs of production. Higher costs of production result in a deterioration of the competitive position of any given hospital vis-à-vis other hospitals in the medical care market. This control over hospitals by the AMA has been used to induce hospitals to abide

[25] "Congress to Probe Doctor Shortage," 33 *Medical Economics* 141 (June 1956).
[26] 162 *Journal of the American Medical Association* 281 (1956).

by the Mundt Resolution.[27] This resolution advises hospitals that are certified for intern training that their staff ought to be composed solely of members of local medical societies.[28] As a result of this AMA control over hospitals, membership in local medical societies is a matter of enormous importance to practicing physicians. Lack of membership implies inability to become a member of a hospital staff.[29]

County medical societies are for all practical purposes private clubs with their own rules concerning eligibility for membership and grounds for expulsion. A system of appeals from the rulings of county medical societies with respect to their members is provided. On the other hand, for non-members attempting to obtain membership in county medical societies, there is no provision for appeal. The highest court in the medical judicial system is the Judicial Council of the AMA. Between this council and the county medical societies are state medical societies. Judicial review is bound by findings of fact made at the local level.[30] For doctors dependent upon hospitals in order to carry out their practice, and presumably this constitutes the bulk of the profession, being cut off from access to hospitals constitutes a partial revocation of

their license to practice medicine. Consequently, more doctors belong to their county medical associations than is true of lawyers with respect to local bar associations. More significantly, doctors are subject to very severe losses indeed if they should be expelled from their local county medical associations or be refused admission to membership. It is this weapon, expulsion from county medical associations, that is probably the most formidable sanction employed to keep doctors from maximizing their personal incomes by cutting prices to high income patients. "Unethical" doctors, i.e., price cutters, can be in large part removed as a threat to a structure of prices that discriminates in terms of income by the use of this weapon.[31] For potential unethical physicians, it pays not to cut prices if cutting prices means being cut off from hospitals.

Thus far we have argued that control over the individual price policies of the members of the medical profession has been achieved by the AMA through its control over post-graduate medical education. By means of its power to certify a hospital for intern training, the AMA controls the source of supply of a crucial agent for the production of hospital care. Control over the supply of interns has been used to induce hospitals to admit to their staffs only members of county medical associations. Since membership in the county medical associations is in the control of organized medicine, and membership in a hospital staff is extremely important for the successful practice of most branches of medicine, the individual doctor can be easily manipulated by those who control membership in county medical associations.

Members of the medical profession are also subject to another type of control,

---

[27] "By a long record of authoritative inspection and grading of facilities, organized medicine has placed itself in a position to deny alternatively the services of doctor and hospital to each other." O. Garceau, *Political Life of the American Medical Association*, p. 109 (1941).

[28] Hyde and Wolff, op. cit. supra note 19, at p. 952. The certification of hospitals for nursing training and the value of nursing training programs to hospitals may be on a par with intern training.

[29] The strike is another instrument for control over hospitals by the AMA. Doctors have refused to work in hospitals that have admitted osteopaths to their staff. Hyde and Wolff, op. cit. supra note 19, at p. 966; M. M. Belli, *Ready for the Plaintiff*, p. 115 (1956). The threat of a strike has also been used to induce hospitals to refuse staff membership to "unethical" doctors. Group Health Etc. v. King Co. Med. Soc., 39 Wash. 2d 586, 624, 237 P. 2d 737, 757–758 (1951).

[30] Hyde and Wolff, op. cit. supra note 19, at pp. 949–950.

[31] "Ethics has always been a flexible, developing, notion in medicine, with a strong flavor of economics from the start." Garceau, op. cit. supra note 26, at p. 106. Also consult the Hippocratic Oath.

derived from AMA control over post-graduate medical education, that is particularly effective over younger members. Membership in a county medical society is a necessary condition for admission to specialty board examinations for a number of specialties, and passing these examinations is a necessary condition for specialty ratings.[32] Non-society members cannot win board membership in these specialties. This is a particularly important form of control over newcomers to the medical profession because newcomers tend to be young doctors who aspire to specialty board ratings.[33] Consequently the AMA has particularly powerful sanctions over those who are most likely to be price cutters. These are young doctors trying to establish a practice.[34]

B. The Evidence

Just as one would expect an all-out war to reveal a country's most powerful weapons, substantial threats to the continued existence of price discrimination ought to reveal the strongest sanctions available to organized medicine. For this reason, the opposition or lack of opposition to prepaid medical plans that provide medical service directly to the patient ought to be illuminating.

Generally speaking, there exist two classes of medical insurance. One is the cash indemnity variety. Blue Cross and Blue Shield plans fall within this class.[35]

Under cash indemnity medical insurance, the doctor and patient are able to determine fees jointly at the time medical service is sold just as if there were no insurance. Therefore, this class of medical insurance leaves unaffected the power of doctors to discriminate between differences in demand in setting fees. If anything, doctors welcome insurance since it improves the ability of the patient to pay. On the other hand, for non-indemnity type plans, plans that provide medical services directly as contrasted with plans that provide funds to be used to purchase desired services, payments are typically independent of income. Costs of membership in such prepayment plans are a function of family size, age, coverage, quality of service, etc., but are independent of the income of the subscriber. Consequently, such plans represent a means for massive price cutting to high income patients. For this reason, the reception of these plans by organized medicine constitutes an experiment for testing the validity of the discriminating monopoly model. If no opposition to these plans exists, then the implication of the discriminating monopoly model—that some mechanism must exist for maintaining the structure of prices—is invalid. On the other hand, opposition to these plans by organized medicine constitutes observable phenomena that support this implication. If such opposition exists, then it supports the discriminating monopoly hypothesis in addition to providing evidence of the specific character of the sanctions available to organized medicine.

A number of independent observers have found that a systematic pattern of opposition to prepaid medical service plans, as contrasted with cash indemnity plans, exists. "In many parts of the county, organ-

---

[32] Hyde and Wolff, op. cit. supra note 19, at p. 952.

[33] A statement of sanctions similar to that noted above appears in Restrictions on "Free Enterprise in Medicine," p. 9 (April 1949), pamphlet, Committee on Research in Medical Economics.

[34] "Other things being equal, old well-established concerns tend to be more hostile to price cutting than younger concerns." G. Stocking and M. Watkins, *Monopoly and Free Enterprise*, p. 117 (1951).

[35] Most of these plans have service provisions; that is, they agree to provide the service required to treat particular ailments only if the subscriber's income is below some preassigned level. Of the 78 plans approved by organized medicine, 58 have service provisions. Of these, only 3 provide service

to all income classes. The remainder provide a cash indemnity to subscribers whose income exceeds the relevant pre-assigned income levels. Therefore, these plans do not interfere with the discriminatory pricing policies of doctors. Consult "Voluntary Prepayment Medical Benefit Plans," American Medical Association (1954).

ized medical bodies have been distinctly hostile to group practice. This is particularly true where the group is engaged in any form of prepaid medical care." [36] "Early groups were disparaged as unethical. But within recent years active steps have been taken only against those groups offering a plan for some type of flat-fee payment." [37] "There is reason to believe that the Oregon, the San Diego, and the District of Columbia cases exemplify a nationwide pattern of behavior by the American Medical Association and its state and county subsidiaries. What has come into the open here is working beneath the surface in other states and counties." [38] This systematic pattern of opposition to single price medical plans has taken two distinct courses. These are (1) using sanctions in an effort to terminate the life of prepaid medical plans already in existence and (2) lobbying for legislation that would abort their birth.

There have been a number of dramatic battles for survival by prepaid non-price discriminatory medical plans resulting from the efforts of organized medicine to destroy them. These struggles have brought into action the most powerful sanctions available to organized medicine for use against price cutters. Consequently, the history of these battles provides valuable evidence of the character of the weapons available to the participants. For this purpose, the experiences of the following organizations are particularly illuminating: Farmers Union Hospital Association of Elk City, Oklahoma, the Kaiser Foundation of San Francisco and Oakland, Group Health of Washington, Group Health Cooperative of Puget Sound, Civic Medical Center of Chicago, Complete Service Bureau of San Diego, and the medical cooperatives in the State of Oregon. These plans are diverse, from the point of view of location, organization, equipment, sponsorship and objective. However, they all have one crucial unifying characteristic—fees or service charges are independent of income.[39] Similarly, the experiences of Ross-Loos in Los Angeles and the Palo Alto Clinic in California are illuminating because these organizations both operate prepayment single price medical plans and nevertheless continue to stay within the good graces of organized medicine.

The founder and director of the cooperative Farmers Union Hospital in Elk City, Oklahoma, Dr. Michael A. Shadid, was harassed for a number of years by his local county medical association as a consequence of founding and operating this price cutting organization. He was ingeniously thrown out of the Beckham County Medical Society; this organization was dissolved and reconstituted apparently for the sole purpose of not inviting Shadid to become a member of the "new" organization. Before founding the cooperative, Shadid had been a member in good standing in his county medical association for over a decade.

[36] "Building America's Health," report to the President by the Commission on the Health Needs of the Nation, V, I, p. 34 (1952).

[37] Hyde and Wolff, op. cit. supra note 19, at p. 977.

[38] Op. cit. supra note 32, at p. 14.

[39] The Health Insurance Plan of New York is not included in the foregoing enumeration because charges are not completely independent of income. For determining premiums, families are divided into two groups, those with incomes above $6,500 are assessed premiums twenty per cent greater than those applicable to the lower income group. Consult M. M. Davis, *Medical Care for Tomorrow*, p. 237 (1955). However, as a threat against the structure of prices for medical services based on income, this plan is almost as potent as those listed. Consequently, the opposition to it ought to be just about as severe and the weapons employed just as interesting for gaining insights into the nature of the sanctions over the behavior of individual doctors by organized medicine.

Available evidence suggests that HIP is under attack. See the testimony of G. Baehr, President and Medical Director of HIP in Hearings, op. cit. note 9, at pp. 1604, 1642, and 1663. Legislation that would outlaw such plans as HIP has been sponsored by organized medicine. Consult *N.Y. Times*, p. 15, col. 5 (Feb. 21, 1954).

The loss of hospital privileges stemming from non-county society membership was not sufficient for the task of putting Shadid out of business, because his organization had its own hospital. Therefore, organized medicine turned to its control over licensure to put the cooperative out of business. Shadid was equal to this challenge. He was shrewd enough to draw members of the politically potent Farmers Union into his organization. Therefore, in the struggle to take away Shadid's license to practice medicine, the farmers were pitted against the doctors. The doctors came out of this political battle the losers because the state governor at the time, Murray, sided with the farmers.[40] However, the Beckham County Medical Society has been powerful enough to keep doctors who were known to be coming to Oklahoma to join Shadid's organization from getting a license to practice, powerful enough to frighten and cause the departure of a doctor who had been associated with Shadid's organization for a substantial period of time, powerful enough to keep Shadid out of a two-week postgraduate course on bone fractures at the Cook County Graduate School of Medicine (the course was open only to members in good standing of their local county medical societies), and was able to get enough of Shadid's doctors drafted during the war to endanger the life of his organization.[41] In recent years, the tide of battle has turned. The Hospital Association brought suit against the Beckham County Medical

Society and its members for conspiracy in restraint of trade. This case was settled out of court. As part of this settlement, the county medical association agreed to accept the staff of the cooperative as members.

The experience of the Kaiser Foundation Plan is parallel to that of the Farmers Union. Both were vigorously opposed by organized medicine. The medical staff in each case could not obtain membership in local county medical societies. In both cases, the plans were able to prosper despite this obstacle, since they operated their own hospitals. In both cases, the doctor draft was used as a tool in an attempt to put these plans out of business.[42]

Control by organized medicine over licensure was used as a weapon in an attempt to kill the Kaiser Plan. Dr. Sidney Garfield, the plan's medical director, was tried by the State Board of Medical Examiners for unprofessional conduct. Garfield's license to practice was suspended for one year and he was placed on probation for five years. However, the suspension was withheld pending good behavior while on probation. This ruling by the State Board of Examiners was not supported in Court. Superior Court Judge Edward P. Murphy ordered the board to rescind all action against Garfield. The judge ruled that the board was arbitrary in denying Garfield a fair trial. Subsequently the appellate court reversed the decision of the trial court on one count but not the second. Nevertheless the judgment of the trial court in rescinding the decision of the board of examiners was upheld. The entire matter was sent back to the board for reconsideration of penalty.[43]

[40] Davis argues that Shadid would have lost his license to practice if he had not had the powerful political support of the farmers. Op. cit. supra note 38 at p. 229.

[41] The story of Shadid and his organization may be found in M. A. Shadid, *A Doctor for the People* (1939), and *Doctors of Today and Tomorrow* (1947). In Two Harbors, Minnesota, doctors associated with a medical society that disapproved the plan could not win admission to their local county medical society and a doctor associated with this plan could not get into the same school from which Shadid had been barred—the Cook County Graduate School of Medicine. 71 Christian Century 173 (Feb. 10, 1954).

[42] For evidence on this point for the Kaiser Plan, see Hearings before a Subcommittee of the Senate Committee on Education and Labor, pt. 1, p. 338 ff., 77th Cong. 2nd Sess. on S. Res. 291 (1942).

[43] P. DeKruif, *Life Among the Doctors*, p. 416 (1949). The last two chapters of this book deal with the activities of organized medicine against the Kaiser Plan. For the decision of the appellate

Subsequently, Garfield was tried by the county medical association for unethical practices, namely advertising, and found guilty. However, he came away from this trial with only a reprimand and not the loss of his license.[44] By virtue of having its own hospitals and legal intervention by the courts against the rulings of organized medicine, the Kaiser Foundation has been able to resist the onslaughts of its foes. However, the battle is not over yet. Although Kaiser Foundation doctors are now admitted to the Alameda County Society, the San-Francisco County Society still excludes them.[45]

Group Health in Washington was not as fortunate as Kaiser or Farmers Union with respect to hospitals. Unlike these other two organizations, Group Health did not have its own hospital and therefore was dependent upon the existing hospitals in the community. Consequently, when Group Health doctors were ejected from the District Medical Society, Group Health was seriously crippled. Nearly all the hospitals in the district were coerced into denying staff privileges to Group Health doctors and bed space to their patients. Moreover, many doctors were deterred from becoming members of the Group Health staff because of fear of punitive action by the District Medical Society. Still other doctors who were members of the Group Health medical staff suddenly discovered attractive employment possibilities elsewhere and resigned their Group Health positions.[46]

It was fortunate for Group Health that it was located in Washington, D.C. and therefore under the jurisdiction of federal laws, in particular the Sherman Act. The tactics of the District Medical Society and the AMA came to the attention of the Justice Department. This led to the successful criminal prosecution of organized medicine under the Sherman Act. The opinion of the Supreme Court delivered by Mr. Justice Roberts pinpoints the primary concern of the petitioners, the District Medical Society and the AMA. "In truth, the petitioners represented physicians who desired that they and all others should practice independently on a fee for service basis, where whatever arrangement for payment each had was a matter that lay between him and his patient in each individual case of service or treatment." [47]

As a result of this victory, consumer sovereignty with respect to Group Health was restored. As might be suspected from the intense opposition of the AMA and the District Medical Society, Group Health has shown unusual survival properties and flourishes in competition with fee-for-service medical care. Since its victory at court, good relations with the District Medical Society have been achieved by the Group Health staff.[48]

In view of the previous cases cited, the experience of the Group Health Cooperative of Puget Sound, Washington, takes on a familiar cast. The King County Medical Association objected to this prepayment plan. They claimed it was "unethical" because under the terms of the plan subscribers could not employ any doctor in the community. Subscribers could use only doctors who were members of the health plan. Staff members of Group Health were expelled from the county medical associa-

---

court, see Garfield v. Medical Examiners, 99 C. A. 2d 219, 221 P. 2d 705 (1950).

[44] Mayer reports that Dr. Louis Schmidt, the urologist, was expelled from organized medicine for advertising his venereal disease clinic. 180 *Harpers* 27 (Dec. 1939).

[45] Means, op. cit. supra note 5, at p. 131. Opposition to Kaiser also exists in Los Angeles area where this plan also operates. "83 Bulletin of the Los Angeles County Medical Society 501" (1953) contains a condemnation of the Kaiser Plan and a call-to-arms.

[46] Hyde and Wolff, op. cit. supra note 19, at p. 990.

[47] American Medical Association v. United States, 317 U.S. 519, 536 (1943).

[48] Becker, President, Group Health Association, Hearings before Senate Committee on Education and Labor, pt. 5, p. 2528, 79th Cong. 2nd Sess. on S. Res. 1606 (1946).

tion and new additions to the Group Health staff were found ineligible for society membership. The local medical society refused to accept transfers of membership from other county medical associations of doctors who expected to join the staff of the cooperative. The Group Health staff was unable to use the existing hospitals of the community, thereby limiting the value of the plan to many members and potential members. Moreover, the staff was cut off from many scientific meetings and was unable to consult with the orthodox members of the profession. However, the cooperative survived despite the hostility of the county medical society.

As a direct consequence of these harassing measures adopted by the King County Medical Society, the cooperative brought action against the county medical society, charging that the defendants had conspired against them in an effort to force the cooperative out of business. This case went to the state supreme court and was won by the cooperative although no damages were allowed.[49] Mr. Justice Hamley said that "The purpose of the Society . . . has been primarily to benefit the members of the Society and its affiliates through the elimination of such competition. The means employed has . . . been oppressive in the extreme. . . ."[50] Subsequently, the justice went on to argue that the activities of the county medical association against Group Health were designed to eliminate competition in the contract medicine field.[51] The court ruled that the defendants should not exclude applicants from membership in the county medical society or hospitals because of their affiliation with Group Health, and should cease discouraging doctors from joining Group Health or consulting with its staff.[52]

In testimony before a Senate Committee, Dr. Lawrence Jacques of the Civic Medical Center in Chicago reported that none of the staff of this medical center (it numbered fifteen at that time) had succeeded in being admitted to the county medical association.[53] Repeated applications for admission had either been ignored or rejected by the Chicago Medical Society. Appeals to the Illinois State Medical Society and the American Medical Association proved to be fruitless. A direct appeal by a committee of patients of the Civic Medical Center to the county medical association on behalf of their doctors was of little avail.

The doctors associated with the Complete Service Bureau of San Diego could not obtain membership in the county medical society and the patients and doctors associated with the plan were barred from the major hospitals of San Diego County. The county society published paid advertisements in the current editions of the San Diego telephone directory designating the members of the San Diego Medical Society among the physicians listed in the directory. These advertisements contained statements that gave the impression that nonsociety members were not qualified to practice medicine for professional and moral reasons. As a result of society opposition, the bureau had difficulty in hiring doctors at the going market price for their services.[54]

In Oregon, doctors serving on the staff of medical cooperatives were expelled from county medical societies and hospital facilities were made available only to doctors and the patients of doctors who were members in good standing of their local medical societies. Moreover, society members systematically refused to consult with nonsociety members and spread false propaganda in an effort to discredit society op-

[49] Group Health Etc. v. King Co. Med. Soc., 39 Wash. 2d 586, 237 P. 2d 737 (1951).

[50] Ibid., at pp. 622 and 757.

[51] Ibid., at pp. 640 and 766.

[52] Ibid., at pp. 664 and 780; Consult Means, op. cit. supra note 5, at pp. 177–181.

[53] Hearings, op. cit. supra note 47, at p. 2630 ff.

[54] Op. cit. supra note 32, at p. 11.

posed plans.[55] The government brought action against the Oregon Medical Society under the Sherman Act and lost.[56]

The Civic Medical Center in Chicago did not have its own hospital. The members of the center were able to practice in only two hospitals in the entire Chicago area, and in neither of these two hospitals did they have full staff privileges. These limited staff privileges seriously hampered the operations of the group in the two hospitals in which they could practice. For example, in one of the hospitals surgical cases could not be scheduled for more than two days in advance by a physician unless he was a full staff member. In the words of Jacques, "The handicaps of nonmembership in the local medical society are serious and far-reaching and in effect amount to a partial revocation of licensure to practice medicine." [57] During the war, some of the men in this group were disqualified for service as medical officers in the Navy, but nevertheless draftable as enlisted men, because applications to serve as medical officers were automatically rejected unless accompanied by a letter certifying that the candidate was a member in good standing of his local county medical society.[58] When Jacques was asked why his group was being excluded from the county medical association, his response was: "The evidence at hand suggests . . . that we are being excluded because of our prepayment plan." [59]

Apparently the value of price discrimination is deemed to be so great that the AMA has opposed "free" medical care to veterans by the Veterans Administration.[60] Free VA care for veterans would increase enormously the quantity of medical services demanded by making the marginal costs of these services zero for veterans.[61] Moreover opposing free care to veterans comes at a great cost to organized medicine.[62]

---

[55] Ibid.

[56] For the reasons for this loss, see United States v. Oregon Med. Soc., 343 U.S. 326 (1952) and the discussion of the case in Hyde and Wolff, op. cit. supra note 19, at p. 1020. One gets the impression from reading this case that the practices of the state society that would have led to victory for the government were discontinued in 1941.

[57] Hearings, op. cit. supra note 47, at p. 2642.

[58] Apparently this rule is no longer in effect. Consult Hyde and Wolff, op. cit. supra note 19, at p. 951 n. 84.

[59] Hearings, op. cit. supra note 47, at p. 2644.

[60] It seems likely that the value of price discrimination has increased in recent years. In the last two decades, there has been a widespread development of consumer credit. This development has made it possible for credit bureaus to collect extensive and reliable data on consumer incomes. Such data are available to subscribers to credit bureau services. Therefore, doctors that belong to credit bureaus are able to price discriminate more precisely than would have been possible if they had to rely on the unsupported testimony of patients for income data. ". . . routine credit check of patient who had always been billed at modest rates—and learned that he was in fact the owner of thirty oil wells!" "Mills, Credit Ratings: How You Can Use Them," 33 *Medical Economics* 171, 172 (May 1956).

[61] AMA opposition to free medical care for veterans constitutes evidence against the hypothesis that the AMA opposes direct service non-indemnity type group plans because they increase the efficiency with which medical resources are employed and therefore effectively increase the supply of doctors.

Still stronger evidence against the rationalization of opposition to direct service prepayment plans as a manifestation of opposition to changes that increase the efficiency with which the existing stock of doctors can be utilized, i.e., increase the supply schedule of physicians' services, is the relative lack of opposition to group practices. Therefore, unless one is willing to postulate that it is the method of payment associated with prepayment medical plans that is a source of efficiency, one cannot argue that opposition to prepayment plans is on a par with the destruction by workers of machines that improve workers' efficiency.

"Group practice of medicine on a fee-for-service basis is tolerated and even admired by most doctors. The entire profession also strongly advocates voluntary medical insurance. Yet many physicians and some local medical societies violently disapprove of the combination of group practice with pre-payment and do everything in their power to prevent or destroy it." Baehr, Hearings, op. cit. supra note 9, at p. 1642.

[62] This opposition has won organized medicine a powerful foe. A. J. Connell, an ex-National Commander of the American Legion has attacked organized medicine as a "most powerful and monopolistic medical guild." *N.Y. Times*, p. 17, col.

If price discrimination is in fact highly valued by organized medicine and prepayment direct service medical plans have been opposed in order to maintain a structure of discriminating prices, doesn't the existence of the prepayment plans unopposed by the AMA constitute an anomaly?[63]

How can the Ross-Loos and Palo Alto Clinic cases be explained?[64] The Ross-Loos plan in Los Angeles is a prepaid medical plan that is a profit-seeking organization. It was started in 1929 and by the end of 1952 had 127,000 members.[65] The Ross-Loos plan does not have hospitals of its own and is therefore forced to rely on the existing hospitals of the community. Consequently, the condemnation of this plan by organized medicine which occurred after it won acceptance from consumers in the medical care market, represented an enormous threat to its continued existence. The Ross-Loos plan doctors were expelled from the Los Angeles County Medical Associa-

tion. Among the doctors to lose their county society membership was a former President of the Los Angeles County Medical Society. As a result of a number of appeals to higher courts, all within the judicial machinery of organized medicine, the decision that would have crippled if not destroyed this plan was reversed.

An excellent reason for this reversal is suggested by the testimony of Dr. H. Clifford Loos, a co-founder of Ross-Loos. In response to the question, "Are you handicapped to any extent by the fact that you are not able to advertise," Dr. Loos replied:

> As far as that goes, we do not care to be big, or bigger. If I had accepted all of the groups who applied to us, we would need our city hall to house us. We have put the brakes on. We can't accept too many. We feel we can't be too big.[66]

This constitutes strange behavior indeed for a profit-seeking institution that certainly ought to have no fears of Justice Department action for either being too large or monopolizing an industry. One cannot help suspecting that the amicable relations with the Los Angeles County Medical Society may have been acquired at the cost of a sharply curtailed rate of expansion.[67]

The Palo Alto Clinic in California provides prepaid medical care that is non-income discriminating to the students, employees, and faculty of Stanford University. This constitutes a small fraction of the clinic's business. Eighty-five per cent of the receipts of the clinic are attributable

---

3 (Jan. 29, 1954). In opposing "socialized medicine" these two groups were allies.

[63] Evidence of opposition to price cutting on a more modest scale exists. Individuals who have cut prices have either encountered the sanctions of organized medicine or a threat to employ these sanctions. Consult, "Medical Group's Protests Stop Polio Shot Project in Brooklyn," N.Y. *Times,* p. 33M (Sept. 12, 1956). The Los Angeles *Times* reports that Dr. Sylvan O. Tatkin filed a complaint in the Superior Court of Los Angeles charging that the local association was engaging in unlawful rate fixing. Tatkin charged that he was refused membership in the local society and therefore dropped from the staff of Behrens Memorial Hospital in Glendale as a result of price cutting. L.A. *Times,* sec. 2, p. 30, col. 4 (June 29, 1956).

Economic theory implies that there would be no point for a monopolist that has control over supply being concerned with prices directly. For a non-discriminating monopolist, control over supply implies control over prices.

[64] There is evidence that opposition to prepayment plans is not merely local society policy. In Logan County, Arkansas, the entire county society was expelled from the state society by means of charter revocation. The local society was dominated by physicians participating in a disapproved plan. 27 *Journal of the Arkansas Medical Society* 29 (1930).

[65] Hearings, op. cit. supra note 9, at p. 1451.

[66] Ibid., at p. 1469.

[67] Loos has also served as an expert witness for the San Diego County Society during its struggle with another prepayment plan. Complete Service Bureau v. San Diego County Med. Soc., 43 C. 2d 201, 212, 272, P. 2d 497, 504 (1954). Hyde and Wolff, op. cit. supra note 19, at p. 985 impute the tolerance of Ross-Loos by organized medicine to the fact that it is physician sponsored as contrasted with being lay or non-physician sponsored. The theory outlined in this paper implies that this is not a relevant distinction.

to conventional fee-for-service practice that lends itself to discriminatory pricing. This clinic continues to stay within the good graces of organized medicine. When questioned about extending the prepaid nondiscriminatory service, Dr. Russel V. Lee, Director of the Clinic and Professor of Medicine in the School of Medicine of Stanford University, threw some light upon this apparent anomaly. "Several of the industries in the area have come to us for such service. We have been trying to get our county medical society approval before we go into these things, and we are doing a little job of county medical education because in general the county medical society will not approve of anything that smacks of a closed panel." [68] This suggests that the Palo Alto Clinic is in the position of having to go to its principal competitors for permission to sell its services to new customers. This is comparable to a requirement that a Ford dealer must first obtain the permission of his competing Chevrolet dealer before he can sell Fords to non-Ford owners who have asked for the opportunity to buy them. Probably the county medical society that includes the Palo Alto Clinic does not feel that the present level of sales of prepaid medical services by this clinic is high enough to justify the costs and risks of punitive action.

Organized medicine, i.e., the AMA and its political subdivisions, has opposed prepaid non-price-discriminatory medical plans not only directly by fighting against them but also indirectly by lobbying for legislation that would make such plans illegal. State medical societies have achieved a fair degree of success in sponsoring legislation designed to prevent price cutting in the medical care market caused by prepaid medical plans. As of 1954, "there are at least 20 states that have had such laws passed at the instigation of medical societies, which are designed to prevent prepaid group practice and to keep medical practice

[68] Hearings op. cit. supra note 9, at p. 1559.

on a fee-for-service solo basis." [69] Another source says: "Most of the states now have restrictive statutes permitting only the medical profession to operate or to control prepayment medical care plans." [70] Hansen lists as one of the primary objectives of this legislation "to preserve the fee-for-service system as far as possible by controlling the financial administration of the plans." [71]

IV. IMPLICATIONS OF THE DISCRIMINATING MONOPOLY MODEL

In the preceding section, this paper has been concerned with establishing the validity of the discriminating monopoly model for understanding the pricing of an important class of medical services—those produced by doctors in hospitals. Evidence of the existence of a pattern of relatively direct and obvious controls was presented. Yet it was argued that maintaining a structure of discriminatory prices for this large number of independent producers represents a fantastically difficult control problem. Does the existence of this difficult control problem shed any light upon other aspects of the medical profession? Our concern is largely with the more subtle or less obvious methods of control over the price policies of individual doctors.

[69] Baehr, Hearings, op. cit. supra note 9, at p. 1594. Very unorthodox lobbying tactics have been successfully employed by distinguished doctors to achieve the legislative goals of organized medicine. See Osler's forthright description in H. Young, *A Surgeon's Autobiography,* p. 407 (1940).
[70] Hansen, "Laws Affecting Group Health Plans," 35 *Iowa L. Rev.* 209, 225 (1950).
[71] Ibid., at p. 209. Yet in his conclusion, Hansen argues that "Farsighted medical societies should find no valid reason for opposing group health enabling legislation. Instead they should welcome experimentation in the field of medical economics with the same spirit they welcome it in the field of medical science," pp. 235–36. It is one of the implications of this paper that the more farsighted medical societies provide the strongest opposition to experimentation in the field of medical economics.

The controls previously discussed are analogous to surgery; the controls to be discussed are analogous to preventive medicine. In particular, we explore the possibilities of a relationship between maintaining a structure of prices based on income differences and: the representation of specialists in power positions within organized medicine; discrimination against minority groups in admission to medical schools; the free treatment by doctors of other doctors and their families; the position of organized medicine on advertising; the defense of county medical association members against malpractice suits; the *no-criticism rules* that forbid unfavorable comment by one physician of another physician's work before a member of the lay public.

Specialists have more to gain from price discrimination than non-specialists because their work is more likely to be associated with hospitals. The power to withhold hospital facilities from doctors constitutes the strongest weapon for maintaining price discipline within the medical profession. Therefore, discrimination in pricing ordinary office visits as compared with services rendered in a hospital is much less pronounced. In fact, prices charged for office visits ought to be relatively independent of patients' incomes. Office care can be provided by doctors with no hospital connections whatsoever. Consequently, specialists, particularly those who do most of their work in hospitals, have a greater interest in maintaining price discrimination than general practitioners. Therefore, the fact that specialists are over-represented, as measured by the ratio of specialists to all doctors, in the AMA hierarchy is no accident.[72] This is precisely the group that has the greatest economic interest in maintaining price discipline and for this reason, are "naturals" for the job.[73]

Newcomers, even if they were formerly presidents of county societies elsewhere, are probationary members when they join some county societies.[74] They achieve full membership only after a successful term as probationary members. Relegating newcomers to a probationary status is a means for segregating from the general membership those who have a relatively high probability of being price cutters.[75] Newcomers represent a group whose members are trying to acquire practices and therefore are more likely to be price cutters than society members who have well established practices. Consequently newcomers require both an extraordinary degree of surveillance and a strong indication of the costs of non-compliance. Probationary membership achieves both of these objectives.[76]

The advertisement of medical services is approved by the medical profession if and only if such advertisements redound to the interest of the profession as a whole. Ad-

---

archy as attributable to their greater incomes. Larger incomes imply that specialists are better able to afford the "luxury" of political activity. This explanation implies that psychiatrists and dermatologists ought to be just as over-represented as surgeons, abstracting from income differences. On the other hand, the argument advanced here implies that surgeons ought to be more strongly represented because membership in the AMA hierarchy can be more useful for advancing the economic interests of surgeons than it can be for those other specialities. This difference stems from the fact that psychiatrists and dermatologists do not use hospitals to the same extent in their practices.

There exists some reason for believing that among specialists, surgeons are over-represented in medical politics. One observer reports, "Our medical societies are not merely specialist-dominated; they are surgeon-dominated." Berger, op. cit. supra note 11, p. 272.

[74] Hyde and Wolff, op. cit. supra note 19, at p. 941 n. 20 and p. 951 n. 83.

[75] Stocking and Watkins, op. cit. supra note 33, at p. 117.

[76] Some societies have indoctrination programs for newcomers. Drennen, "They Help Young Doctors Get Started Right," 32 *Medical Economics* 104 (June, 1955). Drennen observes that for the newcomer such a program ". . . helps keep him on the path of righteousness," p. 108.

---

[72] Garceau, op. cit. supra note 26, at pp. 55–58. Hyde and Wolff, op. cit. supra note 19, at p. 947.

[73] Some observers have explained the over-representation of specialists in the AMA hier-

vertisements in this class are, for example, announcements of the availability for sale of Blue Cross type medical plans. These plans allow their subscribers the choice of any licensed practitioner. Organized medicine consequently takes the position that these advertisements are of benefit to the entire profession. On the other hand, advertisements that primarily redound to the interests of a particular group, for example, advertisements by a closed panel medical group, are frowned upon. Advertisements in this class are, by definition, resorted to only by "unethical" doctors. Why this difference in the position of organized medicine with respect to these two classes of advertising? The approved class, insofar as it achieves its objective, tends to increase the aggregate demand for medical care. On the other hand, the disapproved variety will have the effect of reallocating patients from the profession as a whole to those who advertise. Consequently, advertising in this class constitutes competitive behavior and leads to price cutting. It tends to pit one doctor or one group of doctors against the profession as a whole with respect to shares of the medical care market. Active competition for increased shares of the medical care market by doctors would tend to eliminate price discrimination based on income differences.

The significance of advertising as a means for maintaining free entry is revealed by two bits of interrelated evidence. These are the strong opposition of organized medicine to advertising calling the public's attention to the services of a particular group of doctors and the willingness of some prepaid medical plans to incur the wrath of organized medicine by undertaking such advertising. Kaiser, the Civic Medical Center, and the Complete Service Bureau at one time or another advertised.[77] The use of advertising in the

face of strong opposition by organized medicine implies that advertising plays a crucial role in enabling these groups to capture part of the medical care market. Consequently the ban on such advertising by organized medicine constitutes a barrier to entry into this market and is a means for keeping doctors from competing with one another and thereby incidentally destroying the structure of prices.

County medical societies play a crucial role in protecting their members against malpractice suits. Physicians charged with malpractice are tried by their associates in the private judicial system of organized medicine. If found innocent, then local society members are available for duty as expert witnesses in the defense of those charged with malpractice. Needless to say, comparable services by society members for plaintiffs in such actions are not equally available. By virtue of this monopoly over the services of expert witnesses and the tacit coalition of the members of a society in the defense of any of their members, the successful prosecution of malpractice suits against society members is extremely difficult.

On the other hand, for doctors who are persona-non-grata with respect to organized medicine, the shoe is on the other foot. Expert witnesses from the ranks of organized medicine are abundantly available for plaintiffs but not for defendants. Therefore the position of a plaintiff in a suit against a non-society member is of an order of magnitude stronger than it is for a suit against a society member. Consequently it should come as no surprise that the costs of malpractice insurance for non-society members is substantially higher than it is for society members. Apparently some non-society members have experienced difficulty

[77] "For the first ten months of its existence, with a considerable reluctance it continued the policy of institutional advertising, because it was felt that the clinic could not survive unless it was brought actively to the attention of the public." Jacques, Hearings, op. cit. supra note 41, at p. 2634. Complete Service Bureau v. San Diego County Med. Soc., 43 C. 2d 201, 214–216, 272 P. 2d 497, 504–506 (1954).

in obtaining malpractice insurance at any price.[78]

This coalition among the members of the medical profession not to testify against one another, like structured prices, puts some doctors in a position of pursuing a policy that does not maximize personal returns. Therefore more than just professional ethics makes this coalition viable. As might be expected, the ability of organized medicine to expel doctors from hospital staffs plays a crucial role in keeping doctors from testifying against one another. Belli reports that a doctor who acted as an expert witness in a malpractice suit he tried was subsequently barred from the staff of every hospital in California.[79] It is because of sanctions of this character that we can find reports of patients with strong prima facie evidence of negligence and yet unable to hire expert witnesses from the ranks of the medical profession.[80]

As a result of this coalition among society members for malpractice defense, two effects are achieved. The more direct and obvious consequence is an increase in the monopoly returns to the members of this profession over what they otherwise would be. The other is the welding together of the medical profession as an in-group. In this latter role, the coalition for malpractice defense is a force that has the same effect as a reciprocity, that is, the free treatment by doctors of other doctors and their families, and the rule that doctors are not to criticize one another in public.[81] The function of reciprocity and *no-criticism* is to induce the members of the medical profession to behave toward one another as if they were members of an in-group. Doctors are subtly coerced into personal relations with one another. Insofar as these measures bear fruit, doctors view themselves as a large association in which members deal with one another on a personal level. In relation to the general public, i.e., outsiders, the in-group, doctors, are united.

But what does the medical profession achieve by subtly coercing its members into in-group relations with one another? The relationships among members of a family, an in-group par excellence, reveal the importance of these subtle controls. Members of a family are relatively reluctant to criticize one another before outsiders, tend not to charge each other market prices for services extended to one another, and try to avoid being in direct competition. The essence of in-group behavior is personal relationships among its members. On the other hand, the essential property of market place relationships is impersonality. Consequently insofar as a non-market place attitude can be fostered and maintained within the medical profession, such an attitude constitutes a barrier against doctors thinking of one another as competitors in the medical care market. This in itself constitutes a barrier against such market place activities as cutting prices.[82]

[78] Garceau, op. cit. supra note 26, at p. 103 ff; Jacques, Hearings, op. cit. supra note 47, at p. 2642; Hyde and Wolff, op. cit. supra note 19, at p. 951 n. 86; Belli, op. cit. supra note 28, at p. 109.

[79] Belli, op. cit. supra note 28, p. 98; "The California Malpractice Controversy," 9 *Stanford L. Rev.* 731 (1957).

[80] See the story by Ullman in the *Toledo Blade* of June 12, 1946, about a surgery patient who was unable to hire an expert witness for demonstrating negligence in a case involving a sponge that a surgeon forgot to remove before sewing up the patient. Belli reports no such problem in hiring expert witnesses for legal malpractice cases. Op. cit. supra note 28, at p. 95.

[81] N. S. Davis, *History of Medicine*, ch. 14 (1907); Wylie, "Conspiracy of Silence," 29 *Medical Economics* 167 (1952); "Doctor Fights Expulsion on Slander Charge," 32 *Medical Economics* 269 (Dec. 1954). This is the story of a doctor expelled from his county medical society for expressing opinions about the professional competence of his colleagues, to patients.

[82] If the hypothesis presented here is correct, then it should be possible to observe a difference between the variance of surgical and psychiatric fees after abstracting from variations caused by differences in skills, type of operation and difficulty of particular cases. This difference would be imputable to the strong control over the pricing of surgical services by means of control over hos-

To the extent that the culture of members of an in-group is distinct from that of non-members, this difference reduces the probability that non-members can successfully "join" the in-group. Differences in culture and values constitute a natural barrier to integration. This is particularly important for medicine because it is both a social and an economic club and the returns of the economic club are related to the degree of social cohesion that exists within the social club. Consequently, members of culturally distinct minority groups would be more difficult to assimilate into such an in-group and it is likely that many would never feel that they were completely members under the best of circumstances. This implies that members of such minority groups would be more difficult to control by means of the informal controls characteristic of in-groups. Being thrown out of a country club is not much of a loss if one is only the janitor; for informal controls to be effective, they must be exercised over those who belong. Insofar as some minority groups are more difficult to assimilate, there exists an *a priori* basis for discrimination. It is to keep out those who have a higher probability of not being willing to go along with the majority. Minority groups whose culture and values are different from those of the majority could rationally be discriminated against in admission to medical schools because they are more difficult to control by informal controls after they are out in medical practice than is characteristic of the population at large.

The discrimination against Jews in admission to medical schools has been explained, by both Jews and non-Jews alike, as a consequence of irrational prejudice.[83] Yet Jews might be regarded as the prototype of a minority group with cultural properties that, given the special problems of maintaining internal discipline within the medical profession, would make them undesirable candidates for admission to this profession. These cultural attributes evolved as a consequence of centuries of unparalleled persecution. This persecution, which by and large was economic, took the form of laws that barred Jews from particular product and labor markets in many of the most important countries in the history of western civilization. Cartels such as guilds followed similar policies. This exclusion policy channeled Jews into highly competitive markets, markets characterized by free entry, and forced them to develop their commercial skills to a higher level than was

[83] For direct evidence on discrimination against Jews in admission to medical schools, consult, Hart, "Anti-Semitism in Medical Schools," 65 *American Mercury* 53 (July 1947); Kingdon, "Discrimination in Medical Colleges," 60 *American Mercury* 391 (Oct. 1945); Bloomgarden, "Medical School Quotas and National Health," 15 *Commentary* 29 (Jan. 1953); Goldberg, "Jews in the Medical Profession—A National Survey," 1 *Jewish Social Studies* 327 (1939); Shapiro, "Racial Discrimination in Medicine," 10 *Jewish Social Studies* 103 (1948).

The indirect evidence on this point seems to be more convincing than the direct evidence. Practically all of the Americans who study medicine abroad are Jews. No comparable evidence for the study by American Jews of law, dentistry, accounting, engineering, etc. in foreign countries exists. Therefore, the hypothesis that Jews prefer to study abroad is not tenable. On the other hand, this evidence is consistent with the hypothesis that Jews are strongly discriminated against in this country. Consult Levinger, Jewish Medical Students in America, 2 Medical Leaves 91, 94 (1939) and Goldberg, supra at p. 332.

Some observers have used a Noah's Ark approach to determine whether or not discrimination against Jews in admission to medical schools exists or existed. Because the ratio of Jewish medical students to all medical students exceeds the ratio of all Jews to our total population, some observers have concluded discrimination is absent. D. S. Berkowitz, *Inequality of Opportunity in Higher Education* (1948).

pitals. Since reciprocity and *no-criticism* rules are viable because they help maintain structured prices, they should not be observed as rigorously by psychiatrists as surgeons. On this latter point, there exists evidence consistent with the hypothesis presented here. Psychiatrists have been the first, and thus far the only group within the medical profession to abandon reciprocity. Miller, "Doctors Should Pay for Medical Care!," 30 *Medical Economics* 82, 84 (Jan. 1953).

characteristic of the population at large in order to survive economically. For Jews, a medieval guild type share-the-market attitude was a non-survival property whereas a policy of vigorously competing was a survival property. The process of adaptation by Jews to laws constraining their economic activities led them to develop considerable ingenuity in minimizing the impact of such laws upon their economic well being. Jews developed into robust competitors with little respect for rules, either government or private, that regulated economic activities and with a substantial body of practical experience in implementing this point of view.[84] These attitudes became a part of Jewish cultural tradition and at least in this respect, distinguished Jews from non-Jews. This was particularly true of Jews that came from Czarist Russia and Poland where discrimination against them was particularly strong.[85]

Because of these special cultural properties, which are vestigial in the United States and therefore are in the process of fading away, the discrimination against Jews in admission to medical schools is far from irrational if one is concerned with maintaining price discrimination in medicine. The *a priori* probability of a Jew being a price cutter because of the special attributes developed in an effort to survive in a hostile environment is greater than that for a non-Jew. The Jewish doctor is more likely to have a commercial market place attitude toward other members of his profession than is the non-Jew. From the point of view of the medical profession, as one doctor expressed it, Jews ". . . spoil everything they go into by turning it into a business." [86]

If, as this analysis implies, admission to

[84] The same problem of survival in a hostile world has led a number of observers to argue that the frequency of Jews among alcoholics, dope addicts, and child deserters is low relative to the non-Jewish population. This same argument has been used to conclude that the frequency of Jews among neurotics is higher. Morrison, "A Biologic Interpretation of Jewish Survival," 3 *Medical Leaves* 97 (1940); Meyerson, "Neuroses and Alcoholism Among the Jews," 3 *Medical Leaves* 104 (1940); Liber, "The Behavior of the Jewish and the Non-Jewish Patient," 5 *Medical Leaves* 159 (1943).

There exists evidence that Jews are underrepresented among prison inmates. Levinger, "A Note on Jewish Prisoners in Ohio," 2 *Jewish Social Studies* 210 (1940). This is what the survival hypothesis suggests. It is significant to note, however, that this under-representation is not uniform for all categories of crime. The representation of Jews among prison inmates convicted of crimes of scheming, i.e., fraud, larceny, possession of stolen property, etc., is relatively large. Laws regulating economic affairs, unlike most laws, were directed against Jews. Hence one should expect to find respect by Jews for this category of laws weakest. By this argument a post-war study of prison populations ought to show a relatively large representation of Jews among OPA violators.
[85] J. W. Parkes, *The Jewish Problem in the Modern World* (1946), recognizes the unique experiences of Jews in modern history and the im-

pact of these experiences upon Jewish culture in his first chapter, "Why Is There a Jewish Question?"
[86] Hall, "Informal Organization of the Medical Profession," 12 *Canadian Journal of Economics and Political Science* 38 (1946). This article suggests that young doctors "buy" positions on hospital staffs by providing free medical care in hospital clinics. The older members of the profession have an interest in maintaining this method of admission to hospital staffs because it helps maintain the acceptability of price discrimination with the public.

Similarly there exist controls over the maximum fees charged, price ceilings in effect, in order to minimize the possibility of fees that the public will regard as outrageous and thereby endanger the existence of structured prices. This function is performed by county medical society review committees that deal with the complaints of excessive fees. For an example of the functioning of such a committee, consult Phillips, "Doctor Cancels $1,500 Bill for Hoopers at Medical Group's Urging," *N.Y. Times*, p. 1, col. 2 (June 23, 1957). For a reflection of public attitudes in this case, consult 70 *Time* 34 (July 1, 1957). A. Ruppin suggests that Jews developed modern competitive attitudes in commerce before the industrial revolution as a result of their exclusion from medieval guilds, in an effort to survive commercially in this hostile environment. With the onset of the industrial revolution and the weakening of trade barriers, the relative economic position of Jews improved. *Jews in the Modern World*, p. 110 (1934).

medical schools is influenced by the desire to select candidates who will not become price cutters, then it ought to be possible to observe similar policies for postgraduate education. In particular, it should be possible to observe evidence of bias against Jews in surgical relative to non-surgical specialties. Consequently Jews ought to be under-represented in surgery relative to other fields of specialization. Converse results ought to hold for psychiatry. A study of physicians who were diplomates in various specialties was made for the year 1946 for Jews and non-Jews for the cities of Brooklyn, Newark, Buffalo, and Hartford-Bridgeport. It was found that thirty-two per cent of the surgeons in Brooklyn were Jews, twenty-five per cent in Newark, eight in Buffalo, and six in Hartford. Of the ten specialties considered for Brooklyn, the representation of Jews among the surgeons was lowest. For the other three cities, eleven specialties were considered. For all three of these cities, the representation of Jews among specialists was also lowest in surgery (453 Jewish specialists were considered in Brooklyn, the other three cities added 122). On the other hand, for the category neurology-psychiatry, the representation of Jews among the specialists practicing in this field ranked third for Brooklyn. For the other three cities, the rankings were one tie for fourth place, one first place and one fourth place.[87]

The distinction between psychiatry and surgery is a special case of the general distinction between surgical and non-surgical specialties. Hospital connections are far more important for the practice of surgical than non-surgical specialties. Therefore controls over the members of the medical profession in surgical specialties are stronger. If, as it has been argued, price discrimination is stronger in the surgical specialties, then there should be a significant difference in the frequency of Jews in surgical and non-surgical specialties. Two independent studies provide evidence that is consistent with this implication. For the state of Pennsylvania, one observer found that the frequency of Jews in non-surgical specialties was forty-one per cent larger than in surgical specialties. The probability of a sample of this size, 1,175, of which 190 were Jews, being a random sample of a population characterized by an absence of a difference in the frequency of Jews in the surgical and non-surgical specialties is less than one half of one per cent.[88] For Brooklyn the frequency of Jews in the non-surgical specialties was thirty percent greater than for the surgical specialties. This difference could occur by chance with a probability of less than one percent if this were a random sample of a population that failed to exhibit this property. Similar results hold for a combination of the other three cities.[89] The hypothesis that there exists a difference between surgical and non-surgical specialties with respect to the admission of Jews is consistent with the qualitative observation found in another report. This source observes that "fair play" exists in the admission of Jews to non-Jewish hospitals for training in the non-surgical specialties but not for training in the surgical specialties.[90] Apparently the

[87] Consult Shapiro, op. cit. supra note 82, at p. 125, table IV.

[88] Weinberg, "Jewish Diplomates in Pennsylvania," 4 *Medical Leaves* 159 (1942). The non-surgical specialties were dermatology and syphilology, pediatrics, psychiatry and neurology, internal medicine, radiology, pathology; the surgical specialties were orthopedic surgery, ophthalmology, otolaryngology, obstetrics and gynecology, surgery, and anesthesiology.

[89] Shapiro, op. cit. supra note 82, at p. 125. One entry for all ophthalmologists in Brooklyn is missing and another entry for all radiologists in Hartford was obviously in error. Therefore Hartford radiologists and Brooklyn ophthalmologists, both Jewish and non-Jewish, were not represented in the foregoing calculations. Personal communication with the author of this article failed to elicit a clarifying response.

[90] "Facilities of Jewish Hospitals for Specialized Training," 3 *Jewish Social Studies* 375, 378 (1941).

Jews who do get into medical schools are "dumped" in the non-surgical specialties.[91]

Another piece of evidence consistent with the price cutting explanation of the discrimination against Jews in medicine is the drop in admissions of Jews to medical schools between 1933 and 1938. During that time, there was a decrease in over-all admissions to medical schools of about five per cent and a decrease in admission of Jewish students of about thirty percent.[92] Between 1928 and 1933, the prices of medical services dropped sharply and the real income of doctors as a group decreased. The depression produced a reduction in the size of the pie available to the profession. This smaller pie was contended for quite vigorously by the existing members. The Jews as price cutters were probably relatively successful, and in the process the structure of discriminatory prices was jeopardized. As a result, the threat of Jews to the aggregate income of the profession was brought home in a very forceful way at this time. Therefore the sharp curtailment in admission of Jews to medical schools resulted in an effort to reduce the vulnerability of structured prices to destruction by competitive behavior.[93]

The evidence used to support the proposition that discrimination against certain minority groups results from the desire to maintain price discrimination is also consistent with the implications of simple monopoly theory. If medicine is a monopoly, then it follows that the number of candidates that would like to win entry into the medical profession exceeds the number that in fact are permitted to enter. Therefore unless the number of openings in the profession are sold or auctioned off, a practice that has not been unknown in the American labor movement, non-price rationing is inevitable. This leaves those who have the job of rationing available openings the opportunity to indulge in their tastes for the kind of people that they would like to see in the profession without any effective constraints in the form of costs or positions that must be filled. Under these circumstances, as contrasted with the free entry characteristic of competitive markets, nepotism, discrimination against unpopular cultural groups such as Jews and Negroes, and discrimination against those who hold unpopular ideas such as communists, thrives.[94] Therefore discrimination against

---

[91] These data are also consistent with at least two other hypotheses worth considering. One is that Jews simply lack the physical dexterity required for success in surgery. This seems to be inconsistent with the frequency of Jews in such fields as dentistry. Levinger, "Jews in the Professions in Ohio," 2 *Jewish Social Studies* 401, 430, table XXXIII (1940). The other is that there exists no more discrimination against Jews in surgical specialties than non-surgical specialties but that there does exist at least an additional barrier that must be surmounted in order to get into the surgical specialties that is absent for the non-surgical specialties. No evidence of the existence of such a barrier has been detected.

[92] Goldberg, op. cit. supra note 82, at p. 332. Another distinguished member of the medical profession who has encountered the disapproval of his colleagues for unorthodox views, recognized the economic motivation for this policy and properly describes it as a trade union tactic. He also recognized the conflict of interest position of organized medicine resulting from its control over admissions to the profession. Cabot, op. cit. supra note 7, at p. 263.

[93] A decrease in the frequency of Jews among medical students could occur for reasons other than an increase in the intensity of discrimination. However only an increase in the intensity of discrimination would (1) increase the frequency of Jews in schools of osteopathy, and (2) increase the frequency of Jews among all Americans studying abroad. Between 1935 and 1946, the frequency of Jews in schools of osteopathy more than doubled (9.1 to 20.3%). *A Report of the President's Commission on Higher Education*, pt. II, pp. 38 ff. (1947). This report imputes to the blocking of opportunities in medicine the rise in the frequency of Jews in osteopathic schools. The President's Commission concluded that a substantial part of the responsibility for the discriminatory practices of medical schools belongs to professional associations.

[94] On theoretical grounds, there is a sound basis for the belief that generally speaking, the A.F.L. craft unions have more monopoly power than the C.I.O. industrial unions. Wright, op. cit. supra

Jews and others in admission to medical schools can be rationalized as a manifestation of non-price rationing. Since the surgical specialties are presumed to have more monopoly power than the non-surgical specialties, there is more non-price rationing in the former and as a result, more discrimination.[95] The increase in the tempo of discrimination in the thirties can also be rationalized as a consequence of an increase in the extent of non-price rationing. The demand for medical services is probably highly income elastic and as a result of the depression and admission policies geared to a demand schedule for medical services that existed in the twenties, the monopoly returns in medicine declined during the early depression years. Therefore admissions were subsequently curtailed in order to redress the effects of too liberal admission policies in the past. Consequently the extent of non-price rationing increased.

CONCLUSION

If different prices for the same service exist, then economic theory implies that there must also exist some means for enjoining producers of this service from acting in their own self interest and thereby establishing uniform prices. Observable phenomena abundantly support this implication. Available evidence suggests that the primary control instrument of organized medicine is the ability to cut off potential price cutters from the use of resources complementary to doctors' services for producing many classes of medical care.

---

note 1, pp. 207 ff. Observers of discrimination in the American labor movement find that Negroes are discriminated against more frequently by A.F.L. unions than by C.I.O. unions. H. E. Northrop, *Organized Labor and the Negro*, ch. 1 (1944).

[95] If it were found that the surgical specialties had no more monopoly power than the non-surgical specialties, this would be evidence against the simple monopoly hypothesis, but would be consistent with the discriminatory monopoly hypothesis.

However, techniques other than the withdrawal of staff privileges in hospitals are also employed to maintain discipline in the medical profession. These include *no-criticism rules*, professional courtesy or the free treatment by doctors of other doctors and their families, prohibition of advertising that might reallocate market shares among producers, preventing doctors from testifying against one another in malpractice suits, and the selection of candidates for medical schools and post graduate training in the surgical specialties that have a relatively low probability of being price cutters. All of these sanctions can be rationalized as means for maintaining price discrimination. Therefore the use of these sanctions is consistent with the hypothesis that the medical profession constitutes a discriminating monopoly.

If being cut off from the use of a complementary agent of production, hospital services, is the chief means of disciplining the existing members of the medical profession, then there ought to be a difference in the price discipline maintained in the surgical and non-surgical specialties. Consequently there ought to be a significant difference between the surgical and the non-surgical specialties in the frequency of discriminatory pricing. There are no grounds for believing that there is any difference between the surgical and non-surgical specialties with respect to the effectiveness of the more subtle means of control. Therefore as a result of the relatively weaker impact on the non-surgical specialties of the loss of hospital staff privileges, it should be possible to observe that the non-surgical specialties have not only more price cutters in their midst but also are relatively freer in criticizing other members of the profession, serving as expert witnesses, and violating professional courtesy. Similarly this analysis implies that before the turn of the century, price discrimination in medicine was less pervasive, doctors criticized each other more freely, were more willing to act as expert witnesses against one another, did not as readily provide free medical care to other members of the profession, and did not discriminate against potential price cutters in admission to medical training.[96]

The economic interest of the medical profession in maintaining price discrimination has led to opposition directed against new techniques for marketing medical services that offer promise of utilizing the existing stock of physicians more efficiently than heretofore. Consequently the opposition by organized medicine to prepaid service type medical plans probably has resulted in higher economic costs of medical care for the community than would otherwise have been the case. Similarly the incompatibility of the indemnity principle of insurance and the "what the traffic will bear" principle of pricing medical services has inhibited the development of major, medical catastrophe insurance in this country and consequently has limited the ability of individuals to insure themselves against these risks. Insofar as freer criticism by the members of the medical profession of one another before the public is of value to consumers in helping them distinguish between better and poorer practitioners and in raising standards within the profession, the public has obtained a lower quality of medical service than would otherwise have been obtainable at existing costs. And insofar as being a potential price cutter weeds out candidates from medical schools and post graduate training in the surgical specialties who were better potential doctors than those accepted, then the quality of the medical services that could have been achieved at existing costs was reduced.

Economic theory implies that prepaid medical service plans imperil the existence of price discrimination. Consequently theory also implies that in geographical areas where such plans exist, price discrimination ought to be relatively less prevalent. In California, the Kaiser Plan has captured a substantial fraction of the medical care market and is the largest single producer in the state. In an effort to meet this competition, service-type plans have been offered by orthodox members of the medical profession that are non-discriminatory with respect to income. Competition has had the effect of reducing the extent of discriminatory pricing in the area. This has been true in a number of counties in California where the Kaiser Plan is particularly strong.[97] Therefore both economic theory and empirical evidence suggest that if there were more competition among doctors in the sale of medical services, i.e., if doctors were individually freer to pursue their self-interest, there would be less discrimination in the pricing of medical services.

---

[96] Fee splitting, according to the hypothesis presented in this paper, should have been more prevalent at this time. Splitting fees makes for freer entry into the surgical care market. Newcomers can offer large rebates to referring physicians and thereby win patients away from established surgeons. There seems to be evidence that fee splitting was prevalent in medicine around the turn of the century and it was indeed employed by newcomers as a means for winning entry into the surgical care market. Rongy, "Half a Century of Jewish Medical Activities in New York City," 1 *Medical Leaves* 151, 158 (1937). This implies that the older, more established surgeons oppose fee splitting. This is consistent with the evidence. Williams, "A. C. S. Closes In On Fee Splitters," 31 *Medical Economics* 161 (1954).

Berger, op. cit. supra note 17, at p. 141 contends that surgeons object to fee splitting for economic reasons.

[97] Oakley, "They Met the Challenge of Panel Medicine," 32 *Medical Economics* 122 (Feb. 1955); Olds, "Usual Fee Plan Put to Test," 31 *Medical Economics* 131, but especially p. 206 (July 1954); Andrews, "How They're Fighting the Kaiser Plan," 31 *Medical Economics,* 126 (Sept. 1954).

Part VII

MICROECONOMICS
OF INCOME
DISTRIBUTION

27. Euler's Theorem and the Problem of Distribution*

JOAN ROBINSON

It is characteristic of the development of economic theory that propositions which appear very simple when we have arrived at them should be first sighted through a haze of ambiguities and approached only by a labyrinth of devious controversy. Of this curious process the history of the famous "adding-up problem" provides a striking example.[1]

As soon as it began to be asserted that factors of production are paid in accordance with their marginal products, the problem was posed: How do we know that, if each factor is paid its marginal product, the total product is disposed of without residue, positive or negative? Of course it is obvious that in any case the total product is distributed among the factors of production. The real question is: Can it be true that each and every factor receives a rate of reward equal to its marginal product? To some writers the theory of marginal productivity appeared as a grand moral principle which showed that "what a social class gets is, under natural law, what it contributes to the general output of industry." [2] But others were beset by doubt. It appeared easy enough to show that the self-interest of employers will ensure that the rate of earnings of each employed factor is equated to its marginal product.[3] The difficulty lay with the entrepreneur. How can we be certain that, when the factors have been paid, the residue which is left over measures the contribution of the entrepreneur?

One answer, provided by J. B. Clark among others, was that in static conditions the entrepreneur makes no specific contribution, so that in fact the earnings of en-

* Reprinted from the *Economic Journal* (September 1934) by permission of the publisher, pp. 398–414. A brief biographical sketch of the author can be found in the introduction to Reading 14.

[1] This question, first canvassed in about 1890, is still "the subject of lively controversy." Professor Robbins (Introduction to Wicksteed's *Common Sense of Political Economy and Selected Papers*, Vol. I, p. xi).

[2] J. B. Clark, "Distribution as Determined by a Law of Rent," *Quarterly Journal of Economics*, April 1891, p. 313. See also *Distribution of Wealth*, p. 3.

[3] A necessary assumption which often fails to be made clear is that the supply of each factor to an individual employer is perfectly elastic, so that the price of a factor represents its marginal cost to the employer.

trepreneurship are always tending to approach zero. Another was that since it is always open to an employer to take service as an employee, or for an employee to set up in business as an employer, the earnings of an individual cannot depart from what he would receive as an employee, and what he would receive as an employee is equal to his marginal product. This argument, used in a more or less ambiguous form by many writers, was explicitly stated by Edgeworth[4] only to show that it is not perfectly satisfactory. A similar point of view is to be found in Marshall's application of the "principle of substitution" to the problem.[5]

An entirely different line of attack was adopted by Wicksteed, in the *Co-ordination of the Laws of Distribution*. Using "the mathematical form of statement . . . as a safeguard against unconscious assumptions, and as a reagent that will *precipitate* the assumptions held in solution in the verbiage of our ordinary disquisitions," [6] he set out the theorem derived from Euler that, where $P = f(a,b,c, . . .)$ is a homogeneous function of the first degree, so that

$$mP = f(ma, mb, mc, . . .),$$

then

$$P = a\frac{\partial P}{\partial a} + b\frac{\partial P}{\partial b} + c\frac{\partial P}{\partial c} + \cdots$$

Translated into economic language, this proposition states that the total product is equal to the sum of the amounts of the factors, each multiplied by its marginal product, provided that conditions of constant returns prevail, in the sense that a given proportional increase in the amount of every factor of production would lead to the same proportional increase in the product.

When confronted with the precision of

Euler's theorem, the argument from the principle of substitution is seen to prove at once too much and too little. It amounts to saying that when the employing factor can take service as an employed factor without any loss of advantage, then the normal level of profits for employers is equal to their marginal productivity as employees. Therefore what they actually receive, when profits are normal, is their marginal product. Thus, on the one hand it makes no overt proviso that constant returns prevail, and so appears to be too general. On the other hand, it leaves us in doubt as to what would happen in a case in which the employing factor has only inferior alternative occupations, and equally in a case in which profits are not normal. It was this vagueness which led Edgeworth to say that the theorem that the employer, as well as the employed factors, receives a reward equal to his marginal product "is neither quite true nor very important." [7]

Euler's theorem leaves us in no such doubt. If constant returns prevail, and if each employed factor is paid its marginal product, then the remnant which goes to the employing factor is equal to its marginal product, whether profits are normal or not.

But at the same time the solution by Euler's theorem did not appear to be perfectly satisfactory. It seemed to imply that we are not to be allowed to believe in the principle of marginal productivity unless conditions of constant return can be shown to prevail in the real world.[8] This gave rise

[7] *Papers*, Vol. II, p. 338. See also Chapman, "Remuneration of Employers," *Economic Journal*, December 1906, p. 528.

[8] For most of the contemporaries of Wicksteed (though not, I think, for Marshall) the "theory of marginal productivity" was a formulation of a somewhat mysterious law of nature. For the modern economist it is merely a series of self-evident propositions displaying the implications of the initial assumption that the individual employer acts in such a way as to maximise his profits. It is this fundamental difference in point of view which gives what appears to the modern reader

[4] *Papers Relating to Political Economy*, Vol. I, p. 30.

[5] *Principles of Economics*, Book VI, Chapter VII.

[6] *Co-ordination*, Prefatory Note, p. 4.

to an appearance of conflict between the mathematical and the economic line of reasoning, which, as the sequel will show, was completely illusory.

Wicksteed himself regarded conditions of constant physical returns as universal,[9] but he was perplexed because the "social product" of an industry in terms of satisfaction obviously does not increase proportionately to the factors of production employed by the industry; nor does the "commercial product" of a firm increase proportionately to the factors employed by the firm. He suggested an ingenious method for surmounting the first difficulty. The consumers also might be regarded as a factor necessary for the production of satisfaction.[10] Then, if each factor in an industry, including consumers, is increased in a given proportion, the satisfaction produced will be increased in the same proportion, and the conditions of Euler's theorem will be fulfilled. But even this expedient will not serve to meet the second difficulty, and Wicksteed realised that for a monopoly, or for a firm controlling an appreciable proportion of the output of a commodity, conditions of constant returns in value of product cannot obtain.[11]

He was therefore obliged to confine his discussion to conditions of perfect competition, and he asserted that, assuming competition to be perfect, constant returns to the individual concern must prevail universally "equally in Robinson Crusoe's island, in an American religious commune, in an Indian village ruled by custom, and in the competitive centres of the typical modern industries." [12] This solution of the problem was met by Edgeworth with mockery rather than argument,[13] and by Pareto

with the objection that it is illegitimate to assume constant returns in terms of physical product.[14]

Wicksteed retreated in face of this criticism, withdrew the argument of the *Co-ordination*,[15] and substituted for its heroic precision a very cloudy passage in the *Common Sense of Political Economy*.[16] Professor Robbins has pointed out,[17] however, that at heart he was impenitent and continued to make use of the argument of the *Co-ordination* in his lectures to University Extension classes[18] some time after Pareto's criticisms had appeared.

Meanwhile Walras had published a *"Note sur la réfutation de la théorie anglaise du fermage de M. Wicksteed."* [19] While acclaiming him as a kindred spirit for his use of precise methods, and congratulating him on his refutation of the English theory of rent, Walras complained of Wicksteed's failure to take any notice of his own contribution to marginal productivity theory.[20] Following a suggestion by Barone, Walras criticised Wicksteed for postulating a homogeneous production function of the first degree, but showed that Wicksteed's result follows from the axiom that costs are at a minimum under perfect competition.[21]

such a perverse and fantastic character to the controversies surrounding the "adding-up problem."

[9] *Co-ordination*, p. 33.

[10] *Ibid.*, p. 34.

[11] *Ibid.*, pp. 35–36.

[12] *Co-ordination*, p. 42.

[13] *Papers*, Vol. I, p. 31.

[14] *Cours d'économie politique* (1897), Vol. II, p. 83 note, and "Anwendung der Mathematik auf Nationalökonomie," *Encyklopädie der Mathematischen Wissenschaften* (1904), Vol. I, Part II, p. 1117 note.

[15] *Common Sense*, Vol. I, p. 373 note, and Review of Pareto's *Manuale*, *Economic Journal*, December 1906, p. 554 note.

[16] *Common Sense*, Vol. I, pp. 370–373.

[17] *Ibid.*, p. xi.

[18] *Ibid.*, Vol. II, p. 862.

[19] *Recueil publié par la Faculté de Droit, Université de Lausanne, 1896.*

[20] The peevish egoism of Walras contrasts unfavourably with the modesty and single-mindedness of Wicksteed.

[21] Pareto accused Walras of the same error of which Walras accused Wicksteed. We have here started a hare which it would take too long to pursue. For the history of this dispute, which contains some entertaining incidents, the reader is referred to Professor Schultz, "Marginal Pro-

Walras (like Pareto and many subsequent critics) implies that Wicksteed had merely overlooked the possibility of increasing returns due to economies of large scale to the firm. In the present context "increasing returns" means a state of affairs in which an equal proportional increase in each factor would give a more than proportional increase in the product. Clearly where economies of large scale are present, increasing returns in this sense will prevail. But Wicksteed had not forgotten this obvious fact. His error was far more subtle. He rejects "the crude division of the factors of production into land, capital and labour," and maintains that "we must regard every kind and quality of labour that can be distinguished from other kinds and qualities as a separate factor. . . . Still more important is it to insist that instead of speaking of so many £ worth of capital we shall speak of so many ploughs, so many tons of manure, and so many horses, or foot-pounds of power." "On this understanding," he writes, "it is of course obvious that a proportional increase of all the factors of production will secure a proportional increase of the product." [22] Now economies of large scale can only arise from the existence of an indivisible productive unit which is not being used to its full capacity.[23] On Wicksteed's plan such a unit would be regarded as a single factor of production. Thus a firm which is subject to economies must be employing the whole of at least one indivisible "factor." The smallest increase in output that can then be made without altering the proportions of the "factors" is an increase of a hundred per cent., and the marginal productivity principle cannot be applied. In order to consider the effect upon output of a small change in the amount of a factor, it is

necessary to define the factors in a manner at least sufficiently crude for each factor to be finely divisible.[24] Wicksteed had not gone astray because he had ignored the existence of economies of large scale, but because in his endeavour to define the factors in such a way as to eliminate the possibility of increasing physical returns he had accidentally eliminated the possibility of defining the marginal productivity of a factor. When the factors are divided on a plan which makes marginal analysis applicable to them, the possibility of increasing returns reappears.[25]

Mr. J. A. Hobson, some years later, made the existence of economies of large scale the basis of a grand attack upon the whole marginal productivity principle,[26] which was very inadequately answered by Marshall in the well-known footnote about shepherds.[27] Mr. Hobson constructs a numerical example in which there are increasing physical returns to the individual productive unit up to a certain output, and beyond that output diminishing physical returns. He shows that where increasing returns prevail, the marginal product multiplied by the amount of the factor[28] is greater than the total product, and declares that the notion that factors are paid their

---

ductivity and the General Pricing Process," *Journal of Political Economy*, October 1929.

[22] *Co-ordination*, p. 33.

[23] Cf. E. A. G. Robinson, *Structure of Competitive Industry*, p. 25.

[24] It must, however, be conceded to Wicksteed that, strictly speaking, it is impossible to reduce a group of non-homogeneous productive units to a common term so that they can be treated as a single factor. Any statement about the marginal productivity of a "factor" which is not perfectly homogeneous cannot be perfectly accurate. I should like to take this opportunity of pointing out that the device suggested in my *Economics of Imperfect Competition* (p. 332) for getting over the difficulty by constructing "corrected natural units" is completely worthless.

[25] The reader will perceive that the above treatment of this problem is superficial, but I must beg him to let it pass, for if we were to turn aside now to explore this territory we should certainly be benighted before the end of our journey.

[26] *The Industrial System* (1909), pp. 112–120.

[27] *Principles*, p. 517 note.

[28] His analytical technique being somewhat primitive, he considers only one factor for the sake of simplicity.

marginal products is therefore completely nonsensical. He goes on to argue that the individual concern will consist of such an amount of factors that average productivity is at a maximum, and points out that the earnings of the factor is equal to its average product.

Marshall dismisses this argument with the remark that "he appears to be mistaken." But clearly Mr. Hobson was right; with perfect competition and normal profits (these are postulated, though somewhat vaguely) the average net productivity of each factor is at a maximum, and is equal to the wage of the factor.[29] Where he went wrong was in denying that marginal productivity also is equal to the wage.[30] The reason why he overlooked this fact is rather curious. The following is one of his arithmetical examples (labour is the only factor employed):—

No. of men	Total product.	Average product.	Marginal product.
1	10	10	—
2	22	11	12
3	37	$12\frac{1}{3}$	15
4	60	15	23
5	72	$14\frac{2}{5}$	12

From this he argues that production will be carried on by groups of four men, who will receive a wage, not of 23, which is the marginal product of a fourth man, but of 15, which is the average product. It is the crudity of his arithmetical example that has betrayed him.[31] If the average product of four men is 15, and the marginal product 23, average productivity must still be rising at the point where four men are employed.

The true maximum of average productivity lies somewhere between four and five men, and at the maximum marginal and average productivity are equal.

Thus Marshall and Mr. Hobson are each right in what they assert, and wrong in what they deny,[32] and if Mr. Hobson had been more subtle in his use of arithmetic, or Marshall less unable to suffer fools gladly, the whole controversy would have been cleared up on the spot.

Meanwhile, Wicksell had expanded Walras' account of the problem.[33] He adopts the view that there is no specific economic function for the employer as such, and deduces from this that the supply price of enterprise or normal level of profits must be zero, for if at any moment a positive profit were being earned by employers, it would soon be reduced to zero by the competition of new entrants eager to share this painless method of earning a livelihood.[34] He proceeds to show, by a line of argument similar to that of Wicksteed, that when each employed factor is paid a rate of reward equal to its marginal product to the firm, profits can only be zero if constant physical returns prevail.[35]

He then argues that at a position of competitive equilibrium constant physical re-

---

[29] Cf. my *Economics of Imperfect Competition*, p. 249.

[30] In my opinion, Mr. Sraffa over-estimates Mr. Hobson's insight on this point. See "Sulle relazioni fra costo e quantità prodotta," *Annali di Economia*, Vol. II, no. I (1925), p. 312 note.

[31] Cf. Edgeworth on Prof. Seligman, *Papers*, Vol. II, p. 397.

[32] Marshall's example of the shepherds is not open to this objection if it is taken to apply to what I call the "quasi-long period" (*Imperfect Competition*, p. 47). There is no tendency for normal profits to be established among his sheep-farmers.

[33] *Vorlesungen über Nationalökonomie*, Vol. I, pp. 186–191.

[34] *Ibid.*, p. 187.

[35] Dr. W. L. Valk in criticising Wicksell's argument on this point shows that he fails to mention the difference between the marginal product of the 100th man when 100 men are employed with 100 units of land, and the marginal product when 100 men are employed with 101 units of land. Dr. Valk appears to argue that the fact that marginal productivity analysis requires us to conceive changes in the factors so small that this difference is negligible, is sufficient to render marginal productivity analysis completely valueless. *Principles of Wages*, p. 74. Cf. Edgeworth on Mr. J. A. Hobson, *Papers*, Vol. I, p. 19, note 3.

turns will prevail. Up to a certain output of the firm there will be increasing returns due to economies of large scale, but if increasing returns to the firm prevail, average cost per unit of output will be falling and competitive equilibrium will be impossible. Beyond a certain output rising average cost may occur. This also is incompatible with equilibrium, because if the output of a firm is so large that average costs are rising the firm must be earning a positive profit; consequently new firms will enter the industry, and the fall in price of the commodity will drive the old firms back to the output at which average cost is at a minimum.

The upshot of all this appeared to be that, so long as conditions of perfect competition[36] are postulated, there is no difficulty about constant physical returns to the firm. But it is necessary to be clear as to what exactly we mean by a firm. The problem of providing a formal treatment of the factor "entrepreneurship," which is easy to handle analytically and at the same time is not too remote from actuality, has never been satisfactorily solved. Three possible methods may be considered, each more appropriate to some problems than to others, but none perfectly satisfactory for any.

First, we may postulate (following Wicksell) that there is no specific function of decision-taking for the entrepreneur to perform, and that the owners of one factor—for instance, capital—hire the services of the others. Capital, as well as the other factors, must be assumed to be employed up to the point at which its marginal productivity to an employing unit is equal to its cost to that unit—that is, to what it can earn as an employed factor.[37] Capital is

thus upon exactly the same footing as the other factors. A profit or loss to the employer is then a difference between total receipts and total costs, including the cost of capital. Second, we may postulate that each firm consists of a single indivisible unit of entrepreneurship whose supply price is independent of the amount of output it controls. Or third, we may postulate that each entrepreneur is not a fixed unit, but performs more or less of his decision-taking function according to the reward which he can earn.

In the first two cases clearly there is no meaning to be attached to the notion of "marginal product of entrepreneurship to the firm." When either of these schemes of analysis is adopted, therefore, the employer must not be regarded as a specific factor of production from the point of view of the firm, and constant returns to the firm must be said to prevail when a given proportional increase of every factor except entrepreneurship would give the same proportional increase in output. In the third case the entrepreneur must be conceived to regulate the amount of effort he supplies to the firm by its marginal productivity to the firm, in just the same way as he regulates the amount of the factors he employs. The entrepreneur's effort is therefore upon exactly the same footing as an employed factor. Constant returns are then said to prevail when a given proportional increase of every factor, including the entrepreneur's effort, gives the same proportional increase in output, and profits are reckoned excluding the variable element in the reward of the entrepreneur.

Each of these methods of depicting entrepreneurship is highly unrealistic, but they are adopted merely in order to display the workings of the marginal productivity principle in various types of cases, and are not put forward as an attempt to solve the problem of a realistic treatment of entrepreneurship as a factor of production.[38]

---

[36] Throughout this essay I am using the phrase perfect competition to mean simply that the elasticities of demand and of supplies of factors for a single firm are infinite. This implies no reference to free entry into the trade or normal profits.

[37] The case of imperfectly elastic supply of factors to an employing unit is considered later—see below p. 356.

[38] A large part of the literature of the subject is

Whichever method is adopted, it is clear from Euler's theorem that in conditions where physical returns, in the relevant sense, are constant, profits in the relevant sense must be zero. For when competition is perfect the wage of each factor is equal to the value of its marginal physical product and there is no residue for the employer.

It is now apparent that Wicksell's assumption of zero normal profits is an essential step in his argument. It is impossible to argue in general that because average cost to the firm is at a minimum in competitive equilibrium therefore constant physical returns to the firm prevail; for the cost which is at a minimum in competitive equilibrium is average cost including normal profits. If normal profits are positive the output at which average cost is a minimum is greater than the output at which net economies of large scale give way to net diseconomies, and constant physical returns do not prevail.

The history of the controversy up to this point is summarised in the Appendix to the *Theory of Wages* by Dr. Hicks.[39] He shows, in effect, that even when Wicksteed had taken the drastic step of confining his argument to cases of perfect competition, he was not yet out of the wood, for he had postulated constant physical returns as a universal technical necessity. This postulate is shown by Pareto and by Walras to be inadmissible, but Wicksell contends that, for the output which will be produced in competitive equilibrium, constant physical returns to the firm do prevail whatever the

technical conditions. Thus it appeared that Wicksteed's assumption of perfect competition, required to get him out of a difficulty of which he was aware—diminishing returns in terms of value—incidentally saved him from a difficulty of which he was not aware —increasing returns in terms of physical product.

Wicksteed's problem was that the marginal productivities of the factors, multiplied by the amounts of the factors, absorb the whole product without residue only in conditions of constant returns. Wicksell's argument shows that constant physical returns will prevail under perfect competition. Thus it appears that, so long as we admit Wicksell's postulate of zero normal profits, there is really no problem at all. On the contrary, the result is exactly what we should expect, for it is only if competition is perfect that the earnings of the factors are equal to the value of their marginal physical products, and only when profits are zero that the earnings of the factors absorb the whole product. After all this long debate we reach a self-evident conclusion.

Nevertheless it is impossible to be satisfied with a solution which applies only to the case of zero profits. The condition that the employed factors receive the value of their marginal physical product to the firm under perfect competition must be fulfilled even when profits are positive or negative.[40] But it is an illusion to suppose that this presents any difficulty, for if profits are not zero constant returns do not prevail. In the present context, increasing or diminishing returns must be said to prevail according as a given proportional increase in the amount of every factor would lead to a greater or smaller proportional increase in output. Now, the economist can prove that

---

devoted to debating the proper analytical treatment of entrepreneurship as a factor; see Edgeworth (*Papers*, Vol. I, "Theory of Distribution") and the authors cited by him. The question has recently been revived by Mr. Kaldor: "The Equilibrium of the Firm," *Economic Journal*, March 1934.

[39] I should like to take this opportunity to make my acknowledgments to Dr. Hicks for the helpful guide-map which he provides to this else bewildering territory, and to Professor Robbins as the champion and editor of Wicksteed.

[40] Dr. Hicks is content to confine himself to the case of zero profits since he holds that in conditions of equilibrium there is no function for the entrepreneur (*Theory of Wages*, p. 234). Beyond this point in our argument, therefore, Dr. Hicks' guidance is less helpful.

profits are negative or positive according as returns are increasing or diminishing for the individual firm. For, under perfect competition, marginal cost to the firm, for the output at which profits are a maximum, is equal to the price of the product. When a loss is being made by the employer, price is less than average cost. Therefore marginal cost is less than average cost. Therefore the average cost curve of output is falling, and physical returns are increasing. Conversely, when a profit is being made by the employer physical returns are diminishing. While the mathematician has only to set out the generalised form of Euler's theorem in order to show[41] that

$$P \lessgtr a\frac{\partial P}{\partial a} + b\frac{\partial P}{\partial b} + \cdots$$

according as

$$mP \gtrless + f(ma, mb, \ldots)$$

If the normal level of profits is positive the number of firms will be so limited that diminishing physical returns to the firms prevail to just the extent which is compatible with the required profit. A positive profit of this level will fail to attract in new enterprise, and so fail to drive existing firms back towards the output at which constant physical returns prevail.

Thus it appears once more that there was really no problem, for it is obvious that the total product cannot be absorbed by the earnings of the employed factors when profits are positive, and we already knew that when profits are positive diminishing physical returns prevail.

But all this applies only to marginal productivity from the point of view of a firm under perfect competition. We have as yet thrown no light on the proposition, contested by Edgeworth, that the entrepreneur, as well as the employed factors, receives a reward equal to his marginal product. For the marginal product of the entrepreneur

to the firm has no meaning. The question must therefore be whether the earnings of the entrepreneur are equal to the marginal productivity of entrepreneurship to the industry.[42] Our next task is to consider marginal productivity from the point of view of an industry, retaining the assumption of perfect competition.

From the point of view of an industry, enterprise must be treated on just the same footing as the other factors, for even if we take the view that there is no specific economic function of entrepreneurship, yet it remains true that the productivity of the other factors varies with the number of firms in which they are organised, and the difference which is made to their productivity by adding an entrepreneur is the marginal product of entrepreneurship.[43]

The proposition that, with constant physical returns to the industry, total output is equal to the sum of the amounts of the factors each multiplied by its marginal physical product to the industry, can be very simply proved by means of Euler's theorem. But the economist can supply his own demonstration of it. The self-interest of the entrepreneurs will ensure that, under conditions of perfect competition, the value of the marginal physical product to the firm of each employed factor is equal to its wage. And under constant returns marginal physical product to the industry is equal to marginal physical product to the firm. It only remains to prove, therefore, that the reward of the entrepreneurs is equal to *their* marginal physical product to the industry. The marginal productivity to the industry of entrepreneurship is the

---

[41] Cf. Wicksell, *loc. cit.,* p. 189, and Chapman, *loc. cit.,* p. 526 note.

[42] The relationship of productivity to the industry with productivity to society is not here discussed.

[43] Anyone who rejects altogether the notion of diseconomies of large scale to a firm is at liberty to say that the marginal productivity of entrepreneurship to an industry may be zero or negative, but never positive. The argument which follows is purely formal, and begs no questions about the nature of entrepreneurship as a factor.

difference which would be made to output if one entrepreneur were withdrawn.[44] That is, the output of one firm *minus* the output which the factors employed by that firm would produce if they were dispersed among the remaining firms. Thus, the value of the marginal physical product of entrepreneurship is the value of output of one firm *minus* the amounts of the employed factors each multiplied by the value of its marginal physical productivity. This is equal to the total receipts of the firm *minus* the total cost of the employed factors. And this is the reward of the entrepreneur.

It is to be observed that this proof contains no reference to normal profits. If we are considering Wicksell's case in which there is no supply price of entrepreneurship, so that the level of normal profits is zero, then in full equilibrium the entrepreneurs receive nothing, and their marginal productivity to the industry is zero. If the normal level of profits is positive, their marginal productivity in equilibrium is positive. If profits are more or less than normal, the marginal productivity of entrepreneurs to the industry is correspondingly high or low, owing to the temporary scarcity or superabundance of entrepreneurs which has caused profits to depart from the normal level.[45]

But what of economies of large-scale industry?[46] When there are economies of large scale, the sum of the amounts of the factors each multiplied by its marginal physical product is greater than the total output. But this causes no difficulty, for the simple reason that the rewards of the employed factors are not equal to their marginal physical products to the industry. The marginal product of a factor to the industry is greater than to the firm by the extent of the economies induced by a unit increase in the amount of the factor employed. And it is the marginal product to the firm which is equal to the wage of the factor. Similarly, the marginal productivity of an entrepreneur to the industry is greater than his earnings by the amount of economies which accrue to the other firms when an increment is added to output whose value is equal to the value of his marginal physical product to the industry.[47] Thus once more the economist finds himself in complete accord with Euler. If the factors *were* paid the value of their marginal products to the industry, total cost would be greater than total receipts when increasing returns to the industry prevail. But actually each factor is paid less, and the total product is exactly disposed of among them.

Conversely if there are diminishing returns to the industry, in the sense in which we have been using that term, that is, if there are real diseconomies of large-scale industry,[48] then the factors are paid more

---

[44] The number of firms in the industry being n, it is necessary to assume that n is so large that the difference between the marginal physical productivities of the constant amount of other factors when they are working with n entrepreneurs and when they are working with $n-1$ may be neglected. Cf. above p. 404 n. 4.

[45] When the entrepreneur's earnings vary with the amount of effort which he supplies to his firm the unit of entrepreneurship from the point of view of the industry is best regarded as a single entrepreneur doing that amount of work whose marginal cost to him is equal to its marginal product to the firm.

[46] It is here that we must finally dispense with the guidance of Dr. Hicks, for in this region his map contains nothing but a blank space marked *Terra Incognita. Loc. cit.,* p. 240.

[47] This is upon the assumption that economies of large-scale industry depend solely upon the output of the commodity and not on the proportions of the factors, so that the production function is homogeneous, though of a higher degree than unity. If the economies vary with the amounts of particular factors employed (the production function is not homogeneous) then only those factors which give rise to economies receive less than their marginal physical products to the industry. Cf. Tarshis, *Review of Economic Studies,* February 1934, p. 145.

[48] We are here concerned with the "rare type" of diminishing returns (see *Imperfect Competition,* p. 348). The reader must guard against misleading associations with the "common type" of diminishing returns.

than their marginal product to the industry to a degree exactly corresponding to the extent of the diseconomies.[49]

All this while we have been dwelling in the world of perfect competition. It is time to return to Wicksteed's long-neglected difficulty, and consider the analysis of marginal productivity under imperfect competition. First consider the matter from the point of view of the individual firm, assuming that, while the market for the commodity is imperfect, the supplies of factors to the firm are perfectly elastic. Under imperfect competition, a firm which is earning zero profits must be producing at falling average cost.[50] Therefore conditions of increasing physical returns to the firm prevail. At a hasty glance it might appear that the provisions of Euler's theorem are therefore violated. But this is not the case. For the earnings of a factor are not equal to the value of its marginal physical product, but to the marginal product in value to the firm; and are thus less than the value of the marginal physical product in the ratio of marginal revenue to price.[51] To satisfy the conditions of Euler's theorem it is necessary to show, not that constant returns in terms of physical output prevail when profits are zero, but that constant returns in terms of value prevail. That is to say, a given proportional increase in every factor employed must give the same proportional increase in the total value of the product.

Wicksteed regarded constant physical returns as a universal condition; therefore, since the price of the commodity produced by the firm falls as its output increases, it was impossible for him to conceive of constant returns in value under imperfect competition. For him diminishing returns in value must always rule. But as soon as we introduce economies of large scale to the firm into the picture Wicksteed's difficulty disappears. Constant returns in value will prevail at the output at which technical economies due to an increase of output just offset the accompanying fall in selling price. And it will be proved in a moment that constant returns in value do prevail when the firm is earning zero profits. Once more the methods of economic analysis will be found to lead to the conclusions of Euler's theorem.[52]

Before turning to the general proof let us consider the case in which competition in hiring the factors is not perfect, so that the supplies of factors to the firm are less than perfectly elastic. We know that in such a case the wage of a factor is less than its marginal product in value. For the marginal product must be equated to the

---

[49] The above argument bears some resemblance to that of Sir Sydney Chapman in his article on the "Remuneration of Employers" (*Economic Journal,* December 1906). But his definition of "increasing and diminishing returns" is somewhat obscure, and matters are not much improved by Edgeworth's comments (*Papers,* Vol. I, p. 99). Sir S. Chapman is quite correct in saying that the reward of the entrepreneur is less than the value of his marginal physical product to the industry when there are economies of large scale. What he evidently failed to realise was that his argument applies to the other factors just as much as to entrepreneurship (*loc. cit.,* p. 527 note). His argument was somewhat grudgingly received by Edgeworth (*Papers,* Vol. II, pp. 331–339), who appears to have had a rooted objection to applying the marginal productivity analysis to the case of the entrepreneur.

[50] See *Imperfect Competition,* p. 97. In that passage I am including normal profit in cost, whereas in the present context cost is reckoned excluding profit.

[51] *Ibid.,* p. 237.

[52] The complete harmony between them is well illustrated by the case in which a firm selling in an imperfect market happens to be producing under conditions of constant physical returns. This will occur when, by a fluke, the marginal revenue curve cuts the marginal cost curve at the output at which it in turn cuts the average cost curve. Constant physical returns prevail, but the factors are receiving less than their marginal physical product; consequently there is a positive profit. The factors receive their marginal product in value, but diminishing returns in value prevail; consequently there is a positive profit. By either line of reasoning the conditions of Euler's theorem are seen to be fulfilled.

marginal cost of the factor to the firm, and this *ex hypothesi* is greater than the wage.[53] Once more there appears at first sight to be a contradiction, but once more upon examination the difficulty disappears, for it is no longer appropriate to measure the factors in physical terms; they must be measured in terms of outlay.

The condition of constant returns may now be more generally defined. It obtains when a given proportional increase in the outlay upon every factor employed would lead to the same proportional increase in value of output. Hitherto we have considered cases in which the supplies of the factors to the firm are perfectly elastic, so that up to this point it has been indifferent whether the factors are measured in physical terms or in terms of outlay. But in the general case a given proportional increase in the outlay upon a factor gives a proportional increase in the amount of the factor which is less in the ratio of average to marginal cost of the factor to the firm.[54] Although the wage of a factor may be less than its marginal product in value per physical unit of the factor, it must be equal to the marginal product per unit of outlay. It follows at once from Euler's theorem that profits are zero, positive, or negative according as returns are constant, diminishing or increasing, measured in terms of value and of outlay.

The same proposition can be proved without resort to Euler's theorem. When profits are zero the average cost curve of the firm is tangential to the demand curve for its output.[55] For the output at which the curves are tangential, profits are at a maxi-

mum of zero; any greater or smaller output would yield a loss. Therefore a curve relating value of output to average outlay per unit of value of output would be at a minimum at this point, and constant returns in terms of value and outlay prevail. If a positive profit is being made, the demand curve for the firm lies above its average cost curve. But for the most profitable output, marginal revenue and marginal cost are equal; therefore the demand curve, which is higher, must have a greater slope than the cost curve.[56] Therefore receipts per physical unit of output fall off faster than outlay as output increases, and conditions of diminishing returns in terms of value and outlay prevail. Conversely, when a loss is being made, increasing returns in terms of value and outlay prevail. The harmony between the economist and the mathematician is complete.

It only remains to consider the case of an industry with imperfect competition between the firms composing it. To isolate the effect of imperfect competition, assume constant physical returns to the industry.[57] Then the employed factors receive less than the value of their marginal physical prod-

[53] See *Imperfect Competition*, p. 293.

[54] The above argument applies to the case of an entrepreneur who supplies units of effort to his firm at rising cost (see above, p. 352), a rising subjective cost of effort being reckoned in money terms. The entrepreneur will supply that amount of effort whose marginal cost to him is equal to its marginal product in value to the firm. Cf. Edgeworth on Mill (*Papers*, Vol. I, p. 17).

[55] Cf. *Imperfect Competition*, p. 94.

[56] Let x be output, y price, and z average cost. Then $y + x \dfrac{dy}{dx} = z + x \dfrac{dz}{dx}$ (marginal revenue = marginal cost).

$\therefore$ if $y > z$, $\dfrac{dy}{dx} < \dfrac{dz}{dx}$.

$\therefore$ the negative slope of the demand curve is greater than that of the cost curve. (In perfect competition—see pp. 353–354—we have the special case in which $\dfrac{dy}{dx} = 0$. $\therefore$ when $y > z$, $\dfrac{dz}{dx}$ must be positive. Since the prices of the factors are constant, this entails diminishing physical returns.)

[57] It is to be observed that the kind of falling supply price for an industry that occurs because competition becomes more perfect as the industry expands (*Imperfect Competition*, p. 101) is not due to increasing returns in the sense here relevant but arises from the fact that the proportion of entrepreneurship to other factors becomes more favourable (that is, less) as the industry expands and the firms grow in size.

ucts to the industry, these being equal to their marginal physical products to the firm. Thus it can be shown directly by appealing to Euler's theorem, that the entrepreneurs receive more than the value of their marginal physical product to the industry. Alternatively, adapting the argument developed above for the case of perfect competition, we may say: the marginal physical product of an entrepreneur is equal to the output of a firm *minus* the amounts of the factors employed by a firm each multiplied by its marginal physical product. But the factors are paid less than the value of their marginal physical products; therefore the earnings of the entrepreneurs are greater than the value of the marginal physical product of entrepreneurship. This is a symptom of the fact that under imperfect competition the ratio of entrepreneurs to other factors is higher than that which would give minimum cost,[58] or, in other words, that the size of the firm is uneconomically small.[59]

The fact that under imperfect competition the entrepreneurs receive more than their marginal physical productivity to the

[58] This is true even if the reward of the entrepreneur is zero, for in that case his marginal physical product to the industry must be negative.

[59] The analysis of the effects of increasing or diminishing physical returns to the industry can be superimposed on the analysis of imperfect competition. For instance, it can be seen that if increasing returns prevail, the employed factors will receive less than the value of their marginal products for two reasons, while the entrepreneurs will receive a reward which may be less or more than the value of their marginal product, according as the effect of increasing returns outweighs or is outweighed by the effect of imperfect competition.

industry was perceived by Wicksteed, but, shaken by Pareto's criticisms, he had not sufficient confidence to state it as a definite proposition. In 1905 he wrote that the "general result of investigation so far as it has yet been carried is to make it seem probable that in proportion as we approximate to the state of things usually assumed in the Theory of Political Economy (*i.e.* free competition, in which each individual competitor does only a small fraction of the total business of his market) we approximate to the result indicated [total product equal to the sum of the factors each multiplied by its marginal product]. So far as we recede from these conditions (for instance, in a great monopoly or trust) we recede from this result, and give the persons who control the concern something more than their distributive share in the product as measured by their marginal industrial efficiency." [60]

And already in 1894 he had caught a glimpse of it: "The failure fully to confirm and generalise a property in the productive functions which would yield an admirably compact and complete co-ordination of the laws of distribution need not discourage us. Its suggestions as to the line of attack we must follow in dealing with monopolies, and with the true socialising of production, are so magnificent in their promise that we are more than consoled for the want of completeness in our immediate results." [61] But, after forty years, economists are still debating the adding-up problem and neglecting to fulfil that magnificent promise.

[60] *Common Sense*, Vol. II, p. 862.
[61] *Co-ordination*, p. 38.

28. A Reformulation
of Naive
Profit Theory*

MARTIN BRONFENBRENNER

Martin Bronfenbrenner (A.B., Washington University, St. Louis, 1934; Ph.D., the University of Chicago, 1939) was born in Pittsburgh, Pennsylvania, in 1914. He is now Professor of Economics in the Graduate School of Industrial Administration of the Carnegie Institute of Technology and adjunct Professor of Economics at the University of Pittsburgh. Before assuming his present position at Carnegie Tech, he taught at the University of Chicago, Roosevelt University, the University of Wisconsin, Michigan State University, and the University of Minnesota, and spent a number of years in various government positions. During the academic year 1966–1967, Bronfenbrenner was a Visiting Fellow at the Center for Advanced Studies in the Behavioral Sciences at Stanford University. He has written widely in various fields of economics, including economic theory, income distribution, monetary and fiscal policy, the economy of Japan, and Marxian economics. Bronfenbrenner has published numerous articles in legal and philosophical as well as in economic journals and is, in addition, the author of *Academic Encounter* and *Is the Business Cycle Obsolete?* He is also the editor of a volume entitled *Income Distribution Theory*.

I. NAIVE PROFIT THEORY AND ITS ECLIPSE

This essay is a salvage operation in the economics of distribution under purely competitive conditions. It is concerned with profit—"pure" profit as distinguished from implicit wages and interest, "normal" profit

as distinguished from windfall and imperfectly-competitive components. It is therefore little more than a footnote to the economics of profit in the large—as seen by business-men or by their critics.

The naive profit theory which we think worth reconsideration enjoyed its heyday in elementary textbooks during roughly the first third of this century.[1] It survives as

* Reprinted from the *Southern Economic Journal* (April 1960) by permission of the publisher, pp. 300–309.

[1] In the late forties a survey of 32 English-language elementary economics texts showed 20 presenting some version of this naive theory. (J.

underpinning for policy pronouncements of a "capitalist-apologist" variety—a fate some consider worse than death. It is embodied in a set of propositions which we shall re-state:[2]

1. One of the distributive shares in a

Fred Weston, "Profit as the Payment for the Function of Uncertainty-Bearing," *Journal of Business*, 1949, XXII, p. 106.) The percentage would have been higher had Weston's survey been made a generation earlier.

What makes Weston's result remarkable is that neither Alfred Marshall nor J. B. Clark, from whom the theoretical sections of these texts are predominantly derived, adopted the naive theory of profit. Marshall's position is that profit vanishes in the long run, as per this passage from *Principles of Economics*, 8th ed. (London: Macmillan, 1920), p. 605 f.: "That share of the normal expenses of production of any commodity which is commonly classed as profits, is so controlled on every side by the action of the principle of substitution, that it cannot long diverge from the normal supply price of the capital needed, added to the normal supply price of the ability and energy required for managing the business, and lastly the normal supply price of that organization by which the appropriate business ability and the requisite capital are brought together."

Clark's *Distribution of Wealth* (New York: Macmillan, 1899), p. 70, is even more clear-cut; profit results from dynamic change. As far as static conditions are concerned, he says: "The prices that conform to the cost of production are, of course, those which give no clear profit to the entrepreneur. A business man whose goods sell at such rates will get wages for whatever amount of labor he may perform, and interest for any capital that he may furnish; but he will have nothing more to show in the way of gain."

Over and beyond business "common sense," the source for the naive theories of the textbooks may be the half-forgotten contributions of a half-forgotten American profit theorist of the century's opening decade, F. B. Hawley. On Hawley, see Frank H. Knight, *Risk, Uncertainty, and Profit* (Boston: Houghton Mifflin, 1921), pp. 41–45.

[2] We owe to Weston our most detailed classification of the principal strains of recent profit theory. ("The Profit Concept and Theory: A Restatement," *Journal of Political Economy*, 1954, LXII, p. 152.) In this classification, what we call the naive theory is class "R"—"profits are rewards for bearing uncertainty and risk." (To this position Weston is himself opposed.)

Alternative classifications of profit theories may be found in Knight, *op. cit.*, ch. 2, and in R. A. Gordon, "Enterprise, Profits, and the Modern Corporation" (originally published 1936) in B. F. Haley and William Fellner (eds.), *Readings in the Theory of Income Distribution* (Philadelphia: Blakiston, 1946), pp. 560–565.

competitive economy is normal (pure, net, or necessary) profit.

2. This is usually a positive quantity in the long run, over and above implicit returns to any services or resources supplied by entrepreneurs to their own enterprises. (It may be zero or negative in the short run.)

3. Profit is a return to the related entrepreneurial functions of ultimate decision-making and ultimate uncertainty-bearing. The maker of ultimate decisions (bearer of ultimate uncertainties) is "the entrepreneur" who receives all profit in the long run.

4. The quantity which a firm seeks to maximize in its economic operations is the absolute size of the profit component.

5. In marginal-productivity terms, uncertainty-bearing or decision-making may be looked upon as a separate "factor of production" on the same footing as land, labor, or capital.

The first four of these propositions are the naive ones. They have substantial intuitive appeal, particularly in a world dominated by proprietorships and partnerships. (We shall however end by modifying all but the first.) The fifth proposition, more sophisticated and usually omitted from elementary expositions, attempts to fit profit into the Procrustean bed of marginal distribution theory. (We shall abandon it.)

For all its intuitive plausibility, this edifice has fallen into disrepair and disrepute. We may assemble certain of the principal considerations brought against naive profit theory, and outline certain of the rival positions.

1. In point of time, the initial crack in the structure was implicit in the "adding-up theorem" of distribution theory. This theorem applied the mathematics of the Euler theorem on homogeneous functions to show that there was nothing left over for profit if the production function were linear and homogeneous (with constant returns to scale). A later extension demonstrated the

same theorem under conditions of long-run competitive equilibrium regardless of the form of the production function.[3]

2. The adding-up theorem seemed to require elevation of decision-making or uncertainty-bearing to separate factors of production. The most ambitious effort in this direction was Pigou's, in *Economics of Welfare*.[4] Pigou's artificial construction was highly tentative, and does not seem to have been followed up.

3. As these formal difficulties became apparent, two attacks on naive profit theory developed "within the family" of neoclassical economics, centering about the names of Joseph Schumpeter and Frank H. Knight. The earlier of the two, the Schumpeterian attack, reduced both uncertainty and profit to consequences of innovation, and defined entrepreneurship as the introduction and development of innovation.[5] The normal or necessary profits of the naive theory were replaced by the windfalls of the innovator. Monopoly and similar profits, when not traceable to innovation, are defined out of the picture as rents or surpluses.

Knight's position, as stated in *Risk, Uncertainty, and Profit*, provides the basis for the more sophisticated versions of contemporary orthodoxy in profit theory.[6] If we may paraphrase Knight and his disciples (of whom Weston has spelled out his own position in greatest detail),[7] profit stems from uncertainty or non-insurable risk. It pervades the entire society, being borne not only by a special entrepreneurial class but by everyone in the economy. It results in positive or negative increments to all incomes from whatever source derived;[8] it is these which Knight calls profit. These elements of profit are not only unplanned but unanticipated. Knight therefore regards them as differences between incomes in disequilibrium and at equilibrium, or between incomes *ex post* and *ex ante*, rather than as compensations for uncertainty-bearing. There is in any event no profit component in distribution, only profit elements in all types of income. As a corollary, the attempt to locate within a corporate body any "entrepreneur" with paramount claim to profit is to look in a dark room for a black cat which is not there. As another corollary, it is meaningless in Knightian language to speak of a firm "maximizing profit" except as a shorthand for maximizing "enterprise net in-

[3] The statement and proof of the Euler theorem most available to economists is by R. G. D. Allen, *Mathematical Analysis for Economists* (London: Macmillan, 1938), pp. 317–320. For a history of its application to distribution theory the standard source is George J. Stigler, *Production and Distribution Theories* (New York: Macmillan, 1941), ch. xii. See also J. R. Hicks, *Theory of Wages* (London: Macmillan, 1932), pp. 233–236, and Joan Robinson, "Euler's Theorem and the Problem of Distribution" (originally published 1934), *Collected Economic Papers* (New York: Kelley, 1951), pp. 1–18.

The later extension is due primarily to Hicks (*op. cit.*, p. 237 f.), although the basic insights had been suggested earlier by Walras and Wicksell. Compare also Paul A. Samuelson, *Foundations of Economic Analysis* (Cambridge, Mass.: Harvard University Press, 1947), pp. 81–89.

[4] A. C. Pigou, *op. cit.*, fourth ed. (London: Macmillan, 1932), pp. 161–164, 771–781.

[5] Joseph A. Schumpeter, *The Theory of Economic Development*, originally published 1912 (Cambridge, Mass.: Harvard University Press, 1934), *passim*. In the Weston classification (Note 2) this theory is placed in category E—"profits are payments for the exercise of managerial or entrepreneurial functions." Knight has pointed out in *Risk, Uncertainty, and Profit*, pp. 32–41, and again in an article, "Profit," in *Encyclopaedia of the Social Sciences*, reprinted in Haley and Fellner, *op. cit.*, p. 540, that Schumpeter's profit theory was to some extent anticipated in Clark, *Distribution of Wealth*, ch. vi, xxv f.

[6] In the Weston classification, Knight and his followers are placed in category U—"profits are deviations arising from uncertainty" between earnings *ex post* and *ex ante*.

[7] Weston, "Profit as the Payment for the Function of Uncertainty-Bearing" and "Enterprise and Profit," *Journal of Business*, 1949, XXII, "A Generalized Uncertainty Theory of Profit," *American Economic Review*, 1940, XL, "The Profit Concept and Theory," *Journal of Political Economy*, 1954, LXII.

[8] However, "in the case of the owner of the business the difference is the entire income, since under perfect equilibrium the owner as such would have no functions and receive no income." Knight, "Profit," p. 537.

come" to all implicit (non-purchased) productive services lumped together.

4. The naive theory of profit includes no unequivocal notion of entrepreneurship. Some treat it as primarily a matter of risk- or uncertainty-bearing, others as primarily a matter of decision-making, others as primarily a matter of organization of the factors of production, and yet others as necessary combinations of a number of these activities.[9] None of these concepts proved equal to the task of identifying the entrepreneur in a corporate regime. In a corporate system, ultimate decision-making and organization came to rest mainly on salaried managers with little ownership interest, and ultimate uncertainty-bearing upon absentee stockholders. The distribution of the corporate usufruct, moreover, was difficult to rationalize by any combination of "uncertainty-bearing," "decision-making," or "factor-organization" principles. To use a catch phrase, ownership had become separated from control. The theory of profit and entrepreneurship which assumed the two to be united, now appeared both anachronistic and apologetic, a textbook embalming of the "folklore of capitalism."[10] Nor was a substitute theory helpful, which allocated the entrepreneurial functions to an artificial personage, the firm itself.[11] This theory gives no clue to the allocation or distribution of profit among the natural persons of the firm's ownership and control groups, and leaves this whole issue to the indeterminacy of corporate infighting.

5. Largely as a result of the diffusion of entrepreneurship, there has arisen a set of sociological or institutional profit theories. These have developed in several forms,[12] although no institutionalist Schumpeter or sociological Knight has yet created a school.[13] Writers of these persuasions agree in defining as profits accountants' "business net income,"[14] including all returns to implicit productive services, all corporate income and profits taxes, and all retained earnings. They usually stress, also, the class distinctions between "profit-receivers" in this sense and such other classes as "wage-earners" and "rentiers."[15] From these class considerations arises, in their view, the

[9] Once again we turn to Weston for detailed bibliography. "Enterprise and Profit," p. 158 f.

[10] The inapplicability of traditional profit theory to the corporate regime is the basic argument of, *inter alia*, Gordon's attack upon it. (Gordon, *op. cit.*, pp. 558–570.)

[11] James H. Stauss, "The Entrepreneur: The Firm," *Journal of Political Economy*, 1944, LII, pp. 112–127; Richard M. Davis, "The Current State of Profit Theory," *American Economic Review*, 1951, XLI, p. 251 f. In the Western classification, this strain of thought is related to the category Q—"profits are unimputable quasi-rents." See Weston, "Profit Concept and Theory," pp. 152, 166–168.

[12] What are called here sociological or institutional theories include not only Weston's category A—"profits are the difference between accounting revenues and costs," but also categories MC, MN, and W—"profits are gains from 'contrived' monopolistic and predatory activities," "profits are surpluses or rents resulting from uncertainty, indivisibilities, and other 'natural' barriers to entry," and "profits are payments derived from the ownership of productive assets." "The Profit Concept and Theory," p. 152.

[13] See however Paul Streeten, "The Theory of Profit," *Manchester School*, 1949, XVII; R. G. Hawtrey, "The Nature of Profit," *Economic Journal*, 1951, LXI; Jean Marchal, "Essai de construction d'une théorie nouvelle du profit," *Bulletin des Transports* (1952), of which an English translation appeared in the *American Economic Review* the preceding year (1951); Peter L. Bernstein, "Profit Theory—Where Do We Go From Here?" *Quarterly Journal of Economics*, 1953, LXVII; Anatol Murad, "Questions for Profit Theory," *American Journal of Economics and Sociology*, 1953, XIII. These writers' positions do not coincide, as may be seen by Bernstein's criticism of Marchal (*op. cit.*, p. 409 f.) and Murad's attempts to found an aggregative profit theory on Keynes' *Treatise on Money* (Murad, *op. cit.*, pp. 8–10).

[14] The contemporary Western accountant shuns the controversial term "profit" in favor of more colorless concepts like "earnings" or "income." (Cf. Weston, "Profit Concept and Theory," p. 165.) At the same time, Soviet accountants and economists use the term freely and theorize regarding its role in their own society.

[15] This particular point is made by Knight as clearly as by any of the institutionalist writers. "Under the enterprise system, a special social class, the business men, direct economic activity; they are in the strict sense the producers, while the great mass of the population merely furnish them with productive services, placing their persons and their property at the disposal of this class." (*Risk, Uncertainty, and Profit*, p. 271.)

principal justification for lumping profit-receivers' diverse income types together under the single head of profit. For some writers, too, such notions as entrepreneurship and pure competition smack of apologetics rather than science. Their views of profit accordingly involve exploitation theorizing in a Socialist tradition.[16]

II. A REFORMULATION OF THE NAIVE THEORY

This essay arises from dissatisfaction with Schumpeter, with Knight, and with the institutionalists. Payments most conveniently regarded as profits apparently persist without justification in Schumpeterian innovation. Business men and promoters continue to estimate profits *ex ante* in defiance of Knightian usage, and the public continues to think of profit as largely the special income of a special class of society. Knight's theory can also be criticized as particularly heavily insulated from both empirical testing and empirical relevance. At the same time the accounting category of "net income" combines elements so numerous and weighted so differently as between firms as to cast doubt on the analytical usefulness of the institutional theories. In this predicament, when both sophistication and iconoclasm seem to fail us, let us explore what can be done by naivete and simple-mindedness.

We consider a static society with constant population, tastes, natural resources, social institutions (of a capitalist sort), and an unchanging range of technical alternatives available for use. The society is purely competitive, with complete divisibility of all inputs and outputs, mobility sufficient to assure a single price for most goods and services on each market at any point in time, and full knowledge of all existing prices. The society is not however stationary. Capital may be accumulating or decumulating. The perfection of knowledge does not extend beyond present prices

[16] Marchal and Murad are examples here.

either to cost and production relationships or to the future, although we assume all elasticities of expectations[17] unitary or fractional for the sake of stability. We have in short uncertainty without innovation.

What is this uncertainty about? Fundamentally, about two matters just mentioned: (1) The amount, nature, and consequences of capital accumulation (even with no change in the spectrum of available techniques)[18] and (2) the forms and coefficients of cost and production functions. (There is no need to forget about the vagaries of weather, the breakdown of machinery, the occurrence of illness and accident, or the consequences of variations in morale.) There is assumed to exist no economically efficient method of transforming any significant part of this uncertainty into insurable or otherwise transferable risk.

We follow tradition in considering only a competitive state of things, and only the long run. Imperfect competition and short-run windfalls are admittedly at the heart of concrete problems, but we have no contribution to their unsatisfactory treatment in economic theory. We further eschew the classical commingling of profit with interest, the Marxian commingling of profit with property income generally, and the accountants' commingling of profit with implicit returns to productive services generally.

Starting from this compromising sort of framework, we can outline a compromising sort of profit theory. We divide economic uncertainties into those giving rise to profit and those affecting other resource incomes. This differentiation seems to permit reestablishment of normal profit, positive or

[17] See Hicks, *Value and Capital* (Oxford: Oxford University Press, 1939), pp. 205–207.

[18] We cannot accept a Knightian dictum: "Many changes, such as the steady growth of population and capital, are fairly predictable, and to a corresponding extent do not occasion imperfect competition or profit." (Profit," p. 541; see also *Risk, Uncertainty, and Profit*, pp. 35–38.) This is more true for the statistician dealing with the economy as a whole than for the business man in any particular branch of trade.

negative, as a separate income share. This is a "specialized" uncertainty theory as distinguished from Weston's "generalized" one. It is derived primarily from the confrontation of the naive theories of the textbooks with the sophisticated theories of Knight and his followers in particular. Given this specialized uncertainty theory, it is possible to make peace with marginal analysis and its adding-up theorem, and to consider *en passant* such problems as the meaningfulness of "profit maximizing" and the identification of "the entrepreneur" in a corporate setting.

Of the thousand natural shocks (and uncertainties) that flesh is heir to, those compensated by profit are neither the most pervasive nor the most significant. Considerations of uncertainty alter (in both directions) the supply and demand conditions for all goods and services. The net effect of uncertainty on prices and incomes is itself uncertain. We propose to consider profit as compensation for merely the subset of uncertainties which arises from having no contractual claim to one's income either per hour of labor, per "piece" of product, or per unit of land or capital. We concentrate therefore upon the incomes of those who accept as residual claimants part or all of what is left after contractual claims are honored and contractual claimants paid.[19] This is not to imply, at one

extreme, that contractual claims are always honored or enforced. Varying degrees of uncertainty, called premia rather than profit, attend the fact that particular contracts may be neither honored nor enforceable. Neither is it accurate, at the other extreme, to confine the profit-receiver's risk to the tautological one of not making his profit. He bears in addition the risk of a possible loss on income account, meaning a smaller income than his services or profit would have brought contractually. Further, if property has been contributed noncontractually, the uncertainty-bearer may also lose on capital account by the writing down or wiping out of the value of his assets when a debt investment would have protected him.

For the special purposes of profit theory let us classify productive inputs not into the usual "factors of production" but into "contractual" and "entrepreneurial" categories, according as their remuneration is or is not determined contractually.[20] This terminology identifies entrepreneurship not with managerial, organizational, or innovational responsibilities, but exclusively with the precarious nature of its legal claims. In a partnership entrepreneurship is di-

---

[19] This view is not original. Knight presents it as a "compromise position" between the "theoretical" view of profit (his own uncertainty theory) and the "practical" one which identifies economic profit with the accountant's "business net income." ("Profit," p. 537 f.) Weston likewise considers this view briefly ("Profit Concept and Theory," p. 167 f).

A word regarding these writers' objections to our position is in order. Knight points out that profit (as he defines it) may be concealed in inflated contractual incomes of "insiders." Weston raises the objection that *all* incomes would be gross profit if institutional arrangements should eliminate the possibility of contractual claims to income. Knight's objection seems valid mainly if not exclusively under conditions of imperfect competition, while Weston's non-contractual world seems inconsistent quite generally with the institutions of an enterprise economy.

[20] This classification is no more water-tight than are most others. We may consider certain intermediate cases:

a. The *preferred stockholder* has a contractual claim, albeit a contingent one. In this he is in a position analogous to that of a salesman on commission.

b. The *convertible bondholder* has a contractual claim, with the privilege of exchanging it on stated terms for an entrepreneurial claim at some future time.

c. The *salaried partner* provides entrepreneurial resources so long as the partnership is in existence, since his claim is not enforceable generally until after the partnership is dissolved. If the partnership goes out of business with his salary in arrears, the salaried partner may then shift to a contractual position.

d. The *executive on the bonus list* is in a hybrid position. He has a contractual claim to his salary. His claim to his bonus is entrepreneurial until it has been voted, and contractual thereafter.

e. The *participating preferred stockholder* is also in a hybrid position. As a preferred stockholder he has a contractual claim; his participation involves an entrepreneurial one.

vided between all partners, silent as well as active. In a corporation it is allocated to common stockholders, coupon-clippers included. (We recall the concept of "drone entrepreneurship," devised in a different setting.)[21] Managers and directors are not in this terminology entrepreneurs except as they are also stockholders. Still less is the entrepreneur "the firm" or any corporate entity abstracted from the people connected with it.

An entrepreneurial service has in pure competition a highly imperfect market, on which several different prices may prevail simultaneously. This is not only because these services are unstandardized, but for special reasons peculiar to the entrepreneurial position. Many of the transactions are implicit, with a resource owner dealing with himself in his other capacity of business manager; demand and supply are identical and neutral equilibrium prevails. In addition, the "price" or "rate of return" of the entrepreneurial service cannot be a contracted, set, or recorded market price or rate of return. It is merely a consensus as to the expected price or rate of return. The expectations and the prices are imprecise; when the buyer and seller deal at arm's length, they may not hold the same expectations. To put the matter geometrically, any "equilibrium position" involves a range, a zone, or a set of points, and not a single point. We shall however use the single-point approximation since, to quote Marshall:[22]

> The adjustment of supply to demand in the case of business ability is somewhat hindered by the difficulty of ascertaining exactly what is the price that is being paid for it in any trade. . . . But though it may be difficult to read the lessons of an individual trader's experience, those of a whole trade can never be completely hidden, and

[21] Clarence Danhof, "Observations on Entrepreneurship in Agriculture," cited by Yale Brozen, "Entrepreneurship and Technological Change," in Harold F. Williamson and John A. Buttrick (eds.), *Economic Development: Principles and Patterns* (New York: Prentice-Hall, 1954), p. 205.

[22] Marshall, *op. cit.*, p. 607 f.

cannot be hidden at all for very long. . . . There is a general agreement among business men that the average rate of profits in a trade cannot rise or fall much without general attention being attracted to the change before long. And though it may sometimes be a more difficult task for a business man than for a skilled labourer to find out whether he could improve his prospects by changing his trade, yet the business man has great opportunities for discovering what can be found out about the present and future of other trades; and if he should wish to change his trade, he will generally be able to do so more easily than the skilled workman could.

We consider in turn each panel of Figure 28.1. The left-hand panel [Figure 28.1(a)]

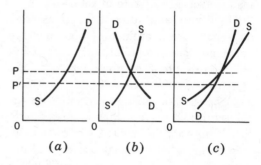

FIGURE 28.1

relates the *internal* supply and demand for an entrepreneurial service or input to its anticipated gross return. The supply and demand functions are identical, since each entrepreneur as demander is buying entrepreneurial services from himself as supplier. The combined supply and demand function is represented by a single curve *DS*. This curve slopes upward in accordance with the general observation that high rates of gross profit result in increased business population, increased internal investment, and similar signs of increased use of productive services under non-contractual conditions.

The center panel [Figure 28.1(b)] represents the *external* supply and demand for the same entrepreneurial service. The demand and supply functions are drawn in conventional shapes. The vertical ordinate

P of their intersection indicates an equilibrium gross profit.

The right-hand panel [Figure 28.1(*c*)] is the horizontal sum of the other two. It is drawn with the internal supply and demand dominant, so that both the aggregate supply and the aggregate demand function for the entrepreneurial service slope upward. The demand function slopes more steeply as a Hicksian stability condition. This is a common state of affairs in unincorporated businesses and closed corporations. For corporations whose securities are traded publicly, the external supply and demand are usually dominant. A company's demand function for equity capital is normally inverse to its rate of return.

The supply and demand functions cross at a point with ordinate *P* (an average value in a zone of equilibrium). This makes *OP* a gross profit or gross return to the entrepreneurial service. Let *OP'* (on Figure 28.1) be the price of the physically identical service in its contractual uses.[23] *OP'* then represents the implicit contractual return to the entrepreneurial service, and *PP'* represents the net or normal profit which we seek to explain.

These diagrams have drawn *P* above *P'*, making the normal profit *PP'* a positive quantity. It may actually be positive, negative, or zero. Its sign depends on many things. What is the relative strength of the "insurance" motive for avoiding uncertainty as against the "gambling" motive for seeking it out?[24] Assuming the former motive to be the stronger at the margin for entrepreneurs as well as for college professors, what are its offsets?

A positive long-run net profit in a competitive industry may mean that the supply of entrepreneurial resources is *not* associated with such putative advantages as empire-building, tax-avoidance, or being one's own boss. (For the ordinary small-scale common stockholder, there is no such association.) If these attractions of "the entrepreneurial way of life" exist, their strength is insufficient to outweigh the dislike for uncertainty-bearing by the suppliers of services on non-contractual terms. The industry may also be believed to be facing deflation, obsolescence, or some other prospect which makes a contractual position attractive as compared to an entrepreneurial one.

On the other hand, nothing in our analysis prevents *P* falling below *P'* (*PP'* becoming a negative quantity) either for another entrepreneurial service in the same industry, for the same entrepreneurial service in another industry, or for all entrepreneurial services in all competitive industries. This may mean that the supply of entrepreneurial services is associated strongly with some or all of the attractions mentioned in the last paragraph.[25] It may mean that entrepreneurs see uncertainty-bearing as a positive pleasure. Or it may mean that the industry (or the economy) is facing some prospect such as price inflation, which renders entrepreneurial positions abnormally attractive by comparison with contractual ones.

The preceding analysis shows how physically uniform productive services, types of labor or property, can command even under competition different remunerations when supplied entrepreneurially than their contractual market prices. These differentials cumulate to net, normal, or necessary profit. It can also be shown, using simple indiffer-

---

[23] We treat *OP'* as a constant, unchanging with the amount of the service used entrepreneurially. Dropping this assumption would require the drawing of the horizontal through *P'* as downward sloping, to allow for the effects of diminishing productivity.

[24] Compare in a different connection Milton Friedman and L. J. Savage, "The Utility Analysis of Choices Involving Risk" (originally published 1948) in George J. Stigler and Kenneth E. Boulding (eds.), *Readings in Price Theory* (Homewood, Ill.: Irwin, 1952), pp. 57–96.

[25] At least one profit theorist can cite personal experience (in commercial banking) to support the familiar proposition that many small business men and farmers accept deliberately, and with full knowledge of alternatives, situations in which normal profit is negative. Bernstein, *op. cit.*, pp. 409–411.

ence analysis, how a firm's budget for a given productive service may be allocated between contractual and entrepreneurial sources of supply.

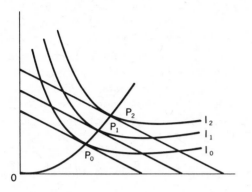

FIGURE 28.2

Both axes of Figure 28.2 measure quantities of a single productive service, available in unlimited amounts to the individual firm on either contractual or entrepreneurial terms.[26] Suppose that we are dealing with money capital, the Keynesian "finance." Funds supplied contractually (debt finance) are measured along the horizontal axis. Funds supplied entrepreneurially (equity finance) are measured along the vertical axis. The straight lines (price lines), drawn with a slope of less than 45 degrees to the horizontal, imply a higher price per dollar of equity than of debt finance. The family of indifference curves (I_0, I_1, . . .) reflect no differences in the liquidity achieved in holding funds raised by the two methods, nor differences in the productivity of goods purchased with funds raised by the two methods. No such differences exist. The indifference curves reflect a variety of considerations in the minds of the management, outgrowths of the pervasiveness of uncertainty. There is a fear of excessive overhead charges for debt service in bad times if too much debt

[26] No allowance is made here for such practical limitations as lack of access to equity capital markets, rationing of debt finance, or the Kalecki "principle of increasing risk."

finance is used ("trading on the equity"). There is fear of dilution of both control and profit if too much reliance is put on equity finance. A firm may prefer a smaller volume of capital in the "right" proportions of debt to equity over a larger volume in the "wrong" proportions. A conventional form of indifference curves, with downward slope and upward concavity, accordingly appears plausible and is adopted on Figure 28.2. The points of tangency (P_0, P_1, . . .) between price lines and indifference curves represent optimal divisions of different outlays budgeted for finance between contractual and entrepreneurial supplies. The expansion path connecting these points of tangency shows how this optimum varies with the size of the budget. For any budget, a weighted average price can be computed for finance as a whole. This weighted average price will be different from the market contractual interest rate. In our example, it will be higher.

We have yet to ask the question—how can normal profit be paid at all? We deal with long-run competitive equilibrium, and with production at minimum average cost. If all productive services receive the value of their marginal products, the entire product is distributed. Yet we have postulated differentials for profit positive or negative. Where do they come from, if they are positive? Where do they go, if they are negative?

Here our weighted averages of contractual and entrepreneurial prices for identical services come to our assistance. The competitive entrepreneur should be looked upon as adjusting the use of productive services so as to equate the values of the marginal products not to their contractual market prices but to weighted averages of contractual and entrepreneurial prices where these diverge and where entrepreneurial inputs are used. This simple device avoids conflict between the persistence of normal profit and the "adding-up theorem." It is consistent with an aspect of the capital market which has aroused comment over the years—the refusal of firms to borrow out to the margin set by contractual interest rates, when their equities earn substantially higher returns. It is equally consistent with the tendency of marginal firms to concentrate on entrepreneurial and avoid contractual inputs whenever possible. This is conventionally criticized as inefficient, but may result from negative normal profit in these enterprises. It may be good marginalism for such firms to consider entrepreneurial services as costing considerably less than the contractual market prices for the same services would suggest.

A welfare complication does however arise from our suggested change in received doctrine. When the competitive firm expands or contracts its output, the proportions normally change in which contractual and entrepreneurial units of identical resources are combined. (The points P_1 on Figure 28.2 need not lie on a single radius vector.) If so, the weighted average price of some productive services to the firm will change with the firm's output, rising or falling as the case may be. Even under pure competition, then, the welfare analysis of the firm's expansion and contraction should involve the considerations now limited to the industry and to imperfect competition —restrictions and over-expansions of output inspired by price changes rather than by "efficiency." The same is true for technological adjustments by which contractual, entrepreneurial, and "mixed" inputs are substituted for each other. Here again firm and industry analysis, pure and imperfectly competitive analysis, move closer to each other in a way which threatens to some extent the conventional welfare economist's preference for pure competition under static conditions.

To present these complications in a form closer to the concrete, suppose that entrepreneurial services for a certain firm cost more than corresponding contractual ones. Suppose also that expansion requires a proportional shift of the firm's input mix in the entrepreneurial direction. This firm's expansion causes its weighted average input prices to rise against it, and vice versa for contraction. The firm will expand less or contract more than is required for optimum resource allocation, always operating below its theoretical optimum scale. Suppose next that the same firm is considering a substitution of machinery for labor at approximately the same level of output, machinery being a mixed and labor a purely contractual input. This substitution would raise the weighted average cost of capital against the firm, which would therefore tend to make it mechanize more slowly and less completely than efficiency would require.

III. ON OPTIMIZING PROFIT

We have listed five propositions which appear to embody the substance of naive profit theory. Proposition 1 we have accepted: "One of the distributive shares in a competitive economy is normal profit." Likewise Proposition 2: "This is usually a positive quantity in the long run, over and above implicit returns to any services or resources supplied by entrepreneurs to their own enterprises," with some doubts as to the positive sign. Proposition 3 defined profit as "a return to the related entrepreneurial functions of ultimate decision-making and ultimate uncertainty-bearing," which might have been combined as ultimate organizing. Our reformulation has modified this proposition considerably. Gone are decision-making and organizing as bases for profit.[27] Limited is uncertainty-bearing, in its relation to profit, to the assumption of non-contractual positions in

[27] Weston puts the case more strongly ("Generalized Uncertainty Theory of Profit," p. 48): "The ultimate decision-makers in a firm need not be compensated as residual income receivers. . . . Judgment is an economic service. The principles explaining the compensation for this service are similar to the principles explaining the compensation for other services. . . . The exercise of judgment may be sold on a fixed-price basis or on a variable-price basis."

the supply of services. As to entrepreneurship, it is scattered among suppliers of various productive services on entrepreneurial terms.[28] Proposition 5 suggests that decision-making or uncertainty-bearing be regarded as a distinct "factor of production," and we have been able to dispense with this proposition entirely. We have as yet said nothing about Proposition 4, that firms seek to maximize total net profit.[29] In this section we shall consider that proposition in the light of our restatement of naive profit theory.

We may state three views baldly. The naive view we have seen already—the rational entrepreneur maximizing his net profit. Sophisticated (Knightian) profit theory has the firm maximizing its net receipts[30]—in our terms, the total return to

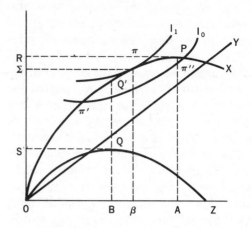

FIGURE 28.3

its entrepreneurial inputs, gross of their contractual input prices. (Some such reformulation follows from the definition of profit as a differential between income *ex post* and *ex ante*, or between disequilibrium and equilibrium situations.)[31] "Organization theory" has the firm trying to maximize no quantifiable variable whatever, but instead to survive comfortably and securely as a good-sized organization.[32]

These three alternatives (which by no means exhaust their field) may lead to quite different results under given conditions, as is shown for example by Figure 28.3.[33] The

[28] Here we part company with Weston, who argues (*ibid.*, p. 47): "Non-contractual income receivers [may be] identified as entrepreneurs. The application of this term with its varied traditional connotations to a use in which functional activities perform no role, is likely to result in confusion. . . . It would be better if [entrepreneurship] were not used to describe various functional types of factors of production whose common attribute is the non-contractual nature of their returns."

[29] Literature on the realism and relevance of "profit maximization" and "maximizing behavior" generally has burgeoned since the late 1930's. Perhaps the earliest in a series of path-breaking articles was R. L. Hall and C. J. Hitch, "Price Theory and Business Behaviour," (originally published 1938), in T. Wilson and P. W. S. Andrews (eds.), *Oxford Studies in the Price Mechanism* (Oxford: Oxford University Press, 1951), ch. 3. A good bibliography of the ensuing controversy may be found in A. G. Papandreou, "Some Basic Problems in the Theory of the Firm," in B. F. Haley (ed.), *Survey of Contemporary Economics*, II (Homewood, Ill.: Irwin, 1952), pp. 205–213.

This writer has profited in this section from the technical contributions of William J. Baumol, Herbert A. Simon, and Tibor Scitovsky, the institutional contributions of Alfred R. Oxenfeldt and Melvin W. Reder, and the "rebuttals" of Armen A. Alchian, James S. Earley, Milton Friedman, and Fritz Machlup. The nature of some of these debts will be clarified below.

[30] Thus Friedman, "The Methodology of Positive Economics," in *Essays in Positive Economics* (Chicago: University of Chicago Press, 1953), p. 21: "Under a wide range of circumstances individual firms behave *as if* they were seeking rationally to maximize their expected returns (generally if misleadingly called 'profits') and had full knowledge of the data needed to succeed in this attempt." And in a footnote to the above passage: " 'Profits' are a result of uncertainty and . . . cannot be deliberately maximized in advance."

[31] Weston puts this point in italics ("Generalized Uncertainty Theory of Profit," p. 54): "*To attribute a central role to profit maximization in static equilibrium analysis must lead to confusion because static analysis abstracts from the very conditions which give rise to profit*" (in Knightian terms).

[32] Compare Simon, *Administrative Behavior* (New York: Macmillan, 1947), ch. 4, and *Models of Man* (New York: Wiley, 1957), ch. 10. A compromise position is presented for oligopoly cases in Baumol, *Business Behavior, Value and Growth* (New York: Macmillan, 1959), chs. 4, 6–8.

[33] This diagram is based on Scitovsky, "A Note on Profit Maximization and Its Implications," (originally published 1943) in Stigler and Boulding, *op. cit.*, Figure 2, p. 354.

horizontal axis of this diagram measures productive services supplied entrepreneurially; the vertical axis measures their income, gross in some cases and net in others. The alternatives open to the supplier of the entrepreneurial services are plotted as though single-valued on three curves OX, OY, and OZ. The curve OX is a path of gross profit; it is drawn with a maximum value OR when OA units are supplied. The ray OY measures the total return to the same service supplied contractually to outside firms under competitive conditions; it is a straight line without extreme values. The curve OZ is the vertical difference between OX and OY. In economic terms, it represents normal profit. It too has a maximum value OS (below OR) where OB units (less than OA) are supplied.[34]

According to the naive theory, the firm will aim at point Q, with co-ordinates (OB, OS) at which net profit is maximized. According to the sophisticated theory, more entrepreneurial services will be used and the firm will aim at point P, with coordinates (OA, OR) at which net revenue or gross profit is maximized. The two theories give the same result when the quantity of entrepreneurial services is fixed. This case may be the one which Knight and his followers have in mind.

Introduce now a set of indifference curves (I_0, I_1, . . .) expressing reluctance to supply services entrepreneurially, at least beyond a certain point, and expressing also a preference for higher income from any quantity of services so supplied. Geometrically, the indifference curves slope upward with upward concavity. In economic terms, this construction may represent not only

aversion to uncertainty-bearing, but tax considerations, devotion to the Hicksian "quiet life," smallness of scale as an end in itself, *rentier* irresponsibility, etc.

In any event, there is generally an "optimizing" tangency point π, with co-ordinates ($O\beta$, $O\Sigma$). This is the point which we maintain that the firm will set as its goal. This point is clearly to the southwest of, and involves smaller supplies of entrepreneurial services than, the point P which the sophisticated theory sets up as the firm's target. We cannot generalize about its relationship to point Q' (the projection of Q on OX) which the naive theory sets up as the firm's target. On the diagram point π lies between points P and Q'.

An interpretation of Simon's organization-theory position may also be presented on Figure 28.3. Suppose that the firm expects to survive with reasonable comfort and security as an organization at any combination of entrepreneurial services and income on or above the indifference curve I_0 (which must cross or touch OX). Suppose further that I_0 crosses OX at two points π' and π'', to the left and right of π. Then according to organization theory any point along OX between the limits π' and π'' is analytically as likely as any other, choice between them being a matter of historical accident. The professional bias of the economist tends to hope for something which will narrow the range of "satisficing" behavior; Baumol's "revenue maximization hypothesis" [35] may be interpreted to suggest that the neighborhood immediately to the left of π'' is more likely than that immediately to the right of π'.

But these are matters for possible empirical testing. At the abstract level of the present discussion, our introductory Proposition 4 (the naive theory of profit maximization) seems to require modification less from sophisticated theories of profit than from notions of "optimizing" rather than "maximizing" profit however defined and isolated.

---

[34] It may be useful to present a generalization of this proposition, which is elementary but has many applications:

Let $u = f(x)$ be a function with negative second derivatives over the relevant range, and let $v = g(x)$ be a monotone increasing function. Let u have a maximum at x_1 such that $f'(x_1) = 0$, and let ($u - v$) have a maximum at x_2 such that $f'(x_2) - g'(x_2) = 0$. Then $x_1 > x_2$, from the negative sign of $f''(x)$.

[35] Baumol, *op. cit.*, ch. 6.

29. The Geometry
of Capital and Interest:
A Suggested Simplification*

DONALD J. DEWEY

Donald J. Dewey (B.A., the University of Chicago, 1943; M.A., Iowa State University, 1947) was born in Solon, Ohio, in 1922. He attended Cambridge University, the London School of Economics, and the University of Chicago. He is now on the faculty of Columbia University. Before assuming this post, he taught at Indiana University and Duke University. Dewey's special interests are microeconomic theory, industrial organization, and monetary theory. He is best known for his two books *Monopoly in Economics and Law* and *Modern Capital Theory*.

In recent years, the study of capital and interest has come to be viewed as a branch of monetary theory. No doubt interest is, in some degree, a monetary phenomenon. (If it is not, central bank policy is an awful hoax.) Unfortunately, young economists who first make the acquaintance of capital and interest through their work in monetary theory often seem to believe that interest is mainly a monetary phenomenon. They are, of course, badly informed.

Since Böhm-Bawerk's day the well-informed economist has known that interest is rooted mainly in the productivity of investment and the economy's preference for present over future consumption. The

effective exposition of this truth, however, has never been easy, and for the last thirty years pedagogical progress has been distressingly slow. Monetary theorists now have a large bag of elegant tricks that demonstrate how changes in the money supply and liquidity preference can affect the interest rate. Advocates of the so-called "real" theory of interest must fall back on a set of teaching aids with a distinctly musty odor—Robinson Crusoe and his fish-catching activities, growing trees, aging wine, the more roundabout method of production, etc. Therefore, there may be merit in describing a pedagogical device that allows the essential properties of capital and interest to be simply, albeit rigorously, conveyed.

Two of the more effective tools available

* Reprinted from the *American Economic Review* (March 1963) by permission of the publisher, pp. 134–139.

423

are Irving Fisher's indifference curves [2, pp. 387–90] and Frank Knight's Crusonia plant—a species of vegetation that supplies all human wants and, though unattended, grows at a constant (geometric) rate "except as new tissue is cut away for consumption" [3, p. 30]. In essence, the pedagogical device described here applies, with modifications, Fisher's geometry to Knight's Crusonia plant.[1]

Consider Figure 29.1. Measure present consumption on the horizontal axis OC. We posit that all consumption for the coming year is done "now." This assumption allows us to treat consumption as having the dimensions of a stock rather than of a flow and, hence, to represent consumption and the stock of capital on the same axis. In Figure 29.1, OC denotes the maximum amount of consumption that is possible now. OC also denotes the present stock of capital (Crusonia) on the assumption that no consumption for this year has yet occurred, and that the whole of the present capital stock can, if it is desired, be consumed this year.

Now measure the stock of capital that will be in existence (and available for consumption) one year from now on the vertical axis OF. If no consumption takes place now, the stock of capital will reach OF by the end of the year. Clearly the size of this future capital stock is a function of (a) the marginal productivity of investment,

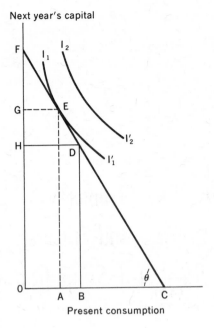

FIGURE 29.1

[1] The Crusonia plant has the great virtue of eliminating three complications in capital theory that are fundamentally unimportant but are, nonetheless, time-consuming in the classroom and a source of confusion to the young. It enables us to ignore the "period of production"—the gestation period of capital assets. (For the view that the period of production is an important idea, see Robert Dorfman's rigorous restatement of Böhm-Bawerk's theory [1].) This period is perforce zero since the Crusonia plant grows continuously. It allows us to avoid all measurement problems. The stock of capital, consumption, and investment per unit of time, can be expressed as quantities of Crusonia. And finally, the Crusonia plant permits an exposition of capital theory in the first instance without any attention to the mechanics of capitalization and discount.

i.e., of not consuming, and (b) the amount consumed now. Every possible combination of present consumption and next year's capital stock is represented by a point on the line CF.

On OF mark off the distance OH equal to OC. The marginal productivity of investment (mpi) is given by the slope of the line CF (minus one). Since this slope is a constant, there are no diminishing returns to investment. The rate of growth of the capital stock is independent of its size, CF is perforce a straight line, and mpi equals $\tan \theta - 1$. We perceive from Figure 29.1 that OB is the amount of consumption compatible with a capital stock that reaches a maximum of OC (or OH) each year. Immediately after consumption OB, the present capital stock is BC. During the year it grows back to OC (or OH). Should consumption exceed OB, the capital stock will be smaller one year from now. Should some part of OB be invested, it will be larger.

In order to reckon investment—and hence capital growth—we must specify the economy's preference for present consumption over future capital. This we do in Figure 29.1 by a set of Fisher-type indifference curves, I_1I_1', I_2I_2'. Present consumption is again measured along the horizontal axis and the stock of capital one year from now along the vertical axis.[2]

From Figure 29.1 we see that the economy attains its highest indifference curve (I_1I_1') by consuming OA now and having a capital stock of OG in one year's time. We may also read off the following information. For a period of one year:

OC = OH = initial capital stock.
OG = final capital stock.
OB = income available for consumption.
OA = actual consumption.
AB = income invested.
HG = growth in capital stock ("net investment").

$\dfrac{HG}{OH}$ = capital stock growth rate.

In Figure 29.1 the marginal productivity of investment during the year is given by any of the following:

$$\tan \theta - 1, \frac{OF}{OC} - 1, \frac{HG}{AB} - 1, \frac{HF}{OB} - 1, \frac{HF}{OH}.$$

Figure 29.1 depicts the "normal" case of an economy that is increasing its capital stock. To derive a zero growth rate we need only revise our diagram to make the indifference curve, I_1I_1' tangent to the line CF at point D. To show capital consumption we would make the point of tangency lie between D and C.

[2] In Fisher's original geometry the vertical axis measures future income and the horizontal axis present income [2, p. 387]. In that context, however, Fisher is not using "income" to denote a flow of goods (or services) in perpetuity. The value of the capital stock in his diagram can only be obtained by discounting the future income by the interest rate and adding the result to present income. Thus it is not immediately clear from Fisher's geometry whether a failure to consume all of present income (as defined by Fisher) serves to increase the capital stock or merely retard its decline. This uncertainty can be resolved by using the data provided by Fisher in his diagram; but the computation is tedious.

The geometry of Figure 29.1 has an additional merit as a teaching aid. It can be used to show that there is no genuine conflict between writers who treat capital as a stock of "real" things that yield incomes in perpetuity and those who define it as a sum of future incomes discounted by the rate of interest. (Given perfect arbitrage, the rate of interest, must, of course, equal the marginal productivity of investment.) For example, let the perpetual annual income be HF; let HF be paid in a lump sum once a year; and let the first payment be due one year from today. The present value of a perpetuity disbursed in this manner is equal to the annual income divided by the interest rate. The interest rate is

$$\frac{HF}{OH}. \quad \text{Therefore,} \quad \frac{HF}{\dfrac{HF}{OH}} = OH.$$

But from Figure 29.1 it is immediately apparent that, when consumption takes place on the last day of the year rather than on the first (as we previously assumed), HF is the annual harvest or income of the capital stock OC or OH.

Our geometry is easily modified to accommodate the case where the marginal productivity of investment declines as the capital stock increases. This is done in Figure 29.2. Let us revert to the assumption that all consumption for the year takes place now. Once again OC denotes the present stock of capital, OB the quantity of present consumption compatible with a constant stock of capital OC (or OH), and the arc FC every possible combination of present consumption and future capital.

However, when diminishing returns to investment are introduced into our model, a complication appears. There is now a different *mpi* for every different capital stock. And, since in the absence of consumption, the capital stock grows continuously, there is a different *mpi* for every moment during the year. (Recall that *mpi* is what the instantaneous growth rate of the capital stock would be if consumption were zero.) Thus one is reduced to speaking of the average value of *mpi* for the year. The greater the fraction of income invested now, the smaller the average value of *mpi*.

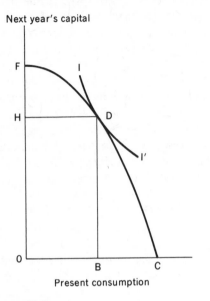

Next year's capital

Present consumption

FIGURE 29.2

Figure 29.2 indicates that the economy has achieved long-run equilibrium. It attains its highest indifference curve *II'* by consuming the whole of its annual income *OB*. Average *mpi* is equal to the slope of *FC* and *II'* at point *D* (minus one). Note that when diminishing returns to investment are posited, average *mpi* is necessarily less than the average rate of return on investment during the year.

In Figure 29.2 the quantity of consumption invested now is *BC*, and the capital stock one year hence will be *OH* (or *BD*). The average rate of return on investment *BC* is therefore $OH/BC - 1$. This last rate

has no special significance in capital theory, except that it is sometimes mistaken for the annual market rate of interest. But the interest rate is tied by arbitrage to average *mpi*—to the slope of *FC* at point *D* (minus one) in the present example. Indeed, the equality of average *mpi* and the interest rate is implied by the proposition that the economy has achieved its highest indifference curve.

What is true is that, as the long-run equilibrium of a stable capital stock is approached, the interest rate and average *mpi* tend toward the average rate of return on *income* invested. For now the quantity of income invested becomes an ever smaller percentage of total investment, i.e., the capital stock. Thus in Figure 29.2, if some minute portion of income *OB* were saved, the average rate of return on income invested would be virtually the same as average *mpi*. In effect, the small fraction of *OB* saved would be the incremental unit of investment.

The essential properties of capital, income, consumption, investment, capital growth, time preference, and capital productivity can be set forth in many ways. The method described above has, I believe, the merit of allowing the delineation to be made clearly, compactly, and with minimum use of cumbersome notation.

REFERENCES

1. R. DORFMAN, "Waiting and the Period of Production," *Quart. Jour. Econ.*, Aug. 1959, *73*, 351–72.
2. I. FISHER, *The Rate of Interest*, New York 1907.
3. F. H. KNIGHT, "Diminishing Returns from Investment," *Jour. Pol. Econ.*, Mar. 1944, *52*, 26–47.

30. The Baseball Players' Labor Market*

SIMON ROTTENBERG[1]

Simon Rottenberg (A.B., George Washington University, 1939; M.A., Harvard University, 1948; Ph.D., 1950) was born in 1916 in Providence, Rhode Island. After serving on the faculties of the University of Chicago, Roosevelt University, and the University of Buffalo, he assumed his present position as Professor of Economics at Duke University in 1965. He is noted, primarily, for his research in the fields of human resources and labor economics, in which he has written widely, and for articles in the areas of medical economics and the economics of education. Many of his writings are concerned with human resource problems of Latin American countries. In addition to his academic affiliations, Professor Rottenberg has also had a distinguished career in government service, and as an adviser to the governments of less-developed countries. In 1970 he served as a senior research economist with the International Labor Organization in Geneva.

Since its inception in the 1870's, organized baseball has developed a market for baseball players and their services in which there is less than perfect freedom to buy and sell. In this paper I shall discuss analytically a number of market problems which are interesting because of some unusual characteristics of the baseball labor market and the organization of the baseball industry.

In the labor market, monopsony is more frank and explicit and less imperfect than in the more common case, in other industries, of covert antipirating agreements. The nature of the industry is such that competitors must be of approximately equal

* Reprinted from *Journal of Political Economy* (June 1956), by permission of The University of Chicago Press. Copyright, 1956, pp. 242–258.

[1] Am indebted to my colleagues and the students of the Department of Economics at the University of Chicago for challenging discussions of this topic which I have had with them. I must lay claim, however, to any errors the paper still contains.

Although I have referred to a large number of different sources in the considerable literature on baseball, I have found no document so valuable by far as the *Hearings before the Subcommittee on Study of Monopoly Power of the Committee on the Judiciary of the House of Representatives* (82d Cong., 1st sess.), Serial No. 1, Part 6: *Organized Baseball* (Washington, D.C.: Government Print-

ing Office, 1952). The materials collected in this volume are massive and are indispensable for the understanding of the economics of this market. The volume will be cited henceforth, for brevity, as *"Celler Hearings,"* after Congressman Emanuel Celler, the committee chairman.

The companion piece to the hearings of the subcommittee is its report, *Organized Baseball: Report of the Subcommittee on Study of Monopoly Power of the Committee on the Judiciary, Pursuant to II. Res. 95, House of Representatives* (82d Cong., 2d sess. [Washington, D.C.: Government Printing Office, 1952]). This document will be referred to henceforth as *"Celler Report."*

"size" if any are to be successful; this seems to be a unique attribute of professional competitive sports.

Before passing to the analytical questions, however, I must describe the structure of the industry and the rules of the market. The structure and the rules of the market for baseball players and their services are defined in seven documents which constitute the constitutional papers of the baseball industry. These documents are the Constitution of the National League of Professional Baseball Clubs, the Constitution of the American League of Professional Baseball Clubs, the Major League Agreement, the Major League Rules, the Major-Minor League Agreement, the Major-Minor League Rules, and the Agreement of the National Association of Professional Baseball Leagues (the minor leagues).[2]

The documents specify the procedures for their own amendment, and they are amended from time to time. They are enormously complex. This complexity arises, in part, from the ingenuity of club owners and business managers in doing violence to the purposes of the rules while obeying their letter. Let a rule be established proscribing a practice and inhibiting gainful action, and teams find some substitute for it, and an amended rule emerges. Complexity also arises from the effort to compromise inconsistent interests within baseball.

Taken all together, the documents constitute baseball as a collusive combination. The parties to this combination have agreed to be bound by rules that inhibit competition and to enforce these rules by extralegal sanctions.

The organized baseball industry[3] consists of two major leagues and a number of minor leagues. The number of minor leagues

varies from time to time in response to changes in product-market conditions. In 1955 there were thirty-three minor leagues operating.[4]

Most leagues are composed of eight teams, but leagues of other sizes, for example, of six teams, are not uncommon. Sometimes a league begins a season with eight teams and will lose a team or two that do not prosper and are abandoned in mid-season.

The major-league season provides for a schedule of 154 games played by each team; 77 games are played at its own home ball park and 77 in those of its opponents. Thus each team plays 22 games with each of the other seven teams in the league, 11 at home and 11 away.

The minor leagues are classified into categories defined by the sum of the populations of the cities of which each is composed. These categories are called Open Classification, AAA, AA, A1, A, B, C, D, and E.[5]

---

the combination bound together by the constitutional documents I have enumerated. Baseball, outside of organized baseball, consists of amateur baseball, in which players receive no compensation for their play; semiprofessional baseball and the industrial leagues (composed of teams representing firms), in both of which a few players are paid for their playing services, but others are not; and a few fully professional leagues and clubs which are independent of organized baseball.

[4] For a record of the number of minor leagues from 1905 to 1951 see *Celler Hearings*, p. 992.

[5] The number of leagues in each category in 1955 was as follows:

Classification	Aggregate Population Requirement	No. of Leagues
Open Classification	10,000,000	1
AAA	3,000,000	2
AA	1,750,000	3
A1	1,450,000	0
A	1,000,000	3
B	250,000	7
C	150,000	8
D	Up to 150,000	9
E	Up to 150,000	0

[2] *The Baseball Blue Book, 1955* (Fort Wayne, Ind.: Bureau of the Blue Book, 1955).

[3] This paper is almost exclusively concerned with *organized* baseball. "Organized" baseball refers to

The minor leagues are made up of teams that are either "independent" or are "farm" teams of a major-league team. Farm teams are either owned outright by a major-league team or controlled by "working agreements" which give the major-league club, in return for financial or other assistance, the right to acquire the services of a specified number of players of the minor-league teams. A farm system makes it possible for a major-league team to accumulate a pool of players from which it can make replacements on its own team, and it provides a place where promising players can be "seasoned" for major-league play.

Of approximately 260 minor-league teams operating in 1955, 155 were farms of the major-league teams, 40 owned outright and 115 controlled by working agreements. Farm teams are not equally distributed among the major-league teams. In 1955, for example, the St. Louis National League team controlled eighteen farm teams, while the Boston and the Chicago American League teams controlled only six farm teams each.[6]

Every team admitted to organized baseball has *"territorial rights"* in the city in which it is located. No team in organized baseball may play in the territory of any other team without the latter's consent.[7] Each team, therefore, monopolizes its own territory within organized baseball, and this monopoly right is a marketable commodity.

An elaborate system of rules has been devised to govern the contractual relationships between players and teams and among teams in the disposition of players' services. This system of rules structures the labor market and imposes restraints upon freedom in the market.

Until he signs his first contract with a

[6] *Baseball Official Guide, 1955* (St. Louis, Mo.: C. C. Spink & Sons, 1955), p. 162.
[7] *Baseball Blue Book, 1955*, p. 712.

team in organized baseball, a player is a *free agent* who may dispose of his services as he wishes, and teams may compete in bidding for him with relative freedom. In the market for free agents, competition is very intense. A star high-school player may have a large number of representatives of different teams prepared to negotiate with him the day after his graduation from school.[8]

When bidding is heavy for the services of a particular free agent, the player is paid a *bonus* for signing a contract with one team rather than another. Bonuses of $100,000 or more to secure a player's signature are not unknown, although they have usually been much smaller.[9] The bonus can be thought of as part of the player's first year's salary or as an income supplement which is distributed over the length of his playing life. The size of the bonus is not the only dimension of bidders' offers. A free agent will also choose among alternative bidders on the basis of his estimates of his lifetime baseball earnings with each bidder, and these estimates are compounded of his estimates of his length of playing life (which may be longer with one team than

[8] The rules do not permit negotiation with a high-school student until the day following his graduation.
[9] In an attempt to reduce the size of bonuses paid to free agents, baseball's rules have recently been changed to impose real costs upon teams contracting bonus players. A bonus player signed to a major-league team, for example, must be kept on the team roster for two years; normally a young player contracted by a major-league team would be sent to the minor leagues for several years of "seasoning." Bonus players, for this purpose, are defined as those who are paid in excess of a stipulated amount for their first year plus an extra sum in compensation for signing their first contracts. To skirt the rule, some teams are said to have paid the player less than this amount but to have employed his father in some nominal capacity at a high salary, although the rules include in their definition of a bonus player payments made to other persons "for the use or benefit" of the player (*Baseball Blue Book, 1955*, pp. 513–14, 613–14, 729).

with another) and his estimates of his average annual earnings.[10]

When a player signs a contract, it must be a *uniform contract*, the terms of which are specified in detail by organized baseball. There is one uniform contract for the major leagues and another for the minors; the two are very similar. No deviation from the terms of the uniform contract is permitted without the approval of the appropriate executive officer of organized baseball, and deviation is rarely permitted.[11]

The uniform contract provides that, in consideration of the payment of the compensation provided for in the contract, the player "agrees to render skilled services as a baseball player." The team may terminate the player's contract if the player should "fail, in the opinion of the Club's management, to exhibit sufficient skill or competitive ability to . . . continue as a member of the Club's team."

Almost all contracts run for a one-year term. However, the uniform player contract contains a renewal clause, conventionally called the *reserve clause*, which permits the team to renew the contract for the following year at a price which the team may fix—subject, in the major leagues only, to the constraint that the salary in the following year shall not be less than 75 per cent of the salary in the current year. In the minor-league uniform contract there is no constraint at all on the price which the

team may fix for the next season's services.

The team with which the player is contracted has exclusive right to the use of his playing services; he may not play baseball elsewhere without its consent. His contract may be assigned by this team to another team, and he is bound to report for play with the asignee team. No other team in organized baseball may employ him.

No team may negotiate with a player already under contract to another team. This is called *tampering* and is prohibited by the rules.[12] If any team wants to secure the services of a player contracted by another, it may negotiate with the team that owns the rights to his services for a purchase, but it may not bid the player away directly by contracting him.

Once a player has signed his first contract in organized baseball, therefore, he is no longer free to dispose of his services. He may withdraw from organized baseball and follow some other calling, but he may not choose freely among bidders for him within baseball.

The market for baseball players has really divided into three markets. One is the market for free agents, in which the player is the seller; another is the market for players who have already signed their first contracts, in which teams are both the sellers and the buyers; the third is the market for current services of contracted players, in which the player is the seller and the team that holds his contract is the buyer.

Some attempts have been made to enforce in the courts the exclusive right to contracted players' services which is conveyed by the uniform contract. On the principle that involuntary servitude is contrary to public policy, the courts have been reluctant to compel players to fulfil their contracts, to restrain them from performing for others, or to restrain others from employing them, and these attempts have met with little

---

[10] Players under contract to Team A or its farm system are a non-competing group vis-a-vis players under contract to Team B or its farm system, because of the operation of the "reserve rule" to be discussed below. Average salaries may therefore vary among teams. On July 1, 1950, the mean salaries of the major-league teams ranged from $18,788 for the New York Yankees to $8,031 for the St. Louis Browns (*Celler Hearings*, p. 965). The range of salaries paid by different teams is also different, and a free agent, in computing his prospective earnings with different clubs, can be expected to consider the salary range of each of the bidders for his services and to estimate where, in the whole course of his playing career, he is likely to fall within it.

[11] *Baseball Blue Book, 1955*, pp. 509, 609.

[12] *Ibid.*, pp. 511, 611.

success.[13] Baseball has therefore resorted to extralegal sanctions to enforce exclusive rights. A player who refuses to play for a team by which he is contracted, or refuses to play for a team to which his contract has been assigned, is suspended; he may not be employed by another team in organized baseball.[14] If he finds employment in baseball outside of organized baseball, he is declared "ineligible" and may not play in organized baseball again until he is restored to eligibility; the length of time after his petition for reinstatement before he will be permitted to resume play will depend upon the evaluation of the gravity of his offense.[15] A team in organized baseball that employs a suspended or ineligible player will find that other teams will refuse to meet it on the field of play; a team outside of organized baseball that employs him will not be permitted to hire the ball park of a team in organized baseball; players who participate in contests in which an ineligible player takes part themselves become ineligible.[16]

The reserve rule is the heart of the limitation on freedom in the baseball labor market. A number of different defenses have been offered for it, some specious and others somewhat stronger.

The defense most commonly heard is that the reserve rule is necessary to assure an equal distribution of playing talent among opposing teams; that a more or less equal distribution of talent is necessary if there is to be uncertainty of outcome; and that uncertainty of outcome is necessary if the con-

sumer is to be willing to pay admission to the game. This defense is founded on the premise that there are rich baseball clubs and poor ones and that, if the players' market were free, the rich clubs would outbid the poor for talent, taking all the competent players for themselves and leaving only the incompetent for the other teams. It will be seen later that the premise is false.

Most of the revenue of baseball clubs comes from admission receipts.[17] A rich club, therefore, is one located in an area where attendance at baseball games is high; a poor club is one whose attendance is low.

Attendance at baseball games, as a whole, is a function of the general level of income, the price of admission to baseball games relative to the prices of recreational substitutes, and the goodness of substitutes.[18] Attendance at the games of any

[17] Combined major-league teams' revenue in 1950 was distributed by source as follows:

	Per Cent
Home-game admissions	57.2
Road-game admissions	14.1
Exhibition games	2.8
Radio and television rights	10.5
Concessions (net)	9.2
Other	6.2

Approximately twenty-five cents of each admission price is paid to the visiting team; the remaining admission revenue is kept by the home team (*Celler Report*, p. 6).

[18] The following estimates show some trends related to baseball attendance:

	1929	1954
Expenditures for recreation as a percentage of total personal consumption expenditures	5.5	5.2
Admissions to specified spectator amusements* as a percentage of expenditures for recreation	21.1	14.0
Spectator sports† as a percentage of admissions to specified spectator amusements	7.2	13.0
Professional baseball as a percentage of spectator sports	25.8	25.1‡

* "Specified spectator amusements" are motion-picture theaters; legitimate theaters, opera, and

[13] On the principle of a case decided in 1852 (*Lumley v. Wagner*) a contracted player may be restrained by a court of equity from making his services available to a third party if (1) the player is unique; (2) the contract is definite; (3) there is mutuality; and (4) the contract is not an unreasonable restraint of trade. There is some question whether players' contracts fulfil these conditions (Peter S. Craig, "Monopsony in Manpower," *Yale Law Journal*, March, 1953, p. 590).

[14] *Baseball Blue Book, 1955*, pp. 538, 636.
[15] *Ibid.*, pp. 540, 637.
[16] *Ibid.*

given team is a positive function of the size of the population of the territory in which the team has the monopoly right to play;[19] the size and convenience of location of the ball park;[20] and the average rank standing of the team during the season in the competition of its league. It is a negative function of the goodness of leisure-time substitutes for baseball in the area and of the dispersion of percentages of games won by the teams in the league.[21]

There is, in fact, a wide variation in attendance among teams. In the period 1931–50 the New York Yankees' aggregate paid attendance was 24,270,000, while that of the St. Louis Browns was 4,160,000.[22]

If, it is argued, other things being equal, a team in an area with a large population has larger revenues than teams in less populous areas, then, in a free players' labor market, the former will get the most capable players, there will be wide variation among teams in the quality of play, contests will become certain, and attendance will decline.

The history of baseball seems, at least superficially, to support the position that

the purpose of the reserve rule was to achieve balance of playing strength among teams. The first professional baseball league was the National Association of Professional Baseball Players, organized in 1870. It did not survive five seasons of play, and A. G. Mills, who first proposed the reserve rule, is reported to have said of its experience:

> This condition was greatly aggravated by the general practice on the part of the richer clubs of stripping the weaker ones of their best playing talent. Then would follow the collapse of a number of these clubs in mid-season, leaving their players unpaid, while the winning clubs, owing to the disbandment of the weaker ones, would also frequently fall from inability to arrange a paying number of games.[23]

The National Association was succeeded by the National League, which was formed in 1876.

To bring the process of unequal distribution of talent to a halt, it was thought necessary to devise the reserve rule to permit the poorer teams to retain the services of players whom they would otherwise lose to teams prepared to pay higher salaries. If this was the purpose of the reserve rule, there seems to be some question whether it has been successful. A number of different measures suggest themselves for testing the equality of distribution of player ability among teams. A simple test is one which counts the number of times each team has won its league pennant. In the period 1920–51 the New York Yankees led the American League in eighteen years, and the Chicago White Sox in none. In the National League, in the same period, the St. Louis Cardinals won in nine years, the New York Giants in eight, and the Philadelphia Phillies and Boston Braves in one year each.[24]

---

entertainments of non-profit institutions (except athletics); and spectator sports.

† "Spectator sports" are professional baseball, football, and hockey; horse- and dog-race tracks; college football; and "others."

‡ 1950; information not available for 1954. (Source: U.S. Department of Commerce, *National Income, 1954 Edition: Supplement to the Survey of Current Business* [Washington, D.C.: Government Printing Office, 1954], Table 30, pp. 206 ff.; *Survey of Current Business*, July, 1955, Table 30, p. 19; *Celler Report*, p. 12.)

[19] Metropolitan area population per major-league team in 1950 ranged from 4,277,000 for each of the three teams in the New York area to 898,000 for Cincinnati and 857,000 for each of the two teams in St. Louis (*Celler Report*, p. 99).

[20] Major-league ball parks ranged in seating capacity in 1955 from 27,523 for Washington to 73,811 for Cleveland (*Baseball Blue Book, 1955*, pp. 18 ff.).

[21] That is to say, the "tighter" the competition, the larger the attendance. A pennant-winning team that wins 80 per cent of its games will attract fewer patrons than a pennant-winning team that wins 55 per cent of them.

[22] *Ibid.*, p. 100.

[23] *Celler Report*, p. 18, quoting *Spalding's Official Baseball Record, 1915*, p. 47.

[24] *Celler Report*, p. 102. Operationally, perfect equality of distribution of players among teams may be made manifest in the following ways: every game ends in a tie; every team wins exactly

Clearly, there has been unequal distribution of talent. The Yankees have had better fortune than the others. By offering higher prices for the purchase of players' contracts from other teams, they have acquired players already under contract; by offering higher first-year salaries and prospects for higher professional lifetime earnings, they have induced the better free agents to sign with them; and by investing heavily in a farm system in the minor leagues, they have had access to a large pool of players from which the most capable could be drawn to the Yankees themselves.

By this simple empirical test, it can be seen that the reserve rule has not distributed players among teams perfectly equally; the teams that were prepared to outbid others for players have not been frustrated by the rule. The reason for this result will be shown later. It will also be shown that a market in which freedom is limited by the reserve rule cannot be expected to equalize the distribution of players among teams more than a market in which there is perfect freedom.

If the reserve rule does not, in fact, equalize the distribution of players, can it have some other result? By confronting each contracted player with an exclusive bidder, the rule can have the effect of depressing salaries, at least for some players. The relevance of salary levels to the rule was clearly seen in an official release of the National League on September 29, 1879, shortly after the adoption of the reserve rule for the first time.

> The financial results of the past season prove that salaries must come down. We believe that players in insisting on exorbitant prices are injuring their own interests by forcing out of existence clubs which cannot be run and pay large salaries except at a large personal loss. . . . In view of these facts,

measures have been taken by this league to remedy the evil to some extent in 1880.[25]

The "measures" taken were a secret agreement among the members of the league that each might reserve five players who could not be contracted by other teams. Over the years the number of players who might be reserved has been revised upward from time to time until now the major-league teams are permitted to reserve forty players and minor-league teams a smaller number, depending on their league classification.[26]

Two other rules affecting the disposition of players should be mentioned. The *draft* or *selection* rule prevents a player from being held indefinitely in a lower classification league if his services are wanted by a team of a higher classification. After a player in the minor leagues has served a stipulated number of years in the minor leagues,[27] he becomes eligible to be drafted (selected) by teams of higher classifications.[28] A player who is drafted has his contract taken up by the team that drafts him. The team that loses him is paid according to a schedule which appears in the constitutional documents; the price depends upon the league classification of the team from which the player is drafted and the classification of the team that drafts him.[29]

---

[25] *Celler Hearings*, p. 139, quoting a release published in the *New York Clipper*, October 11, 1879.

[26] A class AAA team, for example, may reserve thirty-eight players, and a class D team, only twenty-one.

[27] For example, this number is five years in the Pacific Coast League (players in this league, and *only* in this league, may opt to sign a contract which exempts them from the draft; in November, 1955, there were only twenty-seven players in this league who had chosen to sign such a contract); four years in AAA leagues; and two years in D leagues (*Baseball Blue Book, 1955*, pp. 521–22).

[28] In November, 1955, 3,184 players were eligible to be drafted, of a total of about 6,900 players reserved by minor-league teams (*Sporting News*, November 23, 1955, p. 5).

[29] If a major-league team drafts a Pacific Coast League player, it must pay the team losing the player $15,000; if a major-league team drafts a class E player, it must pay the team that loses him $1,500; etc. (*Baseball Blue Book, 1955*, p. 521)

---

half of the games it plays; every team, in an eight-team league, wins the pennant every eighth year.

Thus the draft is a forced sale at a previously stipulated price. A team of classification A or higher may lose only one player in each season by the draft, irrespective of the number of draft-eligible players it has under reserve; in leagues of lower classification than A any number of eligibles may be drafted from any team. Thus only as many players may be drafted from the higher minor-league teams as there are teams.[30]

An elaborate system of rules has been worked out for determining the priority of selecting teams in the draft process. First choice is given to teams of high league classification and last choice to low-classification teams; for teams of any given league classification, first choice is given to those that stood lowest at the end of the previous season, and last choice is given to those that stood highest. The system appears to give the advantage of first choice to the teams of any classification which need talented players most. The advantage, however, is largely illusory. A minor-league team that holds the contracts of, say, three players, each of whom, if sold, would be worth $40,000, will not be prepared to lose any of them for the substantially lower draft price. Since it does not know which of the three will be drafted, it will sell them all before the draft dates.[31] It sells, of course, to the highest bidder, without regard to the previous season's rank position of the bidding teams. In the end, therefore, it seems to be true that the players who are left to be drafted are those who are worth about the draft price. If there are bargains to be had, it is because someone miscalculated the market. As a result, few players are actually drafted.[32]

[30] *Ibid.*, pp. 768–69.

[31] Usually some days are set aside in November of each year for drafting; as soon as drafting by the major leagues is done, the minor leagues begin their own draft, in which teams in each league classification draft from teams in lower classifications.

[32] In November, 1954, of the several thousand eligibles, thirteen players were drafted by major-league teams and forty-four by minor-league teams. Of the thirteen, only seven spent the full

The *waiver*[33] rule limits the freedom of higher-classification teams to dispose of their players to lower-classification teams. A major-league team may freely sell a player's contract to another major-league team of its own league. However, it may not sell the contract to a team of the other major league or to a minor-league team without first asking the other teams of its own league in the first case, and the other teams of both major leagues in the second, to "waive" the player. If one or more of these teams refuses to waive, they say, in effect, that they are prepared to take over the player's contract at a waiver price specified in the rules (currently $10,000).[34]

A major-league player may not have his salary reduced during the season for which he is contracted and may not have it reduced for the following season, if he should stay in the major leagues, to less than 75

following season in the major leagues, none with distinction.

The rule that only one player may be drafted in each year from the higher-classification minor-league teams has permitted the major-league teams with farm systems to protect their reservoir of players by moving draft eligibles among their teams. For example, in November, 1955, the Montreal Royals, an AAA team which is the property of the Brooklyn Dodgers, had a roster of thirty-three players, of whom thirty-two were draft-eligible. By moving its promising draft-eligible players from its other farm teams to Montreal just b fore the draft dates, Brooklyn was assured that it would lose only one of them. The others, who were being protected so that Brooklyn would have a pool of talent from which to get replacements for its players in the future, were reshuffled among the Brooklyn farm teams when the period for drafting had expired. This process is repeated each year.

[33] *Baseball Blue Book, 1955,* pp. 529 ff., 749 ff.

[34] A major-league team may "optionally assign" a player whose contract it holds to a minor-league team within three years of the time it has contracted him without asking waivers. An optional assignment is one which gives the assignor team the right to recall the optioned player into its own service. It differs from an "outright" assignment, which transfers, for a consideration, the right to use or dispose of the player's services. The optional assignment is an exception to the waiver rule.

There is also a waiver rule affecting the assignment of minor-league players between minor-league teams of different classifications.

per cent of its current season level. A team that claims a player for whom waivers have been requested, therefore, says that the exclusive right to the use and disposition of the player's services is worth $10,000, given the salary costs which his contract attaches to him.

A team that has asked other major-league teams for waivers on a player so that it may assign his contract to a minor-league team may, if it wishes, withdraw its request for waivers if any of the major-league teams express an interest in having the player by filing a claim for him. Negotiations then often ensue, in which the team that owns the player tries to get from the team that wants him a price higher than the waiver price. If the negotiations are successfully consummated, the player's contract is assigned outright between the major-league teams; he does not transfer on waivers. The rationale of the waiver rule is that it seeks to keep a player in the highest league classification for which his services are acceptable, if he is worth the waiver price, and despite the fact that he is worth more than this to a lower-classification team.[35]

Only the bare bones of the market rules of the industry have been described in this paper. Their full texts and the exceptions which the rules permit can be found in the constitutional documents themselves. For our purposes the skeletal description given here suffices.

Very little information is available on

player salaries. All contracts are registered with the relevant executive offices of major- and minor-league baseball, but salary information is not made public. The reports of player salaries which appear in the public press are said not to be reliable. Some salary data were divulged, however, by the congressional committee hearings of 1951.

The rules impose a minimum salary in the major leagues of $6,000 per year.[36] No other league has a minimum-salary rule. Neither does any league have a maximum individual player salary rule. All leagues except the two major leagues and the only Open Classification league—the Pacific Coast League—have *team* maximum salary limits.[37]

TABLE 30.1*

AVERAGE SALARIES PER PLAYER-MONTH
AND MONTHLY SALARY RANGES

League Classification	Mean	Median	Range
AAA	$876	$850	$200–$4,000
AA	639	600	300– 4,200
A	391	350	100– 1,555
D	192	165	80– 1,000

* Source: *Celler Hearings*, p. 965.

On July 1, 1950, the range of major-league salaries was from $5,000 [38] to $90,000 per year. The mean was $13,288, and the median $11,000.[39] In the minor leagues salaries were very much lower. Average salaries per player-month and monthly salary ranges in that year were reported to be as shown in Table 30.1.

---

[35] That this is a "fact" may be demonstrated as follows: any major-league team can purchase a player of whom another major-league team wishes to dispose by offering a higher price for his contract than any minor-league bidder and by offering a price which is high enough so that it pays the team owning the player's contract to sell him to the bidding team rather than to employ him on one of its farm teams. The major-league team could do this if there were no waiver rule. If the waiver rule gives it a claim upon a player superior to that of a minor-league team, it is because the former can claim the player at a lower price than the latter is willing to pay for him.

[36] *Baseball Blue Book, 1955*, p. 543.

[37] For example, $7,000 per month per team in A1 leagues; $750 per month per team in E leagues. Each AAA and AA league may set its own team maximum; they were, for example, in 1951, American Association (AAA), $13,800 per team-month; International League (AAA), $14,000 per team-month (*Celler Hearings*, p. 189; *Baseball Blue Book, 1955*, p. 739).

[38] $5,000 was the minimum established by the rules for major-league players at that time.

[39] *Celler Hearings*, p. 965.

The large variation in players' salaries can be expected to attract many players who are hopeful that they will finally fall in the upper levels of the salary distribution. This will cause the average salary of baseball players to be below the level at which it would lie if the dispersion of salaries were smaller.

Baseball-playing skills, at some level of proficiency, are, of course, widely distributed among the young male population of the United States and some other countries of the Western Hemisphere, and the supply of baseball-playing labor must be very elastic to price. In the lower minor leagues players make themselves available at prices which seem to be less than they could earn in some other employment. A congressional committee heard testimony from the former minor-league player that he accepted his first contract with a class D team in 1941 for a salary of $60 a month and that this was the common beginning wage in that classification at the time.[40] The worth of these earnings must surely have been reduced by some of the real costs which baseball players incurred. The same witness, for example, told the committee:

> We used to finish a game in the evening, get on our bus, known as Stucker's Steamer. . . . The man who owned the club was named Ray Stucker. And this was an old, beat-up Ford, a bus, in which we had bunks in the back of the bus, and we used to pile all our suitcases, baseball bats and other things in this bus and then leave Sioux City about midnight and travel to Cheyenne, Wyoming. It is about 600 miles away. We were to get there at 4:30 the following afternoon and play a game in Cheyenne, Wyoming, that night. . . . That is a common practice in all minor leagues. . . . That is the common practice to save hotel bills.[41]

There are other disadvantages of life in the minor leagues. A player under contract may have his salary reduced in midseason

if he is assigned outright to another team of a lower classification, and he may have his contract terminated without notice.[42] Earnings in the lower minor leagues are so low that, at the end of each season, it is a common practice for class D teams to have a "players' night" to raise money that can be given to the players to permit them to pay the expenses of their transportation to their homes.

If players are willing to sell their services for such a wage and under such circumstances, it is perhaps because they derive very large psychic income from playing the game and because, on the average, the players in the lower leagues overestimate the probability that they will excel in play and be chosen to receive a higher salary with a team of a higher-classification league.

Experience diminishes uncertainty and increases knowledge, however, and players recalculate the probabilities which they assign to the occurrence of events. As they find that they have miscalculated, they withdraw from the market. The president of the association of minor leagues testified:

> The turnover in B, C, and D (leagues) is terrific. . . . Boys may be in there a week or maybe 30 days. The turnover in the lower classifications is awfully heavy. . . . I suppose that a good many class D clubs have a turnover maybe five or six times during the season of almost their complete roster.[43]

Especially in the major leagues players have opportunities for earning supplementary income which would not be available to them if they were not baseball players. They may be paid for speaking engagements or for product indorsements; between seasons, if they are employed as salesmen, say, of insurance or automobiles, they will be more successful because they are players;

---

[40] *Ibid.,* p. 349.
[41] *Ibid.*

[42] The president of the association of minor leagues told the Celler Committee of the no-notice rule: "That inspires the player to hustle a little all the time" (*ibid.,* p. 205).
[43] *Ibid.,* pp. 206, 213.

if they invest in retail or service establishments, they are more likely to prosper; if they play well, they may receive gifts from grateful fans; when they retire from baseball, they may teach at baseball schools; if they are engaged in business ventures, they will be rewarded in proportion to the favor in which they were held by the fans during their baseball careers.

The reserve rule, which binds a player to the team that contracts him, gives a prima facie appearance of monopsony to the market. Once having signed a first contract, a player is confronted by a single buyer who may unilaterally specify the price to be paid for his services. Each team and the players under contract to it appear in a labor market specific to them.[44] This market is distinct from those of other teams. No movement among markets, either of buyers or sellers, is permitted. In each market the team operates as buyer; the players, as sellers. While there is no competition on the buying side, there is intense competition on the sellers' side.

In such a market rational maximizing teams[45] might be expected to behave like

[44] In the case of farm systems, the system defines the limits of the market; all the teams in the system coalesce into a single buyer for market purposes.

[45] The question may be asked whether it is sensible to assume that baseball-team owners are rational maximizers of money quantities. Representatives of organized baseball often say that the owners are interested more in providing opportunities for wholesome sport than they are in turning a profit. It was said in 1951 that ten of the sixteen major-league primary owners had their main business interests outside of baseball, and the Celler Committee heard testimony that, as of July, 1951, of 2,287 officers and directors of minor-league teams, only 291 made their living primarily from baseball. If baseball entrepreneurs get large psychic income from their association with the game, they will be willing to pay a price for engaging in the baseball business. This does not mean necessarily that they will be prepared to take a loss on their baseball operations but only that they are prepared to take a smaller return from baseball investment than their capital would earn in some other use. Still, one major-league property is reported to have sold in recent years for three and a half million dollars and another is said to be up for sale, at this

discriminating monopsonists. Each player will have his supply price; if he is offered less than this, he will prefer to work at some other occupation. The supply price will vary among individuals. For each of them it ought to be related to how much he can earn in the next best employment outside of baseball, with the appropriate adjustments made for the plaudits of the crowd, for the supplementary income opportunities baseball provides, for the convenience of seasonal employment and the inconvenience of constant travel, and so on. A maximizing team would be expected to pay different salaries to different players, even though they are of the same quality, but only just about the salaries that are necessary to prevent them from withdrawing their services.

Actually, however, teams seem to pay, in the major leagues, much more than this. Here a paradox emerges. If baseball players have, on the average, no skills other than those necessary to play baseball proficiently, then their next best wage would be relatively low. Why are they paid so much more?

To begin with, it is undoubtedly correct that the player will not be paid more than he is worth to the team, his worth being determined by that part of the team's revenue which is attributable to his capacity to attract patrons to the ball park, net of the price paid for his contract to another team or the cost of his development. Nor will he receive less than his reservation price. The salary he receives, therefore, must fall somewhere between these limits; the question is: Why does it not fall at the bottom of the range?

The answer must be that the player is not without his defenses, even if he is in a

writing, for four million dollars. The most expensive major-league property has been estimated to be worth fifteen million dollars and the average six million dollars. It seems unlikely that people will subject capital of this magnitude to large risk of loss for the pure joy of association with the game.

monopsonistic market. He may withhold his services, and, in fact, each year there are a few holdouts who refuse to sign contracts providing for salaries that are unacceptable to them. In the end they usually sign, either because they become convinced, after a time, that the team will not offer more or because the team raises its offer. But sometimes players hold out for the full season. These may simply be cases of irrational behavior on the part of the player; though he is able to earn only $5,000 in another employment, he may sometimes refuse to accept $15,000 for playing baseball if he believes he is worth $20,000. But, if, in truth, he is worth $20,000, then it pays the team to offer $16,000. Thus the process by which the salary is fixed assumes the characteristics of bargaining, and the level at which it falls is a function of the shrewdness and guile of the parties in devising their bargaining strategies. Moreover, the teams cannot push the salary "too low" even for those who do sign, because it does not pay to have discontented players. Player performance is determined in part by natural abilities like sharpness of eye, perception of space, and muscular co-ordination but also in part by the effort the player exerts. A player who is unhappy about his salary will perhaps not play as well as one who is not.

The solution to the problem of individual salary levels is not, however, completely indeterminate within the limits of the range which has been specified, as it would be in a classic duopoly case. This is so because, while each player has a monopoly of his own services, he is not truly unique, and there are more or less good substitutes for him. His salary is therefore partially determined by the difference between the value productivities and costs of other players by whom he may be replaced.

A rational team will seek to maximize the rent it derives from each player. It will be indifferent between two shortstops, one of whom is worth $30,000 and costs $20,000,

and the other of whom is worth $20,000 and costs $10,000. It will prefer the first if it can have him for $19,000; but it will prefer the second if it must pay the first $21,000 to induce him to play. It will be prepared to pay a Babe Ruth a fabulous salary, simply because there are no very good substitutes for him, and he is worth so much more to the team than any other player. But if a Ruth insisted upon receiving his full worth, it would pay to employ in his stead some other person of less skill on whom some positive rent would be earned. The team would keep a Ruth even if he insisted upon receiving his full value only if all other players also insisted upon receiving theirs and if rents were therefore zero for all of them. Since it is incredible that all players should, in fact, exact their full worth, it follows from this analysis that at least some players are exploited.[46]

It has been suggested,[47] however, that, while major-league players, and especially the star players of the major leagues, may be exploited, it does not follow that all players taken together are. The process by which players are brought to the major leagues can be likened to that by which paying oil wells are brought in or patentable inventions discovered. In all these cases there is heavy investment in the discovery of knowledge. When it is discovered, the returns on it are high, but these returns must compensate for the losses incurred on the attempts which failed. In this schematic conception minor-league players who do not qualify for major-league play are like dry

[46] Representatives of organized baseball testified before the Celler Committee that players receive their full value. "If the players are dissatisfied, they are traded to other teams which will pay them more." This belief is, of course, not consistent with the other, also held by baseball representatives, that the reserve rule has the effect of balancing team strength by permitting poorer clubs, which pay less than the richer clubs, to retain players to whom the latter are prepared to pay a higher wage.

[47] I am indebted for the immediately following idea to Professor Gary S. Becker.

wells and research which does not yield a patent. They are paid more than they are worth because they may turn out to be of major-league caliber. To their cost must be added the cost of scouts and try-out camps and other costs of finding players and assessing their capacities. The monopsony gains in the major leagues are merely compensation for investment losses in scouting and in the operation of farm teams, and returns to investment in baseball, like returns to investment in oil and in research, should be no higher than returns to capital used in other ventures. If they were higher, capital would flow from other uses to investment in baseball.

This suggestion has a great deal of analytical merit. Its power is reduced somewhat, however, by the restraints on freedom of entry in the baseball industry. If the returns on oil investments or on investment in research are very much larger than returns on other investment, new entrants are free to search for oil and knowledge. But the rule of "territorial rights," which gives monopoly rights to desirable locations in the product market to teams currently in organized baseball and the system of private sanctions for the enforcement of the rule put serious disabilities upon prospective new entrants into the baseball industry. If, therefore, there are monopoly gains arising from the characteristics of the baseball labor market, they are reinforced by restraints on competition in the product market.

Is it clear that the reserve rule is necessary to achieve more or less equal quality of play among teams? Assume that teams are distributed among locations, as they are in fact, so that the revenues of some are very much larger than those of others. Assume a free players' labor market, in which players may accept the offer of the highest bidder and teams may make offers without restraint.

At first sight, it may appear that the high-revenue teams will contract all the stars, leaving the others only the dregs of the supply; that the distribution of players among teams will become very unequal; that contests will become less uncertain; and that consumer interest will flag and attendance fall off. On closer examination, however, it can be seen that this process will be checked by the law of diminishing returns, operating concurrently with each team's strategic avoidance of diseconomies of scale.

Professional team competitions are different from other kinds of business ventures. If a seller of shoes is able to capture the market and to cause other sellers of shoes to suffer losses and withdraw, the surviving competitor is a clear gainer. But in baseball no team can be successful unless its competitors also survive and prosper sufficiently so that the differences in the quality of play among teams are not "too great."

If the size of a baseball team is thought of as the number of players under contract to it, each player being weighted by some index of his quality, then diseconomies of scale set in at some point when a team too far outstrips its competitors, and they become larger in proportion to the size of the differences.

Two teams opposed to each other in play are like two firms producing a single product. The product is the game, weighted by the revenues derived from its play. With game admission prices given, the product is the game, weighted by the number of paying customers who attend. When 30,000 attend, the output is twice as large as when 15,000 attend. In one sense, the teams compete; in another, they combine in a single firm in which the success of each branch requires that it be not "too much" more efficient than the other. If it is, output falls.

A baseball team, like any other firm, produces its product by combining factors of production. Consider the two teams engaged in a contest to be collapsed into a single firm, producing as output games, weighted by the revenue derived from admission fees. Let the players *of one team* be one factor and all others (management, transportation, ball parks, *and the players of the other team*), another. The quantity of the factor—players—is measured by making the appropriate adjustment for differential qualities among players, so that a man who hits safely in 35 per cent of his times at bat counts as more than one who hits safely only 20 per cent of the time. Given the quantity of the other factors, the total product curve of the factor—players of one team—will have the conventional shape; it will slope upward as the "quantity" of this factor is increased, reach a peak, and then fall. It will not pay to increase this factor without limit. Beyond some point—say, when a team already has three .350 hitters—it will not pay to employ another .350 hitter. If a team goes on increasing the quantity of the factor, players, by hiring additional stars, it will find that the total output—that is, admission receipts—of the combined firms (and, therefore, of its own) will rise at a less rapid rate and finally will fall absolutely. At some point, therefore, a first star player is worth more to poor Team B than, say, a third star to rich Team A. At this point, B is in a position to bid players away from A in the market. A's behavior is not a function of its bank balance. It does what it calculates it is worthwhile to do; and the time comes when, in pursuing the strategy of its *own* gains, it is worthwhile, whatever the size of its cash balance, to forego the services of an expert player and see him employed by another team.

The wealthy teams will usually prefer winning to losing.[48] If they do, they will prefer winning by close margins to winning by wide ones. If their market behavior is consistent with this objective—that is, if they behave like rational maximizers—playing talent will be more or less equally distributed among teams.

It does not require collusion to bring about this result. It is not senseless to expect it to be produced by a free labor market in which each team is separately engaged in gainful behavior. The position of organized baseball that a free market, given the unequal distribution of revenue, will result in the engrossment of the most competent players by the wealthy teams is open to some question. It seems, indeed, to be true that a market in which freedom is limited by a reserve rule such as that which now governs the baseball labor market distributes players among teams about as a free market would.

Players under contract to a team may be used by that team itself, or they may be sold to another team. Each team determines whether to use a player's services itself or to sell him, according to the relative returns on him in the two uses. If the return will be higher from sale, he will be sold, and vice versa. Now, if he can be sold to another team for a price higher than his worth to his present team, it is because he is worth more to the team that buys him than to the team that sells him. It follows that players will be distributed among teams so that they are put to their most "productive" use; each will play for the team that is able to get the highest return from his services.[49]

---

[48] It should not be thought that wealthy teams will invariably want to assemble winning combination of players, either in a free market or in a market governed by the reserve rule. A team will seek to maximize the difference between its revenue and its costs. If this quantity is maximized, for any given club, by assembling a team of players who are of lower quality than those of another club in its league, it will pay the former to run behind.

[49] The sale of a player's contract occurs in a market in which the seller is a monopolist and the buyer an oligopsonist. The selling price will be not less than the player's capitalized value to the team that owns his contract (the difference between his average yearly product to it and his average yearly salary, multiplied by the estimated number of remaining years of his playing life and appropriately discounted). It will not be more than his capitalized value to the team for which his product would be higher than for any other team. The price will fall between these limits, at a point determined by bargaining strategies and the player's capitalized value to other would-be buyers.

But this is exactly the result which would be yielded by a free market. The difference is only that in a market subject to the reserve rule part of the price for the player's services is paid to the team that sells his contract, and part of his value is kept by the team that holds his contract; in the free market the player gets his full value.

If players were not indentured to teams but were free to accept the offers of the highest bidders, would the amount of investment in the training of players and the quality of play fall? In such a market, players will bear a larger proportion of the cost of training, and the wages they receive will have to compensate for this cost. If it pays now, in a monopsonistic market, to invest in training and development, it will also pay to do so in a free market. There will be cases in which players will reject a higher salary in the major leagues in order to remain longer in the minors and acquire skills that will assure even larger earnings in the future, just as medical students, receiving a negative income, now reject factory work at some positive wage.

Are there other alternatives to the reserve rule? Are there some other rules which would tend to produce a more or less equal distribution of playing talent among teams and which would not be defective on some other criterion?

Let there be a free players' market and let the total revenues of all teams in the major leagues be pooled and shared equally by all teams, perhaps after adjusting for differences in operating costs associated with differences in the size of franchise cities. All teams will then be equal in capacity to bid for talent. There will be no incentive, however, for any single team to win or to assemble a winning combination. Win or lose, play badly or well, it will receive its equal slice of pie. It will pay for all teams, taken together, to play well enough, on the average, so that revenue will not fall off faster than costs. But any individual team, by employing only men whose supply

prices are low, whatever their quality, can then take advantage of the gains yielded by the expenditures of the others. No team will be willing to spend if it cannot be assured that others will also do so. Each team will therefore tend to buy the cheapest playing services in the market. A rule of equal sharing of revenue leads to the equal distribution of mediocre players among teams and to consumer preference for recreational substitutes.

As another possibility, let teams bid for players and players accept offers, subject only to the constraint that a ceiling is imposed on the salaries that may be paid to individual players. The allocational effects of this rule would appear to depend upon the level of the ceiling. If the maximum salary permitted by the rule is higher than the highest wage paid to any player in a free market, the effect can be nothing but zero. It may appear that if the ceiling is sufficiently lower than this, so that more than one team is prepared to pay the specified maximum price to the highest-salaried player, the rule will begin to have some positive effects, and that, the lower the maximum salary, the larger will be the effects. On closer view, this is seen to be not true. Suppose the maximum is placed at some level, x. Players who would be worth more than x in a free market will then distribute themselves among teams on other criteria than the yearly salary, and teams will bid for players by offering other quantities than price; for example, perquisites or the security of long-term contracts.[50]

[50] An interesting subsidiary question is: What effect will long-term contracts, rather than one-year contracts, have on player salaries if the market is free and the contracts are enforceable? Players will accept a lower annual salary if they have the security of a long contract, but they will demand a higher annual salary because it will then be impossible for them to accept a higher offer from another team during the life of the contract. Assuming that players estimate their future prospects correctly, those who expect to do well will sign only a one-year contract. Teams will be prepared to pay a higher annual salary because they have the security of having a player's services for a

Teams which, in the absence of a maximum salary rule, would have outbid other would-be buyers of a player's services with cash will outbid them with non-money offers, and the distribution of players among teams will be left unaffected. If complementary rules are devised and successfully enforced (such as rules forbidding the payment of perquisites, contracts for longer than one year, secret understandings, and employment of players' relatives), so that the cash price is the whole price received by the player, those who receive the maximum will tend to accept, among competing bids, those from the teams which paid the highest average salary, for they will then be combined with higher-priced (and better) players, and the probability that they will share in World Series bonus earnings will be higher.[51] Even if players worth the maximum wage or more are distributed randomly (thus, in the long run, equally) among teams, they will be exploited; the market will not be free for them.

As still another possibility, let there be a free players' labor market and let franchises be distributed so that the size of the product market is equal for all teams. Suppose, for example, that all teams are located in markets whose population is two million. Thus, in the New York area there will be six teams rather than three; in the Chicago area, three rather than two; and so on. If attendance is a unique function of the size of the market, such a distribution of teams may equalize revenues among teams. But,

as has already been shown,[52] attendance is a function of several variables. If psychic income is not zero for all team owners, or if it is larger for some than others, and if consumer income levels, the convenience of reaching the ball park, the taste for recreation relative to other objects of expenditure, or the taste for baseball (within recreational expenditures) is not equal among cities, differences in revenues will occur. When they do, a self-generating process begins to operate to increase the magnitude of the differences. If the revenues of Team A are larger than those of Team B for any of the foregoing reasons, despite the equality of market size, Team A is in a position to contract the better players by offering a higher price,[53] Team A then wins more games than B, and its relative attendance and revenues increase. Now it is in a still better position to outbid B for players. Equal division of markets may, however, tend to result in a somewhat more equal distribution of players among teams than unequal division of markets.

Finally, let teams bid for players and let players accept offers, subject to the constraints that a low ceiling is imposed on the number of players that may be under contract to any team and that the control of players in the minor leagues is prohibited. Suppose no team is permitted to contract, directly or indirectly, more than, say, fifteen players.[54] The smaller the number of players each team is permitted to contract, the more equally will talent be distributed

---

long period; but they will pay a lower annual salary because they run the risk that the quality of his play will decline during the life of the contract. If they estimate a player's future correctly, they will sign a long-term contract with those who will do well in the future and a one-year contract with those who will not. On the assumption of correct estimation of the future on both sides of the market, the outcome seems to be that there will be no difference in the annual salary whatever the length of the contract.

[51] Part of the revenues of each annual World Series is distributed to players of the teams which are in the upper half of the major leagues' rank standings at the season's end.

[52] Above, p. 431.

[53] It may, of course, not do so (see p. 440, n. 48).

[54] The reader is reminded that major-league teams are now permitted by the rules to have an active roster of twenty-five players during the playing season (and, for one year from the date of their discharge from military service, up to five more who have returned from the service); that they may have an additional fifteen players under contract who are out on option to play with minor-league teams, subject to recall; and that they may hold several hundred players indirectly by contracting them to minor-league teams which they own or with which they have working agreements.

among teams. But it must be kept in mind that player limits are inhibitions on freedom to contract and, therefore, inconsistent with market freedom. Like other rules which have been discussed, they lead to exploitation by preventing some players from contracting with a team prepared to pay a higher price for their services; they receive less than they would be worth in a free market uninhibited by rules.

Markets in which the freedom to buy and sell is constrained by the reserve rule or by the suggested alternatives to it do not promise better results than do markets constructed on the postulate of freedom. It appears that free markets would give as good aggregate results as any other kind of market for industries, like the baseball industry, in which all firms must be nearly equal if each is to prosper. On welfare criteria, of course, the free market is superior to the others, for in such a market each worker receives the full value of his services, and exploitation does not occur.

31. The Effects
of Unions
on Resource Allocation*

ALBERT REES[1]

Albert Rees (B.A., Oberlin College, 1943; M.A., the University of Chicago, 1947; Ph.D., 1950) was born in New York City in 1921. Since 1966 he has been Professor of Economics and Public Affairs at Princeton University. Prior to this, he was Professor of Economics at the University of Chicago, where he also served for six years as editor of the *Journal of Political Economy*, and as a member of the staffs of the National Bureau of Economic Research and the Council of Economic Advisors. During 1959–1960, he was a Fellow of the Center for Advanced Study in the Behavioral Sciences at Stanford University. Rees is a specialist in the field of labor economics. His publications include *The Economics of Trade Unions, Real Wages and Manufacturing: 1890 to 1914*, and *Landmarks of Political Economy* (edited with Earl J. Hamilton and Harry G. Johnson).

The purpose of this paper is to suggest in highly condensed form the general order of magnitude of the effects of unions and

* Reprinted from the *Journal of Law and Economics* (October 1963) by permission of the publisher, pp. 69–78.

[1] I am heavily indebted to H. Gregg Lewis for comments on an earlier draft of this paper and for permission to draw freely on two of his works: *Unionism and Relative Wages in the United States* (1963) and "Relative Employment Effects of Unionism," in *Proceedings of Sixteenth Annual Meeting of Industrial Relations Research Association* 104 (1964). However, he is in no way responsible for the opinions expressed here or for the deficiencies of my estimates.

collective bargaining on the allocation of resources. It is widely accepted that unions have the power to raise wages in the establishments where they have bargaining rights. (The term "wages" should be understood to include fringe benefits.) This power comes from their ability to impose costs on management through strikes, slowdowns, or other pressure tactics which, in the short run, are greater than the costs of the wage increases provided through collective bargaining. By changes in relative wages we shall mean changes in wages in establishments covered by collective bargaining relative to wages elsewhere. For the discussion of resource allocation it is not necessary to specify how much of the relative increase arises from an absolute increase in union wages and how much from any possible decrease in nonunion wages. (Such a decrease could occur if labor were displaced from the union sector by rising wages and were therefore in more plentiful supply to the nonunion sector.)

The existence of a relative wage effect implies the existence of a relative employment effect. If blue-collar labor is made more expensive in the union sector, management will have added incentives to save such labor through closer supervision and through the use of additional labor-saving capital investment. Such substitution will minimize, but not eliminate, the addition to cost created by union wage gains. The remaining addition to average unit costs will tend to increase the price of final products and services produced in the union sector and therefore to reduce their consumption. Relative employment in the union sector should therefore decline for two reasons: (*a*) the substitution of other factors of production for union labor and (*b*) the substitution by consumers of cheaper final products and services for the more expensive output of the union sector. Whether these effects are empirically important depends on the size of the relevant elasticities of substitution and of demand.

Empirical estimates of the effect of unions on relative wages and relative employment encounter many difficulties. The basic problem is to correct for factors other than collective bargaining that might have produced differences between the union and nonunion sectors in the movements or levels of wages and employment. The devices used to control for such factors in the estimation of wage effects are discussed in detail in *Unionism and Relative Wages in the United States*.[2]

Lewis' book reviews, criticizes, and amends the previous studies that have estimated union effects on relative wages. In addition, it includes very substantial new work. From all this evidence, Lewis concludes that the effect of unions on relative wages in the late 1950's was about 10–15 per cent (that is, wages of union labor had been raised by unionism 10–15 per cent relative to the wages of nonunion labor). The highest estimate for any part of the period considered is 25 per cent or more at the depth of the Great Depression of the 1930's. In the late 1940's, because of rapid inflation, the union effect is estimated at 5 per cent or less.[3] During rapid inflation, market wages in the nonunion sector tend to rise rapidly, while the rise in union wages is often slowed by rigidities inherent in the bargaining process.

In his paper on *Relative Employment Effects of Unionism*,[4] Lewis estimates that the order of magnitude of the relative employment effect is not significantly different from that of the relative wage effect. In other words, the effect of collective bargaining is to reduce employment in the union sector about 10–15 per cent relative to employment elsewhere. This estimate rests on a less substantial body of work than the estimate of the wage effect.

The effects of unions on resource allocation can be divided into three components: effects via the interindustry wage structure, effects via the intraindustry wage structure, and effects via direct restrictions on output. We shall consider each of these in turn.

Lewis' two works permit us to make a rough estimate of the loss in real output caused by the effects of collective bargaining on the interindustry wage structure. Under certain conventional assumptions, it

briefer and less technical discussion may be found in Rees, *The Economics of Trade Unions*, pp. 73–75 (1962).

[3] These summary figures appear in Lewis, "Relative Employment Effects of Unionism," *op. cit. supra* note 1.

[4] *Ibid.*

[2] Lewis, *Unionism and Relative Wages in the United States, op. cit. supra* note 1, at p. 45. A

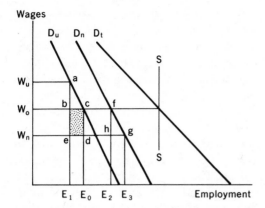

FIGURE 31.1 SS is the supply labor, and D_u, D_n, and D_t are the demand for labor in the union sector, the nonunion sector, and both combined. Before the entry of the union, the wage is W_o. If the union raises the wage in its sector to W_u, employment in the sector declines from E_0 to E_1. This increases the supply of labor to the nonunion sector, raising employment from E_2 to E_3 and forcing the wage down to W_n. The areas under the demand curves are the real net product of labor. The loss in product in the union sector is $E_0 c a E_1$, the gain in product in the nonunion sector is $E_2 f g E_3$. The difference between these areas is the loss of product shown by the shaded rectangle $b\ c\ d\ e$. This is equal to the change in employment times one-half the difference in wages. In the more general case, where the demand curves in the two sectors are nonlinear or do not have the same slope, the equality will be only approximate.

can be shown that the loss of real output is approximately equal to one-half the product of the wage effect and the employment effect (see Figure 31.1). I have used this formula to make a rough estimate for 1957, the last nonrecession year covered in Lewis' estimates. This estimated loss turns out to be approximately 600 million dollars. Since gross national product in 1957 was 443 billion dollars, the loss is approximately 0.14 per cent of national output. This welfare loss is of the same general magnitude as that estimated earlier by Arnold Harberger for enterprise monopoly (0.1 per cent).[5] The method used here is an applica-

tion of that used by Harberger and derived from Harold Hotelling.[6]

The estimated loss is arrived at as follows. Union membership in the United States in 1957 was approximately 17 million. A relative employment effect of 15 per cent implies a transfer of about 1.7 million workers out of the union sector as a result of bargaining, and a relative wage effect of 15 per cent implies an absolute wage effect of about 700 dollars per worker per year. One-half of 700 dollars times 1.7 million is approximately 600 million dollars.

This calculation assumes that the average compensation of union members is equal to the average compensation of all employees in the highly unionized industry divisions: mining, contract construction, manufacturing, transportation, and communications and public utilities. The last assumption involves offsetting errors. Among production workers, union members in these industry divisions have higher compensation than nonunion workers. However, in manufacturing, which accounts for about 70 per cent of total employment in these divisions, the compensation of nonproduction workers is substantially higher than that of production workers, and nonproduction workers are seldom unionized. Moreover, there are some union members in other industry divisions who will on the average have lower compensation than those in the divisions listed above.

In one very restricted sense, the estimate of 600 million dollars as the interindustry component of welfare loss for 1957 is an upper-limit estimate—it uses the upper limits of the ranges of relative wage effects and relative employment effects estimated by Lewis. Nevertheless, there are other assumptions embodied in the estimate that could lead it to be too low. First, since the estimate of employment effects rests on less evidence than that of wage effects, it is

[5] Harberger, "Monopoly and Resource Allocation," *American Economic Association Papers and Proceedings, Am. Econ. Rev.*, May 1954, p. 77.

[6] Hotelling, "The General Welfare in Relation to Problems of Taxation and of Railway and Utility Rates," 6 *Econometrica* 242 (1938).

possible that they exceed the upper limit of the estimated range. An alternative method of estimation would be to combine the estimated relative wage effect with an assumed elasticity of demand for labor. This is the method used by Harberger in his study of enterprise monopoly, in which he assumed an average elasticity of demand for products of −1. The assumption of an elasticity of demand for labor of −1 would not change the estimate given above, since this is the elasticity implicit in the estimates used for the wage and employment effects.

The estimate also assumes that the relative wage and employment effects of unions are uniform within the union sector. The more realistic assumption that the size of these effects varies within the sector will not change the estimate provided that there is no correlation across unionized industries between the size of actual employment and actual wage effects. However, if in general large wage effects are associated with small employment effects, the estimate given above is too high; if large wage effects are associated with large employment effects, the estimate is too low.

In general, it seems reasonable to assume that large wage effects are associated with smaller-than-average employment effects—that is, that unions will raise wages most where the elasticity of demand for labor is smallest and the costs in reduced employment are lowest. There is, however, one important case that does not fit this generalization: the bituminous coal industry, where both the wage effect and the employment effect seem to be unusually large.

The estimated loss under discussion also assumes that no unemployment results from the employment effects of unionization. We should not, of course, charge the unions with the losses arising from general deficiencies in aggregate demand. However, the displacement of labor from one industry to another will give rise to frictional unemployment even under conditions of general prosperity, and the costs of this should be added to the interindustry component of welfare loss. These costs will be smaller if unionization is concentrated in expanding industries, since relative employment effects will then take the form of reducing the rate of hiring rather than requiring the dismissal of present employees. In fact, however, much of the strength of unions has been in contracting or stable industries, so that the unemployment costs of unionization are probably significant.

Professor Lewis has reported to me that he has made an unpublished estimate of the welfare cost of the interindustry component of relative wage and employment effects, using a somewhat more sophisticated method of calculation which allows for the dispersion of the relative wage effect within the union sector. The resulting measure of loss is almost the same as that reported above: 0.15 per cent of national product.

Not much is known about the relative wage effects of unions in particular industries. The available industry studies are summarized by Lewis in *Unionism and Relative Wages in the United States*, chapters iii and v, especially Table 49. These studies suggest that the unions of the following groups of workers had larger than average effects (20 per cent or more): skilled building craftsmen, bituminous coal miners, commercial airline pilots, and East Coast seamen. These estimates refer to the 1950's except that for building craftsmen, which is for 1939. The studies also show that one union, the Amalgamated Clothing Workers, had no appreciable relative wage effect in the period 1946–57, though it did in the years from 1919 to 1939. This loss of power was associated with declining demand for the product.

The list of cases with very large estimated wage effects includes three for craft unions and one for an industrial union. Economic theory suggests that craft unions will have larger relative wage effects than industrial unions because their wages constitute a smaller portion of total costs, except in the unusual case where there are very good substitutes for union craftsmen in production and the elasticity of demand for the product is low.[7] But this advantage holds only if the craft unions in an industry bargain individually. If they bargain as a group, or wage patterns are transmitted to all the occupations in the industry, the case becomes similar to that of industrial unionism.

It is possible to put together the available industry studies, the relevant economic theory, and data on wage movements to make informed guesses on which unions not mentioned in the preceding paragraphs have larger-than-average relative wage effects. My leading candidates would be the skilled craft unions in railroads, entertainment, and the printing trades; the teamsters; and the steelworkers. A list of candidates for additional unions with less-than-average relative wage effects would include the unions of ladies' garment workers, textile workers, shoe workers, and white-collar government workers. The first is included because of the similarity of the industry to men's clothing. The next two are examples of unions that have incomplete organization of industries with national product markets. The government unions are included because their political power is probably an inferior substitute for the use of the strike.

The relative wage and employment effects considered so far arise from the impact of collective bargaining on the interindustry wage structure. We turn next to the effects of collective bargaining on the wage structure within industries, which in some cases may be of considerable importance. Geographical wage patterns are one example. In the absence of collective bargaining, manual labor, and particularly unskilled labor, is appreciably cheaper in the

South than in other regions. This regional wage differential arises from the more abundant supply of unskilled labor in the South. It tends to be reduced by the migration of labor to the North and of capital to the South, but such movements of resources have not been sufficient to offset the greater rate of natural population increase in the South.

Unions that bargain with multiplant employers or with associations of employers operating both in the South and elsewhere have attempted to eliminate regional wage differentials and frequently have succeeded. The union rate for unskilled labor in the southern operations of these employers is therefore further above the market rate than in their northern and western operations.[8] From this may flow a number of consequences: (1) national employers constructing new facilities both in the South and in the North would normally have an incentive to use somewhat more labor-intensive methods in the South; this incentive is eliminated by the uniform wage; (2) where plant location is oriented toward labor costs rather than access to markets or raw materials, an incentive to locate plants in the South is removed; (3) where plant location has been determined by access to southern markets or raw materials, the national employer may be unable to compete with local nonunion employers able to take advantage of low market rates of wages. Factors of this kind are unlikely to be important in the automobile or steel industries but are of considerable importance in meat packing. The displacement of national by local firms could retard the industrialization of the South to the extent that national firms have access to lower-cost sources of capital, both internal and external.

---

[7] See Rees, *op. cit. supra* note 2, at pp. 70–73, and the passages from Marshall and Hicks cited therein.

[8] This is especially true in motor freight, where Hoffa has obtained the same mileage rates from southern as from midwestern truckers, removing traditional differentials. Because of superior weather conditions in the South, these bring higher weekly earnings to southern drivers.

The elimination of regional wage differentials through collective bargaining benefits the southern workers already employed in the unionized sector. However, it injures those workers, not readily identifiable, who would have been employed in industry had incentives for the expansion of industrial employment in the South not been diminished. Equality is achieved within the union sector at the cost of increased disparity between the union plant in the South and the rest of the southern economy.

Another area in which collective bargaining affects the structure of wages is that of skill differentials. Such effects may be readily apparent to personnel people in industry. However, they have not been much studied by academic economists, and the discussion below is therefore somewhat conjectural. The effects seem from existing literature to be mixed and without a dominant pattern.[9]

In several industries represented by industrial unions, the effect of collective bargaining early in the postwar period appeared to be to compress skill differentials. The compensation of the least skilled workers was raised most by unions, that of the most skilled less or perhaps not at all. Such wage compression could affect resource allocation by reducing incentives to undertake training and could lead to shortages of apprentices for the skilled trades. More recently, such compression has been limited or reversed by the actual or threatened secession of skilled workers to form separate unions of their own and by the operation of percentage wage increases such as annual improvement factors.

An opposite effect on skill differentials can occur under craft unionism if the unions representing the most skilled crafts are stronger than those representing the less skilled. This situation may prevail in portions of the railroad and printing industries. In such cases the effect of union-

[9] Reynolds & Taft, *The Evolution of the Wage Structure*, pp. 185–86 (1956).

ism is to prevent skill differentials from narrowing as much as would be expected from the general long-run trend; this provides incentives for employers to economize most in the use of skilled labor. However, the ability of employers to substitute other factors for skilled labor may be severely restricted by union rules.

Since union effects on intra-industry wage structures are more difficult to discern than effects on the interindustry structure, the costs of the former are probably less than those of the latter. This would suggest a combined cost of less than 0.3 per cent of gross national product. If this estimate seems low, it is because the social costs of transferring resources to less productive uses are far less than those of wasting resources altogether. This brings us to the third avenue of union effects on resource allocation: direct restrictions of output through control of manning requirements, the work pace, and work practices, often called "featherbedding." In the course of preparing this paper, I have reached the conclusion that losses of this kind—deadweight losses—probably exceed the social losses from relative wage effects. Indeed, management in a single industry—railroads—claimed in 1959 that obsolete work rules were costing 500 million dollars a year, or over 0.1 per cent of national product. Although this may be an overestimate, particularly through the inclusions of some costs that are in reality higher compensation for necessary work, the comparison between this amount and those mentioned above suggests something about the general magnitudes involved.

The evidence available is not sufficient to permit any numerical estimate of the total costs of union control of manning practices and work rules. The published accounts suggest that a large part of the costs is concentrated in a few industries, especially railroads, printing, longshoring, entertainment, and some aspects of building construction. Costs are especially high in industries with craft union organization where each piece of work, however small, "belongs" to a particular craft, and a member of that craft must be called to do it. On the railroads such practices can result in the payment of a day's pay for a few minutes' work and sometimes in payment to two men for work done by one.[10]

It should be noted, however, that direct union impact on output is not always restrictive. Under some circumstances, unions have made significant contributions to efforts to raise output or productivity, especially where jobs have been threatened by competition from new products or products produced in other locations.

The practices bearing directly on resource use include apprenticeship rules, which can affect the number and quality of people trained, either by their effect on the size and nature of the entering group or by their influence on the percentage of entrants who complete the program. There seems to be general agreement that the number and quality of apprentices in many trades are inadequate to meet probable future needs. Such an effect could arise in any or all of the following ways: (1) the quality of the entering group can be lowered by nepotism or discrimination in the selection of entrants; (2) the number of apprentices can be limited by rules setting the ratio of apprentices to journeymen—this is the best known, but probably not the most important, of the restrictive devices; (3) the numbers of people entering and completing programs will be held down if the programs are unnecessarily long or if the program content is poor; (4) the number entering and completing will be reduced if the apprentice's wage is too low relative to the journeyman's; (5) conversely, the willingness of employers to train apprentices will be reduced if the apprentice's wage rate is too high relative to the journeyman's. All

[10] Slichter, Healy & Livernash, *The Impact of Collective Bargaining on Management,* ch. 11 (1960).

of these observations apply in principle to training programs operated solely by management. However, when management is in sole control of a training program, it has greater freedom to take prompt corrective action if the number or quality of trainees is inadequate.

Union influence on resource allocation that arises from increases in relative wages works unambiguously in the direction of reducing relative employment. Practices that limit output or require unnecessary numbers of men have an unpredictable effect in the long run. In the short run, the effect may be an absolute increase in the employment of the group that institutes the restrictive practices; in the longer run, such practices may encourage types of substitution that the union is powerless to cope with, which will ultimately reduce employment. For example, an effective full-crew law or rule on railroads will increase the number of operating employees per train but may accelerate the substitution of other forms of transportation for rail transportation. In the long run, the number of jobs lost through such accelerated substitution could exceed the number created or preserved by the full-crew rule. The only unambiguous effect is to increase the cost of transportation.

Union restrictions on contracting out work traditionally done in the bargaining unit are less formalized than some other types of restrictions, but may be becoming more widespread. If the work can be done at less cost by the outside contractor, there is an obvious adverse effect on efficiency. In cases where the outside contractor also uses union labor (not necessarily from the same union), any shifts in employment arising from restrictions on contracting out will not be caught by estimates of changes in relative employment in the union sector as a whole.

Throughout the preceding discussion, the implicit comparison has been between the relative wages and distribution of employment existing under unionism and those which would exist under perfectly competitive labor markets. Since the allocation of resources by perfectly competitive markets is known to be optimal, by this standard the impact of the union is necessarily adverse. The standard must be modified to the extent that actual nonunion labor markets are monopsonistic. If nonunion employers, either singly or acting in concert, have the power to hold wages below the levels that would prevail under perfect competition, moderate union effects on relative wages may bring employment closer to an optimal configuration. The scanty available evidence suggests that monopsony power by employers in United States labor markets is small but not nonexistent.[11] However, in some markets where employers have such power (textile-mill towns, for example) there is little unionization, while in others where such power may once have existed (especially coal-mining areas), the union corrective may have gone too far.

If the entire impact of unions on our so-ciety could be subsumed under the heading of resource allocation, there would be little difficulty in reading the conclusions that the over-all impact is adverse and that union power is excessive. The difficulties for policy explored in Professor Meltzer's paper[12] arise because this is not the case. Important aspects of collective bargaining, such as grievance procedure, have only tangential implications for resource allocation, but strong effects on equity in work situations and on the meaning and status of manual work. Union representation of workers in political processes is largely non-economic, yet could be affected by policies designed to deal with problems of resource allocation. The central policy issue is how to design measures that would reduce the adverse effects of collective bargaining on resource allocation while preserving those aspects of bargaining that are socially constructive. There remains much room for debate whether such goals can best be achieved by radical or by cautious measures.

[11] Bunting, *Employer Concentration in Local Labor Markets* (1962).

[12] See Meltzer, "Labor Unions, Collective Bargaining, and the Antitrust Laws," 6 *J. Law & Econ.* 152 (1963).

Part VIII

GENERAL EQUILIBRIUM,
WELFARE ECONOMICS,
AND PUBLIC GOODS

32. The Simple Analytics of Welfare Maximization*

FRANCIS M. BATOR[1]

Francis M. Bator (B.S., Massachusetts Institute of Technology, 1949; Ph.D., 1956) was born in Budapest, Hungary, in 1925. He is, at present, Director of Studies, Institute of Politics, and Professor of Political Economy at the John F. Kennedy School of Government at Harvard University. Formerly, he was Deputy Special Assistant to the President for National Security Affairs and, prior to this, a member of the faculty of MIT, where he served as a senior member of the Center for International Studies. In the fields of economic theory, development, and international economics, Bator has made signal contributions to economic education. Outside the profession he is best known for his book *The Question of Government Spending*.

It appears, curiously enough, that there is nowhere in the literature a complete and concise nonmathematical treatment of the problem of welfare maximization in its "new welfare economics" aspects. It is the purpose of this exposition to fill this gap for the simplest statical and stationary situation.

Part I consists in a rigorous diagrammatic determination of the "best" configuration of inputs, outputs, and commodity distribution for a two-input, two-output, two-person situation, where furthermore all functions are of smooth curvature and where neoclassical generalized diminishing returns obtain in all but one dimension—returns to scale are assumed constant. Part II identifies the "price-wage-rent" configuration embedded in the maximum problem which would ensure that decentralized profit- and preference-maximizing behavior by atomistic competitors would sustain the maximum-welfare position. Part III explores the requirements on initial factor ownership if market-imputed (or "as if"

* Reprinted from the *American Economic Review* (March 1957) by permission of the publisher, pp. 22–59.

[1] The author is indebted to R. S. Eckaus and R. M. Solow for suggestive comment.

market-imputed) income distribution is to be consistent with the commodity distribution required by the maximum-welfare solution. Part IV consists in brief comments on some technical ambiguities, *e.g.*, the presumption that all tangencies are internal; also on a number of feasible (and not so feasible) extensions: more inputs, outputs and households; elasticity in input supplies; joint and intermediate products; diminishing returns to scale; external interactions. The discussion is still stationary and neoclassical in spirit. Then, in Part V, the consequences of violating some of the neoclassical curvature assumptions are examined. Attention is given to the meaning, in a geometric context, of the "convexity" requirements of mathematical economics and to the significance of an important variety of nonconvexity—increasing returns to scale—for "real" market allocation, for Lange-Lerner type "as if" market allocation, and for the solubility of a maximum-of-welfare problem. Finally, Part VI contains some brief remarks on possible dynamical extensions. A note on the seminal literature concludes the paper.[2]

I. INPUTS, OUTPUTS AND COMMODITY DISTRIBUTION

Take, as given:

1. Two inelastically supplied, homogeneous and perfectly divisible inputs, labor-services (L) and land (D). This "Austrian" assumption does violate the full generality of the neoclassical model; elasticity in input supplies would make simple diagrammatic treatment impossible.

2. Two production functions, $A = F_A (L_A, D_A)$, $N = F_N(L_N, D_N)$, one for each

[2] Anyone familiar with the modern literature will recognize my debt to the writings of Professor Samuelson. Reference is to be made, especially, to Chapter 8 of *Foundations of Economic Analysis* (Cambridge, 1947); to "Evaluation of Real National Income," *Oxford Econ. Papers,* Jan. 1950, II, 1–29; and to "Social Indifference Curves," *Quart. Jour. Econ.,* Feb. 1956, LXX, 1–22.

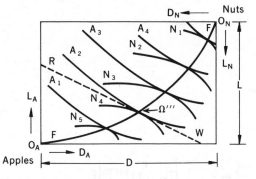

FIGURE 32.1

of the two homogeneous goods: apples (A) and nuts (N). The functions are of smooth curvature, exhibit constant returns to scale and diminishing marginal rates of substitution along any isoquant (*i.e.*, the isoquants are "convex" to the origin).

3. Two ordinal preference functions, $U_X = f_X(A_X, N_X)$ and $U_Y = f_Y(A_Y, N_Y)$— sets of smooth indifference curves convex to the origin—one for X and one for Y. These reflect unambiguous and consistent preference orderings for each of the two individuals (X and Y) of all conceivable combinations of own-consumption of apples and nuts. For convenience we adopt for each function an arbitrary numerical index, U_X and U_Y, to identify the indifference curves. But the functions have no interpersonal implications whatever and for any one individual they only permit of statements to the effect that one situation is worse, indifferent or better than another. We do require consistency: if X prefers situation α to situation β and β to γ, then he must prefer α to γ; indifference curves must not cross. Also, satiation-type phenomena and Veblenesque or other "external" effects are ruled out.

4. A social welfare function, $W = W(U_X, U_Y)$, that permits a unique preference-ordering of all possible states based only on the positions of both individuals in their own preference fields. It is this function that incorporates an ethical valuation of the relative "deservingness" of X and Y.

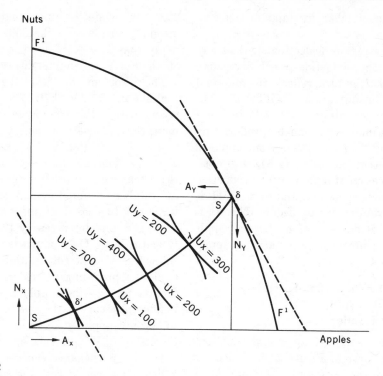

FIGURE 32.2

The problem is to determine the maximum-welfare values of labor input into apples (L_A), labor input into nuts (L_N), land input into apples (D_A), land input into nuts (D_N), of total production of apples (A) and nuts (N), and, last, of the distribution of apples and nuts between X and Y (A_X, N_X, A_Y, N_Y).

A. From Endowments and Production Functions to the Production-Possibility Curve

Construct an Edgeworth-Bowley box diagram, as in Figure 32.1, with horizontal and vertical dimensions just equal to the given supplies, respectively, of D and L, and plot the isoquants for apples with the southwest corner as origin and those for nuts with origin at the northeast corner. Every point in the box represents six variables, L_A, L_N, D_A, D_N, A, N. The problem of production efficiency consists in finding the locus of points where any increase in

the production of apples implies a necessary reduction in the output of nuts (and vice versa). The diagram shows that locus to consist in the points of tangency between the nut and apple isoquants (FF).

From this efficiency locus we can read off the maximal obtainable combinations of apples and nuts and plot these in the output (AN) space. Given our curvature assumptions we get the smooth concave-to-the-origin Pareto-efficient production-possibility curve $F'F'$ of Figure 32.2.[3] This curve, a consolidation of FF in Figure 32.1, represents input-output configurations such that the marginal rate of substitution (MRS) of labor for land in the production of any given quantity of apples—the absolute value of the slope of the apple isoquant—just equals the marginal rate of

[3] This presumes, also, that the intrinsic factor intensities of A and N differ. If they did not, $F'F'$ would be a straight line—a harmless special case. (See V-3-c below.)

substitution of labor for land in the production of nuts.[4]

The slope (again neglecting sign) at any point on the production-possibility curve of Figure 32.2, in turn, reflects the **marginal rate of transformation** (MRT) at that point of apples into nuts. It indicates precisely how many nuts can be produced by transferring land and labor from apple to nut production (at the margin), with optimal reallocation of inputs in the production of both goods so as to maintain the MRS-equality requirement of **Figure 32.1**. It is the marginal nut-cost of an "extra" apple —or the reciprocal of the marginal apple-cost of nuts.

B. From the Production-Possibility Curve to the Utility-Possibility Frontier

Pick any point, δ, on the production-possibility curve of **Figure 32.2**: it denotes a specific quantity of apples and nuts. Construct an Edgeworth-Bowley (trading) box with these precise dimensions by dropping from δ lines parallel to the axes as in Figure 32.2. Then draw in X's and Y's indifference maps, one with the southwest, the other with the northeast corner for origin. Every point in the box again fixes six variables: apples to X (A_X) and to Y (A_Y), nuts to X (N_X) and to Y (N_Y), and the "levels" of satisfaction of X and Y as measured by the ordinal indices U_X and U_Y which characterize the position of the point with respect to the two preference fields. For example, at λ in Figure 32.2, $U_X = 300$, $U_Y =$

200. Note again, however, that this 200 is incommensurate with the 300: it does not imply that at λ X is in some sense better off than is Y (or indifferent, or worse off).

The problem of "exchange-efficiency" consists in finding that locus of feasible points within the trading box where any increase in X's satisfaction (U_X) implies a necessary reduction in the satisfaction of Y, (U_Y). Feasible in what sense? In the sense that we just exhaust the fixed apple-nut totals as denoted by δ. Again, the locus turns out to consist of the points of tangency, SS, and for precisely the same analytical reasons. Only now it is the marginal subjective rate of substitution of nuts for apples in providing a fixed level of satisfaction for X—the absolute slope of X's indifference curve—that is to be equated to the nut-apple MRS of Y, to the slope, that is, of *his* indifference curve.

From this exchange-efficiency locus,[5] SS, which is associated with the single production point δ, we can now read off the maximal combinations of U_X and U_Y obtainable from δ and plot these in utility $(U_X U_Y)$ space ($S'S'$, Figure 32.3). Each such *point* δ in output space "maps" into a *line* in utility space—the $U_X U_Y$ mix is sensitive to how the fixed totals of apples and nuts are distributed between X and Y.[6]

There is a possible short-cut, however.

---

[4] In marginal productivity terms, MRS, at any point, of labor for land in, *e.g.* apple production—the absolute value (drop all minus signs) of the **slope of the apple isoquant (Figure 32.1)**—is equal to

$$\left[\begin{array}{c}\text{Marginal Physical Product of Land} \\ \text{Marginal Physical Product of Labor}\end{array}\right]$$

in apple production at that point. In the symbolism of the calculus

$$\left|\frac{\partial L_A}{\partial D_A}\right|_{\Delta A = 0} = \left(\frac{\partial A}{\partial D_A}\right) \div \left(\frac{\partial A}{\partial L_A}\right).$$

[5] This is Edgeworth's contract curve, or what Boulding has aptly called the "conflict" curve—once on it, mutually advantageous trading is not possible and any move reflecting a gain to X implies a loss to Y.

[6] Each *point* in utility space, in turn, maps into a line in output-space. Not just one but many possible apple-nut combinations can satisfy a specified $U_X U_Y$ requirement. It is this reciprocal point-line phenomenon that lies at the heart of Samuelson's proof of the nonexistence of community indifference curves such as would permit the derivation of demand curves for apples and nuts. The subjective "community" MRS between A and N for given fixed A and N, *e.g.*, at δ in **Figure 32.2**, would surely depend on how the A and N are distributed, *i.e.*, on which $U_X U_Y$ point on SS is chosen. Hence the slope of a "joint" XY indifference curve at δ is not uniquely fixed by AN.

Given our curvature assumptions, we can trace out the grand utility-possibility frontier—the envelope—by using an efficiency relationship to pick just one point from each trading box contract curve SS associated with every output point δ. Go back to Figure 32.2. The slope of the production-possibility curve at δ has already been revealed as the marginal rate of transformation, via production, of apples into nuts. The (equalized) slopes of the two sets of indifference contours along the exchange-efficiency curve SS, in turn, represent the marginal rates of substitution of nuts for apples for psychic indifference (the same for X as for Y). The grand criterion for efficiency is that it be impossible by any shift in production *cum* exchange to increase U_X without reducing U_Y. Careful thought will suggest that this criterion is violated unless the marginal rate of transformation between apples and nuts as outputs—the slope at δ—just equals the common marginal rate of substitution of apples and nuts, as consumption "inputs," in providing psychic satisfaction.

If, for example, at δ one can get two apples by diverting resources and reducing nut-output by one, a point on SS where the (equalized) marginal rate of substitution of apples for nuts along indifference curves is, *e.g.*, one to one, permits the following "arbitrage" operation. Shift land and labor so as to produce two more apples and one less nut. Then, leaving X undisturbed take away one nut from Y and replace it by one apple. By our assumption that MRS = 1 both X and Y are left indifferent: U_X and U_Y remain unaltered. But we have an extra apple left over; since this permits raising U_X and/or U_Y, the initial situation was not on the U_XU_Y frontier.[7]

To be on the grand utility-possibility frontier (BB of Figure 32.3), then, MRT_δ must equal the (equalized) MRS of the

indifference contours along the SS associated with δ. This requirement fixes the single U_XU_Y point on SS that lies on the "envelope" utility-possibility frontier, given the output point δ. Pick that point on SS, in fact, where the joint slope of the indifference curves is exactly parallel to the slope at δ of the production-possibility curve. In Figure 32.2 this point is at δ', which gives the one "efficient" U_XU_Y combination associated with the AN mix denoted by δ. This U_XU_Y combination can then be plotted as δ'' in Figure 32.3.[8]

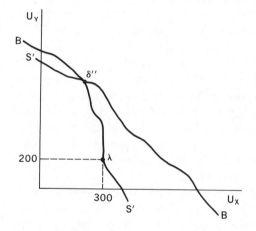

FIGURE 32.3

Repetition of this process for each point on the production-possibility curve—note that each such point requires a new trading box—will yield the grand utility-possibility frontier of Pareto-efficient input-output combinations, BB. Each point of this frontier gives the maximum of U_X for any given feasible level of U_Y and vice versa.

[7] The above argument can be made perfectly rigorous in terms of the infinitesimal movements of the differential calculus.

[8] Never mind, here, about multiple optima. These could occur even with our special curvature assumptions. If, for example, both sets of indifference curves show paths of equal MRS that coincide with straight lines from the origin and, further, if the two preference functions are so symmetrical as to give an SS_δ that hugs the diagonal of the trading box, then either every point on SS_δ will satisfy the MRS = MRT criterion, or none will. For discussion of these related fine points see Parts IV and V.

C. From the Utility-Possibility Frontier to the "Constrained Bliss Point"

But *BB*, the grand utility-possibility function, is a curve and not a point. Even after eliminating all combinations of inputs and outputs that are nonefficient in a Paretian sense, there remains a single dimensional infinity of "efficient" combinations: one for every point on *BB*. To designate a single *best* configuration we must be given a Bergson-Samuelson social welfare function that denotes the ethic that is to "count" or whose implications we wish to study. Such a function—could be yours, or mine, or Mossadegh's, though his is likely to be non-transitive—is intrinsically ascientific.[9] There are no considerations of *economic efficiency* that permit us to designate Crusoe's function, which calls for many apples and nuts for Crusoe and just a few for Friday, as economically superior to Friday's. Ultimate ethical valuations are involved.

Once given such a welfare function, in the form of a family of indifference contours in utility space, as in Figure 32.4, the problem becomes fully determinate.[10] "Welfare" is at a maximum where the utility-possibility envelope frontier *BB* touches the highest contour of the *W*-function.[11] In Figure 32.4, this occurs at Ω.

Note the unique quality of that point Ω. It is the only point, of all the points on the utility frontier *BB*, that has unambiguous normative or prescriptive significance. Pareto-efficient production and commodity-

distribution—being on *F'F'* and also on *BB* —is a necessary condition for a maximum of our kind of welfare function, but is not a sufficient condition.[12] The claim that any "efficient" point is better than "inefficient" configurations that lie inside *BB* is indefensible. It is true that given an "inefficient" point, there will exist *some* point or points on *BB* that represent an improvement; but there may well be many points on *BB* that would be worse rather than better. For example, in terms of the ethic denoted by the specific *W*-function of Figure 32.4, Ω on *BB* is better than any other

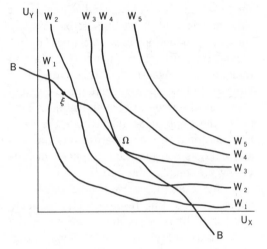

FIGURE 32.4

feasible point. But the efficient point ξ is distinctly inferior to any inefficient point on or northeast of W_2. If I am X, and if my *W*-function, which reflects the usual dose of self-interest, is the test, "efficient" *BB* points that give a high U_Y and a very low U_X are clearly less desirable than lots of inefficient points of higher U_X.[13]

---

[9] Though it may provide the anthropologist or psychologist with interesting material for scientific study.

[10] In the absence of implicit income redistribution these curves cannot be transposed into output-space. They are not community indifference curves which would permit the derivation of demand schedules. See fn. 6 and 13, also IV-3.

[11] If there are several such points, never mind. If the "ethic" at hand is really indifferent, pick any one. If it doesn't matter, it doesn't matter.

[12] Note, however, that Pareto-efficiency is not even a necessary condition for a maximum of just any conceivable *W*-function. The form of our type function reflects a number of ethically loaded restrictions, *e.g.*, that individuals' preference functions are to "count," and count positively.

[13] Note, however, that no consistency requirements link my set of indifference curves with "my"

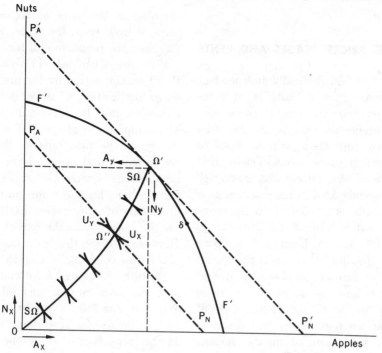

FIGURE 32.5

D. From "Bliss Point" to "Best" Inputs, Outputs and Commodity Distribution

We can now retrace our steps. To Ω on BB in Figure 32.4, there corresponds just one point, Ω', on the production-possibility

---

W-function. The former reflects a personal preference ordering based only on own-consumption (and, in the more general case, own services supplied). The latter denotes also values which I hold as "citizen," and these need not be consistent with maximizing my satisfaction "*qua* consumer." X as citizen may prefer a state of less U_x and some U_Y to more U_x and zero U_Y. There is also an important analytical distinction. X's preference function is conceptually "observable": confronted by various relative price and income configurations his consumption responses will reveal its contours. His *W*-function, on the other hand, is not revealed by behavior, unless he be dictator, subjected by "nature" to binding constraints. In a sense only a society, considered as exhibiting a political consensus, has a *W*-function subject to empirical inference (*cf.* IV-3). The distinction—it has a Rousseauvian flavor—while useful, is of course arbitrary. Try it for a masochist; a Puritan. . . .

curve $F'F'$ in Figure 32.5. (We derived BB, point by point, from $F'F'$ of Figure 32.2: and the $F'F'$ of Figure 32.5 is copied from that of Figure 32.2.) Ω' fixes the output mix: A and N. Then, by examining the trading-box contract curve $S_\Omega S_\Omega$ associated with Ω' of $F'F'$, we can locate the one point where U_X and U_Y correspond to the coordinates of Ω in utility space. The equalized slope of the indifference curves will at that point, Ω'', just equal the slope of $F'F'$ at Ω'. Ω'' fixes the apple-nut distribution implied by the maximum of W: A_X, A_Y, N_X, and N_Y. Further, we can not locate the point Ω''' on the Pareto-efficient input locus, FF of Figure 32.1 that corresponds to Ω' of $F'F'$. It fixes the remaining variables, the factor allocations: L_A, D_A, L_N, and D_N. The maximum-welfare configuration is determinate. We have solved for the land and labor to be used in apple and nut production, for the total output of apples and nuts, and for their distribution between X and Y.

II. PRICES, WAGES AND RENTS

The above is antiseptically independent of institutional context, notably of competitive market institutions. It could constitute an intellectual exercise for the often invoked man from Mars, in how "best" to make do with given resources. Yet implicit in the logic of this purely "technocratic" formulation, embedded in the problem as it were, is a set of constants which the economist will catch himself thinking of as prices. And wisely so. Because it happens —and this "duality" theorem is the kernel of modern welfare economics—that decentralized decisions in response to these "prices" by, or "as if" by, atomistic profit and satisfaction maximizers will result in just that constellation of inputs, outputs and commodity-distribution that our maximum of W requires.[14]

Can these constants—prices, wages, rents —be identified in our diagrammatic representations?[15] Only partially so. Two-dimensionality is partly at fault, but, as we shall see, a final indeterminacy is implied by the usual curvature assumptions themselves.[16] The diagrams will, however, take us part way, and a little algebra will do for the rest.

The exercise consists in finding a set of four constants associated with the solution values of the maximum problem that have meaning as the price of apples (p_A), the price of nuts (p_N), the wage rate of labor (w), and the rental rate of land (r).[17]

First, what can be said about w and r? Profit maximization by the individual producer implies that whatever output he may choose as most lucrative must be produced at a minimum total cost.[18] The elementary theory of the firm tells us that, for this condition to hold, the producer facing fixed input-prices—horizontal supply curves— must adjust his input mix until the marginal rate of substitution (MRS) of labor for land just equals the rent-to-wage ratio. It is easy to see the "arbitrage" possibilities if this condition is violated. If one can substitute one unit of L for two units of D, and maintain output constant, with $w =$ \$10 and $r =$ \$10, it surely reduces total cost to do so and keep doing so until any further reduction in D by one unit has to be matched, if output is not to fall, by adding no less than one unit of L. In the usual diagrammatic terms, then, the producer will cling to points of tangency between the isoquants and (iso-expenditure) lines whose absolute slope equals r/w.

Reversing the train of thought, the input blend denoted by the point Ω''' in Figure 32.1 implies a shadow r/w ratio that just equals the MRS of labor for land in the production of both apples and nuts at that point Ω'''. $\text{MRS}_{\Omega'''}$ is given by the (equalized) slopes of the isoquants at Ω'''. The implicit r/w, therefore, must equal the

[14] Note that this statement is neutral with respect to (1) genuine profit maximizers acting in "real" but perfectly competitive markets; (2) Lange-Lerner-type bureaucrats ("take prices as given and maximize or Siberia"); or (3) technicians using electronic machines and trying to devise efficient computing routines.

[15] To avoid institutional overtones, the theory literature usually attempts verbal disembodiment and refers to them as shadow-prices. The mathematically oriented, in turn, like to think of them as Lagrangean multipliers.

[16] These very assumptions render this last indeterminacy, that of the absolute price level, wholly inconsequential.

[17] Since we are still assuming that all the functions have neoclassical curvature properties, hence that, *e.g.*, the production-possibility curve, as derived, has to be concave to the origin, we can impose the *strong* condition on the constants that they exhibit optimality characteristics for genuine, though perfect, markets. It will turn out, however, that two progressively weaker conditions are possible, which permit of some nonconvexities (*e.g.*, increasing returns to scale), yet maintain for the constants some essentially price-like qualities. More on this in Part V.

[18] In our flow model, unencumbered by capital, this is equivalent to producing the chosen output with minimum expenditure on inputs.

slope of the line *RW* that is tangent to (both) the isoquants at Ω'''.[19]

The slope of *RW* identifies the rent: wage ratio implied by the maximal configuration. Essentially analogous reasoning will establish the equalized slope of the indifference curves through Ω'', in Figure 32.5, as denoting the p_A/p_N ratio implied by the solution. X, as also Y, to maximize his own satisfaction as measured by U_x, must achieve whatever level of satisfaction his income will permit at a minimum expenditure. This requires that he choose an apple-nut mix such that the psychic marginal-rate-of-substitution between nuts and apples for indifference just equal p_A/p_N. He, and Y, will pick Ω'' only if p_A/p_N is equal to the absolute slope of the tangent (P_A/P_N) at Ω''. This slope, therefore, fixes the Ω-value of p_A/p_N.[20]

Note that this makes p_A/p_N equal to the slope also of the production-possibility curve *F'F'* at Ω'.[21] This is as it should be. If $p_A/p_N = 10$, *i.e.*, if one apple is "worth" ten nuts on the market, it would be odd indeed, in our frictionlessly efficient world of perfect knowledge, if the marginal rate of transformation of nuts into apples, via production, were different from ten-to-one. Producers would not in fact produce the

apple-nut combination of Ω' if p_A/p_N differed from MRT at Ω'.

We have identified the r/w and p_A/p_N implied by the maximum of *W*. These two constancies provide two equations to solve for the four unknown prices. Unfortunately this is as far as the two-dimensional diagrammatics will take us. None of the diagrams permit easy identification of the relationship between the input prices and the output prices. Yet such a relationship is surely implied. By the theory of the firm we know that the profit-maximizing producer facing a constant price for his product—the horizontal demand curve of the perfectly competitive firm—will expand output up to where his extra revenue for an additional unit of output, *i.e.*, the price, just equals the marginal cost of producing that output.[22] And marginal cost, in turn, is sensitive to r and w.

It would be easy to show the implied price-wage or price-rent relationships by introducing marginal productivity notions. Profit maximization requires that the quantity of each input hired be increased up to the point where its marginal physical product times the price of the extra output, just equals the price of the added input. Since these marginal physical productivities are determinate curvature properties of the production functions, this rule provides a third relationship, one between an output price and an input price.

Alternatively, given our assumption that production functions show constant returns to scale, we can make use of Euler's "product exhaustion" theorem. Its economic content is that if constant returns to scale prevails, the total as-if-market-imputed income of the factors of production just "exhausts" the total value of the product. This means, simply, that $wL + rD = p_A A +$

---

[19] Again, absolute values of these slopes are implied throughout the argument. Recall from footnote 4 that the labor-for-land MRS, the absolute slope of the isoquants at Ω''' as given by RO_A/WO_A, is equal to the

$$\left[\frac{\text{Marginal Physical Product of Land}}{\text{Marginal Physical Product of Labor}}\right] \text{ratio.}$$

Our shadow r/w, then, turns out to be just equal to that ratio.

[20] The price-ratio relates reciprocally to the axes: $p_A/p_N = P_A O/P_N O$ in Figure 32.5. Along *e.g.*, X's indifference curve (U_X at Ω'') a rise in p_A/p_N, *i.e.*, a steepening of $P_A P_N$, results in a substitution by X of nuts for apples; ditto for Y.

[21] Remember, in choosing the one point on $S_\Omega S_\Omega$ that would lie on the envelope in utility space, we choose the point where the indifference curve slopes just equaled the marginal rate of transformation (see p. 459 above).

[22] Never mind here the "total" requirement—that this price exceed unit cost—if the real-life profit-seeking producer is to produce at all. More on this in Part V.

$p_N N$, and it provides a third relationship between w, r, p_A and p_N for the Ω-values of L, D, A and N.[23]

At any rate, the maximal solution implies a third price-equation, hence we can express three of the prices in terms of the fourth. But what of the fourth? This is indeterminate, given the characteristics of the model. In a frictionless world of perfect certainty, where, for example, nobody would think of holding such a thing as money, only *relative* prices matter. The three equations establish the proportions among them implied by the maximum position, and the absolute values are of no import. If the $p_A:p_N:w:r$ proportions implied by Ω are $20{:}15{:}50{:}75$, profit and satisfaction maximizers will make the input-output-consumption decisions required for the maximum-of-W irrespective of whether the absolute levels of these prices happen to be just $20{:}15{:}50{:}75$, or twice, or one-half, or 50 times this set of numbers. This is the implication of the fact that for the maximum problem only the various transformation and substitution *ratios* matter. In all that follows we shall simply posit that nuts are established as the unit of account, hence that $p_N = 1$. This then makes p_A, w and r fully determinate constants.[24]

Summarizing: we have identified diagrammatically two of the three shadow-price relationships implied by the solution to the welfare-maximum problem and have established, in a slightly more roundabout way, the existence of the third. The purpose was to demonstrate the existence, at

least in our idealized neoclassical model, of a set of constants embedded in the "technocratic" maximum-of-welfare problem, that can be viewed as competitive market prices.[25] In what sense? In the sense that decentralized decisions in response to these constants, by, or "as if" by, atomistic profit and satisfaction maximizers will result in just that configuration of inputs, outputs and commodity-distribution that the maximum of our W requires.

III. FACTOR OWNERSHIP AND INCOME DISTRIBUTION

We have said nothing, so far, of how X and Y "pay" for their apples and nuts, or of who "owns" and supplies the labor and the land. As was indicated above, the assumption of constant returns to scale assures that at the maximum welfare position total income will equal total value of output, and that total revenue from the sale of apples (nuts) will just equal total expenditures for inputs by the producers of apples (nuts). Also, the "solution" implies definite "purchase" of apples and of nuts both by X and by Y. But nothing ensures that the initial "ownership" of labor-hours and of land is such that w times the labor-hours supplied by X, wL_X, plus r times the land supplied by X, rD_X—X's income—will suffice to cover his purchases as required by Ω'', *i.e.*, $p_A A_X + p_N N_X$; similarly for Y. There does exist some Pareto-efficient solution of inputs, outputs and distribution that satisfies the "income = outgo" condition for both individuals for any arbitrary pattern of ownership of the "means of production" —a solution, that is, that will place the system somewhere on the grand utility-possibility envelope frontier (BB in Figure 32.4). But only by the sheerest accident will that point on BB be better in terms of my W-function, or Thomas Jefferson's, or

---

[23] The condition also holds for each firm. In a competitive and constant-returns-to-scale world the profit-maximum position is one of zero profit: total revenue will just equal total cost. It should be said, however, that use of the Euler theorem to gain a relationship between input price and output price involves a measure of sleight of hand. It is only as a consequence of the relationships between price and marginal productivity (*cf.* the preceding paragraph) that the theorem assures equality of income with value of product.

[24] For the possibility of inessential indeterminacies, however, see Part IV-2.

[25] On the existence of such a set of shadow prices in the kinky and flat-surfaced world of linear programming, see Part V, below.

that of a "political consensus," than a multidimensional infinity of other points *on or off BB*. As emphasized above, only one point on *BB* can have ultimate normative, prescriptive significance: Ω; and only some special ownership patterns of land and of labor-services will place a market system with an "as imputed" distribution of income at that special point.[26]

The above is of especial interest in evaluating the optimality characteristics of market institutions in an environment of private property ownership. But the problem is not irrelevant even where all nonhuman means of production are vested in the community, hence where the proceeds of nonwage income are distributed independently of marginal productivity, marginal-rate-of-substitution considerations. If labor-services are not absolutely homogeneous—if some people are brawny and dumb and others skinny and clever, not to speak of "educated"—income distribution will be sensitive to the initial endowment of these qualities of mind and body and skill relative to the need for them. And again, only a very low probability accident would give a configuration consistent with any particular *W*-function's Ω.[27]

Even our homogeneous-labor world cannot entirely beg this issue. It is not enough to assume that producers are indifferent

between an hour of X's as against an hour of Y's labor-services. It is also required that the total supply of labor-hours per accounting period be so divided between X and Y as to split total wage payments in a particular way, depending on land ownership and on the income distribution called for by Ω. This may require that X supply, *e.g.*, 75 per cent of total L; each man working $\frac{1}{2}L$ hours may well not do.[28]

But all this is diversion. For our noninstitutional purposes it is sufficient to determine the particular L_X, D_X, L_Y and D_Y that are consistent with Ω, given market-imputed, or "as if" market-imputed, distribution. Unfortunately the diagrams used in Part I again fail, but the algebra is simple. It is required that:

$$wL_X + rD_X = p_A A_X + p_N N_X,$$

and

$$wL_Y + rD_Y = p_A A_Y + p_N N_Y,$$

for the already-solved-for maximal Ω-values of A_X, N_X, A_Y, N_Y, p_A, p_N, w and r. Together with $L_X + L_Y = L$ and $D_X + D_Y = D$, we appear to have four equations to solve for the four unknowns: L_X, L_Y, D_X and D_Y. It turns out, however, that one of these is not independent. The sum of the first two, that *total* incomes equal *total* value of product, is implied by Euler's theorem taken jointly with the marginal productivity conditions that give the solution for the eight variables, A_X, N_X, A_Y, . . . which are here taken as known. Hence, we have only three independent equations. This is as it should be. It means only that with our curvature assumptions we can, within limits, fix one of the four endowments more or less arbitrarily and still so

[26] It is of course possible to break the link between factor ownership and "final" income distribution by means of interpersonal transfers. Moreover, if such transfers are effected by means of costless lump-sum devices—never mind how feasible—then it is possible, in concept, to attain the Ω-implied distribution irrespective of market-imputations. But no decentralized price-market-type "game" can reveal the pattern of taxes and transfers that would maximize a particular *W*-function. "Central" calculation—implicit or explicit—is unavoidable.

[27] If slavery were the rule and I could sell the capitalized value of my expected lifetime services, the distinction between ownership of labor and that of land would blur. Except in an "Austrian" world, however, it would not vanish. As long as men retain a measure of control over the quality and time-shape of their own services, there will always remain an incentive problem.

[28] All this is based on the "Austrian" assumption that labor is supplied inelastically; further, that such inelasticity is due not to external compulsion, but rather to sharp "corners" in the preference-fields of X and Y in relation to work-leisure choices. More than this, the *W*-function must not be sensitive to variations in the $L_X L_Y$ mix except as these influence income distribution.

allocate the rest as to satisfy the household budget equations.

So much for the income-distribution aspects of the problem. These have relevance primarily for market-imputed income distribution; but such relevance does not depend on "private" ownership of nonlabor means of production. Note, incidentally, that only with the arbitrary "Austrian" assumption of fixed supplies of total inputs can one first solve "simultaneously" for inputs, outputs and commodity-distribution, and only subsequently superimpose on this solution the ownership and money-income distribution problem. If L_X, D_X, L_Y, D_Y, hence L and D were assumed sensitive to w, r, the p's and household income levels, the dimensions of the production-box of Figure 32.1, hence the position of the production-possibility curve of Figure 32.2 and 32.5, etc., would interdepend with the final solution values of L_X, D_X, L_Y and D_Y. We would then have to solve the full problem as a set of simultaneous equations from the raw data: production functions, tastes (this time with an axis for leisure, or many axes for many differently irksome kinds of labor), and the W-function. Three (or more) dimensional diagrams would be needed for a geometrical solution.

IV. SOME EXTENSIONS

We have demonstrated the solution of the maximum problem of modern welfare economics in context of the simplest statical and stationary neoclassical model. Many generalizations and elaborations suggest themselves, even if one remains strictly neoclassical and restricts oneself to a steady-state situation where none of the data change and no questions about "how the system gets there" are permitted to intrude. To comment on just a few:

1. The problem could well be solved for many households, many goods, and many factors: it has received complete and rigor-

ous treatment in the literature. Of course the diagrammatics would not do; elementary calculus becomes essential. But the qualitative characteristics of the solution of the m by n by q case are precisely those of the 2 by 2 by 2. The same marginal rate of transformation and substitution conditions characterize the solution, only now in many directions. Nothing new or surprising happens.[29]

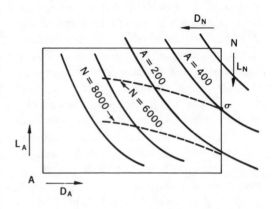

FIGURE 32.6

2. The solution did skirt one set of difficulties that were not explicitly ruled out by assumption. We tacitly assumed that the two sets of isoquants would provide a smooth locus of "internal" tangencies, FF, in the production box of Figure 32.1; similarly, that we would get such an "internal" SS in the trading boxes of Figures 32.2 and 32.5. Nothing in our assumptions guarantees that this should be so. What if the locus of maximum A's for given feasible N's, should occur not at points of strict tangency *inside* the box, but at what the mathematician would call corner-tangencies along the edges of the box? Figure 32.6

[29] Rigorous general treatment of the $m \times n \times q$ situation does highlight a number of analytical fine points that are of interest to the pure theorist, *e.g.*, the difficulties encountered if the number of factors exceeds the number of goods. But the qualitative economics is the same. For a full treatment from a nonnormative point of view, see P. A. Samuelson, "Prices of Factors and Goods in General Equilibrium," *Rev. Econ. Stud.*, 1953–1954, XXI (1), No. 54, 1–20.

illustrates this possibility. The maximum feasible output of A, for $N = 6000$, occurs at σ, where $A = 400$; but at σ the two isoquants are not strictly tangent (they touch but have different slopes). The economic meaning of this is simple. With endowments as indicated by the dimensions of the production box in **Figure 32.6**, and with technology as denoted by the isoquants, it is not possible to reallocate inputs until the MRS of labor for land is the same in apple as in nut production. This is because apple technology (as depicted) is so land-using relative to nut production that the

$$\left[\frac{\text{marginal productivity of land}}{\text{marginal productivity of labor}}\right] \text{ ratio}$$

in apple production exceeds that in nut production even when, as at σ, *all* land is devoted to apples.

Space precludes further analysis of such corner-tangency phenomena. They reflect the possibility that the maximum-welfare solution may require that not every input be used in producing every output (*e.g.*, no land in nut production or no brain surgeons in coal mining), and may even render one of the inputs a "free good," so that its total use will not add up to the total available supply. Let it suffice to assert that by formulating the maximum conditions, not in terms of *equalities* of various slopes, but rather in terms of *inequalities*; by explicit statement of the proper second-order "rate-of-change-of-slope" conditions; and by allowing inequalities in the factor-balance conditions (*e.g.*, $L_A + L_N \leqq L$), such phenomena of bumping into the axes can be handled; further, that only inessential indeterminacies occur in the implied shadow-price configuration.[30]

[30] All this can perhaps be made clearer by two examples. The essential requirement for A_σ, to be at a maximum for $N = 6000$ is that the intersection at the boundary be as in **Figure 32.6** rather than as in **Figure 32.7**. In the latter, σ' gives a minimum of

3. We stressed, above, the nonexistence of *community* indifference contours such as would provide a unique ranking, for the community as a whole, of various output combinations.[31] Individual marginal rates of substitution between, *e.g.*, apples and silk shirts, equalized along a trading-box contract curve to give a "community" MRS, are likely to be sensitive to the distribution of income[32] between gourmets and dandies;

A for $N = 6000$; the true maximum is at σ''. The distinction between σ in 28.6 and σ' in 28.7 is between the relative rates of change of the two MRS's. The price indeterminacy implied by the maximum, *i.e.*, the fact that σ is consistent with an r/w that lies anywhere between the two isoquants, turns out to be inessential. A second example concerns the theory of the firm. It has been argued that if the marginal cost curve has vertical gaps and the price-line hits one of these gaps, then the $MC = p$ condition is indeterminate, hence that the theory is no good. As has been pointed out in the

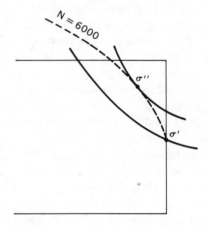

FIGURE 32.7

advanced literature (*e.g.*, by R. L. Bishop, in "Cost Discontinuities . . ." *Am. Econ. Rev.*, Sept. 1948, XXXVIII, 607–17) this is incorrect: What is important is that at smaller than equilibrium output MC be less than price and at higher outputs MC exceed price. It is true, but quite harmless to the theory, that such a situation does leave a range of indeterminacy in the price that will elicit *that* level of output. Such phenomena do change the mathematics of computation. Inequalities cannot in general be used to eliminate unknowns by simple substitution. On all this, see the literature of linear programming (*e.g.*, citations [10] and [13]).

[31] See fn. 6.

[32] In terms of abstract purchasing power.

accordingly, community MRS at a given point in commodity space, *i.e.*, the slope of a curve of community indifference, will vary with movements along the associated utility-possibility curve. However, once the most desirable $U_X U_Y$ combination for a given package of A and N is fixed, MRS at that AN-point becomes determinate. It follows, as recently pointed out and proved by Samuelson,[33] that if the observed community continuously redistributes "incomes" in utopian lump-sum fashion so as to maximize, in utility space, over the W-function implied by a political consensus, then there does exist, in output space, a determinate *social* indifference function which provides a ranking for the community as a whole of all conceivable output combinations. This function, which yields conventionally convex social indifference contours, can be treated as though a single mind were engaged in maximizing it. Moreover, in concept and if granted the premise of continuous redistribution, its contours are subject to empirical inference from observed price-market data.

This existence theorem justifies the use of *social* indifference maps—maps "corrected" for distribution—in handling problems of production efficiency, international trade, etc.—a substantial analytical convenience.[34] More important, it provides a conceptual foundation, however abstract, for prescription based not on just any arbitrary ethic, but rather on the particular ethic revealed by a society as reflecting its own political consensus.[35]

4. It is useful, and in a mathematical treatment not difficult, to drop the "Austrian" assumption of inelastically supplied inputs, and introduce leisure-work choices.[36] The analytical effect is to sensitize the production-possibility curve to the psychic sensibilities—the preference functions—of individuals. Note that the empirical sense of doing so is not confined to an institutional or ethical context of nonimposed choice. A dictator, too, has to take account of such choices, if only because of feasibility limitations on coercion.

5. We assumed away joint-product situations. This is convenient for manipulation but hardly essential; the results can be generalized to cover most kinds of jointness. It turns out, in fact, that in dynamical models with capital stocks, one means for taking account of the durability of such stocks is to allow for joint products. A process requiring a hydraulic press "produces" both stamped metal parts and a "one-year-older" hydraulic press.

6. In our system the distinction between inputs (L, D) and outputs (A, N) could be taken for granted. But the distinction is clear only in a world of completely vertically-integrated producers, all hiring "primary" nonproduced inputs and producing "final" consumable goods and services. In a Leontief-like system that allows for interproducer transactions and intermediate products, many outputs: electricity, steel, corn, beef, trucks, etc., are simultaneously inputs. It is of interest, and also feasible, to generalize the analysis to take account of, *e.g.*, coal being used not only to heat houses, but to produce steel required in the production of mining machines

[33] See citation [11].

[34] Note, however, that none of this eliminates the need for a W-function: social indifference contours are a convex function of individual taste patterns of the usual ordinal variety taken jointly with an implicit or explicit W-function of "regular" content and curvature. Further, no ultimate superiority attaches to the W-function implied by a particular political consensus. One may disapprove of the power relationships on which such consensus rests, etc.

[35] Needless to say, feasibility is not here at issue. Even on this level of abstraction, however, matters become much more difficult once account

is taken of the fact that the world is not stationary.

[36] If we assume only one commodity, say apples, and replace the second good by lesiure (or by negative labor input); and if we let the second-good production function be a simple linear relation, our previous geometry will portray the simplest goods-leisure situation.

designed for the production of coal. Moreover, none of the essential qualitative characteristics of our maximum problem is violated by such generalization.[37]

7. What if instead of assuming that production functions show constant returns to scale, we permit diminishing returns to proportional expansion of inputs? This could be due either to inherent nonlinearities in the physics and topography of the universe, or to the existence of some unaccounted-for but significant input in limited, finite-elastic supply.[38]

Diminishing returns to scale, as distinct from increasing returns, does not give rise to serious trouble, either for the analytical solubility of the system, or for the market-significance of the intrinsic price-wage-rent constants. It does introduce some ambiguities, however. For one thing, the "value" of output will exceed the total of market-imputed income. This makes intuitive sense in terms of the "unaccounted-scarce-factor" explanation of decreasing returns; the residual unimputed value of output reflects the income "due" the "hidden" factor. If that factor were treated explicitly and given an axis in the production-function diagram, returns would no longer diminish—since, on this view, the relative inexpansibility of that input gave rise to decreasing returns to scale to begin with—and the difficulty would vanish.[39]

In a market context, this suggests the explicit introduction of firms as distinct from industries. In our constant-returns-to-scale world the number of apple- or nut-producing firms could be assumed indeterminate. Every firm could be assumed able to produce any output up to A_Ω (or N_Ω) at constant unit cost. In fact, if we had a convenient way of handling incipient monopoly behavior, such as by positing frictionless entry of new firms, we could simply think of one giant firm as producing all the required apples (nuts). Such a firm would be compelled, nevertheless, to behave as though it were an "atomistic" competitor, *i.e.*, prevented from exploiting the tilt in the demand curve, by incipient competitors ready instantaneously to jump into the fray at the slightest sign of profit.

It is, however, natural, at least in a context of market institutions, to think of decreasing returns to scale, as associated with the qualitatively and quantitatively scarce entrepreneurial entity that defines the firm but is not explicitly treated as an input. Then, as apple production expands, relatively less efficient entrepreneurs are pulled into production—the total cost curve of the "last" producer and the associated shadow price of apples become progressively higher—and the intramarginal firms make "profits" due directly to the scarcity value of the entrepreneurial qualities of their "entrepreneurs." The number of firms, their inputs and outputs, are determinate.

[37]Analytically, this is done by designating all produced goods as X_1, X_2, X_3. . . . The gross production of, *e.g.*, X_1 has two kinds of uses: It is partly used up as an input in the production of X_2, X_3 . . . and perhaps of X_1 (the automobile industry is a major user of automobiles). What remains is available for household consumption. The production functions have X's on the right-as well as the left-hand side.

[38]If "output" varies as the surface area of some solid body and "input" as its cubic-volume, a doubling of input will less than double output—this is an example of the first kind. A typical example of the second is the instance where the production function for fishing does not include an axis for the "amount" of lake, hence where beyond a certain point doubling of man-hours, boats, etc. less than doubles the output. There is a slightly futile literature on whether the first kind could or could not exist without some element of the second. If *every* input is really doubled, so say the proponents of one view, output *must* double. The very vehemence of the assertion suggests the truth, to wit, that it is conceptually impossible to disprove it by reference to empirical evidence. Luckily, the distinction is not only arbitrary—it depends on what one puts on the axes of the production-function diagram and what is built into the curvature of the production surface; it is also quite unimportant. One can think of the phenomenon as one will—nothing will change.

[39]The fact that the "hidden scarce factor" view is heuristically useful does not, however, strengthen its pretension to status as a hypothesis about reality.

The last firm just breaks even at the solution-value of the shadow-price.[40]

At any rate, no serious damage is done to the statical system by decreasing returns to scale. When it is a matter of actually computing a maximum problem the loss of linearity is painful, but the trouble is in the mathematics.[41]

8. There is one kind of complication that does vitiate the results. We have assumed throughout that there exists no *direct* interaction among producers, among households, and between producers and households—that there are no (nonpecuniary) external economies or diseconomies of production and consumption. The assumption is reflected in four characteristics of the production functions and the preference functions:

a. The output of apples was assumed uniquely determined by the quantities of land and labor applied to apple production—A was assumed insensitive to the inputs and outputs of the nut industry; similarly for nuts. This voids the possibility that the apple production function might shift as a consequence of movements along the nut production function, *i.e.*, that for given D_A and L_A, A may vary with N, L_N and D_N. The stock example of such a "technological external economy" (or diseconomy) is the beekeeper whose honey output will increase, other things equal, if the neighboring apple producer expands *his* output (hence his apple blossom "supply").[42] The very pas-

toral quality of the example suggests that in a statical context such direct interaction among producers—interaction that is not reflected by prices—is probably rare. To the extent that it does exist, it reflects some "hidden" inputs or outputs (*e.g.*, apple blossoms), the benefits or costs of which are not (easily) appropriated by market institutions.

It should be emphasized that the assertion that such phenomena are empirically unimportant is defensible only if we rule out nonreversible dynamical phenomena. Once we introduce changes in knowledge, for example, or investment in changing the quality of the labor force via training, "external" effects become very important indeed.[43] But on our stratospheric level of abstraction such considerations are out of order.

b. The "happiness" of X, as measured by U_x, was assumed uniquely determined by his own consumption of apples and nuts. He was permitted no sensitivity to his neighbor's (Y's) consumption, and vice versa. This rules out not only Veblenesque "keeping up with . . ." effects, but such phenomena as Y tossing in sleepless fury due to X's "consumption" of midnight tele-

---

[40] More precisely, the "next" firm in line could not break even. This takes care of discontinuity.

[41] It should perhaps be repeated, however, that there remains considerable ambiguity about how the imbalance between income and outlay in decreasing-returns-to-scale situations is best treated in a general equilibrium setup.

[42] The other type of externality treated in the neoclassical literature, the type Jacob Viner labeled "pecuniary," does not in itself affect the results. It consists in sensitivity of input prices to industry output, though not to the output of single firms. External pecuniary economies (as distinct from diseconomies) do, however, signal the existence of either *technological* external

economies of the sort discussed here, or of internal economies among supplier firms. These last reflect increasing returns to scale along production functions—a most troublesome state discussed at length in Part V.

[43] The full "benefits" of most changes in "knowledge," of most "ideas," are not easily captured by the originator, even with strong patent and copyright protection. If, then, the energy and resources devoted to "creating new knowledge" are sensitive to private cost-benefit calculation, some potential for social gain may well be lost because such calculation will not correctly account for cost and benefit to society at large. All this is complicated by the peculiarity of "knowledge" as a scarce resource: unlike most other scarcities, just because there is more for you there is not necessarily less for me. As for training of labor: the social benefit accrues over the lifetime services of the trainee; the private benefit to the producer accrues until the man quits to go to work for a competitor.

vision shows; or X's temperance sensibilities being outraged by Y's quiet and solitary consumption of Scotch. Nobody with experience of a "neighborhood" will argue that such things are illusory, but it is not very fruitful to take account of them in a formal maximizing setup.[44]

c. X and Y were assumed insensitive, also, to the input-output configuration of producers, except as this affected consumption choices. Insensitivity to the allocation of their own working time is subsumed in the "Austrian" assumption, but more is required. Y's wife must not be driven frantic by factory soot, nor X irritated by an "efficiently" located factory spoiling his view.

d. There is still a fourth kind of externality: X's satisfaction may be influenced not only by his own job, but by Y's as well. Many values associated with job-satisfaction—status, power, and the like—are sensitive to one's *relative* position, not only as consumer, but as supplier of one's services in production. The "Austrian" assumption whereby U_X and U_Y are functions only of consumption possibilities, voids this type of interaction also.

Could direct interaction phenomena be introduced into a formal maximizing system, and if so, at what cost? As regards the analytical solubility of some maximum-of-W problem, there is no necessary reason why not. The mathematics of proving the existence or nonexistence of a "solution," or of a unique and stable "solution," or the task of devising a computational routine that will track down such a solution should one exist, may become unmanageable. But the problem need not be rendered meaningless by such phenomena.

Unfortunately that is saying very little indeed, except on the level of metaphysics. Those qualities of the system that are of particular interest to the economist—(i)

that the solution implies a series of "efficiency conditions," the Pareto marginal-rate-of-substitution conditions, which are necessary for the maximum of a wide variety of W-functions, and (ii) that there exists a correspondence between the optimal values of the variables and those generated by a system of (perfect) market institutions *cum* redistribution—those qualities are apt either to blur or vanish with "direct interaction." Most varieties of such interaction destroy the "duality" of the system: the constants embedded in the maximum problem, if any, lose significance as prices, wages, rents. They will not correctly account for all the "costs" and "benefits" to which the welfare function in hand is sensitive.[45]

In general, then, most formal models rule out such phenomena. There is no doubt that by so doing they abstract from some important aspects of reality. But theorizing consists in just such abstraction; no theory attempts to exhaust all of reality. The question of what kinds of very real complications to introduce into a formal maximizing setup has answers only in terms of the strategy of theorizing or in terms of the requirements of particular and concrete problems. For many purposes it is useful and interesting to explore the implications of maximizing in a "world" where no such direct interactions exist.

[45] It should not be concluded, however, that the different types of direct interaction are all equally damaging. All will spoil market performance, almost by definition; but some, at least, permit of formal maximizing treatment such as will yield efficiency conditions analogous to those of Part I—conditions that properly account for full social costs and benefits. So-called "public goods," *e.g.*, national defense, which give rise to direct interaction since by definition their consumption is joint—more for X means not less but more for Y—are an important example. Maximizing yields MRS conditions that bear intriguing correspondence to those which characterize ordinary private-good situations. But these very MRS conditions serve to reveal the failure of duality. (Samuelson's is again the original and definitive treatment. See Citation [12].)

[44] For an important exception, however, see fn. 45.

V. RELAXING THE CURVATURE ASSUMPTIONS: KINKS AND NONCONVEXITIES

None of the above qualifications and generalizations violate the fundamentally neoclassical character of the model. What happens if we relinquish some of the nice curvature properties of the functions?

1. We required that the production functions and the indifference curves have well-defined and continuous curvatures—no sharp corners or kinks such as cause indeterminacy in marginal rates of substitution. Such smooth curvatures permit the use of the calculus, hence are mathematically convenient for larger than 2 by 2 by 2 models. They are, however, not essential to the economic content of the results. The analysis has been translated—and in part independently re-invented—for a world of flat-faced, sharp-cornered, production functions: Linear programming, more formally known as activity analysis, is the resulting body of theory.[46] All the efficiency conditions have their counterparts in such a system, and the existence of implicit "prices" embedded in the maximum problem is, if anything, even more striking.[47]

2. Easing of the neoclassical requirement that functions be smooth is not only painless; in the development of analytical economics it has resulted in exciting new insights. Unfortunately, however, the next step is very painful indeed. In our original assumptions we required that returns to scale for proportional expansion of inputs be constant (or at least nonincreasing) and that isoquants and indifference curves be "convex to the origin." These requirements guarantee a condition that the mathematicians call *convexity*. The violation of this condition, as by allowing increasing returns to scale in production—due, if you wish, to the inherent physics and topography of the universe or to lumpiness and indivisibilities—makes for serious difficulties.

The essence of convexity, a concept that plays a crucial role in mathematical economics, is rather simple. Take a single isoquant such as MM in Figure 32.8(a). It denotes the minimum inputs of L and D for the production of 100 apples, hence it is just the boundary of all technologically feasible input combinations that can produce 100 apples. Only points on MM are both feasible and technologically *efficient*, but any point within the shaded region is *feasible*: nobody can prevent me from wasting L or D. On the other hand, no point on the origin side of MM is feasible for an output of 100 apples: given the laws of physics, etc., it is impossible to do better. *Mathematical convexity obtains if a straight line connecting any two feasible points does not anywhere pass outside the set of feasible points.* A little experimentation will show that such is the case in Figure 32.8(a). In Figure 32.8(b), however, where the isoquant is of "queer" curvature—MRS of L for D increases—the line connecting, *e.g.*, the feasible points γ and ϕ does pass outside the "feasible" shaded area. Note, incidentally, that an isoquant of the linear programming variety, as in Figure 32.8(c), is "convex"—this is why the generalization of (1) above was painless.[48]

What kind of trouble does nonconvexity create? In the case of concave-to-the-origin isoquants, *i.e.*, nonconvex isoquants, the dif-

---

[46] Isoquants in such a setup consist of linearly additive combinations of processes, each process being defined as requiring absolutely fixed input and output proportions. This gives isoquants that look like that in Figure 32.8(c).

[47] A little diagrammatic experimentation will show that the geometric techniques of Part I remain fully adequate.

[48] It is important not to confuse mathematical convexity with curvature that appears "convex to the origin." Mathematical convexity is a property of *sets* of points, and the set of feasible output points bounded by a production-possibility curve, for instance, is convex if and only if the production-possibility curve itself is "*concave* to the origin" (or a straight line). Test this by the rule which defines convexity.

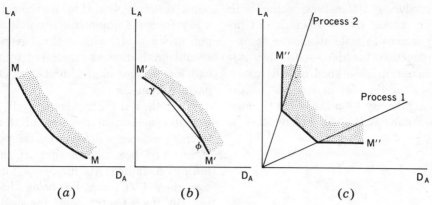

FIGURE 32.8

ficulty is easy to see. Look back at Figure 32.1 and imagine that the old nut-isoquants are really those of apple producers, hence oriented to the southwest, and vice versa for nuts. Examination of the diagram will show that the locus of tangencies, *FF*, is now a locus of minimum combinations of *A* and *N*. Hence the rule that MRS's be equalized will result in input combinations that give a minimum of *N* for specified *A*.[49]

3. This is not the occasion for extensive analysis of convexity problems. It might be useful, however, to examine one very important variety of nonconvexity: increasing returns to scale in production. Geometrically, increasing returns to scale is denoted by isoquants that are closer and closer together for outward movement along any ray from the origin: to double output, you less than double the inputs. Note that the isoquants still bound convex sets in the *LD* plane [they are still as in Figure 32.8(*a*)]. But in the third or output dimension of a two-input, one-output production surface, slices by vertical planes through the origin perpendicular to *LD* will cut the production surface in such a way as to give a boundary such as *VV* in Figure 32.9. It is evident that *VV* bounds a nonconvex

set of feasible points, so the full three-dimensional set of feasible input-output points is not convex.

The effect of such nonconvexity in input-output space can be classified with respect to its possible implications for (a) the slopes of producers' average cost (*AC*) curves; (b) for the slopes of marginal cost (*MC*) curves; (c) for the curvature of the production-possibility curve.

A. Increasing Returns to Scale and AC Curves

It is a necessary consequence of increasing returns to scale that at the maximal configuration of inputs, outputs and input

[49]A minimum, that is, subject to the requirement that no input be "wasted" from an engineering point of view, *i.e.*, that each single producer be on the production function as given by the engineer.

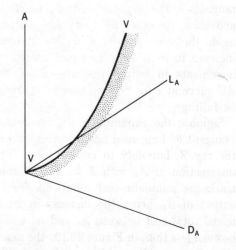

FIGURE 32.9

prices, producers' AC curves decline with increasing output. By the definition of increasing returns to scale at a given point τ of a production function, successive isoquants in the neighborhood of τ lie closer and closer together for movement "northeast" along the ray from the origin through τ (Z in Figure 32.10). As Figure 32.10 is

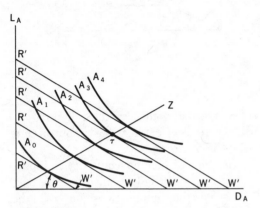

FIGURE 32.10

drawn, the ray Z happens also to correspond to an expansion path for the particular r/w ratio denoted by the family of isocost lines $R'W'$: each $R'W'$ is tangent to an isoquant along Z. Given $r/w = |$ tangent $\theta\,|$, a profit-maximizing apple producer will calculate his minimum total cost for various levels of output from input-output points along Z. But along Z the equal cost $R'W'$ tangents in the neighborhood of τ lie closer and closer together for increasing output, as do the isoquants. This implies that the increase in total cost for equal successive increments in output declines. *Ergo*, the AC curve at τ for $r/w = |$ tangent $\theta\,|$ must be falling.

Suppose the expansion path for $r/w = |$ tangent $\theta\,|$ happened not to correspond to the ray Z, but only to cross it at τ. The intersection of A_4 with Z would not then mark the minimum-cost input-mix for an output of A_4, hence the increase in minimized total cost between A_3 and A_4 would be even less than in Figure 32.10: the negative effect on AC would be reinforced. The

point is, simply, that if for movement along a ray from the origin cost per unit of output declines, AC will decline even more should production at minimized total cost call for changes in the input-mix, *i.e.*, departure from the ray Z.

What, then, if the maximum-of-W input-output combination required of this particular producer is denoted by the point τ? It has just been shown that AC at τ is falling. A falling AC implies a marginal cost curve (MC) that lies *below* the average. But if τ is the Ω'''-point, the shadow-p_A will just equal MC of τ. It follows that the maximum-of-W configuration requires $p_A < AC$, *i.e.*, perpetual losses. Losses, however, are incompatible with real life (perfect) markets; hence where increasing returns to scale prevails correspondence between market-directed and W-maximizing allocation fails. In an institutional context where producers go out of business if profits are negative, markets will not do.[50]

Increasing returns to scale has also a "macro" consequence that is associated with $p < AC$. For constant returns to scale, we cited Euler's theorem as assuring that total factor incomes will just equal total value of output. In increasing-returns-to-scale situations, total imputed factor incomes will exceed the total value of output: $rD + wL > p_A A + p_N N$.[51]

B. Increasing Returns to Scale and MC Curves

Where nonconvexity of the increasing-returns-to-scale variety results in falling AC curves, real-life (perfect) markets will fail. What of a Lange-Lerner socialist bureaucracy, where each civil-servant plant-

---

[50] Needless to say, comments on market effectiveness, throughout this paper, bear only on the analogue-computer aspects of price-market systems. This is a little like talking about sexless men, yet it is surely of interest to examine such systems viewed as mechanisms pure and simple.

[51] The calculus-trained reader can test this for, say, a Cobb-Douglas type function $A = L_A{}^{\alpha} D_A{}^{\beta}$, with $(\alpha + \beta) > 1$ to give increasing returns to scale.

manager is instructed to maximize his algebraic profits in terms of centrally quoted "shadow" prices regardless of losses? Will such a system find itself at the maximum-of-W configuration?

It may or may not. If AC is to fall, MC must lie below AC, but at the requisite Ω-output, MC's may nevertheless be rising, as for example at ϵ in Figure 32.11. If so,

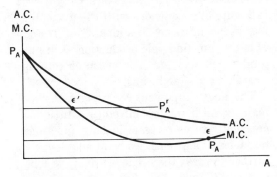

FIGURE 32.11

a Lange-Lerner bureaucracy making input and output decisions as atomistic "profit-maximizing" competitors but ignoring losses will make the "right" decisions, *i.e.*, will "place" the system at the maximum-of-W. Each manager equating his marginal cost to the centrally quoted shadow price given out by the maximum-of-W solution, will produce precisely the output required by the Ω-configuration. By the assumption of falling AC's due to increasing returns to scale either one or both industries will show losses, but these are irrelevant to optimal allocation.[52]

[52] There is an ambiguity of language in the above formulation. If at the maximum-of-W configuration losses prevail, the maximum profit position "in the large" will be not at $p = MC$ but at zero output. Strictly speaking, a Lange-Lerner bureaucracy must be instructed to equate marginal cost to price or profit-maximize "in the small" without regard to the absolute value of profit. "Make any continuous sequence of small moves that increase algebraic profits, but do not jump to the origin." It is precisely the ruling-out of the zero-output position, unless called for by $MC > p$ everywhere, that distinguishes Lange-Lerner systems from "real-life" perfect markets, both viewed as "analogue computers."

What if for a maximum-of-W producers are required to produce at points such as ϵ', where $p = MC$ but MC is declining?[53] The fact that ϵ' shows $AC > MC = p$, hence losses, has been dealt with above. But more is involved. By the assumption of a falling MC-curve, the horizontal price line at ϵ' cuts the MC curve from below, hence profit at ϵ' is not only negative: it is at a *minimum*. A "real-life" profit maximizer would certainly not remain there: he would be losing money by the minute. But neither would a Lange-Lerner bureaucrat under instruction to maximize algebraic profits. He would try to increase his output: "extra" revenue (p_A) would exceed his MC by more and more 'for every additional apple produced. In this case, then, not only would real life markets break down; so would simple-minded decentralized maximizing of profits by socialist civil servants.[54]

Paradoxically enough, the correct rule for all industries whose MC is falling at the Ω-point is: "minimize your algebraic profits." But no such rule can save the decentralized character of the Lange-Lerner scheme. In a "convex" world the simple injunction to maximize profits in response to centrally quoted prices, together with raising (lowering) of prices by the responsible "Ministries" according to whether supply falls short of (exceeds) demand, is all that is needed.[55] Nobody has to know *ex ante*, *e.g.*, the prices associated with the Ω-point. In fact the scheme was devised in part as a counter to the view that efficient allocation in a collectivized economy is impossible due simply to the sheer administrative

[53] This would necessarily be the case, for instance, with Cobb-Douglas type increasing-returns-to-scale functions. Such functions imply ever-falling MC curves, for whatever r/w ratio.

[54] Note that a falling MC curve is simply a reflection of nonconvexity in the total cost curve.

[55] Not quite all. Even in a statical context, the lump-sum income transfers called for by Ω require central calculation. And if adjustment paths are explicitly considered, complex questions about the stability of equilibrium arise. (*E.g.*, will excess demand always be corrected by raising price?)

burden of calculation. With increasing returns to scale however, the central authority must evidently know where MC's will be falling, where rising: it must know, before issuing any instructions at all about the solution.

C. Increasing Returns to Scale and the Production-Possibility Curve

What is left of "duality"? Real-life markets and unsophisticated Lange-Lerner systems have both failed. Yet it is entirely possible, even in situations where the Ω-constellation implies $AC > MC$ with declining MC, that the maximizing procedure of Part I remains inviolate, and that the constants embedded in the maximum problem retain the price-like significance. To see this we must examine the effect of increasing returns to scale on the production-possibility curve. There are two possible cases:

i. It is possible for both the apples and the nut production function to exhibit increasing returns to scale, yet for the implied production possibility curve to be concave to the origin, *i.e.*, mathematically convex (as in Figure 32.2). While a proportional expansion of L_A and D_A by a factor of two would more than double apple output, an increase in A at the expense of N will, in general, not take place by means of such proportional expansion of inputs. Examination of FF in Figure 32.1 makes this clear for the constant-returns-to-scale case. As we move from any initial point on FF toward more A and less N, the L_A/D_A and L_N/D proportions change.[56]

The point is that if, as in Figure 32.1, land is important relative to labor in producing apples, and vice versa for nuts, expansion of apple production will result in

apple producers having to use more and more of the relatively nut-prone input, labor, in proportion to land. Input proportions in apple production become less "favorable." The opposite is true of the input proportions used in nuts as nut production declines. This phenomenon explains why with constant returns to scale in both functions the production-possibility curve shows concave-to-the-origin curvature. Only if FF in Figure 32.1 coincides with the diagonal: *i.e.*, if the intrinsic "usefulness" of L and D is the same in apple production as in nut production, will $F'F'$ for constant returns to scale be a straight line.

The above argument by proportions remains valid if we now introduce a little increasing returns to scale in both functions by "telescoping" each isoquant successively farther towards the origin. In fact, as long as the FF curve has shape and curvature as in Figure 32.1, the production-possibility curve, $F'F'$ in Figures 32.2 and 32.5, will retain its convexity.

In this "mild" case of increasing returns to scale, with a still convex production-possibility curve, the previous maximizing rules give the correct result for a maximum-of-W. Further, the constants embedded in the maximum problem retain their meaning. This is true in two senses: (1) They still reflect marginal rates of substitution and transformation. Any package of L, D, A and N worth $1 will, *at the margin*, be just convertible by production and exchange into any other package worth $1, no more, no less: a dollar is a dollar is a dollar. . . .[57] (2) The total value of maximum-welfare "national" output: $p_A A + p_N N$, valued at these shadow-price constants, will itself be at a maximum. A glance at Figure 32.5 makes this clear: at the price-ratio denoted by the line $P'_A P'_N$, Ω' is the point of highest output-value. As we shall see, this correspondence between the maximum welfare and "maximum na-

---

[56] Only if FF should coincide with the diagonal of the box will proportions not change. The increasing returns to scale would necessarily imply an inward-bending production-possibility curve.

[57] For the infinitesimal movements of the calculus.

tional product" solutions is an accident of convexity.

ii. It is of course entirely possible that both production functions exhibit sufficiently increasing returns to scale to give, for specified totals of L and D, a production-possibility curve such as $F''F''$ in Figure 32.12.[58] This exhibits nonconvexity in output space. What now happens to the results?

If the curvature of $F''F''$ is not "too sharp," the constants given out by the maximum-of-W problem retain their "dollar is a dollar" meaning. They still reflect marginal rates of substitution in all directions. But maximum W is no longer associated with maximum shadow-value of output. A glance at Figure 32.12 confirms our geo-

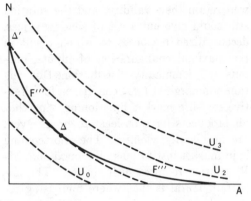

FIGURE 32.13

sharply concave outward, relative to the indifference curves, it may be that the "minimize-profits" rule would badly mislead, even if both industries show declining MC's. Take a one-person situation such as in Figure 32.13. The production-possibility curve $F'''F'''$ is more inward-bending than the indifference curves (U), and the point of tangency Δ is a point of *minimum* satisfaction. Here, unlike above, you should rush away from Δ. The maximum welfare position is at Δ'—a "corner tangency" is involved. The point is that in nonconvex situations *relative* curvatures are crucial: tangency points may as well be minima as maxima.[60]

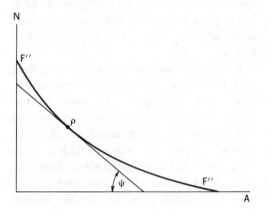

FIGURE 32.12

metric intuition that in situations of nonconvex production possibilities the bliss point coincides with a minimized value-of-output. At the prices implied, as denoted by $|\tan \psi|$, the assumed Ω-point ρ is a point of minimum $p_A A + p_N N$.[59]

But with nonconvexity in output space, matters could get much more complicated. If the production-possibility curve is

---

[58] Try two functions which are not too dissimilar in "factor intensity."

[59] For $p_A/p_N = |\text{tangent } \psi|$, $(p_A A + p_N N)$ is at its maximum at the intersection of $F''F''$ with the A-axis. Recall, incidentally, that in situations of falling MC producers were required to *minimize* profits.

[60] Recall that in our discussion of Part IV corner-tangencies were important in situations where no feasible internal tangencies existed. Here there exist perfectly good and feasible internal tangencies—but they are loci of minima rather than maxima. The second-order conditions, expressed as inequalities, constitute the crucial test of optimal allocation.

It is tempting, but a mistake, to think that there is a unique correspondence between the curvature of the production-possibility curve, and the relative slopes of the nut and apple MC curves. It is true that the $[MC_A/MC_N]$ ratio associated with a point such as Ω' in Figure 32.5 must be smaller than $[MC_A/MC_N]$ at any point of *more A* and *less N* on $F'F'$ (e.g., δ): the absolute slope of $F'F'$ has been shown to equal $p_A/p_N = [MC_A/MC_N]$, and at Ω' the slope is less steep than at δ. It is also true that along a nonconvex production-possibility curve, such as that of Figure 32.12, an increase in A and a decrease in N are associated with a *decline* in $[MC_A/MC_N]$. But it

So much for nonconvexity. In its mildest form, if isoquants and indifference curves retain their normal curvature and only returns to scale "increase," nonconvexity need not violate the qualitative characteristics of the maximum-of-W problem. The marginal-rate-of-substitution conditions may well retain their validity, and the solution still could give out a set of shadow prices, decentralized responses to which result in the maximal configuration of inputs, outputs and commodity distribution. But certain nonmarginal *total* conditions for effective real-life market functioning, *e.g.*, that all producers have at least to break even, are necessarily violated. The shortcoming is in market institutions: the maximum-of-W solution requires such "losses." The important moral is that where increasing returns to scale obtains, an idealized price system is not an effective way to raise money to cover costs. It may, however, still be an effective device for the rationing of scarcities.[61]

does not follow, *e.g.*, in the first case of Figure 32.5, that at Ω' MC_A must be rising for an increase in A sufficiently to offset a possibly falling MC_N. (Remember, in moving from Ω' to δ we move to the right along the A-axis but to the left along the N-axis.) For any departure from Ω' will, in general, involve a change in input shadow-prices, hence *shifts* in the MC curves, while the slopes of the curves at Ω' were derived from a total cost curve calculated on the basis of the given, constant, Ω-values of w and r. The point is that cost curves are partial-equilibrium creatures, evaluated at *fixed* prices, while movement along a production-possibility curve involves a general-equilibrium adjustment that will *change* input prices. Hence it is entirely possible that at say Ω', in Figure 32.5, both MC_N and MC_A are falling, though $F'F'$ is convex.

[61] No mention has been made of the case that is perhaps most interesting from an institutional point of view: production functions that show increasing returns to scale initially, then decreasing returns as output expands further. No profit-seeking firm will produce in the first stage, where AC is falling, and $A\Omega$ and $N\Omega$ may only require one or a few firms producing in the second stage. If so, the institutional conditions for perfect competition, very many firms, will not exist. One or a few firms of "efficient" scale will exhaust the market. This phenomenon lies at the heart of the monopoly-oligopoly problem.

VI. DYNAMICS

We have examined in some detail what conditions on the allocation and distribution of inputs and outputs can be derived from the maximization of a social welfare function which obeys certain restrictions.[62] We have done so, however, using a statical mode of analysis and having ignored all the "dynamical" aspects of the problem. To charge that such statical treatment is "unrealistic" is to miss, I think, the essential meaning and uses of theorizing. It is true, however, that such treament buries many interesting problems—problems, moreover, some of which yield illuminating insight when subjected to rigorous analysis. Full dynamical extension is not possible here, but some indication of the directions which such extension might take is perhaps warranted:

1. The perceptive reader will have noticed that very little was said about the dimensions of A, N, L_A, D_A, L_N, and D_N. The static theory of production treats outputs and inputs as instantaneous time rates, "flows"—apples per day, labor-hours per week, etc. This ignores the elementary fact that in most production processes outputs and the associated inputs, and the various inputs themselves, are not simultaneous. Coffee plants take five years to grow, ten-year-old brandy has to age ten years, inputs in automobile manufacture have to follow a certain sequence, it takes time to build a power station and a refinery (no matter how abundantly "labor and land" are applied). One dynamical refinement of the analysis, then, consists in "dating" the inputs and resultant outputs of the production functions, relative to each other. In some instances only the ordinal sequence is of interest; in others absolute elapsed time, too, matters—plaster has to dry seven days before the first coat of paint is applied.

[62] See fn. 12.

2. Another characteristic of production, on this planet at least, is that service flows are generated by stocks of physical things which yield their services only through time. Turret-lathe operations can be generated only by turret-lathes and these have congealed in them service flows which cannot be exhausted instantaneously but only over time. In a descriptive sense, a turret-lathe's services of today are "joint" and indivisible from some turret-lathe's services of tomorrow. Strictly speaking, this is true of most service flows. But some things, like food, or coal for heating, or gasoline, exhaust their services much faster than, *e.g.*, steamrollers, drill presses, buildings, etc. The stock dimension of the former can be ignored in many problems; this is not true of the latter set of things, which are usually labeled as fixed capital.[63] A second dynamical extension, then, consists in introducing stock-flow relationships into the production functions.

3. Lags and stock-flow relations are implied also by the goods-in-process phenomenon. Production takes place over space, and transport takes time, hence seed cannot be produced at the instant at which it is planted, nor cylinder heads the moment they are required on the assembly line. They have to be in existence for some finite time before they are used.

4. One of the crucial intertemporal interrelations in allocation and distribution in a world where stocks matter and where production takes time, is due to the unpleasant (or pleasant) fact that the inputs of any instant are not manna from heaven. Their supply depends on past output decisions. Next year's production possibilities will depend, in part, on the supply of machine tools; this, in turn, partly depends on the resources devoted this year to the construction of new machine tools. This is the problem of investment. From today's point of view investment concerns choice of *outputs;* but choice of what kinds and amounts of machines to build, plants to construct, etc., today, makes sense only in terms of the *input-uses* of these things tomorrow. Input endowments, L and D, become unknowns as well as data.

5. Tomorrow's input availabilities are also affected by how inputs are used today. The nature and intensity of use to which machines are subjected, the way in which soil is used, oil wells operated, the rate at which inventories are run down, etc., partly determine what will be left tomorrow. This is the problem of physical capital consumption, wear and tear, etc.—the problem of what to subtract from gross investment to get "net" capital formation, hence the net change in input supplies.

How do these five dynamical phenomena fit into the maximum-of-welfare problem? Recall that our W-function was assumed sensitive to, and only to, X's and Y's consumption. Nothing was said, however, about the timing of such consumption. Surely not only consumption of this instant matters. In a dynamic context, meaningful welfare and preference functions have to provide a ranking not only with respect to all possible current consumption mixes but also for future time. They must provide some means for weighing apples next week against nuts and apples today. Such functions will *date* each unit of A and N, and the choice to be made will be between alternative time-paths of consumption.[64]

---

[63] Much depends on arbitrary or special institutional assumptions about how much optimization we leave in the background for the "engineer." For example, machines of widely varying design could very likely yield a given kind of service. "A lathe is not a lathe is. . . ." Further, no law of nature precludes the rather speedy using-up of a lathe—by using it, *e.g.*, as scrap metal. In some situations it could even be economic to do so.

[64] Note how little weight is likely to be given to current consumption relative to future consumption if we pick short unit-periods. This year certainly matters, but what of this afternoon versus all future, or this second? Yet what of the man who knows he'll die tomorrow? Note also the intrinsic philosophical dilemmas: *e.g.*, is John Jones today the "same" person he was yesterday?

Given such a context, the above five dynamical phenomena are amenable to a formal maximizing treatment entirely akin to that of Parts I, II and III. They are, with one qualification,[65] consistent with the convexity assumptions required for solubility and duality. The results, which are the fruit of some very recent and pathbreaking work by R. M. Solow and P. A. Samuelson (soon to be published), define intertemporal production efficiency in terms of time-paths along which no increase in the consumption of any good of any period is possible without a decrease in some other consumption. Such paths are characterized by the superimposition, on top of the statical, one-period or instantaneous efficiency conditions, of certain intertemporal marginal rate-of-substitution requirements. But the statical efficiency requirements retain their validity: for full-fledged dynamical Pareto-efficiency it is necessary that at any moment in time the system be on its one-period efficiency frontier.[66]

Incidentally, the geometric techniques of Part I are fully adequate to the task of handling a Solow-Samuelson dynamical setup for a 2 by 2 by 2 world. Only now the dimensions of the production box and hence the position of the production-possibility curve will keep shifting, and the solution gives values not only for inputs, outputs and prices but also for their period-to-period changes.

There are many dynamical phenomena less prone to analysis by a formal maximizing system than the five listed above. The qualitative and quantitative supply of labor-input in the future is influenced by the current use made of the services of people.[67] There are, also, important intertemporal interdependences relating to the fact of space—space matters because it takes time and resources to span it. Moreover, we have not even mentioned the really "difficult" phenomena of "grand dynamics." Production functions, preference functions, and even my or your welfare function shift over time. Such shifts are compounded by what in a sense is the central problem of nonstationary dynamics: the intrinsic uncertainty that attaches to the notion of future.[68] Last, the very boundaries of economics, as of any discipline, are intrinsically arbitrary. Allocation and distribution interact in countless ways with the politics and sociology of a society . . . "everything depends on everything." But we are way beyond simple analytics.

A HISTORICAL NOTE ON THE LITERATURE

Note: For a short but substantive history of the development of thought in this field, the reader is referred to Samuelson's synthesis (nonmathematical), pp. 203–19 of *Foundations* [1]. See also Bergson, "Socialist Economics," *Survey of Contemporary Economics*, Vol. I [2] and Boulding, "Welfare Economics," *Survey*, Vol II [3].

The foundations of modern welfare theory are well embedded in the soil of classical economics, and the structure, too, bears the imprint of the line of thought represented by Smith, Ricardo, Mill, and Marshall. But in classical writing prescription and analysis are inseparably intertwined, the underlying philosophy is unabashedly utilitarian, and the central normative concern is with the efficacy of market institutions. In contrast, the development of mod-

[65] Capital is characterized not only by the fact of durability, but also by lumpiness or indivisibility "in scale." Such lumpiness results in nonconvexity, hence causes serious analytical troubles.

[66] For possible exception to this, due to sensitivity of the volume of saving, hence of investment, to "as imputed" income distribution, *cf.* my "On Capital Productivity, Input Allocation and Growth," *Quart. Jour. Econ.*, Feb. 1957, LXXI, 86–106.

[67] Although labor is in many respects analytically akin to other kinds of physical capital-resources can and need be invested to expand the stock of engineers, as to expand that of cows and machines. Machines, however, are not subject to certain costless "learning" effects.

[68] While formal welfare theory becomes very silent when uncertainty intrudes, much of economic analysis—*e.g.*, monetary theory, trade fluctuations—would have little meaning except for the fact of uncertainty.

ern welfare economics can best be understood as an attempt to sort out ethics from science, and allocative efficiency from particular modes of social organization.

The classical tradition reached its culmination in Professor Pigou's *Wealth and Welfare* [4]. Pigou, the last of the great premoderns was also, as witness the *Economics of Welfare* [5], among the first of the moderns. But he was not the first. Vilfredo Pareto, writing during the first years of the century, has a pre-eminent claim [6]. It is his work, and Enrico Barone's after him [7]—with their focus on the analytical implications of maximization—that constitute the foundations of the modern structure. Many writers contributed to the construction, but A. P. Lerner, Abram Bergson, and Paul Samuelson come especially to mind [8]. Bergson, in particular, in a single article in 1938, was the first to make us see the structure whole. More recently, Kenneth Arrow has explored the logical underpinnings of the notion of a social welfare function in relation to social choice [9]; T. C. Koopmans, Gerard Debreu and others have tested more complicated systems for duality [10]; Samuelson has developed a meaningful species of social indifference function [11] and derived efficiency conditions for "public goods" [12]; and Robert Solow and Samuelson, in work soon to be published, have provided a dynamical extension [13, 14].

There is, also, an important modern literature devoted to the possible uses of the structure of analysis for policy prescription. Three separate sets of writings are more or less distinguishable. There was first, in the 'twenties and 'thirties, a prolonged controversy on markets versus government. L. von Mises [15] and later F. A. Hayek [16] were the principal proponents of unadulterated *laissez faire*, while H. D. Dickinson, Oscar Lange, Lerner and Maurice Dobb stand out on the other side [17]. The decentralized socialist pricing idea, originally suggested by Barone and later by F. M.

Taylor, was elaborated by Lange to counter the Mises view that efficient allocation is impossible in a collectivized economy due simply to the sheer scale of the administrative burden of calculation and control.

Second, in the late 1930's, Nicholas Kaldor [18] and J. R. Hicks [19] took up Lionel Robbins' [20] challenge to economists not to mix ethics and science and suggested a series of tests for choosing some input-output configurations over others independently of value.[69] Tibor Scitovsky pointed out an important asymmetry in the Kaldor-Hicks test [21] and Samuelson in the end demonstrated that a "welfare-function" denoting an ethic was needed after all [22]. I. M. D. Little tried, but I think failed, to shake this conclusion [23].[70] The Pareto conditions are necessary, but never sufficient.

Third, there is a body of writing, some of it in a partial-equilibrium mode which is concerned with policy at a lower level of abstraction. Writings by Harold Hotelling, Ragnar Frisch, J. E. Meade, W. A. Lewis, are devoted to the question of optimal pricing, marginal-cost or otherwise, in public utility (M.C. < A.C.) situations [24]. Hotelling, H. P. Wald, M. F. W. Joseph, E. R. Rolph and G. F. Break, Little, and more recently Lionel McKenzie, have, in turn, analyzed alternative fiscal devices for covering public deficits [25]. Last, a number of the above, notably Lerner, Kaldor, Samuelson, Scitovsky, Little, McKenzie and, most exhaustively, Meade, as well as R. F. Kahn, Lloyd Metzler, J. de V. Graaf,

[69] The Hicks-Kaldor line of thought has some ties to an earlier literature by Marshall, Pigou, Fisher, etc., on "what is income."

[70] While I find Little's alternative to a welfare function ("an economic change is desirable if it does not cause a bad redistribution of income, and if the potential losers could not profitably bribe the potential gainers to oppose it" [p. 105]) no alternative at all, his is a provocative evaluation of modern welfare theory. For an evaluation, in turn, of Little, see K. J. Arrow, "Little's Critique of Welfare Economics," *Am. Econ. Rev.*, Dec. 1951, XLI, 923–34.

H. G. Johnson and others have applied the apparatus to questions of gains from international trade, optimal tariffs, etc. [26].

BIBLIOGRAPHY

[1] P. A. Samuelson, *Foundations of Economic Analysis* (Cambridge, 1947).

[2] A. Bergson, "Socialist Economics," in H. S. Ellis, ed., *A Survey of Contemporary Economics*, Vol. I (Philadelphia, 1948).

[3] K. E. Boulding, "Welfare Economics," in B. F. Haley, ed., *A Survey of Contemporary Economics*, Vol. II (Homewood, Ill., 1952).

[4] A. C. Pigou, *Wealth and Welfare* (London, 1912).

[5] ———, *The Economics of Welfare*, 4th ed. (London, 1932).

[6] V. Pareto, *Manuel d'économie politique* (Paris, 1909).

[7] E. Barone, "The Ministry of Production in the Collectivist State," transl. in F. A. Hayek, *Collectivist Economic Planning* (London, 1935).

[8] See A. P. Lerner, *The Economics of Control* (London, 1944); A. Bergson (Burk), "A Reformulation of Certain Aspects of Welfare Economics," *Quart. Jour. Econ.*, Feb. 1938, LII 310–14, reprinted in R. V. Clemence, ed., *Readings in Economic Analysis*, Vol. I (Cambridge, 1952); P. A. Samuelson, *op. cit.*, Ch. 8.

For other works, see references in Samuelson, *op. cit.*, p. 219, and in Bergson's and Boulding's *Survey* articles [2, 3].

[9] See K. J. Arrow, *Social Choice and Individual Values* (New York, 1951).

[10] P. A. Samuelson, *Market Mechanisms and Maximization* (unpublished, RAND Corporation Research Memo., 1949).

T. C. Koopmans, *Activity Analysis of Production and Allocation* (New York, 1951); also R. Dorfman, "Mathematical or 'Linear' Programming," *Am. Econ. Rev.*, Dec. 1953, XLIII 797–825.

[11] P. A. Samuelson, "Social Indifference Curves," *Quart. Jour. Econ.*, Feb. 1956, LXX 1–22.

[12] ———, "The Pure Theory of Public Expenditure," *Rev. Econ. Stat.*, Nov. 1954, XXXVI, 387–89.

——— , "Diagrammatic Exposition of a Theory of Public Expenditure," *Rev. Econ. Stat.* Nov. 1955, XXXVII, 350–56.

[13] R. Dorfman, R. M. Solow and P. A. Samuelson, *Linear Programming and Economic Analysis* (New York, 1958), esp. Ch.

11, 12. Ch. 14 contains a most elegant exposition by R. M. Solow of modern welfare theory in linear programming terms.

[14] Four other works should be mentioned: M. W. Reder, *Studies in the Theory of Welfare Economics* (New York, 1947), is a book-length exposition of modern welfare theory; Hla Mynt's *Theories of Welfare Economics* (London, 1948), treats classical and neoclassical writings; W. J. Baumol in *Welfare Economics and the Theory of the State* (London, 1952), attempts an extension to political theory; in a different vein, Gunnar Myrdal's *Political Elements in the Development of Economic Theory*, transl. by Paul Streeten (London, 1953), with Streeten's appendix on modern developments, is a broad-based critique of the premises of welfare economics.

[15] For the translation of the original 1920 article by Mises which triggered the controversy, see F. A. Hayek, ed., *Collectivist Economic Planning* (London, 1935).

[16] See esp. F. A. Hayek, "Socialist Calculation: The Competitive Solution," *Economica*, May 1940, VII, 125–49; for a broad-front attack on deviations from *laissez faire* see Hayek's polemic, *The Road to Serfdom* (Chicago, 1944).

[17] H. D. Dickinson, "Price Formation in a Socialist Economy," *Econ. Jour.*, Dec. 1933, XLIII, 237–50; O. Lange, "On the Economic Theory of Socialism" in Lange and Taylor, *The Economic Theory of Socialism*, B. E. Lippincott, ed. (Minneapolis, 1938); A. P. Lerner, *op. cit.*; M. Dobb, "Economic Theory and the Problem of the Socialist Economy," *Econ. Jour.* Dec. 1933, XLIII, 588–98.

[18] N. Kaldor, "Welfare Propositions in Economics and Interpersonal Comparisons of Utility," *Econ. Jour.*, Sept. 1939, LXIX, 549–52.

[19] J. R. Hicks, "The Foundations of Welfare Economics," *Econ. Jour.*, Dec. 1939, LXIX, 696–712 and "The Valuation of the Social Income," *Economica*, Feb. 1940, VII, 105–23.

[20] L. Robbins, *The Nature and Significance of Economic Science* (London, 1932).

[21] T. Scitovsky, "A Note on Welfare Propositions in Economics," *Rev. Econ. Stud.*, 1941–1942, IX, 77–78.

——— , "A Reconsideration of the Theory of Tariffs," *Rev. Econ. Stud.*, 1941–1942, IX, 89–110.

[22] P. A. Samuelson, "Evaluation of Real National Income," *Oxford Econ. Papers*, Jan. 1950, II, 1–29.

[23] I. M. D. Little, *A Critique of Welfare Economics* (Oxford, 1950).

[24] H. Hotelling, "The General Welfare in Relation to Problems of Taxation and of Railway and Utility Rates," *Econometrica*, July 1938, VI, 242–69, is the first modern formulation of the problem that was posed, in 1844, by Jules Dupuit ("On the Measurement of Utility of Public Works," to be found in *International Economic Papers*, No. 2, ed. Alan T. Peacock *et al.*).

[25] See esp. Little, "Direct versus Indirect Taxes," *Econ. Jour.*, Sept. 1951, LXI, 577–84.

[26] For a comprehensive treatment of the issues, as well as for references, see J. E. Meade, *The Theory of International Economic Policy*, Vol. II: *Trade and Welfare* and *Mathematical Supplement* (New York, 1955).

33. The Problem
of Social Cost*

RONALD COASE[1]

Born in London, Ronald H. Coase (B.Com., London, 1932; D.Sc., 1951) is now a professor at the University of Chicago and Editor of the *Journal of Law and Economics*. Before assuming his post at Chicago in 1964, he was on the faculties of the London School of Economics, the University of Buffalo, and the University of Virginia. Coase, whose research interests are in price theory, the history of economic thought, and the economics of public utilities and industrial organization, is one of the most careful and rigorous scholars in the profession. "The Nature of the Firm" and "The Marginal Cost Controversy", two of his most famous articles, both of which were originally published in *Economica*, have become acknowledged classics in the field.

I. THE PROBLEM TO BE EXAMINED

This paper is concerned with those actions of business firms which have harmful

* Reprinted from the *Journal of Law and Economics* (October 1960) by permission of the publisher, pp. 1–44.
[1] This article, although concerned with a technical problem of economic analysis, arose out of the study of the Political Economy of Broadcasting which I am now conducting. The argument of the present article was implicit in a previous article dealing with the problem of allocating radio and television frequencies ("The Federal Communications Commission," 2 *J. Law & Econ.* [1959]) but comments which I have received

effects on others. The standard example is that of a factory the smoke from which has harmful effects on those occupying neighbouring properties. The economic analysis of such a situation has usually proceeded in terms of a divergence between the private and social product of the factory, in which economists have largely followed the treatment of Pigou in *The Economics of Welfare*. The conclusions to

seemed to suggest that it would be desirable to deal with the question in a more explicit way and without reference to the original problem for the solution of which the analysis was developed.

484

which this kind of analysis seems to have led most economists is that it would be desirable to make the owner of the factory liable for the damage caused to those injured by the smoke, or alternatively, to place a tax on the factory owner varying with the amount of smoke produced and equivalent in money terms to the damage it would cause, or finally, to exclude the factory from residential districts (and presumably from other areas in which the emission of smoke would have harmful effects on others). It is my contention that the suggested courses of action are inappropriate, in that they lead to results which are not necessarily, or even usually, desirable.

II. THE RECIPROCAL NATURE OF THE PROBLEM

The traditional approach has tended to obscure the nature of the choice that has to be made. The question is commonly thought of as one in which A inflicts harm on B and what has to be decided is: how should we restrain A? But this is wrong. We are dealing with a problem of a reciprocal nature. To avoid the harm to B would inflict harm on A. The real question that has to be decided is: should A be allowed to harm B or should B be allowed to harm A? The problem is to avoid the more serious harm. I instanced in my previous article[2] the case of a confectioner the noise and vibrations from whose machinery disturbed a doctor in his work. To avoid harming the doctor would inflict harm on the confectioner. The problem posed by this case was essentially whether it was worth while, as a result of restricting the methods of production which could be used by the confectioner, to secure more doctoring at the cost of a reduced supply of confectionery products. Another example is afforded by the problem of straying cattle

which destroy crops on neighbouring land. If it is inevitable that some cattle will stray, an increase in the supply of meat can only be obtained at the expense of a decrease in the supply of crops. The nature of the choice is clear: meat or crops. What answer should be given is, of course, not clear unless we know the value of what is obtained as well as the value of what is sacrificed to obtain it. To give another example, Professor George J. Stigler instances the contamination of a stream.[3] If we assume that the harmful effect of the pollution is that it kills the fish, the question to be decided is: is the value of the fish lost greater or less than the value of the product which the contamination of the stream makes possible. It goes almost without saying that this problem has to be looked at in total *and* at the margin.

III. THE PRICING SYSTEM WITH LIABILITY FOR DAMAGE

I propose to start my analysis by examining a case in which most economists would presumably agree that the problem would be solved in a completely satisfactory manner: when the damaging business has to pay for all damage caused *and* the pricing system works smoothly (strictly this means that the operation of a pricing system is without cost).

A good example of the problem under discussion is afforded by the case of straying cattle which destroy crops growing on neighbouring land. Let us suppose that a farmer and cattle-raiser are operating on neighbouring properties. Let us further suppose that, without any fencing between the properties, an increase in the size of the cattle-raiser's herd increases the total damage to the farmer's crops. What happens to the marginal damage as the size of the herd increases is another matter. This depends on whether the cattle tend to follow one

[2] Coase, "The Federal Communications Commission," 2 J. Law & Econ. 26–27 (1959).

[3] G. J. Stigler, *The Theory of Price*, 105 (1952).

another or to roam side by side, on whether they tend to be more or less restless as the size of the herd increases and on other similar factors. For my immediate purpose, it is immaterial what assumption is made about marginal damage as the size of the herd increases.

To simplify the argument, I propose to use an arithmetical example. I shall assume that the annual cost of fencing the farmer's property is $9 and that the price of the crop is $1 per ton. Also, I assume that the relation between the number of cattle in the herd and the annual crop loss is as follows:

Number in herd (steers)	Annual crop loss (tons)	Crop loss per additional steer (tons)
1	1	1
2	3	2
3	6	3
4	10	4

Given that the cattle-raiser is liable for the damage caused, the additional annual cost imposed on the cattle-raiser if he increased his herd from, say, 2 to 3 steers is $3 and in deciding on the size of the herd, he will take this into account along with his other costs. That is, he will not increase the size of the herd unless the value of the additional meat produced (assuming that the cattle-raiser slaughters the cattle), is greater than the additional costs that this will entail, including the value of the additional crops destroyed. Of course, if, by the employment of dogs, herdsmen, aeroplanes, mobile radio and other means, the amount of damage can be reduced, these means will be adopted when their cost is less than the value of the crop which they prevent being lost. Given that the annual cost of fencing is $9, the cattle-raiser who wished to have a herd with 4 steers or more would pay for fencing to be erected and maintained, assuming that other means of attaining the same end would not do so more cheaply. When the fence is erected, the marginal cost

due to the liability for damage becomes zero, except to the extent that an increase in the size of the herd necessitates a stronger and therefore more expensive fence because more steers are liable to lean against it at the same time. But, of course, it may be cheaper for the cattle-raiser not to fence and to pay for the damaged crops, as in my arithmetical example, with 3 or fewer steers.

It might be thought that the fact that the cattle-raiser would pay for all crops damaged would lead the farmer to increase his planting if a cattle-raiser came to occupy the neighbouring property. But this is not so. If the crop was previously sold in conditions of perfect competition, marginal cost was equal to price for the amount of planting undertaken and any expansion would have reduced the profits of the farmer. In the new situation, the existence of crop damage would mean that the farmer would sell less on the open market but his receipts for a given production would remain the same, since the cattle-raiser would pay the market price for any crop damaged. Of course, if cattle-raising commonly involved the destruction of crops, the coming into existence of a cattle-raising industry might raise the price of the crops involved and farmers would then extend their planting. But I wish to confine my attention to the individual farmer.

I have said that the occupation of a neighbouring property by a cattle-raiser would not cause the amount of production, or perhaps more exactly the amount of planting, by the farmer to increase. In fact, if the cattle-raising has any effect, it will be to decrease the amount of planting. The reason for this is that, for any given tract of land, if the value of the crop damaged is so great that the receipts from the sale of the undamaged crop are less than the total costs of cultivating that tract of land, it will be profitable for the farmer and the cattle-raiser to make a bargain whereby that tract of land is left uncultivated. This can be made clear by means of an arithmetical example. Assume initially that the value of the crop obtained from cultivating a given tract of land is $12 and that the cost incurred in cultivating this tract of land is $10, the net gain from cultivating the land being $2. I assume for purposes of simplicity that the farmer owns the land. Now assume that the cattle-raiser starts operations on the neighbouring property and that the value of the crops damaged is $1. In this case $11 is obtained by the farmer from sale on the market and $1 is obtained from the cattle-raiser for damage suffered and the net gain remains $2. Now suppose that the cattle-raiser finds it profitable to increase the size of his herd, even though the amount of damage rises to $3; which means that the value of the additional meat production is greater than the additional costs, including the additional $2 payment for damage. But the total payment for damage is now $3. The net gain to the farmer from cultivating the land is still $2. The cattle-raiser would be better off if the farmer would agree not to cultivate his land for any payment less than $3. The farmer would be agreeable to not cultivating the land for any payment greater than $2. There is clearly room for a mutually satisfactory bargain which would lead to the abandonment of cultivation.[4] But the

same argument applies not only to the whole tract cultivated by the farmer but also to any subdivision of it. Suppose, for example, that the cattle have a well-defined route, say, to a brook or to a shady area. In these circumstances, the amount of damage to the crop along the route may well be great and if so, it could be that the farmer and the cattle-raiser would find it profitable to make a bargain whereby the farmer would agree not to cultivate this strip of land.

But this raises a further possibility. Suppose that there is such a well-defined route. Suppose further that the value of the crop that would be obtained by cultivating this strip of land is $10 but that the cost of cultivation is $11. In the absence of the cattle-raiser, the land would not be cultivated. However, given the presence of the cattle-raiser, it could well be that if the strip was cultivated, the whole crop would be destroyed by the cattle. In which case, the cattle-raiser would be forced to pay $10 to the farmer. It is true that the farmer would lose $1. But the cattle-raiser would lose $10. Clearly this is a situation which is not likely to last indefinitely since neither party would want this to happen. The aim of the farmer would be to induce the cattle-raiser to make a payment in return for an agreement to leave this land uncultivated. The farmer would not be able to obtain a payment greater than the cost of fencing off this piece of land nor so high as to lead the cattle-raiser to abandon the use of the neighbouring property. What payment would in fact be made would depend on the shrewdness of the farmer and the cattle-raiser as bargainers. But as the payment would not be so high as to cause the cattle-raiser to abandon this location and as it would not vary with the size of the herd,

[4] The argument in the text has proceeded on the assumption that the alternative to cultivation of the crop is abandonment of cultivation altogether. But this need not be so. There may be crops which are less liable to damage by cattle but which would not be as profitable as the crop grown in the absence of damage. Thus, if the cultivation of a new crop would yield a return to the farmer of $1 instead of $2, and the size of the herd which would cause $3 damage with the old crop would cause $1 damage with the new crop, it would be profitable to the cattle-raiser to pay any sum less than $2 to induce the farmer to change his crop (since this would reduce damage liability from $3 to $1) and it would be profitable for the farmer to do so if the amount received was more than $1 (the reduction in his return caused by switching crops). In fact, there would be room for a mutually satisfactory bargain in all cases in which a change of crop would

reduce the amount of damage by more than it reduces the value of the crop (excluding damage) —in all cases, that is, in which a change in the crop cultivated would lead to an increase in the value of production.

such an agreement would not affect the allocation of resources but would merely alter the distribution of income and wealth as between the cattle-raiser and the farmer.

I think it is clear that if the cattle-raiser is liable for damage caused and the pricing system works smoothly, the reduction in the value of production elsewhere will be taken into account in computing the additional cost involved in increasing the size of the herd. This cost will be weighed against the value of the additional meat production and, given perfect competition in the cattle industry, the allocation of resources in cattle-raising will be optimal. What needs to be emphasized is that the fall in the value of production elsewhere which would be taken into account in the costs of the cattle-raiser may well be less than the damage which the cattle would cause to the crops in the ordinary course of events. This is because it is possible, as a result of market transactions, to discontinue cultivation of the land. This is desirable in all cases in which the damage that the cattle would cause, and for which the cattle-raiser would be willing to pay, exceeds the amount which the farmer would pay for use of the land. In conditions of perfect competition, the amount which the farmer would pay for the use of the land is equal to the difference between the value of the total production when the factors are employed on this land and the value of the additional product yielded in their next best use (which would be what the farmer would have to pay for the factors). If damage exceeds the amount the farmer would pay for the use of the land, the value of the additional product of the factors employed elsewhere would exceed the value of the total product in this use after damage is taken into account. It follows that it would be desirable to abandon cultivation of the land and to release the factors employed for production elsewhere. A procedure which merely provided for payment for damage to the crop caused by the cattle

but which did not allow for the possibility of cultivation being discontinued would result in too small an employment of factors of production in cattle-raising and too large an employment of factors in cultivation of the crop. But given the possibility of market transactions, a situation in which damage to crops exceeded the rent of the land would not endure. Whether the cattle-raiser pays the farmer to leave the land uncultivated or himself rents the land by paying the land-owner an amount slightly greater than the farmer would pay (if the farmer was himself renting the land), the final result would be the same and would maximise the value of production. Even when the farmer is induced to plant crops which it would not be profitable to cultivate for sale on the market, this will be a purely short-term phenomenon and may be expected to lead to an agreement under which the planting will cease. The cattle-raiser will remain in that location and the marginal cost of meat production will be the same as before, thus having no long-run effect on the allocation of resources.

IV. THE PRICING SYSTEM WITH NO LIABILITY FOR DAMAGE

I now turn to the case in which, although the pricing system is assumed to work smoothly (that is, costlessly), the damaging business is not liable for any of the damage which it causes. This business does not have to make a payment to those damaged by its actions. I propose to show that the allocation of resources will be the same in this case as it was when the damaging business was liable for damage caused. As I showed in the previous case that the allocation of resources was optimal, it will not be necessary to repeat this part of the argument.

I return to the case of the farmer and the cattle-raiser. The farmer would suffer increased damage to his crop as the size of the herd increased. Suppose that the size of the cattle-raiser's herd is 3 steers (and that this is the size of the herd that would be maintained if crop damage was not taken into account). Then the farmer would be willing to pay up to $3 if the cattle-raiser would reduce his herd to 2 steers, up to $5 if the herd were reduced to 1 steer and would pay up to $6 if cattle-raising was abandoned. The cattle-raiser would therefore receive $3 from the farmer if he kept 2 steers instead of 3. This $3 foregone is therefore part of the cost incurred in keeping the third steer. Whether the $3 is a payment which the cattle-raiser has to make if he adds the third steer to his herd (which it would be if the cattle-raiser was liable to the farmer for damage caused to the crop) or whether it is a sum of money which he would have received if he did not keep a third steer (which it would be if the cattle-raiser was not liable to the farmer for damage caused to the crop) does not affect the final result. In both cases $3 is part of the cost of adding a third steer, to be included along with the other costs. If the increase in the value of production in cattle-raising through increasing the size of the herd from 2 to 3 is greater than the additional costs that have to be incurred (including the $3 damage to crops), the size of the herd will be increased. Otherwise, it will not. The size of the herd will be the same whether the cattle-raiser is liable for damage caused to the crop or not.

It may be argued that the assumed starting point—a herd of 3 steers—was arbitrary. And this is true. But the farmer would not wish to pay to avoid crop damage which the cattle-raiser would not be able to cause. For example, the maximum annual payment which the farmer could be induced to pay could not exceed $9, the annual cost of fencing. And the farmer would only be willing to pay this sum if it did not reduce his earnings to a level that would cause him to abandon cultivation of this particular tract of land. Furthermore, the farmer would only be willing

to pay this amount if he believed that, in the absence of any payment by him, the size of the herd maintained by the cattle-raiser would be 4 or more steers. Let us assume that this is the case. Then the farmer would be willing to pay up to $3 if the cattle-raiser would reduce his herd to 3 steers, up to $6 if the herd were reduced to 2 steers, up to $8 if one steer only were kept and up to $9 if cattle-raising were abandoned. It will be noticed that the change in the starting point has not altered the amount which would accrue to the cattle-raiser if he reduced the size of his herd by any given amount. It is still true that the cattle-raiser could receive an additional $3 from the farmer if he agreed to reduce his herd from 3 steers to 2 and that the $3 represents the value of the crop that would be destroyed by adding the third steer to the herd. Although a different belief on the part of the farmer (whether justified or not) about the size of the herd that the cattle-raiser would maintain in the absence of payments from him may affect the total payment he can be induced to pay, it is not true that this different belief would have any effect on the size of the herd that the cattle-raiser will actually keep. This will be the same as it would be if the cattle-raiser had to pay for damage caused by his cattle, since a receipt foregone of a given amount is the equivalent of a payment of the same amount.

It might be thought that it would pay the cattle-raiser to increase his herd above the size that he would wish to maintain once a bargain had been made, in order to induce the farmer to make a larger total payment. And this may be true. It is similar in nature to the action of the farmer (when the cattle-raiser was liable for damage) in cultivating land on which, as a result of an agreement with the cattle-raiser, planting would subsequently be abandoned (including land which would not be cultivated at all in the absence of cattle-raising). But such manoeuvres are preliminaries to an agreement and do not affect the long-run equilibrium position, which is the same whether or not the cattle-raiser is held responsible for the crop damage brought about by his cattle.

It is necessary to know whether the damaging business is liable or not for damage caused since without the establishment of this initial delimitation of rights there can be no market transactions to transfer and recombine them. But the ultimate result (which maximises the value of production) is independent of the legal position if the pricing system is assumed to work without cost.

V. THE PROBLEM ILLUSTRATED ANEW

The harmful effects of the activities of a business can assume a wide variety of forms. An early English case concerned a building which, by obstructing currents of air, hindered the operation of a windmill.[5] A recent case in Florida concerned a building which cast a shadow on the cabana, swimming pool and sunbathing areas of a neighbouring hotel.[6] The problem of straying cattle and the damaging of crops which was the subject of detailed examination in the two preceding sections, although it may have appeared to be rather a special case, is in fact but one example of a problem which arises in many different guises. To clarify the nature of my argument and to demonstrate its general applicability, I propose to illustrate it anew by reference to four actual cases.

Let us first reconsider the case of *Sturges v. Bridgman*[7] which I used as an illustration of the general problem in my article on "The Federal Communications Commission." In this case, a confectioner (in Wig-

more Street) used two mortars and pestles in connection with his business (one had been in operation in the same position for more than 60 years and the other for more than 26 years). A doctor then came to occupy neighbouring premises (in Wimpole Street). The confectioner's machinery caused the doctor no harm until, eight years after he had first occupied the premises, he built a consulting room at the end of his garden right against the confectioner's kitchen. It was then found that the noise and vibration caused by the confectioner's machinery made it difficult for the doctor to use his new consulting room. "In particular . . . the noise prevented him from examining his patients by auscultation[8] for diseases of the chest. He also found it impossible to engage with effect in any occupation which required thought and attention." The doctor therefore brought a legal action to force the confectioner to stop using his machinery. The courts had little difficulty in granting the doctor the injunction he sought. "Individual cases of hardship may occur in the strict carrying out of the principle upon which we found our judgment, but the negation of the principle would lead even more to individual hardship, and would at the same time produce a prejudicial effect upon the development of land for residential purposes."

The court's decision established that the doctor had the right to prevent the confectioner from using his machinery. But, of course, it would have been possible to modify the arrangements envisaged in the legal ruling by means of a bargain between the parties. The doctor would have been willing to waive his right and allow the machinery to continue in operation if the confectioner would have paid him a sum of money which was greater than the loss of income which he would suffer from having to move to a more costly or less convenient

---

[5] See Gale on *Easements* 237–39 (13th ed. M. Bowles 1959).

[6] See *Fontainebleu Hotel Corp. v. Forty-Five Twenty-Five, Inc.*, 114 So. 2d 357 (1959).

[7] 11 Ch. D. 852 (1879).

[8] Auscultation is the act of listening by ear or stethoscope in order to judge by sound the condition of the body.

location or from having to curtail his activities at this location or, as was suggested as a possibility, from having to build a separate wall which would deaden the noise and vibration. The confectioner would have been willing to do this if the amount he would have to pay the doctor was less than the fall in income he would suffer if he had to change his mode of operation at this location, abandon his operation or move his confectionery business to some other location. The solution of the problem depends essentially on whether the continued use of the machinery adds more to the confectioner's income than it subtracts from the doctor's.[9] But now consider the situation if the confectioner had won the case. The confectioner would then have had the right to continue operating his noise and vibration-generating machinery without having to pay anything to the doctor. The boot would have been on the other foot: the doctor would have had to pay the confectioner to induce him to stop using the machinery. If the doctor's income would have fallen more through continuance of the use of this machinery than it added to the income of the confectioner, there would clearly be room for a bargain whereby the doctor paid the confectioner to stop using the machinery. That is to say, the circumstances in which it would not pay the confectioner to continue to use the machinery and to compensate the doctor for the losses that this would bring (if the doctor had the right to prevent the confectioner's using his machinery) would be those in which it would be in the interest of the doctor to make a payment to the confectioner which would induce him to discontinue the use of the machinery (if the confectioner had the right to operate the machinery). The basic conditions are exactly the same in this case as they were in the example of the cattle

[9] Note that what is taken into acount is the change in income after allowing for alterations in methods of production, location, character of product, etc.

which destroyed crops. With costless market transactions, the decision of the courts concerning liability for damage would be without effect on the allocation of resources. It was of course the view of the judges that they were affecting the working of the economic system—and in a desirable direction. Any other decision would have had "a prejudicial effect upon the development of land for residential purposes," an argument which was elaborated by examining the example of a forge operating on a barren moor, which was later developed for residual purposes. The judges' view that they were settling how the land was to be used would be true only in the case in which the costs of carrying out the necessary market transactions exceeded the gain which might be achieved by any rearrangement of rights. And it would be desirable to preserve the areas (Wimpole Street or the moor) for residential or professional use (by giving non-industrial users the right to stop the noise, vibration, smoke, etc., by injunction) only if the value of the additional residential facilities obtained was greater than the value of cakes or iron lost. But of this the judges seem to have been unaware.

Another example of the same problem is furnished by the case of *Cooke v. Forbes*.[10] One process in the weaving of cocoa-nut fibre matting was to immerse it in bleaching liquids after which it was hung out to dry. Fumes from a manufacturer of sulphate of ammonia had the effect of turning the matting from a bright to a dull and blackish colour. The reason for this was that the bleaching liquid contained chloride of tin, which, when affected by sulphuretted hydrogen, is turned to a darker colour. An injunction was sought to stop the manufacturer from emitting the fumes. The lawyers for the defendant argued that if the plaintiff "were not to use . . . a particular bleaching liquid, their fibre would not be affected; that their process is unusual,

[10] L. R. 5 Eq. 166 (1867–1868).

not according to the custom of the trade, and even damaging to their own fabrics." The judge commented: ". . . it appears to me quite plain that a person has a right to carry on upon his own property a manufacturing process in which he uses chloride of tin, or any sort of metallic dye, and that his neighbour is not at liberty to pour in gas which will interfere with his manufacture. If it can be traced to the neighbour, then, I apprehend, clearly he will have a right to come here and ask for relief." But in view of the fact that the damage was accidental and occasional, that careful precautions were taken and that there was no exceptional risk, an injunction was refused, leaving the plaintiff to bring an action for damages if he wished. What the subsequent developments were I do not know. But it is clear that the situation is essentially the same as that found in *Sturges v. Bridgman*, except that the cocoa-nut fibre matting manufacturer could not secure an injunction but would have to seek damages from the sulphate of ammonia manufacturer. The economic analysis of the situation is exactly the same as with the cattle which destroyed crops. To avoid the damage, the sulphate of ammonia manufacturer could increase his precautions or move to another location. Either course would presumably increase his costs. Alternatively he could pay for the damage. This he would do if the payments for damage were less than the additional costs that would have to be incurred to avoid the damage. The payments for damage would then become part of the cost of production of sulphate of ammonia. Of course, if, as was suggested in the legal proceedings, the amount of damage could be eliminated by changing the bleaching agent (which would presumably increase the costs of the matting manufacturer) and if the additional cost was less than the damage that would otherwise occur, it should be possible for the two manufacturers to make a mutually satisfactory bargain whereby the new bleach-

ing agent was used. Had the court decided against the matting manufacturer, as a consequence of which he would have had to suffer the damage without compensation, the allocation of resources would not have been affected. It would pay the matting manufacturer to change his bleaching agent if the additional cost involved was less than the reduction in damage. And since the matting manufacturer would be willing to pay the sulphate of ammonia manufacturer an amount up to his loss of income (the increase in costs or the damage suffered) if he would cease his activities, this loss of income would remain a cost of production for the manufacturer of sulphate of ammonia. This case is indeed analytically exactly the same as the cattle example.

Bryant v. Lefever[11] raised the problem of the smoke nuisance in a novel form. The plaintiff and the defendants were occupiers of adjoining houses, which were of about the same height.

> Before 1876 the plaintiff was able to light a fire in any room of his house without the chimneys smoking; the two houses had remained in the same condition some thirty or forty years. In 1876 the defendants took down their house, and began to rebuild it. They carried up a wall by the side of the plaintiff's chimneys much beyond its original height, and stacked timber on the roof of their house, and thereby caused the plaintiff's chimneys to smoke whenever he lighted fires.

The reason, of course, why the chimneys smoked was that the erection of the wall and the stacking of the timber prevented the free circulation of air. In a trial before a jury, the plaintiff was awarded damages of £40. The case then went to the Court of Appeals where the judgment was reversed. Bramwell, L.J., argued:

> . . . it is said, and the jury have found, that the defendants have done that which caused a nuisance to the plaintiff's house. We think there is no evidence of this. No doubt there is a nuisance, but it is not of the defendant's causing. They have done nothing

[11] 4 C.P.D. 172 (1878–1879).

in causing the nuisance. Their house and their timber are harmless enough. It is the plaintiff who causes the nuisance by lighting a coal fire in a place the chimney of which is placed so near the defendants' wall, that the smoke does not escape, but comes into the house. Let the plaintiff cease to light his fire, let him move his chimney, let him carry it higher, and there would be no nuisance. Who then, causes it? It would be very clear that the plaintiff did, if he had built his house or chimney after the defendants had put up the timber on theirs, and it is really the same though he did so before the timber was there. But (what is in truth the same answer), if the defendants cause the nuisance, they have a right to do so. If the plaintiff has not the right to the passage of air, except subject to the defendants' right to build or put timber on their house, then his right is subject to their right, and though a nuisance follows from the exercise of their right, they are not liable.

And Cotton, L. J., said:

Here it is found that the erection of the defendants' wall has sensibly and materially interfered with the comfort of human existence in the plaintiff's house, and it is said this is a nuisance for which the defendants are liable. Ordinarily this is so, but the defendants have done so, not by sending on to the plaintiff's property any smoke or noxious vapour, but by interrupting the egress of smoke from the plaintiff's house in a way to which . . . the plaintiff has no legal right. The plaintiff creates the smoke, which interferes with his comfort. Unless he has . . . a right to get rid of this in a particular way which has been interfered with by the defendants, he cannot sue the defendants, because the smoke made by himself, for which he has not provided any effectual means of escape, causes him annoyance. It is as if a man tried to get rid of liquid filth arising on his own land by a drain into his neighbour's land. Until a right had been acquired by user, the neighbour might stop the drain without incurring liability by so doing. No doubt great inconvenience would be caused to the owner of the property on which the liquid filth arises. But the act of his neighbour would be a lawful act, and he would not be liable for the consequences attributable to the fact that the man had accumulated filth without providing any effectual means of getting rid of it.

I do not propose to show that any subsequent modification of the situation, as a result of bargains between the parties (conditioned by the cost of stacking the timber elsewhere, the cost of extending the chimney higher, etc.), would have exactly the same result whatever decision the courts had come to since this point has already been adequately dealt with in the discussion of the cattle example and the two previous cases. What I shall discuss is the argument of the judges in the Court of Appeals that the smoke nuisance was not caused by the man who erected the wall but by the man who lit the fires. The novelty of the situation is that the smoke nuisance was suffered by the man who lit the fires and not by some third person. The question is not a trivial one since it lies at the heart of the problem under discussion. Who caused the smoke nuisance? The answer seems fairly clear. The smoke nuisance was caused both by the man who built the wall *and* by the man who lit the fires. Given the fires, there would have been no smoke nuisance without the wall; given the wall, there would have been no smoke nuisance without the fires. Eliminate the wall *or* the fires and the smoke nuisance would disappear. On the marginal principle it is clear that *both* were responsible and *both* should be forced to include the loss of amenity due to the smoke as a cost in deciding whether to continue the activity which gives rise to the smoke. And given the possibility of market transactions, this is what would in fact happen. Although the wall-builder was not liable legally for the nuisance, as the man with the smoking chimneys would presumably be willing to pay a sum equal to the monetary worth to him of eliminating the smoke, this sum would therefore become for the wall-builder, a cost of continuing to have the high wall with the timber stacked on the roof.

The judges' contention that it was the man who lit the fires who alone caused the smoke nuisance is true only if we assume that the wall is the given factor. This is what the judges did by deciding that the man who erected the higher wall had a legal right to do so. The case would have been even more interesting if the smoke from the chimneys had injured the timber. Then it would have been the wall-builder who suffered the damage. The case would then have closely paralleled *Sturges v. Bridgman* and there can be little doubt that the man who lit the fires would have been liable for the ensuing damage to the timber, in spite of the fact that no damage had occurred until the high wall was built by the man who owned the timber.

Judges have to decide on legal liability but this should not confuse economists about the nature of the economic problem involved. In the case of the cattle and the crops, it is true that there would be no crop damage without the cattle. It is equally true that there would be no crop damage without the crops. The doctor's work would not have been disturbed if the confectioner had not worked his machinery; but the machinery would have disturbed no one if the doctor had not set up his consulting room in that particular place. The matting was blackened by the fumes from the sulphate of ammonia manufacturer; but no damage would have occurred if the matting manufacturer had not chosen to hang out his matting in a particular place and to use a particular bleaching agent. If we are to discuss the problem in terms of causation, both parties cause the damage. If we are to attain an optimum allocation of resources, it is therefore desirable that both parties should take the harmful effect (the nuisance) into account in deciding on their course of action. It is one of the beauties of a smoothly operating pricing system that, as has already been explained, the fall in the value of production due to the harmful effect would be a cost for both parties.

Bass v. Gregory[12] will serve as an ex-

cellent final illustration of the problem. The plaintiffs were the owners and tenant of a public house called the Jolly Anglers. The defendant was the owner of some cottages and a yard adjoining the Jolly Anglers. Under the public house was a cellar excavated in the rock. From the cellar, a hole or shaft had been cut into an old well situated in the defendant's yard. The well therefore became the ventilating shaft for the cellar. The cellar "had been used for a particular purpose in the process of brewing, which, without ventilation, could not be carried on." The cause of the action was that the defendant removed a grating from the mouth of the well, "so as to stop or prevent the free passage of air from [the] cellar upwards through the well. . . ." What caused the defendant to take this step is not clear from the report of the case. Perhaps "the air . . . impregnated by the brewing operations" which "passed up the well and out into the open air" was offensive to him. At any rate, he preferred to have the well in his yard stopped up. The court had first to determine whether the owners of the public house could have a legal right to a current of air. If they were to have such a right, this case would have to be distinguished from *Bryant v. Lefever* (already considered). This, however, presented no difficulty. In this case, the current of air was confined to "a strictly defined channel." In the case of *Bryant v. Lefever*, what was involved was "the general current of air common to all mankind." The judge therefore held that the owners of the public house could have the right to a current of air whereas the owner of the private house in *Bryant v. Lefever* could not. An economist might be tempted to add "but the air moved all the same." However, all that had been decided at this stage of the argument was that there could be a legal right, not that the owners of the public house possessed it. But evidence showed that the shaft from the cellar to the well had existed for over forty years and that

[12] 25 Q.B.D. 481 (1890).

the use of the well as a ventilating shaft must have been known to the owners of the yard since the air, when it emerged, smelt of the brewing operations. The judge therefore held that the public house had such a right by the "doctrine of lost grant." This doctrine states "that if a legal right is proved to have existed and been exercised for a number of years the law ought to presume that it had a legal origin." [13] So the owner of the cottages and yard had to unstop the well and endure the smell.

The reasoning employed by the courts in determining legal rights will often seem strange to an economist because many of the factors on which the decision turns are, to an economist, irrelevant. Because of this, situations which are, from an economic point of view, identical will be treated quite differently by the courts. The economic problem in all cases of harmful effects is how to maximise the value of production. In the case of *Bass v. Gregory* fresh air was drawn in through the well which facilitated the production of beer but foul air was expelled through the well which made life in the adjoining houses less pleasant. The economic problem was to decide which to choose: a lower cost of beer and wors- ened amenities in adjoining houses or a higher cost of beer and improved amenities. In deciding this question, the "doctrine of lost grant" is about as relevant as the colour of the judge's eyes. But it has to be remembered that the immediate question faced by the courts is *not* what shall be done by whom *but* who has the legal right to do what. It is always possible to modify by transactions on the market the initial legal delimitation of rights. And, of course, if such market transactions are costless, such a rearrangement of rights will always take place if it would lead to an increase in the value of production.

VI. THE COST OF MARKET TRANSACTIONS TAKEN INTO ACCOUNT

The argument has proceeded up to this point on the assumption (explicit in Sections III and IV and tacit in Section V) that there were no costs involved in carrying out market transactions. This is, of course, a very unrealistic assumption. In order to carry out a market transaction it is necessary to discover who it is that one wishes to deal with, to inform people that one wishes to deal and on what terms, to conduct negotiations leading up to a bargain, to draw up the contract, to undertake the inspection needed to make sure that the terms of the contract are being observed, and so on. These operations are often extremely costly, sufficiently costly at any rate to prevent many transactions that would be carried out in a world in which the pricing system worked without cost.

In earlier sections, when dealing with the problem of the rearrangement of legal rights through the market, it was argued that such a rearrangement would be made through the market whenever this would lead to an increase in the value of production. But this assumed costless market transactions. Once the costs of carrying out market transactions are taken into account it is clear that such a rearrangement of

[13] It may be asked why a lost grant could not also be presumed in the case of the confectioner who had operated one mortar for more than 60 years. The answer is that until the doctor built the consulting room at the end of his garden there was no nuisance. So the nuisance had not continued for many years. It is true that the confectioner in his affidavit referred to "an invalid lady who occupied the house upon one occasion, about thirty years before" who "requested him if possible to discontinue the use of the mortars before eight o'clock in the morning" and that there was some evidence that the garden wall had been subjected to vibration. But the court had little difficulty in disposing of this line of argument: ". . . this vibration, even if it existed at all, was so slight, and the complaint, if it can be called a complaint, of the invalid lady . . . was of so trifling a character, that . . . the Defendant's acts would not have given rise to any proceeding either at law or in equity" (11 Ch.D. 863). That is, the confectioner had not committed a nuisance until the doctor built his consulting room.

rights will only be undertaken when the increase in the value of production consequent upon the rearrangement is greater than the costs which would be involved in bringing it about. When it is less, the granting of an injunction (or the knowledge that it would be granted) or the liability to pay damages may result in an activity being discontinued (or may prevent its being started) which would be undertaken if market transactions were costless. In these conditions the initial delimitation of legal rights does have an effect on the efficiency with which the economic system operates. One arrangement of rights may bring about a greater value of production than any other. But unless this is the arrangement of rights established by the legal system, the costs of reaching the same result by altering and combining rights through the market may be so great that this optimal arrangement of rights, and the greater value of production which it would bring, may never be achieved. The part played by economic considerations in the process of delimiting legal rights will be discussed in the next section. In this section, I will take the initial delimitation of rights and the costs of carrying out market transactions as given.

It is clear that an alternative form of economic organisation which could achieve the same result at less cost than would be incurred by using the market would enable the value of production to be raised. As I explained many years ago, the firm represents such an alternative to organising production through market transactions.[14] Within the firm individual bargains between the various cooperating factors of production are eliminated and for a market transaction is substituted an administrative decision. The rearrangement of production then takes place without the need for bargains between the owners of

the factors of production. A landowner who has control of a large tract of land may devote his land to various uses taking into account the effect that the interrelations of the various activities will have on the net return of the land, thus rendering unnecessary bargains between those undertaking the various activities. Owners of a large building or of several adjoining properties in a given area may act in much the same way. In effect, using our earlier terminology, the firm would acquire the legal rights of all the parties and the rearrangement of activities would not follow on a rearrangement of rights by contract, but as a result of an administrative decision as to how the rights should be used.

It does not, of course, follow that the administrative costs of organising a transaction through a firm are inevitably less than the costs of the market transactions which are superseded. But where contracts are peculiarly difficult to draw up and an attempt to describe what the parties have agreed to do or not to do (e.g. the amount and kind of a smell or noise that they may make or will not make) would necessitate a lengthy and highly involved document, and, where, as is probable, a long-term contract would be desirable;[15] it would be hardly surprising if the emergence of a firm or the extension of the activities of an existing firm was not the solution adopted on many occasions to deal with the problem of harmful effects. This solution would be adopted whenever the administrative costs of the firm were less than the costs of the market transactions that it supersedes and the gains which would result from the rearrangement of activities greater than the firm's costs of organising them. I do not need to examine in great detail the character of this solution since I have explained what is involved in my earlier article.

But the firm is not the only possible answer to this problem. The administrative

[14] See Coase, "The Nature of the Firm," 4 *Economica*, New Series, 386 (1937). Reprinted in *Readings in Price Theory*, 331 (1952).

[15] For reasons explained in my earlier article, see *Readings in Price Theory*, n. 14 at 337.

497 The Problem of Social Cost

costs of organising transactions within the firm may also be high, and particularly so when many diverse activities are brought within the control of a single organisation. In the standard case of a smoke nuisance, which may affect a vast number of people engaged in a wide variety of activities, the administrative costs might well be so high as to make any attempt to deal with the problem within the confines of a single firm impossible. An alternative solution is direct government regulation. Instead of instituting a legal system of rights which can be modified by transactions on the market, the government may impose regulations which state what people must or must not do and which have to be obeyed. Thus, the government (by statute or perhaps more likely through an administrative agency) may, to deal with the problem of smoke nuisance, decree that certain methods of production should or should not be used (e.g. that smoke preventing devices should be installed or that coal or oil should not be burned) or may confine certain types of business to certain districts (zoning regulations).

The government is, in a sense, a super-firm (but of a very special kind) since it is able to influence the use of factors of production by administrative decision. But the ordinary firm is subject to checks in its operations because of the competition of other firms, which might administer the same activities at lower cost and also because there is always the alternative of market transactions as against organisation within the firm if the administrative costs become too great. The government is able, if it wishes, to avoid the market altogether, which a firm can never do. The firm has to make market agreements with the owners of the factors of production that it uses. Just as the government can conscript or seize property, so it can decree that factors of production should only be used in such-and-such a way. Such authoritarian methods save a lot of trouble (for those doing

the organising). Furthermore, the government has at its disposal the police and the other law enforcement agencies to make sure that its regulations are carried out.

It is clear that the government has powers which might enable it to get some things done at a lower cost than could a private organisation (or at any rate one without special governmental powers). But the governmental administrative machine is not itself costless. It can, in fact, on occasion be extremely costly. Furthermore, there is no reason to suppose that the restrictive and zoning regulations, made by a fallible administration subject to political pressures and operating without any competitive check, will necessarily always be those which increase the efficiency with which the economic system operates. Furthermore, such general regulations which must apply to a wide variety of cases will be enforced in some cases in which they are clearly inappropriate. From these considerations it follows that direct governmental regulation will not necessarily give better results than leaving the problem to be solved by the market or the firm. But equally there is no reason why, on occasion, such governmental administrative regulation should not lead to an improvement in economic efficiency. This would seem particularly likely when, as is normally the case with the smoke nuisance, a large number of people are involved and in which therefore the costs of handling the problem through the market or the firm may be high.

There is, of course, a further alternative, which is to do nothing about the problem at all. And given that the costs involved in solving the problem by regulations issued by the governmental administrative machine will often be heavy (particularly if the costs are interpreted to include all the consequences which follow from the Government engaging in this kind of activity), it will no doubt be commonly the case that the gain which would come from regulating the actions which give rise to the harmful effects will be less than the costs involved in Government regulation.

The discussion of the problem of harmful effects in this section (when the costs of market transactions are taken into account) is extremely inadequate. But at least it has made clear that the problem is one of choosing the appropriate social arrangement for dealing with the harmful effects. All solutions have costs and there is no reason to suppose that government regulation is called for simply because the problem is not well handled by the market or the firm. Satisfactory views on policy can only come from a patient study of how, in practice, the market, firms and governments handle the problem of harmful effects. Economists need to study the work of the broker in bringing parties together, the effectiveness of restrictive covenants, the problems of the large-scale real-estate development company, the operation of Government zoning and other regulating activities. It is my belief that economists, and policy-makers generally, have tended to over-estimate the advantages which come from governmental regulation. But this belief, even if justified, does not do more than suggest that government regulation should be curtailed. It does not tell us where the boundary line should be drawn. This, it seems to me, has to come from a detailed investigation of the actual results of handling the problem in different ways. But it would be unfortunate if this investigation were undertaken with the aid of a faulty economic analysis. The aim of this article is to indicate what the economic approach to the problem should be.

VII. THE LEGAL DELIMITATION OF RIGHTS AND THE ECONOMIC PROBLEM

The discussion in Section V not only served to illustrate the argument but also afforded a glimpse at the legal approach to the problem of harmful effects. The cases considered were all English but a similar selection of American cases could easily be made and the character of the reasoning would have been the same. Of course, if market transactions were costless, all that matters (questions of equity apart) is that the rights of the various parties should be well-defined and the results of legal actions easy to forecast. But as we have seen, the situation is quite different when market transactions are so costly as to make it difficult to change the arrangement of rights established by the law. In such cases, the courts directly influence economic activity. It would therefore seem desirable that the courts should understand the economic consequences of their decisions and should, insofar as this is possible without creating too much uncertainty about the legal position itself, take these consequences into account when making their decisions. Even when it is possible to change the legal delimitation of rights through market transactions, it is obviously desirable to reduce the need for such transactions and thus reduce the employment of resources in carrying them out.

A thorough examination of the presuppositions of the courts in trying such cases would be of great interest but I have not been able to attempt it. Nevertheless it is clear from a cursory study that the courts have often recognized the economic implications of their decisions and are aware (as many economists are not) of the reciprocal nature of the problem. Furthermore, from time to time, they take these economic implications into account, along with other factors, in arriving at their decisions. The American writers on this subject refer to the question in a more explicit fashion than do the British. Thus, to quote Prosser on Torts, a person may

> make use of his own property or . . . conduct his own affairs at the expense of some harm to his neighbors. He may operate a factory whose noise and smoke cause some

discomfort to others, so long as he keeps within reasonable bounds. It is only when his conduct is unreasonable, *in the light of its utility and the harm which results* [italics added], that it becomes a nuisance. . . . As it was said in an ancient case in regard to candle-making in a town, "Le utility del chose excusera le noisomeness del stink."

The world must have factories, smelters, oil refineries, noisy machinery and blasting, even at the expense of some inconvenience to those in the vicinity and the plaintiff may be required to accept some not unreasonable discomfort for the general good.[16]

The standard British writers do not state as explicitly as this that a comparison between the utility and harm produced is an element in deciding whether a harmful effect should be considered a nuisance. But similar views, if less strongly expressed, are to be found.[17] The doctrine that the harmful effect must be substantial before the court will act is, no doubt, in part a reflection of the fact that there will almost always be some gain to offset the harm. And in the reports of individual cases, it is clear that the judges have had in mind what would be lost as well as what would be gained in deciding whether to grant an injunction or award damages. Thus, in refusing to prevent the destruction of a prospect by a new building, the judge stated:

> I know no general rule of common law, which . . . says, that building so as to stop another's prospect is a nuisance. Was that the case, there could be no great towns; and

I must grant injunctions to all the new buildings in this town. . . .[18]

In *Webb v. Bird*[19] it was decided that it was not a nuisance to build a schoolhouse so near a windmill as to obstruct currents of air and hinder the working of the mill. An early case seems to have been decided in an opposite direction. Gale commented:

> In old maps of London a row of windmills appears on the heights to the north of London. Probably in the time of King James it was thought an alarming circumstance, as affecting the supply of food to the city, that anyone should build so near them as to take the wind out from their sails.[20]

In one of the cases discussed in section V, *Sturges v. Bridgman*, it seems clear that the judges were thinking of the economic consequences of alternative decisions. To the argument that if the principle that they seemed to be following:

> were carried out to its logical consequences, it would result in the most serious practical inconveniences, for a man might go—say into the midst of the tanneries of *Bermondsey*, or into any other locality devoted to any particular trade or manufacture of a noisy or unsavoury character, and by building a private residence upon a vacant piece of land put a stop to such trade or manufacture altogether,

the judges answered that

> whether anything is a nuisance or not is a question to be determined, not merely by an abstract consideration of the thing itself, but in reference to its circumstances; What would be a nuisance in *Belgrave Square* would not necessarily be so in *Bermondsey*; and where a locality is devoted to a particular trade or manufacture carried on by the traders or

[16] See W. L. Prosser, *The Law of Torts* 398–99, 412 (2d ed. 1955). The quotation about the ancient case concerning candle-making is taken from Sir James Fitzjames Stephen, *A General View of the Criminal Law of England* 106 (1890). Sir James Stephen gives no reference. He perhaps had in mind *Rex. v. Ronkett,* included in Seavey, Keeton and Thurston, *Cases on Torts* 604 (1950). A similar view to that expressed by Prosser is to be found in F. V. Harper and F. James, *The Law of Torts* 67–74 (1956); *Restatement, Torts* §§ 826, 827 and 828.

[17] See Winfield on *Torts* 541–48 (6th ed. T. E. Lewis 1954); Salmond on the *Law of Torts* 181–90 (12th ed. R.F.V. Heuston 1957); H. Street, *The Law of Torts* 221–29 (1959).

[18] *Attorney General v. Doughty,* 2 Ves. Sen. 453, 28 Eng. Rep. 290 (Ch. 1752). Compare in this connection the statement of an American judge, quoted in Prosser, *op. cit. supra* n. 16 at 413 n. 54: "Without smoke, Pittsburgh would have remained a very pretty village," Musmanno, J., in *Versailles Borough v. McKeesport Coal & Coke Co.,* 1935, 83 Pitts. Leg. J. 379, 385.

[19] 10 C.B. (N.S.) 268, 142 Eng. Rep. 445 (1861); 13 C.B. (N.S.) 841, 143 Eng. Rep. 332 (1863).

[20] See Gale on *Easements* 238, n. 6 (13th ed. M. Bowles 1959).

manufacturers in a particular and established manner not constituting a public nuisance, Judges and juries would be justified in finding, and may be trusted to find, that the trade or manufacture so carried on in that locality is not a private or actionable wrong.[21]

That the character of the neighborhood is relevant in deciding whether something is, or is not, a nuisance, is definitely established.

> He who dislikes the noise of traffic must not set up his abode in the heart of a great city. He who loves peace and quiet must not live in a locality devoted to the business of making boilers or steamships.[22]

What has emerged has been described as "planning and zoning by the judiciary." [23] Of course there are sometimes considerable difficulties in applying the criteria.[24]

An interesting example of the problem is found in *Adams v. Ursell* [25] in which a fried fish shop in a predominantly working-class district was set up near houses of "a much better character." England without fish-and-chips is a contradiction in terms and the case was clearly one of high importance. The judge commented:

> It was urged that an injunction would cause great hardship to the defendant and to the poor people who get food at his shop. The answer to that is that it does not follow that the defendant cannot carry on his business in another more suitable place somewhere in the neighbourhood. It by no means follows that because a fried fish shop is a nuisance in one place it is a nuisance in another.

In fact, the injunction which restrained Mr. Ursell from running his shop did not even extend to the whole street. So he was pre-

sumably able to move to other premises near houses of "a much worse character," the inhabitants of which would no doubt consider the availability of fish-and-chips to outweigh the pervading odour and "fog or mist" so graphically described by the plaintiff. Had there been no other "more suitable place in the neighbourhood," the case would have been more difficult and the decision might have been different. What would "the poor people" have had for food? No English judge would have said: "Let them eat cake."

The courts do not always refer very clearly to the economic problem posed by the cases brought before them but it seems probable that in the interpretation of words and phrases like "reasonable" or "common or ordinary use" there is some recognition, perhaps largely unconscious and certainly not very explicit, of the economic aspects of the questions at issue. A good example of this would seem to be the judgment in the Court of Appeals in *Andreae v. Selfridge and Company Ltd.*[26] In this case, a hotel (in Wigmore Street) was situated on part of an island site. The remainder of the site was acquired by Selfridges which demolished the existing buildings in order to erect another in their place. The hotel suffered a loss of custom in consequence of the noise and dust caused by the demolition. The owner of the hotel brought an action against Selfridges for damages. In the lower court, the hotel was awarded £4,500 damages. The case was then taken on appeal.

The judge who had found for the hotel proprietor in the lower court said:

> I cannot regard what the defendants did on the site of the first operation as having been commonly done in the ordinary use and occupation of land or houses. It is neither usual nor common, in this country, for people to excavate a site to a depth of 60 feet and then to erect upon that site a steel framework and fasten the steel frames to-

[21] 11 Ch.D. 865 (1879).

[22] Salmond on the *Law of Torts* 182 (12th ed. R.F.V. Heuston 1957).

[23] C. M. Haar, *Land-Use Planning, A Casebook on the Use, Misuse, and Re-use of Urban Land* 95 (1959).

[24] See, for example, *Rushmer v. Polsue and Alfieri, Ltd.* [1906] 1 Ch. 234, which deals with the case of a house in a quiet situation in a noisy district.

[25] [1913] 1 Ch. 269.

[26] [1938] 1 Ch. 1.

gether with rivets. . . . Nor is it, I think, a common or ordinary use of land, in this country, to act as the defendants did when they were dealing with the site of their second operation—namely, to demolish all the houses that they had to demolish, five or six of them I think, if not more, and to use for the purpose of demolishing them pneumatic hammers.

Sir Wilfred Greene, M.R., speaking for the Court of Appeals, first noted

that when one is dealing with temporary operations, such as demolition and re-building, everybody has to put up with a certain amount of discomfort, because operations of that kind cannot be carried on at all without a certain amount of noise and a certain amount of dust. Therefore, the rule with regard to interference must be read subject to this qualification. . . .

He then referred to the previous judgment:

With great respect to the learned judge, I take the view that he has not approached this matter from the correct angle. It seems to me that it is not possible to say . . . that the type of demolition, excavation and construction in which the defendant company was engaged in the course of these operations was of such an abnormal and unusual nature as to prevent the qualification to which I have referred coming into operation. It seems to me that, when the rule speaks of the common or ordinary use of land, it does not mean that the methods of using land and building on it are in some way to be stabilised for ever. As time goes on new inventions or new methods enable land to be more profitably used, either by digging down into the earth or by mounting up into the skies. Whether, from other points of view, that is a matter which is desirable for humanity is neither here nor there; but it is part of the normal use of land, to make use upon your land, in the matter of construction, of what particular type and what particular depth of foundations and particular height of building may be reasonable, in the circumstances, and in view of the developments of the day. . . . Guests at hotels are very easily upset. People coming to this hotel, who were accustomed to a quiet outlook at the back, coming back and finding demolition and building going on, may very well have taken the view that the particular merit of this

hotel no longer existed. That would be a misfortune for the plaintiff; but assuming that there was nothing wrong in the defendant company's works, assuming the defendant company was carrying on the demolition and its building, productive of noise though it might be, with all reasonable skill, and taking all reasonable precautions not to cause annoyance to its neighbors, then the plaintiff might lose all her clients in the hotel because they have lost the amenities of an open and quiet place behind, but she would have no cause of complaint. . . . [But those] who say that their interference with the comfort of their neighbors is justified because their operations are normal and usual and conducted with proper care and skill are under a specific duty . . . to use that reasonable and proper care and skill. It is not a correct attitude to take to say: 'We will go on and do what we like until somebody complains!' . . . Their duty is to take proper precautions and to see that the nuisance is reduced to a minimum. It is no answer for them to say: 'But this would mean that we should have to do the work more slowly than we would like to do it, or it would involve putting us to some extra expense.' All these questions are matters of common sense and degree, and quite clearly it would be unreasonable to expect people to conduct their work so slowly or so expensively, for the purpose of preventing a transient inconvenience, that the cost and trouble would be prohibitive. . . . In this case, the defendant company's attitude seems to have been to go on until somebody complained, and, further, that its desire to hurry its work and conduct it according to its own ideas and its own convenience was to prevail if there was a real conflict between it and the comfort of its neighbors. That . . . is not carrying out the obligation of using reasonable care and skill. . . . The effect comes to this . . . the plaintiff suffered an actionable nuisance; . . . she is entitled, not to a nominal sum, but to a substantial sum, based upon those principles . . . but in arriving at the sum . . . I have discounted any loss of custom . . . which might be due to the general loss of amenities owing to what was going on at the back. . . .

The upshot was that the damages awarded were reduced from £4,500 to £1,000.

The discussion in this section has, up to this point, been concerned with court decisions arising out of the common law relating to nuisance. Delimitation of rights in this area also comes about because of statutory enactments. Most economists would appear to assume that the aim of governmental action in this field is to extend the scope of the law of nuisance by designating as nuisances activities which would not be recognized as such by the common law. And there can be no doubt that some statutes, for example, the Public Health Acts, have had this effect. But not all Government enactments are of this kind. The effect of much of the legislation in this area is to protect businesses from the claims of those they have harmed by their actions. There is a long list of legalized nuisances.

The position has been summarized in *Halsbury's Laws of England* as follows:

> Where the legislature directs that a thing shall in all events be done or authorises certain works at a particular place for a specific purpose or grants powers with the intention that they shall be exercised, although leaving some discretion as to the mode of exercise, no action will lie at common law for nuisance or damage which is the inevitable result of carrying out the statutory powers so conferred. This is so whether the act causing the damage is authorised for public purposes or private profit. Acts done under powers granted by persons to whom Parliament has delegated authority to grant such powers, for example, under provisional orders of the Board of Trade, are regarded as having been done under statutory authority. In the absence of negligence it seems that a body exercising statutory powers will not be liable to an action merely because it might, by acting in a different way, have minimised an injury.

Instances are next given of freedom from liability for acts authorized:

> An action has been held not to be against a body exercising its statutory powers without negligence in respect of the flooding of land by water escaping from watercourses, from water pipes, from drains, or from a canal; the escape of fumes from sewers; the escape of sewage: the subsidence of a road over a sewer; vibration or noise caused by a

railway; fires caused by authorised acts; the pollution of a stream where statutory requirements to use the best known method of purifying before discharging the effluent have been satisfied; interference with a telephone or telegraph system by an electric tramway; the insertion of poles for tramways in the subsoil; annoyance caused by things reasonably necessary for the excavation of authorised works; accidental damage caused by the placing of a grating in a roadway; the escape of tar acid; or interference with the access of a frontager by a street shelter or safety railings on the edge of a pavement.[27]

The legal position in the United States would seem to be essentially the same as in England, except that the power of the legislatures to authorize what would otherwise be nuisances under the common law, at least without giving compensation to the person harmed, is somewhat more limited, as it is subject to constitutional restrictions.[28] Nonetheless, the power is there and cases more or less identical with the English cases can be found. The question has arisen in an acute form in connection with airports and the operation of aeroplanes. The case of *Delta Air Corporation v. Kersey, Kersey v. City of Atlanta*[29] is a good example. Mr. Kersey bought land and built a house on it. Some years later the City of Atlanta constructed an airport on land immediately adjoining that of Mr. Kersey. It was explained that his property was "a quiet, peaceful and proper location for a home before the airport was built, but dust, noises and low flying of airplanes caused by the operation of the airport have rendered his property unsuitable as a home," a state of affairs which was described in the report of the case with a wealth of distressing detail. The judge first referred to an earlier

[27] See 30 Halsbury, *Law of England* 690–91 (3d ed. 1960), Article on Public Authorities and Public Officers.
[28] See Prosser, *op. cit. supra* n. 16 at 421; Harper and James, *op. cit. supra* n. 16 at 86–87.
[29] Supreme Court of Georgia 193 Ga. 862, 20 S.E. 2d 245 (1942).

case, *Thrasher v. City of Atlanta*[30] in which it was noted that the City of Atlanta had been expressly authorized to operate an airport.

> By this franchise aviation was recognised as a lawful business and also as an enterprise affected with a public interest . . . all persons using [the airport] in the manner contemplated by law are within the protection and immunity of the franchise granted by the municipality. An airport is not a nuisance per se, although it might become such from the manner of its construction or operation.

Since aviation was a lawful business affected with a public interest and the construction of the airport was authorized by statute, the judge next referred to *Georgia Railroad and Banking Co. v. Maddox*[31] in which it was said:

> Where a railroad terminal yard is located and its construction authorized, under statutory powers, if it be constructed and operated in a proper manner, it cannot be adjudged a nuisance. Accordingly, injuries and inconveniences to persons residing near such a yard, from noises of locomotives, rumbling of cars, vibrations produced thereby, and smoke, cinders, soot and the like, which result from the ordinary and necessary, therefore proper, use and operation of such a yard, are not nuisances, but are the necessary concomitants of the franchise granted.

In view of this, the judge decided that the noise and dust complained of by Mr. Kersey "may be deemed to be incidental to the proper operation of an airport, and as such they cannot be said to constitute a nuisance." But the complaint against low flying was different:

> . . . can it be said that flights . . . at such a low height [25 to 50 feet above Mr. Kersey's house] as to be imminently dangerous to . . . life and health . . . are a necessary concomitant of an airport? We do not think this question can be answered in the affirmative. No reason appears why the city could not obtain lands of an area [sufficiently large] . . . as not to require such

low flights. . . . For the sake of public convenience adjoining-property owners must suffer such inconvenience from noise and dust as result from the usual and proper operation of an airport, but their private rights are entitled to preference in the eyes of the law where the inconvenience is not one demanded by a properly constructed and operated airport.

Of course this assumed that the City of Atlanta could prevent the low flying and continue to operate the airport. The judge therefore added:

> From all that appears, the conditions causing the low flying may be remedied; but if on the trial it should appear that it is indispensable to the public interest that the airport should continue to be operated in its present condition, it may be said that the petitioner should be denied injunctive relief.

In the course of another aviation case, *Smith v. New England Aircraft Co.*,[32] the court surveyed the law in the United States regarding the legalizing of nuisances and it is apparent that, in the broad, it is very similar to that found in England:

> It is the proper function of the legislative department of government in the exercise of the police power to consider the problems and risks that arise from the use of new inventions and endeavor to adjust private rights and harmonize conflicting interests by comprehensive statutes for the public welfare. . . . There are . . . analogies where the invasion of the airspace over underlying land by noise, smoke, vibration, dust and disagreeable odors, having been authorized by the legislative department of government and not being in effect a condemnation of the property although in some measure depreciating its market value, must be borne by the landowner without compensation or remedy. Legislative sanction makes that lawful which otherwise might be a nuisance. Examples of this are damages to adjacent land arising from smoke, vibration and noise in the operation of a railroad . . . ; the noise of ringing factory bells . . . ; the abatement of nuisances . . . ; the erection of steam engines and furnaces . . . ; unpleas-

[30] 178 Ga. 514, 173 S.E. 817 (1934).
[31] 116 Ga. 64, 42 S.E. 315 (1902).

[32] 270 Mass. 511, 523, 170 N.E. 385, 390 (1930).

ant odors connected with sewers, oil refining and storage of naphtha. . . .

Most economists seem to be unaware of all this. When they are prevented from sleeping at night by the roar of jet planes overhead (publicly authorized and perhaps publicly operated), are unable to think (or rest) in the day because of the noise and vibration from passing trains (publicly authorized and perhaps publicly operated), find it difficult to breathe because of the odour from a local sewage farm (publicly authorized and perhaps publicly operated) and are unable to escape because their driveways are blocked by a road obstruction (without any doubt, publicly devised), their nerves frayed and mental balance disturbed, they proceed to declaim about the disadvantages of private enterprise and the need for Government regulation.

While most economists seem to be under a misapprehension concerning the character of the situation with which they are dealing, it is also the case that the activities which they would like to see stopped or curtailed may well be socially justified. It is all a question of weighing up the gains that would accrue from eliminating these harmful effects against the gains that accrue from allowing them to continue. Of course, it is likely that an extension of Government economic activity will often lead to this protection against action for nuisance being pushed further than is desirable. For one thing, the Government is likely to look with a benevolent eye on enterprises which it is itself promoting. For another, it is possible to describe the committing of a nuisance by public enterprise in a much more pleasant way than when the same thing is done by private enterprise. In the words of Lord Justice Sir Alfred Denning:

> . . . the significance of the social revolution of today is that, whereas in the past the balance was much too heavily in favor of the rights of property and freedom of contract, Parliament has repeatedly intervened

so as to give the public good its proper place.[33]

There can be little doubt that the Welfare State is likely to bring an extension of that immunity from liability for damage, which economists have been in the habit of condemning (although they have tended to assume that this immunity was a sign of too little Government intervention in the economic system). For example, in Britain, the powers of local authorities are regarded as being either absolute or conditional. In the first category, the local authority has no discretion in exercising the power conferred on it. "The absolute power may be said to cover all the necessary consequences of its direct operation even if such consequences amount to nuisance." On the other hand, a conditional power may only be exercised in such a way that the consequences do not constitute a nuisance.

> It is the intention of the legislature which determines whether a power is absolute or conditional. . . . [As] there is the possibility that the social policy of the legislature may change from time to time, a power which in one era would be construed as being conditional, might in another era be interpreted as being absolute in order to further the policy of the Welfare State. This point is one which should be borne in mind when considering some of the older cases upon this aspect of the law of nuisance.[34]

It would seem desirable to summarize the burden of this long section. The problem which we face in dealing with actions which have harmful effects is not simply one of restraining those responsible for them. What has to be decided is whether the gain from preventing the harm is greater than the loss which would be suffered elsewhere as a result of stopping the action which produces the harm. In a world in which there are costs of rearranging the rights established by the legal system, the

[33] See Sir Alfred Denning, *Freedom Under the Law* 71 (1949).
[34] M. B. Cairns, *The Law of Tort in Local Government* 28–32 (1954).

courts, in cases relating to nuisance, are, in effect, making a decision on the economic problem and determining how resources are to be employed. It was argued that the courts are conscious of this and that they often make, although not always in a very explicit fashion, a comparison between what would be gained and what lost by preventing actions which have harmful effects. But the delimitation of rights is also the result of statutory enactments. Here we also find evidence of an appreciation of the reciprocal nature of the problem. While statutory enactments add to the list of nuisances, action is also taken to legalize what would otherwise be nuisances under the common law. The kind of situation which economists are prone to consider as requiring corrective Government action is, in fact, often the result of Government action. Such action is not necessarily unwise. But there is a real danger that extensive Government intervention in the economic system may lead to the protection of those responsible for harmful effects being carried too far.

VIII. PIGOU'S TREATMENT IN "THE ECONOMICS OF WELFARE"

The fountainhead for the modern economic analysis of the problem discussed in this article is Pigou's *Economics of Welfare* and, in particular, that section of Part II which deals with divergences between social and private net products which come about because

> one person A, in the course of rendering some service, for which payment is made, to a second person B, incidentally also renders services or disservices to other persons (not producers of like services), of such a sort that payment cannot be exacted from the benefited parties or compensation enforced on behalf of the injured parties.[35]

[35] A. C. Pigou, *The Economics of Welfare* 183 (4th ed. 1932). My references will all be to the fourth edition but the argument and examples examined in this article remained substantially un-

Pigou tells us that his aim in Part II of *The Economics of Welfare* is

> to ascertain how far the free play of self-interest, acting under the existing legal system, tends to distribute the country's resources in the way most favorable to the production of a large national dividend, and how far it is feasible for State action to improve upon 'natural' tendencies.[36]

To judge from the first part of this statement, Pigou's purpose is to discover whether any improvements could be made in the existing arrangements which determine the use of resources. Since Pigou's conclusion is that improvements could be made, one might have expected him to continue by saying that he proposed to set out the changes required to bring them about. Instead, Pigou adds a phrase which contrasts "natural" tendencies with State action, which seems in some sense to equate the present arrangements with "natural" tendencies and to imply that what is required to bring about these improvements is State action (if feasible). That this is more or less Pigou's position is evident from Chapter I of Part II.[37] Pigou starts by referring to "optimistic followers of the classical economists" [38] who have argued that the value of production would be maximised if the Government refrained from any interference in the economic system and the economic arrangements were those which came about "naturally." Pigou goes on to say that if self-interest does promote economic welfare, it is because human institutions have been devised to make it so. (This part of Pigou's argument, which he devel-

changed from the first edition in 1920 to the fourth in 1932. A large part (but not all) of this analysis had appeared previously in *Wealth and Welfare* (1912).

[36] *Id.* at xii.

[37] *Id.* at 127–30.

[38] In *Wealth and Welfare*, Pigou attributes the "optimism" to Adam Smith himself and not to his followers. He there refers to the "highly optimistic theory of Adam Smith that the national dividend, in given circumstances of demand and supply, tends 'naturally' to a maximum" (p. 104).

ops with the aid of a quotation from Cannan, seems to me to be essentially correct.) Pigou concludes:

> But even in the most advanced States there are failures and imperfections. . . . there are many obstacles that prevent a community's resources from being distributed . . . in the most efficient way. The study of these constitutes our present problem. . . . its purposes is essentially practical. It seeks to bring into clearer light some of the ways in which it now is, or eventually may become, feasible for governments to control the play of economic forces in such wise as to promote the economic welfare, and through that, the total welfare, of their citizens as a whole.[39]

Pigou's underlying thought would appear to be: Some have argued that no State action is needed. But the system has performed as well as it has because of State action. Nonetheless, there are still imperfections. What additional State action is required?

If this is a correct summary of Pigou's position, its inadequacy can be demonstrated by examining the first example he gives of a divergence between private and social products.

> It might happen . . . that costs are thrown upon people not directly concerned, through, say, uncompensated damage done to surrounding woods by sparks from railway engines. All such effects must be included—some of them will be positive, others negative elements—in reckoning up the social net product of the marginal increment of any volume of resources turned into any use or place.[40]

The example used by Pigou refers to a real situation. In Britain, a railway does not normally have to compensate those who suffer damage by fire caused by sparks from an engine. Taken in conjunction with what he says in Chapter 9 of Part II, I take Pigou's policy recommendations to be, first, that there should be State action to correct this "natural" situation and, second, that

the railways should be forced to compensate those whose woods are burnt. If this is a correct interpretation of Pigou's position, I would argue that the first recommendation is based on a misapprehension of the facts and that the second is not necessarily desirable.

Let us consider the legal position. Under the heading "Sparks from engines," we find the following in Halsbury's Laws of England:

> If railway undertakers use steam engines on their railway without express statutory authority to do so, they are liable, irrespective of any negligence on their part, for fires caused by sparks from engines. Railway undertakers are, however, generally given statutory authority to use steam engines on their railway; accordingly, if an engine is constructed with the precautions which science suggests against fire and is used without negligence, they are not responsible at common law for any damage which may be done by sparks. . . . In the construction of an engine the undertaker is bound to use all the discoveries which science has put within its reach in order to avoid doing harm, provided they are such as it is reasonable to require the company to adopt, having proper regard to the likelihood of the damage and to the cost and convenience of the remedy; but it is not negligence on the part of an undertaker if it refuses to use an apparatus the efficiency of which is open to bona fide doubt.

To this general rule, there is a statutory exception arising from the Railway (Fires) Act, 1905, as amended in 1923. This concerns agricultural land or agricultural crops.

> In such a case the fact that the engine was used under statutory powers does not affect the liability of the company in an action for the damage. . . . These provisions, however, only apply where the claim for damage . . . does not exceed £200, [£100 in the 1905 Act] and where written notice of the occurrence of the fire and the intention to claim has been sent to the company within seven days of the occurrence of the damage and particulars of the damage in writing showing the amount of the claim in

[39] Pigou, *op. cit. supra* n. 35 at 129–30.
[40] *Id.* at 134.

money not exceeding £200 have been sent to the company within twenty-one days.

Agricultural land does not include moorland or buildings and agricultural crops do not include those led away or stacked.[41] I have not made a close study of the parliamentary history of this statutory exception, but to judge from debates in the House of Commons in 1922 and 1923, this exception was probably designed to help the smallholder.[42]

Let us return to Pigou's example of uncompensated damage to surrounding woods caused by sparks from railway engines. This is presumably intended to show how it is possible "for State action to improve on 'natural' tendencies." If we treat Pigou's example as referring to the position before 1905, or as being an arbitrary example (in that he might just as well have written "surrounding buildings" instead of "surrounding woods"), then it is clear that the reason why compensation was not paid must have been that the railway had statutory authority to run steam engines (which relieved it of liability for fires caused by sparks). That this was the legal position was established in 1860, in a case, oddly enough, which concerned the burning of surrounding woods by a railway,[43] and the law on this point has not been changed (apart from the one exception) by a century of railway legislation, including nationalisation. If we treat Pigou's example of "uncompensated damage done to surrounding woods by sparks from railway engines" literally, and assume that it refers to the period after 1905, then it is clear that the reason why compensation was not paid must have been that the damage was more than £100 (in the first edition of *The*

Economics of Welfare*) or more than £200 (in later editions) or that the owner of the wood failed to notify the railway in writing within seven days of the fire or did not send particulars of the damage, in writing, within twenty-one days. In the real world, Pigou's example could only exist as a result of a deliberate choice of the legislature. It is not, of course, easy to imagine the construction of a railway in a state of nature. The nearest one can get to this is presumably a railway which uses steam engines "without express statutory authority." However, in this case the railway would be obliged to compensate those whose woods it burnt down. That is to say, compensation would be paid in the absence of Government action. The only circumstances in which compensation would not be paid would be those in which there had been Government action. It is strange that Pigou, who clearly thought it desirable that compensation should be paid, should have chosen this particular example to demonstrate how it is possible "for State action to improve on 'natural' tendencies."

Pigou seems to have had a faulty view of the facts of the situation. But it also seems likely that he was mistaken in his economic analysis. It is not necessarily desirable that the railway should be required to compensate those who suffer damage by fires caused by railway engines. I need not show here that, if the railway could make a bargain with everyone having property adjoining the railway line and there were no costs involved in making such bargains, it would not matter whether the railway was liable for damage caused by fires or not. This question has been treated at length in earlier sections. The problem is whether it would be desirable to make the railway liable in conditions in which it is too expensive for such bargains to be made. Pigou clearly thought it was desirable to force the railway to pay compensation and it is easy to see the kind of argument that would have led him to this conclusion. Sup-

[41] See 31 Halsbury, *Laws of England* 474–75 (3d ed. 1960), Article on Railways and Canals, from which this summary of the legal position, and all quotations, are taken.

[42] See 152 H.C. Deb. 2622–63 (1922); 161 H.C. Deb. 2935–55 (1923).

[43] *Vaughan v. Taff Vale Railway Co.*, 3 H. and N. 743 (Ex. 1858) and 5 H. and N. 679 (Ex. 1860).

pose a railway is considering whether to run an additional train or to increase the speed of an existing train or to install spark-preventing devices on its engines. If the railway were not liable for fire damage, then, when making these decisions, it would not take into account as a cost the increase in damage resulting from the additional train or the faster train or the failure to install spark-preventing devices. This is the source of the divergence between private and social net products. It results in the railway performing acts which will lower the value of total production—and which it would not do if it were liable for the damage. This can be shown by means of an arithmetical example.

Consider a railway, which is *not* liable for damage by fires caused by sparks from its engines, which runs two trains per day on a certain line. Suppose that running one train per day would enable the railway to perform services worth $150 per annum and running two trains a day would enable the railway to perform services worth $250 per annum. Suppose further that the cost of running one train is $50 per annum and two trains $100 per annum. Assuming perfect competition, the cost equals the fall in the value of production elsewhere due to the employment of additional factors of production by the railway. Clearly the railway would find it profitable to run two trains per day. But suppose that running one train per day would destroy by fire crops worth (on an average over the year) $60 and two trains a day would result in the destruction of crops worth $120. In these circumstances running one train per day would raise the value of total production but the running of a second train would reduce the value of total production. The second train would enable additional railway services worth $100 per annum to be performed. But the fall in the value of production elsewhere would be $110 per annum; $50 as a result of the employment of additional factors of production and $60

as a result of the destruction of crops. Since it would be better if the second train were not run and since it would not run if the railway were liable for damage caused to crops, the conclusion that the railway should be made liable for the damage seems irresistible. Undoubtedly it is this kind of reasoning which underlies the Pigovian position.

The conclusion that it would be better if the second train did not run is correct. The conclusion that it is desirable that the railway should be made liable for the damage it causes is wrong. Let us change our assumption concerning the rule of liability. Suppose that the railway is liable for damage from fires caused by sparks from the engine. A farmer on lands adjoining the railway is then in the position that, if his crop is destroyed by fires caused by the railway, he will receive the market price from the railway; but if his crop is not damaged, he will receive the market price by sale. It therefore becomes a matter of indifference to him whether his crop is damaged by fire or not. The position is very different when the railway is *not* liable. Any crop destruction through railway-caused fires would then reduce the receipts of the farmer. He would therefore take out of cultivation any land for which the damage is likely to be greater than the net return of the land (for reasons explained at length in Section III). A change from a regime in which the railway is *not* liable for damage to one in which it *is* liable is likely therefore to lead to an increase in the amount of cultivation on lands adjoining the railway. It will also, of course, lead to an increase in the amount of crop destruction due to railway-caused fires.

Let us return to our arithmetical example. Assume that, with the changed rule of liability, there is a doubling in the amount of crop destruction due to railway-caused fires. With one train per day, crops worth $120 would be destroyed each year and two trains per day would lead to the destruction of crops worth $240. We saw previously that it would not be profitable to run the second train if the railway had to pay $60 per annum as compensation for damage. With damage at $120 per annum the loss from running the second train would be $60 greater. But now let us consider the first train. The value of the transport services furnished by the first train is $150. The cost of running the train is $50. The amount that the railway would have to pay out as compensation for damage is $120. It follows that it would not be profitable to run any trains. With the figures in our example we reach the following result: if the railway is not liable for fire-damage, two trains per day would be run; if the railway is liable for fire-damage, it would cease operations altogether. Does this mean that it is better that there should be no railway? This question can be resolved by considering what would happen to the value of total production if it were decided to exempt the railway from liability for fire-damage, thus bringing it into operation (with two trains per day).

The operation of the railway would enable transport services worth $250 to be performed. It would also mean the employment of factors of production which would reduce the value of production elsewhere by $100. Furthermore it would mean the destruction of crops worth $120. The coming of the railway will also have led to the abandonment of cultivation of some land. Since we know that, had this land been cultivated, the value of the crops destroyed by fire would have been $120, and since it is unlikely that the total crop on this land would have been destroyed, it seems reasonable to suppose that the value of the crop yield on this land would have been higher than this. Assume it would have been $160. But the abandonment of cultivation would have released factors of production for employment elsewhere. All we know is that the amount by which the value of production elsewhere will increase will be less than $160. Suppose that it is $150. Then the gain from operating the railway would be $250 (the value of the transport services) minus $100 (the cost of the factors of production) minus $120 (the value of crops destroyed by fire) minus $160 (the fall in the value of crop production due to the abandonment of cultivation) plus $150 (the value of production elsewhere of the released factors of production). Overall, operating the railway will increase the value of total production by $20. With these figures it is clear that it is better that the railway should not be liable for the damage it causes, thus enabling it to operate profitably. Of course, by altering the figures, it could be shown that there are other cases in which it would be desirable that the railway should be liable for the damage it causes. It is enough for my purpose to show that, from an economic point of view, a situation in which there is "uncompensated damage done to surrounding woods by sparks from railway engines" is not necessarily undesirable. Whether it is desirable or not depends on the particular circumstances.

How is it that the Pigovian analysis seems to give the wrong answer? The reason is that Pigou does not seem to have noticed that his analysis is dealing with an entirely different question. The analysis as such is correct. But it is quite illegitimate for Pigou to draw the particular conclusion he does. The question at issue is not whether it is desirable to run an additional train or a faster train or to install smoke-preventing devices; the question at issue is whether it is desirable to have a system in which the railway has to compensate those who suffer damage from the fires which it causes or one in which the railway does not have to compensate them. When an economist is comparing alternative social arrangements, the proper procedure is to compare the total social product yielded by these different arrangements. The comparison of private and social products is neither here nor there. A simple example will demonstrate this. Imagine a town in which there are traffic lights. A motorist approaches an intersection and stops because the light is red. There are no cars approaching the intersection on the other street. If the motorist ignored the red signal, no accident would occur and the total product would increase because the motorist would arrive earlier at his destination. Why does he not do this? The reason is that if he ignored the light he would be fined. The private product from crossing the street is less than the social product. Should we conclude from this that the total product would be greater if there were no fines for failing to obey traffic signals? The Pigovian analysis shows us that it is possible to conceive of better worlds than the one in which we live. But the problem is to devise practical arrangements which will correct defects in one part of the system without causing more serious harm in other parts.

I have examined in considerable detail one example of a divergence between private and social products and I do not propose to make any further examination of Pigou's analytical system. But the main discussion of the problem considered in this article is to be found in that part of Chapter 9 in Part II which deals with Pigou's second class of divergence and it is of interest to see how Pigou develops his argument. Pigou's own description of this second class of divergence was quoted at the beginning of this section. Pigou distinguishes between the case in which a person renders services for which he receives no payment and the case in which a person renders disservices and compensation is not given to the injured parties. Our main attention has, of course, centred on this second case. It is therefore rather astonishing to find, as was pointed out to me by Professor Francesco Forte, that the problem of the smoking chimney—the "stock instance" [44] or "classroom example" [45] of the second case—is used by Pigou as an example of the first case (services rendered without payment) and is never mentioned, at any rate explicitly, in connection with the second case.[46] Pigou points out that factory owners who devote resources to preventing their chimneys from smoking render services for which they receive no payment. The implication, in the light of Pigou's discussion later in the chapter, is that a factory owner with a smokey chimney should be given a bounty to induce him to install smoke-preventing devices. Most modern economists would suggest that the owner of the factory with the smokey chimney should be taxed. It seems a pity that economists (apart from Professor Forte) do not seem to have noticed this feature of Pigou's treatment since a realisation that the problem could be tackled in either of these two ways would probably have led to an explicit recognition of its reciprocal nature.

In discussing the second case (disservices without compensation to those damaged), Pigou says that they are rendered "when the owner of a site in a residential quarter of a city builds a factory there and so destroys a great part of the amenities of neighbouring sites; or, in a less degree, when he uses his site in such a way as to spoil the lighting of the house opposite; or when he invests resources in erecting buildings in a crowded centre, which by contracting the air-space and the playing room of the neighbourhood, tend to injure the health and efficiency of the families living there." [47] Pigou is, of course, quite right to describe such actions as "uncharged disservices." But he is wrong when he describes these

[44] Sir Dennis Robertson, I *Lectures on Economic Principles* 162 (1957).

[45] E. J. Mishan, "The Meaning of Efficiency in Economics," 189, *The Bankers' Magazine* 482 (June 1960).

[46] Pigou, *op. cit. supra* n. 35 at 184.

[47] *Id.* at 185–86.

actions as "anti-social."[48] They may or may not be. It is necessary to weigh the harm against the good that will result. Nothing could be more "anti-social" than to oppose any action which causes any harm to anyone.

The example with which Pigou opens his discussion of "uncharged disservices" is not, as I have indicated, the case of the smokey chimney but the case of the overrunning rabbits: ". . . incidental uncharged disservices are rendered to third parties when the game-preserving activities of one occupier involve the overrunning of a neighboring occupier's land by rabbits. . . ." This example is of extraordinary interest, not so much because the economic analysis of the case is essentially any different from that of the other examples, but because of the peculiarities of the legal position and the light it throws on the part which economics can play in what is apparently the purely legal question of the delimitation of rights.

The problem of legal liability for the actions of rabbits is part of the general subject of liability for animals.[49] I will, although with reluctance, confine my dis-

cussion to rabbits. The early cases relating to rabbits concerned the relations between the lord of the manor and commoners, since, from the thirteenth century on, it became usual for the lord of the manor to stock the commons with conies (rabbits), both for the sake of the meat and the fur. But in 1597, in *Boulston*'s case, an action was brought by one landowner against a neighbouring landowner, alleging that the defendant had made coney-burrows and that the conies had increased and had destroyed the plaintiff's corn. The action failed for the reason that

> . . . so soon as the coneys come on his neighbor's land he may kill them, for they are *ferae naturae*, and he who makes the coney-boroughs has no property in them, and he shall not be punished for the damage which the coneys do in which he has no property, and which the other may lawfully kill.[50]

As *Boulston*'s case has been treated as binding—Bray, J., in 1919, said that he was not aware that *Boulston*'s case has ever been overruled or questioned[51]—Pigou's rabbit example undoubtedly represented the legal position at the time *The Economics of Welfare* was written.[52] And in this case, it is not far from the truth to say that the state of affairs which Pigou describes came about because of an absence of Government action (at any rate in the form of statutory enactments) and was the result of "natural" tendencies.

Nonetheless, *Boulston*'s case is something of a legal curiosity and Professor Williams makes no secret of his distaste for this decision:

> The conception of liability in nuisance as being based upon ownership is the result, apparently, of a confusion with the action of cattle-trespass, and runs counter both to principle and to the medieval authorities on

---

[48] *Id.* at 186 n.1. For similar unqualified statements see Pigou's lecture "Some Aspects of the Housing Problem" in B. S. Rowntree and A. C. Pigou, "Lectures on Housing," in 18 *Manchester Univ. Lectures* (1914).

[49] See G. L. Williams, *Liability for Animals— An Account of the Development and Present Law of Tortious Liability for Animals. Distress Damage Feasant and the Duty to Fence, in Great Britain, Northern Ireland and the Common Law Dominions* (1939). Part Four, "The Action of Nuisance, in Relation to Liability for Animals," 236–62, is especially relevant to our discussion. The problem of liability for rabbits is discussed in this part, 238–47. I do not know how far the common law in the United States regarding liability for animals has diverged from that in Britain. In some Western States of the United States, the English common law regarding the duty to fence has not been followed, in part because "the considerable amount of open, uncleared land made it a matter of public policy to allow cattle to run at large" (Williams, *op. cit. supra* 227). This affords a good example of how a different set of circumstances may make it economically desirable to change the legal rule regarding the delimitation of rights.

[50] 5 Coke (Vol. 3) 104 b. 77 Eng. Rep., 216, 217.
[51] See *Stearn v. Prentice Bros. Ltd.* (1919), 1 K.B., 395, 397.
[52] I have not looked into recent cases. The legal position has also been modified by statutory enactments.

the escape of water, smoke and filth. . . . The prerequisite of any satisfactory treatment of the subject is the final abandonment of the pernicious doctrine in *Boulston's* case. . . . Once *Boulston's* case disappears, the way will be clear for a rational restatement of the whole subject, on lines that will harmonize with the principles prevailing in the rest of the law of nuisance.[53]

The judges in *Boulston's* case were, of course, aware that their view of the matter depended on distinguishing this case from one involving nuisance:

> This cause is not like to the cases put, on the other side, of erecting a lime-kiln, dyehouse, or the like; for there the annoyance is by the act of the parties who make them; but it is not so here, for the conies of themselves went into the plaintiff's land, and he might take them when they came upon his land, and make profit of them.[54]

Professor Williams comments:

> Once more the atavistic idea is emerging that the animals are guilty and not the landowner. It is not, of course, a satisfactory principle to introduce into a modern law of nuisance. If A. erects a house or plants a tree so that the rain runs or drips from it on to B.'s land, this is A.'s act for which he is liable; but if A. introduces rabbits into his land so that they escape from it into B.'s, this is the act of the rabbits for which A. is not liable—such is the specious distinction resulting from *Boulston's* case.[55]

It has to be admitted that the decision in *Boulston's* case seems a little odd. A man may be liable for damage caused by smoke or unpleasant smells, without it being necessary to determine whether he owns the smoke or the smell. And the rule in *Boulston's* case has not always been followed in cases dealing with other animals. For example, in *Bland v. Yates*,[56] it was decided that an injunction could be granted to prevent someone from keeping an *unusual and excessive* collection of

manure in which flies bred and which infested a neighbour's house. The question of who owned the flies was not raised. An economist would not wish to object because legal reasoning sometimes appears a little odd. But there is a sound economic reason for supporting Professor Williams' view that the problem of liability for animals (and particularly rabbits) should be brought within the ordinary law of nuisance. The reason is not that the man who harbours rabbits is solely responsible for the damage; the man whose crops are eaten is equally responsible. And given that the costs of market transactions make a rearrangement of rights impossible, unless we know the particular circumstances, we cannot say whether it is desirable or not to make the man who harbours rabbits responsible for the damage committed by the rabbits on neighbouring properties. The objection to the rule in *Boulston's* case is that, under it, the harbourer of rabbits can *never* be liable. It fixes the rule of liability at one pole: and this is as undesirable, from an economic point of view, as fixing the rule at the other pole and making the harbourer of rabbits always liable. But, as we saw in Section VII, the law of nuisance, as it is in fact handled by the courts, is flexible and allows for a comparison of the utility of an act with the harm it produces. As Professor Williams says: "The whole law of nuisance is an attempt to reconcile and compromise between conflicting interests. . . ."[57] To bring the problem of rabbits within the ordinary law of nuisance would not mean *inevitably* making the harbourer of rabbits liable for damage committed by the rabbits. This is not to say that the sole task of the courts in such cases is to make a comparison between the harm and the utility of an act. Nor is it to be expected that the courts will always decide correctly after making such a comparison. But unless the courts act very foolishly, the ordinary law of nuisance would seem likely

---

[53] Williams, *op. cit. supra* n. 49 at 242, 258.

[54] *Boulston v. Hardy, Cro. Eliz.,* 547, 548, 77 Eng. Rep. 216.

[55] Williams, *op. cit. supra* n. 49 at 243.

[56] 58 Sol.J. 612 (1913–1914).

[57] Williams, *op. cit. supra* n. 49 at 259.

to give economically more satisfactory results than adopting a rigid rule. Pigou's case of the overrunning rabbits affords an excellent example of how problems of law and economics are interrelated, even though the correct policy to follow would seem to be different from that envisioned by Pigou.

Pigou allows one exception to his conclusion that there is a divergence between private and social products in the rabbit example. He adds: ". . . unless . . . the two occupiers stand in the relation of landlord and tenant, so that compensation is given in an adjustment of the rent." [58] This qualification is rather surprising since Pigou's first class of divergence is largely concerned with the difficulties of drawing up satisfactory contracts between landlords and tenants. In fact, all the recent cases on the problem of rabbits cited by Professor Williams involved disputes between landlords and tenants concerning sporting rights.[59] Pigou seems to make a distinction between the case in which no contract is possible (the second class) and that in which the contract is unsatisfactory (the first class). Thus he says that the second class of divergences between private and social net product

> cannot, like divergences due to tenancy laws, be mitigated by a modification of the contractual relation between any two contracting parties, because the divergence arises out of a service or disservice rendered to persons other than the contracting parties.[60]

But the reason why some activities are not the subject of contracts is exactly the same as the reason why some contracts are commonly unsatisfactory—it would cost too much to put the matter right. Indeed, the two cases are really the same since the contracts are unsatisfactory because they do not cover certain activities. The exact bearing of the discussion of the first class of divergence on Pigou's main argument is

difficult to discover. He shows that in some circumstances contractual relations between landlord and tenant may result in a divergence between private and social products.[61] But he also goes on to show that Government-enforced compensation schemes and rent-controls will also produce divergences.[62] Furthermore, he shows that, when the Government is in a similar position to a private landlord, e.g. when granting a franchise to a public utility, exactly the same difficulties arise as when private individuals are involved.[63] The discussion is interesting but I have been unable to discover what general conclusions about economic policy, if any, Pigou expects us to draw from it.

Indeed, Pigou's treatment of the problems considered in this article is extremely elusive and the discussion of his views raises almost insuperable difficulties of interpretation. Consequently it is impossible to be sure that one has understood what Pigou really meant. Nevertheless, it is difficult to resist the conclusion, extraordinary though this may be in an economist of Pigou's stature, that the main source of this obscurity is that Pigou had not thought his position through.

IX. THE PIGOVIAN TRADITION

It is strange that a doctrine as faulty as that developed by Pigou should have been so influential, although part of its success has probably been due to the lack of clarity in the exposition. Not being clear, it was never clearly wrong. Curiously enough, this obscurity in the source has not prevented the emergence of a fairly well-defined oral tradition. What economists think they learn from Pigou, and what they tell their students, which I term the Pigovian tradition, is reasonably clear. I propose to show the inadequacy of this Pigovian tradition by

---

[58] Pigou, *op. cit. supra* n. 35 at 185.
[59] Williams, *op. cit. supra* n. 49 at 244–47.
[60] Pigou, *op. cit. supra* n. 35 at 192.

[61] *Id.* 174–75.
[62] *Id.* 177–83.
[63] *Id.* 175–77.

demonstrating that both the analysis and the policy conclusions which it supports are incorrect.

I do not propose to justify my view as to the prevailing opinion by copious references to the literature. I do this partly because the treatment in the literature is usually so fragmentary, often involving little more than a reference to Pigou plus some explanatory comment, that detailed examination would be inappropriate. But the main reason for this lack of reference is that the doctrine, although based on Pigou, must have been largely the product of an oral tradition. Certainly economists with whom I have discussed these problems have shown a unanimity of opinion which is quite remarkable considering the meagre treatment accorded this subject in the literature. No doubt there are some economists who do not share the usual view but they must represent a small minority of the profession.

The approach to the problems under discussion is through an examination of the value of physical production. The private product is the value of the additional product resulting from a particular activity of a business. The social product equals the private product minus the fall in the value of production elsewhere for which no compensation is paid by the business. Thus, if 10 units of a factor (and no other factors) are used by a business to make a certain product with a value of \$105; and the owner of this factor is not compensated for their use, which he is unable to prevent; and these 10 units of the factor would yield products in their best alternative use worth \$100; then, the social product is \$105 minus \$100 or \$5. If the business now pays for one unit of the factor and its price equals the value of its marginal product, then the social product rises to \$15. If two units are paid for, the social product rises to \$25 and so on until it reaches \$105 when all units of the factor are paid for. It is not difficult to see why economists have so readily accepted this rather odd procedure. The analysis focusses on the individual business decision and since the use of certain resources is not allowed for in costs, receipts are reduced by the same amount. But, of course, this means that the value of the social product has no social significance whatsoever. It seems to me preferable to use the opportunity cost concept and to approach these problems by comparing the value of the product yielded by factors in alternative uses or by alternative arrangements. The main advantage of a pricing system is that it leads to the employment of factors in places where the value of the product yielded is greatest and does so at less cost than alternative systems (I leave aside that a pricing system also eases the problem of the redistribution of income). But if through some God-given natural harmony factors flowed to the places where the value of the product yielded was greatest without any use of the pricing system and consequently there was no compensation, I would find it a source of surprise rather than a cause for dismay.

The definition of the social product is queer but this does not mean that the conclusions for policy drawn from the analysis are necessarily wrong. However, there are bound to be dangers in an approach which diverts attention from the basic issues and there can be little doubt that it has been responsible for some of the errors in current doctrine. The belief that it is desirable that the business which causes harmful effects should be forced to compensate those who suffer damage (which was exhaustively discussed in section VIII in connection with Pigou's railway sparks example) is undoubtedly the result of not comparing the total product obtainable with alternative social arrangements.

The same fault is to be found in proposals for solving the problem of harmful effects by the use of taxes or bounties. Pigou lays considerable stress on this solution although he is, as usual, lacking in detail and qualified in his support.[64] Modern economists tend to think exclusively in terms of taxes and in a very precise way. The tax should be equal to the damage done and should therefore vary with the amount of the harmful effect. As it is not proposed that the proceeds of the tax should be paid to those suffering the damage, this solution is not the same as that which would force a business to pay compensation to those damaged by its actions, although economists generally do not seem to have noticed this and tend to treat the two solutions as being identical.

Assume that a factory which emits smoke is set up in a district previously free from smoke pollution, causing damage valued at $100 per annum. Assume that the taxation solution is adopted and that the factory owner is taxed $100 per annum as long as the factory emits the smoke. Assume further that a smoke-preventing device costing $90 per annum to run is available. In these circumstances, the smoke-preventing device would be installed. Damage of $100 would have been avoided at an expenditure of $90 and the factory-owner would be better off by $10 per annum. Yet the position achieved may not be optimal. Suppose that those who suffer the damage could avoid it by moving to other locations or by taking various precautions which would cost them, or be equivalent to a loss in income of, $40 per annum. Then there would be a gain in the value of production of $50 if the factory continued to emit its smoke and those now in the district moved elsewhere or made other adjustments to avoid the damage. If the factory owner is to be made to pay a tax equal to the damage caused, it would clearly be desirable to institute a double tax system and to make residents of the district pay an amount equal to the additional cost incurred by the factory owner (or the consumers of his products) in order to avoid the damage. In these conditions,

[64] *Id.* 192–4, 381 and *Public Finance* 94–100 (3d ed. 1947).

people would not stay in the district or would take other measures to prevent the damage from occurring, when the costs of doing so were less than the costs that would be incurred by the producer to reduce the damage (the producer's object, of course, being not so much to reduce the damage as to reduce the tax payments). A tax system which was confined to a tax on the producer for damage caused would tend to lead to unduly high costs being incurred for the prevention of damage. Of course this could be avoided if it were possible to base the tax, not on the damage caused, but on the fall in the value of production (in its widest sense) resulting from the emission of smoke. But to do so would require a detailed knowledge of individual preferences and I am unable to imagine how the data needed for such a taxation system could be assembled. Indeed, the proposal to solve the smoke-pollution and similar problems by the use of taxes bristles with difficulties: the problem of calculation, the difference between average and marginal damage, the interrelations between the damage suffered on different properties, etc. But it is unnecessary to examine these problems here. It is enough for my purpose to show that, even if the tax is exactly adjusted to equal the damage that would be done to neighboring properties as a result of the emission of each additional puff of smoke, the tax would not necessarily bring about optimal conditions. An increase in the number of people living or of business operating in the vicinity of the smoke-emitting factory will increase the amount of harm produced by a given emission of smoke. The tax that would be imposed would therefore increase with an increase in the number of those in the vicinity. This will tend to lead to a decrease in the value of production of the factors employed by the factory, either because a reduction in production due to the tax will result in factors being used elsewhere in ways which are less valuable, or because factors will be diverted to produce means for reducing the amount of smoke emitted. But people deciding to establish themselves in the vicinity of the factory will not take into account this fall in the value of production which results from their presence. This failure to take into account costs imposed on others is comparable to the action of a factory-owner in not taking into account the harm resulting from his emission of smoke. Without the tax, there may be too much smoke and too few people in the vicinity of the factory; but with the tax there may be too little smoke and too many people in the vicinity of the factory. There is no reason to suppose that one of these results is necessarily preferable.

I need not devote much space to discussing the similar error involved in the suggestion that smoke producing factories should, by means of zoning regulations, be removed from the districts in which the smoke causes harmful effects. When the change in the location of the factory results in a reduction in production, this obviously needs to be taken into account and weighed against the harm which would result from the factory remaining in that location. The aim of such regulation should not be to eliminate smoke pollution but rather to secure the optimum amount of smoke pollution, this being the amount which will maximise the value of production.

X. A CHANGE OF APPROACH

It is my belief that the failure of economists to reach correct conclusions about the treatment of harmful effects cannot be ascribed simply to a few slips in analysis. It stems from basic defects in the current approach to problems of welfare economics. What is needed is a change of approach.

Analysis in terms of divergencies between private and social products concentrates attention on particular deficiencies in the system and tends to nourish the belief that

any measure which will remove the deficiency is necessarily desirable. It diverts attention from those other changes in the system which are inevitably associated with the corrective measure, changes which may well produce more harm than the original deficiency. In the preceding sections of this article, we have seen many examples of this. But it is not necessary to approach the problem in this way. Economists who study problems of the firm habitually use an opportunity cost approach and compare the receipts obtained from a given combination of factors with alternative business arrangements. It would seem desirable to use a similar approach when dealing with questions of economic policy and to compare the total product yielded by alternative social arrangements. In this article, the analysis has been confined, as is usual in this part of economics, to comparisons of the value of production, as measured by the market. But it is, of course, desirable that the choice between different social arrangements for the solution of economic problems should be carried out in broader terms than this and that the total effect of these arrangements in all spheres of life should be taken into account. As Frank H. Knight has so often emphasized, problems of welfare economics must ultimately dissolve into a study of aesthetics and morals.

A second feature of the usual treatment of the problems discussed in this article is that the analysis proceeds in terms of a comparison between a state of laissez faire and some kind of ideal world. This approach inevitably leads to a looseness of thought since the nature of the alternatives being compared is never clear. In a state of laissez faire, is there a monetary, a legal or a political system and if so, what are they? In an ideal world, would there be a monetary, a legal or a political system and if so, what would they be? The answers to all these questions are shrouded in mystery and every man is free to draw whatever conclusions he likes. Actually very little analysis is required to show that an ideal world is better than a state of laissez faire, unless the definitions of a state of laissez faire and an ideal world happen to be the same. But the whole discussion is largely irrelevant for questions of economic policy since whatever we may have in mind as our ideal world, it is clear that we have not yet discovered how to get to it from where we are. A better approach would seem to be to start our analysis with a situation approximating that which actually exists, to examine the effects of a proposed policy change and to attempt to decide whether the new situation would be, in total, better or worse than the original one. In this way, conclusions for policy would have some relevance to the actual situation.

A final reason for the failure to develop a theory adequate to handle the problem of harmful effects stems from a faulty concept of a factor of production. This is usually thought of as a physical entity which the businessman acquires and uses (an acre of land, a ton of fertiliser) instead of as a right to perform certain (physical) actions. We may speak of a person owning land and using it as a factor of production but what the land-owner in fact possesses is the right to carry out a circumscribed list of actions. The rights of a land-owner are not unlimited. It is not even always possible for him to remove the land to another place, for instance, by quarrying it. And although it may be possible for him to exclude some people from using "his" land, this may not be true of others. For example, some people may have the right to cross the land. Furthermore, it may or may not be possible to erect certain types of buildings or to grow certain crops or to use particular drainage systems on the land. This does not come about simply because

of Government regulation. It would be equally true under the common law. In fact it would be true under any system of law. A system in which the rights of individuals were unlimited would be one in which there were no rights to acquire.

If factors of production are thought of as rights, it becomes easier to understand that the right to do something which has a harmful effect (such as the creation of smoke, noise, smells, etc.) is also a factor of production. Just as we may use a piece of land in such a way as to prevent someone else from crossing it, or parking his car, or building his house upon it, so we may use it in such a way as to deny him a view or quiet or unpolluted air. The cost of exercising a right (of using a factor of production) is always the loss which is suffered elsewhere in consequence of the exercise of that right—the inability to cross land, to park a car, to build a house, to enjoy a view, to have peace and quiet or to breathe clean air.

It would clearly be desirable if the only actions performed were those in which what was gained was worth more than what was lost. But in choosing between social arrangements within the context of which individual decisions are made, we have to bear in mind that a change in the existing system which will lead to an improvement in some decisions may well lead to a worsening of others. Furthermore we have to take into account the costs involved in operating the various social arrangements (whether it be the working of a market or of a government department), as well as the costs involved in moving to a new system. In devising and choosing between social arrangements we should have regard for the total effect. This, above all, is the change in approach which I am advocating.

34. The Anatomy of Market Failure*

FRANCIS M. BATOR[1]

What is it we mean by "market failure"? Typically, at least in allocation theory, we mean the failure of a more or less idealized system of price-market institutions to sustain "desirable" activities or to estop "undesirable" activities.[2] The desirability of an activity, in turn, is evaluated relative to the solution values of some explicit or implied maximum-welfare problem.

It is the central theorem of modern welfare economics that under certain strong assumptions about technology, tastes, and producers' motivations, the equilibrium conditions which characterize a system of competitive markets will exactly correspond to the requirements of Paretian efficiency.[3]

Further, if competitively imputed incomes are continuously redistributed in costless lump-sum fashion so as to achieve the income-distribution implied by a social welfare function, then the competitive market solution will correspond to the one electronically calculated Pareto-efficient solution which maximizes, subject only to tastes, technology and initial endowments, that particular welfare function.[4]

Many things in the real world violate

* Reprinted by permission of the publishers from Francis M. Bator, *The Quarterly Journal of Economics* (August 1958). Cambridge, Mass.: Harvard University Press. Copyright, 1958, by the President and Fellows of Harvard College, pp. 351–379. A brief biographical sketch of the author can be found in the introduction to Reading 32.
[1] I am much indebted to R. S. Eckaus and R. M. Solow for detailed comment and discussion.

[2] "Activities" broadly defined, to cover consumption as well as production.

[3] I.e., to the conditions which define the attainable frontier of maximal utility combinations with given preference functions, resource endowments and technology. A community is on its

Paretian frontier if it is impossible to make anyone better off (in terms of his own ordinal preference function) without making someone else worse off. Associated with the utility possibility frontier, in turn, is a production possibility frontier denoting maximal alternative output combinations. (Cf. my "Simple Analytics of Welfare Maximization," *American Economic Review*, XLVII [(Mar. 1957), 22–59, and references therein. Reprinted supra. pp. 455–483.])

[4] In other words, given the "right" lump-sum taxes, markets will match the allocation called for by the point of tangency of the relevant W-function with the utility-possibility frontier, i.e., by the "bliss point." The W-function need not, of course, be explicit—it could be implicit in the political power-configuration which characterizes a community. On the other hand, it cannot be just any kind of function. It has to have some special characteristics which reflect a number of ethic-loaded restrictions, e.g., that individuals' preference functions are to count, and to count positively (cf., *ibid.*, and Section V below).

such correspondence: imperfect information, inertia and resistance to change, the infeasibility of costless lump-sum taxes, businessmen's desire for a "quiet life," uncertainty and inconsistent expectations, the vagaries of aggregate demand, etc. With most of these I am not here concerned: they have to do with the efficiency of "real life" market institutions operated by "real life" people in a nonstationary world of uncertainty, miscalculation, etc.

What follows is an attempt, rather, to explore and order those phenomena which cause even errorless profit- and preference-maximizing calculation in a stationary context of perfect (though limited) information and foresight to fail to sustain Pareto-efficient allocation. I am concerned, in other words, with the decentralizing efficiency of that regime of signals, rules and built-in sanctions which defines a price-market system.[5]

Specifically, Section I sets out the necessary conditions for efficiency of decentralized price-profit calculations both in a "laissez-faire" and in a "socialist" setting of Lange-Lerner civil servants. Section II is a brief digression on an often discussed mode of failure in these conditions: neoclassical external economies. It is concluded that the modern formulation of the doctrine, in terms of "direct interaction," begs more questions than it answers; further, that the usual emphasis on "divorce of scarcity from effective ownership" is misplaced. Section

III, then, suggests a comprehensive ordering of types of market failure, with generalized indivisibility, public goods, and, last and least, nonappropriability as the villains of the piece. Section IV consists of some comments on the Meade and Scitovsky classifications of external economies; on the analytical link between indivisibility and public goods; on the significance of "exclusion"; on organizational arrangements designed to offset externality; and on blends of the various types of market failure. Section V concludes with some cautionary notes on the relevance of market-efficiency for choice of institutions.

I. THE CONDITIONS OF MARKET EFFICIENCY

The central theorem of modern welfare economics, the so-called *duality theorem*, asserts a correspondence between Pareto efficiency and market performance. Its analytical essence lies in the remarkable fact that with all-round convexity, independence of tastes, etc., the technocratically formulated, institutionally neutral, Paretian maximum-of-welfare problem has embedded within it a set of constants: "duals," Lagrangean multipliers, shadow-prices, which have all the analytical characteristics of prices, wages, rents, interest rates.[6] Correspondence between Pareto-efficiency and market performance implies, at the least, that decentralized decisions in response to these "prices" by atomistic profit- and satisfaction-maximizers sustain just that

[5] In most of what follows, I shall assume that individual preferences, though not necessarily sensitive only to own-consumption, are representable by strictly convex indifference surfaces [i.e., by an ordering (one for each individual)] such that all points on a straight line connecting two equivalent points x and y are preferred to x (hence to y)). But convexity is too restrictive. It excludes not only such characteristics of man's psyche as violate the "usual" regularities—these I do want to exclude—but also such physical and topographical facts as lumpy consumption-goods. Rather than attempt a specification of preferences with convex-like properties where choice must be made among discrete bundles, I dodge the problem by attributing lumpiness only to inputs (including, however, inputs that are intermediate outputs).

[6] The theorem holds for the statical steady-state flow model of the Walrasian sort where the solution values are stationary time-rates; it holds, also, for dynamical systems involving capital formation (given, still, convexity throughout). For these last, the solution values are time paths of inputs, outputs, prices, etc. (A set of points is convex if, and only if, the straight lines connecting all possible pairs do not anywhere pass outside the set. The set of feasible output points bounded by a production possibility curve is convex, for instance, if the curve itself is concave-to-the-origin or a straight line. On all this, see Section V of "Simple Analytics," *ibid.*)

constellation of inputs, outputs and commodity-distribution, that the maximum of the specified social welfare function calls for. It implies, in other words, that decentralized market calculations correctly account for all "economic" costs and benefits to which the relevant W-function is sensitive.[7]

Duality can fail in many ways. Specifically, and in a statical and "laissez-faire" context:[8]

1. Duality will fail unless the Pareto-efficient (a) input-output points (production) and (b) associated commodity distribution points (exchange) which associate with the maximum of the welfare function in hand are characterized by a complete set of marginal-rate-of-substitution (MRS) equalities (or limiting inequalities) which, in turn, yield a set of price-like constants. Where no such constants exist, reference will be to *failure of existence*.[9]

[7] Given, again, optimal lump-sum redistribution of as-imputed incomes. While I make use of the lump-sum transfer device throughout this paper to abstract from the income distribution problem and permit exclusive attention to Pareto efficiency, it is well to note that this involves a measure of sleight-of-hand. No decentralized price-market type "game" can reveal the pattern of taxes and transfers that would maximize a particular welfare function. "Central" calculation—implicit if not explicit—is unavoidable. Moreover, since distribution (hence correct redistribution) of numeraire-incomes interdepends with allocation in production and exchange, the supposedly automatic, nonpolitical character of market mediation is a myth on the strictest neoclassical assumptions. This is not to say, even on our stratospheric levels of abstraction, that markets are "useless." Where they do compute well we are saved an awful lot of calculation.

[8] With optimal redistribution.

[9] We could consider, instead, the configuration which associates with the initial pattern of ownership of endowment. Or we could play it safe and extend the conditions to cover each and every Pareto efficient configuration. But this would be overly strict, since many efficient situations have no relevance either to any interesting W-functions or in terms of the initial distribution of scarcities. It may be worth noting, incidentally, that "existence," as used above, is not the same as existence in the sense of, e.g., Arrow and Debreu (in "Existence of an Equilibrium for a Competitive Economy," *Econometrica*, Vol. 22 [July

2. Should such an associated set of Lagrangean parameters exist, duality would nevertheless fail, specifically in production, unless the bliss configuration of inputs and outputs, evaluated in terms of these price parameters, will yield: (a) a local profit-maximum position for each producer, rather than, as possible, a profit minimum; (b) non-negative profits for all producers from whom production is required; (c) maximum profits-in-the-large for each producer. Failure on counts (a) and (c) will be labeled *failure by signal*, that on count (b) *failure by incentive*.[10]

3. Even if all efficient production configurations, or the one which maximizes a particular welfare-function, coincide with points of maximum and non-negative producers' profits, market mediation may fail in production. If prices are determined by market forces, they will not correspond to a Paretian maximum unless self-policing perfect competition obtains in all markets. Self-policing competition requires "very many" producers in every market.[11] If, then, for whatever reason, some markets are saturated by a few firms of "efficient" scale, the full welfare-maximum solution of inputs, outputs *and prices* will not be sustained. There will be *failure by structure*.

4. Finally, even if all above is satisfied, market performance could still fail, and fail in a statical sense, due to arbitrary legal and organizational "imperfections," or feasibility limitations on "keeping book,"

1954), pp. 265–90]. They use the term to denote the complete set of conditions which defines competitive equilibrium, and this includes, in addition to all that is implied by (1) above, conditions akin to my conditions (2), and some analogous conditions on consumers.

[10] This is slightly misleading: as we shall see, failure on count (c) leads both to signaling and to incentive troubles. Anyway, the labels are only for expository convenience.

[11] Or at least the potentiality of very many producers, ready and able to "enter the fray" instantaneously. This may be sufficient in the constant-cost case, where the equilibrium number of firms per industry is indeterminate.

such as leave some inputs or outputs "hidden," or preclude their explicit allocation or capture by market processes (e.g., the restriction, unless I go into baseball, on the sale of the capitalized value of my lifetime services). Failure is *by enforcement*.

All the above are germane to duality in its usual sense, to the statical Pareto-efficiency of laissez-faire markets with genuine profit- and satisfaction-seekers.[12] Conditions (1), (2) and (4) are relevant, also, to the decentralizing efficiency of a Lange-Lerner type organizational scheme. In its "capitalist" version, with profit-motivated operation of privately-owned means of production where it is simply an anti-monopoly device to assure parametric take-prices-as-given behavior, conditions (1), (2) and (4) are all necessary for efficiency. Of course condition (3): self-policing competition, no longer matters.

In its true socialist version, a Lange-Lerner system can afford to "fail" also "by incentive," (2b). Socialist civil servants, under injunction to maximize profit (in the small) in terms of fixed centrally-quoted prices, care or should care not at all about absolute profitability. By assumption the scheme can dispense with the built-in incentive of positive profit: the lure of bureaucratic advancement, the image of Siberia, or the old school tie presumably substitute for the urge to get rich. But if prices and the injunction to maximize profit are to be used to decentralize, condition (1): existence, and (2a) and (2c): correct and unambiguous signals, remain crucial.[13]

So does condition (4): the solution of quantities and prices need not be profitable and self-enforcing, but it does have to be enforceable. If the nectar in apple blossoms is scarce and carries a positive shadow price, it must be possible to make every beekeeper pay for his charges' meals.

It warrants repetition that this has to do with whether a decentralized price-market game will or will not *sustain* a Pareto-efficient configuration. The word sustain is critical. There exists a host of further considerations which bear on dynamical questions of adjustment, of "how the system gets there." (E.g., will some "natural" price-market type computational routine of price-quantity responses with a meaningful institutional counterpart tend to track the solution?) These are not here at issue. We shall be concerned only with the prior problem of whether a price-market system which finds itself at the maximum-welfare point will or will not tend to remain there.[14]

---

[12] The mathematically minded will object that (3) and (4), at least, do not really violate "duality" in its strict mathematical sense; the dual minimum problem still yields Lagrangean constants. True, yet I think it suggestive to use "duality" rather more loosely as a label for the general welfare theorem, particularly as this does not lead, in this context, to any ambiguity.

[13] It is tempting, but wrong, to suggest that in a true Lange-Lerner world totals do not matter and only margins count. It is true that the non-negativeness of profits is immaterial. Where there is any sharing of shadow-price sets by two or more production points, however, totals necessarily become a part of the signaling system and if

(2c) does not hold they may lead down the garden path.

[14] More precisely, whether the point of maximum welfare is or is not a point of self-policing and "enforceable" market equilibrium, where, following common usage, equilibrium is defined to subsume both the first-order and the second-order inequalities for a maximum. A firm, for instance, is taken to be in equilibrium only at a point of maximum profit. This way of defining equilibrium does bring in issues of stability hence some implicit dynamics. In particular, the word "sustain" is taken to imply some scanning or reconnaissance by producers and consumers at least in the neighborhood of equilibrium. But I do not think it does any harm to subsume this much stability in the equilibrium notion. The possibility of a firm in *unstable* "equilibrium," i.e., in equilibrium at a point of minimum profit, is hardly likely to be of import.

On the other hand, correspondence between Pareto-efficiency and the equilibrium state of perfectly competitive markets is not sufficient to insure market efficiency. It is the burden of "failure by structure" that markets may fail to be competitive, and of "failure by enforcement" that legal or institutional constraints may prevent competitive markets from allocating efficiently, even though there does exist a competitive equilibrium for each Pareto-efficient configuration. "Existence" in the sense of Arrow and Debreu (*op. cit.*) is necessary but not sufficient for market-efficiency in the present context.

The relevant literature is rich but confusing. It abounds in mutually reinforcing and overlapping descriptions and explanations of market failure: external economies, indivisibility, nonappropriability, direct interaction, public goods, atmosphere, etc. In a sense, our problem is simply to sort out the relations among these. In doing so, it is appropriate and useful to begin with a brief review of the neoclassical doctrine of external economies and of its modern formulation in terms of "direct interaction."

II. NEOCLASSICAL EXTERNAL ECONOMIES: A DIGRESSION

By Way of Some History

Marshall, as has often been pointed out, proposed the external economy argument to explain, without resort to dynamics, the phenomenon of a negatively sloped ("forward falling") long-run industry supply curve in terms consistent with a horizontal or rising marginal cost curve (MC) in the "representative" firm. The device permits—in logic, if not in fact—long-run competitive equilibrium of many firms within an industry, each producing at its profit-maximum price-equal-to-a-rising-MC position, without foreclosing the possibility of a falling supply price with rising industry output.[15]

The mechanism is simple. It is postulated that an expansion in the output of the industry as a whole brings into play economies which cause a downward shift of the cost curves of all the component firms. These economies, however, are not subject to exploitation by any one of the myriad of tiny atomized firms. Their own MC curves, at $p = MC$, rise both before and after the shift, due, presumably, to internal diseconomies associated with the entrepreneurial function which defines the firm.

Even the modern formulation is not entirely without ambiguity—institutional ambiguity is intrinsic to the device of parametrization: how many firms does it take for the demand curve of each to be perfectly horizontal?—but it does provide a means for "saving" the competitive model, of ducking the monopoly problem.

Marshall, and also Professor Pigou, "preferred," as it were, the other horn of what they perhaps saw as a dilemma. The external economy device, while saving competition, implies a flaw in the efficacy of the "invisible hand" in guiding production.[16] "Price equal to MC" is saved, but wrong. Market forces, they argued, will not give enough output by industries enjoying external economies and will cause industries with rising supply curves to overexpand. Hence the Marshall-Pigou prescription: to harmonize private production decisions with public welfare, tax the latter set of industries and subsidize the former.

It took the better part of thirty years, and the cumulative powers of Allyn Young, and Messrs. Robertson, Knight, Sraffa, and Viner, to unravel the threads of truth and error which run through the Marshall-Pigou argument.[17] The crucial distinction, which provides the key to it all, is between what Viner labeled technological external economies, on the one hand, and pecuniary external economies on the other. The latter, if dominant, cause the long-run supply curve of an industry, say A, to decline because the price of an input, B, falls in response to an increase in A's demand for it. The technological variety, on the other hand, though also a reversible function of industry output, consists in organizational

---

[15] This refers to a so-called Marshallian supply curve. It has nothing whatever to do with the Walrasian "maximum quantity supplied at a given price" type schedule.

[16] That there are difficulties also with income distribution was by that time generally recognized.

[17] The strategic articles, with the exception of Young's ["Pigou's *Wealth and Welfare*," this *Journal*, XXVII (1913), 672–86], as well as Ellis and Fellner's 1943 treatment, have all been reprinted in American Economic Association, *Readings in Price Theory*, ed. Stigler & Boulding. For an excellent modern discussion, see R. L. Bishop, *Economic Theory* (to appear).

or other improvements in efficiency which do not show up in input prices.[18]

As regards pecuniary external economies, Robertson and Sraffa made it clear that in a sense both the Marshall-Pigou conclusions were wrong. For one thing, no subsidy is called for. The implied gains in efficiency are adequately signaled by the input price, and profit-maximizing output levels by the A-firms are socially efficient. Second, monopoly troubles may be with us, via, as it were, the back door. For what causes the price of B to drop in response to increased demand? We are back where we started: a declining long-run supply curve.

In the end, then, if *internal* technological economies of scale are ruled out, we are left with only *technological* external economies. All pecuniary external economies must be due to technological economies somewhere in the system.[19] It is true—and this is what remains of the original Marshall-Pigou proposition—that technological externalities are not correctly accounted for by prices, that they violate the efficiency of decentralized market calculation.

The Modern Formulation[20]

In its modern version, the notion of external economies—external economies proper that is: Viner's technological variety —belongs to a more general doctrine of "direct interaction." Such interaction, whether it involves producer-producer,

consumer-consumer, producer-consumer, or employer-employee relations, consists in interdependences that are external to the price system, hence unaccounted for by market valuations. Analytically, it implies the nonindependence of various preference and production functions. Its effect is to cause divergence between private and social cost-benefit calculation.

That this is so, is easily demonstrated by means of a simplified variant of a production model suggested by J. E. Meade.[21] Assume a world of all-round perfect competition where a single purchasable and inelastically supplied input, labor $(\overline{L})$, is used to produce two homogeneous and divisible goods, apples (A) and honey (H), at nonincreasing returns to scale. But while the output of A is dependent only on L_A : $A = A(L_A)$, honey production is sensitive also to the level of apple output: $H = H(L_H, A(L_A))$. (Professor Meade makes pleasurable the thought of apple blossoms making for honey abundance.)[22]

By solving the usual constrained maximum problem for the production-possibility curve, it can be shown that Paretian production efficiency implies

$$p_H \frac{\partial H}{\partial L_H} = w \tag{1}$$

$$p_A \frac{dA}{dL_A} + p_H \frac{\partial H}{\partial A} \frac{dA}{dL_A} = w \tag{2}$$

where p_H, p_A, and w represent the prices, respectively, of honey, apples and labor.[23]

---

[18] Note, however, that there need be nothing about an organizational improvement to make it obvious in advance whether it will turn out to be technological or, through "internalization," pecuniary. Many trade-association type services which are justified by the scale of an industry could as well be provided commercially, and vice versa.

[19] Pecuniary diseconomies, in contrast, need have no technological counterpart. Finite-elastic supplies of unproduced inputs are a sufficient cause. Recall, incidentally, that only narrowly statical reversible phenomena are admissible here.

[20] While this section makes some slight use of elementary calculus, the reader uninterested in technicalities may avoid, without loss of continuity, all but some simple notation.

[21] *Economic Journal*, LXII (Mar. 1952). Meade uses a two factor model and, while he does not explicitly solve the Paretian maximum problem, shows that market imputed rates of remuneration will not match marginal social product.

[22] Both functions are assumed homogeneous of degree one. Moreover, apple blossoms (or the nectar therein) are exhaustible, rationable "private" goods: more nectar to one bee means less to another. On the need for this assumption, see Section III-3 below.

[23] Assuming internal tangencies and all-round convexity (the last is implicit in constant returns to L: the A-effect on H reinforces convexity), as well as nonsatiation and nonredundancy $(\overline{L} = L_A + L_H)$, the maximization of $p_A A + p_H H$, subject to the

Equation (1) is familiar enough and consistent with profit maximizing. Each competitive honey producer will do for profit what he must for efficiency: hire labor until the value of its social as well as private marginal product equals the wage rate. Not so the apple producers; unless $\frac{\partial H}{\partial A} = 0$—unless the cross effect of apples on honey is zero—their profit-maximizing production decisions will be nonefficient. Specifically, if apples have a positive external effect on honey output, market-determined L_A will be less than is socially desirable.[24]

A different way to see this is to examine the relations of private to social marginal cost. The marginal money cost of apples to the competitive apple producer is $\frac{w}{dA/dL_A}$; that of honey to the beekeeper, $\frac{w}{\partial H/\partial L_H}$.

It is the ratio of the two: $\frac{\partial H/\partial L_H}{dA/dL_A}$, that competitive market-mediation brings into equality with the equilibrating configuration of relative prices. Markets will be efficient if, and only if, this *private* marginal cost ratio reflects the true marginal cost to society of an extra apple in terms of foregone honey: the marginal rate of transformation between H and A.

What is MRT in the model? Differentiating (totally) the two production func-

tions and dividing the value of one derivative into the other, we get, in absolute (cost) terms:

$$MRT \equiv \left| \frac{dH}{dA} \right| = \frac{\partial H/\partial L_H}{dA/dL_A} - \frac{\partial H}{\partial A}.$$

If, then, $\frac{\partial H}{\partial A} > 0$, the true marginal *social* cost of an "extra" apple, in terms of honey foregone, is less than the market-indicated private cost. It is less precisely by the amount of positive "feedback" on honey output due the "extra" apple.

By combining (1) and (2), eliminating w, and dividing through by p_H and $\frac{dA}{dL_A}$, we get the condition for Pareto efficiency in terms of private MC's:

$$\frac{\partial H/\partial L_H}{dA/dL_A} = \frac{p_A}{p_H} + \frac{\partial H}{\partial A}.$$

Clearly, price equal to private marginal cost will not do. Further, if prices are market-determined, they will diverge from true, *social* marginal cost.

Any number of variations on the model suggest themselves. As Meade pointed out, interactions can be mutual and need not be associated with the outputs. Even in the above case, it is perhaps more suggestive to think of L_A as producing some social value-product both in the A industry and the H industry. In the most general formulation, one can simply think of each production function as containing all the other variables of the system, some perhaps with zero weight. Moreover, by introducing two or more nonproduced inputs one can, as Meade does, work out the consequences for income distribution and input proportions.[25]

---

production functions and the supply of labor, is equivalent to finding a critical value for the Lagrangean expression, $F = p_A A(L_A) + p_H H[L_H; A(L_A)] + w(\bar{L} - L_A - L_H)$. To do so, differentiate F with respect to L_A and L_H, treating p_A, p_H and w as arbitrary constants and set the resulting first order partial derivatives equal to zero. This will give exactly (1) and (2). (Needless to say, the value weights can be varied at will, or taken as given.)

[24] To see this, rewrite (2) to read $\frac{dA}{dL_A} = \frac{w}{p_A + p_H \frac{\partial H}{\partial A}}$ and match it against the profit-maximizing rule, $\frac{dA}{dL_A} = \frac{w}{p_A}$. Clearly,

$$\frac{\partial H}{\partial A} \lesseqgtr 0 \longrightarrow \left(\frac{dA}{dL_A} \right)_{\text{Private}} \lesseqgtr \left(\frac{dA}{dL_A} \right)_{\text{Social}}.$$

[25] The question of whether technological external economies involve shifts of each other's production functions, or mutually induced movements along such functions, is purely definitional. If one chooses so to define each producer's function as to give axes only to inputs and outputs that are purchased and sold, or at least "controlled," and the effects of everything else impinging on production (e.g., of humidity, apple

Some Queries

The modern formulation of the doctrine of external economies, in terms of direct interaction, is not only internally consistent: it also yields insight. Yet one may well retain about it some dissatisfaction. There is no doubt that the Robertson-Sraffa-Viner distinction between the technological and the pecuniary sort gets to the nub of what is the matter with the original Marshallian analysis. It cuts right through the confusion which led Marshall and Pigou to conclude that the price mechanism is faulty in situations where in truth it is at its best: in allocating inputs in less than infinitely elastic supply between alternative productive uses. It also facilitates unambiguous formulation of the more difficult "falling supply price" case. But in a sense it only begs the fundamental question: what is it that gives rise to "direct interaction," to short circuit, as it were, of the signaling system?

Most modern writers have let matters rest with the Ellis-Fellner type explanation: "the divorce of scarcity from effective ownership." [26] Does nonappropriability then explain all direct interaction? In a sense it does, yet by directing attention to institutional and feasibility considerations which make it impracticable for "real life" market-institutions to mimic a price-profit-preference computation, it diverts attention from some deeper issues. Surely the word "ownership" serves to illuminate but poorly the phenomenon of a temperance leaguer's reaction to a hard-drinking neighbor's (sound insulated and solitary) Saturday night, or the reason why a price system, if efficient, will not permit full "compensation," in an age of electronic scramblers, for an advertisement-less radio program, or for the "services" of a bridge.[27]

It may be argued, of course, that at least the two latter examples are out of order, that radio programs and bridges do not involve "direct," i.e., non-price, interaction. But is this really so? Does not the introduction of a new program directly affect my and your consumption possibilities, in ways other than by a change in relative prices? Does not a bridge, or a road, have a direct effect on the production possibilities of neighboring producers, in precisely the sense in which apples affect the possibilities of beekeepers? [28]

True, perhaps bridges and roads are un-

---

blossoms, etc.) are built into the curvature of the function, then it follows that externalities will consist in shifts of some functions in response to movements along others. On the other hand, if, as in our apple-honey case, it seems useful to think of the production function for H as having an A-axis, then, clearly, induced movement along the function is a signal of externality.

[26] *Op. cit.*

[27] Moreover, in the one sense in which nonappropriability fits all cases of direct interaction, it explains none. If all it denotes is the failure of a price-market game properly to account for (to appropriate) all relevant costs and benefits, then it is simply a synonym for market failure (for generalized externality), and cannot be used to explain what causes any particular instance of such failure. I use it in a much narrower sense, to mean the inability of a producer of a good or service physically to exclude users, or to control the rationing of his produce among them. In my sense not only bridges but also, say, television programs are fully appropriable: it is always possible to use scramblers.

[28] It is possible, of course, to interpret these examples as involving very large changes in price: from infinity to zero. But it does not help to do so. The shared characteristic of bridges and programs is that there is no price which will efficiently mediate both supply and demand. I have puzzled over ways of limiting the notion of "direct interaction" to something less than all instances where there is some interaction not adequately signaled by price. Robert Solow has suggested to me that this might be done by distinguishing situations where something is not subject to a market test at all from instances where no single price constitutes a correct test for both sides of a transaction (e.g., where the correct ration price for the services of an expensive facility is zero). I am inclined, rather, to drop the attempt to use "direct interaction" as an explanation of market failure; it is best used, if at all, as yet another synonym for such failure.

fair: they violate the neo-classical assumption of perfect divisibility and nonincreasing returns to scale. But they surely do involve non-price interaction. In fact, lumpiness and increasing returns are perhaps the most important causes of such interaction. Are they to be denied status as externalities? More generally, are we to exclude from the class of externalities any direct interaction not due to difficulties with "effective ownership," any failures other than "by enforcement"?

It would be, of course, perfectly legitimate to do so—tastes are various. But I think it more natural and useful to broaden rather than restrict, to let "externality" denote any situation where some Paretian costs and benefits remain *external* to decentralized cost-revenue calculations in terms of prices.[29] If, however, we do so, then clearly nonappropriability[30] will not do as a complete explanation. Its concern with the inability of decentralized markets to sustain the solution-prices and quantities called for by a price-profit-preference type calculation, as computed by a team of mathematicians working with IBM machines, tends to mask the possibility that such machine-calculated solution q's may well be nonefficient.[31] It explains failure "by enforcement," but leaves hidden the empirically more important phenomena which cause failure by "nonexistence," "signal," and "incentive." Section III is designed to bring these deeper causes of generalized externality into the foreground.

[29] Recall that it is the existence of such "externality," of residue, at the bliss-point, of Pigouvian "uncompensated services" and "incidental uncharged disservices" that defines market failure. It may be objected that to generalize the externality notion in this way is to rob it of all but descriptive significance. But surely there is not much to rob; even in its strictest neoclassical formulation it begs more than it answers. In its generalized sense it at least has the virtue of suggesting the right questions.

[30] As defined in fn. 27, p. 525 above.

[31] Or that the algorism may break down for lack of a consistent set of p's.

III STATICAL EXTERNALITIES: AN ORDERING

If nonappropriability is, by itself, too flimsy a base for a doctrine of generalized (statical) externality, what broader foundation is there? Section I's hierarchy of possible modes of market failure suggests a fivefold classification. If, however, one looks for an organizing principle not to modes of failure but to causes, there appear to be three polar types: (1) Ownership Externalities, (2) Technical Externalities,[32] and (3) Public Good Externalities. These are not mutually exclusive: most externality phenomena are in fact blends. Yet there emerges a sufficient three-cornered clustering to warrant consolidation.[33]

Type (1): Ownership Externalities

Imagine a world which exhibits generalized technological and taste convexity, where the electronically calculated solution of a Paretian maximum-of-welfare problem yields not only a unique set of inputs, outputs and commodity-distribution, but where initial endowments plus lump-sum transfers render income distribution optimal in terms of the community's social welfare function. Assume, further, that everything that matters is divisible,

[32] I should much prefer "technological," but since this would necessarily confuse my Type (2) with Professor Viner's "technological" I fixed on "technical."

[33] In effect, we end up with a five-by-three ordering of types of "failure": five "modes" vs. three "causes." Its relation to Meade's categories (*op. cit.*) and to Tibor Scitovsky's classification (in "Two Concepts of External Economies," *Journal of Political Economy*, LXII, April 1954) is discussed in Section IV below. I have had the benefit of reading, also, William Fellner's "Individual Investment Projects in Growing Economies," *Investment Criteria and Economic Growth* (Proceedings of a Conference, Center for International Studies, Massachusetts Institute of Technology, 1955) and an unpublished paper by Svend Laursen, "External Economies and Economic Growth."

conventionally rational, and either available in inelastic total supply,[34] or producible at constant returns to scale; also that tastes are sensitive only to own-consumption. We know, then, from the duality theorem, that the bliss point implies a unique[35] set of prices, wages and rents, such as would cause atomistic profit- and preference-maximizers to do exactly what is necessary for bliss. In particular, all required production points give maximum and non-negative producer's profits.

This is an Adam Smith dream world. Yet it is possible that due to more or less arbitrary and accidental circumstances of institutions, laws, customs, or feasibility, competitive markets would not be Pareto-efficient. Take, for instance, the Meade example of apples and honey. Apple blossoms are "produced" at constant returns to scale and are (we assumed) an ordinary, private, exhaustible good: the more nectar for one bee, the less for another. It is easy to show that if apple blossoms have a positive effect on honey production (and abstracting from possible satiation and redundancy) a maximum-of-welfare solution, or any Pareto-efficient solution, will associate with apple blossoms a positive Lagrangean shadow-price.[36] If, then, apple producers are unable to protect their equity in apple-nectar and markets do not impute to apple blossoms their correct shadow-value, profit-maximiz-

ing decisions will fail correctly to allocate resources (e.g., L) at the margin. There will be failure "by enforcement."

This is what I would call an *ownership* externality. It is essentially Meade's "unpaid factor" case. Nonappropriation, divorce of scarcity from effective ownership, is *the* binding consideration. Certain "goods" (or "bads") with determinate non-zero shadow-values are simply not attributed. It is irrelevant here whether this is because the lake where people fish happens to be in the public domain, or because "keeping book" on who produces, and who gets what, may be impossible, clumsy, or costly in terms of resources.[37] For whatever legal or feasibility reasons, certain variables which have positive or negative shadow-value are not "assigned" axes. The beekeeper thinks only in terms of labor, the orchard-owner only in terms of apples.

The important point is that the difficulties reside in institutional arrangements, the feasibility of keeping tab, etc. The scarcities at issue are rational and finely divisible and there are no difficulties with "total conditions": at the bliss-configuration every activity would pay for itself. Apple nectar has a positive shadow-price, which would, if only payment were enforceable, cause nectar production in precisely the right amount and even distribution would be correctly rationed. The difficulty is due exclusively to the difficulty of keeping accounts on the nectar-take of Capulet bees as against Montague bees.[38]

---

[34] The supply of such nonproduced scarcities need not, of course, remain constant. On the other hand, their ownership distribution must not be so concentrated as to preclude competitive rationing. There must exist no "indivisible" lake full of fish, etc., such as might be subject to monopolization, but thousands of lakes, all perfect substitutes.

[35] Or, where there are corners, only inessentially indeterminate.

[36] Set up a variant of the Apple-Honey model of Part II, introducing apple blossoms, B, explicitly. Add a production function, $B = B(L_A)$, and substitute $B(L_A)$ for $A(L_A)$ as the second input in honey production. The solution will give out a positive Lagrangean shadow-price for B, and profit-maximizing producers of the joint products: A and B, will push L_A to the socially desirable margin.

[37] Though on this last, see Section IV, first paragraph.

[38] More generally, it could as well be due to difficulty in knowing who "produced" the "benefit"—oil wells drawing on the same pool are an example. The owner cannot protect his own; in fact it is difficult to know what one means by "his own." Moreover, in the case of *diseconomies*, at least, it may be that both the source and the recipient of the "bad" are identified: one factory producing soot and nothing but one laundry in the neighborhood, yet it is difficult to see how a price can be brought to bear on the situation. Presumably the laundry can pay for negative units of smoke.

Many of the few examples of interproducer external economies of the reversible technological variety are of this type: "shared deposits" of fish, water, etc.[39] Much more important, so are certain irreversible dynamical examples associated with investment. For instance, many of Pigou's first category of externalities: those that arise in connection with owner-tenant relationships where durable investments are involved, have a primarily organizational quality.[40] Perhaps the most important instance is the training of nonslave labor to skills—as distinct from education in a broader sense [which partakes more of Type (3)]. In the end, however, and in particular if restricted to reversible statical cases, it is not easy to think of many significant "ownership externalities" pure and simple. Yet it turns out that only this type of externality is really due to nonappropriability.

Type (2): Technical Externalities

Assume, again, that all goods and services are rationable, exhaustible, scarcities, that individual ordinal indifference maps are convex and sensitive only to own-consumption and that there exist no ownership "defects" of Type (1). If, then, the technology exhibits indivisibility or smooth increasing returns to scale in the relevant range of output, these give rise to a second and much more important type of market failure: "technical externality."[41]

The essential analytical consequence of indivisibility,[42] whether in inputs, outputs or processes, as well as of smooth increasing returns to scale, is to render the set of feasible points in production (input-output space) nonconvex. A connecting straight line between some pairs of feasible points will pass outside the feasible set. Nonconvexity, in turn, has a devastating effect on duality.[43]

In situations of pure "technical externality" there does, of course, still exist a maximal production possibility frontier (FF); and with a Samuelson-type social indifference map (SS)—i.e., a map "corrected" for income distribution which provides a ranking for the community as a whole of all conceivable output combinations[44]—it is

[39] Though indivisibility elements enter into some of these. Why can't somebody "own" part of a lakeful of fish?

[40] When not simply due, in a world of uncertainty, to inconsistent expectations.

[41] Again, this is not the same as Viner's "technological." Note, incidentally, that the above formulation unabashedly begs the question of whether smooth increasing returns to scale could or could not arise without indivisibility somewhere. The issue is entirely definitional: it is conceptually impossible to disprove either view by reference to empirical evidence. (Cf. "Simple Analytics," *loc. cit.*, fn. 37 and references.)

The pioneer work on decreasing cost situations

is Jules Dupuit's remarkable 1844 essay, "On the Measurement of Utility of Public Works," translated in *International Economic Papers,* No. **2,** ed. A. T. Peacock, *et al.* Harold Hotelling's "The General Welfare in Relation to Problems of Taxation and of Railway and Utility Rates," in the July 1938 issue of *Econometrica,* is the originating modern formulation. Cf., also, references to work by R. Frisch, J. E. Meade, W. A. Lewis and others in Nancy Ruggles' excellent survey articles on marginal cost pricing [*Review of Economic Studies,* XVII (1949–50), 29–46, and 107–26].

[42] Indivisibility means lumpiness "in scale" and not the kind of indivisibility-in-time we call durability. (Durability, as such, does not violate convexity.) Lumpiness has to do with the impossibility to vary continuously, e.g., the capacity service-yield per unit time of such things as bridges.

[43] The best known and perhaps most important variety of nonconvexity occurs where isoquants are properly convex, but returns to scale are increasing, hence the full set of feasible input-output points is nonconvex. [In a two-input, one-output situation, slices by (vertical) planes through the origin perpendicular to the input plane will cut the production surface in such a way as to give a nonconvex boundary.] A production point lying in an "increasing returns" region of a production function implies that (1) the associated average cost curve (AC) is downward sloping at that level of output; (2) the associated marginal cost curve (MC), while it may be rising, could as well be falling and will certainly lie below AC; and (3) the production possibility curve of the community may be nonconvex. On all this, see Part V of "Simple Analytics," *loc. cit.*

[44] Cf. P. A. Samuelson, "Social Indifference Curves," this *Journal,* LXX (Feb. 1956), 1–22.

possible, in concept, to define a bliss point(s).[45] Also, where indivisibility is exhibited by outputs, and only outputs, or, stronger, where smoothly increasing returns to scale is the only variety of nonconvexity—isoquants for one, are properly convex—the locus of efficient output combinations can be defined in terms of conditions on marginal-rates-of-input-substitution.[46] Moreover, bliss could possibly occur at a point where SS is internally tangent to FF, perhaps to a convex FF. But even in the least "pathological," most neoclassically well-behaved case, where there exists a meaningfully defined set of shadow-prices associated with the bliss point, genuinely profit-seeking competitive producers, responding to that set of prices, would fail to sustain optimal production. At best, even if at the bliss-configuration all MC's are rising, some producers would have to make continuing losses, hence would go out of business; market calculations would necessarily fail "by incentive." If, in turn, prices are not centrally quoted but permitted to set themselves, monopoly behavior will result. There will be failure "by structure."

Further, bliss may require production at levels of output where losses are not only positive, but at a constrained maximum;[47] $p = MC$ may be correct, though MC at that point is falling. If so, the embedded Lagrangean constants may still retain meaning as marginal rates of transformation, but they will fail to sustain efficient production even by Lange-Lerner civil servants who care only about margins and not about absolute totals. There will be failure

"by signal": producers under injunction to maximize profit (in the small) will not remain where they ought to be.

If, moreover, we drop the assumption of smooth increasing returns to scale and permit indivisibilities such as give scallop-like effects and kinks in cost curves and in the production-possibility curve, things get even more complicated. Bliss could require production at points of positive but locally minimum profit, where MC exceeds AC but is falling. Worse, even if bliss should occur at points where production functions are locally convex and MC (greater than AC) is rising, prequoted prices may still not sustain the solution unless production functions are in fact convex throughout. Though positive and at a local maximum, profits may not be at their maximum-maximorum: other hills with higher peaks may induce producers with vision at a distance to rush away from bliss. Alternatively, if prices are not administered, competition may not be self-policing and markets could fail "by structure." [48]

On the other hand, given our assumptions, the Paretian contract locus of maximal (ordinal) utility combinations which is associated with any one particular out-

---

Such a function presumes that *numeraire*-incomes are continuously redistributed so as to maximize in utility space over the community's operative social welfare function.

[45] This is saying very little, of course, except on the level of metaphysics.

[46] Inequalities due to kinks and corners are as good as equalities where all is smooth.

[47] Subject to the requirement that total cost for that level of output be a minimum, i.e., that each producer be on his least-cost expansion path.

[48] Where sharp indivisibility gives a nonconvex production possibility curve with corners and kinks, duality may fail even if there exists a price vector in terms of which decentralized producer-calculations would sustain the bliss-point output mix. The existence of such a vector does not assure that it will coincide with the price-vector which would efficiently ration that bill of goods among consumers. The point is that there may not exist a *single* set of prices which will at the same time keep both consumers and producers from rushing away from where they ought to be. The prices which will effectively mediate production may cause consumers' calculations to go wrong and vice versa.

It should be noted, incidentally, that none of the above takes space and distance considerations into account. For some interesting effects of plant-indivisibility where there are interplant flows and transport takes resources, see T. C. Koopmans and M. Beckmann, "Assignment Problems and the Location of Economic Activities," *Econometrica*, Vol. 25 (Jan. 1957).

put point is defined, as in the trouble-free neoclassical model, by the usual subjective, taste-determined, marginal-rate-of-substitution equalities (or, at corners, inequalities). These *MRS* equalities, in turn, imply a set of shadow-prices which, if centrally quoted, would efficiently ration among consumers the associated (fixed) totals of goods. In the sphere of exchange, then, a decentralized price system works without flaw.

In what sense do these Type (2) situations exhibit "externality"? In the (generalized) sense that some social costs and benefits remain external to decentralized profitability calculations. With Type (1) externalities, though it is not feasible to police the bliss values of all quantities and prices, there exists embedded in the solution a set of prices whose use for purposes of decentralized signaling would sustain, if only appropriation or exclusion were feasible, both itself and the maximum welfare configuration of inputs, outputs, and distribution. This is not the case here. In Type (1) situations, at the bliss point there is complete correspondence between social and private pay-off, both at the margin and in totals.[49] Profits are at their maxima and non-negative throughout. Here there is no such correspondence; there may well be divergence, either at the margin: bliss-profits may be at a "minimum," or in *totals*. The private totals in terms of which producers in an (idealized) market calculate—total revenue minus total cost—will not reliably signal the social costs and benefits implied by the relevant social indifference curves.[50] Hence at the set of prices which

would correctly ration the bliss point bill of goods, that bill of goods may not be produced by profit seekers, or even by Lange-Lerner civil servants.[51]

A point to note, in all this, is that in relation to "technical externalities" the nonappropriability notion, as generally conceived, tends to miss the point. Strictly speaking, it is, of course, true that price mediation, if efficient, cannot be counted on to "appropriate" the full social benefits of activities showing increasing returns to scale or other types of indivisibility to those engaged in them. But the existence of such "uncompensated services" has in this case nothing whatever to do with "divorce of scarcity from ownership," with feasibility limitations on "exclusion." It is entirely feasible to own a bridge and profitably ration crossings; indeed, a private owner would do so. The point is, rather, that such profitable rationing, such "compensation" for services rendered, would inefficiently misallocate the "output" of bridge crossings. If in terms of scarce resource inputs the marginal cost of an additional crossing is zero, any positive toll will, in general, have the usual monopolistic effect: the resulting output configuration will not be efficient.[52]

[49] More correctly, there would be such correspondence, if only the *p*'s could be policed.

[50] This is particularly awkward since the very nonconvexities which cause a divergence between private and social total conditions render output-mix calculations based on margins alone wholly inadequate. Even if bliss gives all local profit maxima, there may be several such open to any one producer, hence he must make total calculations in order to choose.

[51] There is one qualification to be made to the above. It may be that the bliss configuration gives unique and positive profit maxima throughout, though some production functions exhibit nonconvexities at a distance. It was to exclude this case that we assumed that increasing returns or indivisibility obtain in the "relevant ranges." Should this happen, no "externality" divergence of social and private calculation will occur, at least in a statical context. But unless all is convex throughout, the existence of such a locally stable tangency cannot be taken as evidence that the point is in fact the bliss-point—a difficulty of considerable significance for dynamical efficiency.

[52] Of course, if at bliss the bridge were to be used "to capacity," it is possible that the Lagrangean ration price (now positive) would make commercial operation profitable. If so, an administered price setup would efficiently mediate the demand and supply of crossings. But while a Lange-Lerner sytem would work fine, laissez-faire markets would fail "by structure."

This, incidentally, is where most pecuniary external economies lead: a supplier is required to produce in a range of declining AC due to internal technological economies of scale and hence cannot make "ends meet" at the socially correct price. The crucial associated difficulty at the level of social organization is monopoly.

Can we leave matters at that? Not quite. There is a third kind of externality, recently emphasized by Professor Samuelson, caused by so-called "public goods."

Type (3): Public Good Externalities

In some recent writings on public expenditure theory, Samuelson has reintroduced the notion of the collective or public good. The defining quality of a pure public good is that "each individual's consumption of such a good leads to no subtractions from any other individual's consumption of that good . . .",[53] hence, "it differs from a private consumption good in that each man's consumption of it, $X^1{}_2$ and $X^2{}_2$ respectively, is related to the total X_2 by a condition of *equality* rather than of summation. Thus, by definition, $X^1{}_2 = X_2$ and $X^2{}_2 = X_2$."[54]

As Samuelson has shown, the form of the marginal rate of substitution conditions which define the Pareto-efficient utility possibility frontier in a world where such public goods exist, or at least where there are outputs with important "public" qualities, renders any kind of price-market routine virtually useless for the computation of output-mix and of distribution, hence, also, for organizational decentralization. Where some restraints in the maximum problem take the form: total production of X *equals* consumption by Crusoe of X *equals* consumption of X by Friday, Pareto efficiency requires that the marginal rate of transformation in production between X and Y

equal not the (equalized) MRS of each separate consumer, but rather the algebraic *sum* of such MRS's. This holds, of course, in what in other respects is a conventionally neoclassical world: preference and production functions are of well-behaved curvature, all is convex.

If, then, at the bliss point, with Y as numeraire, Px is equated to the marginal Y-cost of X in production (as is required to get optimal production), and X is offered for sale at that p_x, preference-maximizing consumers adjusting their purchases so as to equate their individual MRS's to p_x will necessarily under-use X. Moreover, a pricing game will not induce consumers truthfully to reveal their preferences. It pays each consumer to understate his desire for X relative to Y, since his enjoyment of X is a function only of total X, rather than, as is true of a pure private good, just of that fraction of X he pays for.

The two Samuelson articles[55] explore both the analytics and the general implications of "public goods." Here the notion is of relevance because much externality is due precisely to the "public" qualities of a great many activities. For example, the externality associated with the generation of ideas, knowledge, etc., is due in good part to the public character of these "commodities." Many interconsumer externalities are of this sort: my party is my neighbor's disturbance, your nice garden is any passerby's nice view, my children's education is your children's good company, my Strategic Air Command is your Strategic Air Command, etc. The same consumption item enters, positively or negatively, both our preference functions. The consumptions involved are intrinsically and essentially joint.

[53] P. A. Samuelson, *Review of Economics and Statistics,* XXXVI (Nov. 1954), 387.

[54] P. A. Samuelson, *Review of Economics and Statistics,* XXXVII (Nov. 1955), 350.

[55] And a third unpublished paper, which was read at the 1955 American Economic Association meetings and to a copy of which I came to have access while this paper was being written. For earlier writings on public goods, by Wicksell, Lindahl, Musgrave, Bowen and others see references in the above cited Samuelson articles.

This kind of externality is distinct from either of the other two pure types. Here technological nonconvexities need in no way be involved. In fact the $MRT = \Sigma MRS$ condition is certain to hold true precisely where production takes place at constant or non-increasing returns, and hence where the production possibility set is necessarily convex. Further, there are no decentralized organizational rearrangements, no private bookkeeping devices, which would, if only feasibility were not at issue, eliminate the difficulty. It is the central implication of the Samuelson model that where public good phenomena are present, there does not exist a set of prices associated with the (perfectly definable) bliss point, which would sustain the bliss configuration. The set of prices which would induce profit-seeking competitors to produce the optimal bill of goods, would be necessarily inefficient in allocating that bill of goods. Moreover, even abstracting from production, no single set of relative prices will efficiently ration any fixed bill of goods so as to place the system on its contract locus, except in the singular case where at that output and income-distribution MRS's of every individual are identically the same (or zero for all but one). There is failure "by existence."

IV. COMMENTS

Type (1)   In a sense, Type (1) is not symmetrical with the other two categories. One can think of some nontrivial instances where the institutional element does appear to be "binding": skill-training of people, for example. But even there, it could be argued that the crucial elements are durability, uncertainty, and the fact that slavery as a mode of organization is itself in the nature of a public good which enters people's preference functions, or the implicit social welfare function, inseparably from the narrowly "economic" variables. In those instances, in turn, where bookkeeping feasibility appears to be the cause of the trouble,

the question arises why bookkeeping is less feasible than where it is in fact being done. In the end, it may be that much of what appears to partake of Type (1) is really a compound of Types (2) and (3), with dynamical durability and uncertainty elements thrown in. At any rate, a deeper analysis of this category may cause it substantially to shrink.

Nonproduced scarcities   One particular instance where what appears like Type (1) is really Type (2) warrants special mention. Public ownership of nonproduced resources, e.g., the lakes and mountains of national parks, may make it appear that externality is due to statutory barriers to private ownership and commercial rental. But this is missing the point. Take, for instance, a community which has available a single source of fresh water of fixed capacity. Assume that the bliss solution gives out a positive ration-price per gallon such as would make sale of the water commercially profitable. Yet a laissez-faire system would fail, "by structure," to sustain bliss. A private owner of the single indivisible well, if given his head, would take advantage of the tilt in the demand curve. The real cause of externality is not the arbitrary rapaciousness of public authority but the indivisibility of the source of supply. This case, by the way, is akin to where indivisibility or increasing returns to scale within a range allow profitable scope for one or a few efficient producers, but for no more. At the bliss price all will do the right thing, but if prices are not administered, oligopoly or monopoly will result. A capitalist Lange-Lerner system with private ownership but administered prices would work fine, but laissez-faire markets would fail.

Meade's "atmosphere"   The relation of my tri-cornered ordering to Meade's polar categories is of interest.[56] His first category, "unpaid factors," is identical to my Type

[56] *Op. cit.* (This and the next section can be omitted without loss of continuity.)

(1). But his second, labeled "atmosphere," is a rather curious composite. Meade's qualitative characterization of "atmosphere": e.g., of afforestation-induced rainfall, comes very close to the public good notion.[57] He links this, however, as necessarily bound up with increasing returns to scale in production to society at large, hence a J. B. Clark-like overexhaustion, adding-up problem.[58]

If, following Meade, one abstracts from shared water-table phenomena (let rain-caused water input be rigidly proportional to area) then Farmer Jones' rain is Farmer Smith's rain and we have my Type (3). But nothing in this situation requires that either farmer's full production function (with an axis for rain) need show increasing returns to scale. It may be that returns to additional bundles of non-rain inputs, with given constant rainfall, diminish sharply, and that it takes proportional increases of land, labor *and rain* to get a proportional effect on output. If so, Meade's overexhaustion problem will not arise. But all would not be well: the public good quality of rainfall would cause an independent difficulty, one that Meade, if I understand him correctly, does not take into account, i.e., that rain ought to be "produced" by timber growers until its MC is equal to the sum of all the affected farmers MRS's for rain as an input, whatever may be the curvature of the latter's production functions.[59]

On the other hand, Meade's formal mathematical treatment of "atmosphere," as distinct from his verbal characterization and his example, suggests that it is a non-appropriable, and therefore unpaid, factor which gives rise to increasing returns to scale to society though not to the individual producer. At least this is all he needs for the effect he is looking for: a self-policing though nonoptimal competitive situation, where, because the full production functions (i.e., with an axis for rain) are of greater than first degree, the correction of externality via subsidies to promote the creation of favorable atmosphere requires net additions to society's fiscal burden. If this is the crucial consequence of "atmosphere," then it need have no "public" quality. All this would happen even though Smith and Jones were "competing" for the water from the shared water-table under their subsoil, just like bees competing for nectar.

Scitovsky's "two concepts" [60] Professor Scitovsky, in turn, in his suggestive 1954 article, distinguishes between the statical direct interactions of equilibrium theory and the kinds of pecuniary external economies emphasized in the economic development literature. He classifies the former as consumer-consumer, producer-consumer, and producer-producer interactions, labels

---

[57] See esp. bottom of p. 61 and top of p. 62, *op. cit.*

[58] Since his argument is restricted to competitive situations, hence necessarily excludes increasing-returns-to-paid-factors such as would require production at a loss, Meade specifies constant returns to proportional variation of labor and land in wheat farming, though the full production function for wheat, including the atmosphere input (rain), exhibits increasing returns to scale. But the individual farmer does not pay for rain, hence his factor payments just match his sales revenue, by the Euler Theorem.

[59] Formally, Meade denotes "atmosphere" as a situation where the production function, e.g., of farmers takes the form $X_1 = H_1(L_1,C_1)A_1(X_2)$,

with L as labor, C as capital and A the atmosphere effect on X_1 of X_2. The full function exhibits increasing returns to scale but the H function alone, with A constant, is homogeneous of first degree. But why can't this be put in terms of Meade's unpaid factor type function where $X_1 = H_1(L_1,C_1,X_2)$? Example: $X_1 = L_1^a C_1^{1-a} X_2$. All this has nothing to do with whether $A = A_1 + A_2$ or rather $A = A_1 = A_2$. Unfortunately, the example itself tends to mislead. The fact that exclusion of rain-users (farmers) by producers (timber-growers) is hardly feasible, i.e., that rain is like Type (1), distracts attention from the important point that *if* rain is, as Meade tells us, a public good, then rationing it by price would be inefficient even if it were feasible. (It should be said that Meade concludes his article: "But, in fact, of course, external economies or diseconomies may not fall into either of these precise divisions and may contain features of both of them.")

[60] *Op. cit.*

the last as external economies and asserts that they are rare and, on the whole, unimportant.

While Scitovsky does not raise the question of what gives rise to such producer-producer interactions, both his examples, and his conclusion that they are of little significance, suggests that he is thinking primarily of Type (1): nonappropriability. But this is to ignore public goods—surely a more important cause of interaction. Moreover, by taking full account of these, Scitovsky's "fifth and important case, which, however, does not quite fit into . . . (his) . . . classification . . . , where society provides social services through communal action and makes these available free of charge to all persons and firms," can be made nicely to fall into place.[61]

Samuelson on Types (2) and (3) While the public good model helps to sort out the phenomena Meade lumped under "atmosphere," Samuelson himself emphasizes the analytical bond between indivisibility and public good situations. In both an explicit "summing in" is required of "all direct and indirect utilities and costs in all social decisions." [62] In Type (2) situations it is the intramarginal consumer's and producer's surpluses associated with various all or nothing decisions "in-the-lump" that have to be properly (interpersonally) weighted and summed, while in Type (3) it is only utilities and costs at the margin that require adding. But, and this is the crucial shared quality of the two categories, both make it necessary to sum utilities over many people.[63]

Exclusion One more comment may be warranted on the significance, in a public good type situation, of nonappropriability. "Exclusion" is almost never impossible. A recluse can build a wall around his garden, Jones can keep his educated children away from those of Smith, etc. But if thereby some people (e.g., the recluse) are made happier and some (e.g., the passers-by) less happy, any decision about whether to "exclude" or not implies an algebraic summing of the somehow-weighted utilities of the people involved. And if the wall requires scarce resources, the final utility sum must be matched against the cost of the wall. When Type (3) blends with indivisibility in production, as it does in the case of the wall, or in the case of a lighthouse, the comparison has to be made between intramarginal totals. Where no lumpiness is involved (e.g., the decibels at which I play my radio) only MRS and perhaps MC calculations are called for. But the really crucial decision may well be about how much perfectly feasible appropriation and exclusion is desirable.

---

[61] *Ibid.*, fn. 3, p. 144. Scitovsky, following Meade, restricts his "first concept" of external economies to phenomena consistent with competitive equilibrium. He treats indivisibilities and increasing returns to scale as belonging to his "second concept" which has to do with disequilibrium, investment decisions, and growth. It is, of course, entirely legitimate to restrict analysis to competitive situations. But the Scitovsky treatment must not be taken to imply that lumpiness is irrelevant to statical analysis of stationary solution points. If one is interested in the statical efficiency of decentralized price calculations, they are crucial. But this is carping. Scitovsky's important contribution lies in emphasizing and clarifying the point first hinted at by P. N. Rosenstein-Rodan that in a world of disequilibrium dynamics pecuniary external economies may play an independent role —one distinct, that is, from simply being an unreliable signal of monopoly troubles (*Economic Journal*, LIII, 1943, 202–11).

[62] *Ibid.*, p. 9.

[63] There is one qualification to be made: if all public good and increasing returns to scale industries produce only intermediate products, all externalities may cancel out in intra-business-sector transactions. If so, only total revenues and total costs have to be summed. Incidentally, the exposition may misleadingly suggest another symmetry between Types (2) and (3). In a pure Type (3) situation, *if* there are no public producers' goods, then while prices cannot be used to ration the bliss point output-mix, they can be used efficiently to mediate production. In Type (2), on the other hand, *if* all final consumables are divisible, price calculations, while failing in production, will work in exchange. This symmetry breaks down, of course, as soon as one violates, as does the real world, the two "if's."

Arrangements to offset   It is of interest to speculate what, if any, organizational rearrangements could offset the three categories of externality and avoid the need for centrally calculated tax-subsidy schemes.[64] In concept, Type (1) can be offset by rearrangements of ownership and by "proper" bookkeeping, such as need not violate the structural requirements of decentralized competition. Further, no resort to non-market tests would be required.[65]

Types (2) and (3) are not so amenable to correction consistent with decentralized institutions. The easiest possible case occurs where increasing returns obtain on the level of single producers'-good plants, much of whose production can be absorbed by a single user firm. Here vertical integration takes care of the problem. Not every process inside a well-run firm is expected to cover its cost in terms of the correct set of internal accounting (shadow) prices. Total profits are the only criterion, and it may pay a firm to build a private bridge between its two installations on opposite sides of a river yet charge a zero accounting price for its use by the various decentralized manufacturing and administrative divisions; the bridge would make accounting losses, yet total company profits will have increased. As long, then, as such integration is consistent with the many-firms requirement for competition, no extra-market tests are required.[66] The private total conditions: TR less TC, correctly account for social gain.

Where a producers'-good firm, required to produce at a stage of falling AC, sells to many customer firms and industries, an adding up of all the associated TR's and TC's at the precalculated "as if" competitive prices associated with the bliss point would again effectively "mop up" all social costs and benefits.[67] But the institutional reorganization required to get correct decentralized calculation involves horizontal and vertical integration, and the monopoly or oligopoly problem looms large indeed. The Type (3) case of a pure *producers'* public good belongs here: only input MR's along production functions require summing.

In the general case of a mixed producer-consumer good (or of a pure consumer good) which is "public" or is produced under conditions of increasing returns to scale, it is impossible to avoid comparison of multiperson utility totals. Explicit administrative consideration must be given, if you like, to consumer's and producer's surpluses for which no market-institution tests exist short of that provided by a perfectly discriminating monopolist. But to invoke perfect discrimination is to beg the question. It implies knowledge of all preference functions, while as Samuelson has emphasized,[68] the crucial game-theoretical quality of the situation is that consumers will not correctly reveal their preferences: it will pay them to "cheat."

Blends   Examination is needed of various blends of Types (2) and (3), such as Sidgwick's lighthouse;[69] or for that matter,

---

[64] For illustrative derivation of the formulas for corrective taxes and subsidies in Type (1) situations, see Meade (*op. cit.*).

[65] The Emancipation Proclamation could constitute, of course, a substantial barrier.

[66] If, however, the "break even" scale of operation of the integrated firm (i.e., where MC cuts AC from below) is much greater than if the river had not been there to span, or could be spanned by some means of a lower fixed-cost-to-variable-cost ratio, the monopoly problem may simply be "pushed forward" to consumer markets.

[67] Assuming that all consumer goods are finely divisible and require no lumpy decisions by consumers.

[68] Cf. any of the three "Public Expenditure" articles (*supra*).

[69] Sidgwick, by the way, as also Pigou, thought of a lighthouse as of Type (1). It is, of course, "inconvenient" to levy tolls on ships, but it is hardly impossible to "exclude," for instance by means of "scrambling" devices (though poor Sidgwick could hardly have known about such things). The point is, rather, that it would be inefficient to do so: the marginal cost to society of an additional ship taking directional guidance from the beacon atop the Statue of Liberty is zero, *ipso* price should be zero. In the case of a lighthouse

and as suggested by Samuelson, of blends of public and private goods even where all production functions are fully convex. There are many puzzling cases. Do bridge crossings differ in kind from radio programs? Both involve indivisibility and, where variable cost is zero for the bridge, zero MC's. The correct price for an extra stroller, as for an extra listener, is clearly zero. Yet bridge crossings have a distinctly private quality: bridges get congested, physical capacity is finite. This is not true of a broadcast. There is no finite limit to the number of sets that can costlessly tune in.[70] Radio programs, then, have a public dimension. Yet, in a sense, so do bridges. While your bridge crossing is not my bridge crossing, in fact could limit my crossings, your bridge is my bridge. What is involved here is that most things are multidimensional and more than one dimension may matter.

V. EFFICIENCY, MARKETS AND CHOICE OF INSTITUTIONS

All the above has to do with the statical efficiency of price-directed allocation in more or less idealized market situations. Relevance to choice of institutions depends, of course, on the prevalence of the phenomena which cause externality and on the importance to be attached to statical efficiency. Space precludes extensive discussion of these important issues, but a few casual comments, in the form of *dicta,* are perhaps warranted.

How important are nonappropriability, nonconvexity and public goods? I would be inclined to argue that while nonappropria-

bility is of small import,[71] the same cannot be said of the other two. True enough, it is difficult to think of many examples of pure public goods. Most things—even battleships, and certainly open air concerts and schools (though not knowledge)—have an "if more for you then less for me" quality. But this is of little comfort. As long as activities have even a trace of publicness, price calculations are inefficient.[72] And it is surely hard to gainsay that some degree of public quality pervades much of even narrowly "economic" activity.

Lumpiness, in turn, and nonlinearity of the increasing returns sort, while in *most* instances a matter of degree, and, within limits, of choice, are also in the nature of things. The universe is full of singularities, thresholds and nonproportionalities: speed of light, gravitational constant, the relation of circumference to area, etc. As economists we can cajole or bully engineers into designing processes and installations that save on congealed inputs and give smaller maximal service yields, especially when designing for low-income communities. But the economically perhaps arbitrary, not completely physics-imposed quality of indivisibilities associated with standard designs and ways of doing things should not blind. Nonlinearity and lumpiness are evident facts of nature.[73]

More important, at this level of discourse[74]—though perhaps it hardly need be said—is that statical market efficiency is neither sufficient nor necessary for market institutions to be the "preferred" mode of social organization. Quite apart from insti-

this is twice true: because the beacon is in the nature of a public good: more for the Queen Mary means no less for the Liberté; and because a lighthouse is virtually an all-fixed-cost, zero variable-cost facility.

[70] Richard Eckaus has suggested to me that it is possible to exhaust the space to which the broadcast is limited and that this makes the situation a little more like that of a bridge. Neither of us is entirely satisfied, however.

[71] Except for labor skills—and these would take us beyond the bounds of reversible statics.
[72] This is not to say that there exist other feasible modes of social calculation and organization which are more efficient.
[73] Their quantitative significance is, of course, very sensitive to scale, to "size" of markets. This explains the particular emphasis on the role of "social overheads" in low income countries.
[74] Where recourse to strategic considerations of feasibility, crucial though they be, is quite out of order.

tutional consideration, Pareto efficiency as such may not be necessary for bliss.[75] If, e.g., people are sensitive not only to their own jobs but to other people's as well, or more generally, if such things as relative status, power, and the like, matter, the injunction to maximize output, to hug the production-possibility frontier, can hardly be assumed "neutral," and points on the utility frontier may associate with points inside the production frontier.[76] Furthermore, there is nothing pre-ordained about welfare functions which are sensitive only to individual consumer's preferences. As a matter of fact, few people would take such preferences seriously enough to argue against any and all protection of individuals against their own mistakes (though no external effects be involved).

All this is true even when maximization is subject only to technological and resource limitations. Once we admit other side relations, which link input-output variables with "noneconomic" political and organizational values, matters become much more complicated. If markets be ends as well as means, their nonefficiency is hardly sufficient ground for rejection.[77] On the other hand, efficient markets may not do, even though Pareto-efficiency is necessary for bliss. Even with utopian lump-sum redistribution, efficiency of the "invisible hand" does not preclude preference for other efficient modes of organization, if there be any.[78]

Yet when all is said, and despite the host of crucial feasibility considerations which render choice in the real world inevitably a problem in the strategy of "second best," it is surely interesting and useful to explore the implications of Paretian efficiency. Indeed, much remains to be done. There is need, in particular, for more systematic exploration of the inadequacies of market calculation in a setting of growth.[79]

---

[75] That it is never sufficient is, of course, well known. Of the infinite Pareto-efficient configurations at best only one: that which gives the "right" distribution of income in terms of the W-function that is to count, has normative, prescriptive significance. Moreover, most interesting W-functions are likely to be sensitive to "noneconomic" factors, such as are, if not inconsistent, at least extraneous to Paretian considerations. Where such additional values of a political or social nature are separable from input-output values (i.e., where the two sets can be varied independently of each other) one "can" of course separate the overall W-function into a "political" and an "economic" component and maximize separately over each.

[76] This is different from the usual case of consumer sensitivity to the input-output configuration of producers, e.g., factory soot or a functional but ugly plant spoiling the view. Such joint-product "bads" can be treated as inputs and treated in the usual Paretian fashion. It is a different matter that their public quality will violate duality, hence render market calculation inefficient.

[77] This is too crude a formulation. It is not necessary that markets as such be an "ultimate" value.

Political and social (non-output) values relating to the configuration of power, initiative, opportunity, etc., may be so much better served by some form of noneficient market institutions than by possible alternative modes of more efficient organization as to warrant choice of the former. The analytical point, in all this, is that the outcome of a maximization process and the significance of "efficiency" are as sensitive to the choice of side-conditions as to the welfare-function and that these need be "given" to the economist in the same sense that a welfare function has to be given.

[78] The above is still strictly statical. For related dynamical problems, e.g., possible conflict between one-period and intertemporal efficiency, cf., "On Capital Productivity, Input Allocation and Growth," this *Journal*, LXXI (Feb. 1957).

[79] The development literature on market failure, while full of suggestive insight, is in a state of considerable confusion. Much work is needed to exhaust and elucidate the seminal ideas of Young, Rosenstein-Rodan, Nurkse and others. For important beginnings, see Scitovsky (*op. cit.*), M. Fleming, "External Economies and the Doctrine of Balanced Growth," *Economic Journal*, LXV (June 1955), and Fellner (*op. cit.*).

The view that we should not turn social historian or what not, that the logic of economizing has some prescriptive significance, rests on the belief that narrowly "economic" efficiency is important in terms of many politically relevant W-functions, and consistent with a wide variety of power and status configurations and modes of social organization. On the other hand, some may feel that the very language of Paretian welfare economics: "welfare function," "utility-frontier," in relation to choice of social institutions, is grotesque. What is at stake, of course, is not the esthetics of language, on which I yield without demur, but abstraction and rigorous theorizing.

35. Diagrammatic Exposition of a Theory of Public Expenditure*

PAUL A. SAMUELSON

Paul A. Samuelson (B.A., Chicago, 1935; M.A., Harvard, 1936; Ph.D., 1941) was born in Gary, Indiana, in 1915. He is one of the world's most distinguished economists, having made outstanding contributions both at the most advanced and abstruse levels, and at the level of the economic novice. The 1970 Nobel Memorial Prize citation lauded his efforts "to raise the level of scientific analysis in economic theory." His book *Foundations of Economic Analysis* is a highly mathematical and sophisticated treatment of dynamic theory and general equilibrium economics. His introductory textbook, *Economics*, which has gone through eight editions since it was first published in 1948, is the most widely used "principles" book in America. Samuelson's professional writings, covering an incredibly wide sweep of economic research, have been reprinted in the two volume work, *Collected Scientific Papers of Paul A. Samuelson*. Since 1940, Professor Samuelson has been on the faculty of the Massachusetts Institute of Technology.

In the November 1954 issue of this RE-VIEW my paper on "The Pure Theory of Public Expenditure" presented a mathematical exposition of a public expenditure theory that goes back to Italian, Austrian, and Scandinavian writers of the last 75 years. After providing that theory with its needed logically-complete optimal conditions, I went on to demonstrate the fatal inability of any decentralized market or voting mechanism to attain or compute this optimum. The present note presents in terms of two-dimensional diagrams an essentially equivalent formulation of the theory's optimum conditions and briefly discusses some criticisms.

A Polar-Case Model of Government

Doctrinal history shows that theoretical insight often comes from considering strong or extreme cases. The grand Walrasian model of competitive general equilibrium is

538

one such extreme polar case. We can formulate it so stringently as to leave no economic role for government. What strong polar case shall the student of public expenditure set alongside this pure private economy?

One possibility is the model of a groupmind. Such a model, which has been extensively used by nationalists and by Romantic critics of classical economics, can justify any, and every, configuration of government. So there is perhaps little that an economic theorist can usefully say about it.

My alternative is a slightly more sophisticated one, but still—intentionally—an extreme polar case. It is consistent with individualism, yet at the same time it explicitly introduces the vital external interdependencies that no theory of government can do without. Its basic assumption is an oversharp distinction between the following two kinds of goods:

(i) A *private* consumption good, like bread, whose total can be parcelled out among two or more persons, with one man having a loaf less if another gets a loaf more. Thus if X_1 is total bread, and X_1^1 and X_1^2 are the respective private consumptions of Man 1 and Man 2, we can say that the total equals the sum of the separate consumptions—or $X_1 = X_1^1 + X_1^2$.

(ii) A *public* consumption good, like an outdoor circus or national defense, which is provided for each person to enjoy or not, according to his tastes. I assume the public good can be varied in total quantity, and write X_2 for its magnitude. It differs from a private consumption good in that each man's consumption of it, X_2^1 and X_2^2 respectively, is related to the total X_2 by a condition of *equality* rather than of summation. Thus, by definition, $X_2^1 = X_2$, and $X_2^2 = X_2$.

Obviously, I am introducing a strong polar case. We could easily lighten the stringency of our assumptions. But on re-

flection, I think most economists will see that this is a natural antipodal case to the admittedly extreme polar case of traditional individualistic general equilibrium. The careful empiricist will recognize that many—though not all—of the realistic cases of government activity can be fruitfully analyzed as some kind of a blend of these two extreme polar cases.

Graphical Depiction of Tastes and Technology

The first three charts summarize our assumptions about tastes and technology. Each diagram has a private good, such as bread, on its vertical axis; each has a public good on its horizontal axis. The heavy indifference curves of Figure 35.1 summarize Man 1's preferences between public and private goods. Figure 35.2's indifference curves do the same for Man 2; and the relative flatness of the contour shows that, in a sense, he has less liking for the public good.

The heavy production-possibility or opportunity-cost curve AB in Figure 35.3 relates the total productions of public and private goods in the usual familiar manner: the curve is convex from above to reflect the usual assumption of increasing relative marginal costs (or generalized diminishing returns).[1]

Because of our special definition of a public good, the three diagrams are not independent. Each must be lined up with *exactly the same horizontal scale*. Because increasing a public good for society simultaneously increases it for each and every

[1] Even though a public good is being compared with a private good, the indifference curves are drawn with the usual convexity to the origin. This assumption, as well as the one about diminishing returns, could be relaxed without hurting the theory. Indeed, we could recognize the possible case where one man's circus is another man's poison, by permitting indifference curves to bend forward. This would not affect the analysis but would answer a critic's minor objection. Mathematically, we could without loss of generality set $X_2^i =$ any function of X_2, relaxing strict equality.

man, we must always be simultaneously at exactly the same longitude in all three figures. Moving an inch east in one diagram moves us the same amount east in all.

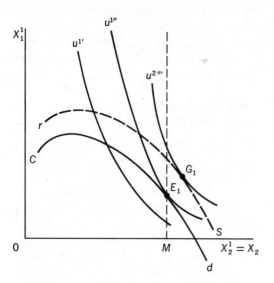

FIGURE 35.1 INDIFFERENCE CONTOURS RELATING MAN 1's CONSUMPTION OF PUBLIC AND PRIVATE GOODS

The private good on the vertical axis is subject to no new and unusual restrictions. Each man can be moved north or south on his indifference diagram independently. But, of course, the third diagram does list the total of bread summed over the private individuals; so it must have a larger vertical axis, and our momentary northward position on it must correspond to the sum of the independent northward positions of the separate individuals.

Tangency Conditions for Pareto Optima

What is the best or ideal state of the world for such a simple system? That is, what three vertically-aligned points corresponding to a determination of a given total of both goods and a determinate parcelling out of them among all separate individuals will be the ethically preferred final configuration?

To answer this ethical, normative question we must be given a set of norms in the form of a *social welfare function* that renders interpersonal judgments. For expository convenience, let us suppose that this will be supplied later and that we know in advance it will have the following special individualistic property: leaving each person on his same indifference level will leave social welfare unchanged; at any point, a move of each man to a higher indifference curve can be found that will increase social welfare.

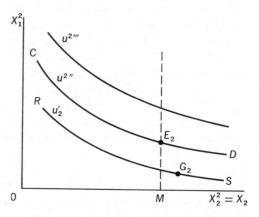

FIGURE 35.2 INDIFFERENCE CONTOURS RELATING MAN 2's CONSUMPTION OF PUBLIC AND PRIVATE GOODS

Given this rather weak assurance about the forthcoming social welfare function, we can proceed to determine tangency conditions of an "efficiency" type that are at least necessary, though definitely not sufficient. We do this by setting up a preliminary maximum problem which will eventually necessarily have to be satisfied.

Holding all but one man at specified levels of indifference, how can we be sure that the remaining man reaches his highest indifference level?

Concretely, this is how we define such a tangency optimum: Set Man 2 on a specified indifference curve, say his middle one CD. Paying attention to Mother Nature's scarcity, as summarized in Figure 35.3's AB curve, and following Man 1's tastes as given by Figure 35.1 indifference curves, how high on those indifference curves can we move Man 1?

The answer is given by the tangency point E_1, and the corresponding aligned points E_2 and E.

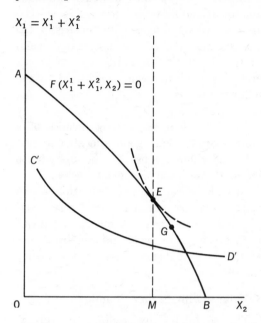

$$X_1 = X_1^1 + X_1^2$$

$$F(X_1^1 + X_1^2, X_2) = 0$$

FIGURE 35.3 TRANSFORMATION SCHEDULE RELATING TOTALS OF PUBLIC AND PRIVATE GOODS

How is this derived? Copy CD on Figure 35.3 and call it $C'D'$. The distance between $C'D'$ and AB represents the amounts of the two goods that are physically available to Man 1. So subtract $C'D'$ vertically from AB and plot the algebraic result as cd in Figure 35.1. Now where on cd would Man 1 be best off? Obviously at the tangency point E_1 where cd touches (but does not cross) his highest attainable indifference contour.[2]

[2] The reader can easily derive rs and the tangency point G_1 corresponding to an original specification of Man 2's indifference level at the lower level RS rather than at AB. He can also interchange the roles of the two men, thereby deriving the point E_2 by a tangency condition. As a third approach, he can *vertically add* Man 2's specified indifference curve to each and every indifference curve of Man 1; the resulting family of contours can be conveniently plotted on Figure 35.3, and the final optimum can be read off from the tangency of AB to that family at the point E—as

How many such Pareto-optimal points are there? Obviously, for each of the infinite possible initial indifference curves to put Man 2 on, we can derive a new highest attainable tangency level for Man 1. So there are an infinity of such optimal points —as many in number as there are points on the usual contract curve. All of these Pareto-optimal points have the property that from them there exists no physically-feasible movement that will make every man better off. Of course we cannot compare two different Pareto points until we are given a social welfare function. For a move from one Pareto point to another must always hurt one man while it is helping another, and an interpersonal way of comparing these changes must be supplied.

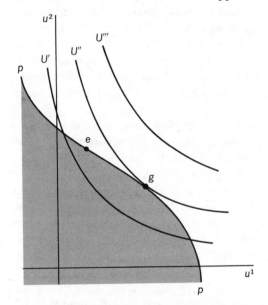

FIGURE 35.4 UTILITY FRONTIER OF PARETO-OPTIMAL EFFICIENCY AND ITS TANGENCY TO HIGHEST ATTAINABLE SOCIAL WELFARE CONTOUR

Figure 35.4 indicates these utility possibilities on an ordinal diagram. Each axis provides an indicator of the two men's re-

shown by the short broken-line indifference curve at E. It is easy to show that any of these tangencies are, in the two-good case, equivalent to Equation (2) of my cited paper; with a single private good my Equation (1) becomes redundant.

spective indifference curve levels. The utility frontier of Pareto-optimal points is given by pp: the double fold infinity of "inefficient," non-Pareto-optimal points is given by the shaded area; the pp frontier passes from northwest to southeast to reflect the inevitable conflict of interests characterizing any contract locus; the curvature of the pp locus is of no particular type since we have no need to put unique cardinal numbers along the indifference contours and can content ourselves with east-west and north-south relationships in Figure 35.4 without regard to numerical degree and to uneven stretchings of either utility axis.

The Optimum of All the Pareto Optima

Now we can answer the fundamental question: what is the best configuration for this society?

Use of the word "best" indicates we are in the ascientific area of "welfare economics" and must be provided with a set of norms. Economic science cannot deduce a social welfare function; what it can do is neutrally interpret any arbitrarily specified welfare function.

The heavy contours labelled U', U'', and U''' summarize all that is relevant in the provided social welfare function (they provide the needed ordinal scoring of every state of the world, involving different levels of indifference for the separate individuals).[3]

---

[3] These social welfare or social indifference contours are given no particular curvature. Why? Again because we are permitting any arbitrary ordinal indicator of utility to be used on the axes of Figure 35.4.

An ethical postulate ruling out all "dog-in-the-manger phenomena" will make all partial derivatives of the social welfare function $U(u^1, u^2, \ldots)$ always positive. This will assure the usual negative slopes to the U contours of Figure 35.4. However, without hurting the Pareto part of the new welfare economics, we can relax this assumption a little and let the contours bend forward. If, at every point there can be found at least one positive partial derivative, this will be sufficient to rule out satiation points and will imply the necessity of the Pareto-optimal tangency condition of the earlier diagrams.

Obviously society cannot be best off inside the utility frontier. Where then on the utility frontier will the "best obtainable bliss point" be? We will move along the utility frontier pp until we touch the highest social indifference curve: this will be at g where pp tangentially touches, without crossing, the highest obtainable social welfare level U''. In words, we can interpret this final tangency condition[4] in the following terms:

(i) The social welfare significance of a unit of any private good allocated to private individuals must at the margin be the same for each and every person.

(ii) The Pareto-optimal condition, which makes relative marginal social cost equal to the sum of all persons' marginal rates of substitution, is already assured by virtue of the fact that bliss lies on the utility frontier.[5]

Relations with Earlier Theories

This completes the graphical interpretation of my mathematical model. There remains the pleasant task of relating this graphical treatment to earlier work of Bowen[6] and others.

To do this, look at Figure 35.5, which gives an alternative depiction of the optimal tangency condition at a point like E.

---

[4] This tangency condition would have to be expressed mathematically in terms of numerical indicators of utility that are not invariant under a monotonic renumbering. However, it is easy to combine this tangency with the earlier Pareto-type tangency to get the formulation (3) of my cited paper, which is independent of the choice of numerical indicators of U, u^1, or u^2.

[5] A remarkable duality property of private and public goods should be noted. Private goods whose totals add—such as $X_1 = X_2{}^1 + X_1{}^2$—lead ultimately to marginal conditions of simultaneous equality—such as $MC = MRS^1 = MRS^2$. Public goods whose totals satisfy a relation of simultaneous equality—such as $X_1 = X_2{}^1 = X_2{}^2$—lead ultimately to marginal conditions that add—such as $MC = MRS^1 + MRS^2$.

[6] Howard R. Bowen, "The Interpretation of Voting in the Allocation of Economic Resources," *Quarterly Journal of Economics*, LVIII (November 1943), 27-49. Much of this is also in Bowen's *Toward Social Economy* (New York, 1948), ch. 18.

I use the private good X_1 as numeraire, measuring all values in terms of it. The MC curve is derived from the AB curve of Figure 35.3: it is nothing but the absolute slope of that production-possibility schedule plotted against varying amounts of the public good; it is therefore a marginal cost curve, with MC measured in terms of the numeraire good.

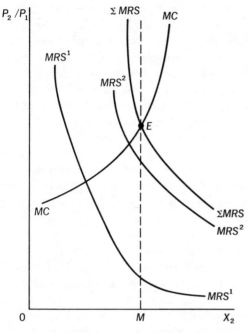

FIGURE 35.5 INTERSECTION OF PUBLIC GOOD'S MARGINAL COST SCHEDULE AND THE VERTICALLY-SUMMED INDIVIDUAL'S MARGINAL RATES OF SUBSTITUTION, AS ENVISAGED BY LINDAHL AND BOWEN

The marginal rate of substitution curves MRS^1 and MRS^2 are derived in a similar fashion from the respective indifference curves of Man 1 and Man 2: thus, MRS^1 is the absolute slope of the $u^{1'''}$ indifference curve plotted against varying amounts of the public good; MRS^2 is the similar slope function derived from Man 2's indifference curve CD. (All three are "marginal" curves, bearing the usual relationship to their respective "total" curves.)

These schedules look like demand curves. We are accustomed to adding horizontally

or laterally the separate demand curves of individuals to arrive at total market demand. But this is valid only for private goods. As Bowen rightly says, *we must in the case of public goods add different individuals' curves vertically.*

This gives us the heavy ΣMRS curve for the whole community. Where is equilibrium? It is at E, where the community MC curve intersects the community ΣMRS curve. Upon reflection the reader will realize that the equality $MC = \Sigma MRS = MRS^1 + MRS^2$ is the precise equivalent of my mathematical equation (2) and of our Pareto-type tangency condition at E_1, E_2, or E. Why? Because of the stipulated requirement that Figure 35.5's curves are to depict the absolute slopes of the curves of Figures 35.1–35.3.

Except for minor details of notation and assumption, Figure 35.5 is identical with the figure shown on page 31 of the first Bowen reference, and duplicated on page 177 of the second reference. I am happy to acknowledge this priority. Indeed anyone familiar with Musgrave's valuable summary of the literature bearing on this area[7] will be struck with the similarity between this Bowen type of diagram and the Lindahl 100-per-cent diagram reproduced by Musgrave.[8]

Once the economic theorist has related

[7] Richard A. Musgrave, "The Voluntary Exchange Theory of Public Economy," *Quarterly Journal of Economics*, LIII (February 1939), 213–17. This gives citations to the relevant works of Sax, De Viti de Marco, Wicksell, and Lindahl. I have greatly benefited from preliminary study of Professor Musgrave's forthcoming treatise on public finance, which I am sure will constitute a landmark in this area.

[8] Musgrave, *op. cit.*, 216, which is an acknowledged adaption from Erik Lindahl, *Die Gerechtigkeit in der Besteuerung* (Lund, 1919), 89. I have not had access to this important work. This diagram plots instead of the functions of Figure 35.5 the exact same functions after each has been divided by the MC function. The equilibrium intersection corresponding to E now shows up as the point at which all persons will together voluntarily provide 100 per cent of the full (unit? marginal?) cost of the public service. (If MC is not constant, some modifications in the Musgrave diagram may be required.)

my graphical and mathematical analysis to the Lindahl and Bowen diagrams, he is in a position, I believe, to discern the logical advantage of the present formulation. For there is something circular and unsatisfactory about both the Bowen and Lindahl constructions: they show what the final equilibrium looks like, but by themselves they are not generally able to find the desired equilibrium. To see this, note that whereas we might know MC in Figure 35.5, we would not know the appropriate MRS schedules for *all* men until we already were familiar with the final E intersection point. (We might know MRS^2 from the specification that Man 2 is to be on the AB level; but then we wouldn't know MRS^1 until Figure 35.1's tangency had given us Man 1's highest attainable level, $u^{1'''}$.) Under conditions of general equilibrium, Figures 35.1–35.3 logically contain Figure 35.5 inside them, but not vice versa. Moreover, Figures 35.1–35.3 explicitly call attention to the fact that there is an infinite number of different diagrams of the Lindahl-Bowen type, one for each specified level of relative interpersonal well-being.[9]

Concluding Reflections

I hope that the analytic model outlined here may help make a small and modest step toward understanding the complicated realities of political economy. Much remains to be done. This is not the place to discuss the wider implications and difficulties of the presented economic theory.[10] However, I should like to comment briefly on some of the questions about this theory that have been raised in [the *Review of Economics and Statistics*].[11]

(i) On the deductive side, the theory presented here is, I believe, a logically coherent one. This is true whether expressed in my original mathematical notation or in the present diagrammatic form. Admittedly, the latter widens the circle of economists who can understand and follow what is being said. The present version, with its tangencies of methodologically the same type as characterize Cournot-Marshall marginal theory and Bergson-Pigou welfare theory, should from its easily recognized equivalence with the mathematical version make clear my refusal to agree with Dr. Enke's view that my use of mathematics was limited "to notation."

(ii) In terms of the history of similar theories, I hope the present paper will make clear relationships to earlier writers. (In particular, see the above discussion relating my early diagrams and equations to the Bowen-Lindahl formulation.) I shall not bore the reader with irrelevant details of independent rediscoveries of doctrine that my ignorance of the available literature may have made necessary. Yet is it presumptuous to suggest that there does not exist in the present economic literature very much in the way of "conclusions and reasoning" that are, in Dr. Margolis' words,

---

[9] The earlier writers from Wicksell on were well aware of this. They explicitly introduce the assumption that there is to have been a *prior* optimal interpersonal distribution of income, so what I have labelled E might better be labelled G. But the general equilibrium analyst asks: how can the appropriate distribution of income be decided on a prior basis *before* the significant problems of public consumptions have been determined? A satisfactory general analysis can resist the temptation to assume (i) the level of government expenditure must be so small as not to affect appreciably the marginal social significance of money to the different individuals; (ii) each man's indifference curves run parallel to each other in a vertical direction so that every and all indifference curves in Figure 35.1 (or in Figure 35.2) give rise to the same MRS^1 (or MRS^2) curve in Figure 35.5. The modern theorist is anxious to free his analysis from the incubus of unnecessarily restrictive partial equilibrium assumptions.

[10] At the 1955 Christmas Meetings of the American Economic Association and Econometric Society, I hope to present some further developments and qualifications of this approach.

[11] Stephen Enke, "More on the Misuse of Mathematics in Economics: A Rejoinder," [*Review of Economics and Statistics*], xxxvii (May 1955), 131–33; Julius Margolis, "On Samuelson on the Pure Theory of Public Expenditure," this issue, p. 347.

"familiar"? Except for the writers I have cited, and the important unpublished thoughts of Dr. Musgrave, there is much opaqueness in the literature. Much of what goes by the name of the "voluntary exchange theory of public finance" seems pure obfuscation.[12]

(iii) Far from my formulation's being, as some correspondents have thought, a revival of the voluntary exchange theory —it is in fact an attempt to demonstrate how right Wicksell was to worry about the inherent political difficulty of ever getting men to reveal their tastes so as to attain the definable optimum. This intrinsic "game theory" problem has been sufficiently stressed in my early paper so that it has not been emphasized here. I may put the point most clearly in terms of the familiar tools of modern literary economics as follows:

Government supplies products jointly to many people. In ordinary market economics as you increase the number of sellers of a homogeneous product indefinitely, you pass from monopoly through indeterminate oligopoly and can hope to reach a determinate competitive equilibrium in the limit. It is sometimes thought that increasing the number of citizens who are jointly supplied public goods leads to a similar determinate result. This is reasoning from an incorrect analogy. A truer analogy in private economics would be the case of a bilateral-monopoly supplier of joint products whose number of joint products—meat, horn, hide, and so on—is allowed to increase without number: such a process does not lead to a determinate equilibrium of the harmo-

nistic type praised in the literature. My simple model is able to demonstrate this point—which does have "policy implications."

(iv) I regret using "the" in the title of my earlier paper and have accordingly changed the present title. Admittedly, public expenditure and regulation proceed from considerations other than those emphasized in my models. Here are a few:

a. Taxes and expenditure aim at redistributing incomes. I am anxious to clear myself from Dr. Margolis' understandable suspicion that I am the type of liberal who would insist that all redistributions take place through tax policies and transfer expenditures: much public expenditure on education, hospitals, and so on, can be justified by the feasibility consideration that, even if these are not 100 per cent efficient in avoiding avoidable dead-weight loss, they may be better than the attainable imperfect tax alternatives.[13]

b. Paternalistic policies are voted upon themselves by a democratic people because they do not regard the results from spontaneous market action as optimal. Education and forced paces of economic development are good examples of this.

c. Governments provide or regulate services that are incapable of being produced under the strict conditions of constant returns that go to characterize optimal self-regulating atomistic competition.

d. Myriad "generalized external economy and diseconomy" situations, where private pecuniary interest can be expected to deviate from social interests, provide obvious needs for government activity.

I am sure this list of basic considerations underlying government expenditure could be extended farther, including even areas where government probably ought not to operate from almost anyone's viewpoint.

(v) This brief list can end with the most

[12] See Gerhard Colm, "The Theory of Public Expenditure," *Annals of the American Academy of Political and Social Sciences,* CLXXXIII (January 1936), 1–11, reprinted in his *Essays in Public Finance and Fiscal Policy* (New York, 1955), 27–43 for an admirable criticism of the Graziani statement, "We know that the tax tends to take away from each and all that quantity of wealth which they would each have voluntarily yielded to the state for the satisfaction of their purely collective wants" (page 32).

[13] See my "Evaluation of Real National Income," *Oxford Economic Papers,* N.S. II (January 1950), 18 ff. for analytic discussion of this important truth.

important criticism that the various commentators on my paper have put forth. They all ask: "Is it factually true that most—or any!—of the functions of government can be properly fitted into your extreme category of a public good? Can education, the courts, public defense, highway programs, police and fire protection be put into this rigid category of a 'public good available to all'? In practically every one of these cases isn't there an element of variability in the benefit that can go to one citizen *at the expense* of some other citizens?"

To this criticism, I fully agree. And that is why in the present formulation I have insisted upon the polar nature of my category. However, to say that a thing is not located at the South Pole does not logically place it at the North Pole. To deny that most public functions fit into my extreme definition of a public good is not to grant that they satisfy the logically equally-extreme category of a private good. To say that your absence at a concert may contribute to my enjoyment is not to say that the elements of public services can be put into homogeneous additive packages capable of being optimally handled by the ordinary market calculus.

Indeed, I am rash enough to think that in almost every one of the legitimate functions of government that critics put forward there is to be found a blending of the extreme antipodal models. One might even venture the tentative suspicion that any function of government not possessing any trace of the defined public good (and no one of the related earlier described characteristics) ought to be carefully scrutinized to see whether it is truly a legitimate function of government.

(vi) Whether or not I have overstated the applicability of this one theoretical model to actual governmental functions, I believe I did not go far enough in claiming for it relevance to the vast area of decreasing costs that constitutes an important part of economic reality and of the welfare economics of monopolistic competition. I must leave to future research discussions of these vital issues.

Economic theory should add what it can to our understanding of governmental activity. I join with critics in hoping that its pretentious claims will not discourage other economic approaches, other contributions from neighboring disciplines, and concrete empirical investigations.

36. An Economic Theory of Clubs[*]

JAMES M. BUCHANAN[1]

James M. Buchanan (B.S., Middle Tennessee State College, 1940; M.A. Tennessee, 1941; Ph.D. the University of Chicago, 1948) was born in Murfreesboro, Tennessee, in 1919. Presently, he is at Virginia Polytechnic Institute where he is University Professor and General Director of the Center for the Study of Public Choice. Prior to this he served on the faculties of the University of Tennessee, Florida State University, the University of Virginia, and University of California, Los Angeles. Buchanan, whose primary research has been in the fields of public finance and collective decision making, has contributed significantly to the profession's understanding of the relationship between individual preferences and public choice. His many publications include *Public Principles of Public Debt, The Public Finances, Fiscal Theory and Political Economy, The Calculus of Consent* (with Gordon Tullock), *Public Finance in Democratic Process, The Demand and Supply of Public Goods, Cost and Choice,* and *Academia in Anarchy* (with Nicos E. Devletoglou). He is a past president of the Southern Economic Association and a past member of the Executive Committee of the American Economic Association.

The implied institutional setting for neo-classical economic theory, including theoretical welfare economics, is a régime of private property, in which all goods and services are privately (individually) utilized or consumed. Only within the last two decades have serious attempts been made to extend the formal theoretical structure to include communal or collective ownership-consumption arrangements.[2] The "pure theory of public goods" remains in its infancy, and the few models that have been most rigorously developed apply only to polar or extreme cases. For example, in the fundamental papers by Paul A. Samuelson, a

[*] Reprinted from *Economica* (February, 1965) by permission of the publisher, pp. 1–14.
[1] I am indebted to graduate students and colleagues for many helpful suggestions. Specific acknowledgement should be made for the critical assistance of Emilio Giardina of the University of Catania and W. Craig Stubblebine of the University of Delaware.

[2] It is interesting that none of the theories of Socialist economic organization seems to be based on explicit co-operation among individuals. These theories have conceived the economy either in the Lange-Lerner sense as an analogue to a purely private, individually oriented social order or, alternatively, as one that is centrally directed.

sharp conceptual distinction is made between those goods and services that are "purely private" and those that are "purely public." [3] No general theory has been developed which covers the whole spectrum of ownership-consumption possibilities, ranging from the purely private or individualized activity on the one hand to purely public or collectivized activity on the other. One of the missing links here is "a theory of clubs," a theory of co-operative membership, a theory that will include as a variable to be determined the extension of ownership-consumption rights over differing numbers of persons.

Everyday experience reveals that there exists some most preferred or "optimal" membership for almost any activity in which we engage, and that this membership varies in some relation to economic factors. European hotels have more communally shared bathrooms than their American counterparts. Middle and low income communities organize swimming-bathing facilities; high income communities are observed to enjoy privately owned swimming pools.

In this paper I shall develop a general theory of clubs, or consumption ownership-membership arrangements. This construction allows us to move one step forward in closing the awesome Samuelson gap between the purely private and the purely public good. For the former, the optimal sharing arrangement, the preferred club membership, is clearly one person (or one family unit), whereas the optimal sharing group for the purely public good, as defined in the polar sense, includes an infinitely large number of members. That is to say, for any genuinely collective good defined in the Samuelson way, a club that has an infinitely large membership is preferred to all arrangements of finite size. While it is evident that some goods and services may be reasonably classified as purely private, even in the extreme sense, it is clear that few, if any, goods satisfy the conditions of extreme collectiveness. The interesting cases are those goods and services, the consumption of which involves some "publicness," where the optimal sharing group is more than one person or family but smaller than an infinitely large number. The range of "publicness" is finite. The central question in a theory of clubs is that of determining the membership margin, so to speak, the size of the most desirable cost and consumption sharing arrangement. [4]

I

In traditional neo-classical models that assume the existence of purely private goods and services only, the utility function of an individual is written,

$$U^i = U^i(X_1{}^i, X_2{}^i, \ldots, X_n{}^i), \qquad (1)$$

where each of the X's represents the amount of a purely private good available during a specified time period, to the reference individual designated by the superscript.

Samuelson extended this function to include purely collective or public goods, which he denoted by the subscripts, $n + 1, \ldots, n + m$, so that (1) is changed to read,

$$U^i = U^i(X_1{}^i, X_2{}^i, \ldots, X_n{}^i; \\ X_{n+1}{}^i, X_{n+2}{}^i, \ldots, X_{n+m}{}^i). \qquad (2)$$

This approach requires that all goods be initially classified into the two sets, private and public. Private goods, defined to be wholly divisible among the persons, $i = 1, 2, \ldots, s$, satisfy the relation

---

[3] See Paul A. Samuelson, "The Pure Theory of Public Expenditure," *Review of Economics and Statistics*, vol. xxxvi (1954), pp. 387–89; "Diagrammatic Exposition of a Theory of Public Expenditure," *Review of Economics and Statistics*, vol. xxxvii (1955), pp. 350–55.

[4] Note that an economic theory of clubs can strictly apply only to the extent that the motivation for joining in sharing arrangements is itself economic; that is, only if choices are made on the basis of costs and benefits of particular goods and services as these are confronted by the individual. In so far as individuals join clubs for camaraderie, as such, the theory does not apply.

$$X_j = \sum_{i=1}^{s} X_j{}^i,$$

while public goods, defined to be wholly indivisible as among persons, satisfy the relation,

$$X_{n+j} = X_{n+j}{}^i.$$

I propose to drop any attempt at an initial classification or differentiation of goods into fully divisible and fully indivisible sets, and to incorporate in the utility function goods falling between these two extremes. What the theory of clubs provides is, in one sense, a "theory of classification," but this emerges as an output of the analysis. The first step is that of modifying the utility function.

Note that, in neither (1) nor (2) is it necessary to make a distinction between "goods available to the ownership unit of which the reference individual is a member" and "goods finally available to the individual for consumption." With purely private goods, consumption by one individual automatically reduces potential consumption of other individuals by an equal amount. With purely public goods, consumption by any one individual implies equal consumption by all others. For goods falling between such extremes, such a distinction must be made. This is because for such goods there is no unique translation possible between the "goods available to the membership unit" and "goods finally consumed." In the construction which follows, therefore, the "goods" entering the individual's utility function, the X_j's, should be interpreted as "goods available for consumption to the whole membership unit of which the reference individual is a member."

Arguments that represent the size of the sharing group must be included in the utility function along with arguments representing goods and services. For any good or service, regardless of its ultimate place along the conceptual public-private spectrum, the utility that an individual receives from its consumption depends upon *the number of other persons with whom he must share its benefits.* This is obvious, but its acceptance does require breaking out of the private property straitjacket within which most of economic theory has developed. As an extreme example, take a good normally considered to be purely private, say, a pair of shoes. Clearly your own utility from a single pair of shoes, per unit of time, depends on the number of other persons who share them with you. Simultaneous physical sharing may not, of course, be possible; only one person can wear the shoes at each particular moment. However, for any finite period of time, sharing is possible, even for such evidently private goods. For pure services that are consumed in the moment of acquisition the extension is somewhat more difficult, but it can be made none the less. Sharing here simply means that the individual receives a smaller quantity of the service. Sharing a "haircut per month" with a second person is the same as consuming "one-half haircut per month." Given any quantity of final good, as defined in terms of the physical units of some standard quality, the utility that the individual receives from this quantity will be related functionally to the number of others with whom he shares.[5]

Variables for club size are not normally included in the utility function of an individual since, in the private-goods world, the optimal club size is unity. However, for our purposes, these variables must be explicitly included, and, for completeness, a club-size variable should be included for each and every good. Alongside each X_j there must be placed an N_j, which we define as the number of persons who are to participate as "members" in the sharing of

[5] Physical attributes of a good or service may, of course, affect the structure of the sharing arrangements that are preferred. Although the analysis below assumes symmetrical sharing, this assumption is not necessary, and the analysis in its general form can be extended to cover all possible schemes.

good, X_j, including the ith person whose utility function is examined. That is to say, the club-size variable, N_j, measures the number of persons who are to join in the consumption-utilization arrangements for good, X_j, over the relevant time period. The sharing arrangements may or may not call for equal consumption on the part of each member, and the peculiar manner of sharing will clearly affect the way in which the variable enters the utility function. For simplicity we may assume equal sharing, although this is not necessary for the analysis. The rewritten utility function now becomes,

$$U^i = U^i[(X_1{}^i, N_1{}^i), (X_2{}^i, N_2{}^i), \ldots, (X_{n+m}{}^i, N_{n+m}{}^i)].^6 \quad (3)$$

We may designate a numeraire good, X_r, which can simply be thought of as money, possessing value only as a medium of exchange. By employing the convention whereby the lower case u's represent the partial derivatives, we get $u_j{}^i/u_r{}^i$, defined as the marginal rate of substitution in consumption between X and X_r for the jth individual. Since, in our construction, the size of the group is also a variable, we must also examine, $u_{N_j}{}^i/u_r{}^i$, defined as the marginal rate of substitution "in consumption" between the size of the sharing group and the numeraire. That is to say, this ratio represents the rate (which may be negative) at which the individual is willing to give up (accept) money in exchange for additional members in the sharing group.

We now define a cost or production func-

⁶ Note that this construction of the individual's utility function differs from that introduced in an earlier paper, where "activities" rather than "goods" were included as the basic arguments. (See James M. Buchanan and Wm. Craig Stubblebine, "Externality," *Economica*, vol. xxxi (1962), pp. 371–84.) In the alternative construction, the "activities" of other persons enter directly into the utility function of the reference individual with respect to the consumption of all other than purely private goods. The construction here incorporates the same interdependence through the inclusion of the N_j's although in a more general manner.

tion as this confronts the individual, and this will include the same set of variables,

$$F = F^i[(X_1{}^i, N_1{}^i), (X_2{}^i, N_2{}^i), \ldots, (X_{n+m}{}^i, N_{n+m}{}^i)]. \quad (4)$$

Why do the club-size variables, the N_j's, appear in this cost function? The addition of members to a sharing group may, and normally will, affect the cost of the good to any one member. The larger is the membership of the golf club the lower the dues to any single member, given a specific quantity of club facilities available per unit time.

It now becomes possible to derive, from the utility and cost functions, statements for the necessary marginal conditions for Pareto optimality in respect to consumption of each good. In the usual manner we get,

$$u_j{}^i/u_r{}^i = f_j{}^i/f_r{}^i. \quad (5)$$

Condition (5) states that, for the ith individual, the marginal rate of substitution between goods X_j and X_r, in consumption, must be equal to the marginal rate of substitution between these same two goods in "production" or exchange. To this acknowledged necessary condition, we now add,

$$u_{N_j}{}^i/u_r{}^i = f_{N_j}{}^i/f_r{}^i. \quad (6)$$

Condition (6) is not normally stated, since the variables relating to club size are not normally included in utility functions. Implicitly, the size for sharing arrangements is assumed to be determined exogenously to individual choices. Club size is presumed to be a part of the environment. Condition (6) states that the marginal rate of substitution "in consumption" between the size of the group sharing in the use of good X_j, and the numeraire good, X_r, must be equal to the marginal rate of substitution "in production." In other words, the individual attains full equilibrium in club size only when the marginal benefits that he secures from having an additional member (which may, and probably will normally be, negative) are just equal to the marginal costs that he incurs from adding a member (which will also normally be negative).

Combining (5) and (6) we get,

$$u_j{}^i/f_j{}^i = u_r{}^i/f_r{}^i = u_{Nj}{}^i/f_{Nj}{}^i. \qquad (7)$$

Only when (7) is satisfied will the necessary marginal conditions with respect to the consumption-utilization of X_j be met. The individual will have available to his membership unit an optimal quantity of X_j, measured in physical units and, also, he will be sharing this quantity "optimally" over a group of determined size.

The necessary condition for club size may not, of course, be met. Since for many goods there is a major change in utility between the one-person and the two-person club, and since discrete changes in membership may be all that is possible, we may get,

$$\frac{u_j{}^i}{f_j{}^i} = \frac{u_r{}^i}{f_r{}^i} > \frac{u_{Nj}{}^i}{f_{Nj}{}^i}\bigg|_{Nj=1};$$

$$\frac{u_j{}^i}{f_j{}^i} = \frac{u_r{}^i}{f^r} < \frac{u_{Nj}{}^i}{f_{Nj}{}^i}\bigg|_{Nj=2} \qquad (7A)$$

which incorporates the recognition that, with a club size of unity, the right-hand term may be relatively too small, whereas, with a club size of two, it may be too large. If partial sharing arrangements can be worked out, this qualification need not, of course, be made.

If, on the other hand, the size of a cooperative or collective sharing group is exogenously determined, we may get,

$$\frac{u_j{}^i}{f_j{}^i} = \frac{u_r{}^i}{f_r{}^i} > \frac{u_{Nj}{}^i}{f_{Nj}{}^i}\bigg|_{Nj=k} \qquad (7B)$$

Note that (7B) actually characterizes the situation of an individual with respect to the consumption of any purely public good of the type defined in the Samuelson polar model. Any group of finite size, k, is smaller than optimal here, and the full set of necessary marginal conditions cannot possibly be met. Since additional persons can, by definition, be added to the group without in any way reducing the availability of the good to other members, and since additional members could they be found, would presumably place some positive value on the good and hence be willing to share in its costs, the group always remains below optimal size. The all-inclusive club remains too small.

Consider, now, the relation between the set of necessary marginal conditions defined in (7) and those presented by Samuelson in application to goods that were exogenously defined to be purely public. In the latter case, these conditions are,

$$\sum_{i=1}^{s} (u_{n+j}{}^i/u_r{}^i) = f_{n+j}/f_r, \qquad (8)$$

where the marginal rates of substitution in consumption between the purely public good, X_{n+j}, and the numeraire good, X_r, summed over all individuals in the group of determined size, s, equals the marginal cost of X_{n+j} also defined in terms of units of X_r. Note that when (7) is satisfied, (8) is necessarily satisfied, provided only that the collectivity is making neither profit nor loss on providing the marginal unit of the public good. That is to say, provided that,

$$f_{n+j}/f_r = \sum_{i=1}^{s} (f_{n+j}{}^i/f_r{}^i). \qquad (9)$$

The reverse does not necessarily hold, however, since the satisfaction of (8) does not require that each and every individual in the group be in a position where his own marginal benefits are equal to his marginal costs (taxes).[7] And, of course, (8) says nothing at all about group size.

The necessary marginal conditions in (7) allow us to classify all goods only after the solution is attained. Whether or not a particular good is purely private, purely public, or somewhere between these extremes is determined only after the equilibrium values for the N_j's are known. A good for which the equilibrium value for N_j is large can

---

[7] In Samuelson's diagrammatic presentation, these individual marginal conditions are satisfied, but the diagrammatic construction is more restricted than that contained in his earlier more general model.

be classified as containing much "public-ness." By contrast, a good for which the equilibrium value of N_j is small can be classified as largely private.

II

The formal statement of the theory of clubs presented in Section I can be supplemented and clarified by geometrical analysis, although the nature of the construction implies somewhat more restrictive models.

Consider a good that is known to contain, under some conditions, a degree of "public-ness." For simplicity, think of a swimming pool. We want to examine the choice calculus of a single person, and we shall assume that other persons about him, with whom he may or may not choose to join in some club-like arrangement, are identical in all respects with him. As a first step, take a facility of one-unit size, which we define in terms of physical output supplied.

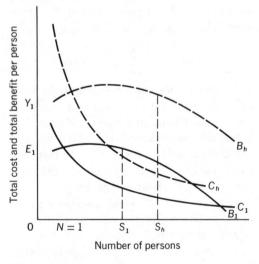

FIGURE 36.1

On the ordinate of Fig. 36.1, we measure total cost and total benefit per person, the latter derived from the individual's own evaluation of the facility in terms of the numeraire, dollars. On the abscissa, we measure the number of persons in possible

sharing arrangements. Define the full cost of the one-unit facility to be Y_1, and the reference individual's evaluation of this facility as a purely private consumption good to be E_1. As is clear from the construction as drawn, he will not choose to purchase the good. If the single person is required to meet the full cost, he will not be able to enjoy the benefits of the good. Any enjoyment of the facility requires the organization of some co-operative-collective sharing arrangement.[8]

Two functions may now be traced in Fig. 36.1, remaining within the one-unit restriction on the size of the facility. A total benefit function and a total cost function confronting the single individual may be derived. As more persons are allowed to share in the enjoyment of the facility, of given size, the benefit evaluation that the individual places on the good will, after some point, decline. There may, of course, be both an increasing and a constant range of the total benefit function, but at some point congestion will set in, and his evaluation of the good will fall. There seems little doubt that the total benefit curve, shown as B_1, will exhibit the concavity property as drawn for goods that involve some commonality in consumption.[9]

The bringing of additional members into

---

[8] The sharing arrangement need not be either co-operative or governmental in form. Since profit opportunities exist in all such situations, the emergence of profit-seeking firms can be predicted in those settings where legal structures permit, and where this organizational form possesses relative advantages. (Cf. R. H. Coase, "The Nature of the Firm," *Economica*, vol. IV (1937), pp. 386–405.) For purposes of this paper, such firms are one form of club organization, with co-operatives and public arrangements representing other forms. Generally speaking, of course, the choice among these forms should be largely determined by efficiency considerations.

[9] The geometrical model here applies only to such goods. Essentially the same analysis may, however, be extended to apply to cases where "congestion," as such, does not appear. For example, goods that are produced at decreasing costs, even if their consumption is purely private, may be shown to require some sharing arrangements in an equilibrium or optimal organization.

the club also serves to reduce the cost that the single person will face. Since, by our initial simplifying assumption, all persons here are identical, symmetrical cost sharing is suggested. In any case, the total cost per person will fall as additional persons join the group, under any cost-sharing scheme. As drawn in Fig. 36.1, symmetrical sharing is assumed and the curve, C_1, traces the total cost function, given the one-unit restriction on the size of the facility.[10]

For the given size of the facility, there will exist some optimal size of club. This is determined at the point where the derivatives of the total cost and total benefit functions are equal, shown as S_1 in Fig. 36.1, for the one-unit facility. Consider now an increase in the size of the facility. As before, a total cost curve and a total benefit curve may be derived, and an optimal club size determined. One other such optimum is shown at S_h, for a quantity of goods upon which the curves C_h and B_h are based. Similar constructions can be carried out for every possible size of facility; that is, for each possible quantity of good.

A similar construction may be used to determine optimal goods quantity for each possible size of club; this is illustrated in Fig. 36.2. On the ordinate, we measure here total costs and total benefits confronting the individual, as in Fig. 36.1. On the abscissa, we measure physical size of the facility, quantity of good, and for each assumed size of club membership we may

trace total cost and total benefit functions. If we first examine the single-member club, we may well find that the optimal goods quantity is zero; the total cost function may increase more rapidly than the total benefit function from the outset. However, as more persons are added, the total costs to the single person fall; under our symmetrical sharing assumption, they will fall proportionately. The total benefit functions here will slope upward to the right but after some initial range they will be concave downward and at some point will reach a maximum. As club size is increased, benefit functions will shift generally downward beyond the initial non-congestion range, and the point of maximum benefit will move to the right. The construction of Fig. 36.2 allows us to derive an optimal goods quantity for each size of club; Q_k is one such quantity for club size $N = K$.

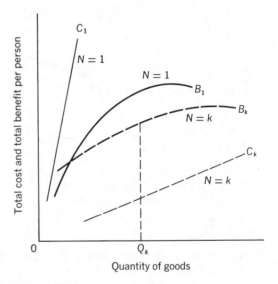

FIGURE 36.2

The results derived from Figs. 36.1 and 36.2 are combined in Fig. 36.3. Here the two variables to be chosen, goods quantity and club size, are measured on the ordinate and the abscissa respectively. The values for optimal club size for each goods quantity, derived from Fig. 36.1, allow us to

[10] For simplicity, we assume that an additional "membership" in the club involves the addition of one separate person. The model applies equally well, however, for those cases where cost shares are allocated proportionately with predicted usage. In this extension, an additional "membership" would really amount to an additional consumption unit. Membership in the swimming club could, for example, be defined as the right to visit the pool one time each week. Hence, the person who plans to make two visits per week would, in this modification, hold two memberships. This qualification is not, of course, relevant under the strict world-of-equals assumption, but it indicates that the theory need not be so restrictive as it might appear.

plot the curve N_{opt}, in Fig. 36.3. Similarly, the values for optimal goods quantity, for each club size, derived from Fig. 36.2, allow us to plot the curve, Q_{opt}.

The intersection of these two curves, N_{opt} and Q_{opt}, determines the position of full equilibrium, G. The individual is in equilibrium both with respect to goods quantity and to group size, for the good under consideration. Suppose, for example, that the sharing group is limited to size, N_k. The attainment of equilibrium with respect to goods quantity, shown by Q_k, would still leave the individual desirous of shifting the size of the membership so as to attain position L. However, once the group increases to this size, the individual prefers a larger quantity of the good, and so on, until G is attained.

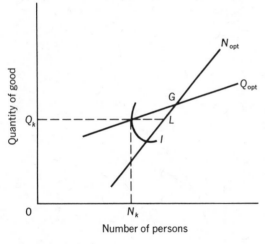

FIGURE **36.3**

Figure 36.3 may be interpreted as a standard preference map depicting the tastes of the individual for the two components, goods quantity and club size for the sharing of that good. The curves, N_{opt} and Q_{opt}, are lines of optima, and G is the highest attainable level for the individual, the top of his ordinal utility mountain. Since these curves are lines of optima within an individual preference system, successive choices must converge in G.

It should be noted that income-price con-

straints have already been incorporated in the preference map through the specific sharing assumptions that are made. The tastes of the individual depicted in Fig. 36.3 reflect the post-payment or net relative evaluations of the two components of consumption at all levels. Unless additional constraints are imposed on the model, he must move to the satiety point in this construction.

It seems clear that under normal conditions both of the curves in Fig. 36.3 will slope upward to the right, and that they will lie in approximately the relation to each other as therein depicted. This reflects the fact that, normally for the type of good considered in this example, there will exist a complementary rather than a substitute relationship between increasing the quantity of the good and increasing the size of the sharing group.

This geometrical model can be extended to cover goods falling at any point along the private-public spectrum. Take the purely public good as the first extreme case. Since, by definition, congestion does not occur, each total benefit curve, in Fig. 36.1, becomes horizontal. Thus, optimal club size, regardless of goods quantity is infinite. Hence, full equilibrium is impossible of attainment; equilibrium only with respect to goods quantity can be reached, defined with respect to the all-inclusive finite group. In the construction of Fig. 36.3, the N curve cannot be drawn. A more realistic model may be that in which, at goods quantity equilibrium, the limitations on group size impose an inequality. For example, in Fig. 36.3, suppose that the all-inclusive group is of size, N_k. Congestion is indicated as being possible over small sizes of facility, but, if an equilibrium quantity is provided, there is no congestion, and, in fact, there remain economies to scale in club size. The situation at the most favourable attainable position is, therefore, in all respects equivalent to that confronted in the case of the good that is purely public under the more restricted definition.

Consider now the purely private good. The appropriate curves here may be shown in Fig. 36.4. The individual, with his income-price constraints is able to attain the peak of his ordinal preference mountain without the necessity of calling upon his fellows to join him in sharing arrangements. Also, the benefits that he receives from the good may be so exclusively his own that these would largely disappear if others were brought in to share them. Hence, the full equilibrium position, G, lies along the vertical from the $N = 1$ member point. Any attempt to expand the club beyond this point will reduce the utility of the individual.[11]

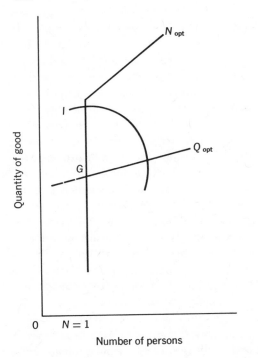

FIGURE 36.4

goods quantity and club size. This involves an oversimplification that is made possible only through the assumptions of specific cost-sharing schemes and identity among individuals. In order to generalize the results, these restrictions must be dropped. We know that, given any group of individuals who are able to evaluate both consumption shares and the costs of congestion, there exists some set of marginal prices, goods quantity, and club size that will satisfy (7) above. However, the quantity of the good, the size of the club sharing in its consumption, and the cost-sharing arrangements must be determined simultaneously. And, since there are always "gains from trade" to be realized in moving from non-optimal to optimal positions, distributional considerations must be introduced. Once these are allowed to be present, the final "solution" can be located at any one of a sub-infinity of points on the Pareto welfare surface. Only through some quite arbitrarily chosen conventions can standard geometrical constructions be made to apply.

The approach used above has been to impose at the outset a set of marginal prices (tax-prices, if the good is supplied publicly), translated here into shares or potential shares in the costs of providing separate quantities of a specific good for groups of

III

The geometrical construction implies that the necessary marginal conditions are satisfied at unique equilibrium values for both

[11] The construction suggests clearly that the optimal club size, for any quantity of good, will tend to become smaller as the real income of an individual is increased. Goods that exhibit some "publicness" at low income levels will, therefore, tend to become "private" as income levels advance.

This suggests that the number of activities that are organized optimally under co-operative collective sharing arrangements will tend to be somewhat larger in low-income communities than in high-income communities, other things equal. There is, of course, ample empirical support for this rather obvious conclusion drawn from the model. For example, in American agricultural communities thirty years ago heavy equipment was communally shared among many farms, normally on some single owner-lease-rental arrangement. Today, substantially the same equipment will be found on each farm, even though it remains idle for much of its potential working time.

The implication of the analysis for the size of governmental units is perhaps less evident. In so far as governments are organized to provide communal facilities, the size of such units measured by the number of citizens, should decline as income increases. Thus, in the affluent society, the local school district may, optimally, be smaller than in the poor society.

varying sizes. Hence, the individual confronts a predictable set of marginal prices for each quantity of the good at every possible club size, independently of his own choices on these variables. With this convention, and the world-of-equals assumption, the geometrical solution becomes one that is relevant for any individual in the group. If we drop the world-of-equals assumption, the construction continues to hold without change for the choice calculus of any particular individual in the group. The results cannot, of course, be generalized for the group in this case, since different individuals will evaluate any given result differently. The model remains helpful even here, however, in that it suggests the process through which individual decisions may be made, and it tends to clarify some of the implicit content in the more formal statements of the necessary marginal conditions for optimality.[12]

IV

The theory of clubs developed in this paper applies in the strict sense only to the organization of membership or sharing arrangements where "exclusion" is possible. In so far as non-exclusion is a characteristic of public goods supply, as Musgrave has suggested,[13] the theory of clubs is of limited relevance. Nevertheless, some implications of the theory for the whole excludability

[12] A note concerning one implicit assumption of the whole analysis is in order at this point. The possibility for the individual to choose among the various scales of consumption sharing arrangements has been incorporated into an orthodox model of individual behaviour. The procedure implies that the individual remains indifferent as to which of his neighbours or fellow citizens join him in such arrangements. In other words, no attempt has been made to allow for personal selectivity or discrimination in the models. To incorporate this element, which is no doubt important in many instances, would introduce a wholly new dimension into the analysis, and additional tools to those employed here would be required.

[13] See R. A. Musgrave, *The Theory of Public Finance*, New York, 1959.

question may be indicated. If the structure of property rights is variable, there would seem to be few goods the services of which are non-excludable, solely due to some physical attributes. Hence, the theory of clubs is, in one sense, a theory of optimal exclusion, as well as one of inclusion. Consider the classic lighthouse case. Variations in property rights, broadly conceived, could prohibit boat operators without "light licenses" from approaching the channel guarded by the light. Physical exclusion is possible, given sufficient flexibility in property law, in almost all imaginable cases, including those in which the interdependence lies in the act of consuming itself. Take the single person who gets an inoculation, providing immunization against a communicable disease. In so far as this action exerts external benefits on his fellows, the person taking the action could be authorized to collect charges from all beneficiaries under sanction of the collectivity.

This is not, of course, to suggest that property rights will, in practice, always be adjusted to allow for optimal exclusion. If they are not, the "free rider" problem arises. This prospect suggests one issue of major importance that the analysis of this paper has neglected, the question of costs that may be involved in securing agreements among members of sharing groups. If individuals think that exclusion will not be fully possible, that they can expect to secure benefits as free riders without really becoming full-fledged contributing members of the club, they may be reluctant to enter voluntarily into cost-sharing arrangements. This suggests that one important means of reducing the costs of securing voluntary co-operative agreements is that of allowing for more flexible property arrangements and for introducing excluding devices. If the owner of a hunting preserve is allowed to prosecute poachers, then prospective poachers are much more likely to be willing to pay for the hunting permits in advance.

Index

(Italicized number indicates starting page of author's paper included in this volume)

A

Abramovitz, Moses, 159

Additivity assumption, 114

Advertising expenditure, 235-247; and average production costs, 243; and Chamberlin's theory of selling costs, 236; and condition of constant cost, 241; and cost per unit, 242; and decreasing returns, 239, 257-258; and demand curves, 245; and group equilibrium, 240; and increasing returns, 239; and locus of average revenue, 243; and marginal revenue curve, 236, 237, 239; and maximum maximorum, 245; and monopolistic competition, 240; and optimum advertising cost outlays, 243; and optimum rate of output, 242; and optimum rate of production, 242, 243; and optimum selling prices, 238; and production costs, 241; and price elasticity of demand for product, 246; and selling costs, 235

Alchian, Armen A., 33, 34, *57*, *131*, 150, 153, 154, 155, 156, 158, *159*, 370, 371, 421

Alessi, Louis De (*see* De Alessi, Louis)

Alexander, Sidney S., 41

Allen, G.C., 148

Allen, R.G.D., 73, 102, 209, 413

Allen, R.M., 377

Allen, W.R., 158

Allocation, 455-537

Allocation of resources, and effects of unions, 444-451

American Medical Association, and approval of hospitals, 379; and control of medical education, 378; and Council on Medical Education, 376; as discriminating monopoly model (*see* Price discrimination in medicine); and Judicial Council, 379; and medical insurance, 380; powers of, 377; *See also* Medical monopoly: Organized medicine; Price discrimination in medicine

Andrews, P.W.S., 40, 396, 421

Antitrust law, 38, 360-361

Arrow, Kenneth J., 368, 481, 482, 520, 521

Asher, H., 168

Ashton, T.S., 144

Asset size, 132

Assumptions, in analysis, crucial, 37; realism of, 54; of a theory, 31, 32, 34-41; unrealistic, 53; use of, 37; *See also* Economic theory; Hypothesis